FROM SCOTTSBORO TO MUNICH

my young
brilliant
colleague —
another
student of
a past
empire

Love

[signature]
2009.

FROM SCOTTSBORO TO MUNICH

RACE AND POLITICAL CULTURE

IN 1930s BRITAIN

Susan D. Pennybacker

PRINCETON UNIVERSITY PRESS   PRINCETON AND OXFORD

Requests for permission to reproduce material from this work should be sent to Permissions, Princeton University Press

Published by Princeton University Press, 41 William Street, Princeton, New Jersey 08540

In the United Kingdom: Princeton University Press, 6 Oxford Street, Woodstock, Oxfordshire OX20 1TW

Library of Congress Cataloging-in-Publication Data

Pennybacker, Susan D. (Susan Dabney), 1953–
    From Scottsboro to Munich : race and political culture in 1930s Britain / Susan D. Pennybacker.
        p.   cm.
    Includes bibliographical references and index.
    ISBN 978-0-691-08828-0 (cloth : acid-free paper)—ISBN 978-0-691-14186-2 (pbk. : acid-free paper)   1. Great Britain—Race relations—History—20th century.   2. Politics and culture—Great Britain—History—20th century.   3. African Americans—Great Britain—History—20th century.   4. Scottsboro Trial, Scottsboro, Ala., 1931.   5. African Americans—Relations with British—History—20th century.   6. African Americans—Relations with Germans—History—20th century.   7. Blacks—Great Britain—History—20th century.   8. Blacks—Great Britain—Politics and government.   9. Racism—Great Britain—History—20th century.   10. United States—Race relations—History—20th century.   I. Title.
    DA125.N4P46 2009
    305.800941′09043—dc22   2008041123

British Library Cataloging-in-Publication Data is available

This book has been composed in Minion

Printed on acid-free paper. ∞

press.princeton.edu

Printed in the United States of America

10 9 8 7 6 5 4 3 2 1

CONTENTS

LIST OF FIGURES

ACKNOWLEDGMENTS

A ROCKEFELLER FOUNDATION HUMANIST-IN-RESIDENCE Arturo Schomburg Fellowship at the City College of New York and a subsequent award from CCNY's Simon Rifkind Center for the Humanities, made it possible for me to begin this book in the New York Public Library's Schomburg Center for Research in Black Culture over the course of two years in the early 1990s. Diana Latchatanere and Andre Elizee kindly connected me with Marika Sherwood in London, the first of many sorts of help that they offered. Sherwood led me to the archival consultant and translator Liudmilla Selivanova, and with the assistance of the Rockefeller award, I made the first two trips of three to Moscow, in 1994 and 1996. Selivanova's grasp of the evolving project and her comprehensive knowledge of the Comintern archives proved indispensable, as they have for others who followed.

The Notes on Sources and Bibliography attest to my use of many other collections and materials. I thank the personnel of the Russian, American, British, Dutch, and French research institutions noted in these sections, and especially the following persons, institutions, and organizations for all nature of archival and library assistance: Oleg Naumov and Kirill Anderson of the Russian State Archive for Social-Political History in Moscow; the Manuscripts, Archives and Rare Books Division of the New York Public Library and the Astor, Lenox and Tilden Foundations, for permission to cite the Ralph Bunche Papers, the International Labor Defense Records and the Richard B. Moore Papers at the Schomburg Center for Research in Black Culture; Dr. Joyce Turner for permission to cite the papers of Richard B. Moore; Marcel van der Linden and the staff of the International Institute for Social History in Amsterdam; Jeffrey M. Flannery, John Michael Haynes, Beverly Brennan, David J. Kelly, Judith Robinson, and Elgin Reid of the Library of Congress, the longest home of this project; the family of Naomi Mitchison and the Trustees of the National Library of Scotland for permission to cite Mitchison's papers at the Library, where I was assisted by Sheila Mackenzie and Robin Smith; Lisa Dowdeswell and The Society of Authors in London, on behalf of the Bernard Shaw Estate, for permission to cite letters of George Bernard Shaw; Elizabeth Wells of the Churchill Archive Center, Churchill College, Cambridge; Kate E. Boyce of Hull University Archives; Maureen Waltry of the Sydney Jones Library of the University of Liverpool, for permission to cite the papers of Eleanor Rathbone; Jeff Howarth of Anti-Slavery International for permission to cite the papers of Lady Simon within the Anti-Slavery Society collection at Rhodes House, Oxford; the Department of Special Collections of the Charles E. Young Research Library, UCLA, for permission to quote the Ralph Bunche Diary, and Lilace Hatayama and Genie

Guerard of the Library; Tim Baker, formerly of the research library of the United States Holocaust Memorial Museum in Washington, D.C.; Sue Donnelly and Graham Camfield of the London School of Economics Archives; Lucy Mc-Cann of Rhodes House, Oxford, and her colleagues, including the historian Amalia Ribi; Helen Roberts and Darren Treadwell of the Labour History and Study Center in Manchester, and their former colleagues Stephen Bird and Jo Robson; Donna Hetherington, researcher, and Fiona Courage, manager, of the University of Sussex Special Collections; Dorothy Sheridan, the great director emeritus of the Mass Observation Archive; the Curtis Brown Group Ltd., London, on behalf of the Trustees of the Mass Observation Archive at the University of Sussex, for permission to cite its files; Sarah Lewis of Curtis Brown, London; Maureen Wilbraham and Irene O'Brien of the Mitchell Library in Glasgow; Rukshana Singh of the Southern California Library for Social Studies and Research; the Fabian Society for permission to cite the papers of the Fabian Colonial Bureau; Juanita van Zyl of the Library of the South African Parliament, Cape Town; and Jennifer Block of the Firestone Library, Princeton University.

For assistance with images, I thank all those who tracked information and routes of access, and especially, Anne-Marie McNally of GettyImages; Arnaud Balvay in Paris and the Cliché Atelier photographiques des Archives nationales; Thomas Lisanti of the New York Public Library; Donald Manning, Ruth Long, Lynda Unchern, and Les Goody of the Cambridge University Library; George Barrow for the estate of Joseph Southall; Murdo Macleod for the use of his photographic portrait of Naomi Mitchison; the *Morning Star* for permission to use images taken from the pages of the *Daily Worker*; Blyden Nurse Cowart for permission to use George Padmore's photograph; Lynette Cawthra and Mike Weaver of the Working Class Movements Library in Salford; Robert Blair in Johannesburg; Emma Smith of the University of Western Australia Press; and, Ellen Sandberg of the Granger Collection in New York City. David Sutton and Nicholas Hiley also assisted.

During a sabbatical year in 1997–98, I was a visitor at King's College of the University of Cambridge; I thank the College Fellowship for their invitation and the privilege of working among them. In 2002 I received further support for the writing of this book from the Virginia Foundation for the Humanities and Public Policy at the University of Virginia, matched by the Dean of Faculty's office at Trinity College. I thank Roberta Culbertson and those who worked as fellows alongside me at the VFH and on the staff of this important center for public history, scholarship, and social action, which boasts the resources of UVA's Alderman Library and the university's excellent historians and literary scholars so close to hand. The VFH made the completion of crucial parts of the text possible in a productive and respectful environment.

My previous coauthors Eve Rosenhaft and James A. Miller, worked with me on the first pictures we painted together of the international Scottsboro campaign. Both were among the closest readers of the book-in-progress. Eve's breadth of knowledge and quiet, dogged intellect are formidable. Jim remains my first reader, whose profound and life-sustaining sense of irony I admire, but cannot hope to capture. Consummate, lifelong students of the 1930s, and veteran practitioners of language, each has enriched this book in many visible ways, bringing an activist's sense of engagement to bear upon our common efforts: the inheritance of experience, not just information. David Montgomery of Yale University was the inspiration for my first Moscow foray, and for much of the shape of this work as a whole. His insistence that the newly opened Russian archives be examined by scholars unburdened by blinding prejudice, and his unrivaled knowledge of the history of internationalism, opened paths for me even as he lent a critical ear to my contentions. I am forever in his debt. Wendy Goldman's presence made each journey to Russia possible and exciting, and offered an example of the integrity of committed and pioneering scholarship of the first order. Dorothy Thompson, John Saville, and Eric Hosbawm spoke with me of their past political commitments; I was honored to have the time and company of each and, in Dorothy's case, over many years. James Livingood in Chattanooga, Miriam Sherman in Los Angeles, Lloyd Brown (while on a trip to the Robeson Centenary in London), and Si and Sophie Gerson in Brooklyn—all five now deceased—offered their own riveting accounts of the period. Those living of their generation may not recognize or countenance the rendition herein, but I thank them no less for their efforts to help me understand. I thank Ellen and Ken Spuul, who arranged a visit with Naomi Mitchison on the Mull of Kintyre, just before her death. I was delighted to meet Blyden Nurse Cowart in Trinidad.

Two anonymous readers for Princeton University Press provided blueprints for submission that were erudite and persuasive. Ian Patterson, Eve Rosenhaft, Jan Lambertz, Ani Mukherji, Kevin Grant, Vijay Prashad, James A. Miller, and Woodford McClellan undertook close and learned readings of particular sections of the text, each embodying grace under pressure. Like all others mentioned here, none bears a shred of responsibility for the weakness of argument or empirical errors that readers may find within; they have only my deepest thanks for rescue, knowledge, challenges, and suggestions. Fellow historians Eve Rosenhaft, Jan Lambertz, and Richard Mitten, my colleague Kenneth Lloyd-Jones, and Anja Macher in Cape Town all provided translations as fluent readers of the several languages that the text engages. Raj Chandavarkar argued patiently with me about this project from its inception; not being able to present this book to him still shocks in its sadness and sense of loss. Gareth Stedman Jones, Denise Riley, Jennifer Davis, Deborah Epstein Nord, Philip Nord, Ian Patterson, Tom Jeffery, Deborah Thom, and David Feldman have discussed with me many matters related to this work over more than three decades, offering sharp and unsparing intelligence, experience, fact, and argumentation, but also lasting friendship; they are my first critics. Andrew Thompson served as an early research assistant at Cambridge.

I thank those who invited me to speak; commented upon my work in settings formal and informal; brought their work to bear upon mine; and offered readings, archival tips, and contacts. They include Paul Sherwin, Marcus Rediker, Yassen Zassoursky, Adrienne Edgar, James Barrett, Geoff Eley, Penny von Eschen, Kevin Gaines, Susan Ferber, Thomas Lebien, Steven Sage, Pascal Gross, Bill Schwarz, David Cannadine, John Lonsdale, Bruce Berman, Alison Drew, Ira Katznelson, Rick Halpern, Michael Zuckerman, David Jaffee, Barbara Brooks, Larry Greene, Delia Jarrett-Macauley, Carla Capetti, Peter Stansky, Paul Deslandes, Elizabeth Prevost, Chris Waters, Antoinette Burton, David Roediger, Hakim Adi, John Marriott, Kevin Morgan, Carolyn Brown, Anson Rabinbach, Clifford Rosenberg, Brent Edwards, Christopher Brown, Alex Bain, Paul Kershaw, Yaël Fletcher, Ian Fletcher, Daniel Anker, Barak Goodman, Robbie Aitken, Atina Grossmann, Mary Nolan, and Gordon Pirie. Lora Wildenthal served with me as cochair of the Race in Europe seminar at the Minda de Gunzburg Center for European Studies at Harvard-MIT, her impeccable professionalism advancing our common agenda with a host of gifted speakers. At the University of the West Indies, both in St. Augustine and in Cave Hill, I was welcomed by the late Fitzroy Baptiste, Rodney Worrell, Alan Cobley, Aaron Kamugisha, and the precious network of Caribbean scholars and specialists who are among Padmore's heirs there and abroad. I thank Ani Muhkerji and Barrymore Bogues, and all others present, for the privilege of participating in an excellent graduate students' symposium on Early Twentieth-Century Black Radicalism at Brown University in April 2008, whence much promising work is yet to come.

Many others assisted me in ways known to them, in the locales that were my archival haunts or places where I lived, visited, and worked on this long journey. They include Biancamaria Fontana, Lynn Szwaja, Margaret Mitchell Smith, Sophia Kishkovsky, Tatiana Venediktova, Pavel Balditsyn, Diane Neumaier, Wendy Lower, Lisa Zaid, David Chanin, Doreen Saar, Naomi Amos, Will Thomas, Heather Thomas, Andrew Freeman, Hazel Mills, Joanna Innes, Alison Jeffery, Julian Bell, Basim Musallam, Anna Hont, Istvan Hont, Nigel Swain, Miri Rubin, Polly Moran, Dina Copelman, Larry Poos, and Jennifer Houle.

At Trinity College in Hartford, Connecticut, every last member of the History Department has expressed collegial support for my work, including my brilliant youngest colleagues. I especially thank my fellow modern Europeanists Kathleen Kete and Samuel Kassow for their example, counsel, trust, and insight. Sam's knowledge of much of the era in question is unrivaled, and even more so his capacity to render it intelligible and memorable. I thank Borden W. Painter, Jr., for his support for the honor granted me in assuming a position that bears his name. I thank all those who came to my inaugural lecture at which I first sketched the final outline of this book. I thank my other Trinity colleagues, past and present: Stephen Valocchi, Pablo Delano, W. Frank Mitchell, Sandra Wheeler, Anne Lundberg, Tony Hall, Vijay Prashad, Louis Masur, Berel Lang, Robert Palter, Lisa Pleskow Kassow, Andrew Walsh, Paul Lauter,

Johanna Fernandez, Monica van Beusekom, and Laurel Baldwin-Ragaven for extending expertise, friendship, and collegiality to me in ways that assisted my research and writing, and my well-being. The Dean of the Faculty Rena Fraden, the Associate Academic Dean David Robbins assisted by Nancy Horton, and President James Fleming Jones, Jr., have in recent years created a climate of support for scholarly production at Trinity that allowed the manuscript of this book, and the acquisition for publication of the images that appear in it, to come to completion with unprecedented institutional commitment and interest. My students encouraged this project, even checking up on me in other parts of the country and the world, and some of them becoming historians.

I thank the staff of Trinity Library, and especially Doris Kammradt, Mary Curry, Patricia Bunker, and my academic computing colleague David Tatem for all their labors on my behalf. I thank my former student assistants Ashesh Prasann, Hamza Chaudary, and Kay Bassen. Gigi St. Peter's role in directing the everyday work of Trinity's History Department extended into vigilant support for this project over many years. Sandra Andrews brought her intelligence, steadfastness and intuition to the tasks associated with the long production of the manuscript for submission. In the inner circles of the Hartford Studies Project, the weight of my commitments to this book were honored by Elizabeth Rose, Stephen McFarland, Glenn Orkin, Charles and Virginia Lewis, and others who share with us a common vision of documentary history and film. I thank them for their interest, understanding, and companionship.

In 2005 I first came to work and write in Cape Town through the kind invitation of the History Department of the University of the Western Cape, and a Trinity College sabbatical. Once again, another entire department of creative and committed individuals supported and encouraged me. I especially thank Uma Mesthrie my UWC Chair, and my friends and colleagues Leslie Witz and Josephine Frater, Subithra Moodley-Moore and Basil Moore, and Stephen and Andrew Marquard. While introducing me to South Africa in tandem with others, they provided the essential framework that allowed me to work serenely on three extended visits lasting ten months, in an urgent and unforgettable context.

At Princeton University Press, Brigitta van Rheinberg accepted, refined, and championed this project well beyond its planned lifespan. Her canny understanding of its challenges and possibilities was informed by her own scholarly knowledge of the twentieth-century. Clara Platter brings a quick intelligence to her desk. I have benefited beyond measure from work with both of these editors, and likewise the fine production editor Ellen Foos and the professional staff with whom all three work. I thank them for their trust and patience. Marsha Kunin's copyediting has been unsurpassed in its rigor and depth of understanding.

In the lost childhood summers of the 1950s and early 1960s, I spent many hot nights tossing in the close Tennessee air, and watched the daylight sun envelop the magnificent mountains in hazy vapors. A few minutes away lived Ada Wright, so near that we could have passed each other even in that world, and it transpired that some of our relations had done so. My final thanks must go to my Tennessee-rooted family and friends now flung across the American South and Southwest, and to Ada Wright's descendants. All know the inheritance of the 1930s, the twilight of Jim Crow and how much of it endures; they remember others now gone who lived it on all sides. Martha Hackney Pennybacker and Albert M. Pennybacker, Jr., Janet P. Scott and David William Pennybacker, the Mitchell-Smith clan, the Wright extended family and their wider community have borne witness to much more than this book tells. I thank them for their insights and their tenacity, their candor and their narratives. My parents sought with hearts and souls to break the barriers, to push across the line and to live differently, finally crossing the oceans into the larger world. This work of mine is a small part of that legacy, received each day as the stars begin to fall.

Susan Dabney Pennybacker
Cape Town and Princeton, 2008

ABBREVIATIONS

ACE	League of Nations Committee of Experts on Slavery
ACLU	American Civil Liberties Union
AME	African Methodist Episcopal church
AN	*Archives Nationales*, National Archives of France, Paris
ARAF	*Anti-Slavery Reporter and Aborigines' Friend*
ASE	Amalgamated Society of Engineers
BLP	British Labour Party
CGT	French General Confederation of Labor
CI	Comintern, the Communist International
CID	Criminal Investigation Division, United Kingdom
CP	Communist Party
CPGB	Communist Party of Great Britain
CPI	Communist Party of India
CPUSA	Communist Party of the United States
DBN	Papers of Reginald Bridgeman, Hull
DCL	Archives of Liberty (Formerly The National Council for Civil Liberties), Hull University
ECCI	Executive Committee of the Communist International
FEBR	Papers of Fenner Brockway, Churchill Archives Center, Cambridge
FCB	Papers of the Fabian Colonial Bureau, Rhodes House, Oxford
FO	The British Foreign Office, Whitehall, London
IAO	*International African Opinion*
IASB	International African Service Bureau
IISH	International Institute of Social History, Amsterdam
ILD	International Labor/Labour Defense
ILP	Independent Labour Party
ILO	International Labour Organization
ITUCNW	International Trade Union Committee of Negro Workers
JMP	Papers of James Maxton, Mitchell Library, Glasgow
KC	King's Counsel
KMP	Kingsley Martin Papers, University of Sussex
KPD	German Communist Party
KUTV	Communist University of Toilers of the East, Moscow
LAI	League against Imperialism
LCC	London County Council
LHASC	Labour History and Study Center, University of Central Lancashire

LNU	League of Nations Union
LOC	Library of Congress, Washington, D.C.
LOCP	League of Coloured Peoples
LSE	London School of Economics and Political Science
LSI	Labor and Socialist International
LSP	Lady Simon Papers, in the Anti-Slavery Society Papers, Rhodes House, Oxford
LWP	Leonard Woolf Papers, University of Sussex
MI5	Military Intelligence, Section 5, United Kingdom
MO	Mass Observation project
MOPR	Russian Red Aid
NA	National Archives of the United Kingdom, Kew Gardens, London
NAACP	National Association for the Advancement of Colored People
NATO	North Atlantic Treaty Organization
NKVD	People's Commissariat for Internal Affairs, Soviet Union
NLS	National Library of Scotland, Edinburgh
NMP	Naomi Mitchison Papers, National Library of Scotland
NSPCC	National Society for the Prevention of Cruelty to Children
NWA	Negro Welfare Association
PCF	French Communist Party
PEN	Worldwide association of writers
RAF	Royal Air Force
RBD	Ralph Bunche Diary, UCLA Library
RGASPI	Russian State Archive of Socio-Political History, Moscow
RP	Papers of Eleanor Rathbone, University of Liverpool
SAP	German Socialist Workers Party
SC	Schomburg Center for Research in Black Culture, New York Public Library
SCLS	Southern California Library for Social Studies and Research, Los Angeles
SFIO	French Section of the Workers' International
SPD	German Social-Democratic Party
TVA	Tennessee Valley Authority
UCLA	University of California at Los Angeles
UNIA	United Negro Improvement Association
USDJ	U.S. National Archives, U.S. Department of Justice, Central Files
WASU	West African Students' Union
WILF	Women's International League for Peace and Freedom

FROM SCOTTSBORO TO MUNICH

INTRODUCTION

A SKELETAL RAILROAD crossing at Paint Rock, Alabama, in the mountainous terrain near Scottsboro is the unlikely starting point for a journey into the political culture of imperial Britain in the 1930s—a journey that continues across the English Channel to the plains north of the Bavarian Alps and Munich. The metropolitan British and German rail centers dwarfed the sparse Alabama settlement that was too small to have a courthouse; those picked up in Paint Rock on suspicion of foul play had to be carried in flatbed trucks to the county seat. How did "race" figure in the 1930s? This history of the decade is comprised of unanticipated travel, unjust trials, and tangled and ragged networks of people living in dark times. The nine young defendants in the Scottsboro rape case were arrested in March of 1931, and Munich was the scene of the conference in September 1938, at which representatives of the British and French governments, with fascist Italy's assistance, attempted to appease Adolf Hitler's drive for war, sacrificing peoples and lands in the balance. The paths of many of those who responded to these events crossed in Britain, where London served as an unofficial center of colonial and antifascist exile. The imperial capital on its rain-swept islands—between the European continent, the ports of the Caribbean, and the North American seaboard—remained the seat of a parliamentary democracy that continued to allow entry to some people in flight. Britain was the final and first stop for many coming and going across oceans and seas. This story unfolds in the interconnections of activist lives, and is about the ideas and purposes to which those lives were dedicated.

Why was Ada Wright, a domestic worker from Chattanooga, Tennessee, walking so determinedly on Fleet Street in the summer of 1932? How does her story find a connection to the designs for peace that led to war staged in Munich? The answers to these questions foster a reconfigured narrative of the 1930s, whose protagonists formed a diffuse "front" of radicals and liberals, many of them socialists and communists, passionately involved in racial politics, who for the most part knew one another between the wars. The persons at the center of this story visited or worked, in Britain, or exercised influence over a strand of British-based activism, yet each came from somewhere else—Tennessee, Trinidad, Ireland, India, and Germany—and achieved notoriety in one political circle or another in the era.

In the 1930s, the Empire was a central foundation of Britain's life and through the operations of what some have termed her "gentlemanly capitalism," a source of much of her wealth, covering a quarter of the globe and governing a quarter of the world's population, over 350 million of whom lived on the Indian subcontinent alone.[1] London was not the only theater of imperial control, but from it flowed much of the Empire's power, investment, and governance. The myriad forms of metropolitan racial politics of the 1930s and the very different individuals who voiced them, formed an essential part of the vast interwar imperial order, and inherited various transatlantic connections—from the Atlantic world of merchant and slave vessels, colonization, revolution, and civil wars. These took many observable forms. We turn to the capital of the "other Britain," land of the Scots, in the year before Munich.

In August of 1937, Bishop William Heard, 35th bishop of the African American AME (African Methodist Episcopal) Church, traveled by steamship to Edinburgh with his niece to attend the Second World Conference on Faith and Order of the progressive, international ecumenical movement. He was the conference's oldest delegate and the oldest AME bishop, a former slave who had organized black railroad workers in the American South before entering the ranks of the clergy, winning a major court battle against segregation in 1877 and serving as U.S. consul-general in Liberia in the 1890s. Now ninety, Heard was one of many hundreds of African Americans increasingly visible in Britain and on the European continent. W.E.B. Du Bois attended the University of Heidelberg before 1914, and black troops fought in the Jim Crow U.S. military in France during World War I. When the fighting ceased, those African Americans who could afford to do so came to see the sights of Europe, some famously making their homes in Paris and London.

Even the leading U.S. African American newspapers—the *Chicago Defender*, *Pittsburgh Courier*, and the *Baltimore African-American*—had offices and journalists in London in the thirties. The Heards were in these respects unexceptional visitors. But the bishop and his niece were denied a hotel room on that summer day in Edinburgh, the hotel's owner pleading that white American tourists had pressured him not to let rooms to blacks, asking that the segregationist practices that obtained in the United States prevail in Scotland so that they might feel entirely at home. This prohibition was still common in Britain and Europe, and within the law. The African American actor Paul Robeson had been refused entry to the Savoy Hotel Grill in a celebrated case a few years earlier. Quick to act on behalf of his fellow clergyman, no less a personage than the Archbishop of York William Temple offered his own home to the Heards. Temple was a radical cleric, a professed socialist who had taught in workingmen's educational clubs in the 1920s and whose *Christianity and the Social Order* and other works, championed a fervent antifascist and pro-labor doctrine. He was active in Jewish refugee relief work, was elected Archbishop of Canterbury in 1942, and became a chief architect of the World Council of Churches. Italy, Germany, and now Spain were engulfed by fascism and the kinds of racial policies that Archbishop Temple loathed. Guernica was bombed in April of that year, and in this month of August, the Vatican recognized Franco. Scotland could little afford the embarrassment of its American ecumenical guest, a former slave no less, being spurned accommodation on racial grounds.

But Archbishop Temple's hospitality was not required; the Heards went to a smaller hotel where they were made welcome, their booking reportedly secured by other "influential whites." Nevertheless, the home secretary Sir John Simon, a Liberal party MP who was now part of Britain's National Government (the rightward-leaning coalition first elected in 1931), felt personally compelled to come and convey his apologies to the black bishop. He was accompanied by his wife, Lady Kathleen Manning Simon. Irish by birth, Lady Simon was a leader of the Anti-Slavery and Aborigines' Protection Society, the venerable organization based in London that claimed advocacy of millions of global victims of incarcerated labor. The Simons rushed north from the metropolis to Edinburgh to pay their respects. Bishop Heard died two weeks later after returning home to Philadelphia, his visit and death covered in the *New York Times*. The *Chicago Defender* reported the episode under the headline "British Regret Jim Crow Insult."[2] His anxious hosts in Britain breathed a sigh of relief that they had not been the cause of his passing and had instead eased his way home. Liberal tolerance had prevailed. Simon wrote to W.E.B. Du Bois.

> I do not know if you saw any account of my husband's and my action in Scotland because of the treatment meted out to Bishop Heard and his great-niece Miss Caldwell. My anger was raised to white heat at the refusal of a hotel to accommodate them because of their color. We invited them out and showed them publicly with us and I learned that the poor old man was comforted by our action. Curiously enough several people in Edinburgh whom I did not know, came and thanked me for my action which "took the slur from our city."[3]

But Bishop Heard may have regarded the episode in another way. He had first visited Britain in 1895, and in the 1920s wrote that "in certain parts of London and Liverpool the prejudice is as great as in New York."[4] Britain's interwar communities of color numbered 20,000–30,000, comprised largely of maritime workers, domestic servants, and low-paid or migrant laborers. There were small middle-class and professional contingents of blacks, Asians, and those from the Middle East, including two Asian MPs who served before 1914, Parsis Dadabhai Naoroji and Mancherjee Bhownagree, and several black London borough officials including John Archer and Henry Sylvester Williams. The sons of some wealthy colonials of color attended Eton and Oxbridge. British Jewry, commonly referred to as members of the "Jewish race," numbered 300,000 or more, both Anglo-Jewry and recent immigrants constituting a community ten times the size of the groups of "nonwhites," even apart from the largely European immigrants and their descendants of non-Jewish backgrounds, and the Irish. Blacks, including African Americans, had long featured on the

London cultural scene, and Londoners who had not seen them perform in person were accustomed to their depiction on the music hall stage, and in the variety theater and the cinema. The popular minstrel routines of the 1930s served as metaphors for racial assumption, racial attitude, and for "race" as it informed this particular historical conjuncture. The words and performances of black entertainers and their impersonators constituted a familiar, streetwise, transatlantic interwar idiom. Bishop Heard could not escape common presumption and he knew that. Those who spoke on his behalf lived within the cultural moment and terms of their times.

The Heard episode was unsurprising for its era. Racial exclusion was common and lawful in many parts of the United States. American tourism was on the upswing in Europe, the dollar fiercely coveted in the dangerous straits of the later thirties. But the visit of the bishop and his niece, and the apology they received from a Cabinet member whose name would shortly be linked to the attempted appeasement of Hitler by the British government, are not part of the routine histories of the interwar years. The fact of an African American press office in London, the transatlantic travels of an aging black church official, the importance attached to Simon's apology in his and Lady Simon's circles and her witnessing of it are details left aside in the dominant stories of the thirties: economic depression, lynching in America, the rise of fascism, democracy's late mobilization, and the longer story of the eventual pursuit of "Civil Rights," only when the time came and in America—on the bridge at Selma, Alabama, and after. A fixed image of the decade and what followed, especially in its assumptions about racial politics, acts as a vise on knowledge and on the imagination. This book is committed to the release of that constraint.

The leap from the music hall and variety stage to the lynch mob of the Jim Crow South was assisted by many British travelers' accounts of life in America, and the British press carried lurid and graphic accounts of many a lynching. The Scottsboro, Alabama, trials began in 1931, when the nine young black defendants were summarily found guilty of raping two white women hobos on a train that was stopped at Paint Rock—a crime that they did not commit. Their supporters used the vernacular of the music-hall stage to portray the defendants as pathetic and unsuspecting racial outcasts pleading for their lives. The print culture emanating from the events of the case promoted the stereotypes of stage and screen. Communists, socialists, and liberals who participated in the Scottsboro campaign that arose internationally in the wake of capital sentences being handed down in Alabama also employed this minstrel vernacular, routinely interwoven with the language of communist appeals to the proletariat.[5]

Each chapter that follows pursues a figure who appeared in the international Scottsboro campaign—Ada Wright, George Padmore, Shapurji Saklatvala, Willi Münzenberg, and Lady Simon, who donated funds to the campaign and committed herself to other racial causes that placed her within its orbit. Padmore, Saklatvala, and Münzenberg knew one another and had seen or met Ada

Wright. They knew of Lady Simon and the antislavery movement; she had knowledge of them and their milieus. Knowledge of the lives and perceptions of these actors contributes to a new understanding of what transatlantic and imperial racial politics looked like to the man and woman of conscience and even to the more casual observer in the thirties. These individuals acted as lightning rods for antiracism in an era whose written history often does not admit them as full players or acknowledge their mutual connections. Their awkward presences upset historical convention and pose some little-asked questions of the decade that spanned the distance between the outbreak of the Scottsboro case and the disruption and sacrifice of lives that lay in the aftermath of the Munich agreements. London sat uncomfortably poised between Jim Crow and the Third Reich. What did it mean to be an antiracist at this time? What did it mean to oppose empire or fascism, or both, on grounds of racial inhumanity and racial injustice, or to articulate a vision of an interracial world culture?

The story begins with the relationship between the American Jim Crow South and the Anglo-European world that was fascinated with Southern ways, and repulsed by them. A mirror of the racial animosities witnessed by Europeans in their own global intrigues, and a prophetic vision of the violence that would come with mounting racial hatreds on the European continent, the South was "read" and perceived as beyond a boundary of white civilization, any trace of which increasingly compelled an apology from the Simons and others of their liberal persuasion. Those who saw the Scottsboro rape trials of the nine African Americans as symbols of the most horrific outcome of that boundary's crossing—the legal execution of the innocent—were passionately mobilized around the defendants' release. This is an account of individual lives known to one another through this case and other similar, often related endeavors, from liberal antislavery politics and humanitarian refugee activism, to liberalism, socialism, and communism. How did these persons address the racial episodes of the 1930s and with what common and discordant languages? What were their visions of the future? How did they reconcile the struggle against a growing fascism with their sympathies for the victims of Jim Crow? When war grew nearer, how did "racial politics" change?

Ada Wright, the mother of two of the defendants, Roy and Andy Wright, crossed the Atlantic to Germany in the summer of 1932; the Scottsboro case occasioned her life's first travels outside of the Jim Crow South. She sat with her companion, International Labor Defense leader and American communist Louis Engdahl, among white passengers on the liner that docked at Hamburg, the center of European communist work among black and Asian seafaring laborers who made up significant numbers of the harborside population of the city. Along with Liverpool, Bristol, Cardiff, London, Marseille, and Paris, Hamburg had one of the most visible communities of color in the European world of the thirties. Wright, a member of a Primitive Baptist congregation in

Chattanooga whose mother was born in slavery, made her way across Britain and Europe through the offices of what was termed Red Aid, a very large network of mass relief and propaganda organizations with direct affiliation to the Communist International (Comintern)—the international association, directorate, and secretariat of worldwide communist parties headquartered in Moscow. But Wright also saw many other Europeans that summer who were not communists. And when she spoke, the dialect of Tennessee conveyed images of the South, including harsh depictions of slavery that enforced the propaganda cry to free her sons and the other defendants. In 1932 Wright spent ten days in London, the shires, Scotland, and Wales. The photograph from the Russian archives on this book's cover, was taken as she departed a press conference on Fleet Street, the British International Labour Defense leader and trade unionist Bob Lovell by her side. In the wake of Wright's visit, the British writer Nancy Cunard and others worked with many kinds of political organizations and associations across London to mount a spirited defense campaign. One of the anchors of the "Scottsboro front" was the small communist-led League against Imperialism (LAI), the successor to the League against Colonial Oppression, a global association founded in Berlin in 1926, and first convened in Brussels in 1927, by German communist Willi Münzenberg. Among the LAI's early members were the British socialist MP James Maxton of the Independent Labour Party (ILP) and a small group of anticolonial activists from across the empire, including the future Kenyan president Jomo Kenyatta.

Nancy Cunard's involvement in Scottsboro brought many notables on board as signatories, from London's chief rabbi to Cunard's literary and artistic cronies. They included poet Ezra Pound, artist Augustus John, Charlie Chaplin, and Albert Einstein. Many public figures from arts, literary, and political circles embraced a campaign featuring dances, fêtes, and concert fund-raisers in which expatriate African Americans also participated. Wright's intrepid journey, her "translated" speech and interactions with her supporters, introduce the chapters that follow—a visit uncharted in most accounts of the interwar British and European left.

Among Nancy Cunard's close associates was the Trinidadian intellectual George Padmore (the adopted name of Malcom Nurse), who headed the Comintern's Negro Committee in Hamburg. Padmore met Ada Wright when she arrived in Europe in 1932. The grandson of a slave and son of a schoolmaster, Padmore completed a medical board certificate in Trinidad in 1916. In 1924 he left Port of Spain for New York and joined the American communist party. He journeyed on to the Soviet Union and lived among an international circle of exiled activists in Moscow, including figures like the young Ho Chi Minh. Padmore was sent to Germany from Russia. His fellow European organizer of Comintern relief and defense campaigns was the sensational communist impresario and publishing magnate Willi Münzenberg, a former German youth leader who participated in the German revolution of 1918–19. Münzenberg and Padmore worked in Europe alongside other activists in and around the communist movement in the early thirties, including African American James Ford, a veteran of the First World War in France, and the Soudanese former schoolteacher Garan Kouyate.

Padmore became the editor of the *Negro Worker*, a shipboard publication that was sold in bookstores and smuggled in Bibles and other literature across the globe from New York to Port of Spain, Cape Town, Nairobi, and Paris. Padmore's writing focused on the exploitation of labor in the British and European empires. He was a wry and visionary critic of imperialism in all its guises, who adopted Lenin's purported querulous description of the League of Nations as the "thieves' kitchen." Padmore is a central figure in this portrait of the 1930s whose pen, voice, and trenchant analytical ability, constituted the decisive intervention of a brilliant intellectual of color in his time in British and European political culture; he was recognized by and known as such to many who appear in this story. Padmore's presence in London over the next twenty years defied the minstrel vernacular in all its versions, including the communist rendition. His perceptions of racial attitudes and interactions in the communist movement appear in his correspondence. The Soviet claim that the Soviet Union was a racially harmonious entity that transcended ethnic differences was a powerful one for fellow travelers of the thirties, and especially for visitors and activists of color, and the insistence upon the celebration of multiracial assimilation and racial progress a mainstay of Soviet doctrine—this depiction of the Soviet Union was often wielded against portraits of the racist American South. Padmore made this claim as a propagandist while privately insisting upon the hypocrisies of comradely practice.

In February of 1933, weeks after Hitler came to power, Padmore was arrested in Hamburg, imprisoned for several months, and then deported to the United Kingdom where he was entitled to the rights of an imperial British subject. The irony of this guarantee of safe refuge did not escape the Home Office, and no sooner had he disembarked than British security agents began to trail him. It took him weeks to find anyone in London prepared to rent to a black man. The last issue of the *Negro Worker* under his editorship led with a piece on German fascism, and discussed the Nazi opposition to Wright's 1932 visit to Germany. Padmore soon severed his ties with the Comintern authorities and they with him, inaugurating a new era of his own independence as a writer and organizer in which he extended his connections to the fragile movements for independence and social justice in Britain's colonies and especially in Africa and the Caribbean, condemning Stalinist neglect of anticolonial work and challenging fascist consolidation.

Padmore traveled between London and Paris, working closely with Garan Kouyate and others around the black publications *Étoile nord-africaine* and *Le Cri des nègres*. In London, his roommates, peers, and companions included the activist Dorothy Pizer, who became Dorothy Pizer Padmore, Jomo Kenyatta, and Padmore's former Howard University professor and the future United Nations diplomat Ralph Bunche, who passed through en route to Africa. These and others, including Lady Simon's colleague, the Anti-Slavery Society leader John Harris, came to form the International Friends of Ethiopia and the African Friends Service Bureau. They collaborated with the former suffrage leader Sylvia Pankhurst, whose publication, the *Ethiopian Times and Orient Review* was a central organ of the opposition to Mussolini's October 1935 invasion of Abyssinia (Ethiopia). Addis Ababa fell in May of 1936, and this group welcomed Haile Selassie in his London exile. Padmore struggled to redefine his political project in the light of the Soviet Union's decision to enter the League of Nations and Soviet oil deals with Mussolini, spending the period just before the war as a crack journalist writing for the African American press and serving as an editor of the ILP newspaper the *New Leader.* Padmore remained an important advocate for anticolonial oppositionists throughout the empire.

Padmore's 1950s memoir *Pan-Africanism or Communism?* acknowledges Lady Simon's earlier work on behalf of black people, dodging the Simons's views on Africa and British diplomacy.[6] John Simon was a key player in the negotiations with Mussolini that preceded Munich, and an architect of the final summit. He and Lady Simon were both antislavery advocates, and she enjoyed an avid correspondence with Du Bois and visits from American NAACP leaders. For years, the Italian antislavery society had also corresponded with Simon and her colleagues. The British antislavery forces, critics of Abyssinian involvement in slavery, monitored Italy's desire to occupy Ethiopia, some vesting hopes in Mussolini as a reformer in Africa. Though Emperor Haile Selassie had vowed to curb the warlords' traffic in human life, Mussolini's army sought to enforce a more resolute ban on slavery, simultaneously exploiting other forms of coerced labor after their victory in 1935. During the fascist subjugation of the only independent state in Africa apart from Liberia, the cause of "antislavery" continued to serve as a pretext for British support of Mussolini, allowing the Simons's mutual interests to converge.

In the months before Munich, some in the British political community proposed that land in the empire could be swapped for peace. This activated Padmore and many other commentators including Willi Münzenberg's friend Jawaharlal Nehru. Former British Foreign and Colonial Office appointees Reginald Bridgeman and Leonard Barnes also protested against this notion, and the Independent MP Eleanor Rathbone spoke out against "colonial transfers." Indian activists decried the implied compromise of their fight for independence against the backdrop of a decade of British attempts at co-option, prosecutions, imprisonment, and the harsh treatment of strikes in India, occurring during the years of the Civil Disobedience movement and the proliferation of other forms of Indian political activity. In the late 1920s Sir John Simon had led the all-white Simon Commission to India, encountering repeated protests; Nehru was struck by the police while he demonstrated against Simon. The

Commission's attempt to promulgate an agenda of imperially governed "home rule" was followed in 1932 by the Round Table discussions in London attended by Gandhi and other dignitaries.

In this context, the British conducted a major trial for treason in India, rounding up thirty-one activists of diverse political backgrounds and imprisoning them at Meerut, a garrison town northeast of Delhi. The militants, organizers, and trade union leaders, including three white British communist agents, were seized in raids at their homes just after the fledgling Indian communist party was implicated in a large textile strike in Bombay and other cities. The Meerut Trial and its appeals, lasting from 1929 to 1932, constituted the largest and costliest treason prosecution in British imperial history. Meerut became a western cause célèbre, with Münzenberg, Padmore, and hundreds of others organizing Scottsboro protests that linked the Alabama case with the Meerut case, and demanding freedom for all on a global scale.

A leading metropolitan spokesman for the Meerut cause in Britain was the former MP for the South London borough of Battersea, Shapurji Saklatvala. Born in 1874 to the wealthy Parsi elite, his mother a member of the powerful family of Tata, Saklatvala abandoned his family's chosen career in order to become a socialist, after experiencing racism in India and seeing London's poverty firsthand. Before World War I he worked with Sylvia Pankhurst in the suffrage movement, eventually joining the British communist party. He was an unabashed parliamentary critic of British India and an orthodox communist who idealized the Transcaucasian republics of the Soviet Union. An anticolonialist who took exception to many forms of nationalism, Saklatvala voiced commitments that were common among Indians of the communist left. In the era of the First World War a variety of Indian activists with Comintern affiliations operated out of Berlin, among them Virendranath "Chatto" Chattopadhyaya and his American companion, the writer Agnes Smedley. The Ghadr Party of exiled Indian revolutionaries was based in San Francisco.

Saklatvala was among those who greeted Ada Wright when she came to London in 1932, and he saw her again at the international Amsterdam Anti-War Congress that August. He harbored private views of British communism's failures with persons and communities of color that lay unremarked in archival documents in Moscow for more than half a century after his death in 1936, though his last public writings hinted at his frustrations with internal party racial attitudes. Three years before, he had rallied Londoners to the cause of the staged "Reichstag Fire Trial" that challenged the Nazi persecution of three defendants on trial in Leipzig for setting fire to the German parliament building in 1933. In this "mock" trial, he and others represented a vital link between opposition to empire and opposition to fascism.

The deep repression aimed explicitly at the broad left in Germany, and then in much greater and overwhelming numbers at the Jews of Europe, took on new force with Hitler's assumption of power in 1933. Willi Münzenberg, still an important German communist leader and propagandist extraordinaire at the time of the Nazi coup, fled Germany with his wife Babette Gross and made his way to Paris, like many others on the left. Some chose the Saarbrücken as their first destination, which was then a supervised mandate under Versailles, and still others chose Prague. As the next years passed, the three safe havens for members of the German left, many among them Jewish, all proved to be danger zones of surveillance and assassination, and eventual pickup points for the journey to the camps of the Reich. Münzenberg and Gross sought the company of other exiled communists and socialists including their fast friend the Hungarian journalist Arthur Koestler, writer Manès Sperber, and communist organizer Otto Katz. Münzenberg made two trips to Moscow from Paris and continued to report to Comintern authorities while remaining close to many former Bolshevik leaders, his oldest comrades, in the Soviet Union. On a visit made from Paris, he and Gross visited a labor camp near Moscow whose conditions Gross recalled as shocking. The Germans, like many other exiles from India, China, and across Europe, believed that Moscow was another safe haven. Gross's brother-in-law and the exiled Indian Chattopadhyaya, were among those who died in the Gulag.

As the repression intensified in Germany, thousands of Germans and Austrians also fled to London. The numbers of those in Britain grew from a few thousand in the earlier years, to 80,000 at the War's outset. Ninety percent of refugees who fled Nazi Germany for Britain were German-Jewish in background. Their numbers swelled after the British authorities lifted tight emigration restrictions in the wake of *Kristallnacht*.[7] In the mock "Reichstag Fire Trial," those whom the Nazis had accused of setting fire to the Reichstag were "tried" in a mock legal proceeding held in the Law Society offices off the Strand, despite Sir John Simon's efforts as foreign secretary to thwart its opening. None other than Münzenberg, Koestler, and their followers in Paris planned the events in cooperation with their British contacts and supporters, prominent among them the former British naval commander and radical Lord Marley, the communist film maker Ivor Montagu, and the Labour MP Ellen Wilkinson. Among the "judges" serving was the attorney Arthur Garfield Hays, an American who had worked with Clarence Darrow in the Scopes trial in Tennessee and who had attended one of a series of European Pan-African Congresses. The mock trial was the occasion for Münzenberg to publish, with British assistance, *The Brown Book of the Hitler Terror*, despite all its factual errors the most important early exposé of Nazi policy, including the brutal racial policies of the Reich.[8] After the publication of *The Brown Book*, the irrepressible Münzenberg continued to pursue various alliances in Paris that raised suspicions in Moscow, and to lead the World Committee of the Victims of German Fascism, which had an American affiliate. Much larger Jewish relief organizations sprang up almost immediately in Britain, and as more and more Jews and other central Europeans streamed into London, refugee work overwhelmed the organizations drawn from the religious and cultural communities as well as those allied to secular activist organizations in the political community. Münzenberg led a small fraction of this work from afar, and in 1934, the Comintern took action to undermine him during an absence from Paris; this last effort led to his resignation and expulsion from the Comintern, though he departed in a less-assured and principled way than Padmore. His most trusted confidants in Moscow were executed over the next few years. He had no defender left, and his doubts about Stalinism increased accordingly and persuasively.

Münzenberg and his intimates briefly published an independent German language paper *Die Zukunft* in Paris, which developed wide-ranging contacts, its pursuit of readers extending to Churchill's inner circle and the liberal personnel of the Roosevelt administration in Washington. The paper's galaxy of contributors from the three major British political parties bore testament to Münzenberg's zeal just before the outbreak of war. Across the channel in London, those who had started out organizing around Scottsboro, with the American racial divide at the heart of their complaint, now spent endless and anxious days finding shelter and work permits for Europeans streaming across the waters caught in the conundra of the murderous racial politics of the Nazi regime. After 1934, Scottsboro all but disappeared from the scene in the face of the enormity of fascism's imposition; for many, there were simply not enough hours in the day, nor enough will to connect all the issues resolutely. Global conditions overwhelmed the transatlantic sensibility. When Nehru came to London in 1938 he spoke at a rally of the Left Book Club to a room of three thousand. "No true anti-Fascist could ignore imperialism, as some of them tried to do."[9] Munich lay just ahead.

The reader new to the thirties may wonder whether historians have attacked these questions before. Wide and separate if not equally known histories, hail one another from across many divides. This narrative leaps across barriers, asking that the approaches of each academic literature shed new light on the thirties *in ensemble*, irreverently asserting the connections among "independent" lines of historical inquiry. In order to answer the questions it asks, these disparate kinds of histories must come together, give up ground, and accept facts in order to reconsider the shape of the era. Conventional explorations of politics and diplomacy, and the biographies and memoirs of statesmen are essential to its substance, yet each genre is inattentive to racial politics, treating these politics as foreign and secondary to the central events. Prime Minister Gordon Brown's biography of the ILP leader James Maxton never mentions Maxton's colleague Padmore, to cite one instance among many.[10] The history of anti-imperialism, including venerable studies of opposition to imperial rule in the colonial settings and territories,[11] overlaps with a fluid "Black British" canon that encompasses many postcolonial, diaspora, and subaltern studies works that are related to movements in disciplines other than history, especially in the social sciences and literature.[12] African American studies and new kinds of Southern American history have contributed to the pioneering work on the Scottsboro case and its subsequent interpretations.[13]

This book also engages the discordant new histories of communism.[14] Its archival base includes Comintern sources recently investigated by non-Russian scholars. Studies of communist practices and beliefs emphasize the specificity of local and national experience and seek to define "Stalinism" in a variety of complex ways, some judging the development of popular communist activism without assuming either absolute top-down control from Moscow, or the possibility of complete autonomy for external communist parties, while others examine domestic events through a new lens.[15] Three of the five central figures of this book were elite communist cadre; they were not rank and file activists, but leaders. They made conscious choices about how to respond to the practices and culture of the Comintern and the national parties and international organizations in which they participated, and possessed broad and detailed knowledge of these practices, both internal and external.

Those new communist histories that revolve around the "revelations" that national and local parties had funds from Moscow simply restate the problem without addressing it, alighting on a plain already occupied in the 1930s. Playwright George Bernard Shaw, in some respects a Soviet sympathizer, wrote to ILP leader Fenner Brockway in 1933. "The Communist Party made the grave tactical mistake of affirming the international character of the Socialist principle by accepting money from a foreign Government and placing itself under its direction."[16] The question of whether external communist parties allied themselves with and were directed and funded by Moscow begs the more pressing question of what the parties did or did not do as a consequence. At a time when the quantity and detail of Stalinist practices in the Soviet Union and externally are matters of new historical reconstruction, historians are also gathering testimony from those who were teenagers and young adults in the thirties; their recollections can be juxtaposed with a fuller documentary historical record.[17]

As the history of the Scottsboro case bears out, there was significant doubt surrounding the Communist call to aid the cause of racial justice in the 1930s. The skeptics included the critic George Schuyler, whose column in the African American *Pittsburgh Courier*, saluted Padmore, proclaiming in 1934: "The Negro seems to be the Communist Jonah. Whenever carrying him along proves burdensome or embarrassing, the Reds can always be depended upon to throw him overboard to the sharks." A month later, Schuyler wrote candidly of the "few hundred thousand political prisoners in Siberia."[18] In the context of a Soviet foreign policy that sought Western allies, the profound NKVD repression, and the forced collectivization of Russian agriculture, the Comintern increasingly failed to sustain an antiracist and anti-imperialist stance on a global scale. Paradoxically, those ideas passé in Moscow attracted many individuals to communist banners and membership in the West, at least for a few months or years of the thirties, serving as deterrents to criticism of the Soviet Union on other grounds, as if to contend that one could exonerate the Kremlin's domestic policy in the light of Soviet and Comintern posturing about the injustices of the British Empire and the abuses of Jim Crow.

The hierarchical, meritocractic post-Bolshevik Soviet elite could appeal to mandarin British sensibilities like those of Fabian Society founders and Labour party strategists Beatrice and Sidney Webb, or liberals like Eleanor Rathbone, who intermittently contributed to popular-front and coalition endeavors under communist sponsorship, including the early Scottsboro campaign.[19] From African American writer Langston Hughes to Scots writer Naomi Mitchison, dozens of well-disposed fellow travelers and the curious were wined and hosted in the USSR. Even when returning visitors and political opponents voiced complaints about observed and documented Soviet conditions and policies, many found the West so wanting that they pushed aside the realities of the Comintern and Kremlin practices, otherwise engaged. Padmore and Nehru were not alone in condemning imperialism and fascism in the same breath. While some saw this language as propping up Stalin or Hitler by refusing to rank the evils, others saw it as the appropriate mode in which to discuss Roosevelt, Churchill, Neville Chamberlain, or Édouard Daladier—as handmaidens to fascism in their roles as perpetrators of imperialism. The coming war's deepest challenges and most profound atrocities knew few clairvoyants, though Padmore arrestingly described the fascists in 1937 as "planning to make a holocaust of humanity."[20] The portrayal of the multiplicity of political voices of the thirties is consigned to Caribbean, Indian, African, and African American specialists; Holocaust studies brilliantly marks out its own terrain. "Never the twain shall meet," yet one hopes for better as the new archival openings that inform this book are more deeply plumbed and as older collections are newly interrogated. A conceptual leap is also required. This is not compensatory history, but instead a drive for a deeper understanding of the origins of the global dilemmas of twenty-first-century life.

Death followed quickly for many portrayed here in their last vital years of unceasing energy. Their ambitions are most often associated with a later period, if with Britain and Europe at all. Mention of the civil rights movement and the era of national independence and Third World liberation—years of the "decline of Empire" and "decolonization"—connote the postwar era, the starting gate for the great sea change in racial politics that marked the ensuing decades.[21] These postwar histories should not be disentangled from the interwar era. Racial politics as a category of inquiry allows for new understandings of the bedrock history of Britain and its global relationships in the years before the war that in turn inform and broaden understandings of what came next.

The monstrous global economic crisis of the 1930s, like the cinematic terror King Kong, seemed determined to thrust humankind into oblivion. Nothing but a global solution could stop the monster and yet, no single solution arose.[22]

Instead, individuals and groups, nations and "races" competed to lead different kinds of battles. Some leaped toward fascism or entered the blind alleys of Stalinism. Others were lost on side roads to peace, socialism, and world unity that defied realpolitik. This tale of contest can be told as a story of the triumph of democratic will over racial hatred. In that version, when the Allied armies landed at Normandy and the bombs dropped over Japan, a new era of freedom began. In 1989 this freedom was extended to most of the world as the statues of Lenin tumbled. Yet injustices persisted. Did they not constitute an inheritance of the years before the war?

A different story, the one told here, pauses instead to lighten the pathways traveled in the 1930s, searching for elusive figures and lost words. The fears and predicaments of the world after the second global war were visible in the years immediately before it. Clues have been overlooked. One can begin in the metropolitan center that ruled an empire, in whose streets walked the characters of this book, even as Samuel Pepys and Dr. Johnson had: *London before the Blitz*, before the *Luftwaffe*. Another starting point is the very poor African American community at the foot of Lookout Mountain in the verdant, towering reaches of the Tennessee Smokies, in a city whose textile mills and train yards cluttered landscapes and townscapes whose names came from their first inhabitants, the city's own name the Native American word for the towering mountain above—*Chattanooga seventy years after slavery*.

The misunderstood origins of these southern American "Indians" suggest a third starting point in a second city of textile mills, a harbor of merchant vessels, and a port of departure for young aspirants who as subjects of the Crown made their way to London at the start of the new twentieth century, some hoping to change the world and others their fortunes to seek: *Bombay before Independence and Partition*. Another harbor appeared—one could gaze from it upon the splendor of the Chrysler building and find Armstrong and Ellington in midtown and uptown. Union Square witnessed red flags flying: *New York City before the civil rights movement*. One could take a ship along the coast to the Antilles, striking southeast to Port of Spain: *Trinidad one hundred years after Emancipation*. Ships from here headed back to the imperial metropolis across the Atlantic—to the "Mother Country."

From London, still more ships sailed back down the ocean crossings to Cape Town, and from there, trains ran haphazardly north. Some reached Lake Victoria, and still others, Addis: *Africa after Versailles*. From the northern coast of the continent one could cross the sea, departing from one region of "metropolitan France" for Paris. From here, tracks stretched west to Freidrichstrasse: *Berlin during Weimar, after the failed German revolution and before the Nuremburg Laws*. Still more trains traveled farther east to redbrick towers and Byzantine domes that adorned buildings that had been converted to washrooms and dining halls: *Moscow in the age of the Comintern*. Back across tracks that lay very far west were the Pyrenees and on the other side, the Republic: *Spain before the battle of Madrid.* Beyond the plains was the Atlantic again, and across it North America. More train lines stretched from Chicago to New Orleans; trains traveled across northern Alabama and on to Memphis in April of 1931. Here in the tiny mountain town of Paint Rock—just a railroad crossing in what was once a "slave state"—begins *this* story of the 1930s.

Chapter 1

ADA WRIGHT AND SCOTTSBORO

Camptown Races
De Camptown ladies sing dis song—Doodah, Doo-dah!
De Camptown Race-track five miles long—Oh, doodah-day!
I come down dah wid my hat cav'd in—Doodah, Doo-dah!
I go back home wid a pocket full ob tin—Oh, doodah-day!
Gwine to run all night! Gwine to run all day.
I'll bet my money on de bobtail nag—Somebody
bet on de bay . . .

I'se Gwine Back to Dixie
I'se gwine back to Dixie.
No more I'se gwine to wander;
My heart's turned back to Dixie,
I can't stay here no longer,
I miss de old plantation.
My home and my relation.
My heart's turned back to Dixie.
And I must go
—*The Labour Party Songbook: Everyday Songs for Labour Festivals*

****

Doo-Dah-Day
We march along with a merry song,
Doodah, Doodah
We-re all going strong and we shan't be long.
Doodle, doodle, doo-dah-day
We're out to see that an end shall be
Doodah, Doodah,
Of poverty and tyranny,
Doodle, doodle doo-dah-day.

Going to work all night,
Going to work all day,
Till the profit system's all washed up,
Doodle, doodle doo-dah-day.
—*Workers' Music Association*

PRELUDE: FELLOW TRAVELERS

The British press of the 1930s often carried news of Southern lynchings. Dramatic tales of racial violence across the Atlantic appeared on breakfast tables and Jim Crow hovered over tea breaks. African American servicemen who came to Europe during the Great War offered the English a glimpse of organized segregation, and after the war a growing stream of African American travelers passed through London. Ivan H. Browning, London stringer for the *Chicago Defender* enthused, "The West End will look like Harlem for a hot minute. Americans always attract immediate attention, much more than other Colored people, and as the different ones stroll in and around town they are not exactly laughed at but looked at with great curiosity. I have enjoyed so very much lately seeing so many of my people."[1] British travelers below the Mason-Dixon Line wrote in turn of their American encounters with sharecroppers, miners and shoe shine "boys"—the word used by whites to address black men of any age. The British *Labour Songbook* excerpted above boasted "Old Folks at Home," "Old Black Joe," "Camptown Races," and "I'se Gwine Back to Dixie" along with Eugene Pottier's "The Internationale," while the communist version of "Camptown Races" that appears below it, proletarianized and cleansed the wording, leaving in "Doo-dah" for good measure. These songs casually nurtured versions of a "plantation stereotype," identified and defined by African American writer James Weldon Johnson, and revisited by Alain Locke in Nancy Cunard's 1934 anthology, *Negro*.[2]

In April 1931, a month after the Scottsboro case began, King George V and Queen Mary attended a royal command music hall performance at the London Palladium that featured black-faced minstrels Alexander and Mose. In the royal party was the U.S. ambassador's wife, Mrs. Charles Gates Dawes, whose husband was the recipient of the 1926 Nobel Peace Prize and a key figure in the reparations politics of interwar Germany and the League of Nations, and the Earl of Athlone, recently back from serving as governor-general of South Africa.[3] One did not have to be a Labour party member to hum the *Camptown Races*, which appeared on the bill that night. A 1930s radical took political exception to the lyrics and replaced them with the version that appears above, retaining the crucial refrain "Doo-dah," a rejoinder meant to capture African American dialect, and part of the dominant version of the song heard in childhood, when the new lyricist was not likely to have been a communist. The tune remained, signifying racial assumptions and racial attitudes. Many other forms of discrimination existed. In 1932, the year that Scottsboro Mother Ada Wright came to Britain, a color bar was imposed on the British Empire heavyweight championship, stipulating that contenders must be "born of white parents."[4]

Labour MP Jennie Lee wrote of her trip to the American South that year, in the *New Leader*. She later recalled the era. "Long before my time labour notables,

Figure 1.1. "At the Palladium" (London). Ivy Anderson (1905–1949) singing with Duke Ellington in May, 1933, on the Duke's first trip to England, a two-week engagement with drummer/bassist Max Miller from Chicago. The Prince of Wales, the future Edward VIII, attended Ellington's run. Anderson is regarded as Ellington's best vocalist; she appeared with him from 1931 to 1942 (Frank Driggs/GettyImages).

large and small, had established a regular trade route between Great Britain and the States."[5] She remarked on "the vast and politically incoherent American scene" in an English vernacular, identifying "settlers" rather than farmers, and "missionaries" rather than evangelists.

It is a very pleasant experience to stumble backwards into summer, and doubly luxurious against an unfamiliar background of cotton and tobacco plantations, smiling darkies, and a skyline of picturesque forest land. . . . even in the most trivial matters strict separation of the two races is rigidly maintained. . . . The passing stranger cannot hope to form any reliable opinion regarding the relative capacities of the white and colored children, but a white settler . . . originally a missionary teacher . . . [gave] as his serious opinion that the colored children are quite as intelligent as those of his own race. . . . the negro is an easy-going fellow, not inclined to trouble so long as he has enough to eat and is not too brutally overworked and has plenty of sunshine.[6]

Lee observed " . . . the colored people with their unaffected ways and their quick laughter and their brown skins and their plentiful picaninnies and their voice and their songs. And, tying us in close fraternity, the pathos of their tentative first efforts to organize industrial unions." She remembered a man presiding at a meeting after a union official was killed as "an Old Uncle Tom himself—just as I had pictured him in my children's story book."[7] British writer Sylvia Townsend Warner, another of the Southern travelers in the thirties, wrote for the *New Statesman and Nation* about her trip to research Appalachian folk songs. "The quality of the tunes shows no variation, save a natural fragmentariness of the jogs, and in the hymns a degeneration into something akin to the pious *fol-de-rol* of the negro spiritual."[8]

Scots writer Naomi Mitchison entered the American racial scene in another way, on an extensive Fabian Society trip to the Soviet Union in 1932. She approached two African American travelers whose group met hers.

> I took my courage in both hands and went up to a table where two of the colored people were, one quite dark and one lighter. . . . They were more charming and cultured and more generally sympathetic than I can well express. I hadn't talked books and highbrows to anyone with much of a point of view for some weeks, and I enjoyed it. But they were also politically and socially solid and sure of their ground in a way that few English highbrows are. And they were gentle and friendly, and yet with a certain good toughness, just as the Russians are.

Although Mitchison did not identify her companion in conversation, the writer Loren Miller was traveling with Langston Hughes.[9] They spoke of writers John Dos Passos and Edna St. Vincent Millay.

> I discovered that the other one was Langstone [*sic*] Hughes, whom I knew by name (as they knew me). He was pleased at being recognized at all, I think; they both purred quite a lot when one was nice to them. They talked a good deal about the Scottsboro case and said nobody would have heard about it—they themselves [would have paid] little attention to it, thinking it was only one more injustice out of a hundred—if the local Communists hadn't taken it up. They also told about traveling across the States in a Ford car, how they'd tried ordinary restaurants, and the general attitude of the proprietors had been "Get out, you ought to know better!" I said it seemed to me quite impossible—it really does—but I found out that one of the American parties had refused to eat in the same dining room with them here! I can honestly say that I feel no color antagonism at all, if anything a slightly romantic feeling toward them, because they have so lately been slaves, and are still terribly oppressed. I went up to their room afterwards, while they packed, and we talked, and Hughes gave me a copy of his Scottsborough poem, which is not very good as a poem (though not bad at all) but which must have made a fine thing when acted. Something rather awful has occurred to me! I believe there is a party of Indian students in Moscow. Would I—could I—have felt so friendly towards them? Would I have found them so sympathetic? Could I have said honestly that I felt no color bar? If not, why not? Can there possibly be an ECONOMIC reason?[10]

The decade was marked by a literary curiosity about African American habits and rituals in the face of continuing racial violence. "Negroes" might be benevolently portrayed as incapable of concerted action and undeserving of brutal punishment, but for the fellow traveler like Mitchison the intellectual Negro was an amiable, momentary, and reassuring companion. The week that Ada Wright arrived in Britain to plead the case of her sons, the papers gave pride of place to the murder of the rogue lover of a prominent socialite, Thomas William Scott Stephen. His assailant was his mistress, twenty-seven-year-old Mrs. Dolores Elvira Barney, daughter of Sir John and Lady Mullens.[11] Mrs. Barney and Wright appeared very near one another on the news pages in the summer of 1932. In the case of Mrs. Barney, who claimed the gun had fired accidentally, the London courts were generous and she was let off, risking the disappointment of a spellbound public, and earning her the communist press label of "wealthy parasite."[12] Mrs. Wright's sons faced harder luck.

THE SCOTTSBORO CASE

On March 25, 1931, the journey of nine black youngsters who boarded a train at the rail center of Chattanooga, Tennessee, in the Smokey Mountains, came to an abrupt halt at the station in Paint Rock, whose location in the Alabama hill country across the Tennessee line would forever mistakenly cast the defendants as Alabama residents.[13] Despite its location deep in the Bible Belt, most travelers would have called it "godforsaken," and so it must have appeared to the forlorn group of young men whose only blessing that night was not being lynched. Instead, they were taken by truck to Scottsboro. The inhabitants of the poor mountain towns suffered the deprivations of the Depression, their racial prejudices in part an inheritance of the American Civil War, a conflict that had ended less than seventy years earlier and in some respects in name only.

A series of trials in Scottsboro led within sixteen days to all but one of the defendants, the youngest—Leroy Wright—being convicted of capital offenses, and their execution date set for July 10, 1931. They were pronounced guilty of raping two white women found on the train dressed as male hobos, who had accused the youngsters only after a pointed talk with the local authorities. It was illegal to ride the rails without a ticket, and the defendants' supporters would always claim that the whites, Ruby Bates and Victoria Price, had "been bulldozed" into the accusations.[14] A group of white male vagrants thrown off their rail gondola at an earlier point that night had alerted the local police to the presence of the black youths. It later transpired that a melee had occurred on the train as it passed down the line toward Memphis. Someone stepped on a white youth's hand and he was hurled from the train in the fight. Why such an episode had not led to lynching remains a matter of speculation. Chattanooga historian James Livingood attested that a 1906 experience with federal roundups of local sheriffs who let a black defendant in a rape case go to his death at the hand of a mob on the Walnut Street bridge in Chattanooga, and the local memory of jail terms up in Washington had spread fear in the region of further

reprisals from the "Feds," serving as a deterrent to violence that would otherwise have been routine.[15]

The nine Scottsboro defendants included brothers Roy and Andy Wright
and their fellow Chattanoogans Eugene Williams and Haywood Patterson.
They hailed from a city with a large, stratified African American community
whose brick churches, separate YMCA's, black medical institutions, philan-
thropic groups, educational facilities, and traditions of self-organization grew
up in the midst of widespread unemployment and deep poverty. Those defendants who were from Chattanooga were not from families prominent in this
milieu, but in the small-city atmosphere their relatives did not remain unknown to most African Americans for very long.[16] The Georgians among the
defendants were strangers to one another; each had slipped across the northern
border of his home state to Chattanooga—the largest rail center in proximity to
Atlanta. They were Ozie Powell, Clarence Norris, Olen Montgomery (partially
blind), Charlie Weems, and Willie Roberson, who had syphilis. The accused
had Southern lawyers during the first set of trials held in Scottsboro in 1931,
sixty miles from Chattanooga. Their first, Stephen Roddy, an incompetent with
a Ku Klux Klan record, was hired by the black Interdenominational Minsters'
Alliance. An International Labor Defense (ILD) lawyer later stated that Roddy
was given to the ministers by a crooked black city politician, W. M. James.[17]

Chattanooga remained the center of family activity on the defendants' behalf. The widowed mother of Roy and Andy Wright was quickly approached by
the regional communist party headquartered there, the Tennessee border city
being a safer town for communist activity than Birmingham; it boasted a significant Jewish population that included the family of Adolph Ochs who owned
two newspapers—the *Chattanooga Times* and its celebrated northern cousin,
the *New York Times*.[18] Chattanooga had a history of labor organizing in the
midst of Klan and segregationist violence and was the American Communist
Party's (CPUSA) "best foothold in the South."[19] In 1930 the communists held a
conference there of its front, the Trade Union Unity League, and five or six
hundred people reportedly came to the odd demonstration or public meeting
called in the city. Yet that summer, the district CPUSA organizer, Tom Johnson, wrote candidly to the distant New York leadership of the party. "Our forces
here in general altho all good comrades and hard workers, are hardly experienced enough for the tasks set them." It was tough to cover Tennessee, Georgia,
and Alabama from a base in Chattanooga, and "impossible to handle the three
states in this district on thirty dollars per week without a car," especially when
the regional communist paper *Southern Worker* was also published and distributed from the city.[20] Johnson had just been released from jail after an arrest
for vagrancy. In July he wrote to New York, "We must get guns at once. This is
no joke but might turn out to be a life or death matter to us. . . . we might have
to leave town ahead of a lynch mob."[21] And when arrests came in the region,
legal help was slim. Johnson wrote of a sympathetic attorney named Rosenthal,

Figure 1.2. "The Scottsboro' Boys in Decatur Jail. Left to right (standing): Clarence Norris, Ozie Powell (now seriously ill after being shot in the head by a guard), Haywood Patterson, Roy Wright, Charlie Weems, Eugene Williams. Sitting: Andy Wright, Olin [*sic*] Montgomery, Willie Roberson." This photo taken in Decatur, Alabama, appeared in the ILP's *New Leader*, April 12, 1935, with an article entitled "The Scottsboro Negroes: They Must Be Saved" (reproduced by kind permission of the Syndics of Cambridge University Library).

that it was "impossible to get another man in Birmingham who is worth a whoop in hell to take our cases."[22]

Johnson was picked up by a car of plainclothes officers who drove him from a demonstration to the city line of Birmingham, stripped him, dumped him, and told him that if he set foot in the city again, he was a dead man. He crawled naked, to uncertain safety.[23] It was so risky for the women communist organizers, green and from the North, to live among African Americans, that they had to make their homes separately lest a black man suffer the consequences of being seen with them in the segregated and impoverished no-go zones of the African American neighborhoods. In 1932 with the case already in full swing, comrade Martha Hall wrote despairingly to the central committee in New York: "It is difficult for a woman to work among negro workers in the South, because of their fear of being framed. I do not think it impossible, but it is certainly much more difficult for a woman."[24]

Fears of miscegenation and opposition to any type of mixed company resonated that night in Paint Rock, providing a pretext for the defendants' accusers, the found "hoboes" Ruby Bates and Victoria Price, to cut a deal. The defense lawyers and the campaign organizers described them as "prostitutes" in a professional sense, but Price and Bates were ordinary, largely unemployed mill workers, who had occasionally taken cash from male companions with whom they enjoyed an evening out. In keeping with new Comintern doctrine that emphasized the Negro's plight and centrality to its causes, the communist party was quick to respond to the case.[25] Its persistent legal counsel team, first represented in a visit to the defendants in the Birmingham jail by prominent left attorney Joseph Brodsky, necessarily caught the interest of the defendants' families. Lawyers Allen Taub and Lowell Wakefield reported to New York on their progress: "On our instructions all families have been visited and welcome our coming into the case."[26] Tom Johnson struggled with the national leadership to soften the algebraic language of party slogans, urging them to recognize the need to establish their clients' innocence and to acknowledge the white poverty and ignorance of the region, rather than to paint an illusory portrait of the context in which the defendants found themselves. Johnson directed his venom at Southern elites: "The white landlords and bosses care nothing for the protection of the 'virtue of white women' but this is an excuse to incite racial hatred."[27]

The less radical NAACP, whose national African American membership far outnumbered black communists, initially held back indecisively from the case after attempting to compete for the attention of the families. National field secretary William Pickens pulled no punches in reporting what he had seen in the South: "Now as to those parents and relatives—and maybe this will make you think like lying down and quitting. They are the densest and dumbest animals it has yet been my privilege to meet. But I have been exceedingly patient. . . . I told them of the peril [of the communist ILD]." But to Pickens's dismay, the parents again fell under the sway of his rivals: "I went straight up into the apartments [of defendant Eugene Williams's family], a sort of slave-pen row. . . . The red who was leading them away did not dare even look in my direction. . . . Have you ever in your life seen dumb cattle so hopelessly entrapped?"[28] After charging that the ILD brought imposter Scottsboro mothers to campaign events in various parts of the country, and wrangling repeatedly with the defendants over their clear choice of the ILD as their legal arm, the NAACP begrudgingly stood back from the case in dissent until December 1935, continuing through the early years of the campaign to presume that a communist defense meant death for the defendants.

A GLOBAL DEFENSE CAMPAIGN

As the legal defense achieved initial stays of execution for the defendants, a massive international defense campaign led by the communists grew, and its American arm in concert with their European supporters persuaded Ada Wright to come to Britain and Europe in 1932 to represent her sons. This campaign used several written languages and a host of spoken vernaculars as part of a universal attempt to free the defendants. Communist organizers reassigned the youths to a global struggle against "imperialism"—a word that the defendants had most likely never heard before the case; they had probably never heard of communists. Yet many hundreds of thousands—including the Russians who attended officially convened protests, demonstrated on their behalf. Ada Wright's visit to Britain was one episode of this extraordinary journey. Her reception there drew upon the legacy of the nineteenth-century antislavery movement. In Germany the propaganda message of the campaign relied upon the history of the American South. "Hers is a background of Negro slavery days in the U.S. . . . the right of the slave owner to murder his own slaves links him to the lynch murder today."[29] The left press echoed the coverage given by the establishment news services to racial violence in the South. The same lynching photographs of the era now so well known in the United States, and circulated as postcards and memorabilia, also made their way to British and European readers through the channels of the ILD and its fraternal organizations in Europe.[30]

George Padmore was editing the *Negro Worker* from Hamburg at the time of Wright's visit. In an essay entitled "Lynch Justice in America: Story of the Scottsboro Case," Padmore explained American ways: "As they are unable to provide themselves with railroad fare, the practice of 'stowing away' on freight trains is quite widespread . . . 'riding the rails.'" Padmore condemned the defense of "'Nordic superiority' and 'white womanhood'" by the Southern ruling class, admonishing, "Proletarians of Germany—form a red united front with your Negro class brothers in America in order to rescue these nine young workers from the electric chair. . . . [It is] time to show solidarity with your black and yellow brothers."[31]

International Workers' Aid, Willi Münzenberg's front, comprised of a group of nationally based mass organizations, assisted striking workers and their families, ran soup kitchens, and provided legal advice of the sort that had brought the communists to the aid of the Scottsboro families in the United States. Red Aid, the network of European affiliates of Russian Red Aid (MOPR) was a chief conduit of the Scottsboro campaign, whose advocates worked with and overlapped with Münzenberg's operations, and especially with the League against Imperialism (LAI).[32] Though the British communist movement was small and sectarian compared to most communist parties on the Continent, during the 1920s its front organization, the British International Labour Defense, claimed thousands of members and ran "class-war prisoners" campaigns with similar goals.[33] In 1930 the overarching Red Aid Secretariat, and the Münzenberg-led groupings in Europe, spoke in a language of assistance to those suffering.

> The Negro masses are beginning to awaken. In America they fight shoulder to shoulder with white workers in strikes and political demonstrations. In the black Colonies,

Figure 1.3. "Communist Meeting." Supporters of the League against Imperialism, Trafalgar Square, London, August 1, 1931. One sports a star, another, a hammer and sickle (GettyImages).

the revolutionary wave is rising even higher and growing ever more intense. . . . In East, West and South Africa the blood of the Negro masses has flowed in rivers. . . . In the United States, 36 horrific lynchings were carried out on Negroes in the first nine months of 1930.[34]

This organizational culture meant that an apparatus was in place to greet and escort Ada Wright. Demonstrations at U.S. embassies in Europe grew in number. In June 1931 protestors smashed windows at the U.S. embassy in Berlin.[35] The German response to Scottsboro was especially large and vocal. Despite the conflicts that many independent radicals and liberals had with organized communism and the Soviet state, Scottsboro protests began to spread globally, as if all the critics of Jim Crow America suddenly shouted with one voice, "reaching from California to Sydney, from Montreal to Cape Horn, from Shanghai to Buenos Aires."[36] Illinois congressman Oscar DePriest submitted a petition to President Herbert Hoover from Americans living in Paris in April 1932. The signatories included the American cabaret singer and salon hostess Ada Smith, known as Bricktop.

[I]n the name of JUSTICE, HUMANITY and FAIR PLAY . . . [we] humbly beseech you to use the influence of your high office and make intervention on behalf of these eight

American children. . . . how can the land of liberty tolerate legalized lynching? . . . how can [this] be countenanced by people who profess [the] religion of our Lord? . . . For an ALLEGED "rape" of two females of doubtful character in company with seven vagabonds in a box car. The disrespect for law caused by prohibition, the reign of bandits and the Lynch law cause us to hang our heads in shame when other nationals say that America, our America—the land of WASHINGTON and LINCOLN—is actually the most lawless and barbarous country on earth.[37]

Three days after DePriest forwarded the statement, the U.S. secretary of state received a report from his representative in Beirut stating that six or seven men passing the U.S. embassy in a car had hurled stones at its windows attached to handbills protesting against the Scottsboro verdicts and signed by the "Central Commission Assistant Committee of Syrian Reds."[38] In Latin America, supporters rallied in Mexico, Cuba, Panama, Chili, Peru, Argentina, and Uruguay. From its Moscow offices, International Red Aid continued to inspire its sections to work on Scottsboro and on the defense of the San Francisco socialist Tom Mooney, also falsely imprisoned and also represented by his mother. Mother Mooney toured with the Scottsboro mothers before her death.[39] In early 1932, the head of the U.S. legation in Riga, Latvia, monitoring Soviet developments, reported "the campaign carried on in Soviet Russia for the liberation of the Negro defendants is being conducted on a massive scale."[40] Many Scottsboro supporters, and Ada Wright herself, came to believe that the Soviets and all those who protested against the court decisions under communist influence altered the course of history and stayed the executions several times in the thirties. The extensive evidence of the campaign suggested that this was correct in many respects. The Scottsboro families' pragmatic attempts to adhere to the principles of the ILD and Red Aid, as explained to them, advanced from that assumption.

In the spring of 1932, when the American ILD proposed the tour of Europe to enhance the possibilities of raising funds there, Wright agreed to go, and spent some time in New York City under communist auspices, training for her journey through interventions in rival NAACP meetings in Harlem.[41] The Justice Department received news of her plans from an informer, W. J. Morris of Brooklyn, who recorded that the Comintern had declared May 7, 1932, a day for global Scottsboro demonstrations. Morris tipped the Department that ILD leader Louis Engdahl would accompany Wright; his expenses were to be paid by the Red Aid organization.[42] On May 2, 1932, U.S. ambassador Andrew Mellon refused to see a group of British Scottsboro petitioners in London.[43] The next day, the FBI notified State Department personnel abroad of the trip. "It is understood that L. Engdahl, National Secretary of the International Labor Defense of the International Red Aids, is going abroad with Ada Wright, mother of two of the convicted negroes, to take part in the demonstration, going first to Germany. It is stated that the demonstrations will be violent."[44]

ADA WRIGHT COMES TO EUROPE

Born in rural Tennessee close to 1890, and the granddaughter of a slave, Ada Wright was a domestic servant to a Chattanooga Irish American family of anti-slavery heritage, in whose employ she remained after the initial furor surrounding the case. She was a forceful, committed fighter for her sons, and a Primitive Baptist congregant with no political ties other than those prompted by the case.[45] Her sojourn with communism made a lasting impression; she was foisted onto a ship, taken across the ocean with the freedom of the decks that was denied her in her own country, moved by train across Europe in the days of the last great strike of Weimar Berlin, taken farther east into Moscow and throughout much of eastern and western Europe and the British Isles—all in order to serve as the authentication and personification of her sons' struggle. Still, she kept her own counsel and her religious devotion. She was her own person.

Wright and Louis Engdahl disembarked at Hamburg on May 7, 1932. They journeyed each day only at the pleasure of the authorities in the regions where their supporters engaged them. The trip was often uneasy. Ada Wright was soon recognized all over Germany "to the extent that on trains, in streetcars, and even on the public highways, the Negro mother, her likeness being made familiar by pictures and publicized everywhere, was continuously asked by those interested, 'What can we do to help?'" Thousands of German schoolchildren wrote letters to President Herbert Hoover. The Comintern's organizations in Germany boasted of their successes.

> This is the first time such a spokesman has come from America. . . . it is particularly fitting that a Negro Mother should have been the first to be invited to Europe by the German Red Aid, raising sharply the actual picture of class oppression and mass misery in the US against the usually accepted and rainbow-hued glories of "the land of prosperity and democracy."[46]

Despite this avowed popularity, Wright and Engdahl were often turned away from halls under legislation that barred agitators from addressing meetings. Not as much money was raised as the ILD had hoped—small wonder given the economic crisis—yet Engdahl was pressed to justify his trip by the European Red Aid comrades who said they would not pay his expenses as only Wright had been invited. Engdahl defended his presence: "As for Mrs. Wright, I am having her write her own statement, as best she can, stating her own viewpoint. My own opinion is that it would have been a catastrophe to have sent her alone," and she had admitted as much after the first day.[47] Throughout the journey, State Department informants continued to observe Wright's movements and filed reconnaissance reports to Washington. Government agents were not alone on Wright's trail. Engdahl reported that the NAACP's William Pickens and his wife had arrived in Germany by ship in order to shadow Mother Wright's tour.[48]

As the two proceeded through Europe, British Scottsboro supporters began to mobilize for her arrival there. The fledgling community of black radicals and their followers, among small and dispersed black and Asian communities in London, included several Indian organizations, colonial students' associations, and the politically moderate League of Coloured Peoples (LOCP) led by physician Harold Moody. Activists organized among black and Asian dockworkers in the British port towns and in East London. The communist-led Negro Welfare Association (NWA), and its Barbadian organizer Arnold Ward, were exceptional in their communist affiliation.[49] A 1930 internal Comintern memo to the British communist party (CPGB) mentioned the "most inexcusable passivity and neglect," characterizing what was termed Negro work, "especially when there are colonial outbursts." It suggested that the party was in need of a "campaign against white chauvinism," as in America. White members had denounced themselves in a ritualized, healing series of "trials," sometimes leading to expulsions, a step not taken in Britain. The memo affirmed the fight against "increasing discrimination in England," but apart from the waterfront, the party reported that there was no trade-union base for organizing black workers given their absence from the industrial workforce. Further, a band of reformists, including the Jamaican leader of the Negro Improvement Association, Marcus Garvey, who resided in London, were charged with "misleading" potential black recruits.[50] Ada Wright was a rare inspiration to action for the few black communist supporters who joined her on her ten-day British sojourn.

The activist and writer Nancy Cunard, an estranged member of the Cunard shipping-line family, visited the United States in May 1931, within weeks of the Scottsboro case breaking in Alabama, and met many personalities who figured in the wrangles and coalitions that constituted the campaign's defense front over the years to come. They included Walter White and William Pickens of the NAACP, and Langston Hughes and his fellow African American writer Countee Cullen.[51] In mid-July African American communist leader James Ford wrote to Padmore of his recent trip to Europe. Cunard was not entirely alone in pursuing black leaders. At a Geneva conference on forced labor, Ford had met a forty-five-year-old American, "a white woman from Liberia" who had been expelled from the troubled African nation in an intrigue involving her display of documents to a Russian. She wanted to get to the USSR to broadcast what she knew about forced labor over radio and was friendly with the political opposition in Liberia. "She pretends a great interest in the Scottsboro case, although she is not much interested in the Negro question in the USA. She is a clever woman and I am unable to fathom her purpose. . . . what should be done?" Ford thought she might be useful.[52] But Cunard proved to be more than a fleeting contact. She was not yet a major actor in the Scottsboro campaign, but she would befriend Padmore through her engagements with the circle to which he still belonged.

As the front of people working on Scottsboro began to take shape, Countee Cullen wrote to Walter White from Paris, where the communist campaign was beginning.

Dear Walter,

Thanks very much for your telegram and the letter explaining the Scottsboro case. There had been no news here until your telegram came. It may not please you, because of your troubles with the American communists, to know that I wanted the news for use by some communist friends here. They have been the only ones, as far as I know, who have shown an actual interest in the case here in France. I hope you don't mind my having given your communication to them.[53]

The London Friends' leader John Fletcher, also wrote to Walter White in his capacity as secretary of the "Joint Council to Promote Understanding between White and Coloured People in Britain," a Quaker group that included Harold Moody of the LOCP on its executive. Fletcher had seen a notice from White about the case. "So far nothing has appeared in our Press about it, but yesterday I learnt that the International Labour Defense people are talking about it a good deal amongst colored people and others in London." Fletcher asked that White send literature to him and to his friend Arnold Ward of Whitfield Street. "He is about the most influential of the resident Negroes in London. He is a working man but is very well informed and speaks in Hyde Park and other places on the Negro question. Indeed any information at any time that you can send to him will be used very well." White replied to Fletcher as if the NAACP's legal team was the only one working for the defendants. He indicated that he was already writing to Ward, making no mention of Ward's communist affiliations.[54]

London communists and their supporters successfully engaged organizations and associations across the metropolis to become interested in the campaign in the year leading to Wright's visit. They fanned out across London, obtaining signatures on petitions and protest letters that were sent to the American embassy. A group, including thirty-three MPs and the writer H. G. Wells, signed a letter opposing the death sentence as "apparently influenced by mob passion," and called for a retrial or appeal.[55] But the organizational conflicts that divided the U.S. campaign traveled to Britain in the mail packets. Harold Moody wrote to Walter White about the LOCP's association with the former Jamaican governor-general Lord Sydney Olivier—a figure whom the communists did not embrace.[56] Moody subsequently remarked upon White's published diatribe against the U.S. communist-led defense team.

I am instructed by my executive . . . to thank you most warmly for all your communication to hand including your excellent account in *Harper's Magazine*. We are watching with interest this case, and hope you will be successful in all your efforts on behalf of these unfortunate boys. . . . I will be sending to you in due course a report of Lord Olivier's address.[57]

The street activist Arnold Ward wrote to Padmore two weeks later in a dissenting mode, castigating a moderate South African trade unionist who was visiting London: "We got coming over here from South Africa men like Jabavu telling the British public He prefer British rule than any other invited to Lord and Lady Saunders and they were jumping around like a lot of nanny Goats no Manhood at all about them."[58] Ward found Sydney Olivier "disgruntling . . . telling grand things done for the Negroes in Jamaica."[59]

In 1932 Nancy Cunard returned to this London scene from abroad. Her arrival prompted J. S. Headley, a black seaman who spoke at Scottboro rallies and was an organizer for the NWA to write excitedly to Padmore:

Comrade, there is by the way a supposed countess who is here who is supposed to have some kind of interest in Negroes: whether it is Bourgois Liberalism or Humanitarianism or nor I do not know: but the fact is that she was here and her name is Nancy Cunard she is tall, thin, and is usually dressed in Red. She was present at the club recently, and also attended the protest that we held at 59 Cromer St. Her present address is Vignette, Tervuren, Belgium. Of course I cannot say for certain who she is, but I will ask Ward if he knows anything of her. I understand that she usually hangs out up town with the boys.[60]

In February 1932, on the same day that Langston Hughes visited the Scottsboro defendants in jail in Alabama, a 2,000-strong march from the Thames to Hyde Park dispatched a Scottsboro protest delegation to the U.S. embassy. The organizers read telegrams from India, Australia, and South Africa.[61] In April campaign supporters marched from Poplar and Bermondsey in East London, to the embassy. In Hamburg, as he prepared to travel to London to speak about the case in Poplar, East London, Padmore received word from the West African activist I.T.A. Wallace-Johnson of successful Scottsboro meetings in Lagos, Nigeria, where the *Negro Worker* had spread news of the case.[62] In Britain Cunard contributed a piece entitled "Black Injustice" to the journal *Everyman*, and appealed for funds in the pages of the *Daily Mirror*.[63] The Hull City Trades Council demanded the immediate release of the Scottsboro defendants, while the Battersea Cooperative Comrades' Circle resolved against "legal lynching," condemning what they termed an "attempt to create racial feelings, in an effort to break the growing solidarity of the Negro and white workers."[64]

In May 1932 Wright and Engdahl were still in their first days on the Continent. They laid wreaths in Altona, at the graves of those killed in antifascist demonstrations, and attended the conference of the International Union of Seaman and Harbor Workers at Hamburg, in which Padmore played a leading role. The Altona police supplied the American consul in Hamburg with the names of the American delegates: "Engdahl and Wright . . . are the subjects of the [Justice] Dept.'s telegraphic instructions of May 2, 1932." Wright spoke at the conference, but all traces of her vanished when she and Engdahl left for Cologne, giving those trailing them the slip. "Their trip to Cologne is believed to have been a blind, and . . . Mrs Wright returned to Hamburg."[65] Soon after, a Scottsboro demonstrator was killed in the industrial city of Chemnitz in Saxony.[66]

But in London, Ward reported that only five blacks marched on May Day, the largest demonstration Ward had seen.

> [F]or the last week the press here is giving plenty of publicity to Nancy Cunard. The Negroes are like a lot of lost dogs hoping that this rich white woman will deliver them out of <u>Bondage</u> a useless Godforsaken Bunch of Fools instead of coming in with us and help to raise some funds to help the woman in her endeavor in pushing the case to the State Supreme Court.

Padmore replied, still skeptical of Cunard: "By the way, I am sending you a Negro newspaper with news about Nancy—also a clipping from the *New York Times*. What's wrong with her? She certainly makes herself cheap with all this newspaper notoriety."[67]

Ward became more frustrated with black leaders outside of his own NWA group, as Wright's scheduled arrival date in Britain grew closer.

> [Adrian Cola] Rienzi must bring in his West Indian self-government and Federation twaddle. . . . You see the demerrara Tribune what Moody and Cinnamon [Sinanan] wrote what they did for the Scottsboro boys. Such damned liars. The Mother of one of the boys is coming over here . . . so they are all trying to make a good showing when she comes to say what they have done for Her son . . . how is the fight in America. Nancy wrote that [James] Ford is going South raising Hell with the cra[c]kers the fight I like to be in. . . . don't bother about Nancy. She is rich and don't know what to do with Herself.

Ward derided Jomo Kenyatta, then a student at LSE, as a traitor for passing materials to the Friends (despite Quaker John Fletcher's claim to be Ward's associate). Only James Maxton of the ILP received Ward's blessing because he had tried unsuccessfully to press the House of Commons to rescind a ban on the *Negro Worker* in the colonies.[68]

In June, the *New Leader* carried an account of Scottsboro by fellow traveler and former diplomat Reginald Bridgeman, who emphasized the corruption of the accusers and the guileless incompetence of the defendants. The communists' propaganda had not been lost on him; he stated that Ruby Bates and Victoria Price "were known to eke out their entirely insufficient wages by prostitution." Bridgeman cited material that referred to the accused as "little more than children" and twice quoted the kind of artifical dialect of statements popular in the campaign's publications: "Help us, boys. . . . we ain't done nothing wrong. We are only workers like you are. Only our skin is black." Bridgeman inserted a comma and turned the phrase into an appeal, rather than using the ungrammatical plural possessive—"help us boys"—with no intervening comma. "Help us, boys," was colloquial British usage, meaning "assist us, mates." If he had absorbed the original attempt at dialect at all, he did not wish to repeat it.[69]

Nancy Cunard became Ward's close associate. When she revisited New York, he wrote to Padmore of her movements.

> . . . receive a letter from Nancy very interesting. She has met a comrade from Jamaica an He wants to come here and work. She mention he is a very Capable Comrade member of the C.P. but he has no money—kind of comrade we want here . . . <u>Bob Lovell</u> the Secretary of the ILD was planning to have a big collection from Trafalgar Square [Scottsboro] meeting on Sunday . . . you see that is the reason He wanted to keep us in the background. But the forty thieves fell out and <u>Busted</u> Lovell head with an iron bar, man those fellows have not sent one penny to America for the Boys and I have address lots of meetings for them and appeal for funds and sold their pamphlets for them and turn in the money to them and that is what happens after Sunday I am finish with these people. I can say now our future look a little brighter after the Children's Outing [an annual NWA event for black youngsters] . . . we can laugh at them [Harold] Moody, [John Alexander] Barbour James, [Beresford] Gale and the whole lot of them. These white comrades women—[Carmel Haden] Guest, Hare and Birch are doing there best to make it a success. It is a shame but these people seems to do with us as they like, never mind old boy. Someday we will beat them.[70]

In a subsequent letter to James Ford in Hamburg, Ward further bemoaned the "political backwardness" of Negroes in Britain, stating that they needed advice on issues like insurance and housing. "Cruel" unemployment in the shipping industry was common. Only a single shipping line would take black workers below deck and only with an alien registration card, prejudicing other kinds of employers against them. British workers were ignorant of them and looked upon them as outsiders. Yet Ward experienced success with workers in his audiences at Hyde Park Corner and other venues.

> We can't find many Negroes who likes the platform for instance the Nine Negro Lads of Scottsborough [sic] Alabama. I could not get one Negro to come on the platform and speak on behalf of the Lads, and the Friends (the old Quakers) and Lady Simon from the Anti-Slave Aborigines Society with the [Charles Roden] Buxton and [Robert] Cecil that gang parading up and down the country as the Saviours of the Negro race these people like to see the Negroes in the background it does there business good . . . Kenyatta, Dr. Moody and Mr. Barber James these are the type of Negro leaders that is always at the people disposal and now comes the Elks with Mr. Gale makes it very difficult for us with the help of the CP or LAI to organize.[71]

Ward's frustrations did not abate.

MOTHER WRIGHT IN BRITAIN

The British government banned Louis Engdahl from entering Britain, allowing Ada Wright to visit unaccompanied. It was not a catastrophe. Wright's use of English was not that of her hosts, and they altered the renditions of her "quoted" words to suit their readers' usage, as those in other countries working in other languages had done. The trade unions, the Women's Cooperative Society, the communists, and others lodged protests against the denial of entry rights to both Wright and Engdahl in the weeks leading to her arrival. When the government finally granted Wright entry, her advocates took the credit. But the Foreign Office file on Wright suggests that the government had been under pressure to raise an official complaint and had demurred from doing so, fearing that the defendants would suffer the fate of the American anarchists Sacco and Vanzetti, executed in the face of protest. The government feared not Wright, but an American backlash against the defendants, whatever its attitude toward Engdahl's communist affiliation. The Sheffield branch of the Transport and General Workers' Union prompted the Sheffield Trades and Labor Council to write to Sir John Simon protesting against "anti-racial tyranny in the State of Alabama," requesting that representations be made to the U.S. government: "We believe the evidence was unreliable and demand their immediate release. We also demand full equal civil and political rights for all colored races."[72] An official responded in an internal memo, stating that such protests would be unsuccessful: "The pressure brought to bear in the Sacco and Vanzzetti [sic] case did no good and even considerable harm. . . . How much more harmful would the intervention of a foreign Government be! . . . there is no need to explain publicly our inability to do anything." An official recorded the news that "A negress named Wright" was on her way to Britain: "I told the H.O. [Home Office] that I did not think there was any special ground necessitating instructions for her to be refused admission."[73]

Ada Wright came to Britain in June of 1932, wearing the same raincoat in which she appeared in most of the photographs of her European trip. Her descendants posit that she may have been "packing"—carrying a concealed weapon in an era without metal detectors or hand searches. Wright reportedly was met by an indeterminate "large number of white and colored workers," as described in a phrase typical of the communist press coverage of her trip.[74] Shapurji Saklatavala and Bob Lovell led the arrival delegation. She was pleased to work without a translator, though her interpreters were ever present; Nancy Cunard, who played such a major role in the British Scottsboro campaign, was absent abroad.

Once on British soil, Wright was also able to speak more freely in other ways, untethered by Engdahl and uninhibited by British government authorities. She attributed the recent stay of execution granted the lawyers at home to the success of the worldwide campaign. Her sons now awaited their first Supreme Court hearing.[75] In the *Daily Worker* and other papers Andy Wright became a one-time "rag-picker" and "lorry driver," terms unfamiliar to Americans. Just after her arrival from Paris, Wright gave an evening talk at the Clerkenwell Club and Institute, dramatized by the *Daily Worker*: "Mrs. Wright rose to speak, a toil-worn woman . . . [who said] . . . We . . . know that white boys would never have been sentenced to death for an alleged assault on black girls. The Scottsboro boys have been condemned to death because they are black. That is their only crime." Saklatvala spoke of the "Scottsboro's of India" and of hundreds of Bengali boys held in Hijli prison, three of whom had been shot in a jail protest over food. He reported that the trade unions had not assisted the defendants in the United States and predicted little trade-union support for Indians in Britain. Isobel Brown, a prominent and able communist fund-raiser, was among the other speakers.[76] Wright's trip figured only sporadically in the establishment and popular press alongside other kinds of coverage of the racial politics of the day. Winston Churchill contributed a piece against Indian self-rule to the *Daily Mail* during the week of Wright's visit. The caption for the image that accompanied the essay identified its Indian subjects as "humble, primitive folk, who have been incapable of evolving, even in a most rudimentary form, a village government."[77] If Europe could not achieve sound local government, how could India? The *North London Recorder*'s featured "recipe of the week" was "Nigger Blanc-Mange."[78]

Wright's visit to the House of Commons to see trade unionists and Labour MPs Seymour Cocks and Tom Williams received little mention in the press, though party leader George Lansbury embraced the campaign. That evening, Wright addressed both the League of Coloured Peoples, and a gathering of Deptford and Greenwich workers at Greenwich Borough Hall, one hundred of whom reportedly joined the ILD.[79] In the outer London district of Willesden, she spoke before a crowd estimated at five hundred, most of whom were schoolchildren. Wright was introduced by a militant from the communist-led Unemployed Workers Movement, and spoke about the attempts on the part of her neighbors at home in Chattanooga to prevent her from consorting with the "Reds." The local paper announced "Mother of Condemned Boys Makes a Pathetic Appeal to Stonebridge Audience," expressing shock at reports from the American South of "notorious third degree methods of extracting information from potential witnesses. . . . when Mrs. Wright . . . arose . . . the sympathy of the meeting went out to this pathetic figure."[80]

Her first days in London were followed by a tour through parts of Britain. After a stop at Temple Meads, Bristol, Wright took the night train through to speak in Albert Square in Dundee. In both cities, crowds came to the stations and greeted her, singing the "Internationale." The *Dundee Free Press* observed the visit by running the writer Louis Golding's syndicated piece "Nine Niggers on a Train: The Color Problem in the U.S.," its title taken from the children's song "Ten Little Niggers." Golding recalled being distressed as a child at the disappearance of the ten black children in the lyric—he imagined them now as the Scottsboro Boys.

> It might have been possible to convince an old-time "coal-black mammy" that what Uncle Sam was doing was for the good of the black man's soul, or that it was bound to be right anyway, but that does not work with the modern well-read Negro.... There is a great opportunity for those in charge of the Scottsboro negroes' demand for a re-trial to bring into being a long-needed new conception of freedom.[81]

In Kirkcaldy, Lockerbie, Springburn, Glasgow, and Manchester, Wright spoke in places where a communist struggle was under way, the local events inspiring the map of her journey. The *Fifeshire Advertiser* announced the "American Negress at Kirkcaldy" where there had been arrests of demonstrators at rallies against unemployment.[82] In Manchester she met activists recently released from jail and Mrs. Gladys Knight, whose son Lester Hutchinson was one of the three white trade unionists on trial at Meerut, India. The *Daily Worker* published a letter from a woman reader in Manchester: "My own two sons are out of work and the eldest has walked down to London to look for work like your boys were doing."[83] But more typically, the *Glasgow Evening News* ran stories of a lascar murderer in Dock Row and the tale of a youngster stealing a coffin: "Willie is an innocent little nigger boy of twelve years old."[84]

While Wright was visiting northern England, Scotland, Wales, and the Midlands, London activists held corner Scottsboro rallies in sites like Portobello Market. Five LSE faculty members—historians R. H. Tawney, Harold Laski, and Eileen Power; the scientist and physiologist Lancelot Hogben; and the sociologist Morris Ginsberg—signed a protest letter along with seventeen of their colleagues, more than fifty graduate students, and nearly two hundred undergraduates. "We regard this travesty of justice, the result of the gravest race prejudice, as an intolerable abuse of the basic principles of civilization, and demand immediate repeal of the sentence."[85] The resolution passed by the Leyton Trams Transport and General Workers Union branch that week, was more blunt: "The very fact that the two white girls were known to be prostitutes proves the whole case to be unfounded. Also the fact that the white girls themselves declared that the Negroes had not touched them and that it was only under pressure from the police did these girls make this false confession." While Wright's British tour continued, Irish prime minister Eamon de Valera prohibited Wright's entry into Ireland. He and nationalist James Larkin, Jr., had been approached by the ILD about a visit. De Valera was an anticommunist and sought to sustain a modus vivendi with the United States.[86] His opposition to visits by Indian nationalist and pacifist speakers, including Gandhi, was a matter of record for the Comintern. Reginald Bridgeman, the convener of Wright's London press conference, wrote to Padmore. "Valera refuses to allow Mrs. Wright to visit the Irish Free State in order to win a little credit with the

United States Government at the expense of the Negroes."[87] The *Irish Times* did not cover the decision, but reported on the visit of the Princess Ubangi "of a rapidly dwindling pigmy tribe . . . one of the many attractions at the Cork Industrial Fair. . . . ignorant of English and African dialects, she still holds the ancient belief that the earth is flat. In her dances, she portrays the human emotions, and this renders them rather puzzling to Western minds."[88]

The English and Scots press continued to highlight the socialite Mrs. Barney's acquittal in her trial for murder. CPGB leader Harry Pollitt condemned the court's decision and the fact that no firearms charge had been pressed. He admonished both the short-lived Labour government of the late twenties, and the present National Government of 1931, for assaulting and even killing Negroes in South Africa and Nigeria.[89] The *Daily Herald* announced a "race riot" in Bombay that the police had not stopped. The *City and East London Observer* ran "Nine Niggers" by Golding, and it also appeared in Dundee: "Should not every American citizen choke over his national anthem? . . . Is it not about time that the working of the brain of the Negro should be understood?" The paper simultaneously reported that two "colored seamen," Abrahams Shadwell and Berie Boyne, were let off on charges of theft in a London court because the judge observed that their accuser was "a girl whose character was such that he would not think of accepting [her testimony] without some corroborative evidence."[90]

On July 8 Wright spoke at her London press conference of the moment in Paint Rock that sparked the trials, avowing that her sons' accusers, "being prostitutes, were intimidated" by the Sheriff: "[T]he girls said they were forced to tell a lie because the boys were Negroes. They had been examined by the doctors, who said that they were all right." Bridgeman chaired the press conference, and emphasized the severity of the punishment: "I do not think that rape is an action which calls for a death sentence in any country." Bridgeman tried to satisfy the moral argument offering a way to support the defendants no matter what actions they may have taken. Wright added that she had not done public speaking before the case arose, "not even in church," and spoke of her family.[91]

Saklatvala addressed Wright's farewell ceremony at Shoreditch Church: "The British workers have shown by their reception to Mrs. Wright that they have broken down the barriers dividing them from the Negro races." A thousand marchers reportedly took her to Liverpool Street Station where she departed for Scandinavia. Wright had spoken to crowds of at least a few hundred in a host of British cities, her visit a success if judged by communist sources.[92] It was an adventure that had not led to arrest and was the only part of the long journey that summer in which she conducted her own business unaccompanied by Engdahl. Word about the case had reached Britain in limited but visible press coverage, and many ordinary people across a wide sweep of the country had seen its living representative. Arnold Ward was elated: "Since Mrs. Wright been here the International Solidarity has taken on a deeper and greater hold on the workers. Here more than I have ever seen before and I think it is for the best. Boy we are moving. Cherio."[93] But Ward warned that George Padmore's new work on the global position of black workers, *The Life and Struggles of Negro Toilers*, had not sold in Britain and occupied a low place in the communist pantheon, regrettable in light of the enthusiasm shown Mother Wright by whites:

[A]ll through the . . . campaign not one Negro Toiler was sold and hundreds ought to be sold. Look here Padmore, you have to face the Situation as it is these people don't like us and they only use us for a tool . . . but as long as we always have to be running to them cap in hand like a little lap dog, there [*sic*] will treat us like one. . . . the Scottsboro Campaign was great—Bob Lovel worked Mrs. Wright like a Slave but poor woman She is Good and the white comrades the Women did all they could for Her. She had a better send off from Here than the Royal family.[94]

A month after Wright's departure from Britain, Ward praised Nancy Cunard's zeal and again identified black Londoners as retrograde: "I like [Nancy]— she is a fighter. . . . [Y]ou will soon experience how it is impossible to work with Negroes over here you think London is New York. So you would soon find out."[95] Ward imagined New York's greater possibilities, but in the United States, white communist comrades' behavior toward other visiting Scottsboro mothers was called out by party leaders:

Mrs. Powell . . . was placed with the rankest sort of white chauvinist who put her to work washing dishes, scrubbing floors, washing dyties, etc. . . . if our enemies had found out that we handled the mothers liké we did, what would have been the result? Take it another way. If we knew these mothers were handled like this by the NAACP, would we not jump at their throats in meetings, conferences, etc.?[96]

WRIGHT RETURNS TO THE CONTINENT

Ada Wright visited Norway after departing London, and those who observed her continued to emphasize the sexual deviance of Price and Bates as a reassuring component of her sons' defense. A sympathetic press report appeared in *Tidens Tegen*, and reached the office of the American Secretary of State: "There is something tragic in the touring of Europe by Mrs. Ada Wright. . . . Mrs. Wright shows a tenacity, courage and devotion in her restless journey which should silence all talk of an inferior race. . . . She is Black . . . and it was not difficult to find her at the railway station last evening when she arrived." Her sons were the victims of "two prostitute factory girls."[97] A report that the accusers were "almost imbecile girls, prostituted . . . and supposedly not entirely disinclined to advances on behalf of the negroes," was forwarded from Copenhagen.[98] The unquestioned assumption that the defendants had felt compelled to assault the two "loose" women underlay the press portraits. The black defendants were excused for uncontrollable behavior through the character assault on the two white accusers, their own "characteristic" racial identities reinforced, not challenged.

Wright's journey continued to draw supporters. The U.S. legation received over two hundred cards of protest from Danish trade unionists. But not all of her European observers were as convinced. The *Journal d'Alsace* bluntly reported Wright's appearance before an impassive crowd on a hot day in Strasbourg.

> At the risk of passing for an unfeeling heart, I must confess that her attitude, her voice, her speech, had nothing very maternal. Perhaps we are accustomed to feeling mothers, especially when they have two children to wrest from death. Or is it that forced resignation which, from generation to generation, has made the American negroes fatalists without reaction? There is one sure thing: if Eda Wright did not move us by her "recitation" in that dreadful English of the rural districts of the southern parts of America, she did not seem either to move the audience. The applause was just polite.

The *Dernières Nouvelles de Strasbourg* curtly described "a speaker, an authentic Negro woman, who, in very bad English, protested against the imprisonment of young negroes in England. Evidently nobody understood anything from her long speech."[99] In November Padmore's friend, Soudanese activist Garan Kouyate led a delegation to the American embassy in Paris on behalf of the Scottsboro cause. Nancy Cunard later reported that the U.S. officials expressed chagrin "at Negroes talking correct French."[100]

Wright appeared on the platform at the Amsterdam Anti-War Congress, a gathering of three thousand pacifist, socialist, and communist representatives from twenty-seven countries, who passed a resolution on Scottsboro amid their protests against imperial war. Isobel Brown, Saklatvala, writer John Strachey, and filmmaker Ivor Montagu formed the British communist delegation.[101] The ILP and the Cooperative Guild sent delegates from Britain.[102] Wright again met Mary Knight, the mother of Meerut defendant Hutchinson in Amsterdam.[103] Women's delegates from Switzerland took up Wright's cause, and delegations from Vassar and Wellesley colleges in the United States were inspired by her presence to pressure Alabama senator Hugo Lafayette Black, the future U.S. Supreme Court Justice, about the case.[104] Wright and Engdahl subsequently visited Austria and Switzerland, and were expelled from Belgium, where a women's delegation approached the Belgian government on Wright's behalf.[105]

In Paris, her hosts at the *Salle Wagram* were the writer and Trotskyist organizer Magdeleine Paz and the socialist party leader, the future prime minister Léon Blum. The event was part of a multifaceted French campaign that touched both salon and factory floor. Paz wrote, "Ada's presence and speech produced great feeling. . . . In a general fashion, this affair has revived a live interest in the race question. I have been asked for articles and for conferences."[106] Wright toured the Netherlands and spoke on platforms with anticolonial Indonesian activists.[107] But in Germany, the Nazi paper *Der Angriff* denounced the Wright visit as a *coup de théâtre* and targeted Scottsboro signatories Thomas Mann and Albert Einstein, admonishing Mann to limit his attentions to Germany's affairs rather than those of the rest of the world, and dismissing Einstein as a Jew.[108]

In September Wright was arrested at the coal mining center of Kladno, Czechoslovakia. She spent three days in jail; the communists charged that the American ambassador had urged the government to arrest her and Engdahl for disrupting public order and compromising state security. In Budapest the authorities prohibited her from speaking, but in Sofia she met with supporters at the train station.[109] A letter ostensibly written from Vienna by Wright, visibly doctored by Red Aid, mentioned the plight of the Bulgarian children she had seen. "There were many countries in Europe we could not even enter because all forms of working class activity are prohibited—Italy, Romania, Poland, Greece, Portugal, Finland and other countries I never heard of before." Her statement about the upcoming World Conference on Red Aid in Moscow was typical of those drafted for her. "I think I understand a little about it—how it seeks to unite the down-trodden of all races and nationalities for struggle against their oppressors against the war and for the defense of the Soviet Union."[110]

Wright had minor surgery in a Berlin hospital, and she and Engdahl went on to Moscow. Miriam Sherman, a communist youth activist from Los Angeles, accompanied Wright back to the United States. Sherman kept a diary of her days at the Red Aid world conference. She noted hearing reports on the imprisonment of Warsaw militants, on the hundreds of children detained by the nationalist regime in China, and on the deaths of more than a hundred antifascist fighters in Germany. Sherman heard members of MOPR, the Russian Red Aid organization, discuss their own weaknesses in a session of self-criticism. Comintern Red Aid director Elena D. Stassova criticized the British ILD for organizing along "nonpolitical" lines, suggesting that its work had been too broad based to suit Moscow.[111] Within two years, the Comintern shift toward the application of its "popular front" line allowed for a much less critical stance toward noncommunist "progressive forces," but in 1932, the derision of socialist platforms and practices, especially in Germany, was still in full swing.[112] Even though the British Labour party eschewed any supportive organizational role in Scottsboro, many rank-and-file Labour party members followed the fortunes of the case and lent their individual support. In this respect the early Scottsboro defense campaign in Britain anticipated some of the features of the Popular Front, especially in the broad base of its signatories of Scottsboro petitions and manifestos.[113]

Sherman heard George Padmore address the Moscow conference on the subject of Africa. He was typically outspoken, declaring that Red Aid's Negro work was its "weakest link." He and other speakers offered news on activism in Madagascar and the French Empire, El Salvador, Trinidad, and other parts of the Caribbean.[114] A CPUSA speaker complained of not being able to recruit Negroes. Sherman mused, "Scottsboro is still in a state where we can agitate but [there are] no organizational results . . . [and] few Negroes in the [American] ILD," adding that the Dutch were "asleep in doing colonial work."[115] She recalled turning a corner in the nighttime Moscow streets to find Langston Hughes before her; he took her and her companions to a party in a private apartment. It was on this trip that Hughes and Loren Miller encountered Naomi Mitchison.

Then Louis Engdahl died suddenly of pneumonia in a Moscow hospital, and young Miriam Sherman was delegated to take Ada Wright back across Europe by train. Long after, she remembered Wright as politely unapproachable and steadfast. The box of Engdahl's ashes swayed back and forth across the railcar shelf. As their train approached the German border, Wright told Sherman of being taken by the Russians to see Engdahl's body cremated. In Wright the Russians had an irreproachable witness lest there be a diplomatic question raised about the circumstances or even the occurrence of her companion's death.[116] As the two women crossed Europe, a State Department agent alerted Washington that an article published in Algeria had reached American offices on the Continent, stating that if the Supreme Court went against the defendants "in the case of the negro boys . . . an attempt will be made to assassinate President Hoover, the Ambassador at Paris, and the Governor of Alabama." The FBI forwarded this news on to the Secret Service, giving the security forces more to worry about for the moment than the return of the "Scottsboro Mother."[117] A crowd of twelve thousand mourned Louis Engdahl at a Bronx Coliseum memorial in November 1932—a measure of the ILD's public profile in New York, after Sacco and Vanzetti and the Scottsboro case had both attracted new supporters.[118] Ada Wright returned to Chattanooga bereft of her friend, both her sons still prisoners of the State of Alabama.

PORTRAYAL IN LANGUAGE

In Britain the success of the Scottsboro campaign depended on portraying the defendants in sympathetic language that made use of the idioms familiar to its onlookers and readers, commensurate with the usage of the left press. For communists, the "boys" often became "workers."[119] The April 1931 issue of *Anti-Imperialist Youth* carried the headline "Save Nine Young Negro Workers from the Electric Chair in the USA," also referring to the defendants as "Nine Negro Boys."[120] "Translations" and expressions of solidarity relied upon stereotypic images of America. In August 1931 the *Daily Worker* referred to the "Negro plantation workers" of Alabama in a piece about both lynching and the Limehouse supporters of the Scottsboro defendants.[121] Some campaign propaganda took on a "darkie" intonation, using pejorative minstrel, vaudeville, and Hollywood take-offs on African American speech. "Authentic" letters written by the defendants from their jail cells appeared, rendered in each European tongue as translated from the first American propaganda rendition. These practices emerged in words whose origins had no "spoken" authenticity and no credible "original" version except as ascribed, imitative forms of entertainment. In this respect, the Scottsboro lingoes joined the riffs already known to Europeans from the stage, the cinema, and the variety hall.

Under Padmore's editorship, the *Negro Worker* published different kinds of material, written in a hybrid of dialect and political message and sometimes in the "voice" of the defendants. "What we guilty of? Nothing but being out of a job. . . . So we hopped a freight—just like any one of you workers might a done. . . . We was taken off the train by a mob and framed up on rape charges. . . . Only ones helped us down here been the International Labor Defense. . . . We's only poor working class boys whose skin is black."[122] It is striking that the paper assumed that all its disparate readers on all continents would promptly recognize the form and that no particular road map was needed. In his contribution to Nancy Cunard's massive anthology *Negro*, the African American writer Alain Locke invoked the work of James Weldon Johnson in describing the prevailing idiom: "[D]ialect is an organ with only two stops— pathos and humor."[123] Ada Wright's defenders most often chose pathos in their representations of her and the defendants. Humor issued from the pen of the Afro-Caribbean Arnold Ward in his personal letters to Padmore, and likewise dotted the African American press. His correspondence suggested a freer, more ironic sense of private communication among blacks. John Wexley's Scottsboro play *They Shall Not Die* was briefly satirized in the pages of the *Pittsburgh Courier*, when a piece on another subject appeared under the heading "They Shall Not Dine."[124] But most attempts to lighten the typical British reader's burdens bore the indelible stamp of 1930s "do-dah" and jungle characters with bones in their heads like those in radical cartoonist David Low's contributions to the *Evening Standard*.[125] A year before the case broke, one *Daily Worker* reader, "William Wilson," wrote an open letter to the paper asking that it change its house style to appeal to more black readers.

> One of the first steps . . . is the discontinuance of the use of any term which would cause a member of the working class engaged in a struggle against imperialism to feel that he had been offered an affront, that insult had been offered him, that his brothers in the struggle had asserted their "superiority." . . . we are more than surprised to find in the columns of the *Daily Worker* the term nigger.

Wilson pointed out that the "bourgeois" press was changing its usage in relation to "Indian and Negro" subjects, "but not our *Daily*," asking for the term "Negro" to appear with an upper-case "N."[126] By the time Scottsboro arose, the paper had ceased to use "nigger," while similarly derogatory cartoon images remained.[127] The propaganda campaign around Scottsboro was dour and stern, with little that emanated from its print culture finding a space in which to land, in Alain Locke's metaphor, between "the ditches of minstrelsy and the trenches of race propaganda."[128] Ada Wright's utterances were virtually never recorded verbatim. Her sons and the other defendants were poorly educated, Southern black youngsters, only Andy Wright having completed even the sixth grade. To write their speech for them was a task of calculation, sympathy, and, inevitably, of fabrication that risked misrepresentation—literalness that risked ridicule. Each choice of wording could evoke responses encompassing pity, solidarity, and racial prejudice. In an era of minstrelsy and Shirley Temple, of *Gone with the Wind* and Louis Armstrong's London debut at the Palladium, the Scottsboro defendants landed "in context," intruding upon images and speech already seen and uttered.[129]

Two letters from the files of the American communists suggest the complexity of approximating the "actual" speech of the defendants or of their mothers, and illustrate the common gap between expression by word and the greater range of oral expression that the defendants and their families had at their disposal. A Scottsboro defendant's mother wrote to African American communist leader William Patterson of the ILD in November of 1932: "You don't know how glad I was, and so glad that you'll done win the Supreme Court. ILD best in the world. . . . They isn't strong here but I am doing the best here, sell books and papers and talking to them." A second mother wrote from Mobile, Georgia: "Received money and help me out a lots if it wasn't for the ILD I don't know what would become of we mothers and the boys ether. . . . Just two or three dollars mean a whole lot to me." Defendant Olen Montgomery wrote to Patterson from jail:

> I am so happy over it until I don't hardly know exactly how to thank them for their kindness love of us poor ones. But I do appreciate it to the very highest respect. And Mr. Patterson, sence you all are going to have us . . . I will ask you to have some one send me a pair of . . . slippers dark tan and size seven english toed. Now . . . I don't want you to thank I am choicery because I can't be because of the circumstances I am under. But really my feet is small and keen an boney. And a broad toed shoe don't fit my feat."[130]

The Scottsboro campaign also depended on making a sharp distinction between "rape," the capital charge leveled against the defendants, and "prostitution," the charge informally made against Ruby Bates and Victoria Price in the courts and by the campaign's supporters. By asserting that the women were prostitutes, the defense and the campaign not very subtly dismissed the notion that they could have been "violated" under any circumstance, thereby suppressing idle discussion of the defendants' guilt or innocence, though the *official* communist line on this issue waffled for only a few days immediately after the case began.[131] Speculation surrounding this issue continues to the present day, not least among the communities in which the defendants and their families were known before and after the trials. Ada Wright herself took refuge in an attack on prostitution as a measure of protection for her sons. The Leyton trade-union resolution had typically declared "the very fact that the two white girls were prostitutes proves the whole case to be unfounded."[132] In October 1932, the *Daily Worker* referred to the accusers as "known prostitutes with police records."[133] This remained so, even after the fabled spring 1933 Decatur, Alabama, retrial of defendant Haywood Patterson, in which the pedigreed Southerner, Judge James E. Horton, ruled against the appeal jury's decision on grounds of unfairness, and saved the defendants' lives for a few more months, abruptly and irrevocably ending his own career in the Alabama judiciary. Horton partly relied upon incontrovertible and newly offered medical testimony that the women had not had intercourse on the night in question.[134] In the midst of the trial, Ruby Bates, one of the accusers, appeared in the courtroom, called as a witness for the defense, now claiming she had not been raped after all. But Judge Horton's decision to challenge the jury did not allay the insistence upon denigrating both women's characters or diminish the comfort that the general charge of prostitution allowed those who otherwise feared the energy and appetite of "black manhood" in relation to white women. Though the semen discovered by the doctor on the night of the arrests was simply too old to be that of the defendants, its presence was a sign of "loose living." The campaign took on the notion of the accusers' feminine sanctity, deriding the Old South's claim to protect white women as a cover for the defense of undeserving harlots, a tack that failed, despite Judge Horton's salvaging of the defendants.

When Ruby Bates "went over" to the defense and was appropriated by the communists as a new recruit, her reputation was in some respects doubly sullied; neither side—detractors nor supporters of the defendants—was much taken with her. The African American writer Lloyd Brown, who went to Russia as a 1930s Scottsboro organizer, recalled that he was "not impressed" by Bates, and described her as "ignorant, uncultured ... not an admirable person."[135] This reputation survived despite Bates's attempted cultivation by communist cadre and her own earnest efforts at rehabilitation. She closed a letter to organizer Richard B. Moore with "Give my love and best regards to ... Mrs. Patterson [mother of defendant Haywood Patterson]. I hope our struggle for the boys will be successful. I close with my love and best regards to you and best wishes for the meetings. Comradely greetings, Ruby Bates."[136] After the NAACP rejoined the defense efforts, when the campaign finally broadened into a wider coalition, the organization's leader Walter White recalled meeting "tough hard-boiled Victoria Price, a cotton mill worker and part-time prostitute, and a younger mill worker, also free with her favors for a price, Ruby Bates."[137] In 1937 attorney Roger N. Baldwin, a chief architect of the American Civil Liberties Union, stated "whatever the evidence, no Negro can be acquitted when a white woman, even of the lowest character, accuses him. . . . so deep-rooted is southern prejudice, in favor of the word of any white woman, whatever her character, that no defense can overcome it."[138] He recalled the defendants as "just a bunch of unlettered Negroes."[139]

Conventional political division also colored the language surrounding the case. There was a broad, shared set of images and words, but many dissented from those that bespoke a doctrinaire communist commitment. The NAACP had serious contacts in Europe prior to Scottsboro, including those of W.E.B. Du Bois.[140] His correspondent Lady Kathleen Simon also hosted Walter White in England.[141] The British and European liberal and socialist communities kept in touch with their American political counterparts and were formally linked to the British Labour party through the Second International of world socialism. When Du Bois came to London for the 1921 second Pan-African Congress, he visited Fabian Sidney Webb and Harold Laski. Fabian and Labour party personalities also attended the 1923 Third Pan-African Congress held in both Lisbon and London, which called for the abolition of white rule in Kenya, South Africa, and Rhodesia in its resolutions.[142] The NAACP was never far away from the case. The *Daily Worker* reported that Pickens and his wife and a group of two dozen others, sailed to Germany on the *Leviathan*, singing spirituals on the boat deck as they journeyed to follow Ada Wright's path. Pickens sometimes spoke for groups that Wright had just addressed.[143] Despite the NAACP's deep aversion to communism, African American journalist Homer Smith spied Walter White's book on sale in a shop window while attending a Moscow Scottsboro rally. The Soviet interest in African Americans did not preclude attention to the enemies of the CPUSA.[144]

The divisions between communists, socialists, and liberals that plagued many European interwar political communities manifested themselves repeatedly in the Scottsboro campaign. Magdeleine Paz, Ada Wright's host in Paris, corresponded with Walter White early in the Scottsboro case:

> I have learned that the Communists (*Sécours Rouge*) [French Red Aid] (ILD), have taken over the campaign of defense. While having hardly any illusions on the efficacy of the Communists, in general we have responded, Maurice Paz [her husband and fellow Trotskyist] and I, to the appeal that was made to us to join in their efforts; but at the meeting of the Committee, the first thing that we asked was the broadening of the campaign. . . . only great manifestations in which individuals representing all phases of social life would participate could carry much weight. We argued that political divisions must be put aside and an appeal must be made principally to the sentiments of humanity and justice, and not to adhere to the handful of converts who are influenced by the Communists. We must try to touch public opinion in its entirety, so to speak.

Paz reported that those in the French Scottsboro campaign had decided not to appeal to the socialists or even the CGT, the national communist trade union organization, wishing instead to restrict participation to their own distinct constituency. So Paz asked those involved in the support committee that she organized for the imprisoned American socialist Tom Mooney, including writer Henri Barbusse and English philosopher Bertrand Russell, to become active in the Scottsboro case. She wrangled with the communists after taking independent action, but succeeded in attracting four thousand to her meeting, visited at the final hour by Mother Wright and her comrade-escorts: "Her presence and her speech produced great feeling. Engdahl (ILD) took the opportunity to say, among other things, that if the Negroes were executed, the fault would lie with the Socialists, and he also attacked the NAACP—I refused to translate this part of his speech." [145] White's response to Paz's success at bringing out such a large crowd in the face of communist attempts to deter her audience from attending, was implacable, his own agenda paramount. "Terrible as is the plight of these nine helpless young boys, an even greater tragedy is the terrible mismanagement of the case by the American Communists." [146]

The veracity of Ada Wright's self-presentation and of her convictions was also questioned by critics of the communist campaign. The *Birmingham Post* of Alabama, the leading newspaper of the state in which her sons were incarcerated, referred to Wright as an "ignorant, gibbering negro woman."

> Ada Wright does not and cannot represent any issue of human rights. She has no real knowledge of the guilt or innocence of her boy. She knows little of the meaning of legal rights or of the Communist doctrine of her sponsors. Her sole qualification is that she speaks strange racial dialect which permits of whatever translation a designing interpreter may wish to give. [147]

Wright's supporters emphasized her modesty, presenting her as pitiable rather than sophisticated. The *Daily Worker* described her as a

> toil-worn woman from far away Tennessee, who had undertaken this long journey of suffering in order to save the lives of her sons. . . . she spoke quietly in the soft, pleasant drawl of the South. The audience strained to catch every word. Intense interest and sympathy was written on every face and tears welled into many eyes. The Negro mother told her story as only a mother can. Just a simple story of life at home, the departure of the boys in search of work and then—prison, the menace of the electric chair.

In another edited remark, Wright reportedly added that her sons were linked to "class war prisoners all over the world." She spoke of her grandmother's life as a slave who was sold for three hundred dollars and whipped on an auction block, and recounted her mother's life working in the fields for a quarter a day. In Scotland,

> Cries of indignation rent the air as she told in simple, poignant language of the brutal savagery of the drunken, lynching mob outside the [Alabama] Court House,

demanding death for the boys. . . . the Dundee workers will not quickly forget the visit which has forged new bonds of unity between British workers and their colored comrades.[148]

This expression of solidarity required several leaps of imagination. Ada Wright was born in a rural area but worked and lived in a city. She was a domestic servant engaged in the single most prevalent form of women's employment in Britain in the 1930s. She had not witnessed slavery. There was a small black presence in Scotland, but the "colored comrades" mentioned in the paper were mostly present in greater numbers in other cities. The defendants were even less political than was Wright herself, who had no known political ties, her church membership constituting her clearest public associational identity.

AFTER ADA WRIGHT: 1933

In 1930 the literary scholar Lascelles Abercrombie published *The Sale of St. Thomas, Six Acts*, an investigation into antiquity that portrayed St. Thomas's incarceration in unremitting terms, prompting the critic Oliver Elton to observe of the work, "On the ship and in the slave-sheds he has suffered from cruel sights, which are described without flinching."[149] Abercrombie was soon to play the leading administrative role in the new Scottsboro campaign defense committee. Nancy Cunard recruited many of the literary figures to the committee's work. Their lives reflected an earnest revulsion with social oppression and a common preoccupation with racial injustice. They knew each other, and their political work on many fronts dovetailed one another's. Naomi Mitchison was a contributor to Abercrombie's *Revaluations: A Study in Biography*, constituting a connection typical among the group.[150] London was the campaign's headquarters, and the London Scottsboro Defense Committee included in various incarnations Jomo Kenyatta; writers Abercrombie, Vera Brittain, and Mitchison; Eleanor Rathbone; and radical scientist Julian Huxley. In its heyday, it was led by the energetic Cunard, who once more appeared on the London scene in early 1933, and who, like most of the others, never joined the communist party.[151]

In August 1932 the campaign observed a day in support of the Scottsboro defendants and the African American communist Angelo Herndon, on trial for incitement to riot, in Atlanta. "Scottsboro-Herndon Day" was also dedicated to the campaign for the release of Ernst Thälmann, jailed German communist leader. The observance received critical commentary in the *Manchester Guardian*; it suggested that the communist-inspired defense efforts had resulted in longer jail terms for the Alabama defendants and broached the usually unuttered question of their possible guilt. "Whatever the truth about this may be, the most important question now is not whether the negroes may have been guilty but whether they receive a fair trial. . . . In both cases [American socialist Tom Mooney's was the other], the Radicalism of the defenders is used as an excuse to keep them incarcerated."[152] The communists were not pleased with the tenor of the piece.[153] But three months after Wright's departure, the October 1932 *Week-end Review* carried a manifesto of support for the Scottsboro defendants, sent from Boar's Hill, Oxford, and signed by writers Mitchison, Vera Brittain, Louis Golding, H. G. Wells, Stephen Spender, Leonard and Virginia Woolf, and Hugh Walpole; scientist Julian Huxley; historian Raymond Postgate; and Bertrand Russell and other luminaries, adding gravitas and greater inclusiveness to the campaign.[154]

In January 1933, Paul Robeson, the most sought-after and best-known African American personality in Britain, first appeared on Scottsboro rounds in a matinee of Eugene O'Neill's *The Emperor Jones*, offered as a benefit for the campaign. He and Cunard fought negative publicity in New York City in 1932, and Cunard seized the limelight to promote Scottsboro.[155] In 1933 she issued a press notice to over one hundred news agencies from her office in Chandos Street. It informed its readers that Ruby Bates had defected to the defense, stating that Bates had previously been "terrorized into false statements. . . . But this will not necessarily be considered sufficient and not indeed suffice for [the defendants'] unconditional liberation." Cunard's cosigners included painter Augustus John; French writer André Gide; American writer Upton Sinclair; poets Ezra Pound, Robert Graves, and Laura Riding; and British writers Rebecca West, J. B. Priestley, and Storm Jameson—a plethora of arts figures signifying Cunard's influence and recruiting powers in the context of growing global appeals.[156]

In April 1934 the British Scottsboro Defense Committee included Abercrombie who served as secretary, Gladys White, and the writers Carmel Haden Guest (wife of liberal MP Leslie Haden-Guest), Norman Collins, and Mitchison, who may have been responsible for Eleanor Rathbone's name appearing on the letterhead. Ashanti Prince Cobina Kessie joined anthropology student Jomo Kenyatta and the African American musical performer Isaac Hatch to comprise the committee's three black members. Hatch helped to create the vogue of Scottsboro. He often presided over donor events featuring minstrelsy, jazz, and a cross section of London's black entertainment community.[157] The enlarged defense committee's membership bore the full imprint of Cunard's networks of friends and fellow literati, many active in fellow travelers' circles. She directed the writer Edgell Rickword and a small staff, who undertook the clerical work of the committee. Cunard recalled one of her fund-raisers. "You would have liked one of my voluntary helpers in collecting funds for the legal defense: George Burke sometimes unemployed and sometimes a pedlar—the way he threw his heart into everything that interested him, a cockney princeling rather than a down and out."[158]

In June 1933 Arnold Ward wrote to African American communist William Patterson, enclosing news clippings on Africa with his note: "You have benefit from it. I mean Scottsboro. . . . [the black] comrades wonder what role they can play. . . . Alun Thomas, secretary of the ILD is trying to jolly them along to get another concert out of them, but I believe you can help us in this matter." Ward felt that Cunard, Hatch, Bridgeman and others could secure funds.

> We must coax the Negroes here. There here are different to what you have in different parts of the World. What might help us over here a lot is an experience . . . woman. One who could do some canvassing also type a letter and help us to organize. There is plenty of office room here for her to work. Could the Party in USA or the CI [Comintern] help in this direction for six months. It is not money chuck away. It is a real sound investment.
>
> Our forces is so scattered and so divided. But Scottsboro, Kenya, Nigeria, is beginning to make the Negroes think here. Color bar in the Seamen's Union, 100's of ships leave the London Docks every month and only seven ships of this company gave work to Negro seaman a year. Stokers only coal ships oil burning ships the company will not employ Negro stokers in other profession such as music hall artists, 90% is out of work. Some American Negroes have been over here 40 years and know they are looking forward to the work house.
>
> I could write you pages of hardships the Negroes suffer here. I have been talking and debating arguing with men to come together and let us try to do something that would benefit the whole and help the CP who is working for all but my pleading always fall on deaf ears.

Ward felt there was a large group who would help but needed to see something they could respond to. "Consider this letter carefully. I have think it out long before writing you and write to you because I personally believe you grasp the International Negro question better than the other Negro leaders." Patterson replied, recommending George Padmore to Ward and suggesting that the communist party needed to make a specific request for assistance to the Political Bureau (executive of the CPUSA): "He [Padmore] has . . . a very clear understanding of this question and is at the same time a relentless fighter for the intensification of our work in this direction." Patterson suggested that Ward work to develop a concrete program of relief, in concert with Padmore and London communist Hugo Rathbone. "Every effort should be made to utilize these Negroes who are now employed as seamen as an acting link with the colonies. Through them we should try to get our literature and other correspondence into such colonial countries as they have contact with."[159]

The Scottsboro campaign widened its propaganda reach. The Nigerian activist I.T.A. Wallace-Johnson was moving between London and Africa in early 1933, and reported to the *Negro Worker* on his trip to the Lagos Girls Model School at the invitation of the city's Women's League. Over three hundred were present to hear him speak about the defendants' arrest and trials, "for an act which the whole European world maintains that they are not only innocent of but an act that was never committed at all." He supported his statements by "letters, photographs of Mrs Ada Wright . . . as well as newspaper publications in England and other places."[160] But Wallace-Johnson's freedom of movement was soon jeopardized. After spending a week in Britain that spring, he wrote to inform Padmore that upon his return to Lagos he had been greeted by an "embargo." The colonial administration declared the Nigerian trade unions illegal and banned meetings like those he had attended.[161]

Then in the early summer of 1933, the Labour party czar of international affairs, William Gillies, received a defensive missive from Bertrand Russell, who felt swindled by the Scottsboro campaign—Gillies had recently identified it as deeply influenced and directed by the communists. Russell wrote to Gilles, "I am a Socialist and as much opposed to Communism as you are. I do not intentionally associate myself with any movement inspired by the Communists."[162] Herbert Morrison, the leader of the London Labour party and Gillies's chief collaborator in the surveillance and outing of communist fronts, was also responsible for the pamphlet that provoked Russell and many others. It was entitled *The Communist Solar System: the Communist International*, and its cover depicted a planetary system of British communist front groups with Moscow at its center, eerily anticipating the language and imagery of the Cold War.[163] But Labour party censorship did not seem immeditaly to daunt the Scottsboro Defense Committee, which was busy promoting a musical gala fund-raiser at the Phoenix Theater. Ike Hatch hosted the eclectic program, featuring black vaudeville acts like the Mississippi Page Boys; the Black Flashers ("Can they flash oh boy"); the Gold Coast Quartet; and Black Bottom Johnny; along with the classically trained clarinettist Rudolph Dunbar; dance-band leader John Payne; and a dancer from Guiana, Ken Johnson, later known as "Snakehips." The Barbadian seamen's organizer Chris Jones from Liverpool addressed the music scene's notables and the assembled crowd. Cunard and the African American actor Beresford Gale were among the event's sponsors.[164]

William Gillies's correspondence indicates that his efforts to finger communists did bear fruit. The Cooperative Union of Manchester was concerned that he had identified their organization nationally as a fertile bed for secret communist cells.[165] Typically, Gillies wrote a Cooperative Society supporter to confirm that the Negro Welfare Association was a communist endeavor.[166] By late 1934, Labour was threatening the expulsions of those involved in communist-related activity, in a period when the CPGB sought a united front with Labour.[167] Many Labour party supporters were involved in the Scottsboro campaign, and in the growing antifascist activities. Yet Gilles avidly pursued his "outing" mission, fueled by increased communist-related and inspired activism.[168]

George Padmore's departure from the ranks of the Comintern eliminated a powerful spokesman for the official London Scottsboro campaign. Padmore was accused of being an opponent of the CPGB, and his close associate and friend Arnold Ward took cover in the characterization of Padmore as a "race man," chastising Padmore's orientation as premised upon the notion that

"Everything is no good only Negroes is good." But Ward also wrote despondently to William Patterson in New York:

> I don't get the *Liberator* [a CPUSA publication] no more and I am isolated over here. The ILD here seems to drop the Scottsboro campaign and they are such a storm in the colonies at the moment and we can't get a single thing going.... so comrade, where do I come in, comrade write us a line and cheer us up. Let's know about Scottsboro and also Ada Wright.[169]

In the years following Padmore's departure from the Comintern, the ILP's *New Leader* continued its coverage of the case, and in December 1933 published "All God's Chillun"—its title taken from Eugene O'Neill's successful West End play of the 1933 season and named for the Negro spiritual "All God's Chillun' Got Shoes"—it was a year since the Nazi seizure of power in Germany:

> The negroes in the USA, are today fighting their way to economic and social emancipation in a struggle in which mob law reigns and the favorite weapon is lynching. Inflamed nationalism, stirred-up racial bigotry, the superiority of white races over the exploited colored peoples: all these are condoned, to put it mildly, by the present ruling class in America under the "progressive" President Roosevelt. And, just as many a British worker will devour the Imperialist propaganda churned out by Fleet Street under flaming headlines against Ireland, and ignore the class struggle going on around him, so the American worker is being played on in the anti-Negro campaign, and the bread-lines are given scanty space. Change the wording again, make Germany the country, read Nordic for white races and Jews for colored people, and the picture is again complete.

The unidentified author drew upon examples from Kenya and other parts of Africa. "Even the South African Labour Party maintains the color-bar." The article condemned both the Meerut trial in India and developments in America: "[Haywood] Patterson, the Scottsboro negro, is under sentence of death—one more life to be taken by Imperialism."[170] The Scottsboro defendants' British advocates encompassed many outside of communist circles. Padmore's departure from the communist movement beckoned a greater ecumenism of purpose on the antiracist left, one that prefigured the realignments soon fostered by a growing "antifascism."

1934–35: CUNARD AND MITCHISON

The Scottsboro campaign in Britain, and Ada Wright's visit there, achieved a different kind of literary celebrity in 1934 with the publication of Nancy Cunard's learned, sensational, and oversized anthology *Negro*, the first of its kind to emerge out of contemporary, multiple black global cultures and a boon to the campaign in the select circles in which it was read.[171] Though Cunard's

Figure 1.4. Nancy Cunard, Paris, 1927, bearing the inscription "To the friends of 1 from the friends of 2 your loving Nancy, 1927, as before, since," from a scrapbook owned by the Parisian-based writers and editors Janet Flanner and Solita Solano. Cunard moved to Paris in the 1930s, where she collaborated with George Padmore (Papers of Janet Flanner and Solito Solano, Library of Congress).

publishers, Wishart and Co., issued a limited first run of a thousand copies at a cost of fifteen hundred pounds, and the iconic status of *Negro* was only achieved decades later, those who read it in the midthirties, some in syndicated accounts, were treated to a full and factual portrayal of the case and the campaign. Cunard had not been in London for Ada Wright's visit, and almost certainly never met her, yet the editor's unnamed photographer colleagues made many images of the London personalities whom Wright encountered, available for publication in *Negro.* The stir and passion of the visit comes through on each page of the account, unmistakably culled from the pages of the *Daily Worker.* *Negro* presents Wright's "life story," referring to her early employment at age twelve without pay, in exchange for clothes and food. *Negro* went on sale in the United States and the Caribbean not long after its London release and in syndicated form delivered detailed news about Scottsboro that many readers did not otherwise possess.[172] Many of the signatories of the campaign were identified in the volume, ranging from London's chief rabbi Joseph H. Hertz to Ezra Pound.[173]

Cunard dramatized her message: "The Scottsboro frame-up is more than an attempt to electrocute 9 innocent Black Alabamians—it is part of the effort to

force into the dumbest and most terrorized form of subjection all Negro workers who dare aspire to live otherwise than as virtual slaves." But she also wrote
of black self-awareness, and "[t]he spirit and determination in the Negro to
break through the mountain of tyranny heaped on him." She uncritically hailed
the role of the communists, even though by 1934, Cunard's strong ties to Comintern renegade Padmore and her maverick behavior were irritants to party
insiders. Her solicitous attitude toward Garan Kouyate, also a dilettante in the
eyes of the Comintern, demonstrated the eclecticism of her comradeship.[174]
Other unorthodox personalities populated the anthology; Cunard's own political line, as represented in the text, remained shrill: "[I]t is Communism alone
which throws down the barriers of race. . . . The Communist world-order is the
solution of the race problem for the Negro." She proclaimed, "To-day in Russia
alone is the Negro a free man, a 100 per cent. equal," and in a flight of fancy,
called for "an all-Communist Harlem in an all-Communist United States!"[175]
The African American Pauli Murray provided an essay on "riding the rails"
that explored the pattern of hopping trains, and the dilemma that led to the
Scottsboro defendants' arrest. Cunard took on the NAACP's false charges that
the Scottsboro mothers had been invented, but also included essays on other
subjects by NAACP leaders Du Bois and Walter White, not shirking from offering them a showcase for their own writings, despite their distance from
communism. Even the droll, anticommunist columnist of the *Pittsburgh Courier*, George Schuyler, whose acid pen lambasted the Soviet Union, had space
in *Negro*.[176] The pantheon of contributors belied any doctrinal fidelity. Racial
achievement was the hallmark of the collection. Many of its pages were filled
with a pictorial presentation of African art. Political antagonists from James
Ford to William Pickens appeared alongside one another, the latter writing on
lynching. Much of the anthology was devoted to the study of language including a controversial piece on dialect by the young Columbia University student
of anthropology Zora Neal Hurston.[177]

Cunard's exploits into African American life engaged a form of romantic
and sexual tourism. Her recent lover, African American musician Henry
Crowder (also a contributor to *Negro* to whom Cunard dedicate the anthology), accompanied her on a highly-publicized voyage to New York from London and stayed with her in a Harlem hotel, the occasion for the charge that she
had been with Paul Robeson instead.[178] Iris Tree, an actress and Cunard's writer
friend, narrowly asserted years later that "one much disputed loyalty to an
American Negro . . . fired her to battle for recognition of his people, compiling
and publishing her *Negro Anthology*." But Cunard's travels and relationships
amounted to many more engagements than her affair with Crowder; there was
an anthropological dimension to her modus operandi. She accumulated a lexicon of African American vernacular, and provided a glossary of terms for *Negro*'s readers, translating American street idioms for the speaker of British English: "*Brother*: equivalent to old chap . . . *Feelin' as low as whale's dung*: feeling

very low indeed."[179] In 1935 she commented in *Left Review* on writer Anatoli Vinogradov's *The Black Consul*, "we find the Negro written off as an historical equal—it has taken the revolutionary point of view to do justice to plain facts," suggesting the ways in which politics informed her personal encounters.[180] Cunard refashioned her own history in ways that claimed a lifelong core of racial consciousness. She recalled Crowder:

> I was intensely interested—amazed too—at what I learned from him about the life of the American Negro. . . . My feeling for things African had begun years ago with sculpture, and something of these anonymous old statues had now, it seemed, materialized in the personality of a man partly of that race. My sympathy with the Afro-American had, obviously, begun with music.[181]

In childhood she had dreamed of Africa, "the 'Dark Continent'—with Africans dancing and drumming around me, and I one of them, though still white, knowing mysteriously enough, how to dance in their own manner."[182] Cunard toured the German ethnographic museum collections with Crowder, and much of her self-presentation as a racial investigator and amateur ethnographer continued to celebrate the "exotica" of blackness, even as she strove to connect her interests to a more conventional political discourse—one with which she was never entirely *au fait*.[183] The result was a success of a rare and pioneering kind, full of contradiction and idiosyncracy. The distinguished ex-patriate American writer Janet Flanner, wrote of *Negro*, "It was the first book of such scope—of such unlimited immediate hopes for the Negroes—and it had an unusual list of distinguished contributors."[184] Cunard's wider American contacts assisted her development of this list, including the New Jersey physician and master poet William Carlos Williams, who offered a prose fragment, and whose home address Cunard used as her own when visiting in the United States.[185]

Scottsboro was central to the anthology, even though *Negro* drifted to many subjects. A number of campaign signatory-contributors appeared throughout. A painting by Augustus John, and Ike Hatch's photographs figured among images of work by or about a few dozen black artists. The members of Padmore's immediate circle were also contributors; the anthology featured his photograph and his essays on Ethiopia, the British Empire, and South Africa. A likeness of Kenyatta, and an essay by Padmore's colleague from his former Comintern Negro work, Nigerian Benjamin Nnamdi Azikiwe further represented his influence.[186] The volume's contents were considered explosive enough to warrant its ban from sale in the West Indies by government order.[187] Cunard wrote to her friend W. J. Strachan in 1961 about the belated growth of her American readership: "I am so glad that at last Afro-America is taking more interest in its antecedents than it did when I was there in 1932."[188]

The publication of *Negro* elicited some critical responses in Britain, but most Londoners would have been more aware of the ongoing public work of the Scottsboro Defense Committee and of its allied organizations and grouplets

than of the anthology, if they knew of the case at all. There were marches in
Hyde Park in 1934, more demonstrations at the American embassy, and more
joint work between the ILD and groups like the socialist freethinkers.[189] Amy
Ashwood Garvey, the Afro-Caribbean activist and first wife of Marcus Garvey,
appeared on the campaign platform at a Hyde Park demonstration that summer alongside Reginald Bridgeman and Arnold Ward.[190] *We Were Framed*, the
Scottsboro Defense Committee's first published account of the case in pamphlet form, appeared in June, its publication the occasion for a concert of
"Negro artists," which raised one hundred pounds in donations to the ILD.
One of the event's sponsors was the Amalgamated Engineers Union, long active in Scottsboro.[191] The American playwright John Wexley's drama about the
case, *They Shall Not Die* was performed in branches of the Left Theater in Hol-
born, Greenwich, and East Ham. The radical Catholic activist Monica Whately
addressed audiences during the play's intervals.[192] On June 29, 1934, the *Times*
broke the news that Haywood Patterson's and Clarence Norris's convictions
had been upheld in the U.S. courts, followed by more stays of execution.[193] The
Old Trafford branch of the ILP near Manchester sent letters of protest to President Roosevelt that characterized the death sentences as "merely a reflection of
racial prejudice, and a gross travesty of justice." The Women's Cooperative
Guild of Rochdale wrote to the president pleading for the lives of the defendants, "believing they have suffered sufficiently for any crime they are supposed to have committed."[194] Later that year, the secretary of education for the
Salop County Council, E. B. Ross, also wrote to Roosevelt.

> You may feel it not our business in England. But many men and women of goodwill
> are working hard for the complete abdication of the Death penalty here, as, I believe,
> in some of your own States, even in conclusively proved cases of actual murder. . . .
> will you intervene . . . in accordance with your strength, goodness, and [as] a gesture
> of wisdom and guidance to the World ? The World needs a lead in clemency and
> justice.[195]

The defense campaign was changing, both in Britain and in the United
States. It was a precursor to the "popular front" era, associated with the Comintern's decision to drop the disastrous "class against class line" of Stalin's
Third Period and end a time of violent contempt for the noncommunist left,
including the Labour party and the ILP.[196] In Britain, the defense campaign
had been a coalition from the outset, in a context in which no European-style
mass political parties of the left existed. The zany presence of Cunard with her
off-beat paeans to the Soviets, coupled with her literary populism and willingness to bring many into the fold, was eventually matched by developments
in the United States that ultimately engaged the NAACP with the ILD apparatus, as well as other organizations.[197] In the Soviet Union, ordinary Russians
were still mobilized in defense of the "Scottsboro Boys." In 1934 the case still
served as an exemplar of the NAACP's "reformist" betrayal, an exposé of

American hypocrisy. In February 1934, African American journalist Henry Lee Moon published, "A Negro Looks at Soviet Russia" in the pages of *The Nation*.

> Interest in the final outcome of the Scottsboro case is far keener in the Soviet Union than in America. Despite the wide publicity given the case, no group in this country [the USA] has ever been able to assemble 40,000 people in a single meeting to protest. . . . Yet I saw such a crowd in an unforgettable demonstration one evening in the vast open-air amphitheater in Moscow's Park of Rest and Culture. Row after row of eager faces of men, women and children listening attentively as Negro and white, Russian and American, told the story. . . . There was a Union Square ring in the speeches of the Americans. There were the usual cherished denunciations of the capitalist courts and the bourgeois press, and a tirade, sounding rather irrelevant at that distance from the scene, against the NAACP. A dramatic picturization in fireworks of the fall of [Alabama's] Kilby Prison before the onslaught of an aroused working class concluded the demonstration.[198]

Whatever its political fortunes, the campaign continued to enhance and to contribute to a fascination with the American South among both the British public and radical activists. Naomi Mitchison journeyed to America in 1935 with her friend Zita Baker, taking up the conversation that had started in her earlier encounters in the Soviet Union, as recorded above. But her American contacts were followers of the Second International—socialists not communists. She was led to friends in Memphis, Tennessee, by the aging American socialist leader Norman Thomas, whom she visited in Boston not long after her arrival. The American socialist party hosted her at a series of events involving the Southern Tenants' Farmers Union, for which she became a spokesperson, and in so doing she crossed paths with Jennie Lee whose writings opened this chapter.[199] Mitchison's trip is another instance of the profound impact of Southern exposure upon British *marxisant* and liberal circles, and her revelations of racial encounters characterize the genre. Her diaries and writings recorded the experience.

Coming to Memphis

This-here is the end of the world,
Full of the gloomy and endless walking
Of the property-less great-grandchildren of slaves.
Poverty here tooths the eroded banks,
Rots through the soaking timber,
Picks at the boards of cabins.
This is the end of my kind of world.
Oh Challengers,
Oh Movers of the new thing in the human spirit,
Is it the beginning of yours ?[200]

She had not anticipated the seriousness of the trip, but perhaps had taken a cue from Loren Miller and Langston Hughes in Russia.

> I am going to America by a cargo liner which also takes passengers: £36 return. It looks rather fun, and takes ten days to get to New York. . . . I shan't stay in New York long. Then Zita Baker and I will pass (I hope) the US driving test, buy a Ford and set off south. . . . I want to see the cotton growing country, also if possible the Tennessee [TVA] dam, and we may get as far as New Orleans. The roads are good and there are car camps everywhere. . . . I need a holiday . . . and I also need to get a perspective on Europe and present-day events. Whether it's a good thing or not, I am one of the leaders now and I have to keep my mind supple.[201]

Her manuscript diary records their exploits.

> We bought a second-hand Ford; people said we should take guns, but we said no, no they might go off. Well, they said, at least never give lifts. . . . we gave lifts to all sorts of delightful people, white and black, some of whom helped us put our car together when bits fell off it, while others sang to us. . . . Zita and I got involved with the sharecroppers in the black soil, one-crop, cotton country the far side of the Mississippi. . . . not yet having seen Howrah or the Palestinian refugee camps, I had never met such poverty, the houses built of old pieces of tin and cardboard, the children obviously suffering from pellagra, American children who didn't know a chocolate bar when they saw one: poor whites and poor blacks living equally badly and determined to struggle together for a slightly fairer share of the cake and also perhaps for *freundschaft* and *freiheit*. We went to packed meetings in candle-lit rooms with boarded windows in case there was shooting. . . . Very few had socks. It made me think of Tolpuddle [where nineteenth-century labor protestors were arrested] and I told my new friends about the martyrs and then about Vienna [where she visited during political conflict in the 30s] and comradely solidarity. . . . I was asked to speak. . . . my poor Chairman at one meeting had bad trouble, for he put his hand on my shoulder introducing me: I was a white woman, he a black man. Someone duly shot in his house. . . . both being personable young women, [we] were good publicity for the sharecroppers.

Mitchison described the law officers of the region.

> . . . two wicked sheriffs, like characters in a movie. . . . there was the chaplain to the Union, coal-black Mr. Brookins. Wanting above all to leave him with a taste of happiness and encouragement, I dodged my anti-religious principles and knelt on the sidewalk for his blessing. We corresponded with one another until 1939. . . Zita . . . told me rightly, I think, that it was time I started wearing a bra, which I had not done so far. . . . We had decided that we must go to Washington and tell those in power about the sharecroppers . . . but found . . . worse than indifference.

Mitchison and Baker wrote directly to Roosevelt, receiving only a perfunctory acknowledgment. But when new legislation relieved some of the sharecroppers, Mitchison ventured "Perhaps we helped a little."[202]

Mitchison and others involved in the Scottsboro campaign were unorthodox fellow travelers, not hardened party stalwarts. When the British ILD collapsed in late 1934, the Comintern charged "organizational incompetence . . . [the] failure to understand the growing fascism and tasks that grow out of that for the ILD." Instead, a new plan was needed, of "strictly non-party independent character." Scottsboro had widened in its appeal, and the defendants were supported by celebrities and notables. Tones altered; communist activists tried to make the transition and to place the Scottsboro mothers in rhetorical ascendancy two years after Ada Wright returned home. The Negro families of the defendants were now considered educated to the struggle, so to speak, and possessed of a worldliness in their new incarnation, as viewed from Moscow:

> From the depths of despair into which they were first plunged they have been lifted to high levels of hope and of understanding. More than they have ever known before or hoped to know of life has been crowded into their lives in a period of three short years. Now it is clear to them that the struggles for the lives of their young ones is an inseparable part of the struggle of the liberation of humanity from war and from oppression. . . . Their roots are deep in the soil. They are being steeled in the struggle. They are growing. They have spoken against war and fascism.[203]

But a month later, Janie Patterson, Haywood Patterson's mother, wrote to President Roosevelt in a very different language: "You know how mother love is, for my boy is innocent he was just only looking for a job, to help his father my child was a Christian he went to church every Sunday at the Church of Christ."[204] The gap between the "real" mothers and the "communist" mothers widened as all sides searched for new angles.

When Naomi Mitchison returned to Britain flushed from the sharecroppers' struggles, she received a missive from Eleanor Rathbone:

> *Dear Mrs. Mitchison,*
> I did reluctantly consent to join the Scottsboro' Committee, but didn't know it had Communist affiliations. Not that I would object to that myself, but I do think it a bad connection for anyone who wants to influence general public opinion as it would be more likely to alienate it. I think my best plan is just to send you a cheque for £5 and ask you to be good enough to pass it on to the Association for the Advancement of Colored People, or whatever other body you find is dealing with the matter, either now or when you get to the USA. I don't know the address of the Association and I expect you do, so I hope this is not giving you too much trouble.

Rathbone added a postscript indicating her intention to take up the matter with "some of the Labour leaders and stir them up about it."[205] Rathbone's letter is in the files of the NAACP; Mitchison did as she was asked. Walter White's office replied in a letter addressed to "Eleanor *Rathborn*," stating, "Mrs. Mitchison has handed us your very generous contribution of five pounds for the Scottsboro cases. . . . your interest is appreciated." This exchange indicates the

NAACP's continuing ties to many diverse circles in London and the ease with which it could seek legitimation as a new arm of the legal defense of the later campaign.[206] Many of Rathbone's associates were increasingly publically connected to Scottsboro and, like herself, were not taken for communists; they preferred a wider brief and participated avidly in less partisan events. A May 1935 Garrick Theater gathering featuring "Famous Negro Artists" boasted the patronage of Liberal MP and antislavery advocate Lord Noel-Buxton, and Lady Marley, the spouse of Dudley Leigh Aman, the Labour member of the House of Lords. Lord Marley was Willi Münzenberg's chief establishment contact in London and wrote the introduction to the *Brown Book of the Hitler Terror*.[207]

Later that year, Ike Hatch attended the regional "Blackfaced Minstrel Picnic" in London at the time of the visit of a singing group from Kentucky. The *Daily Worker* reunion that autumn featured a "carnival Dance Band" and a performance by the Kentucky minstrels.[208] In May 1935 Paul Robeson appeared in the London run of Paul Green's *Stevedore* at the Embassy Repertory Theater. George Padmore was one of those who helped him recruit black actors for the production, which depicted interracial labor organizing.[209] Nancy Cunard reviewed it for the NAACP's journal *The Crisis*, a clear manifestation of her intent to reach all parties involved in the case just as Padmore's work with Robeson, after his ties with Moscow ended, signaled his willingness to do work among circles close to the CPGB. Cunard wrote of the "mosaic" of actors taking the parts of African Americans, and then of the response of the London audience:

> [A]s everywhere it is the main body of the stalls which understands least the true import of such plays on social or racial themes. . . . this part, particularly, of English audiences, knows very little of the Negro's situation in USA. That lynchings take place is known—not much, if anything beyond that. To be stirred by the action, the story and the vivid black personalities, yes—but not *shattered* by the facts presented, as has happened with American audiences. The other parts of the theater grasp it all better. The applause is long and sincere.

Cunard believed that if *Stevedore* toured, it would get full and appreciative working-class audiences. The play's guiding force, the film and theater critic Marie Seton, had complained to Cunard that blacks did not attend the show. Cunard eschewed objection to the script's use of "nigger" in the lines of the Southern white lynch-mob characters, praising the play's treatment of what she termed the "racial-social question."[210]

At the end of the year, Cunard departed London and chaired a Paris gala in defense of Ethiopia, now threatened by Mussolini's regime.[211] The Negro Press Association in the United States sent her to Geneva to report on the League of Nations, and in April she left for Barcelona to cover the war in Spain. Padmore saw her off at the station in Paris. She freelanced over the next three years, contributing to the *Manchester Guardian* and Sylvia Pankhurst's *New Times and Ethiopia News*. The weakening Scottsboro campaign in London held a dance at

Bush House, just as the sixth anniversary of the *Daily Worker* was being celebrated at City Hall. Palme Dutt, the leading communist theoretician, was the keynote speaker for the *Daily Worker* event, which featured the William Morris Choir performing Stanford Robinson's arrangement of "Swanee River" and "L'il Liza Jane."[212] In the United States, *The Crisis* hailed the Supreme Court's decision to defy Alabama's all-white jury in the Scottsboro case. The rejection of two earlier decisions had set the stage for the upcoming new trials of the defendants.[213] *The Crisis* attempted to seize the moral high ground in the case by complimenting the communists and challenging them in the same breath:

> The Scottsboro defendants ... never heard of Communists or radicals or liberals or conservatives. They had no political beliefs. Out of a clear sky they found themselves in the worst spot a Negro can find himself in the South: charged with rape by a white woman.... the exploitation of Negroes by the South has been pitilessly exposed to the world. An important legal victory has been won against the lily-white jury system. As far as propaganda is concerned the whole Negro race is far ahead of where it would have been had the Communists not fought the case in the way that they did. But what about the Scottsboro youths? They stand today in precisely the same danger.... The lives and freedom of these boys is more precious to them than the future of the Negro race.... Shall we fight to free the defendants ... or use them as pawns?[214]

1936–39: SPAIN TO MUNICH

In 1936 Cunard was in Spain, and Lascelles Abercrombie, like many former leading Scottsboro activists, had other pressing preoccupations. In February, he contributed a letter to the *Times* entitled, "Persecution of the Jews, Cultural Relations with Germany" on behalf of the Academic Freedom Committee. "The Vortex of Spain: Issues of the Conflict" appeared in the August *New Statesman and Nation*, signed by the same group who had cosigned his earlier manifesto entitled "Britain and the Spanish War."[215] Scottsboro sentiment flowed toward the civil-liberties and civil-rights concerns posed by the war in Spain waged against a democratically elected republic. Robeson cut a record in aid of the refugee Basque children, which included a reading of Langston Hughes's "Minstrel Man."[216] October witnessed the largest antifascist march ever mounted in London, and the issues it raised absorbed the attentions and energies of many whose eyes had turned for years and months across the Atlantic and south to Madrid. Now, they turned toward central Europe.

A month after this demonstration, Ada Wright wrote from Chattanooga to one of her patrons among the ILD women in New York City. She referred to Anna Damon, one of the leaders of the ILD.

> Your letter didn't find me so well nor my family. I am tell you what I need in clothing line. Underwear not so long underwear, stocking. Lucile [her daughter] needs

sweater and shoes big you can find them in shoes line, Size 30 in skirt. Are not you all not going to send us down and see the boys anymore. Please give Annie Damon my best wishes and love and all the comrade in all the offices my best wishes and love. Next times you write Please send me some stamps. We all send love to you all u I be looking for my thing. Please, please don't send Mrs. Patterson [Haywood Patterson's mother] all the best thing. Lucile is going to school everyday but don't have any good shoes go in. Yours truly, Mother Wright[217]

In January 1937 she wrote and insisted, "Most things fix Lucile and not myself. . . . when are the boy trial come up I would like very much to go when it come up." A week later, ILD leader Rose Baron, replied, "we sincerely hope that you receive as much pleasure from the contents as we did in sending them to you."[218]

In February 1937 the *Times* continued its frequent coverage of American lynchings. "A young Negro is reported to have been lynched near Headland, Alabama. A crowd of armed men seized him from the jail where he was detained on a charge of attacking a white girl, and his bullett-riddled body was afterwards found hanging in a wood."[219] Thereafter the paper dutifully recorded the new developments in the slow-moving, despairing Scottsboro case. In July 1937 the Alabama Supreme Court upheld the death sentence for Clarence Norris and lengthy sentences for four other defendants, but the four youngest, including Roy Wright, Ada's son, were freed after six years of incarceration.[220] The *Times* offered an explanation for the length of time that had passed since the case began. "One of the two women . . . long ago confessed that her charge against them was false, but the other has never altered her testimony."[221] A month later, the newspaper misleadingly declared, "End of Scottsboro Cases: Four Negroes Set Free."[222] Roy Wright's brother Andy and four others remained in custody.

The four freed youths from the South had a tumultuous reception in New York's Pennsylvania Station, orchestrated by Samuel Leibowitz, the spectacular and controversial criminal lawyer who had remained with the case since the first Decatur trial, despite his anticommunism.[223] The *Chicago Defender* wryly observed Leibowitz telling all four, "while speeding northward" by train, "that they were moving toward a richer, fuller life," after which they "assumed the appearance of four collegians."[224] Lucile Wright wrote to Leibowitz, "Mother shouted and cry out that 'Oh my baby boy is free.'"[225] But ten days later the newspaper also reported that Mother Wright and Olen Montgomery's mother, Viola Montgomery, had been housed at a separate Brooklyn address from the freed youngsters and given very little time with their sons. Their mothers did not travel with the four young men to defense engagements, remaining off the platforms, in the audience. Willie Roberson and Eugene Williams joined Brooklyn's Holy Trinity Church at the behest of their clergyman host. By the end of the month, long before the freed defendants' lives slipped back into the anonymity of poverty and even bouts of imprisonment, CPUSA leader William Patterson arrived in London to claim victory in his terms. The *Daily Worker* reported that he attributed "the success of the campaign to win freedom for the Scottsboro boys to the united front of Race organizations with the white working class and liberal movements of the world." His change of line was evident. Hitler was in power; Stalin was sabotaging the Spanish Republican forces, and five of the defendants sat in their cells in Alabama as the war approached—the others were declared free courtesy of the Popular Front.[226]

Paul Robeson's involvement in Spain was a focus of racially conscious politics until the defeat of the Republic, and many from the Scottsboro circles mobilized around the British defense of Spain. Angela Guest, the daughter of Dr. Leslie Haden-Guest MP and Carmel Haden Guest of the Scottboro committee, returned from Spain where her brother had been killed fighting, and offered a public narrative of the events there. In May 1938 Robeson visited Spain, where he was followed by reporters into the ranks of the U.S. Lincoln Brigades, for a visit with its African American members.[227] This activity continued to leave the "Scottsboro Boys" behind. With the fate of Europeans increasingly at issue, the urgency attached to the defendants' case in Alabama waned and the case felt old.

Nancy Mitford's *The Pursuit of Love*, set in the late thirties, portrays a heroine whose communist lover takes her to "exotic" political parties:

> "Czechs at the Sacco and Vanzetti Memorial Hall in Golders Green, Ethiopians at the Paddington Baths . . . and the Scottsboro boys at some boring old rooms or other. You know." . . . "The Scottsboro' boys," I said. "Are they really still going? They must be getting on." "Yes, and they've gone downhill socially," said Linda, with a giggle. "I remember a perfectly divine party Brian gave for them. . . . it was fun. . . . next Thursday won't be the least like that. . . . I bet the Scottsboro boys will be electrocuted in the end, if they don't die of old age first, that is. One does feel so much on their side, but it's no good."[228]

In June 1938, in a short burst of energy, D. N. Pritt, lead counsel in the mock Reichstag Fire Trial; H. G. Wells, who had been investigating Roosevelt's America for himself; and Paul Robeson, released a statement that was picked up by the *Pittsburgh Courier*.

> Despite the present tragic turn of world events and the constant war rumors which are spreading, there are still some people who are determined to press for the recognition of human rights [and who] appeal to draw folks to the case again. . . . How is it that five can still be guilty if four are innocent? Justice should be international and we ask British opinion to show its practical sympathy.

They requested that readers send telegrams to Alabama governor Bibb Graves and the Alabama Kilby Prison warden, demanding the transfer of Ozie Powell from chain-gang labor, referring their supporters to Arnold Ward in Islington, who could supply speakers on the case.[229] That month, the Alabama Supreme Court upheld the decision to execute Clarence Norris, but Governor Graves commuted the sentence to life imprisonment in July. Haywood Patterson and Ozie Powell petitioned the court for pardons, which were denied in August. Clarence Norris, Charlie Weems, and Andy Wright, Ada Wright's elder son, were denied pardons in October. All five defendants still serving time were again denied pardons in November 1938, two months after Munich.[230]

Aftermath and Reflections

For Ada Wright, times remained hard as the war approached. She wrote to ILD leader Rose Baron in New York during Thanksgiving 1939.

> Rosa have they cut me off all way off look like you would have wrote and told me. . . . Please send me something big enough for me . . . a coat size 46. I need one so bad. Do you all think you will get Andy them a pardon for xmas I hope so. Rosa you no I have got $5.00 for this month. If you see Ben Davis [of the ILD] you tell him for me please that Lucile said she was looking for a box of candy he promised her. Give him my love also all the comrades my love. Time is awfully hard down here. I am not working.[231]

These were not the words of a hardened recruit. Wright's audiences in Britain were unlikely to have imagined her sons as proletarian heroes. The prevailing British antislavery movement of the 1930s attested to the widespread sympathy for victims of slavery wherever they were in the world; this sentiment and a ready identification with injured motherhood, seemed to transform the defendants into "slaves who should be set free," in the eyes of Wright's beholders, and her own speeches anticipated those perceptions. Even for adherents of the more committed left, the graphic exposure of the flaws of American democracy conjured up the post–Reconstruction South—not so much the "class struggle" of the urban North, but the race war of the Southern states so often conveyed by the travel literature of the day. Glasgow's *Forward* wrote of James Ford running for vice president of the United States on the communist ticket: "They are running a negro . . . who remembers the lynching of his grandfather, away down in Georgia."[232]

Empire reformers found solace in this violent rendition of their American cousins. The myth that the Empire did not behave in the same way, and its supporting claim that the civility of domestic England witnessed no lynchings, were comforting examples of the rule of law, not lynch law. The reformers avidly sought to distinguish themselves from a Southern mentality, and Scottsboro provided an arena in which to do so. Both the glamour and the terrifying spectacle of 1930s America fed the Scottsboro stories. In the syndicated "Nine

Niggers on a Train," Louis Golding identified the two white girls "who certainly had no nodding acquaintance with Ceasar's wife."[233] Elizabeth Lawson declared in her campaign pamphlet *Scottsboro's Martyr*, "As they stood there and gave their message, the curtain of ignorance and illusions concerning America was rent asunder and millions of European workers saw the Black Belt! They saw that Uncle Sam was a twentieth-century slave-driver—a modern Simon Legree."[234]

Yet for all the rendering of the "black masses" and all the anonymity embedded in the picture of "Southern toilers," the Scottsboro campaign paradoxically still relied upon outstanding, self-respecting, and independent personalities of color—among them Wright herself. The defendants emerged with individual faces, with names on placards and their photographs in the mass European and ILD press, sometimes docile, other times menacing. The Continental campaign also used blackface performers in Scottsboro skits. The tension between promoting leading black figures as charismatic and prepossessing individuals and the theatrical control exercised over the public life of the campaign, surfaced in the internal correspondence between black participants, including between Padmore and his incongruous, autodidact comrade Arnold Ward. Ada Wright's visit was a focal point for speculation and private gossip, even as it gave ground for white mischief.

In 1933, as above, Ward wrote to Padmore of a new vigor: "Since Mrs. Wright been here the International Solidarity has taken on a deeper and greater hold on the workers. Here more than I have ever seen before and I think it is for the best. Boy we are moving. Cheerio." His proprietary sense of how the lady ought to have been treated and advised shines through as he chides the ILD leader Lovell.

> The Scottboro [*sic*] campaign was a big success overflowing meetings everywhere, Bob Lovell the Swine He work Mrs. Wright like a Slave but this woman is a Good woman and will do anything for the party cause and Her two Children comes next. I really think that the party should take her in hand and train her because she is a gallant Fighter."[235]

The tales of transatlantic comradely "enslavement" of the defendants' mothers at the hands of their communist hosts bespoke the sustaining power of racial attitudes in personal behavior, a pattern not lost on the fascist movements that overtook Europe. After Hitler's assumption of power in 1933, Scottsboro continued alongside many other intertwined campaigns for forms of social justice—some communist led, others not. The British ILD, sponsors of Mrs. Wright's visit, was not reconstituted after 1934—its leader, Alun Thomas, resigned to its collapse. "This is a hell of country to be in just now. Things seem so docile in comparison with everywhere else. We have the tremendous number of five class war prisoners and all of those will be out, except two, some time this month." Still, protests continued on the part of groups like the West

African Students Union (WASU), an organization of young colonial activists living in Britain, and Moody's LOCP, whose ties to the NAACP remained.[236] The Labour party persisted in monitoring the left as war grew nearer.

Scottsboro continued as a communist case, even as many noncommunists and anticommunists became more involved in the advocacy of the defendants. But in the end, the larger "fight against fascism" overtook and swallowed up the antiracist language and purpose of the Scottsboro movement. It appropriated the cause of racial justice, refocused it, and reinterpreted it. Support for China transfixed many British activists. Opposition to the Italian invasion of Abyssinia embodied the Scottsboro spirit for some, as Italy attacked and sought to subjugate a black African nation.[237] The Comintern's approachs to anticolonial and anti-imperial causes were often reset and recalibrated though the later thirties, imposing other contradictions upon those activists who still sought its leadership.

The legal wrangling, war's imminence, the suspicions leveled at the defense, and the air of urgency attached to other matters, forced a fade-out of Scottsboro work in Europe. Ada Wright's tour of Britain was a piece of the challenge that the campaign posed for interracialism, public witness, and for racial understandings and misunderstandings, revisited in the postwar world.[238] If Ada Wright did not upstage Paul Robeson or Louis Armstrong in the Anglo-European imaginary, she brought their experience into focus on another plain. Not an entertainer by profession, Wright nevertheless satisfied the curiosity of many in the crowds. One need not have advocated an end of empire, nor promoted a communist or any other kind of revolution in order to chant "free the Scottsboro Boys." The communist and broader left gained some credibility by its championing of the defendants and lost some by its failure to win the clear victory of their full release and exoneration. The role of the case in terms of legal precedent was still hazy as the thirties came to an end.[239]

The power of Ada Wright lay in her crossing of borders, but the black tourists whose hotel preferences grace the pages of the *Chicago Defender* and *Pittsburgh Courier* did that as well. She was the most unlikely of tourists, the least likely of mothers, to bring a story of her sons across the Atlantic. But the fact that she did so, uniquely in the pantheon of African American imagery, brought the broader American experience of Jim Crow and its opponents into view in a new way for Europeans who heard about her. As an element of her course of action, Wright sought and found a way to speak in several languages and her words were reinterpreted and presented in other words, by other voices. The Southern speech of her birth was refined by her religious training and limited formal education. She incompletely assimilated the slogans and epithets of the Comintern and meandered through "black vernaculars" imposed by her editors in the retellings. Her Primitive Baptist commitment to a devout and absorbing sect on the fringe of the black Baptist congregations steeled her for her communist sojourn. Its discipline, both mental and physical, offered counsel and redemption. Whatever happened on this Atlantic crossing, a crossing that her family said she found exciting and exhilarating, Wright understood herself as destined for an even better place, not of this world. Her shrewdness projected modesty. Her former employer's son bellowed, "Ada didn't know a communist from an elephant," but those who knew her best said she told them that "there are people she met over there, white people, who treated her better than some of her own kind ever had at home."[240] Her letters to New York greet readers in a schooled, feminine hand, her grammar and syntax askew. The white communist ladies could not have easily forgotten her, and she did not let them do so.[241] She was a quintessential "mother" whose defiance of the limits imposed on mobility by the category of "motherhood," was her hallmark, even as her promoters sought to project the docility of pathos. She was a pioneer of humanitarianism in a lexicon that reserved that label for persons of notoriety and trained intellect. She forced the jaws of "African American experience" to widen awkwardly and some of Europe's troubled peoples to dare to receive the visitor at an inopportune moment. Not only bourgeois convention was disrupted and not only a complicated and forbidding political map traversed. The racial etiquette of the left was closer to its establishment origins than it cared to acknowledge. There was no sure place for Ada Wright, and precious little for those outwardly resembling her, yet she found a slight foothold, and some listened. Her adjudged authenticity was "more real" than that of the communists. There was no musicians' union to throw her from the Savoy's bandstand so that white artists might try to imitate her unchallenged.[242] Her physicality was unusual in those times in Britain, especially in the provincial areas where some had never seen a black person, and her verbiage was unmistakably "uncolonial" and African American. Scottsboro became larger, more humane, more suggestive and more intrusive when she appeared on the scene. In her hands so used to work, the plight of "her boys" lit another kind of fire.

Chapter 2

GEORGE PADMORE AND LONDON

In 1924 THE YOUNG STUDENT Malcolm Nurse traveled by ship up the eastern coast of the United States from his native Trinidad and disembarked in New York City. The Ellis Island immigration authorities classified him as an "African Black" on sight, though he had not yet journeyed to the continent that drew much of his life's interests and commitments. Malcolm Nurse lived briefly on West 135th Street in Harlem and took a sociology course at Columbia University fifteen blocks south before heading across the Mason-Dixon Line. Though he was a black man living under Jim Crow, only two hours' drive from Chattanooga, his life was in most ways very different from that of Ada Wright and her family. He had come to Nashville to pursue his medical studies at African American Fisk University. Born in the Arouca District of Trinidad and raised in Port of Spain, Nurse completed the Cambridge Local Examinations at secondary school and was awarded a medical board certificate in 1916. When he came to America, he left his wife Julia Semper, pregnant with their daughter, at home. The child symbolized their identification with the cause of Trinidadian emancipation from the British, named as she was for Edward Blyden, a seminal figure for pioneers of Carribean independence.[1]

Nurse's political commitments grew and the prospect of remaining at Fisk dimmed for the young schoolmaster's son, grandson of a slave, rumored to be a relative of the celebrated Caribbean activist Henry Sylvester Williams.[2] Instead, he began speaking out regularly on the problems of colonial rule and the British Empire, participating in a symposium on China at nearby, segregated Vanderbilt University in 1927. His political activities in Nashville may have gained him notoriety with the local Ku Klux Klan. Four years before the Scottsboro case broke, he left the region for America's radical political center, arriving in New York for the last sustained visit of his lifetime. The study of law briefly beckoned Malcolm Nurse, but his increasingly demanding political commitments led him to withdraw from New York University in late 1927. He joined the American communist party in 1928 and took his cousin's name as a pseudonym. An American official in Liberia appeared a decade later with that same name; the coincidence created more than a little confusion. But Nurse never relinquished the alias and was now "George Padmore." He found employment as a janitor at the *New York Times* building and as a crewman on Hudson riverboats, an anonymous West Indian who sought out the country's greatest newspaper and one of her greatest waterways as a common laborer-observer. Former communist youth activist Miriam Sherman recalled him visiting her parents' home in upstate New York; an important and welcomed black man talked in low tones after dinner with his comrades who were her parents, just before they and other families were scheduled to leave to help form a communal laundry in the Soviet Union. When that plan fell through they moved en masse to Los Angeles whence she journeyed to Moscow and met her traveling companion Ada Wright.[3]

But the party soon assigned Padmore to the nation's capital to organize at Howard University. The future American diplomat Ralph Bunche met him for the first time when Padmore enrolled in his class. Alain Locke lived in Washington with his mother and was part of the Howard circles, as was the future Nigerian president Benjamin Nnamdi Azikiwe, whom Padmore had approached while still at Fisk to seek his help in agitation around the issues facing Liberia.[4] Padmore readily exhibited strong leadership skills and a charismatic intelligence. But in what is perhaps the most interesting recorded admission of his American years, he wrote in a letter to his sister-in-law, "Life, habits, customs and institutions of this country are entirely different to ours and never appeal to one who has had a decent British training."[5] His biographer attributes his success as a youth leader to the experience of hearing and seeing dissent in the West Indian context, but Padmore's speech, etiquette, and a cogent writing style owed a great deal to his rigorous formal education, whatever the contributions of free thinking.

While Padmore was traveling back and forth between New York and Washington, Willi Münzenberg was busy organizing his Comintern-funded, anticolonial work in Europe. The League against Colonial Oppression, first convened in 1927 at Brussels, and its rump successor, the communist-dominated LAI, cultivated sympathizers among liberals, radicals, and humanitarian opponents of empire.[6] The British section of the LAI, so active in Scottsboro, was formed in April.[7] Delegates to the Sixth Congress of the Comintern, held in Moscow between July and September 1928, affirmed a more concerted dedication to anticolonialism and the "Negro question" in the United States. These were the organizational and doctrinal steps that strengthened the web of American ILD connections that assisted Ada Wright and Louis Engdahl to move around Europe. Padmore made his name in these networks as early as 1928 by writing for the American *Daily Worker* alongside leading Harlem communist Richard B. Moore, an advisor and escort of Wright and her family in the thirties.

Moscow, Hamburg, and the Comintern Days

Padmore boarded a ship bound for Germany in the summer of 1929 and made his way to Frankfurt to attend the second conference of Münzenberg's LAI, held near the city's zoo. The organization embraced a broad coalition of global fighters for freedom and justice, yet in the years that followed, fewer and fewer of those present would gather communally.[8] Internecine strife ripped away the pacifists from communists, socialists from liberals, labor advocates from Stalin's defenders, and nationalists from internationalists. William Pickens of the NAACP served on the LAI Executive but voted against a key resolution calling for the overthrow of the colonial empires in Africa.[9] His communist detractors did not let him forget this faux pas on European soil.

Padmore met Jomo Kenyatta in Frankfurt and they traveled together to Moscow. He also met ILP leader James Maxton, a great parliamentary orator who would become one of Padmore's white allies, and Reginald Bridgeman, who would serve as Ada Wright's host in London. Padmore and the Soudanese activist Garan Kouyate, who was also on the LAI Executive, also became fast friends.[10] After the conference, Padmore briefly returned to New York to join his wife; he told her that the American party leader William Z. Foster demanded his presence in Moscow. Never would the couple share a roof again. As a result of his Moscow sojourn, he was refused entry to the United States five years later. Padmore now began his career as a polemicist and organizer for the Comintern, an organization whose branches and fledgling affiliates were barely formed or united when he graduated from the College of the Immaculate Conception in Trinidad two years before the Russian Revolution, a brilliant young writer and speaker. The Red International of Trade Unions (also known as the Profintern), an amalgam of communist fractions in the labor movement that sought to create alternatives to the official "reformist" trade organizations, appointed him head of its tiny Negro Committee. Under Padmore, the Bureau became a more vocal, noticeable, and mixed confederation of those of African descent. It is no exaggeration to suggest that Padmore himself *became* the Negro Committee in the few short years of its greatest prominence, years encompassing the early campaign around Scottsboro.[11]

On his next trip to Russia, Padmore wrote for the *Moscow Daily News*, and performed various interventionist tasks for the Comintern leadership including the adjudication of Chinese factional matters. The party supported his lavish lifestyle in circumstances having little in common with those of ordinary Muscovites. Padmore journeyed to London where he met the British communist leader Harry Pollitt in Euston Station, adjacent to neighborhoods where he was to spend most of the rest of his life.[12] The historian Woodford McClellan has established that Padmore visited Africa very briefly at this time, setting out from Liverpool, visiting Dakar, Sierra Leone, Liberia, and Gold Coast in an attempt to recruit delegates for his 1930 Hamburg conference.[13] But his efforts did not fare well. Police agents and intelligence forces sought to inhibit all those who might attend the Conference.[14] There is no record of his traveling to Africa again at any other point until after the war, and his movements in the 1930s were restricted to Europe as—in Kenyatta's words— "a commercial traveler of sorts," what Americans would term a "traveling salesman." [15] Padmore carried with him a deep and familiar knowledge of life in the Caribbean and parts of America as his writings always demonstrated, even though his meetings with West Indians, Asians, African Americans, and Africans occurred almost exclusively in Germany, Vienna, Moscow, Paris, and London.

Padmore had withdrawn from Howard University before leaving the United States but not to a life entirely removed from academic pursuits. In 1930 he taught at KUTV (communist), University of the Toilers of the East, in Moscow where there were perhaps a dozen black students. [16] Padmore later boasted of his own intervention in a dispute over the racist behavior of visiting American workers toward blacks. His correspondence revealed a nuanced and critical perspective on racial etiquette and a watchful and skeptical eye trained on his white European comrades. While remaining outwardly loyal in his public writings during the few years in which he was a Comintern functionary, Padmore's private correspondence often recorded his displeasure with race relations inside of the organization.

Sometime that year, he relocated to Vienna where a former comrade recalled him sharing an apartment with an Austrian communist and her two children. [17] His energies were devoted to analyzing the British Empire. Palme Dutt, the British communist theoretician with a keen interest in imperialism, was convalescing in Vienna where he met Padmore. [18] Meanwhile, African American communist leader James Ford raised the call to action of the first International Conference of Negro Workers now planned for Hamburg, where one of Europe's largest contingents of African, Caribbean, and Asian maritime workers lived and visited. The city was also the stronghold of the German communist party leader Ernst Thälmann, but it had not been the organizers' first choice for the conference venue. Ramsay MacDonald's Labour government in London refused to allow them to meet in the imperial capital. [19] The organizers issued an ambitious call to action:

> We must take up organizational questions relating to the economic situation and working conditions of the Negro workers—industrial and agricultural workers; we must discuss lynching, terrorism, police and soldier massacres, pass-laws and restrictions, racial discriminations, forced labor, the coming imperialist war and a number of other questions and problems . . . take China, take India, take Indonesia, take Korea and Latin America, take the forcible industrialization of the African masses who through poll and hut taxes and other forms of taxation are forced off their lands to become industrial slaves for the imperialists, and the United States where the capitalists have an internal army of millions of Negro toilers who are no less exploited and on whose labor billions in profits are piled up. [20]

Ford predicted the coming of an interimperialist war in which black troops would play a major role. His writings on the conference stressed the threat posed by Marcus Garvey's movement, "Pan-Africanism" then being associated with the American NAACP-sponsored Pan-African Congresses, and with what he perceived as nonrevolutionary reformism.[21] He was entirely resistant to accommodation with factions that inhibited a global anti-imperial struggle, stressing the connections of Negroes' causes with events in Asia.

Padmore came to Hamburg in early July for the conference. Kenyatta and Kouyate were present, as was Frank Macaulay of Nigeria, who died a year later. Delegates from the United States and southern Africa were among the participants.[22] Padmore's private views of the conference displayed an exasperated skepticism, suggesting a bedraggled and disorganized effort:

> [It was] . . . conducted poorly and with unsatisfactory representation. . . . [It featured] . . . the refusal of visas, lack of civil rights, arrest of delegates from Panama, losing of delegates from South Africa by what methods we do not as yet know, the banning of the conference by the British Labour Government, the Jim Crow practices on steamships resulting in late arrival of the American delegation, the backward[ness] and isolation of the Negro organizations from the International labor movement.[23]

Padmore had hoped for better. A few dozen delegates attempted to travel across the seas, some arriving and others prevented from doing so, with many subject to discrimination not only at the behest of the authorities but at their comrades' hands. This all conformed to a pattern that continued through Padmore's short time with the Comintern. Could he close the gap between "black organizations" and the "larger world of labor"? Could he help the world population of people of African descent and their allies transcend "backwardness"? These ways of forming the questions assumed that communism was still worth striving for. The conference was a disheveled attempt to unite forces.

Padmore leaped to the task of unification, using his pen as his weapon, assisting with the publication of the *Negro Worker*, the organ that carried the news of Scottsboro throughout the British Empire and to several continents. The twin preoccupations of fighting reformist black leaders and organizations, and of spreading news of struggles and conditions were evident from the first issues published under his direction.[24] The offices of the International Trade Union Committee of Negro Workers, the front organization for what was colloquially known both as the Negro Bureau and the Comintern's Negro Committee (here, Committee), was opened at 8 Rothesoodstrasse, near the docks, serving as a seamen's club for black sailors, a house still standing at this writing. Its agents smuggled the *Negro Worker* into the offices hidden in bound volumes of religious tracts. African American communist James Ford preceded Padmore as editor and was hounded by the German police.[25] Though West Indian, New York–based communist Otto Huiswoud was passed over by the Comintern as leader of this work, he was brought to Moscow by the Profintern to direct "red trade union" efforts, and in January 1931, he and Padmore jointly authored a confidential report on conditions in the West Indies from their respective offices.[26]

Figure 2.1. American Communist leader James Ford, League against Imperialism founder Willi Münzenberg, and the Soudanese former schoolteacher Garan Kouyate of the League for Defense of the Negro Race (a Comintern affiliate), from Münzenberg's German weekly, *Arbeiter Illustrierte Zeitung* ("Die schwarze Rasse stösst vor," *Arbeiter Illustrierte Zeitung*, summer, 1931, special number, *Leben und Kampf der schwarzen Rasse*, "The Life and Struggle of the Black Race") (New York Public Library).

Negro Committee agents black and white used the Channel ferry and North Sea crossings to Britain from Europe. On the London end, varied forms of activism, one step removed from the communist party, formed the context in which the *Negro Worker* circulated, as the agitation around Scottsboro confirmed. When Jomo Kenyatta returned from Russia to London in 1931, he shared a flat with Paul Robeson and stayed in touch with Padmore. The *Negro Worker* had a small readership that reflected its domestic British, imperial, and transatlantic drop points. The de facto "Scottsboro front" mobilized an eclectic, partly communist but mostly unaffiliated group of black intellectuals and artists who mingled with their white counterparts in other circles and were rarely exclusivist in their work, always seeking to address concerns in the wider European-led organizations and conferences of the time. In June 1931 the International Labour Organization in Geneva convened a "Save the Children" conference, which both Ford and Kenyatta attended.[27] At the end of 1931, Reginald Bridgeman wrote to Padmore to alert him that Nancy Cunard was living in Paris; the durable collaborative relationship they formed was a further connection to Scottsboro for both.[28] Padmore also traveled to Russia that summer, and in one of his last public appearances in the Soviet world, spoke at a Fourth of July Leningrad rally in support of the Scottsboro defendants.[29] Padmore found the Negro Committee's seamen's club in disarray when he returned to Hamburg. He noted the existence of internal tensions; a German comrade related badly to his coworkers and he wrote that "conduct with regard to all African comrades, not only to these people, [was] no good at all," involving behavior that seemed endemic to party circles.[30] Yet his own close contact with friends and allies did not seem to mirror these tense internal relations in the work of the Bureau.

In 1931 Padmore completed *The Life and Struggles of Negro Toilers*, whose themes were those of the wider communist movement that characterized the conference reports and pamphlet literature of the Comintern agencies of its time. Padmore described the global conditions of peoples "of African descent." Omitting no region of the world from his detailed case studies, he "set forth some of the conditions of life ... enumerate[d] some of the struggles," and "indicate[d] in a general way the tasks of the proletariat in the advanced countries," calling for an international working-class presence in these chosen conflicts.[31] Strong narratives of the black proletariat's contributions in the past and forecasts of imperialist wars to come supported his arguments. He focused upon Liberia under American imperialism and labor and political exploitation throughout the African colonies of Europe's empires,[32] praising the 1930 Hamburg conference, nothing of its shambles making its way into these pages. He delivered his data and illustrative material in a detached and informal style of réportage, describing the situation in the United States bluntly—"no civilized country ... was ... worse," and recounting a series of American lynchings in graphic detail, using lengthy eyewitness testimonies taken from the Southern press. "Inch by inch the Negro was fairly cooked to death. ... As the flames were eating away his abdomen, a member of the mob stepped forward and saturated the body with more gasoline." These were "Roman holidays," fêtes that allowed the ruling class to keep blacks and whites apart. Padmore wrote of "slaves" still working in coal mines and road construction, and of ghettoes, segregation, and Jim Crow. He told explicit and dramatic stories of exploitation, violence, and torture in the imperial possessions. He quoted Londres's *Land of the Black*, on the Belgian Congo. "We started to hunt the Negroes. Our men caught them as best they could with the help of lassoes. ... We put 'collars' on them, as they are called here. The human material recruited in this way was not of the best. ... The death-rate increased."[33] In South Africa, the "police, reinforced by armed bands of white fascists" returned and shot five workers and wounded seventeen. Twenty-three of those who succeeded in escaping were afterwards arrested and thrown into jail." In Basutoland, he reported, "revolts have frequently occurred among these tribesmen in recent years, and have only been suppressed by the use of military planes attacking the villages with bombs." Such images combined with hard statistics served as education and agitation. Large sections of the text admonished "misleaders"

Figure 2.2. "A group of miners with safety lamps in the Robinson Deep Gold Mine at Kimberley South Africa," May 3, 1939 (*sic*). The British seized the mines and annexed the area in the former Cape Province, when diamonds were discovered on Boer farms in the 1870s. They named the town, now in the Northern Cape, for the Secretary of State for the Colonies, Lord Kimberley. In the *Life and Struggles of the Negro Toilers* (1931), Kimberley was the site of an infamous British "concentration camp" in which Boer women and children were held during the South African War. But the Robinson Deep mine was on the Rand, in present-day Gauteng. The mislabeled photograph may have been taken there and not in the Kimberley mines. (Reg Speller, GettyImages).

but the argument for a unified struggle and the exposé of conditions remained most arresting.

> The Negro workers must not be deceived by the demagogic gestures of [Marcus] Garvey and his supporters. They must realize that the only way in which they can win their freedom and emancipation is by organizing their forces millions strong, and in alliance with the class-conscious white workers in the imperialist countries, as well as the oppressed masses of China, India, Latin America and other colonial and semi-colonial counties, deliver a final blow to world imperialism.[34]

At the thousands-strong World Congress of Red Aid in Germany in October 1931, the illusion that the "final blow" was not far off might have seemed very real. Münzenberg's Russian-financed event was convened in the cause of "class war prisoners," antifascism, and internationalism.[35] The nine young black men from Tennessee and Georgia had the support of the conference. Yet within a matter of a few years, many in the room would themselves be imprisoned or executed. The Scottsboro defendants outlived most of their European advocates. The *Negro Worker's* offices in Hamburg were raided by the authorities on January 1, 1932, and ten thousand pamphlets seized. The Berlin police stormed the LAI offices. In the aftermath of the raid, its editors wondered aloud if the Weimar Government sought favor with the British and French authorities.[36]

SCOTTSBORO AND 1932

In 1932, the last year before the triumph of Nazism, Padmore continued to dedicate his time fully to Comintern work. On a short trip to London after someone thought they should be "introduced," he tried unsuccessfully to interest his childhood friend from Trinidad, Trotskyist C.L.R. James, in his operations. At this first reunion in many years, the two "finally parted at four in the morning, speaking the whole time about the revolutionary movement." James was a member of the ILP, as a "deep entry" interventionist on behalf of a Trotskyist tendency, but had come to London from a recent background in the provincial Labour party.[37] Whatever James told him of anti-Stalinism, Padmore remained steadfastly a Comintern man in 1932. His readers in the *Negro Worker's* network numbered in the thousands and he remained publicly and privately committed to the view that the existing, indigenous black leadership was inadequate to the task of the international proletarian struggle. In February Padmore wrote to Reginald Bridgeman about his fellow Trinidadians, including the trade-union leader Ashford Sinanan:

> I presume you have had enough experience with colonial intellectuals to know their limitations. We cannot base our work primarily upon them, nevertheless they can help you to get connections with many organizations with a mass following in the West Indies. . . . The psychology of most colonials is that they like to have connections with organizations in the "mother" countries. . . . when they get back—[their] illusions will be shattered.[38]

Padmore sought to pose an alternative framework for action through the circulation of the *Negro Worker* to ports all over the world. The paper advertised sales in shops from the People's Bookstore in Harlem to Cape Town, Johannesburg, Paris, Nairobi, and London. Its distribution in the United States was especially broad, with copies sold in many cities, including Pittsburgh, Buffalo, Seattle, and Chicago. Padmore did not speak German, and he planned to publish bilingual leaflets. Josef Bilé of Cameroon was a stronger choice for German Red Aid platforms.[39] The Committee's English-language literature went to Ward's Negro Welfare Association in London and to the black press in Africa and the West Indies. Padmore pleaded with the Comintern offices in Moscow for more funds to support engagements in London, Liverpool, and Cardiff.[40]

Scottsboro was launched as a campaign, and this was in no small part due to Padmore's work and that of the Red Aid organizations. Huiswoud's biographer notes the case of a shipboard seamen's discussions of Scottsboro that resulted in many signatures to a statement of support for the campaign.[41] On March 16 philosopher Bertrand Russell, sexologist Havelock Ellis, and Charlie Chaplin published their Scottsboro defense statement in the *Manchester Guardian*. Bernard Shaw, H. G. Wells, Gandhi, Gorki, and the Indian philosopher Rabindranath Tagore appeared as Scottsboro signatories in *Le Monde* a week later. How frustrating it must have been for Padmore to receive regular news of the British government's banning of his own work just as the Scottsboro campaign took hold. The wider political vision of the *Life and Struggles* threatened British imperial authorities. The book was banned from distribution in West Africa while Padmore sought further inroads for the *Negro Worker* in South Africa and Basutoland, present-day Lesotho.[42] He was committed to the distribution of materials in Africa and to the recruitment of blacks for training in Russia, and certain that the Comintern was not doing enough on these fronts. Even blacks from Britain were scarce in Moscow: "We are waiting for 100% Bolsheviks to come out of Central Africa. No, Comrades, it is our task to get hold of the raw people and send them *back* [his emphasis] 100% Bolsheviks." In this letter to an unknown correspondent, Padmore noted that his future friends in the British ILP had mobilized around colonial issues. These "fakirs had done more in their way than the Party or the LAI."[43]

Padmore could well have been frustrated by reports of the Scottsboro campaign's tactics that flowed from Arnold Ward's pen, words from a comrade with his ears to the ground. Saklatvala was helping to convene London meetings, and he and Ward were both members of the LAI executive. At one gathering, the English communist organizer Isobel Brown had put the case to delegates from an Indian worker organization, "[W]e asked, what are they doing for the nine boys?" Ward reported few blacks in attendance when a Scottsboro resolution was read at an unemployment demonstration.[44] Still, Padmore came to speak at Poplar Town Hall in London's Docklands in April, and met both with C.L.R. James, and with the future ILP chairman, and Trotskyist C. A. Smith.[45]

The increasing repression of the publications for which Padmore was most responsible, and in which Scottsboro was often cited, continued over the months of Ada Wright's visit. In May, the authorities banned the *Negro Worker* in Nigeria. James Maxton fought the proscription on the floor of the Commons to no avail.[46] Then the authorities banned the paper in Trinidad and Tobago, and again Maxton fought unsuccessfully.[47] Ada Wright and Arnold Ward both appeared at the Anti-War Congress in Amsterdam, and though issues like the South African exploitation of blacks were raised at this important gathering, Ward again wrote to Padmore that there were "few colonials there"[48] and continued to disparage other black activists, especially his fellow West Indians.[49] Ward's confidences alerted Padmore to the roadblocks to communist black and colonial work. In early July the Liverpool activist William Brown complained to Padmore of divisive behavior: "The light skin boys around and you would not believe the Names they give me."[50] African American James Ford wrote to Padmore from New York about the "bourgeois liberal woman Nancy Cunard" and her contacts in the United States with the ILD and Scottsboro attorney Joseph Brodsky. Ford admonished Padmore for his compromising denunciations of liberals at a moment when the English publication *Everyman* had willingly carried Nancy Cunard's Scottsboro plea. But Ford also acknowledged that the Negro Welfare Association had been excluded from greeting Wright upon her arrival in London, a "blunder . . . [with] bad effects for [the] NWA with colored workers . . . using Negroes when wanted, discarding when unwanted."[51]

Padmore traveled once more to Moscow that summer with Kenyatta, whom Arnold Ward referred to as the "dog without a tail," in order for both to attend a Comintern executive meeting. He spoke at the subsequent Red Aid conference, recounted by Miriam Sherman, and this meeting afforded him a last glimpse of Ada Wright.[52] Padmore then visited London, where he met up with Nancy Cunard, who had just returned from her trip to New York with musician Henry Crowder.[53] Cunard was sending British Scottsboro donations on to the United States, and she sought Padmore's collaboration on *Negro*, later recalling that he had suggested other contributors for the volume even before they met.[54]

On his return to Germany, Padmore wrote to an unidentified colleague of an "emergency situation" in Berlin, complaining that a key comrade was absent there. He had been unable to acquire any for his work and feared for the safety of the African students whose passage he sought. They were to travel to Haiti and Liberia. He needed both sterling and "gold dollars," and complained that their Liberian affiliate was in jeopardy.[55] His communiqué is especially interesting in light of his claims at the time of his expulsion from the Comintern not to have been involved in Liberian matters since 1931.[56] But his letter was also about organizational priorities and the chaos involved in servicing "Negro work," a missive written on the eve of Nazism about a related but separate problem. He suffered from a spiraling pattern of frustration with Comintern arrangements or their absence, which coincided with the failure of the Comintern strategy to defeat Hitler and the era of Stalin's increasing accommodation with the European powers and their accommodations with him.[57] In this and similar letters, Padmore referred to Münzenberg's indisposition, and of Comintern functionary Clemens Dutt's poor health and "bad state of mind."[58] Across the Channel, in Sheffield, a weak and temporary alliance was forged between the ILP and the British communists.[59] On October 8, 1933, *Weekend Review* published its Scottsboro appeal signed by many liberals and fellow travelers, two days before Red Aid's global international Scottsboro celebration.

Padmore Leaves the Comintern

In January, 1933, a fateful month for Germany, the Meerut conspiracy-trial sentences were handed down in India, closing a chapter in global communist agitation. Africa remained a constant preoccupation for Padmore. In what may have been his first encounter with WASU, he wrote to its president, the Nigerian Ladipo Solanke, in London, and urged him to keep abreast of African affairs.[60] Terrible repression continued against the left in Germany with the ascension of the Nazis to power in January. Whither Padmore? He had been arrested in Hamburg by the German police, just after the Nazis assumed power. When the police released him from jail, they deported him to Britain as a British subject. He was greeted by Criminal Investigation Department (CID) agents, who, as he recalled, "searched ... even my a ..." and continued to shadow him.[61] Arnold Ward looked after him when he arrived in London, but Padmore soon made his way on to Paris, where he shared an address with Kouyate in the rue de la Grange-aux Belles.

The April–May 1933 issue of the *Negro Worker* still listed Padmore as its editor from a base in Copenhagen, a cover for Paris, and named Kenyatta as an editorial board member. In sharp contrast to most of the communist Scottsboro literature emanating from the United States and Britain in this moment, Padmore's writings explicitly linked the Alabama case with what he had observed in Germany in the final months of Weimar and the first days of the new Nazi regime. The *Negro Worker* led with "Fascist Terror against Negroes in Germany."

> Most Negroes in Europe and America as well as in the colonies do not yet fully realize that fascism is the greatest danger which confronts not only the white workers, but it is the most hostile movement against the Negro race. The most glaring manifestation of this anti-Negro feeling is to be seen in the attitude of the Hitler movement in Germany. Even before the fascists came into power in Germany, they carried on the most violent agitation against Negroes, Jews, and all so-called non-Nordics. But since Hitler has become Chancellor, this Nazi agitation has taken on the form of open physical violence against all colored peoples. . . . the fascists are preaching race hatred and advocating lynch law. . . . [from the fascist organ, *Nationalsozialistische Monatshefte*:] "All assimilation, all education is bound to fail on account of the racial inborn features of the blood. One can therefore understand why in the Southern States of America, sheer necessity compels the white race to act in an abhorrent and perhaps even cruel manner against the Negroes. And, of course, most of the Negroes that are lynched do not merit any regret." . . . on the occasion of Mrs. Ada Wright's ... tour ... the *Angriff*, the leading paper of the Nazi party in Berlin, demanded her arrest and expulsion from Germany. The editors of the *Angriff* openly expressed solidarity with the lynchocrats of Alabama and said that the only way to keep Negroes in their place is to lynch them.[62]

The same issue contained a long account of fascist terror "against the revolutionary working class as well as the Jewish minority" from the *Manchester Guardian*, offered as confirmation of the *Negro Worker*'s editorial line. A photo accompanying "Mob Rule in Germany," depicts "A Jew who has been shaved and trousers cut at the knees made to walk through the street bare-footed with a card around his neck which reads, 'I am a Jew, but will not complain about the Nazis,' " immediately followed by a long account of the Scottsboro case.[63] In the summer of 1933, the *Negro Worker* published a communication to an anti-fascist congress held in Paris in June that condemned conditions in Africa and the United States, and expressed solidarity "on behalf of the toiling masses of Africa, America, and the West Indies." The article directly compared the global conditions faced by Negroes to those endured by victims of fascism, invoking lynching and Scottsboro. The Anglo-Belgian imperial collaboration in the Congo, in which social-democrats were implicated, was, for Padmore, an instance of "terrorism and forced labor." The Union of South Africa was "one of the most classical colonies of fascism." India, Madagascar, and Indochina were sites of injustice. The Meerut prisoners and other Indian prisoners, and those the RAF bombed in India, did not enjoy the civil rights extended to national minorities in the Soviet Union.

> It is also well to remind the British Labour Party that fifty Negro women were shot down with machine guns in Nigeria under the administration of the so-called Labour Government.... Because of the conditions, the Negro peoples of the world welcome the opportunity to demonstrate their solidarity with the European proletariat, the Jews and anti-fascist intellectuals, and all other persecuted representatives of advanced culture.[64]

The manifesto called for racial unity and for the "Freedom of All Persecuted Humanity." It opposed both fascism and "Racial Oppression" and "any attempt to turn over the former African colonies to the Nazi slave drivers."[65] This material captured Padmore's sense of urgency in addressing the twin evils of exploitation on the European continent and in the empires. The fascist crisis was presented as a global crisis, embracing and inclusive in its ambition, and disruptive of the present imperial-racial order. This understanding was key to Padmore's discursive combat of the next few years.

Britain did not forbid the domestic distribution of the *Negro Worker*. Padmore's associates from the anticolonial work were in London, among them the Barbadian seamen's organizer Chris Jones, with whom he would remain friends until Jones's death. But a month after Padmore arrived in London, the Scottsboro gala at the Phoenix Theater featured minstrel musical acts, and urged support for the campaign in language that would never have been his, contending that one should do so "because this great Empire believes in impartial justice and fair play for all men, regardless of creed or color." These terms were alien to Padmore's outlook and arguments.[66] If the *Negro Worker* was on sale at the event, its approach would certainly have seemed anomalous in that company. A month later, Padmore resigned his offices and was expelled from communist membership; the work of the Negro Committee was curtailed, the publication of the *Negro Worker* continuing in various incarnations until the later thirties. The LAI offices in London sought to maintain some colonial work among seamen. Port committees were active for a time in Belgium and in the Netherlands. There was a highly visible Dutch Scottsboro campaign, and the *Étolie nord-africaine* pursued an anticolonialist politics in Paris.[67]

Padmore, a lone wolf without a party, living between Paris and London, searched out his friends. He found Kenyatta who had returned from Moscow at the end of the summer. In September 1933 many of his former close associates organized the mock trial of the Reichstag fire defendants. But Padmore was a pariah, a purged, ex-communist uninvolved and excluded from these activities. As if to symbolize the closure of the kind of anticolonial organizing work that had been his vision and forté, his friend, the Sierra Leonean and former seaman I.T.A. Wallace-Johnson, who had worked in Hamburg and in Moscow and had taken the story of Scottsboro to Africa, was arrested and deported from the Gold Coast for his agitation around the case.[68] He did not attend the Comintern's thirteenth plenum of December 1933, and in 1934, in a new twist of policy, the Soviet Union entered the League of Nations—a capitalist club that had excluded the "bloody Bolsheviki" and the vanquished German plenipotentiaries after Versailles, and to which the US did not belong. Lenin had reportedly called it the "thieves' kitchen," a characterization that Padmore avidly embraced, even while continuing on his own steady diet of League publications.[69]

Padmore's departure from the Comintern has led historians to assert his adoption of "Pan-Africanism" immediately on the tails of his communist membership. "George Padmore was editor of *Negro Worker* until his expulsion by the Comintern in 1934. He then became a leading figure in Pan-African politics in Britain."[70] A second narrative is as certain. "His had been a politics which had always been sympathetic to the ultimate aims of Pan-Africanism, even when sectarian denunciation had been in order. But from this time onward, organizationally, he swiftly moved from communism to Pan-Africanism."[71] Yet "Pan-Africanism" was a moveable feast.[72] It may be dated from 1900 when Du Bois and a few dozen delegates met in London for the Pan-African Conference, or, from the first Pan-African Congress convened in 1919, which had a wider constituency and sought help from London liberals, including the anti-slavery leaders.[73] Most adherents of the "movement" that was not yet a movement were not communists, and although it was in the circles *outside* of the communist sanctum that Padmore was to remain for the rest of his life, he did not immediately gravitate to those more politically moderate than he, including those who had led the Pan African Congresses, nor did he immediately articulate an alternative to the politics of Comintern Negro work. The South

African writer Peter Abrahams observed of the man he met at the end of the thirties, "For him the fault was not in the party and its principles but in the men who ran it," while Ras Makonnen (Padmore's friend George Thomas Griffith) quipped, "he never became a party man."[74] A small step in his transition out of the dogmatic Comintern world to a kind of African-liberationist eclecticism was Padmore's involvement in Cunard's *Negro*, which saluted many communist-inspired efforts and for which he wrote about Ethiopia and republished some verbatim excerpts from the *Negro Worker* and from his own *The Life and Struggles of the Negro Toilers*, work previously produced under the aegis of the Comintern.[75]

Only in his new activities over time, did his own sober, working definition of "Pan-Africanism" slowly emerge. He set about mending fences, opening doors, and reaching out to sectors with which his previous contacts had been circumscribed by party discipline or by the demands of sustaining a publication and an apparatus from Germany. He wrote enthusiastically to W.E.B. Du Bois about his friend Garan Kouyate and the circle of French Africans in Paris grouped around another publication that had been fraternally tied to Hamburg, *La Race Nègre*.[76] Kouyate and others had met to proclaim the need for a "Negro World Unity Congress," a proposition foreign to contemporary Comintern norms. "The Negro problem was discussed relative to the present economic and social crisis the world over, and the fascist danger which threatens our racial extermination. It was the most serious political discussion which I have ever listened to among Negroes." This comment reflected both Padmore's global concerns and his preoccupation with the onset of a war that would, he believed, stimulate and affirm racially supremacist politics. He wanted to alert Du Bois to this organizational development and to put him in touch with the French-based activists and with WASU in London. But he was so unpracticed in an easy nonparty vernacular that he used the acronym "NACP" for NAACP.[77] Padmore moved to Paris again briefly, sharing rooms with Kouyate for three months, and wrote *How Britain Rules Africa*. His formal date of expulsion from the communist movement came on February 23, 1934.[78]

Padmore's departure from the Comintern remained a subject of speculation among both his followers and his detractors into the postwar era, fanned by the publication of his memoir, *Pan-Africanism or Communism?* two years before his death in 1959.[79] His former comrades made much of his "antiparty" activity in the thirties. He admonished that he would not venture back to Moscow without guarantees of safety and these he never received. He joked about the Comintern bosses asking him to cease his criticisms of the imperialists.[80] The British labor historian John Saville, a member of the communist youth organization in London at this time, recalled that party youth were told not to engage Padmore, and remembered him being regarded as an outcast. He recalls seeing Padmore lingering about at events, and being placed under discipline not to speak with him.[81]

The formal party charges against Padmore were slow to air and revolved around his insistence on working with Kouyate, of whom Comintern leaders were suspicious, and who was also expelled from the French party. Padmore also faced charges about his ostensible ties to Liberian nationalism.[82] West Indian communist Otto Huiswoud was sent by Moscow to review and criticize the work of Padmore and Kouyate in Paris in August and September of 1933, shortly before the Comintern decision to expel Padmore.[83] It is also noteworthy that in late 1932, Padmore had written to anticommunist African American editor George Schuyler, "When all is said and done, Liberia and all her little autocrats are merely one of the pawns in the big game of world imperialism."[84] His critics made the charge that Padmore favored "blackness first, the Comintern second." By April 1934 he was at the address that Kenyatta used when he studied with Bronislaw Malinowski at LSE.[85] The *Negro Worker* continued after Padmore's departure, first edited by Padmore's former Moscow ally and Comintern agent Huiswoud, under the assumed name Charles Woodson.[86] The Negro international trade union representation of the Committee in print shifted from Copenhagen to Brussels to Harlem, and the fall 1934 issue of the *Negro Worker* was datelined New York, while the Huiswouds moved around Europe.[87] As Nazism engulfed Germany and the larger Reich, the Italians' steady gaze upon North Africa intensified. Taking these events as his starting points, Padmore recouped in London and began to work as a journalist, "well-dressed . . . always . . . spic and span like a senator, and his shoes shown so you could see his face in them; his trouser creases could shave you," wrote Makonnen.[88]

The British Labour party, the League of Nations, and the international diplomatic community were locked in debate about the Italian invasion of Abyssinia during October, when Mussolini's troops advanced into its territory from Eritrea and Italian Somaliland. In October 1935 Padmore became deeply engaged by the conflict, critical of the Comintern's stance, and committed to the support of Emperor Haile Selassie's regime in exile. Sylvia Pankhurst, along with her lover Silvio Corio, played a major role in this struggle, founding *New Times and Ethiopia News* in April 1936; émigrés Austrian Ruth Schulze and Hungarian Bela Menczer assisted her. They maintained a distribution network in the Caribbean and Africa. Her circle overlapped considerably with Padmore's and included his African and Asian associates and many Scottsboro signatories like Cunard and the attorney Prince Cobina Kessie, the latter a member of the original British defense committee. Pankhurst also had ties to Du Bois and the *Chicago Defender*.[89]

Mussolini's invasion of Abyssinia thrust Padmore into black activism. He had two London addresses apart from Kenyatta's residence—one in the Vauxhall Bridge Road and another in Guildford Street near Russell Square. His closest circle included the Afro-Caribbean café owner T. Ras Makonnen; Oxford student Eric Williams from Trinidad, the country's future president; Ceylonese radical T. B. Subasinghe; white ILP friends like novelist Ethel Mannin and her husband, Reginald Reynolds, and various expatriates and ex-communists.[90] Reynolds described the origins of this group, and his reasons for joining it.

> The Communist somersault of 1934 left radical pacifists like myself in a political Cave of Adullam, but not for long. The Independent Labour Party, though split by the usual dissensions, still held in the main to a line that we could support. Some Labour Party rebels, now well to the left of the Communists, were also willing to join in forays against imperialism. But most important was the effect of the new Soviet policy on the colonial peoples. When the Popular Front came into power in France, with the full support of the C.P., any move against French imperialism was regarded as a betrayal of Russia, since France was now her ally. The "League Against Imperialism" abandoned all propaganda relating to the French colonies. . . . French colonials in revolt were denounced as "fascists"—or at least as inspired or provoked by fascist agents. Quite clearly . . . the French Communists could not . . . support the Popular Front Government and condemn those who revolted against it. Their betrayal . . . had a prompt reaction . . . even on many of the colonial intellectuals in Britain. . . . Padmore . . . was an outstanding example. Mainly through George I was rapidly drawn into a circle of colored people in London.[91]

In collaboration with C.L.R. James, Padmore helped to form the International Friends of Ethiopia (International African Friends of Ethiopia). Jomo Kenyatta served as secretary. Chris Jones and Ras Makonnen were among the leaders. They worked closely with activist Amy Jacques Garvey, who hosted a reception for Haile Selassie when he arrived in London in exile.[92] Ras Makonnen met Selassie's entourage at Waterloo Station at the first moment of his welcome.[93] The historian Dorothy Thompson recalls attending a tea party for Selassie's daughter as a young activist, and indeed many on the left and among liberals (including Lady Kathleen Simon) had encounters with the family, who were salon celebrities of a sort.[94] Padmore also maintained close contact with the Gold Coast students' organization and his friends in WASU.[95]

The Comintern was more lax in its propagandistic response to the Ethiopian crisis than were these small organizations of Africans, West Indians, and their allies, and Padmore charged that this was because of oil deals between the Soviets and the Italians; he later contended it was also "because the Italo-Ethiopian war was a racial one."[96] Even an internal confidential Comintern memo written to the communist parties of France, Britain, the United States, Spain, and Switzerland charged that, "Our press and our parties again do not react adequately to the threatening war against Abyssinia at the present phase. The Social Democratic press deals with these events much more than our press, with the exception of *L'Humanité*."[97] Reginald Bridgeman recalled that Padmore refused to work with other organizations on the Abyssinian crisis because of the acrimony between him and some groups that were communist-affiliated or predominantly white.[98]

Figure 2.3. "Fenner Brockway." ILP leaders C. A. Smith, James Maxton, and Fenner Brockway, arriving at the Foreign Office in Whitehall, London, January 31, 1933 (GettyImages).

Padmore's friends in the ILP had broken with the communists over the Soviet entry into the League of Nations, and in May 1934 James Maxton issued a *Liberty and Democracy Leadership Manifesto*. The title conveyed the third way sought by the diminishing band of independent, anticolonial British socialists.[99] Padmore saw these ILPers as increasingly legitimate allies and began to write for the ILP's *New Leader*, later serving as one of its editors. His antagonism with Moscow grew after the 1935 Seventh Congress of the Comintern that summer, the Congress that abandoned "third period" sectarianism in favor of a "united front" against fascism. This was Moscow's belated response to the failure of German socialist and communist forces to build a coalition against Nazism. It also expressed a policy already in practice in some places, as in the idiosyncratic British Scottsboro campaign that included Nancy Cunard and many individual Labour party supporters. This new policy became the face of Stalinism in a desperate pursuit of new global allies; no recantation of fundamental outlook occurred. The Soviet "labor camps," Spain, the betrayals of radical opponents, and the murderous pursuit of Trotsky and his followers—all were subsumed within this practice. Padmore's alienation was complete. He had not renounced "communism" as a guide to action but he expressly rejected its contemporary Soviet manifestations.

The 1935 Comintern Congress also witnessed his ostracization and dismissal by former comrades. In a farcical subplot, Cunard decided to attend the Congress, but the Russians denied her a visa. She attributed this decision to her defense of Padmore. French poet Louis Aragon and African American journalist Homer Smith intervened on her behalf and she finally secured the document. Presumably, her work with the party on Scottsboro and her cooperation with African American communist leader William Patterson, whom she visited (and berated) in Moscow, both influenced Soviet acquiescence.[100] She must have seemed a strange, self-styled advocate for Padmore, who proved himself generally capable of fighting his own battles. The Russians may also have had their worst suspicions of him confirmed once they encountered Cunard.

Padmore struck in the pages of the NAACP's *The Crisis*, submitting his "Open Letter to Earl Browder," the American communist-party chairman, and noting the liquidation of the over-arching Comintern Negro Bureau as early as August 1933. He accused Moscow and its parties of being reluctant to offend the British Foreign Office in ways that might have brought diplomatic pressure to bear on the Soviet Union. The Comintern had, he said, riled its African and West Indian supporters in the colonies. The *Negro Worker*, he charged, had been effectively liquidated, a claim that its continued publication did not bear out. He protested against the accusation that he had colluded uncritically with Liberia. Why had the censors not raised this issue earlier? He had not recently commented on the Liberian situation. He wrote defiantly, "Early Browder, Negroes are not grown up children as many whites still think; although we are still in chains we can nevertheless do a little thinking for ourselves."[101] He further charged that the Comintern had been "outdoing the Nazis and the lynchocrats of Alabama."[102] Padmore asserted that he had not been given a trial or the opportunity to defend himself. He could not resist asking why, in any case, the Comintern had not defended Liberia against the machinations of the Americans. With a stroke of vanity for which he was widely known, he asked if other Negroes whom the communists courted, were not covetous of his skills. "You get support from petty little Negroes who I know are envious and jealous of my capacities. But the world is there for you to conquer; surely I am not standing in their way." In the fifteen years of its existence, the party had made no headway among American Negroes, said Padmore. In the *Negro Worker*, Otto Huiswoud, he charged, had gone so far as to accuse him of giving four thousand seamen's names to the German police. The party had required him to abandon his studies at Howard University. He pleaded that he had given a great deal. How could African Americans James Ford and William Patterson be silent and not rally to him? Padmore closed with a declaration of his "youthful indignation," he who was now just thirty.[103] C.L.R. James recalled Padmore being unwilling to offer support for "democratic capitalists" in the Caribbean. "They said to him, 'Well George, sometimes you have to change the line.' His answer was, 'Well, boys, this is one line I can't change.'"[104]

Arnold Ward detached himself from his friend, presumably understanding that, otherwise, the resources of the London communists would not be at his disposal. Ward wrote to William Patterson that Padmore and his supporters were agitating for "race politics for Africa and Africans. . . . The Negro workers in Europe or elsewhere have no money and the Garvey days are over. Padmore will soon fade out, of this I am sure." But he had also seen him with the Barbadian Chris Jones and reported that Padmore "told [his] story in a way that comrades believe him still," adding, "frankly I believe the Party here is too weak to deal effectively with these people. They have to close their eyes to a lot of things and in some ways work with them." Ward shamelessly reported that his former friend and mentor was sowing seeds of dissension "among the colonials" and "plotting grand schemes."[105] Sure enough, Ward's name appeared on the reconfigured editorial board of the *Negro Worker* in the late thirties.[106]

In another act of denunciation the African American communist Angelo Herndon, on trial in Georgia, answered Padmore publically. He claimed that Padmore believed that black communists were "Uncle Toms" and that Padmore could not conceive of white and black workers involved together in a proletarian struggle. Herndon ridiculed Padmore's rhetoric and action as "lower than the Alabama and Georgia lynchers":

> A frog could not put his belly any closer to the ground than this. . . . I want to point out that had it not been for the militant fight of the American Communist Party, the Scottsboro boys would have long been fried in the electric chair and I would have been done to death on the murderous Georgia Chain-gang. . . . So use your own vicious and slanderous words. . . . Negroes are not just grown-up children.[107]

The most prominent of African American communists, James Ford, did not keep silent, and in September wrote to Patterson of Padmore's purported "International Negro Liberation Committee."[108]

Surely the bickering and one-upmanship that accompanied Padmore's disgrace at the hands of the Comintern now appear less important than the overriding problem of Padmore's outlook and its profound incompatibility with what he had observed and experienced as communist practice. His expulsion also came on the heels of the fissures created by the catastrophic policies undertaken by radical movements in Europe in the early thirties and the communists' unconditional defense of the Soviet state. The charge that he was an agent provocateur could not stick. It was unfounded; it derived in part from his insistence on working with Kouyate, whom the communists did not trust, and who was also a black anticolonial expatriate.[109] The Comintern objections to Padmore's "defection" to the Liberians and his reputation as a "race man" deserve attention. Padmore understood that the German débacle of 1933 had dealt an incapacitating blow to communist aspirations. He had a steadfast belief both in the need for proletarian revolution and the impending Armageddon of "racial extermination," which he believed would be shared by both Europeans and the colonized world. He literally believed that the "black masses" were politically and militarily necessary to the victory over fascism and to any successful proletarian uprising in the new global context. He could not envision a victorious antifascism that perpetuated the racist imperial system. In these terms, he had perceived the conduct and efficacy of the Comintern Negro work as his litmus test for the conduct and efficacy of the communist movement as a whole, and in that respect, he *was* a "race" man, whether his critics understood his outlook or not.

Padmore had many grounds for frustration apart from Comintern dicta. From his perspective, the "liquidation" of Negro work was not merely part of Soviet foreign policy. It was the culmination, the "last straw," in a series of chaotic or botched endeavors that had neither produced sufficient results, nor assured him of the commitment of white comrades to the cause of racial justice. Such a judgment was self-propelled; he might not have claimed the role for himself retrospectively, but he was a singularly important force in the "nonwhite" mobilization of communist sympathizers and black party members outside of the United States in the years up until his expulsion. No one replaced him. And no one ever really forgot him; he unknowingly enjoyed grudging respect in many communist and sympathizer circles for many years to come, in the face of the charges made in 1934. Finally, his preoccupation with the central role to be played by people of African descent in the struggle for human liberation was not a sentimental perception, or a conceit. He did not flaunt rhetoric. He saw his worldview and guide to action as structural necessities, believing that for all the wide spectrum of behavior and opinion among blacks in Europe, America, the colonies, and among the wider Asian and Latin American populations, there could be a special form of solidarity galvanized best and first by black activists like himself. He had taken a concerted interest in Liberia in this regard, but this author has seen no evidence of any fronting for the Liberian government that would substantiate the Comintern charges.[110]

Padmore never excluded whites from his intimate circle or his projects. He embraced alliances with them for the remainder of his life, but he also never joined another radical party or organized political faction, the short-lived International African Service Bureau excepted. To evaluate communist work among black populations after Padmore is in many respects, even within the United States, to look at a vastly changed and diminished possibility. The repression of ideas and of persons inside and outside of organized communism, not only contributed to a failed vision, but helped to create the political space for the triumphs of the organized right. The absence of clear and committed antiracist and anticolonial policies enhanced the authority of the right, just as American lynchings were fodder for Nazi charges of American hypocrisy. Padmore's analysis was most flawed in his assumption that one set of European-based dilemmas could not be even temporarily solved without the full participation of black and other global populations of color. The remainder of the

1930s would prove this a false assumption in the first instance, and yet the preservation of the vision that it implied fueled Padmore's work, sustained his fertile intelligence, and structured an inheritance for the postwar world of the later twentieth century that finally could not be dismissed or ignored.

AFTER THE COMINTERN

Padmore's sharp critique of Moscow formed an integral part of the political vision that he articulated in his second career as a radical journalist, largely in the African American and ILP press, his compromises in the style and tone of his writing notwithstanding.[111] In May 1935, Du Bois's *The Crisis* published "Ethiopia and World Politics," in which Padmore decried Moscow's recent betrayals, lumping the Soviet Union together with the Western powers.

> Soviet leaders have changed their foreign policy . . . .[W]ith the object of safeguarding the Revolution … Russia can … be considered a member of the Versailles camp. . . . It is very important for Negroes to understand this, for the failure of France and the other Allies to live up to their promises today has direct bearing on the Ethiopian situation. In other words, as war is again being prepared, France is trying to pay Italy her arrears by giving her a free hand to grab Ethiopia so as to win her support in the future.[112]

This was his approach until the outbreak of war. Padmore typically judged the behavior of the imperialists, the fascists, and the Soviets in terms of their treatment of Africa, a few months later comparing the British in Uganda to Mussolini in Ethiopia.[113] He influenced African American perceptions of Soviet policy, at least to judge from a 1935 editorial in *The Crisis* which caustically weighed the effect of Soviet self-interests.

> Of course, close students of Soviet Russia discovered long ago that the great idealism of the so-called Communist nation was in reality hard-boiled opportunism, as shameless as that of any nation not professing the high idealism preached from the Kremlin. Therefore it is only recording one more inconsistency and not one more surprise to set down that the Soviets are raking in good capitalist profits selling wheat and coal tar to Italy for use in the war against Ethiopia. . . . since their Moscow masters are opportunists in the matter of war profits, who would dare criticize the American followers for opportunism in a little thing like race segregation? Who, indeed, except the segregated American Negro?[114]

British communism had never depended on Padmore. In late October 1935 the Negro Welfare Association held a conference at Conway Hall in London on the situation of blacks in Britain and developments in the colonies. It addressed topics from indirect rule in Gold Coast and the banning of literature in Nyasaland to complaints about the extent of black unemployment in Britain and the absence of housing for black students. It made no mention of Padmore, who instead appeared at a National Peace Council conference on Africa also attended by Leonard Barnes and William Macmillan, radical writers whose works on the colonies were highly influential in anticolonialist circles.[115] Padmore rebuked the conference from the floor, stating that Africans themselves had not been asked their opinions of what to do about their own territories. He was a lone interventionist now, no longer a party agent. He kept counsel with some of the figures from the Indian Congress movement. He liked Nehru and had met other Asian activists, though he was an opponent of nationalism. He visited the Swaraj Freedom House in Percy Street where he encountered its founder K. M. Kumria, and the lawyer, borough councillor and India League secretary Krishna Menon.[116] But he was still floating, and shortly returned to Paris. In 1936 Padmore shared his last residence in France before the War with Edgar André, a German activist to whom he dedicated *Africa and World Peace*.[117] The Nazis beheaded André in Hamburg in early November for his involvements in antifascism.[118] Padmore continued his Abyssinian commitment.

In Britain a broad spectrum of labor and left opinion existed on the Abyssinian question. The ILP called for sanctions against Italy, and for British neutrality. C.L.R. James urged support for Abyssinia against Mussolini, challenging the moral pacifism of James Maxton, who supported the armed defense of the Spanish Republic but had demurred on the issue of intervention on behalf of Abyssinia.[119] Meanwhile, the National Government, led by Neville Chamberlain, courted Mussolini in ways that constituted one of the "green lights" that Hitler now saw flashing on the Anglo-European diplomatic landscape. The debates about Africa engaging radicals had more than fringe, sectarian implications. The Ethiopian situation also politicized African Americans in sectors where Scottsboro had made its mark.[120] In June the International Friends of Ethiopia hosted a London reception for Emperor Haile Selassie. Sylvia Pankhurst's *New Times and Ethiopian News* was a force for knowledge and organization. Paul Robeson was a supporter of the Friends of Ethiopia and appeared in the West End production of C.L.R. James's *Black Jacobins*, a narrative of black liberation in eighteenth-century Haiti, its message welcomed by Abyssinia's supporters.

In August Padmore's *How Britain Rules Africa* was published in London ahead of its Swiss edition. Cunard had typed it for him when he visited her in France, and he acknowledged her and Kouyate, James, Azikiwe, and Kenyatta.[121] The book begins with an epigraph by the American poet James R. Lowell, "They are slaves who fear to speak."[122] Padmore expressed his despair at the prevailing racial etiquette. "Even in London, the heart of the Empire, men and women of color are often ostracized and humiliated in such a way as to destroy whatever early love and affection they might have had for the Commonwealth of which they are supposed to be citizens." Padmore described the European world, gripped by "a desperate struggle for expansion and re-division,"

Figure 2.4. "Abyssinia Map." Fleet St. onlookers examine a map of Abyssinia, titled *Abyssinia Day by Day* in the window of the *Daily Express* building, London, October, 1935 (GettyImages).

much as he had two years earlier. Africa desired not simply self-rule but the abolition of racial hierarchies. "Young Africa believes in the democracy of men and not the aristocracy of color." He underlined the necessity of black involvement in what he termed the European settlement. Imperial powers, like the French, needed "the military and economic support of colonial peoples" to face "another European crisis." He referred to the National Peace Council's demand for Britain to "share colonies" with other friendly nonfascist powers as a scheme of "collective imperialism." But he did not deride whites who sought to help Africa and "out of religious sentiments, humanitarian reasons or political convictions, sympathize[d] with the hopes and aspirations of subject races."[123] His contempt for what he characterized as "Fascist-Imperialism"—the "new slavery"—was complete. His analysis reversed the familiar colony-to-mother country relationship, instead claiming that the working classes of the metropole needed the "fraternal support of the colonial peoples" to emancipate themselves. He increasingly drew analogies between racism in the European context, and its colonial manifestations, introducing the book as one in which,

> Everywhere we shall see stark imperialist oppression and exploitation, allied with racial ignorance and arrogance, swaggering about without the least sign of shame. This

is especially so in countries like South Africa, Southern Rhodesia, South-West Africa and Kenya. Such brutality and barbarity remind us of conditions in Germany today. It is therefore no accident that General Goering, the leader of the notorious Nazi Secret Police, addressing his own men at a meeting of ex-colonials in Berlin, solemnly declared them heirs to the traditions of the former German-East African armed colonial force.[124]

With this book, Padmore staked out a position that challenged liberal, radical, and imperial reform currents among white activists. But he also challenged much that constituted contemporary black wisdom about revolutionary social change whether articulated in Marxist, liberal, academic, or social-democratic circles of black activists. One response came from Ralph Bunche, who reviewed *How Britain Rules Africa* for the *Journal of Negro Education*.

Padmore's intense feeling for nationalism tends to make him somewhat insensitive to the fact that the surest road toward liberation of the African masses is not through Pan-Africanism, but rather that road which leads inevitably to a fundamental reconstruction of the political and economic systems of the imperialistic nations at home.[125]

Bunche elevated "Pan-Africanism" in coherence and stature in ways that it did not possess institutionally or organizationally, and Bunche identified Padmore as an incipient nationalist, an adherent to a creed and practice that Padmore rejected; he increasingly disavowed the distinction between "home" and "empire" in regard to the global crisis, calling instead for a mutually supportive global mobilization, not a national or nationalist solution. For Bunche, the advanced world was to redeem the backward world. Padmore had already jettisoned the notion of "backwardness" as a brake on revolutionary transformation, pondering the reconfiguration of the world in wartime instead. The tables would be turned, he thought. Africa might lead the West.

Ralph Bunche sailed to England in February 1937. His London diary attests to the lifestyle and modus operandi of Padmore and his associates before the war. In March 1937 both he and Padmore were involved in the founding of the International African Service Bureau (IASB), built on the remnants of C.L.R. James's Friends of Ethiopia. The IASB had strong ties to the ILP, and Sylvia Pankhurst served as a patron of the new organization and its organ, *International African Opinion*, edited by I.T.A. Wallace-Johnson, who quickly ceded control to Padmore. Wallace-Johnson identified the journal's central issues as the proposed transfer of British colonies to the fascists, the pursuit of collective alternatives to the imperial mandate system, and the growth of repressive legislation such as the sedition laws, then being enacted in the colonies. The IASB campaigned for civil rights and political representation, and opposed the alienation of land and mineral resources in Africa. It called for "the establishment of a stronger and more intimate feeling of international solidarity and inter-racial unity" among regions, including the United States.[126] It was formed "in order to cooperate with all peace-loving, democratic and working class forces who desire to help the advancement of Africans,"[127] conveying a broad, populist and inclusive Pan-African outlook accessible to whites but centered among the group's intelligentsia of color. The work of the IASB brought new clarity of meaning to the term "Pan-African."

In March Bunche arrived fresh on the London scene and attended a meeting on the Abyssinian question chaired by Padmore. The IASB issued a declaration. "Never since the emancipation of the slaves have Africans and other subject races been so awake to a realization of the wrongs and injustices inflicted upon weak and defenseless peoples as in the brutal Italian fascist war against Abyssinia." Padmore lived in St. Bride's after his return from Paris, and then moved to Cranleigh Gardens in northwest London where he met the Jewish Londoner Dorothy Pizer, who became his life partner. She was an activist who served the movement partly as a stenographer and writer, soon known as Dorothy Padmore.[128] Padmore's Comintern prophecies seemed to be coming to fruition as he prepared to publish *Africa and World Peace*.[129] His friend Reginald Bridgeman formed the Colonial Information Bureau from remnants of the LAI, centering his work around the defense of Chinese activists whose cause was familiar to Padmore from his Moscow days. Events in China were as important in politicizing many individual communists and other activists as the Spanish Civil War. Chinese involvement in the 1927 Brussels conference and Madame Sun Yat-sen's support for the Brussels gathering and her early commitment to the LAI, brought Padmore, Münzenberg, Nehru, and others close to Chinese developments at the start of their political sojourns in Europe. The American writer Agnes Smedley also became deeply involved in this work.[130] As the Comintern curtailed its involvement in the anti-imperial and anticolonial work that had first cemented friendships among members of this group, each chose whether to remain in touch with one another. Bridgeman and Padmore were in contact. Willi Münzenberg visited Nehru. Those who remained communists increasingly devoted time to coalition building with liberals and radicals, in "united front" style, and could not avoid Padmore in London.

Labour party renegade Stafford Cripps penned the foreword to Padmore's *Africa and World Peace*.[131] He responded to the debate over pacifism, rearmament, internationalism, and empire that would rage until Munich, calling Africa "one of the greatest danger points in the world," whose colonization was directly linked to the shape of European politics. Each region was subjected to a great power's "extension at the expense of another power." Cripps urged abstention from an interimperial conflict, the view that had recently cost him his Labour party membership, stating "whether Fascist or Imperialism [sic], the problem will remain," while Africans would "remain substantially the exploited slaves of one or other group of western nations, and Africa will provide a continual basis for quarreling between those nations." Padmore bluntly declared at the start of the text, "Everywhere statesmen are openly speaking of Armageddon." His underlying theme was simply the "issue of war and peace."[132]

Padmore now occupied a new base in Alderney Street, Pimlico. He invited Ralph Bunche to meetings and conclaves, apprising him of his contacts in Calthorpe Street who had participated in the 1935 Pan African Congress.[133] He invited Bunche to meet his friend Ethel Mannin, writer and columnist for the ILP's *New Leader*. Mannin was coming "to his digs," and Padmore suggested that "[W]e may all go to a concert for Spain at which Robeson is singing." He told Bunche that he had recently read and liked a pamphlet written by Bunche's friend and colleague Alain Locke, adding, "I get a kick out of life and feel certain that the future is OURS."[134] Bunche's account of such an evening reveals his own powers of observation and sense of propriety.

> Took cab to Padmore's. . . . Ethel Mannin had sent regrets. But Wallace-Johnson, Griffin [Makonnen], Chris Jones (from Barbados and N.Y., organizer of seamen here) and two ofay gals present. More conferring on plans for a journal on Africa. . . . W. Johnson quite a blatant "I" man. He's no shrinking violet, whatever good work he may have done on the W. Coast [of Africa], given to exaggeration I think. Claims to have W. African Natives in the palm of his hand, etc., and about "raising thousands of pounds" . . . Jones is very interesting—says Englishmen are most subtle g____d____d prejudiced . . . people in the world. Thinks U. S. is the best country. Interesting that tho Padmore, e.g., is a perfervid pan-africanist and a racial chauvinist, he ignores the principle in regard to his choice of woman. Says Englishmen don't want Negroes to fool with their women—even the radicals.[135]

Much of Bunche's time spent with Padmore, Wallace-Johnson, and Kenyatta was devoted to discussions of the International African Service Bureau, which was taking up offices in St. George's Square, NW1, despite its need for funds.[136] Bunche was also thrown into a heady social scene in which fund-raising, celebrity, and political gatherings merged:

> Dashed over to Padmore's for tea. Ethel Manin [*sic*], Reginald Reynolds (author) "The White Sahibs of India" . . . young Tagore, grandson of the poet were present. . . . Rode back to Victoria Palace to attend benefit Concert for Homeless Women and Children of Spain. [Paul] Robeson was big gesture on otherwise all white and non-Spanish program. Robeson sang Negro and Finnish folk songs and received smashing ovation. Big crowd out. [Lithuanian-born anarchist] Emma Goldman made a big anti-fascist pro Spanish government talk in the intermission.[137]

Radical politics in 1937 revolved around Spain, and if the Padmore circle was more involved with Africa, it still moved with many others who were deeply immersed in the defense of the Spanish Republic. Franco's use of Moorish troops added a particular racial dimension to the discussion. The

Moors—Bedouin and Arab troops—were the butt of caricature and racial invective.[138] The left was pressing for the British government to drop its stance of neutrality and "Aid Spain." Caught up in the spirit of it all, Bunche assessed the united front.

> Went to Hyde Park and saw a colorful and huge May Day parade—this was the radical group's day the CP, SP and ILP etc. The *Internationale* was sung up and down the line. Youth predominantly, Oxford and Cambridge and sections. Red flags plentiful. Unity with Spanish workers. "Scholarships not battleships." Few dark people represented. One small Indian section. Saw Chris Jones and few other Negroes at the tail-end but no impressive anti-imperialist section or slogans. . . . [On Labor Day, May 2, he wrote], not so colorful or noisy as that of radical groups yesterday. Saw no black men at all tho there may have been.[139]

That month Bunche journeyed to the Wimbledon household of Mannin and Reynolds to find Reynolds sporting a Spanish POUM button.[140] Padmore and Makonnen (whom Bunche called Padmore's "man Friday") were there, and all discussed various instances of left hypocrisy and betrayal. They did not just beat up on the communists, but expressed contempt for Labour party turncoat Ramsay MacDonald and for Lord Philip Snowden; both MacDonald and Snowden were expelled from the Labour party for their participation in the coalition National Government. They derided Léon Blum's *Front Populaire* in France.[141] On other occasions, Bunche met Indian Swaraj League activists: Ishar Dass from the Kenyan Legislative Council, the League's secretary K. M. Kumria, and trade unionist and Labour MP Arthur Creech Jones, a Swaraj League member. Bunche moved around town fluidly, encountering many former Padmore associates. He met the communist trade-union leader Ben Bradley, a Meerut Trial defendant. Bradley boasted to Bunche of Paul Robeson's donation to the Negro Welfare Association's annual "outing for colored children," then complained of Padmore as an "an obstacle" to his and Reginald Bridgeman's work, criticizing "his inconsistencies."[142]

Padmore's continuing influence on communist circles was evident. His own small, independent following had no party structure at its disposal in these years just before the war. Ethel Mannin described her participation in Padmore's work, which received the financial support of Frances Evelyn Greville, Countess of Warwick, for what was evidently the Colonial Liberties Group.

> I became involved in activities of an anti-Imperialist organization, a group consisting mainly of railway workers—restaurant car stewards—and colored people. Through this work I met that beautiful and charming woman the late Frances Warwick, and George Padmore. . . . The Countess . . . occasionally graced a meeting in the rooms taken by the group in a dingy square in Chalk Farm. . . . I would take the chair; George Padmore or some other vigorous colored anti-Imperialist would lecture, and

for such occasions the room would be packed and money raised to keep the group going.

Mannin reported that the group's fortunes fell, its dance and lecture money insufficient to support it while the study group it spawned "had begun to fall off."[143]

The question of where to place one's sympathies in the impending global conflict seriously divided Padmore's West Indian and African associates. White British circles of dissenters, liberals, and critics of Empire had their own agendas in this debate, and most would choose to defend the Empire in time of war. In 1937 contention on this issue rippled though various sectors of incipient Pan-African sentiment. In small ways and ultimately in large and shattering ones, the issue was whether those of African descent with a vested interest in the collapse of the Empire had an obligation to the struggle against fascism if that struggle was itself to be waged by the imperialists. Black responses varied and were often fractious.

In early June 1937 Bunche saw Padmore again at a meeting apparently called in solidarity with Abyssinia.

> Padmore told us of his debate with Garvey last Sunday. Said Marcus boasted that he was for Mussolini; called Selassie a coward, dumb and a trickster; Padmore had to protect him from the white proletarian audience when Garvey attacked them as riff-raff pointing out that the Great Empire would be lost if it weren't for the "great men" at the head of the Government—[Prime Minister Stanley] Baldwin, *et al*, attacked Selassie for having white advisors.[144]

Bunche traveled to the Paris World Exposition of 1937, and Padmore urged him to contact Kouyate at #5 Cité Paradis.[145] Among his fellow visitors were the New York communists William and Louise Thompson Patterson, who toured the Exposition en route to Spain. Bunche returned to London to continue his anthropological studies, but politics repeatedly intervened, and his own appetite for academic undertakings lessened. As Padmore jibed in a note at the end of the summer, "I conclude from your letter that British anthropology is worse than the race relations program of the Society of Friends."[146]

In May 1937 *The Crisis* inaugurated an ambitious diplomatic and foreign-policy series written by Padmore that provides a record of Padmore's thinking just before he wrote of having undertaken a surreptitious trip back to Nazi Germany. It also demonstrates the populist power of his pen, and his capacity to render the global situation in terms that activist black readers in the United States could find insightful and clear. In May 1937 he began with an investigation of the exploitation of Abyssinia by the Allies, the "so-called defenders and champions of 'Collective Security.'" He called attention to Italy's role as guarantor of the "Cape to Cairo" dream of Ceceil Rhodes at the start of the century, and its pact with France against Germany in 1935.[147] In June 1937 he followed

Figure 2.5. "Beauty Competition in the Great Boom Country" (James Friell, aka "Gabriel," *Daily Worker*, London, July 23, 1937) appeared above an article condemning the government for opposing the miners' trade-union demand for a decrease in working hours commensurate with a drop in global coal consumption and similar to measures being enacted in Europe and the Soviet Union. The miners, led in part by the communist trade unionist Arthur Horner in South Wales, had just passed resolutions on other aspects of pay and pension issues. Here, the white British cannibals inspect competitors for the "stock exchange," each of whom is bloated by the "swollen" price of goods. The upper left-hand-corner reference suggests that some "uncivilized regions" regarded fat as a sign of beauty, a "spreading" custom. The white "wage earner" is perplexed by the "native potentate" who wishes to barter the beauty parade (*Morning Star*, reproduced by kind permission of the Syndics of Cambridge University Library).

this piece with an article on the British betrayals of Abyssinia that had occurred while the government was "posing before the Electorate at home as champions of peace, justice and heaven knows what":

> At no time did the British imperialists ever intend to defend Abyssinia. And when they failed to get what they wanted, they just scurried away like rats from a drowning ship. . . . But little did they realize that when Addis Ababa fell the peace of Europe would go down with it. And soon the European peoples will be called upon to pay the bitter price for the duplicity of these imperialist brigands.[148]

Africa was the key to exposing the designs that would lead to the coming war, for Padmore. The League of Nations was a prop for war, not a hindrance to it. He wrote that the League "merely creates pacifist illusions in the minds of the workers and toiling masses of the world—who ardently desire peace—and in this way masks the diplomatic maneuvers and military plans of the great imperialist powers." He identified Britain's primary interests as the defense of empire, the preservation of the "integrity of France and Belgium," and the maintenance of free passage through the Mediterranean to India, Australia, and the Far East. He accused Britain of never wanting an Italian defeat. A defeated Italy would have served as inspiration for the "antifascist forces" and "anti-imperialist movements," anathema to British interests. He lambasted the socialists and communists for not assisting Abyssinia, congratulating the "liberal humanitarians" for their greater commitment. "These great 'champions' and stalwart fighters for the rights of the colonial peoples and subject races did not provide one gas mask, one ambulance outfit, much less financial assistance, to help these Abyssinians.... Yesterday it was Abyssinia. Today Spain. And tomorrow . . . ?"[149]

War Approaches

Padmore's desire for activism and intervention reached a new zenith in the era of Munich. He increasingly contributed to the African American press and continued to do so throughout the war. He supplemented his income by paid tutorials and collected welcome fees from the *Pittsburgh Courier* and the *Chicago Defender*. In the late thirties, he burrowed further into the inner life of the ILP. He never actually joined the party, but wrote more for *New Leader* and participated in activities like an ILP school on "Imperialism and War" with Fenner Brockway and others. He and Kenyatta coauthored an essay that appeared in a special "Empire" supplement of *New Leader*.

> We have deliberately devoted the greater part of this May Day issue . . . to the subject of Imperialism. We have done this because there is a great danger at the present time that our hatred of the tyranny of Fascism may cause us to forget the tyranny of Imperialism. . . . the truth is that four-fifths of the British empire is as much a dictatorship as the Fascist countries. . . . It is the exploitation of the millions in the Empire which gives the British Isles the economic stability which permits the British ruling class to govern here without Fascism.[150]

New Leader's "Empire Special" provided raw data on the colonies. Reginald Reynolds contended that in India, "British Imperialism [was] in no respect different from Fascist Terrorism in Italy." An article cited the Arabist and socialist ex–Colonial Office member H. St. John Philby on the issue of aerial bombings and military force in British possessions in the Middle East. Another cited conservative MP Leo Amery, who would become secretary of state for India and

Burma during the coming war. "Our whole policy in India, our whole policy in Egypt, stands condemned if we condemn Japan." The statements of Captain J.R.J. Macnamara, conservative MP, on aerial bombing in the northwest territories of India provided useful testimony. "Talking about murder from the air, we must once more take ourselves to task over what we smugly call 'police bombing.'" Other articles described British guns turned on striking women in Nigeria, under the previous Labour government, and Brockway cited testimony from Lady Kathleen Simon in an account of forced labor in the colonies. He compared the repression against Jews under fascism to colonial racial policies, citing South Africa's rules for "colored" citizens. "Even in Fascist countries 'non-Aryans' are not treated with more continual suggestions that they belong to an inferior race." Padmore wrote on Trinidad, expressing solidarity with ousted Governor-General Murchison Fletcher who had denounced the rates of malnutrition among the island's workers and whose 1937 defense of the militant oil trades-union leader Uriah Butler, wanted by the imperial authorities under Fletcher's command, had cost the governor-general his posting. Kenyatta's piece in the subsequent issue of *New Leader*, whose publication coincided with the celebration of Empire Day, was entitled "Hitler Could Not Improve on Kenya."[151]

Padmore's rehabilitation as a political figure and commentator in his own right, was undeniable. Even Reginald Bridgeman, who was close to the communists, acknowledged that Padmore's writings on the use of Moorish troops by the right in Spain had influenced and chastened British radical opinion about the nature of that episode of the Civil War. Padmore strived to connect the use of North Africans by the fascists with the Abyssinian question, consistent with his wider approach, noting that the Allies had used black troops in the First World War.[152] His lectures emphasized these views. He spoke for the Gold Coast Student Association on "Africa, a Pawn in European Politics."[153] At the same time, he articulated the links between Spain and Abyssinia, as in Cunard's literary petition, *Authors Take Sides*.[154] Padmore and 144 writers were signatories; each wrote a short statement of support for, or opposition to, the Spanish republic's fight. Padmore's contribution was unmistakable.[155] "The sympathy of Africans and other colonial peoples naturally goes out to the toiling masses of Spain. . . . they have not forgotten Abyssiania. . . . it is so regrettable that democratic Spain, by failing to make an anti-imperialist gesture to the Moors, played into the hands of France. . . . 'No people who oppress another people can themselves be free."[156] Padmore collaborated with Harold Moody and the League of Colored Peoples on a response to the government's Bledisloe Commission report on Rhodesia. As always, Africa and its global connections commanded much of his attention. A May rally in London protested against colonial and territorial transfers and specifically against the High Commission Territories of Bechuanaland, Basutoland, and Swaziland being ceded to South Africa.[157]

The global nature of the crisis of 1938–39 was exemplified by the challenges to the British Empire mounted in the Caribbean. Pleas for democracy and for economic justice spawned rebellions, and Padmore hurled himself into the work of responding to these movements from London. Strikers in his native Trinidad were arrested and tried by judges whose number included Labour party supporters. Padmore condemned their role.[158] In May, the opening of an Empire Day anticolonial exhibition at Conway Hall, sponsored by the International African Service Bureau was a point of mobilization, and late that summer he and others led a demonstration to protest against the Empire Exhibition in Glasgow.[159] In June Padmore, C.L.R. James, Chris Jones, and others spoke on the Jamaican disturbances at a Trafalgar Square rally, even as Rhodes House, Oxford, observed the centenary of Jamaican emancipation. Harold Moody and Creech Jones participated in the festivities.[160] Robeson lent his service to the Committee for West Indian Affairs while the government established a Royal Commission on the West Indies.[161]

The pressure on the government from diverse groups, the celebrity of some of the individuals involved, and the perfunctory responses from Westminster each reflected an element of the discussion of Africa and India from within Britain in the last months of the thirties. A myopia about the future of empire, and the delusion that Britain could somehow alone decide global outcomes, pervaded the wider discourse on the fate of the colonial world and its peoples. In September 1938 the pro-appeasement wing of the government struck deals with Hitler for the rescue of Britain through a negotiated peace. This was secured through Chamberlain's concession of Czechoslovakia, and the question of British possessions and their fate at the hands of the brokers, arose in the climate of negotiation. Padmore chided, "Europe's difficulty is Africa's opportunity."[162] He was to claim that he returned to Germany in November of 1938 and even attended a rally in Berlin.[163]

The threat now posed so sharply to the possession and life of the colonies was Padmore's preoccupation in the final approach to war. In January 1939 he helped to host an IASB conference at the Quaker headquarters, Friends House, near Euston Station. Among the participants were French Trotskyist sympathizer and anarcho-syndicalist Daniel Guérin, who spoke of the situation in France, and C.L.R. James's associate, Arthur Ballard, from the Center against Imperialism.[164] Labor rebellion continued in the Caribbean with demonstrations in Port of Spain. Repression and the surveillance of dissent increased in Britain. A Colonial Office report on "Colonial Students in Britain" called for greater government supervision of their groups.[165] More coalition work ensued, though in July a Memorial Hall conference on "African Peoples, Democracy and Peace" witnessed Padmore attacking the communist party. The conference sponsors were drawn from a spectrum of black organizations including the LOCP, the NWA, the Colored Film Artistes' Association, and the Gold Coast students' group.[166] *International African Opinion's* motto, "Educate, Cooperate,

GEORGE PADMORE is probably the best known of Negro Socialist leaders. He was the Negro representative on the Executive of the Communist International, but resigned when ordered by Moscow to tone down his anti-Imperialist activities in order not to prejudice the Franco-Soviet Pact and the Liberal elements in the French Popular Front. He is now the chairman of the International African Bureau.

Figure 2.6. "Negro Leader: George Padmore is probably the best known of Negro Socialist leaders. He was the Negro representative on the Executive of the Communist International, but resigned when ordered by Moscow to tone down his anti-imperialist activities in order not to prejudice the Franco-Soviet Pact and the Liberal elements in the French Popular Front. He is now the chairman of the International African Bureau [sic]." *New Leader*, October 20, 1939. The caption refers to the International African Service Bureau (courtesy Blyden Padmore Cowart; reproduced by kind permission of the Syndics of Cambridge University Library).

Emancipate," suggested a spirit of collaboration, yet its writers mocked and derided the hesitant responses of West Indian elites to the strikers on their doorsteps in the Caribbean. Its words recalled Padmore's skepticism toward "colonial intellectuals" when he was still a Comintern official. "Today, after years of comparative obscurity, the British West Indian islands have forced themselves into the consciousness of the people and rulers of the British Empire and the whole world, and the method by which this has been done is at once a reproach and a sign-post to the better-educated people of African descent in these colonies."[167]

The journal presented the struggle against fascism as one between the propertied and propertyless.

Fascism, which is the most brutal form of imperialism, puts a firm brake on all liberal ideas, all freedom, on every concept of human equality and fraternity. In Germany, it bases itself on a fanatical nationalism, and exaggerated racial arrogance. Its inhuman persecution of the Jews is a sop to national discontent and a convenient distraction from the real issues at stake.[168]

This essay articulated the vision of a coalition in the anglophone Caribbean that would forge ties with the region's Indian community on an equal footing. The IASB would not cater to notions of racial privilege.

> We preach no narrow race doctrine. It is the business of the Intellectuals of African descent to work in the closest harmony with the East Indians, to make the cause of the Indian working masses their own and to strive for unity of action between these two racial groups so closely allied by a common poverty. To those of other races who wish genuinely to participate in the struggle, the West Indian Intellectuals will extend the hand of friendship. But the large majority of people in the West Indies are of African descent. . . . while all of every race and creed will be welcome as friends and allies, it must be on the rigid understanding that the days for superior claims on the score of race are over and that such impertinence will be mercilessly driven out of the movement.[169]

Rearmament prompted deep reflection. The global imperialist and fascist ambition, coupled with the prevailing interpretation of Munich as a primarily "European" rather than a global crisis, fostered self-assertion and a desire for racial independence among IASB circles. Padmore traveled to Europe in the summer of 1939, to attend an international socialist conference.[170] His affiliation with the followers of the social-democratic Second International was never formalized but his close ties to the ILP were made manifest by this journey. Ada Wright had spoken nine years earlier on the same platforms as socialist leaders Léon Blum of France and Emil Vendervelde of Belgium. At that time, the relations between communists and socialists were already fraught, but the German defeat, the acrimony and murderous antagonisms that beset communists and Poumists in Spain, were yet to come. There was less debate then about Russian domestic incarceration and the disappearances of German communists who fled fascist terror only to rot in Soviet prisons or to meet deaths before firing squads. Now the possibilities of left alliances at the national and municipal level being affirmed again internationally lay abandoned. Stalin had not yet agreed to the Non-Aggression Pact with Hitler but the deal lay just ahead. Socialist vacillation on rearmament and pacifist opposition to war alienated many patriotic trade unionists and sat poorly with communists who defended the Soviet fatherland as a first commitment. In 1939 *International African Opinion* wistfully ran J. R. Casimir's "O Africa," sung to the tune of the labor movement's English anthem, "Jerusalem." "O Africa, our Motherland, We long to come to thee. To rest on thy sweet loving breast. And no more homeless be." But borders were sealed and ships' passages forbidden.

Padmore assessed his life in *Pan-Africanism or Communism?*, published in 1957, the year he left London for newly independent Ghana. In this volume, whose epigraph was taken from Tagore, Padmore expressed resentment of Europeans *both communists and anticommunists*, for the "arrogance of white 'loftiness' . . . an unwarranted interference and unpardonable assumption of superiority." He insisted that "Africans do not want to wait for Communists to 'incite' them. The realities of their status have infused their determination to be free." The African American writer Richard Wright introduced the volume: "Black people primarily regard American, British and French anti-Communists as *white people* . . . The Negro's outlook is basically determined by his economic and social position, by his color, and racial oppression." Even in the Comintern, Padmore had worked for "freedom for black people."[171]

Then Padmore retraced his steps. He recalled that the 1930s Hamburg Negro Committee had been committed "to help enlighten public opinion, particularly in Great Britain . . . as to the true conditions in the various colonies, protectorates and mandated territories in Africa and the West Indies." His evaluation of the thirties British communist party was unforgiving, scathing in its commentary on its members' racial attitudes, and on black reactions to the paternalism of the era. He acknowledged his work with the Negro Welfare Association as an exception to these practices, disingenuously calling it a "leftish welfare organization" and emphasized the failure of the communists or organizations such as the LAI to attract blacks. Praise was reserved for the ILP; he referred to it as "the only British political party which has consistently opposed colonialism." He alluded to the cavalier tactics of the propaganda campaigns of the Moscow-financed Red Aid years. "Mr. Münzenberg once told the writer that it was the easiest thing to get signatures of famous Europeans, providing the right approach was used." He described a pattern in which "anti-imperialism made way for anti-fascism and anti-war," contending that Münzenberg fell out of Russian favor when he opposed the Stalin-Hitler pact, a generous reconstruction of the demise of his former comrade.[172]

In his analysis of the collapse of Comintern internationalism, Padmore placed weight upon both Soviet entry into the League of Nations in 1934 and Soviet oil sales to Mussolini in 1935, consistent with his earlier writings on Abyssinia. In a gesture toward the tradition that he found most appealing, he concluded this memoir with a tribute to his white allies. "Africans have so many 'friends' today that it is well to recall those who championed their causes at a time when it was not considered so fashionable to denounce colonialism and racism." He named among them several figures that appear in this story: Lady Simon, to whom we turn in the chapter that follows; Leonard Woolf; Sylvia Pankhurst; James Maxton; Leonard Barnes; Reginald Bridgeman; and Nancy Cunard. He also wrote of Saklatvala: "He denounced British imperialism. . . . He was one Indian who had no time for opportunistic trimmers and sycophants. The most independent-minded Communist ever. A Titoist before Tito!"[173]

Padmore did not portray himself as at odds with his own past. To understand the views he expressed in *Pan-Africanism or Communism?* as governed simply by his involvement in support of national independence struggles in Africa, or as byproducts of the global McCarthyism of the 1950s, is to deny his careful weighing of the commitments he undertook during the 1930s. Padmore gave communism its fair chance, and he faithfully carried out a painstaking agenda of "Negro work" in Europe during the era of Scottsboro to the best of his ability, given his organizational and doctrinal choices. The Marxist movement was integral to the person he was in the twenties and early thirties, and his later evolution rested upon the realization of that movement's failings in the 1930s. He witnessed them and participated in them as they transpired. His passion for journalism, which engaged the very largest "white" establishment diplomatic and economic issues of his day, separated him from others who also called themselves Pan-Africanists. His concern for the central role that he believed people of African descent had to play in world events in order for justice to triumph was unwavering. He saw them traversing the *world* stage, not just the African, Caribbean, or Harlem theaters of struggle. He spent more than two decades of his later life in a propaganda-group existence because of his understanding of what global revolutionary politics required, not because he had abandoned those politics. His talents would readily have been appropriated by other movements and for other goals had he made himself available, had his vision been weaker than his ambition. His wit and brilliance as a journalist alone would have made him a ready contender for celebrity had he adopted a more moderate outlook. Britain remained his home until 1957. When he left for Accra with his life partner, Dorothy Padmore, it was meant to be for a long journey. But his health declined. In 1959 he died on a medical visit to London. Like so many other émigré and refugee activists, his forebears from Marx to Garvey, London was an undesired but familiar final destination. After one last flight from Britain to the Continent of his dreams and passions, his ashes were interred in independent Ghana.

Chapter 3

LADY KATHLEEN SIMON AND ANTISLAVERY

"Workers of the World Unite"; I thought of the wide shallow slogans of political parties, as the thin bodies, every rib showing, with dangling swollen elbows or pock-marked skin, went by me to the market; why should we pretend to talk in terms of the world when we mean only Europe or the white races? Neither the I.L.P. nor Communist Party urges a strike in England because the platelayers in Sierra Leone are paid sixpence a day without their food. Civilization in West Africa remains exploitation; we have hardly improved the natives' lot at all.
—*Graham Greene*, Journey without Maps, *1936*

In 1956 GEORGE PADMORE acknowledged Lady Kathleen Simon's role in the struggle for rights of those of African descent.[1] Kathleen Manning Simon, the Irishwoman and doctor's widow who married the politician and cabinet minister Sir John Simon, was an ardent antislavery advocate and, from 1927, a leader of the venerable British and Foreign Anti-Slavery and Aborigines' Protection Society (the "Society") that claimed the legacy of early abolitionist William Wilberforce. Her life's work was deeply engaged with the Society in many respects.[2] Simon's opposition to lynching in the era of Scottsboro was steadfast. Her call for freedom for the more than 6 million persons, whom she and her associates deemed "living in bondage" in the 1930s, forced a relentless gaze upon many parts of the globe, in the hope of eradicating the evil of slavery as a basis for both trusteeship and the enlightened preservation of empire.[3] In so doing, the Society challenged Parliament's failure to press the issue forward in the peace negotiations at Versailles. Lady Simon affected a memorable presence and was an indefatigable orator and fund-raiser. It would have been cruel to undermine achievement with a search for greater motive beneath her magnanimous and liberal exterior. Padmore may have judged that he ventured there at his own peril and instead left Lady Simon on the brighter side of posterity. But his fellow activist Sylvia Pankhurst and her colleagues had not demurred from such dissent in the thirties, challenging "the propaganda emanating from what they called the 'antislavery enthusiasts,' the 'welfare of natives group,' and denounc[ing] them as Roman Catholics and Fascist sympathizers."[4]

The League of Nations, closely allied to the Society in its promulgation of the Slavery Convention of 1926, had already failed to galvanize the post-Versailles world to take up a struggle against human incarceration in its many forms by the time the Scottsboro case broke. Scottsboro's communist connections were brakes upon the Society's engagement with the case and it was never directly involved in the campaign, though Lady Simon made a contribution to the defense fund. Apart from the orthodox left, Lady Simon's and the Society's work overlapped and coexisted with various currents in humanitarian and early human-rights advocacy, including those identified with the Christian mission and YMCA leader J. H. Oldham, whose ecumenical career crossed that of Archbishop William Temple. Despite the institution of the International Labour Organization (ILO), the Geneva Protocol, and other measures undertaken by the League of Nations, Simon and the Society filled their lives with unfinished and often futile work on behalf of those enduring and diverse forms of incarcerated labor.[5]

Kathleen Manning came from County Wexford. When her husband died she made her way to London and worked as a midwife in the East End. Her observation of dire poverty at the heart of England's wealth left an indelible imprint on a colonial heart. She did not mince words on the issue of Irish independence any more than on many conditions of human degradation, wherever in the world she happened to find or hear of them. One of John Simon's biographers unkindly conjectured that Sir John sought her out in desperation when socialite Mrs. Ronnie Greville refused the lonely widower.[6] But for Kathleen Manning, the reunion with her former employer offered something more than romance. Her son was a POW, captured while serving with the Irish Guards in the Great War. Manning went to RAF major John Simon to seek assistance. They were already well known to each other, as Manning had served as governess to Simon's children after his first wife's death, unable to support herself by midwifery alone. The supplicant became Sir John Simon's fiancée and after their wartime wedding in France, Lady Simon remained there as a Red Cross worker. John Simon welcomed her skills as an organizer in the 1918 election campaign in which the raging war in Ireland figured prominently. He wrote of his "plucky little Irish wife":

> [F]uture contests . . . were to show that no M.P. ever owed more to a comrade than I did to her. Her courage and her humor, with a wonderful power of moving appeal in support of the causes in which we both believed, transformed the atmosphere in which my electoral campaigns were conducted and was even thought to mellow the cold austerity of the candidate![7]

In that khaki contest, which took its name from the uniforms still being worn by many electors, the Simons told crowds that the government should not pursue the war in Ireland and called for peace, condemning the tactics of both the Protestant Black and Tans paramilitaries, and Sinn Fein, the political movement of the Irish Republican Army. Lady Simon encouraged her husband in the face of his own physical exhaustion, reminding him of "those dreadful things . . . being done in [her] country."[8] She conducted countless meetings over the coming years in the homes of Liberal dowagers and ordinary electors. Even though the Liberal party's support diminished under David Lloyd George's rocky postwar leadership, Simon held onto his seat from 1922 onward, not least because of his wife's dynamic energy. Had she had no impulse toward the eradication of what she regarded as the world's foremost evil, her reputation might simply have remained that of an overzealous spouse of the more reserved and better-bred Simon. As one of his colleagues so bluntly put it, "Money did not like her." Prime Minister Neville Chamberlain, destined to end the thirties as the Englishman most hated by his own people, said quizzically of his partner in crime, "How can he come to marry that wife I don't know. She doesn't seem the part of a *grand-dame*."[9] Even without the antislavery crusade that made her reputation, the accolades she received as Simon's wife stood as a kind of recognition—her Indian host Susie Sorabji named the College at Poona's "Lady Simon Hostel" after her.[10] Lady Simon accompanied her husband twice when he led a controversial and, for many, notorious parliamentary investigative commission on Indian government and education in 1928 and 1929.[11] But her first opposition to slavery grew in territory unknown to him. The road she traveled ran from Ireland through Georgia and Tennessee, long before it reached London or Calcutta.

Antislavery: A Life Commitment

The Society, more than a hundred years old, was Lady Simon's vehicle of protest and mass education.[12] At a 1927 gathering of Liberal women in Blackpool, the Liberal party supporter Violet Bonham Carter and Lady Simon resolved to support the League of Nations' (the "League's") antislavery convention and the ILO, declaring that in territories under British control "no color barrier should be erected which would [prevent] people from reaching positions for which their capacities and merits should fit them."[13] The *Times* published the Simons's exposé of the practice of slavery in the British protectorate Sierra Leone, a byproduct of the first campaign in League circles for support of abolition.[14] In 1928 she appeared with NAACP leader Walter White, at a Wilberforce monument dedication in Hull, signifying the connection between Simon and African American sympathy and activism. But it was the publication of her highly successful 1929 work *Slavery* that revealed Lady Simon's deeper indebtedness to the American scene. Sir John Simon introduced the volume, but it was dedicated to "Amanda of Tennessee and to all those who have suffered and still suffer in slavery." This popular text documented contemporary global slavery and sought "to complete the work of Wilberforce." John Simon explained, "For just as Lincoln declared that a nation cannot be half-free, half-slave so in the new international order the liberties which some communities enjoy make it intolerable that there should be men, women and little children of other races who

Figure 3.1. "Antislavery protest meeting." A placard of the Anti-Slavery and Aborigines Protection Society, on display in Hull, circa 1927, announcing the visit of Society leaders Lady Kathleen Simon and John Harris, and Masha Katish (upper left), a former slave. Whips, knives, and chains are attached (courtesy of University of Oxford, Bodleian Library and Antislavery International).

are still in actual bondage." Now slavery could "be swept away by the League. . . . one ground for hope is the immensely increased sensitiveness of each part of the world to what is going on elsewhere." In an eerily familiar paean to the new communications technologies, Simon wrote,

> It seems incredible today that so little time should have elapsed since public executions were a holiday spectacle. We now prefer that unpleasant things should happen at a distance. But even distance is ceasing to provide a screen. "Delhi is far off" ran the Indian proverb, but now we know that the wireless wave travels fast enough to put a girdle round the earth seven times in a single second. And once the inhumanity of slavery as practiced today in different parts of the earth is, as the saying is, "brought home," the conscience of the world, working through the instrument of international action, will not rest until it be ended.[15]

This kind of optimism embraced the endeavors of the decade. The failures of various forms of internationalism now appear just as irreducible as the hopes invested in their successes appeared before Munich. Human bondage—incarceration, ownership, and enforced peonage—were Lady Simon's chief concerns. Conditions in China, Abyssinia, Saharan Africa, and the territories of the Persian Gulf especially gripped her. Four to six million people had been seized "since the days when Admiral Hawkins in the *Jesus of Lubeck* sailed from West Africa to America." Historical reenactment was a mainstay of Simon's repertoire, and she offered readers many narrative renditions of the Atlantic slave trade and its gradual supersession by recent and continuing forms of labor exploitation termed "slavery" in the 1930s. Undergirding this narrative was the proposition that "even amongst primitive peoples" each person possessed rights.[16] The large discourse of slavery and freedom was fraught with conceptual and political difficulty.[17] She felt that the League should serve as the international coordinator of contemporary antislavery efforts, based upon its 1926 antislavery convention. The abolition of American and imperial slavery were benchmarks for more "backward" nations.

In line with British foreign policy, Lady Simon especially focused on the case of slavery in the only Christian nation in which it still obtained—Abyssinia—a case that the British had pursued since the end of the Great War. "The whole of Abyssinian life is overshadowed by slavery."[18] Abyssinia had joined the League in 1923 and was subject to the antislavery convention. The Italians were attempting to police the Abyssinian trade, and Simon suggested that a European power might have to take over the country in order to secure an end to the abomination.[19] She compared neighboring Sudan's practices with those revealed in *Uncle Tom's Cabin*.[20] In its turn, Liberia had become a site of denial. "All well-wishers of the negro race would like to believe that the Liberian Government, composed as it is of American Negroes, had succeeded so well in its efforts to build up a modern Republic that it had been able to abolish slavery."[21] Padmore quoted her statements on Liberia a short time later in *American Imperialism Enslaves Liberia* and mentioned her antislavery colleague John Harris's charges against Liberia, which Harris had presented to the League.[22] Abolition had occurred in Burma and Nepal only very recently, while peonage persisted in Latin America. Abolitionist Katherine Mayo had written for the American press about practices in the Phillippines.[23] The Portuguese territories were notorious offenders.[24]

Simon largely exempted the British Empire from view, but she cited forced labor practices recently defended by the Church hierarchy, including those in Kenya and Tanganyika.[25] In a clear statement of the Society's aims, she forcefully declared, "In our position of trustees for the natives in the colonies over which we rule, the endeavor of the white races should be to help the native to use his own land and make it productive, rather than to exploit him for the benefit of the settler," recalling the role assumed by the great powers in the colonies as mandated under the League charter at Versailles and thereafter.[26] The nineteenth-century abolitionist movement had spawned the first model international effort from which the League took inspiration. Simon saluted the Society's predominantly Quaker legacy and presented its heros: early abolitionist, litigant, and classicist Granville Sharp (who also founded a settlement in Sierra Leone); parliamentary leader of the campaign for the 1807 Slave Trade Act,

Wilberforce, and his fellow activist and essayist Thomas Clarkson; former plantation manager and agitator Zachary Macaulay; slave rebellion supporter and missionary John Smith (who died in a Demerara jail); the iconic David Livingstone, medical missionary and African explorer, and Wilberforce's successor in Parliament; and Thomas Fowell Buxton, whose descendants were Simon's colleagues.[27]

The history lesson was remonstrative: "Sales of slaves had still sometimes occurred on English soil and no one seems to have challenged the proceeding."[28] But she felt that things had improved. From the agreements of the Congress of Vienna in 1815 at the close of the Napoleonic Wars, to the Berlin Conference in 1885, at which the powers addressed claims upon Africa, Europeans had repeatedly closed in on the slave trade albeit in an effort to make imperialism function more smoothly and inclusively, with less moral opprobrium. In the face of the Empire's profound involvement in the historic slave trade, Britain claimed a superior moral record as compared to other slaving powers, placing Simon near the helm of a new era of imperial leadership, and her book was meant to spur public opinion to promote government support for inclusive, renewed antislavery activity on a global scale.

The *Manchester Guardian*'s editor C. P. Scott was a Society vice president, and his newspaper praised *Slavery*'s "impressive array of fact and argument."[29] Both the *Times* and the *Daily News* emphasized its challenge to the widespread ignorance of slavery's continued existence, "one of the comfortable beliefs of those whose lives are cast in pleasant places that slavery passed away at some unstated but distant time." The *Star* presumed a special role for women in the antislavery movement, one that Simon embraced, and its review prompted images of childlike victims—undomesticated, abject and orphaned. "Lady Simon has written a book on slavery which is a challenge to Liberals throughout the world, and especially to women. Slavery, not in any modified form, but with all its grim realities of torture, emasculation and the denial of any family rights, exists today."[30] The Society claimed that *Slavery* received as much press coverage as any other book on the market in its first year of publication, a year of enormous activity for Lady Simon, crowned by John Simon's tour of North America, sponsored by the American Bar Association, which provided her with an extraordinary audience in Canada as well as in the land of Lincoln. Walter White wrote to thank her for praising his own book, asking for a copy of hers to send to his contact at Viking Press in the unrealized hope that there would be an American edition.[31] The Society's *Antislavery Reporter and Aborigines' Friend* (the *Reporter*), carried regular bulletins of American lynchings, noting that in 1930 "in only a few (three)—was rape the alleged cause." There was a report of a Louisiana peonage case "pure and simple"—a planter who chained up recalcitrant croppers.[32]

Though Liberal interests dominated the Society, all political parties were represented on its board and executive over the course of the thirties. Women played a central role in the Society's work—led most importantly by John and Alice Harris, who brought the involvement of mission organizations to their long commitment.[33] In this context of shared leadership, Lady Simon's book was a publishing triumph that established her as an instant world authority, affording her carte blanche in many settings. Her independence from Sir John Simon was seldom at issue; he continually appeared by her side and she by his, not on official business so much as in their avid participation in antislavery events. Her book's ostensible universalism lay in its transparent appeal for support for the League, but it also bore a strong tie to a documentary tradition practiced by the left in the thirties. Steeped in empiricism, its method of argument by the facts, figures, press cuttings, interviews, testaments, case studies, eyewitness accounts, and travelogues conveyed a documented social reality, in the stark terms also used by Padmore. Melodrama, and a preoccupation with the physicality of slavery, assisted narratives like those appearing in eighteenth- and nineteenth-century antislavery literature. The selection of locales and of issues had a political agenda but the emotional appeal of suffering substantiated by "fact" was its first and most salient element. Lady Simon devoted the rest of her life to this method and the hope of its efficacy. She helped to order and to articulate a cosmos of feelings and opinions not simply about a set of exploitative practices but about wider issues of racial politics.

No evidence suggests that Lady Simon intermingled intimately with black communists or their supporters like Padmore or Robeson (of whom she was a fan) in the thirties, and communist Arnold Ward derided her. But she did correspond with African American leaders, and even taped a radio series with C.L.R. James. In July 1930 writer Alain Locke wrote to her from Paris, thanking her for arranging interviews for him on a recent trip to London, regretting that he would not be in his Washington home when she and Sir John Simon arrived there to visit Howard University, where Locke had provided them with a letter of introduction to Mordecai Johnson, the university's president. Locke was writing on the problem of "forced labor" and awaiting a shipment of literature from John Harris.[34] Locke sent a copy of his *The New Negro* to her, professing his "personal esteem" for Simon.[35] She thanked him, expressing approval of a recent article by Du Bois. "Books such as these tell us of the yearnings of your race towards the improvement of their lot, and their endeavor to take their place on an equality with the rest of the world."[36] Simon shared with the communists a belief in the leading role in racial achievement for "Westernized" Negroes as models for Africa and other "primitive" zones, though her standard was that of educated African Americans, not the advanced inhabitants of the new Soviet republics.[37]

On the other side, Africa presented an unremitting gallery of horrific episodes upon which Simon drew for her antislavery oratory. These anecdotes were rarely modified by references to cultural achievement, instead identifying Africa and Asia as unmitigated living hells for which their European overlords could be held responsible. The *Reporter* announced an expedition to Burma to investigate the existence of slavery, head-hunting, and human sacrifice. In Durban, South Africa, poll-tax riots invited brutal responses by the police, who appeared adorned with gas masks, unmistakable symbols of warfare after Verdun and the Somme. From the office of the undersecretary of state for the colonies came reports of executions carried out in Nigeria without recourse to defense counsel. Liquor flowed too freely while political rights remained circumscribed. The journal protested against the restricted franchise in Fiji and the child traffic of domestic servants in Ceylon.[38] Society members were also involved in rescue operations nearer to home. In 1930 they established a "Welfare of Africans in Europe War Fund," which received over six hundred letters on behalf of Africans personally known to their advocates. The Society's membership lists suggest a high collective consciousness about certain selected patterns of injustice. The rolls included Mrs. Herbert Gladstone, widow of the Liberal cabinet minister and a governor-general of South Africa; Sydney Olivier, former colonial secretary in Jamaica; descendants of William Wilberforce, David Livingstone, and Josiah Wedgewood; and liberal critics like C. P. Scott, and H. W. Nevinson.[39] This was the modern currency of abolitionism, its eyes directed toward the evils of the other empires and "correctable" abuses within British territories. The Society explained American failings both in terms of slavery's lingering aftereffects, so well challenged by the Society's forebears in their time, *and* in terms of the progress that democracy could foster among the enlightened and acquisitive specimens of "post-African" Negro life.

Lady Simon was an unrivaled crusader, and she and the antislavery movement drew more popular audiences than many drawn by the left. In 1930 a demonstration at Central Hall, Westminster, was addressed by the Archbishop of Canterbury, Cosmo Gordon Lang; League statesman Robert Cecil, and Charles Roden Buxton, who, with John Harris, took a leading role in antislavery.[40] The League of Nations Union (LNU), acted as co-sponsor, reaching layers in both provincial and metropolitan life that the Society would not have reached alone.[41] The pace and range of Simon's yearly engagements and correspondence was staggering, and in the later thirties her ill health became an evident source of anxiety for her husband. In May Simon unveiled a plaque in Bath at a home that had belonged to Wilberforce and addressed the Women Liberals' Conference. "I want a war on slavery" she cried, proclaiming a recent shift in public attitudes. This "great evil ha[s] to be abolished" in places like Hong Kong, where under the flag, "women and girls were men's property."[42] Two days later she spoke on "Christianity and Slavery: the case for Abyssinia." She could better understand murder than she could owning another human being, and estimated that 2 million were held in bondage in Abyssinia, where a slave who had stolen an orange had had his right hand cut off. Those fortunate enough to escape across the desert into British Sudan were not hunted down and returned. In the Red Sea, ships patrolled for traders and set men free.[43]

Transatlantic Crossing

Lady Simon's 1930 whirlwind North American journey offers clues to the varied transatlantic racial-political exchanges of the thirties. In mid-August, Simon spoke on Abyssinia for the Toronto Imperial Order, Daughters of the Empire. She described the dramatic flight of slaves into Sudan and their first gaze upon the Union Jack, identifying instances of slavery "as it was when *Uncle Tom's Cabin* was written."[44] The North American press featured her book as the most riveting account of slavery since English writer Harriet Martineau's study published in the 1830s.[45] In Chicago Simon spoke for the Women's International League for Peace and Freedom (WILF), condemning American lynchings. In a talk on Abyssinia, Arabia, and China, she drew connections. "While slavery has been abolished in America . . . another shocking evil had grown up . . . a blot on our national education. . . . I cannot condemn America enough for tolerating such barbarity.'"[46] The very next day the British press reported the horrific lynching of Abram Smith and Tom Shipp in Marion, Indiana, which had occurred two weeks earlier on August 7, and may have fueled Simon's attack. The photographs of this episode spread throughout the globe, later appearing in the German and Dutch Red Aid organs on the Continent alongside images of the Scottsboro case.[47]

Two days later, Oliver Green was lynched at Tarboro, North Carolina, in the first reported episode in the state since 1921. In New York Lady Simon spoke for a gathering hosted by the radical journal the *Nation*. The ecumenical Federal Council of Churches, which took a lead in collecting and disseminating lynching data to the Society, hosted her at the Town Hall in Manhattan.[48] In Washington, D.C., she addressed the English Speaking Union, and the Simons viewed the new art gallery at Howard University, just as Alain Locke had suggested they should. At journey's end, the *New York Sun* called Lady Simon "the modern Harriet Beecher Stowe."[49] On her return to London she told the *Manchester Guardian*, "I love Chicago." Instead of gangsters, she had witnessed people bathing along Lake Michigan—"healthy people" and "new buildings." She had seen "the great Negro settlement." She had met W.E.B. Du Bois and taken in the wildly popular stage play of black life, *Green Pastures*, in New York.[50]

> I thought it rather wonderful. . . . it represented the Negroes' idea of the Diety. The actor who took that part was very good. As a girl I lived in Tennessee and in Georgia . . . and I know the Negroes very well. That is why I like them. "Green Pastures" represented exactly what the negro feels about the Deity as a good pal who is with him in all his troubles and looks after him. It would seem natural to the negro that this friend should have a frockcoat and the "ten-cent seegar" which is the negro idea of great wealth.[51]

British Propaganda

After the return of the Simons to Britain, the Portuguese representatives successfully resisted a British-led attempt at Geneva to strengthen the League's antislavery convention. Italy, Liberia, and France took umbrage and supported Portugal in defiance of Britain, leaving the organization hamstrung in its efforts to curb slavery more rigorously. The decisions taken at Geneva were challenged by an international commission of inquiry that included the naturalist Cuthbert Christie and African American sociologist Charles Johnson of Fisk University. Liberia was under increasing scrutiny for its practices of slavery and compulsory labor, reported in abundance and acknowledged by the Liberian government. Four hundred thousand of the country's population of 2.5 million reportedly were slaves in the Society's terms.[52] Though the American rubber firm of Firestone, the country's key employer, was not implicated in the trade per se, there were many instances of other employers whose male slave laborers were reportedly lured to work by women posing as procurers, then finding themselves incarcerated. Indeed, Firestone was accused of using "forced labor," and this influenced the United States to accuse Liberia of complicity in slavery. When the Liberian government suddenly freed many such coerced workers, the *News Chronicle* smirked, "Picanninies in Pawn. 400,000 Slaves Freed In Liberia Sold Like Cattle."[53] The only black republic on the Continent provided grim fodder for those who decried the possibility of African self-rule. George Padmore was not the only critic snared in its proxy politics.

In a parallel development, growing concern over the rumors of forced labor conditions and testimonies of victims in the Soviet Union reached a clamourous level in London in November 1930. Parliamentary debate on the subject merited wide press coverage, and in 1931, the Society decided to conduct an inquiry into the complaints.[54] The news on conditions in Soviet "timber camps" came in part from ethnic Germans who had found themselves within the borders of the new Soviet entity at the end of the Great War. A collection of some of their prison letters was edited and published by writer and Scottsboro signatory, Hugh Walpole.[55] There was also significant skepticism about the motives for a British attack upon the Soviet Union. In 1920 prominent antislavery advocate and journalist Charles Roden Buxton traveled as a translator with the Labour and Trade Union Delegation to Russia, and dozens of other political visitors from Britain followed suit in the interwar years, including writer Naomi Mitchison. His sister wrote of the trip's persuasive importance for Roden Buxton.

> The visit was a milestone in his life. In spite of the evidences that he saw of the suffering caused by civil war and blockade with their accompanying violence and cruelty, Charlie everywhere detected signs that the Communists had achieved one vastly

important object: they had given new political and social power to the masses of men and women who owned no property.[56]

There was sympathy for the Russians in many quarters. The former prime minister Ramsay MacDonald, Buxton's companion on his Russian trip in 1920, regarded the pursuit of the case of Russian timber camps "as a political stunt." Some in Parliament sought to apply the Foreign Prison–Made Goods Act of 1897, against Soviet timber, because of the conditions of incarceration faced by Soviet workers.[57] The journal *Time and Tide* eschewed the hypocrisy of the debates, citing Lady Simon's disclosures of atrocities in China and peonage in South America as analogous to the treatment of Germans in Ukraine: "The man who shrinks horrified from tales of brutal handling of Indian pickets shrugs an indifferent and incredulous shoulder at stories of Soviet prison camps." In Ireland those appalled by wartime German actions in Belgium had asked of every British soldier that he function impeccably while on duty. *Time and Tide* reasoned that there was "little left for those whose suffering [was] inconvenient. . . . Nothing pleases the Soviets more today than an act of minor tyranny on the part of an imperial power; nothing would disappoint Mr. Churchill more than that the Russian Government should declare tomorrow a humanitarian amnesty to its political prisoners."[58]

Lady Simon and her associates were not friends of communism. Sir John Simon and other Society members participated in the parliamentary debate and commentary on Russian conditions and they commissioned a Society report.[59] The Soviet Union's failures to live by the principles claimed at its founding constituted a form of political capital, as did the exposures of corruption in the case of Liberia. If freed slaves or their descendants and the revolutionary Soviet empire, could not guarantee the abolition of conditions of slavery, then did the British Empire not have legitimacy? The *Reporter* summarized Charles Roden Buxton's Merttens Peace Lecture for 1931, published by the Hogarth Press as *The Race Problem in Africa*.

> He emphasizes the grave responsibilities of Great Britain for her colonial subjects, pointing out that the economic life of the industrial peoples is more than ever before dependent on the products of the tropics, and as a consequence there is greater danger of the exploitation of the native worker on a large scale. . . . the principle of national sovereignty . . . must give place . . . to that of international solidarity. The backward races must be developed . . . for the world in general, for whom the Powers which have Colonial possessions are Trustees. . . . it is the people of Great Britain . . . upon whom responsibility rests "for seeing that justice is done to the dumb unrepresented millions of tropical Africa."[60]

This was not the purported internationalism of Stalin's Comintern, or Padmore's call for international proletarian solidarity with those of African descent. It was not the biracial trade unionism advocated by American communists. But it was a powerful paternalist internationalism that reached beyond an apologia for empire's failings. Buxton and others like him sought to preserve empire within the stewardship of interwar, international law. In the years immediately following, these tenets were profoundly tested in the case of slavery in Abyssinia. In late spring 1931, a month after the Scottsboro case broke, the Parisian daily *Le Matin* published a series of investigative articles on Abyssinian slavery, containing interviews with traders who carried slaves out of Abyssinia into Arabia in large caravans, herding them onto ships. The slaves marched with pilgrims on their way to Mecca, spurred on by drivers who made merciless use of chains. A German traveler who witnessed these practices reported his findings, venturing that the trade was hard to regulate.[61] The *International Labour Review* published similar information.[62] John Harris advised Lady Simon on the coming Lords debate on the subject. It was believed that there were 2 million slaves in Abyssinia where slave raiding was frequent. Slaves were sold in exchange for weapons and reprisals for misconduct included the chopping off of limbs and the use of arms as ritual drumsticks. The prices of slaves had recently quadrupled and the caravan traffic had dried up and been replaced by smaller gangs.[63]

In early 1931 the Society corresponded with Haile Selassie, an avowed opponent of slavery whose capacity to challenge indigenous regional rulers was severely limited. Lord Noel-Buxton visited Abyssinia, and in September 1932 Selassie issued a full proclamation of freedom specifically manumitting the slaves of his opponent, Ras Hailu. But a League report on conditions in the same year stated that "in Abyssinia there would be special difficulties in seeking to abolish serfdom otherwise than gradually."[64] It noted the end of slavery in Afghanistan, Iraq, Nepal, Kelt, Transjordan, Persia, and Bahrein, adding that unless it was still practiced in Tibet or Central Asia, regions for which few data were in hand, the only regions still allowing slavery included Hejaz, Nejd (both in Saudi Arabia), Yemen, Hadramaut (in Yemen), Oman, Kuwait, and Abyssinia, and Abyssinia alone professed Christianity. British, French, and Italian ships were patrolling the Red Sea.[65] Robert Cecil had disconcertingly admitted in the League Assembly that the League's antislavery convention was ineffectual. The report insisted that Britain must stand for the creation of real international authority. The *Times* pressed for a League commissioner to supervise Selassie.[66]

The United States was not a League member but had signed the antislavery convention at the end of the War, as a gesture of support for abolition. As news of American lynchings continued to stream into the British and antislavery press, the time of reckoning with the Scottsboro case approached. At first, there was no mention of the case in the Society's *Reporter*. Lady Simon never spoke of it publically or if she did, there is no record of her doing so among her personal papers, nor a record of John Harris or Charles Roden Buxton acting as Scottsboro signatories. None was without contacts within the growing circles

Figure 3.2. "Abyssinian slaves" circa 1930 (GettyImages).

of those who had signed on behalf of the defendants. Virginia Woolf recorded dining with her friend Buxton during the Labour Party Conference of 1933.

> And then the Rodent ... reminiscent of my early youth—a rather thin, water-blooded kind of man, with hair parted and steel grey eyes—& a mouth like a spinsters [sic] reticule, but of course humane, vitalized by his humanity, sufferings of negroes, son who goes to Russia, vegetarian, once every 3 weeks overcome with lust for beef—ate fish—he gave us lunch at Frascati's [at Hastings, East Sussex], or some such place. I had a vast plate of beef. L. [Leonard Woolf] fed Pinka [their dog] on the bone of his cutlet.[67]

Leonard Woolf would become secretary of both of the Labour party's Advisory Committees on International and Imperial Affairs, in which Buxton also served.

But unlike the Woolfs, the liberal and Tory establishment that dominated the leadership of the Society did not much want to touch a case so clearly tied to communism—ties that Labour officially rejected as well. Further, Lady Simon's NAACP African American colleagues were not those active in the first wave of Scottsboro supporters. But this did not prevent her from keeping private track of the defense case even as the Society monitored the more "supportable" outcry over American lynchings. In 1932 the *Reporter* published the lynching data gathered by the NAACP and the American Southern Commission on the

Study of Lynching. It told the story of the Maryville, Missouri, case in which African American Raymond Gunn was dragged three miles and chained to the roof of a schoolhouse, then burned to death with gasoline for the murder of a white schoolmistress, Velma Colter. Gunn laid his jacket out below his body and was ordered to lie face down to die while the crowd formed a ritualistic circle around the house: "The shameful spectacle was witnessed by a mob of 2000, including hundreds of women." There was a "long string of motor cars holding hundreds more. The National Guard and sheriff's forces put up no resistance."[68]

Lady Simon gathered many such stories for her files. One of her American correspondents wrote, "The intolerance here regarding religion, race and other things is appalling."[69] A few weeks before Scottsboro broke, Sir John and Lady Simon spoke at the Oxford League of Nations Union meeting, presided over by Professor Gilbert Murray, Society member and future Scottsboro signatory. Sir John's speech typified an influential, imperial reform perspective. "Don't let us suppose that we here are merely patronizing critics of others. . . . We have an immense opportunity, not as patrons or superiors, but as members of the greater society of mankind, to change the face of the world." When his wife rose to speak, she revealed her deep affinity for the American scene, recounting her girlhood at school in the South.

> I passed through the Hall of the College . . . and sitting alone was a beautiful girl with a blonde complexion and blue eyes. Not a soul spoke to her. I asked my companion, Why is she isolated? Hush, was the reply. No one must speak to her; she's the child of liberated slaves. In a moment . . . the blood was up, and I went and sat by her as a companion. The seed lay buried for years, but I think I can say that I owe my enthusiasm to Amanda of Tennessee.[70]

Lady Simon's rendition of the free, light-skinned Amanda, implied that she had appeared to be white and would have been treated better if she "really were so." The story asked that listeners imagine the consequences of "being mistaken" as black. Lady Simon often spoke of Amanda in order to reassure her listeners of the veracity and authenticity of her own rhetoric.[71] The press similarly focused upon stories of individual victims of lynch mobs when a case lent itself to a compassionate reading. In December 1931 the papers featured ninety-four-year-old Cudjo Lewis of Mobile, Alabama, the last living person brought to the United States in slavery. In 1859 he had been among those who arrived on a freebooter that landed with a cargo of Africans on the Alabama coast, where they were soon sold into bondage in the fields. After the Civil War, Lewis worked in the shipyards, less than a day's drive from where Ada Wright's sons were passing their eighth month in jail. The physical proximity of a living person who had been transported in slavery was a fascinating anomaly. One-hundred-year-old former slaves, identified as still alive in the early thirties, were most likely living in the United States and Brazil rather than in Britain.[72]

The Society used various media to convey its data and its message. In 1931 Simon, Robert Cecil, John Harris, Professor Reginald Coupland, and Margery Perham contributed to a BBC radio series on slavery and the work of the League, with special attention given to the recent exposé of Liberian slavery. The Central Council for Broadcast Adult Education organized group listening sessions."[73] The Society created a series of lantern slide shows that reinterpreted Eldon Rutter's historic passion play *The Holy Cities of Arabia*, among other narratives. Lady Simon proclaimed "the task is to get all nations to accept the British view."[74] In the spring of 1933, *Pageant on Slavery* was performed by the Hampstead Imperial Players at the Rudolf Steiner Theater. It reenacted eleven historical scenes including Pope Gregory and the "British" slaves in A.D. 500, William Wilberforce and the Somerset case, T. F. Buxton's antislavery quest, an interview with Emperor Haile Selassie, a Mecca slave market, and Wilberforce's apotheosis—his conversion to the antislavery cause. Its closing scenes featured personifications of Public Opinion, and Liberty, a young woman on a Grecian urn.[75] A reviewer enthused, "The flogging scene . . . in the Mecca market, was really thrilling. . . . Mr. Cecil Melvin—as a slave, was man-handled by his master in a way which delighted his friends in the audience." Not all the tableaux were as impressive. "H.I.M. Hailé Selassie is a very handsome man, but the unfortunate Mr. L. Roberts, who took his part, was made to look like a fourth-rate nigger minstrel on Margate beach."[76] The play traveled to local churches, schools, and social institutes. Lady Simon rose to offer remarks at the closing performance in Hampstead.

News from Alabama kept coming. Simon saved a series of articles in October 1932, seven months after the Scottsboro case broke, suggesting her more than casual private attention to the story. The first was the *Weekend Review* petition that offered a graphic and persuasive account of the episode in Paint Rock, framed "in cooperation with Theodore Dreiser's committee in New York City and a similar committee in Germany" and "urgently" supporting an "appeal for funds," as above.[77] Most of its signatories were not Simon's intimates, but Gilbert Murray was among them, and Eleanor Rathbone, who joined the Society's executive that month, and was also on the Scottsboro Defense Committee executive at that early date. Three days later, Simon saved a piece entitled "Condemned Negroes' Appeal in USA," mislabeling it, "Lynching: Scottsboro Case Trial." It described the Washington, D.C., police routing of a communist demonstration in support of the defendants: "The race and youth of the prisoners and the circumstances of their trial have led Radicals and Liberals here and abroad to come to their defense and start up an international propaganda campaign for their release, or failing that, for a new trial for them."[78] The *Times* story "Seven Youths to Die" told of Judge James E. Horton's overturning of the jury's decision in the Decatur, Alabama, trial, on the basis of medical testimony that supported the defendants' claim that they had not raped the two women. The réportage continued "After the original trial, German intellectuals interested themselves in the case, and German Communists held protest meetings."[79]

Despite all this material in Simon's personal possession, the *Reporter* still fell shy of covering the case. "Convict Labor in the US," contained stories of shocking conditions in U.S. prisons taken from the *Manchester Guardian*. Most prisoners were Negroes, kept in "virtual peonage" by "cruel and brutal men, who rule[d] strictly by the use of leg-irons, revolvers, and the whip." American public opinion would not "denounce these horrors" nor object to the leasing out of convict labor.[80] Simon's friends in the NAACP may have encouraged her to distance herself from communist advocacy, while her marriage was a prohibition upon involvements with the organized left, though Roden Buxton's early interest in postrevolutionary Russia suggests the permeability of political camps and tendencies. Lord Sherfield recalled John Simon's "anxiety when he was obliged to receive his wife formally as a representative of the antislavery movement."[81] In the months between the train passing through northern Alabama and the Decatur trial of the defendants, Ada Wright's case had come before those who reported to Sir John Simon as foreign secretary. He knew of the case, and the publicity surrounding it had already caught Lady Simon's attention; in a few years' time, she would write of this to Du Bois.

In December 1932 the *London Star* published the American Wickersham Commission's (the National Commission on Law Observation and Enforcement's) lynching statistics of a type already familiar to readers of the *Reporter*. The same issue told of the Salisbury, Maryland, lynching of a black man who was dragged from his hospital bed by a mob of two thousand after killing his employer in a dispute over wages. He had attempted suicide and was receiving treatment for his wounds when he was seized.[82] The London arts venues also continued to popularize notions of American racial violence. W. Angus MacLeod produced *Gallows Glorious* at the Shaftesbury Theatre in the spring of 1933. Just after Hitler assumed power in Germany, London audiences saw this dramatic rendition of the life of militant abolitionist leader John Brown.[83] For some, Scottsboro spoke for all these issues. But Lady Simon soon threw herself into the celebration of a cause that was unambiguous in its more conventional liberal politics.

THE WILBERFORCE CENTENARY

During 1933 and 1934 the British imperial world observed the Wilberforce centenary, marking the passage of parliamentary legislation banning slavery, and honoring both William Wilberforce's legislative triumph and the promulgation of emancipation in 1834. This was the crowning moment of Lady Simon's career as an antislavery activist. All of the contemporary issues of the movement were revisited within the context of the celebration. The Society justly claimed incontestable rights to the legacy of Wilberforce. His authority hung in the air like a vapor of sanctity, disavowing complexity, simplifying purpose, and shrouding political motive. In February 1933 Lady Simon and John Harris announced that the centenary would be co-sponsored by the League of Nations Union, inaugurating a series of speaking and touring commitments unrivaled in Lady Simon's repertoire. She toured the country from the Bradford Mechanics Institute to the Kensington Catholic Council, from the Women's Freedom League, the Bethnal Green Public Library, the Bedford Physical Training College, the Swindon Workers Education Association, to the Peel Institute in Finsbury. When the men of the Derby Unemployed Men's Brotherhood read her book and saw her lantern slide show, their leader wrote to say, "May I thank you for giving us such an important and startling document as *Slavery*? I wish it could be placed in the hands of every deep-thinking citizen."[84]

The centenary materials were suffused with propaganda in support of the League of Nations.[85] And in October 1933 resolutions were passed at Geneva authorizing the establishment of a slavery commission, the Committee of Experts on Slavery (ACE) with representatives from Britain, Belgium, Malay, Spain, Eritrea, the Netherlands, and a single woman member from Portugal. John Simon appointed barrister Sir George Maxwell to the ACE over Lady Simon, in order to avoid any appearance of impropriety.[86] In March Lady Simon spoke at Barry on the 1885 Berlin Conference at which German Chancellor Otto von Bismarck had endorsed an antislavery provision, her mention a taunt to the new Nazi regime but a notice of Germany's past good intentions, as well.[87] The Society's executive now included two great liberal progressives, former high commissioner for Palestine and Liberal party leader Herbert Samuel, and theologian and social reformer J. Scott Lidgett, joined its vice presidents; the claim to a legacy of progress and even liberal collectivism was considerable, and the Society's leadership roster made such claims more credible. Lidgett's first involvements dated from the Congo Reform Association agitation and Samuel's from the campaign against Chinese slave labor in South Africa.[88] Lady Simon even approached Winston Churchill after he published an article on *Uncle Tom's Cabin*. Churchill authorized its reproduction and assisted her in clarifying the early edition's accompanying documents, which listed names of slave-owning clergy, and referred her to Beecher Stowe's Everyman's edition.[89]

Simon told and retold the story of the transatlantic slave trade. She described the "Middle Passage" to a meeting of the Women's Freedom League: "So closely packed were they in the hold of the vessel that they tore one another to pieces in their agony. Survivors were brought onto the deck and for exercise were made to dance under the lash of the whip. If they refused to eat, hot cinders were forced down their throats."[90] At Cardiff, she explained that "men grew rich on it, and actually built churches on the money they had gained by bartering in human souls."[91] An air of confession and redemption infused these gatherings.

The visceral renderings of the treatment of the human body, the acknowledgment of past complicity, and the moment of redemptive release were all elements of her stock presentation. Simon asked that past sins be exonerated by present action. The Catholic Archbishop of Liverpool spoke before his brethren in April 1933, identifying their city as the "chief slaving port of England," an example of antislavery catharsis.[92] The English had a duty to share the lessons of emancipation with the unenlightened powers. Simon wrote for the *Cleakheaton Guardian* that "the cause" had seemed dead after 1833, but the 1922 League of Nations inquiry into slavery had "discovered . . . its persistence in the dark corners of the earth." Forty nations had signed the League antislavery convention since then. "Every child born of slave parents [in Abyssinia] is now declared free." Slavery now belonged to "backward and non-progressive countries. . . . China . . . with its 2,000,000 little girl slaves. . . . and Mahomedan countries are not easy to convert, as they claim they have the decree of Jehovah from the Koran to carry on slavery."[93] The markets and locales may have altered, but the brutality had not diminished. Chattel and plantation forms of ownership were collapsed into one. Many forms of bondage and serfdom constituted slavery in her vision.

> The same cruelties are still inflicted—with whips, branding-irons, shackles, chains and yokes. The same well-authenticated accounts are available of flogging, torture, amputation and murder. The same concomitants still obtain: slave raids, the slave gang, the overseas traffic, breeding for the market, open, as well as private, markets, for the sale of slaves.[94]

Simon's capricious use of history, and the collapsing of regions and eras and modes of property and polity into one large miasma of suffering, made the story overwhelmingly accessible, rendering it a question of belief rather than a mass of arguable or documented detail. This was not the style of the sober *Reporter*, or the empirical style of parts of her own *Slavery*, but it was her stump style. Though there were exceptions, like Reginald Coupland's cool-headed attempt to attribute the 1833 victory to the abolition of corrupt "pocket boroughs" promulgated by the Great Reform Act of 1832, pedantic narratives did not ignite in the same way.[95] Journalist Henry W. Nevinson, a veteran opponent of Angolan slavery, made an equally noble gesture at erudition in "Why We Honor the Name of Wilberforce," even knocking the old man down a peg or two. "But on the whole one must call him a Tory for his strong belief in authority and his fear of extending power to the working classes. He supported the Laws against Combinations and excused the bloodshed of Peterloo."[96] John Harris conflated the old Wilberforce with the new League of Nations in a speech at Bingley, West Yorkshire.

> He wanted to see the abolition of the slave mentality in the minds of the stronger races, to see "native races" given a chance in his world to develop their own countries

and their own interests. In short, he wanted the civilized nations to regard the child races of the world, not as objects of exploitation, but as a sacred trust given to [their advocates] so that [they] could help them forward on the plane of civilization.[97]

On July 23, 1932, the first of the great fêtes to commemorate William Wilberforce was held at his memorial at Hull. A group of civic and academic dignitaries led a crowd of twenty thousand. The lord mayor and Viscount Cecil placed wreaths on the monument.

> The stillness as they did so was impressive. The only movement visible was that of pigeons flying overhead and some returning seagulls heading for the Humber. The bishop of Hull offered prayer, "Giving heartfelt thanks for those who have worked for Thee here, especially William Wilberforce of this city," and then from forty-five masts, there broke flags of the Empire and other nations.
>
> There was a delightful incident toward the close. Following a blessing by the Bishop of Hull, a fanfare of trumpets preceded a salute by three airplanes.[98]

In London the festivities included those identified as "African and West Indian Negroes," making pilgrimages to Clapham to another of Wilberforce's homes, accompanied by Girl Guides, Boy Scouts, local government officials, and the clergy.[99]

Sir John and Lady Simon visited Brazil that summer. She spoke before the English communities of Rio de Janiero and Sao Paulo at the archdeacon's home, boldly asking her listeners if they could imagine men being lynched on the Avenida: "The future of the world is going to depend entirely upon the influence of instructed humane public opinion."[100] She returned to England to receive a despondent letter from W.E.B. Du Bois, who was just about to depart the NAACP and was absorbed by the news of repression against political activism occurring in the colonial world. Tight labor markets and economic dislocation were engendering dissent that was met with the coercive reactions of the police and military. He told his story to Lady Simon, a sympathetic if uninformed reader. "We have made, as perhaps you know, several attempts to get the colored groups into alliance through the Pan-African Congresses but have met all sorts of difficulties from the Colonial powers. We have not given up. The depression here is pretty hard and I do not know whether we are going to keep *The Crisis* alive or not."[101]

Within weeks of this exchange, London's *Daily Express* reported on the American Great Migration. "Great Exodus of Negroes Begins; Flight from Lynch Terror: Black Folk Take to the Hills; Human Head Sent to Governor," claiming that if a crime befell a white girl, a Negro was invariably charged.[102] In Princess Anne, Maryland, a group of lynching suspects had just been released who "dug up the grave of the negro for whose lynching the four men had been arrested, cut off the buried man's head and presented it as a 'Thanksgiving present' to Governor [Albert C.] Ritchie."[103] After the incident, three hundred people fled in caravans and cars. "Similar caravans are leaving the little towns and villages scattered all over the extensive South where the Negro, still in effect a slave, is unable to travel in the white folks' train or even buy his ticket from the white folks' booking office."[104] The *Times* described the four perpetrators being carried away in victory.[105]

Coverage of events in the United States escalated. In April 1934 the American ecumenical body the Federal Council of Churches responded to the *Reporter*'s review of a widely read muckraking study of the treatment of blacks in the South, John Louis Spivak's *Georgia Nigger*. They sought support for a bill to abolish chain gangs in Georgia. Spivak offered graphic descriptions of routine practices including "the use of spikes applied to the ankles of prisoners . . . bloodhounds to follow up fugitives . . . tortures ruthlessly applied."[106] The *Reporter* drew attention to the similarity between these techniques of torture and incarceration and those being used in the penal systems of Togoland and Cameroon, drawing parallels between "Western" and "primitive" contexts, even claiming that the majority of abuses that the Society discovered and documented were occurring in the "civilized world," and referring to Willi Münzenberg's publication of *The Brown Book of the Hitler Terror*. The *Reporter* compared Nazi tactics with those of the Soviets. "The *Brown Book* and much other evidence have recently been published to show what is being done in Germany today and similar charges have been made and substantiated, to a large extent, against Russia."[107] This reference revealed the intersection of communist-led antifascism with the antislavery forces of the establishment; the *Brown Book* led unwitting readers into political spaces they had not occupied before.

GLOBAL WILBERFORCE

Sierra Leone honored the centenary with a series of special sermons and a procession of denominational authorities including Anglicans, Methodists, Catholics, clerics of the United Baptist Convention and African Methodist Episcopal churches, and an imam leading an Islamic contingent. Special postage stamps appeared and concerts and garden fêtes were held. The largest ceremony featured a preacher who was a descendant of slaves and a 350-person black choir. The general secretary of the Sierra Leone All Muslim Congress declared, "Mohammed our Prophet . . . was the first man in the history of the world who felt commiseration for the slave class. . . . Islam was the first creed which made the liberation of slaves a matter of great virtue, thus changing the whole world in this respect." In Johannesburg, a more modest ceremony at Ebenezer Congregational Church included "Eurafrican or colored members and children of the London Missionary Society [whose] forefathers [were] set free." John Harris was visiting this southernmost zone of the African Continet, and he attended these rites, observing the "very poor and suffering."[108]

The greatest London centenary event took place in July at St. Botolph's, Bish-opsgate, exactly a century after the day upon which the Emancipation Procla-mation had been read in the West Indies before tens of thousands of attentive, liberated slaves who lit great bonfires. The occasion began with a late evening reception to which fifty "representative colored people" were invited.[109] A larger service followed, attended by workers from the nearby City of London, includ-ing young and old, antislavery celebrities like the Wilberforce descendants, and many community leaders who sat alongside ordinary Londoners, black and white. "The whole function was poignantly mixed. I sat between an inspector of the NSPCC [National Society for the Prevention of Cruelty to Children] and a negress in European clothes and stud earrings."[110] Harold Moody of the LOCP spoke. This centenary brought antislavery advocates the possibility of sparking interest among the thousands of Africans and West Indians residing in the capital. Apart from Moody, the program featured the peace activist Rev. H.R.L. Sheppard; Henry Nevinson; Lady Simon; and black singer, John Payne, whose quartet performed "Didn't My Lord Deliver Daniel, Then Why Not Every Man?" and "Ride Up in de Chariot."

Scottsboro signatory, preacher, and feminist leader, Maude Royden, sent a message of solidarity. Lady Simon's own leaflet advertising the occasion began with the call, "Let us all, white and dark people together . . ."[111] Isabel de Vere, a descendant of Grenadian slave owners, wrote to the *Daily Mail* about the in-habitants of her homeland who were now "suffering from poor prices for its staple products. . . . there is much poverty and distress."[112] The Wilberforce days became moments of exposure and confession that begged the question of how much had changed in a century. The scene at St. Botolph's was extraordinary.

> Floodlights lit up the outside of the church and the gardens, but the scene inside was one which few present will ever forget. Every seat was taken. Sir John and Lady Simon sat in one of the front pews and all round the brightly-lit church were Domin-ion and Colonial flags. Dozens of colored people were among the congregation and sang heartily the old "Battle Hymn of the Republic" to the tune of "John Brown's Body" to which the armies of the Northern States marched to war. That and Blake's "Jerusalem" and "God Save the King" sung at the beginning of the service, were the only hymns.[113]

A Bethnal Green church warden led those gathered in two minutes of si-lence at midnight. In his hands was the same watch that his Methodist grand-father had held to mark emancipation in the West Indies one hundred years earlier. The original copy of the decree from Antigua adorned the lectern. "It is a case of extremes meeting and mixing. Lady Simon is a diminutive Tiperarry woman [Simon scrawled the correction, "Wexford" on her file copy], highly-emotional and her husband is, pretty obviously, neither diminutive nor emo-tional." After all, the reporter averred, his wife had coaxed Sir John Simon into the Anglo-Irish peace campaign at the time of the Black and Tan disorders.[114]

The *News Chronicle* described the Simons kneeling "in prayer shoulder to shoulder with Negroes whose grandparents were slaves."[115] The reading was from Isaiah: "Liberty to the captives and the opening of the prison door to them that are bound . . . "[116] Drama ensued: "Slowly the church lights fade out. The exterior flood-lighting breaks through the side windows and falls into the darkened nave. From the darkness by the altar comes the Voice of the Slave yearning for spiritual and political freedom."[117] Harold Moody appeared in crimson and purple academic robes. He spoke forthrightly.

> Although the material shackles have gone, a mental slavery still exists which subjects my people to terrible disabilities here and in other lands. The Premier of Southern Rhodesia said quite recently that there can be no equality between black and white. Let it be clearly understood on this centenary day that we here stand for the full emancipation of our race in the British Empire and throughout the world. Let the white man who persists in living in the atmosphere of fear understand that history gives him no grounds for such fear as far as my race is concerned . . . and that it is a libel against my fair-minded race to think that the black man, in spite of all his sufferings at their hands, will ever deal unkindly with the white man if he gives him this freedom and equality.[118]

The nighttime event had a mystical quality. Both aura and audience were little known to a metropolis in which black and white mixed awkwardly if at all, but the Wilberforce centenary had proven unexpectedly scintillating. Still, realpolitik was exercised. Lady Simon wrote to the *Times* for its Monday edition with urgency. "Free men and women should never be content unless they have helped the League of Nations to the utmost of their power to wipe the dark stain of slavery from the face of the world."[119] She did not pause to debate the ironies of the Italian antislavery society's statement of support for the Wilberforce celebrations. International politics had protruded at many turns during the festivities, as when Charles Roden Buxton addressed Moody's LOCP on "Impressions of Liberia."[120] The centenary did not distract from the business of diplomacy.

On November 15 many months of remembrance ended at Mansion House with a great public meeting at which the Lord Mayor and the Archbishop of Canterbury presided. The site was near where Wilberforce was said to have experienced the epiphany that led him to join in the cause alongside the classicist and abolitionist leader Granville Sharp. The archbishop intoned, "They were met to commemorate a body of men who set both the slaves and the conscience of the British Empire free." On the first day of the ensuing month, guns were fired in Cape Town in Wilberforce's honor. There were services in the mission churches for the city's "Colored" population. These modest rites included a pageant play performed exclusively by "Colored" players, billed as a history of "non-Europeans from early times."[121] It is unlikely that anyone mentioned that in 1816, when Wilberforce entertained African and Asian guests, they had been required to sit behind a screen and to eat separately from whites at dinner.[122] His hospitality had its strict limits.

In late 1934, the end of the first year of Nazi rule in Germany, the Society expressed its sympathy for "Interracial Committees" being formed in each American state. The *Reporter* printed statements by Hannah Clothier Hull, president of WILF, made before the Wagner-Costigan Congressional hearings on lynchings—hearings that ultimately failed to result in an antilynching bill that would have imposed fines on jurisdictions where the violent acts occurred. The United States faced international disgrace. Clothier Hull said that no crime was more difficult to explain than "the lack of adequate protection by the federal government of the US of a minority race which has so long been a victim of the crime of lynching." She bemoaned the practices of Liberia:

> We are trying to lead people toward civilization. . . . Members of our organization traveling in such remote places as old Bokhara, and Tashkent, in Indo-China and in all parts of Europe, have found that the good name of the United States has been doubted because of this total lack of federal responsibility in lynchings. This fact, we believe, has a very real and unfortunate effect on our international relations. It often weakens the perfectly sincere and honest efforts on the part of our Government to throw its influence on the side of humanity and justice when racial outrages occur in other parts of the world.[123]

Walter White wrote to Simon of the NAACP's campaign in support of the antilynching bill, ruthlessly opposed by Southern senators who successfully blocked its passage.[124] He sent her some literature from Jesse Ames's Southern Women's Anti-Lynching Association. Simon replied:

> I have received the literature which you so kindly sent to me on Lynching. . . . I wish we could do something in the matter over here, but I think it rests more with the white women of America to get up a crusade against such a hideous crime. I feel as much about it as I do about my own crusade against slavery. Having lived so much in the Southern States perhaps I realize more than the casual person I speak to in this country. I know you are working as hard as you can against it and you have all my sympathy and desire for an improvement of conditions.[125]

Simon commented upon the recent resignation of W.E.B. Du Bois from the NAACP:

> There is no use in asking you your opinion about the situation which made Mr. Du Bois resign—I suppose there is something to be said on both sides. I hope he is happy in his new position, but I am afraid he is a man who does not see eye to eye with many people. I often recall that first memorable meeting when you and I were on the platform in Hull. We had a wonderful emancipation meeting in London, which a great many of your people attended in July and my husband, Sir John Simon, read the lesson in the Church; it was a most impressive celebration.[126]

Simon contacted Jesse Ames in the face of White's warning that Ames had not been a strong advocate of the proposed antilynching legislation. Ames and her association's support for "due process" in instances in which a potential lynching victim was "rescued" and tried before what many others perceived as unjust courts and prejudiced white juries, bore striking resemblance to Simon's and the Society's notion that the British Empire offered "fair chances" as compared to those afforded the colonial subjects of other powers. In a talk at Bedford, Simon boasted, "No one in the British Empire was a slave," referring to the trail leading from Abyssinia to Sudan.[127] Simon was also attracted to Ames's insistence upon white women's mobilization. She replied enthusiastically to Ames's entreaties, asking if an "Irish woman" could be added to the list of names of Ames's supporters, rather perversely invoking her own Southern experience: "If the black people had turned to lynching the white men who seduced the colored girls, they would have been as much within their rights as the suggested outrages on white girls by black men, which I think are often quite exaggerated." Simon referred to lynching as a "crime of white people."[128] Her reference to sexual crimes reflected the pervasive influence of cases like Scottsboro upon the wider discourse of lynching, even though a range of alleged "offenses" reportedly inspired lynchings, and African American women as well as white men and women were present among the victims.

In all these ways, Simon remained a player in transatlantic racial politics.[129] Her comments to Walter White about Du Bois demonstrated her shrewdness in the guise of Lady Bountiful. She displayed a desire to stay in good odor with the NAACP at Du Bois's expense. In early 1935 she wrote to Jesse Ames, "I presume you know Mr. Walter White. I have a great regard for him and have spoken on the same platform as him. I know he works hard for the betterment of his people and I admire him for not trying to pass off—white as he is—as a white man when he is really colored." Her emphasis upon White's light complexion recalled the "Amanda" encounter that lay at the threshold of her racial consciousness. "You may be interested to know that through an episode in my life in Tennessee I decided to dedicate my book on recent slavery to a young girl whom I met there, and who was so white that she would have passed easily in this country, but there she was completely ostracized."[130]

ABYSSINIA: PRELUDE TO MUNICH

It was in southern Europe and northern Africa, rather than the southern states of the United States that Simon and her associates invested their greatest energies in the wake of the Wilberforce celebrations. The apogee of 1930s British antislavery commitment was the Abyssinian crisis and it was this crisis that led inexorably toward Munich with Sir John Simon right at its center. If historians have not seen the connection between the cause that he shared with his wife and the ploy undertaken with Hitler, it is not for want of sources that indicate a flow in clear and commensurate directions. In 1935 Sir John Simon visited Berlin, two years after the Nazi assumption of power and two years after the dislocation of the communist, socialist, and opposition movements that had in some quarters adopted Scottsboro as an "antifascist" cause. Here, Simon learned a great deal about German rearmament and arrived at the conclusion that Hitler would not limit arms production under any circumstance. Simon did not recognize him as a dictator. Instead, he seemed fervently to believe in what Simon's biographer David Dutton refers to as the opportunity for the "moral rehabilitation" of Germany in the post-Versailles world. Simon doubted the possibility of a pact of mutual aid between the Nazis and the Soviets. He was entirely wrong in this assumption, but his demonstrated anticommunism fed the notion that the West ought to be grateful for Hitler's desire for a deal with Britain instead. These views thrust toward appeasement, as historian Niall Ferguson has described it, "trusting that Hitler's protestations of goodwill toward the British Empire were sincere, and letting him have his wicked way with Eastern Europe." [131] In the meantime, Hitler's condition for joining the League, the kind of "rehabilitation" that Simon sought in the early thirties, was the restoration of Germany's colonies. Simon's views on this proposition were negative: "All this is pretty hopeless; for if Germany will not cooperate for confirming the solidarity of Europe, the rest of Europe ought not to cooperate to preserve it in spite of Germany." [132] He resolved to pursue delaying tactics with the Germans as the better part of valor.

April 1935 brought a notorious meeting with Mussolini at Stresa on Lago Maggiore, where one can still view the Duce's chair and promenade along the lakefront past the same Edwardian hotels that hosted Simon and his colleagues. Simon recalled that at the time of this visit, "Germany's attitude made solidarity between France, Italy and ourselves more important than ever." Simon asked that the lone Abyssinian who had come to warn of the Italian arms buildup on his country's borders be heard, but the man was silenced. Though Simon had earlier defended Abyssinia's rights in conversation with Dino Grandi, the Italian representative to the League, he did not raise the issue again at Stresa. Later that year, British Foreign Secretary Anthony Eden convinced the House of Commons that Britain ought to act as arbitrator between Italy and Abyssinia, a quixotic endeavor, but not for lack of trying. The idea was to trade part of British Somaliland to Italy in exchange for Italy backtracking away from Abyssinia. By September of 1935, all of this had collapsed as an option. Mussolini rejected Eden's attempts in Rome. France balked at the diminution in status implied for her own port city of Djibouti on the Gulf of Aden in what is now a republic, and wanted to deal with Italy separately. There was significant public outcry in Britain about the thought of giving her own colonies away. When the League met in September, it decided to strengthen the communal naval presence in the Mediterranean. In a letter to the King, Simon

Figure 3.3. "Mussolini in Africa." Ethiopians salute an image of Mussolini, during the Italian occupation, 1935 (Granger Collection).

stated that "a primitive African nation could not stand in the way of the need to bloc Hitler," cynically advising that "League rituals were hard to avoid."[133]

In October the Italian invasion of Abyssinia began in earnest. France followed the League's ruling in support of sanctions against Italy to the letter, and did not offer assistance to the British navy or the RAF. The American oil companies meanwhile increased their sales to Italy. Padmore, a keen commentator on these developments, claimed that Soviet oil sales to Italy were also at stake and that Comintern policy was stipulated increasingly upon this economic commitment at the expense of African and other anti-imperial interests.[134] Violet Bonham Carter spoke at an Albert Hall rally in support of League sanctions being leveled against Italy.

> One law for the strong, and another for the weak, one law for the white and another for the black, one law for ex-allies and another for ex-enemies. We cannot make licensed brigandage in Africa the price of peace in Europe. We cannot toss backward peoples into the expansionist maw to save our own skins. Abyssinia, her wrongs, her sufferings, and her dead are very far away, but to those who have eyes to see they are our own. In Abyssinia's fate let every nation read its own destiny, and let those who

seek to break or blunt the sword of justice now realize, that if they succeed today, it may never again be drawn to their defense.[135]

Some Labour and ILP politicians opposed British intervention in the conflict on pacifist grounds, including George Lansbury and the ILP leader James Maxton. The sanctions crisis was also the occasion for Stafford Cripps's proscription from Labour party circles.[136] The General Election Manifesto, signed by Conservative leader Stanley Baldwin, Ramsay MacDonald, and Sir John Simon for the National Government coalition, espoused the League principles and called for a prohibition against unilateral action.[137] Though Simon was reelected to his parliamentary seat with a reduced majority, there was clearly strong national sentiment in favor of what appeared to be the negotiating and cooperative spirit of the government.

At the same moment, the London conference "The Colonial Problem and Peace" jointly sponsored by the Society and the National Peace Council and attended by Padmore as well as League administrator Baron Arthur Salter, called for a new definition of trusteeship for the industrial powers. The Conference agreed that the colonies ought to be administered cooperatively, so none would go without; they mandated—without unilateral control—a new conception adopted at Versailles.[138] The notion of cooperative administration was no longer seen as a far-off and utopian goal. Lord Norman Bentwich, a veteran of Egyptian and Palestinian mandate administration, clamored, "The maxim which should govern the new colonial order would be 'Seek equality and avoid greed.'" Lone voices tested the proposition, including the ex-Colonial Office member, and radical Leonard Barnes: "The natives of Africa are the people who ought to be doing the development of Africa under one guidance."[139]

Charles Roden Buxton was more optimistic and viewed the Italian crisis as involving "the whole question of the repartitioning of the world's resources." John Harris felt that the West Africans were outpacing themselves and were going to have to be given a lot of voice in determining the region's future.[140] But the machinations at Geneva were hardly subject to a popular referendum or officially sanctioned public debate beyond the election results that placed the policy makers in power. In early November 1935 Harris had attempted to pressure Sir Samuel Hoare, Simon's successor as foreign secretary, and a key figure in the blundering diplomacy of his day, to include antislavery provisions in the terms being debated as a basis for a peaceful settlement of the Abyssinian crisis. Hoare's secretary replied that the League was in charge.[141] Three days later in a speech at a peace meeting in Tunbridge Wells, Harris attributed the war between Italy and Abyssinia to slave raiding and slavery. He chastised Italy for her hypocrisy, contending that poor conditions also obtained in the Italian-controlled regions of the country.[142] When Hoare traveled to France en route to an alpine vacation three days later, he met secretly with French minister Pierre Laval, engaging in "secret" talks that would soon bear their names in infamy; Laval was executed in 1945 for his subsequent engagement with the Nazis as a Vichy government collaborator. Here a "secret peace" between the belligerents was arranged. But the press got hold of it before the politicians. Italy's new colonial possession would exchange land with Abyssinia, ceding Italian control of a large area of the southern part of the country.

Without support in Britain for Italian acquisition, Hoare was forced to resign his post in the glare of the press exposé, and was replaced by Anthony Eden. This left the League flat and dry, since any such deal was clearly in defiance of its Charter. British protestations to the contrary, the outcome showed the thinness of the League's actual influence. Simon later defended this attempt at resolution as better for Abyssinia than what came after, but who was then to know?[143] The Society's ranks were riven over the moves with Italy. Harris's words captured the fears of those who did not trust a fascist "slave power" to end slavery. In January Sir John Simon defensively informed the Society that the "dispute with Italy has not so far led to the suspension of the Emperor's efforts to combat slavery." He reported that the practice had been abolished in various regions of the country, but this view was not sustained over time among his own membership.[144] In February 1936 Lord Noel-Buxton stated in Parliament that a League settlement of the dispute was the only one that would not result in a "regime which preserves slavery." His own journey to the region and his subsequent *Times* coverage of the sale of children in Abyssinia provoked him to speak out.[145] It was as if the cause of antislavery was somehow aided by British side deals with Italy. The pro-fascist *British-Italian Bulletin* circulated propaganda that asserted Italy's commitment to antislavery in the wake of the invasion.[146]

The idea of internationally supervised mandates was catching on among the League powers. In February Norway claimed that this option might work; surely it appealed to nations who feared a new contest between larger powers and who desired the access to raw materials and labor that newly mandated territories would provide. The Society's discord prevailed. In April a *Reporter* review explicitly stated that while Selassie had made "genuine efforts" at abolition, these had been "hampered and frustrated by the aggressive action of Italy, whose newly-discovered zeal against slavery is a specious pretext for their political policy." This defied the ministrations of Sir John Simon.[147] Lady Simon was feeling the heat. In April she spoke in an interview about the conflict in an unprecedented way: "I am not discussing, and I am not called upon to discuss the international question to which Italy's action gives rise. But on the single question—whether the cause [antislavery] was advanced—I have no doubt at all." On that day, an Italian edict had abolished slavery in the conquered territory, she claimed. It afforded native workers a daily wage and freed children,

> who, instead of growing up as little slaves are undoubtedly developing a freedom and are getting education in schools provided by the Italian Government. . . . in a world where so much is happening that is cruel and horrible, and reactionary I think we

should honestly register the fact that a great advance has been made for the antislavery cause during the last few years in Abyssinia.[148]

The split in the rhetoric of the Society's leadership was evident. Was Lady Simon pressed on by Sir John Simon? An appetite for the European possession of the two "free" territories of Africa had been expressed for some time in relation to Liberia as well as Abyssinia.[149] In 1935 when writer Graham Greene offered parliamentary testimony on his own trip to Liberia, as described in his prose work *Journey without Maps*, he stated that the first question that Liberian president Edwin Barclay had asked him was whether he knew Lady Simon and John Harris. He stressed the single-handed control that the Firestone Rubber Company enjoyed, denying that Liberia necessarily needed "white civilization."[150] Liberia was a case with more than regional implications in the light of Abyssinia.[151] The possibility that the force exerted in Abyssinia by Italy could be extended in the region reinforced opposition to the fascist drive for other colonies, yet Italian fascism did not figure in the Society's internal debates. Sir John Simon had found a way to defend both the art of courting Italy *and* the foremost plank of the Society in the same breath—it was the Italian fascists who were most prepared to end slavery in Abyssinia, and the League best not tarry by engaging in distracting "rituals," as his private letter to the King termed them. Lady Simon followed suit, portraying Abyssinia as a "disgrace to civilization" in a speech before a local Liberal Association meeting a month later. She reminded her listeners that British aggression had brought civilization's benefits to the Sudanese. Yet former slaves faced serious inequities in Sudan and it had taken many years to free them. As if to confirm the wide sweep of this kind of apologia, the *Suffolk and Essex Free Press* carried a letter from one J. MacNab protesting against the absence of League action in the cases of purported Japanese, Polish, and Lithuanian abuse—cases where he averred that the League had "no axe to grind." He asked why sanctions were then being imposed, when "ninety-nine out of every hundred persons in Abyssinia would be benefitted out of all knowledge by the removal of slavery, terrorism, plunder, arson and anarchy, and the substitution of white man's justice and protection?" MacNab identified himself as a member of the British Union of Fascists.[152] Irene Fisher of the Women's Committee of the British-Italian Council for Peace and Friendship wrote to Lady Simon, "Before I had to give up my membership of the Women's Freedom League, you spoke to us and I was greatly impressed by your noble efforts to change a barren egotistic feminism into fruitful labor for the liberation of women who are still actually enslaved."[153]

The opposition also spoke. At the Society's annual meeting of June 1936, Lord James Meston, a League administrator, deplored "the remorseless use of the most inhumane methods known to modern warfare against a relatively defenseless people." He suspected that Italy's statesmen sought its "place in the Sun," and that the drive for "prestige," as an Italian administrator had expressed it to him, was the central element in Italian aggression: "We are concerned with . . . a maintenance of a proper standard of international ethics in the treatment of the backward races." He was faithful to the twin principles of benevolent paternalism and racial superiority coupled with sound, reasoned management, protesting against the thought that, "In this twentieth century, it is conceivable that any nation or any people, however helpless or backward, can be bought and sold like groceries across the counter." He spoke against the "handing over of a dependant people to another Power." The subjects' own wishes needed to be taken into account and mandate status could serve as a bulwark against ill treatment; it was necessary to prohibit slavery while "moral and material conditions" advanced. Norman Angell, League activist and president of the advocate group, the Abyssinia Association, warned of the potential "seizure of the peoples to be used as pawns in a European quarrel." Lord Edward Robert Lytton rose to question the Italian capacity to abolish slavery in Abyssinia without a broad expenditure of funds. The League should pursue this duty of sovereignty instead. Finally, in an astounding statement, Lord Noel-Buxton forecast what for many of his listeners must have been the ultimate repressed nightmare—race war: "And above all, there is the danger that if we have no control by League influence, we shall see black armies arise in Abyssinia."[154] Here, George Padmore's predictions emerged in a revered establishment drawing-room. The speakers banked upon the power vested in the non-Western fighting forces now prostrate in Africa just as Padmore forecast. Such a potent army, its advocates argued, needed molding and supervision by the world's greatest powers, for to leave the fate of the colonials in the hands of the Italians was a first step toward racial suicide.

Parliament explicitly entertained the suspicion of British connivance in stabilizing Italian control in Abyssinia. In July Eleanor Rathbone raised the issue of whether British authorities in the Sudan had prevented Selassie from returning to his country.[155] This was a reversal of the progressive role assigned to Sudan in Lady Simon's past rhetorical flourishes. Rathbone mused as to why it was that the emperor's messages had made their way into the hands of the Italians. In a parallel discourse that ran right to the heart of the matter, MP Duncan Sandys, Churchill's son-in-law, queried William Ormsby-Gore on the floor of the Commons as to the nature of Britain's policy with regard to returning mandated colonial territories to Germany, pointing to the "serious effect on the settlers and native inhabitants and their uncertain futures."[156] The *Reporter* noted the Italian propaganda on the freeing of slaves in Tigre, an act whose stated purpose was to "stamp out barbaric customs."[157] The tug between the immediate gratification that the Society sought in its struggle to end abuses, and the pull of longer-term international solutions and schemes, continued unabated.

Lady Simon continued her lectures and lantern shows as the war in North Africa took the "slavery question" right out of her hands. The notes for her slide show of March 1935 appear anachronistic—she recorded mention of the slave trade, Constantinople, Angola, child slaves liberated by the Society, David Livingstone, John Wesley, a whip, Uncle Tom, and the exhibition of her own photograph. But the detachment of this style of white advocacy from the world of black activism was narrowing. C.L.R. James spoke alongside the West Indian cricket player Leary Constantine before the Sunday Lecture Society at Colne near Nelson, Lancashire, site of Constantine's home club. Lady Simon was in the audience. He spoke of American lynchings and of Kenya and South Africa. He indulged his listeners by stating that "British administration in Africa" was the "best of all European countries," but also pointed to the "freer" areas of Central Africa in which women served as territorial representatives. James saluted Lady Simon, exclaiming that he was honored to find that "as active a woman as the wife of the Chancellor of the Exchequer could find either time or the inclination to attend so humble a function."[158] But his politics were not hers.

1936–37

All manner of cultural practices continued to engage slavery in the later thirties. The National Portrait Gallery featured an antislavery exhibition in the spring of 1935. Stowe's *Uncle Tom's Cabin* reached sales figures of 6.5 million, and the Palladium featured a year-long run of a dramatic rendition of its story. Lady Simon addressed one of the performances on the theme "Present Day Slavery."[159] She assisted the producers of an anticipated Hollywood movie entitled *Slaver*, as she had done for the epic *Cape to Cairo*.[160] In this broader context, Scottsboro momentarily pierced the censor that cloaked the Society's presentation of America. In January 1936, the *Reporter* carried news of a cable from the *Sunday Dispatch* of Decatur, Alabama, entitled: "Five Years of Hate Case Reopens Tomorrow," and did not hesitate to attribute responsibility for the Scottsboro defendants' ordeal. "Financial support from defense supplied by Socialists and Communists has added to the flame of hatred raging round the trial."[161] No other extensive mention of the case appeared in the official Society press for the remainder of the decade, even after the NAACP and the American communists had formed a stronger unified front to support the defendants.

In October 1936 Marcus Garvey reported to Lady Simon on a racially mixed meeting held in Kensington under the auspices of the West London Mission, a venerable Methodist establishment, committed to temperance and women's suffrage, whose director was Donald O. Soper. Garvey condemned the screening of a series of cinematic attractions depicting blacks for what Garvey termed a "burlesque on races and peoples. . . . the Negro has been filmed for ridicule and contempt," and castigated Paul Robeson's *Emperor Jones*, *Sanders of the River*, and *The Song of Freedom* for "creating undue and unreasonable prejudice against the Negro race."[162] He announced a petition campaign to the home secretary to prevent the American production of *Green Pastures* from coming to

England.[163] This remarkable letter attests to Simon's capacity to win the confidence of many black activists of different views, including those who sought a route to her husband. Ralph Bunche notably followed the Society's activities at the same time that he consorted with the Padmore group in London in 1937.[164]

There was also an increasing interest taken at this moment in the presence of blacks in Britain. Several MPs questioned Parliament about resident aliens among the multiracial maritime workforce in the port towns.[165] In February 1936 Arthur Evans, Welsh Labour MP for Cardiff South, asked the House for the number of "colored" men, women, and children, including British-protected subjects and aliens, living in Cardiff. Sir John Simon replied that 2,319 were registered under the 1925 Special Restriction (Coloured Alien Seamen Order). The numbers who were British subjects were unknown and there were no current, aggregate records of resident aliens listed by locale. David G. Logan, Labour MP for the Scots constituency of Liverpool, pushed Simon, asking whether the police ought to know who was about. "Is it not a fact that aliens stay here for a time, get married and acquire British citizenship and then leave the country?"[166] Behind this query was the specter of miscegenation, upon which Lady Simon had made unswerving negative commentary throughout the thirties. She was opposed to interracial unions for what she saw as the suffering that they brought. Her "Amanda narrative" conformed to this view.

The issue of a diminution of maritime jobs and the legacy of racial discrimination in the ports had blown up in 1919 in port-side "race riots" in which white mobs attacked inter-racial couples.[167] In June 1936 a deputation headed by the Rev. G. F. Dempster visited Home Secretary Sir John Simon on behalf of the British Sailors Society, which offered refuge and pastoral services for sailors, protesting against the "evil effects of co-habitation between white women and colored men." The delegation eschewed the depravity of mixed cafes and accommodation. They alleged that persons of color paid off trade-union officials in order to obtain work.[168] Evans asked on the floor of the House if the government knew that many "coloreds" wanted to return home. He felt that the shipping companies ought to provide free passage for some.[169] In late 1936 Lt. Col. John Sandeman Allen, Conservative MP for Liverpool West Derby, asked the minister of labor about Cardiff, Liverpool, and, Glasgow, and what "steps [were] being taken to meet the difficulty which occurs in finding employment for boys and girls who are the result of miscegenation in these ports."[170] He did not wish to see their presence contribute to a lower standard of living; for him, "half-caste" most importantly meant "half-fed." An interdepartmental committee of the Home Office, the Board of Trade, and the Colonial Office ought to oversee the problem. There was further debate and a series of questions posed on the problem of obtaining passports and nationality certificates. This eugenicist language and the impulse toward repatriation and expulsion reflected the fit between racial prejudice and economic grievance following upon the passage of the Aliens Order of 1920, which forced the alien registration of

African, Indian, and Caribbean sailors, even if they were British nationals.[171] But it also reflected a specific aversion to interracial sexual encounters and the wider discursive context in which charges of rape were perceived. Support for the Scottsboro defendants was in part a rejection of an act of miscegenation. It involved a revulsion with Scottsboro accusers Ruby Bates and Victoria Price, in part a revulsion with women whose sexual histories involved a suspicion of consensual relations with black men even prior to the case breaking.

In 1937 Sir John Harris attended a Quaker convention in Philadelphia. He traveled through the American South with black sociologist Charles Johnson, who had served on the League's 1930 Liberia Commission. They visited cotton fields and saw blacks "still inhabiting slave cabins." Harris called the sharecropping system a form of "debt bondage" resulting in "a condition of degradation and economic bankruptcy which constitutes a great problem for the President to deal with." Harris contributed a series to the *Manchester Guardian*, including articles entitled "In the Cotton Belt," "Destitution," "Poor Whites," and "Negroes." His 2,000-mile journey started in Tennessee; "For my part I have never seen such poverty and squalor—not even in Central Africa." When the locals were quoted by the newspaper, it was in the familiar idiom of a contrived Negro dialect: "It ain't no use to grumble so we shows our smiles to de white boss and we shows our tears to de Lord."[172] Lady Simon was not to be outdone in her own contact with Americans. In early 1938 she wrote again to Du Bois, and her letter contained an interesting revelation, couched in the memory she so often referred to.

> Are the Scottsboro boys out yet? I sent my contribution toward their defense. My husband's legal mind is appalled at the case. . . . I have been at Altanta when in my early years I was in Athens, Georgia and later in Tennessee-Knoxville, the latter place being where I saw what burned into my childhood's mind—injustice to Amanda—when I was told not to speak to her as she was descended from slaves. I went out and took her hand in mine for, child as I was the thing struck me as cruel and wrong. The white man could do as he liked but the colored man must be lynched for the same sin.[173]

Here was the crux of the matter again: Amanda was the result of a white raping a black, an act that went unpunished. Scottsboro represented the desire to punish unfairly those who had simply done the same to white women; this was one way in which Simon may have justified her contribution. By this late stage in the case, Judge Horton's decision to defy the white Alabama jury was also on the record.

ABYSSINIA: COLONIAL TRANSFERS

In 1937 transcontinental unity around the opposition to the Italian invasion of Abyssinia crystallized. A series of strikes in Trinidad, part of the general labor upheaval in the West Indies in the years just before the war, were attributed to fury over Abyssinia by a journal as unconcerned with militant political dissent as the *Reporter*. In January a London conference on Africa brought together whites and blacks of different outlooks, all concerned with the fate of the imperial continent. There was a wide discussion of native labor and migration. The African chiefs who attended George VI's coronation supported a resolution protesting against a series of massacres at Addis Ababa when the Italian regime refused to allow an international inquiry.[174] Parliament reacted to reports of serious death and reprisals in Abyssinia exerted against the domestic population in the wake of the attempt upon the life of Italian Marshall Graziani. Lt. Commander John Fletcher asked his parliamentary colleagues if they understood that these were the "worst atrocities in Africa since the Congo atrocities," referring to the 1903 revelations of abuse and terror in the Belgian territory of the Congo.[175] Eleanor Rathbone, now involved with Abyssinian refugees, chastised these acts as constituting a "breach of international practice."[176] MP Emmanuel Shinwell of the ILP, demanded, "is this what is meant by spreading civilization to Africa?"[177] In March, Society secretary Charles Roberts and John Harris, protested against the massacres.[178] John Fletcher hectored Foreign Secretary Anthony Eden: "Is the Right Honorable Gentleman aware of how closely our action with regard to this matter will be followed by the colored population in Africa under our government or control?"[179] In June Harris called for "Fair Play for Britain's Black Subjects" and supported Noel-Buxton's call for an imperial conference to render more equal the rights possessed by indigenous populations in the various tiers of the Empire, responding to colonial subjects' vulnerability in the face of the threat of population transfers "whatever may be their religion or color."[180] In Kenya only whites had landowning rights while in West Africa, land holdings accrued according to custom; historian Frederick Cooper noted that by the 1920s "the myth of African backwardness and tradition conceded the fact that the leading colonial powers had neither transformed nor exploited Africa as their earlier promises had implied." In some territories, "color" was a bar to rights; in others, there were assured "Native rights."[181] The Abyssinian question focused energies around a panoply of colonial issues; German aspirations played a small role in this rhetorical battle.

But in November 1937 Padmore's friends at the West African Students Union issued a resolution that broke the deadlock on the German question for those who were listening, neatly tying together all recent developments in an explicable argument. Their statement mentioned the prewar experience in the Cameroons, Togoland, and Southwest Africa,

> and also the treatment by Germany of the Jews and persons of non-Aryan descent.... [WASU] strongly protests against any proposal plan or scheme whereby any portion or portions of African colonies, British, French or otherwise, shall be handed over now or at any future date, to Germany."[182]

This was a timely intervention. Two days later, Prime Minister Neville Chamberlain reported to the Commons on an Anglo-French communiqué stating that colonial issues could not be discussed without talks involving other countries.[183] Many perceived the League as having no influence. John Harris called for the release of the former German colonies from mandate status and for their communal administration. A press account of his statements was accompanied by a school photograph of German youngsters drawing a blackboard map of Germany's lost empire, with a caption, "They have taken all our colonies away from us."[184] Here was a springboard for cooperative action with the Germans, articulated by an antislavery advocate of reformist internationalism. The two positions, that of WASU and of Harris, were directly counterposed. In the spring of 1938, in a gesture that also suggested accommodation, Franklin Roosevelt attempted a peace initiative with Italy and spoke of his "conciliatory plans to improve our relations," quoting Harris in his speech.[185]

Society members increasingly adopted a prevaricating rhetoric as the possibility of colonial transfers seemed to increase. In a letter to Chamberlain, the Society's leadership affirmed the notion of the "full acquiescence" of the colonial populations who might come into play for transfers, and for impartial commissions and indigenous assemblies, as practiced in Basutoland and Bechuanaland: "It may be possible to devise a form of international control by expanding some of the provisions contemplated in existing systems, such as the Mandatory system or the Convention of Saint Germain," the treaty of 1919 which restricted private arms trafficking. The hypocrisies of compromise knew few limits now that Britain was at risk. "We must earnestly oppose the view that the prime motive of colonial expansion should be the exploitation of material benefits in the interests of the metropolitan Government and the establishment of redundant white populations in tropical areas quite unsuited for white settlement."[186]

In 1938 the mathematician and education reformer Philippa Fawcett published "The Colonial Problem" under the aegis of the League of Nations Union, advocating "international exchanges" and the restoration of access to raw materials. She pointed to the "overpopulation" of Germany, Italy and Japan, and the concerns of prestige and defense. She expressed the need for a "general settlement" in the context of world trade. Radical opinion was hardly opposed to transfers.[187] The notion of "redundancy" was already taking on a pernicious connotation in the context of an expanding Reich. Here, it was invoked as a problem that posed an affront to the process of luring African peoples to accept transfers of power. A less-adulterated Africa would seem more "purely African," and control from afar less threatening and more democratic and perhaps less German or Italian. Abyssinia's dilemma was a cautionary tale. Sir John Simon's reply to a parliamentary question about how much of Abyssinia was in Italian control was firm: "There have been sporadic outbursts of disaffection amongst the native population especially in western Abyssinia. The Italian military authorities are understood to be taking steps to deal with these; and to be in general control of virtually the whole country. So far as we are aware, civil administration is established in the main centers of population."[188]

For the Simons, by March 1938 the Italian-Abyssinian crisis was assimilated into the crisis of British appeasement manifested in the Munich agreement and connected in vital ways to antislavery. In this month, the British refused to join France in offering a guarantee of the sovereignty of Czechoslovakia. Simon's biographer believes that Sir John "did not see Czechoslovakia as real," as a sovereign entity, but instead "as a fiction of Versailles." He believed that French prime minister Édouard Daladier and the French were not outfitted for a defense effort or profoundly committed to it.[189] German claims to colonies, as stated in Parliament, involved over a million square miles of territory presently under the control of Britain, Australia, New Zealand, the Union of South Africa, France, Belgium, and Japan. Liberal MP Geoffrey Mander challenged the government to clarify whether Noel-Buxton's recent trip to Germany to discuss the return of the colonies had been made with official endorsement. A week later the prime minister said that the *Anschluss*, the German annexation of Austria, rendered any discussion of colonial transfers moot, and stated that the issue would not arise in forthcoming discussions with the Italians.[190] Significantly, given the former "secret" Hoare-Laval talks and their role in the debate over the future of the colonies, the Simons and Hoare sat together as hosts of the annual Society luncheon in April 1938. W.E.B. Du Bois wrote to Lady Simon from Atlanta five days before his seventieth birthday, recounting his own enigmatic trip to Nazi Germany in 1936 on a fellowship award and unabashedly commiserating with her: "I note the burden which your husband is bearing."[191]

Perhaps Lady Simon's most revealing public appearance in these auspicious days was as the keynote speaker at the July opening of WASU's Africa House, a men's hall of residence near Camden Square. She did so on behalf of the African Welfare Committee which had strong ties to the Society. The [Cecil James] Rhodes Trust and some of the shipping companies had helped to finance the hostel, and its opening contributed to the ongoing controversy about the legal presence of Africans, West Indians, and Asians in the metropolis.[192] Ladipo Solanke, Padmore's colleague, hosted the event and "spoke of the value of such contacts [trusting] that they would lead to yet a further widening of the circle of friends of the Hostel."[193] Lady Simon was implacable. "We are all glad to be British citizens and this Hostel is to help us be better citizens. The greatest thing about the British Empire is that it stands for equal citizenship."[194] But the occasion also led her to an interview with the enterprising Jamaican journalist Gwen Edwards: "Mussolini, said Lady Simon, had assured her himself that efforts would be made to abolish slavery in Abyssinia and she was convinced that only under European rule would Abyssinia be better off." Simon advised Edwards:

> She did not have enemies. . . . she made it clear that she was not speaking of America as it was well known that there is an intense antagonism against colored people in that country. Then she made reference to miscegenation. She told me she did not believe in intermarriage. She did not mean to imply that there was anything inherently wrong with it, but she believes that the children of inter-marriage are the ones who suffered the most.

Simon was coy on the subject of disturbances and upheavals in the Caribbean. "The matter had to be judged on its own merits as the standard of living was different among the different peoples in the world. The colored people will take their place in the world but only by the virtue of their own efforts." Simon discussed her admiration for Du Bois, Paul Robeson, and one of Haile Selassie's daughters, now a student nurse in London, to whom she said she was "greatly attached."[195] The candor and sweep of this interview attested to Simon's mood; she was absorbed by the politics of appeasement, yet she admired Robeson. There was no contradiction for her, but many others were insistent on the importance of dealing critically with Italian aggression.

Arthur Henderson accused the Italians of recruiting Africans into the British territories of Avon and British Somaliland for the Italian army, while Rathbone continued to press harder on the needs of refugees, even as she was calling for assistance to the Germans flooding into London, terming the refusal to pursue repatriation issues as "the last betrayal of the unfortunate Abyssinians," and promoting the Abyssinian Refugees Relief Fund.[196] Simon's views were not those of all the members of the Society. John Harris was forming closer relationships with the Padmore and Kenyatta group, and the International African Service Bureau, which now counted Fenner Brockway and Harold Moody as members. That autumn, he and his wife traveled to South Africa for a Quaker conference, where he supported the opposition to colonial transfers, still a very live issue in radical circles despite the government in London's disclaimers. From Africa he wrote to Leonard Woolf and others in a private memo directed to those who were part of the Labour Party Advisory Committee on International Questions.[197] He characterized the South African situation as one of an "increase in native discontent." He had witnessed "avowed discrimination" and a "prevalence of the notion [that blacks] were by creation . . . altogether different from the white man." He believed that this concept did not "necessarily imply 'race hatred' or even 'race prejudice.' Indeed, it is probably most firmly held by people of the deepest religious convictions. It is really a kind of 'slave mentality' and its danger lies in the fact that it is based on color alone."[198]

On September 28, 1938, Hitler agreed to a meeting with Mussolini and two days later, Britain signed the Munich agreement, authorizing the transfer of the Sudetenland to Germany, a "transfer" on the European Continent, not in

Africa after all. John Simon never budged from a defense of Munich. He wrote, self-evidently, that if the Czech lands had been Hitler's last claim, a European war could have been avoided, and offered clear evidence of his dismissal of Czech sovereignty. If Neville Chamberlain had "threatened war" it would have been over "the claim to adjust a boundary which had worked injustice and to rescue people of the German race who were suffering under an alien jurisdiction." Simon was at his most candid in his retrospective remarks on the fear of war. He persisted in arguing that Munich bought the British time and helped to whip a fractious Commonwealth into shape. This was a cynical inversion of Padmore's line. Rather than seeing the need to garner the support and strength of the colonies and the Dominions through a reckoning with the expressed views and needs of their peoples, Simon invoked the example of the sacrifice of Czechoslovakia as a useful indication of what could have happened to the British colonies if they had not fallen in line behind unquestioned imperial rule. "Hitler's violation of the Munich pact, which Chamberlain exposed, secured that the British Commonwealth, twelve months later, entered into the struggle united, until, under Churchill's incomparable leadership, the forces of liberty won."[199] He and others also defended "liberating" ethnic Germans from Czech rule as a commitment to the principle of opposition to alien rule.[200] In the moment, the other side used the imperial record as part of its propaganda against Britain. In November 1938 the German press insisted that the concentration camps of the Reich were places where "those held for their criminal opinions or criminal minds are trained to work." This dodged British complaints about the treatment of the Jews, regarded as "meddling with the affairs of another people for the sake of a few synagogues which were burned down as a reprisal for a beastly murder," referring to the assassination in Paris of the German diplomat Ernst vom Rath, in which the accused perpetrator was Jewish. The British, it was claimed, had resorted to violent abuse in order to protect their Empire—in Palestine, in Waziristan (contemporary northwest Pakistan), in Mesopotamia (contemporary Iraq and western Iran), and against the Boers in the Transvaal (South Africa). The Indian Rebellion of 1857, and the 1919 mass killing of Indian civilian protestors at Amritsar by a British army squad, were evidence of British aspirations.

> In India, England's reply to incidents was to make 150 Hindus crawl along the streets on hands and knees, to whip naked girls, to have 200 Hindus flogged and their leaders tied to the mouths of guns which were then fired. . . . Every page of British history reports the facts that guns, machinery guns and of late, bombing planes have always been the means used by great Britain to make it clear to other people living in their own countries that not they, but the English people were the masters.[201]

The *New York Times* referred to Germany being "outside the society of civilized nations" and characterized the Nazi seizure of power as "violent revolution. . . . There is little doubt now that the Munich victory played a great part in defeating the moderates and booming the stock of the radicals. . . . nor can Europe expect any real appeasement." A U.S. senator referred to the Nazi practices as "hideous crimes" in a radio broadcast, and Lady Simon kept abreast of these American developments.[202]

Parliament clamored against the transfer of colonies in the wake of Munich, demonstrating support for the view that it was one thing to trade Slavs and another to trade the inhabitants of British territories. Conservative MP Vyvyan Adams stressed the widespread opposition to such a plan.[203] Four days later, Conservative MP Brendan Bracken pressed Chamberlain about his terms of compensation for entrepreneurs and investors whose businesses were failing in the former German colony of Tanganyika, then a British-controlled mandate. Chamberlain replied that no mandate transfers would occur without taking into account "the interests of all sectors of the population in the territory concerned." Tanganyika was a domain of intense Nazi propaganda. The German threat was depriving English settlers of their livelihoods. Conservative MP Richard Pilkington demanded, "Does the Prime Minister not think that recent happenings in Germany have made it abundantly clear that Germany is not yet fit to undertake the welfare of other populations?" Chamberlain refused to reply to Labour MP Frederick Bellenger's questions as to whether a transfer of former German African territories was being contemplated. Adams pushed again on whether Parliament was being properly consulted on the government's visits to Berlin in which he felt that issues had arisen "which vitally affect[ed] the future of the Empire."[204]

In subsequent debate with Chamberlain, there were direct references made to Hitler's demands for colonies at Bad Godesberg, where Chamberlain met with Hitler to discuss the Sudetenland crisis. Would he accede to these demands?[205] Geoffrey Mander further pressed Sir John Simon (then, the chancellor of exchequer), asking whether "the Colonial problem [was] only to be considered as part of a more general settlement." Simon replied simply, "Statements have been made on that subject." Mander pressed further, pointing to "anxieties" among peoples in the territories in question. He asked Malcolm MacDonald, secretary of the colonies, if there were indeed to be no transfers of territories to Germany. Simon then finally stated that Chamberlain had replied earlier to Bellenger on this question, as above, and Simon rendered Chamberlain's answer to Bellenger as a negative, stating that no transfers were being contemplated, confoundedly adding that the government "must, of course give full attention to the views of the population of any territory concerned." This last caveat suggested ambiguity and was more faithful to the prime minister's equivocation in the earlier exchange with Bellenger. Ramsay MacDonald disavowed that transfers were in the offing. Simon answered yet again that no transfers were contemplated in response to Mander's forthright interrogative: "Will the Minister make it clear, in view of the great anxiety among all classes of the population there are at the present time, that they do not contemplate in any foreseeable period handing over territory to the bullies of Berlin?"[206] Just two weeks later, the press reported passage of the Nazi regulation that Jews wear yellow stars.[207]

Then John Harris began to introduce a "progressive" plan for the transfer of colonies. On November 2, he spoke before a Manchester luncheon club, stating that Germany wanted more than just the mandated territories. Nazi leader Joseph Goebbels wanted raw materials from each of the colonies that had reverted back to German rule. There would not be sufficient imports to sustain German hopes and the domestic costs to German taxpayers would be high. In Harris's vision, a reasonable and successful domain of international control could be established in Central Africa. The inhabitants of the region would also have to want this plan. There could be no unfairness, no racial discrimination. International not British rule was needed. Harris claimed that the Berlin Treaty of 1885 and the Treaty of Saint Germain in 1919, which contained the Covenant of the League of Nations, had contemplated such a utopia "from the Nile to Zambesi and from the Atlantic to the Indian Ocean." He spoke of this kind of usurpation as "an instrument with which to begin a new era in colonial affairs."[208] The notion of the international control of Central Africa was not new. The journalist and politician E. D. Morel advanced such a framework in 1920 that had its critics. But neither treaty had advocated a form of international sovereignty to states.[209] Harris did suggest an understanding of the urgency to contest the global design of fascism, and his proposal encouraged optimism in Britain's imperial future and in her role as a sensible, adjudicating power. It severely compromised any notion of independent African agency and fostered illusions.

In early December the Society approached Chamberlain with a manifesto meant to avoid the terrain of high politics and to oppose controversial plebiscites in possessions that were potentially transferable. Instead, it called for the formation of a commission of inhabitants of any territory under consideration for transfer, whose decisions a council of chiefs might ratify in keeping with the kind of colonial arrangements suggested by Lord Arthur Balfour at the end of the Great War, whose terms for the Zionist state in the Middle East were encased within the "Balfour Declaration." Without such provisions, transfers "could hardly fail to lead to widespread victimization or bloodshed, or both." Neither national interests nor "Native" interests need be jeopardized. All depended upon the conditions of transfer. Existing treaties should be honored. There should be "collective control." The already-existing mandates proved that rigidities in governance were unworkable, and flexibility was needed. Conquest and exploitation were not acceptable purposes for transfers. Moral grounds formed the basis of trusteeship. An "international charter" was desirable. This was a grand statement of hubris and prevarication, signed by many notables, including many of the Society leaders, with Harris among them—but not the Simons. From Labour—Sydney Olivier, Arthur Henderson, and Arthur Creech

Jones signed, as did Independent MP Eleanor Rathbone. The Methodist cleric Scott Lidgett, the anthropologist Anathnath Chatterjee, and the journalist who wrote of Kenya, Norman Leys, were also signatories.[210]

It was as if they were saying that at the eleventh hour, they too had something to give away and could be team players for Britain. An appendix drafted much earlier added that race, creed, and color were not to stipulate policy in the "new mandates," nor slavery be permitted. In the Commons debate the very next day the treatment of German Jews and non-Aryans was cited as grounds for refusing the unconditional hand-over of British territories. Instead, the new mandate system as proposed would set a new ethical tone for colonial subjects and their new masters: "[It] would give to the peoples, including the people of Germany, a new vision of colonial trusteeship."[211] In the end, the Commons motion did not call for an extension of mandates. Colonial Secretary Malcolm MacDonald demurred that Britain's colonial peoples could not be reconstituted as mandated peoples if they were not "ripe for self-government." They remained "glad to be British subjects." The government had been compelled to reassure the Nigerian colonial government by telegram that transfers were not threatened. A "slow, evolutionary process to freedom" was needed. This was the "purpose of the Empire." A majority agreed that the colonial subjects would not fare better under another jurisdiction. So, as if something had been taken away and restored, as if something new had been given, the debate reached uneasy consensus. The Society's supporters had failed to influence a change in policy and their varied individual profiles on questions of race offered evidence of the limitations of the Society's efficacy and the narrowness of national debate on the issue of global and imperial slavery.[212]

A week later, Conservative MP R.A.B. Butler, a new member of the Society who would become an architect of the postwar welfare state, announced on the floor of the Commons that the British government had recognized both de jure and de facto Italian control over Abyssinia. It would not repatriate refugees now resident in Britain.[213] On March15, the army of the Third Reich invaded Prague, and Sir John Simon was disparaged and discredited for the time being, losing authority in the face of the failed results of sham compromise and sham peace. Communist MP Willie Gallacher spoke of Simon's utter "political bankruptcy" while Liberal MP Archibald Sinclair called him the "evil genius of British foreign policy." Labour leader Hugh Dalton remembered him as "the snakiest of them all."[214] Few would speak well of Chamberlain or Simon in the coming months.[215] In an effort at internal education, Sir John Harris wrote to Lady Simon of what he had learned from his reading of *Mein Kampf.* "The effect of this on the minds of natives is beyond belief, except to those who know them. They will stand flogging and shooting but this is a vastly different matter; it puts their race outside the human pale."[216] A celebration of the centenary of the Society was held at Bath in April, not a month after the invasion. African and West Indian guests sat with the descendants of abolitionists, among them the appeaser Sir Samuel Hoare whose forebear Gurney Hoare had been a founding Society member. Wilberforces and Buxtons were there.[217]

International African Opinion, the IASB journal, covered the celebrations at which Sir Samuel Hoare and John Harris spoke:

> Sir Samuel Hoare as chairman, referred to the existing slavery in Abyssinia, observing that the Society recognized the difficulty of the Italians in abolishing the system in a short time. As Sir Samuel—of Hoare-Laval fame—was largely responsible for substituting the fascist slavery of Mussolini for the feudal slavery which Haile Selassie was making honest attempts to eradicate, his sympathies are obvious and his interpretation of the term dishonest.

Harris's views of Africa came under scrutiny as well, and the retort had the unmistakable feel of Padmore's bite:

> Sir John Harris . . . referred to the Color Bar which operates so insidiously in the Union of South Africa. . . . The whites don't like the color of the black man's skin so they don't want him to vote. These half-truths are a conscious deception. The Color Bar operates to keep the black man in Africa in a servile position, politically and economically, in relation to the white ruling groups. If it was not that the Africans were essential to the economic functioning of the industrial and agricultural enterprise, they would long ago have suffered the same fate as the North American Indians and the Australian aborigines—extinction.

Harris reportedly stated that the Color Bar did not exist in the Rhodesias or East Africa, a disputed claim for the British Empire as opposed to the independent South African Republic. "Imperialists, Liberal, Labour or Conservative, have a pretty knack of exposing the faults of rival imperialisms, while conveniently ignoring the glaring brutalities within their own. . . . Hence Sir John [Harris's] apology for Southern Rhodesia, whose native policy is modeled after that of the Union [of South Africa], and is becoming increasingly harsh."[218] This réportage suggests the breadth of one extraparliamentary discourse on the eve of the war, few participants though there may have been.

Lady Simon redefined her legacy and reshaped her history, even as she had rewritten the history of slavery and redefined it over and over. She was able to do so much more readily than was her husband. Her behavior in the thirties had proven "increasingly embarrassing" to John Simon. A colleague of his knew her as "a good-hearted creature . . . with a tousled Irish head and a great gift for saying the wrong thing. . . . the exterior can only be described as vulgar." Austen Chamberlain, the brother of the prime minister, recalled going to a friend's residence simply to "escape . . . from Lady Simon." She was remembered for "drinking to excess." Conservative MP Leo Amery called her an "incredible woman" in the literal-minded usage of his day, lacking in believability. His colleague on the Tory benches, Henry "Chips" Channon referred to her as a "simple *haus frau*," and her colleague, Society leader Richard Holt as "quite inferior," while Neville Chamberlain found her "a sore trial."[219] Her shrewdness, whether intentional or unwitting, was to maintain that she herself could not have come up with a plan to cede Africans to the Italians or the Germans. She proved durable as an icon of virtue in a world of schemers at the center of which stood her husband. Padmore's claims for her in the 1950s upstaged the appeasers and allowed her rehabilitation on selective, independent terms. In this new, expurgated version, she had cared about Africa and Africans when it had been unfashionable, disabused of the links to colonial transfers and the fascist project. But Lady Simon seemed to have had a premonition of what was coming. She wrote to a friend in 1938 as ingenuously as the times and language permitted: "You are quite mistaken in thinking that my work for the cause of the abolition of slaves is anything but humanitarian—it is purely so, and politics do not enter into it in any form whatsoever."[220]

Chapter 4

SAKLATVALA AND THE MEERUT TRIAL

The Meerut Trial . . . is a grim incident in the history of British India. Men were torn from civil life for long years whose only crime was to carry out the ordinary work of trade union and political agitation after the fashion of everyday life in this country. Not merely socialist opinion in Great Britain recognized that it was a prosecution scandalous in its inception and disgraceful in its continuance. . . . A government which acts in this fashion indicts itself. It acts in fear; it operates by terror; it is incapable of that magnanimity which is the condition for the exercise of justifiable power. The Meerut trial belongs to the class of case of which the Mooney trial and the Sacco-Vanzetti trial in America, the Dreyfus trial in France, the Reichstag Fire Trial in Germany are the supreme instances. Because they are foreign, we regard them with pious horror.
—*Harold Laski, 1935*

SHAPURJI SAKLATVALA met Ada Wright in the summer of 1932 long after leaving his native Bombay. Years before, those who controlled his family's business enterprises in India had chosen a commercial future for him, well away from political controversy at home and, in so doing, launched the career of a legendary London radical.[1] By the 1930s Saklatvala had established himself among the London electorate and in the political community. Mahatma Gandhi and Jawaharlal Nehru also became recognizable to the English eye and ear in the thirties, as the growing strength of the Indian Congress party (hereafter, Indian Congress) and the emergence of the 1930–34 Civil Disobedience movement in India troubled and preoccupied English policymakers, including John Simon.[2] A fluttering sympathy for Indian independence grew in the English popular imagination. It was enhanced by the causes of Spain and Abyssinia even as the situation in India increasingly daunted Britain's ruling circles and financial elites. The few Indian activists of personal celebrity in London inhabited a political landscape dominated by the Labour party governments of the 1920s, and the 1931 National Government and its successor regimes, whose members desired to curb nationalist and communist agitation, to divide movements against each other, to visit fierce repression upon known opposition leaders, and to conspire to preserve exploitative, fragile economic relationships. In this context and during the very first years of the decade, a small group of committed British left and liberal activists who were cognizant of

Figure 4.1. "Saklatvala, the first worker prosecuted during the General Strike, he received two months' imprisonment for a speech he made at the Great May 1 demonstration in Hyde Park, preceding the strike" (*Daily Worker*, April 27, 1932) (courtesy *Morning Star*; reproduced by the kind permission of the Syndics of Cambridge University Library).

India, focused upon the trial of those known as the "Meerut prisoners," and like Scottsboro, Meerut became a global passion among the committed, the presence of three Englishmen among the defendants eliciting special curiosity and sympathy among anticolonialists in the metropole. The nine African American youths passing time in jail in Alabama were celebrated in tandem with thirty-three leaders of a sophisticated and diverse Indian labor and political cadre, incongruous as their mutual juxtapositions may have seemed. The names of the Meerut and Scottsboro defendants also began to appear alongside those of antifascist martyrs in central Europe.

In the later thirties, rapid developments among Indian political movements congealed to force a growing recognition of India's leverage at the tables of her overlords. Her army's dispersal throughout the imperial system signified India's colonial status, demographic weight, and geographic advantages. The sophistication of Indian labor activity and of the country's electoral politics, as well as the increasing capacity to enlist so many to the parties' banners, overwhelmed English politicians and some people at home. Here was a cogent example of passionate political mobilization at the ground level. England appeared smaller and more vulnerable as war approached, but not just because of German, Soviet, or American might. Her prodigal colony and Asian protégé was engaged in its own reckoning with communism and fascism. On one terrain of this struggle strode a diminutive Parsi born to wealth, scion of a leading industrial Bombay family, who found a political mission in Fabian London at the turn of the century, who followed it into the ranks of the ILP, and landed among the Bolshevik sympathizers of the new British communist party. Now three decades later Saklatvala was at once the rare success story of British communism on the colonial-recruitment front—a Stalinist; a party orator; an emissary of Soviet Asia, which enraptured him; *and* an elusive figure of complex private doubt and preoccupation. His conflicts are in some respects obvious—how could the fate of his country be dissolved entirely into that of the "British proletariat," or made synonymous with a Soviet or European transformation? The anomie of exile rendered Saklatvala part of a de facto collectivity of persons not primarily identified with communism. He harbored aspirations for India that were accommodated neither by forms of nationalism, civil disobedience nor the sectarianism of the CPGB, even though he acted on behalf of communism in opposing Gandhi and Indian Congress supporters in London. His Zoroastrian religious commitments were at utter variance with official communist-party skepticism and atheism, and he carried certain independent aspirations and the doubts and disappointments that they bred unto death. His enigmas now appear not as eccentricities or "deviations," but as signs of a larger imperial problematic.

IMPERIAL DESIGN

The British Empire was refashioned in the aftermath of the Great War, its design shifting in the face of economic losses. The political impact of the Russian Revolution of 1917 upon central Asia and India, and Britain's subsequent accommodation with the desire for national legislative autonomy in India, influenced the shape of the new era. At home, Labour's Advisory Committee on Imperial Questions became a centerpiece of "legitimate" dissent from empire, its secretary Leonard Woolf embodying a spirit of sober, Fabian advancement for the colonies. The Committee's members supported evolutionary growth toward political maturity for the British possessions, a form of what historian Anil Seal termed "anti-imperialism" as "an intellectual vogue." They raised objections to the various ways in which the British administered their possessions, but not the fact of rule itself.[3] The 1920s was a time of "diminuendo" for others in the ruling political circles and among official pundits. The United States was beginning its struggle for control of the oil reserves of the Middle East. The fear of Russian ambitions, so influential in the 1930s, was confined to the prospects for expansion posed by Afghanistan, Turkey, and Persia, all of which shared borders with the new Soviet empire. Japanese aggression in China drew global anti-imperial sentiment toward agitation. The international commitments of the British Labour governments of the twenties and the National Government of the thirties, rested upon the League, the "high-style façade of internationalism."[4] Incapable of resolving most colonial issues and inhibited by the nonmember states, the League's failure to achieve diplomatic ends and to prevent war were also failures to achieve and to promulgate racial justice, in many instances failures involving the British Empire.

India was the most celebrated, if often the most misrepresented arena of anti-imperial advocacy. Saklatvala was only one of many personalities operating in the West from a variety of Indian political tendencies, and the relationships of exiles to struggles at home were complex. Independence societies and associations had existed in England for decades, including the Swaraj League and the Workers Welfare League of India (hereafter, Workers Welfare League). The communist party boasted the brothers Clemens and Rajani Palme Dutt of partly Indian descent, the latter the leading international theoretician of imperialism in the British communist movement. A few Indians joined the ILP as Saklatvala did, and left student circles included significant Indian contingents at Oxford, Cambridge, and especially the London School of Economics.[5]

The British desire to "keep India" was enshrined in Liberal parliamentarian E. S. Montagu's 1917 declaration that the Raj should foster "responsible government" for India within the existing imperial framework, including through the practice of dyarchy, the splitting of responsibilities between the central government at Delhi and local ministers who reported to local legislatures. The India Act of 1919 promulgated limited franchise reform, but capital and labor remained in conflict. In 1918 a wave of textile strikes was followed by the strengthening of repressive legislation and the infamous acts of the British army at Amritsar in the Punjab in which 370 protestors were killed and 1,000 wounded.[6] A year later, when the first of the two interwar electoral reforms enfranchised a tenth of the adult male population, the reshuffled legislative and municipal bodies still possessed precious little money for social and economic investment, and prices rose nearly 50 percent between 1917 and 1920.[7] Climatic disorder and the devastating influenza global pandemic ravaged many areas of the country. The All-India Trades Union Congress was founded in 1920, and Manabendra Nath Roy and others launched one wing of the communist party of India (hereafter, the CPI),[8] a party that had at least two "founding" dates, the second in 1925. Roy had returned to India from Mexico and the West via Moscow and Tashkent, and briefly served as head of the Eastern section of the Comintern.[9] Soviet involvement in the Indian party's establishment was decisive in terms of leadership, training, and money. The British communist party soon began to act as the Comintern link for the CPI, while the Workers Welfare League represented the All-India Trades Union Congress in London. Saklatvala spent nearly two decades involved with these organizations. But communism was only one movement among many in India. The surrender of Jerusalem at the end of the Great War elicited deep anti-British feeling in the Islamic world. There were many Indian enthusiasts of the subsequent Afghan revolt against the British, and the Afghan ruler Amanullah Khan welcomed 36,000 anti-British Muslims into his country. "At this time there was a movement among the Muslims either to take to *jehad* (holy war) against the British or to immigrate to an Islamic state and make preparations there for such a war. This movement came to be known as the *hirat* movement."[10] Kabul also served as the early base of CPI operations, but the British began to maneuver to expel those involved in communist activism in Afghanistan.

The growing independence efforts in India, the growth of "terrorism" and communism, and the concerted energies of labor activism, marked the Indian 1930s. A group of young Bengali supporters of militant labor revolt attacked the British armory at the Bengal port city of Chittagong, claiming the action in Gandhi's name. The British hunted, arrested, imprisoned, and in some instances executed members of a new generation of educated young Indian militants, convicted of acts of terror. The martyrs were celebrated for years afterward. Some of those whose lives were spared were recruited to Indian communism in prison.[11] In 1925 the British Labour government revived the repressive Bengal Ordinance that allowed for arrests of individuals on suspicion of terrorism, without evidence. In 1926 British communist George Allison arrived in India to serve as a trade-union organizer, but the government soon deported him. British activist Philip Spratt also came to set up a bookstore, and British communist trade unionist Ben Bradley worked with Spratt to forge contacts in the cotton mills and among railway workers. In 1928 a six-month-long textile strike engulfed Bombay followed by a series of "lightning strikes" that were partly communal riots, and among the most significant religious conflicts since the 1890s.[12] These events witnessed the height of communist interwar authority in popular organizing. The trial of the Meerut prisoners followed in the wake of these disturbances.

In November 1930 Labour party prime minister Ramsay MacDonald convened the liberal-imperialist Round Table talks (Indian Constitutional Round Table Conferences) in London. The Indian Congress did not participate in the first series of meetings. These disputed gatherings extended through three sessions until December 1932 and were unsuccessful in achieving an Indian settlement. But they served to ensure a broad princely and diplomatic Indian presence in London different from that of the radicals. Nehru referred to the Round Table sessions as conversations among "an obvious collection of . . . representatives of vested interests," while Gandhi attended the second series in 1931, pronouncing upon the "dumb millions" of his countrymen. In India civil disobedience grew between 1930 and 1934. The youth of the Congress movement now read communist tracts, and after providing leadership of the 1929 strike in Bombay, some communists also became nationalists.[13] Historian Raj

Chandavarkar portrayed the Gandhi movement's "attempt to control not merely to lead, their followers," as a response to the "potential for working class violence" perceived by its leadership. He attributed this potential to the very real duress that labor faced. "Labor was cheapened and more fully subordinated to capital."[14]

Overall economic conditions worsened. The competition for oil picked up, and India was the pathway to the Iraqi oilfields. In September 1931 the Japanese invasion of China posed a warning to India of possible incursions from her Asian neighbor. Deflation accompanied a drop in protectionist practices, lessening the market for finished textile goods without a concomitant domestic price hike to assure continued profit levels. The price falls for the era resulted in a 50 percent decline in the value of rural crops and the closing of markets abroad. The import-export ratios dropped in ways that disadvantaged India's food supply and the ability to extract raw materials. Land taxes and debt remained static in rural areas, causing the peasantry's net cost of living to double. There was a decline in food-grain production relative to population growth.[15] These were the fulcrums of dissent for many workers, and labor policy became the most visible extension of imperial design, even in rural areas. In 1935, just before Saklatvala's death, Britain promulgated the second great Indian Reform Bill, which enfranchised 30 million, one-sixth of the population. Elections became slightly more democratic; there was greater local autonomy and provincial legislatures were empowered through the abolition of dyarchy. The passage of the act fulfilled some electoral ambitions on all sides of the political spectrum, so much so that Winston Churchill's opposition to the bill placed him at a disadvantage in his bid for British rearmament in the coming years.[16] The inculcation of many Indians into diverse echelons of the structure of industrial management helped to maintain public order in equally important ways. The government banned the textile workers' Girni Kamgar Union, the largest communist-led trade union, whose membership had reached 60,000 in 1933 and 1934.

FROM WEALTH TO COMMITMENT

Saklatvala was born in 1874, the son of a Parsi merchant. His mother was a member of the very prominent Tata family, the leading industrialists who had invested wisely in China and who fostered a multireligious ethos among their staff. His father became a partner in the commercial ventures of his mother's family. In the 1890s Saklatvala emerged from a Jesuit and Parsi education with a fervent interest in the millions who were less fortunate.[17] Between 1896 and 1902, a fierce bubonic plague brought him to work with a Russian-Jewish émigré doctor, who had studied Louis Pasteur's techniques. During this stint of relief work, Saklatvala was barred from entering a European club and remembered that moment of frisson when he experienced racism in a visceral and personal form. The plague years also instilled in him the search for an end to poverty. In 1901 he joined the Tata firm, working on the exploration teams that helped to establish India's iron and steel industry. But this assignment brought him into conflict with the occupying British forces in remote regions of the country. In 1905, in a protective move, his employers sent him on to England and to the business community in Manchester. There he met his future wife and lifelong companion, Sarah Marsh of Tansley, Derbyshire. They married in 1907 and moved to London permanently, where Saklatvala joined the Liberal party just as John Morley, Liberal MP, succeeded in leading the parliamentary struggle for an Indian electoral reform that stipulated separate elections for Hindus and Muslims.

Saklatvala's fellow Indian activists were nearby. Nehru attended Harrow and entered Trinity College, Cambridge, in 1907, and was admitted to the London bar in 1912. In little more than a dozen years he assumed the general secretaryship of the Indian Congress. The future Berlin Comintern operative Chattopadhyaya enrolled at Oxford and joined the cultural nationalist Majlis Society. "Chatto" met Shyamaji Krishnavarma, whose London-based journal *Indian Sociologist* supported the newly formed Indian Home Rule Society. Its name suggested an identification with Irish struggles prevalent among Indian radicals. Krishnavarma and his collaborator Madame B. R. Cama, were linked to the New York–based Friends for Freedom of India and the California-based Ghadr party of ex-patriate Punjabis, including Lala Har Dayal, who founded the Indian Independence League in California. Chattopadhyaya led exiled Indian nationalists in Berlin during the Great War and attended the 1927 Brussels conference led by Willi Münzenberg.[18]

Saklatvala's ties to England deepened through his marriage, the raising of his five children, and the transformation of his politics. A disenchantment with prewar Liberalism led him to the East Finchley socialists in North London, the left-wing Social-Democratic Federation, and the Indian Reform Group. He knew Sylvia Pankhurst and participated in the early suffrage campaign. In 1908 he sold the mill machinery that he maintained for Tata, and went to work in the socialist Clarion Club movement of communal hiking, rambling, and collective education. During 1909–10 he joined the ILP, in which he saw the best hope for the unity of British and Indian workers.[19] Saklatvala attended the November 1912 congress of German socialists (SPD) and other parties at Basel. The congress took an anti-imperial international stance that was abandoned in 1914 amid the patriotic fervor of war.

The Russian Revolution inspired Indian radicals partly because it occurred in a largely agricultural economy with a small and advanced industrial sector. The rapid Soviet absorption of Asian territories that shared its borders challenged Indian revolutionaries. Saklatvala was in wartime London at the Revolution's outbreak, serving as the National Union of Clerks' Central London branch delegate to the ILP national conference. He worked closely with the Workers Welfare League in its fight to gain support from British trade unions for Indian trade-union organizing efforts. The movement supported the right to vote, to organize, to demand wage increases, and the abolition of child labor. In his organizing efforts among Lascar seamen, Saklatvala envisioned the formation of an Indian labor party that would adopt the Bolshevik goals of mass education and rapid industrialization. He intervened in ILP meetings on the issues of India and South Africa, comparing the needs of these societies to those of the Soviet Union, and attended very small, wartime Soho meetings of fellow Indian militants in which he reportedly expressed a desire "to kill as many Englishmen as possible" and contemplated tactics like poisoning the water supply of British troops in India with a cholera infection, talk that alienated some of his associates in its ferocity.[20] But Saklatvala was committed to international political action rather than a clandestine world of revolutionary violence. The Berne conference of the Second (Socialist) International held in February 1919 called for full nationalizations in India, and the ILP expressed solidarity with Indian and Egyptian anticolonial sentiments. Many on the British Labour and socialist left increasingly sought an accommodation with the nationalist cause of Indian independence.

The British intelligence services began to monitor the efforts of Indian militants more carefully, and in their first searches of Saklatvala's London home, they uncovered his passionate correspondence with various nationalist figures. Yet Saklatvala's support for trade-union rights also disappointed his contacts among Congress supporters who saw labor struggles as a diversion from the decisive importance of political activity. He remained loyal to social-democratic internationalist views, but his political options in Britain narrowed when the ILP declined affiliation to the Comintern in 1918. Though he spent several more years repeatedly intervening within the ILP on behalf of a radical internationalism, he and many others finally left the ILP to join the ranks of British communism. He helped to establish an information bureau on Russian affairs as a member of the City Branch of the League against Imperialism,[21] and met Palme Dutt in the party's internal international group. In these early years of the CPGB, he first encountered the Glaswegian Helen Crawfurd, who would share many platforms with him.[22] Saklatvala entered the world of international communism, in which the parties of the Comintern competed with organized terrorist cells and the various strands of Indian nationalism to recruit followers over the subsequent decade. Some militants received technical training and sought arms. Indian exiles studied at Moscow's University of the Toilers of the East, including the Meerut trial defendant Shaukat Usmani.[23] Usmani met M. N. Roy and his wife at Moscow's Hotel Lux. The Japanese communist who had helped to found the American communist party, Sen Katayama (Yabuki Sugataro), the British trade unionist Tom Quelch, and the Finnish leader Otto Wilhelm Kuusinen all stayed there with him. Usmani recalled his contact with

"Willi Münzenberg, the communist youth leader from Germany ... also a fellow-student ... at the Lux."[24]

SAKLATVALA AS A BRITISH COMMUNIST

In the early 1920s, despite press attacks upon him for being a supporter of terrorism, Saklatvala established an electoral base in the "red borough" of Battersea, a district south of the Thames that had a strong artisan and labor-left tradition. The ILP and the Battersea Labour Party and Trades Council supported his successful bid as a Labour candidate for Battersea North, the seat vacated by John Burns, a former Liberal cabinet member and leader of the Great Dock Strike of 1889. But a year later Saklatvala's communist affiliation became a larger issue, and in 1924, he was expelled from the Labour party. He continued to serve on committees of the House of Commons with Labour MPs, and the Labour government consulted him on Indian affairs. His ecumenism was a strong element of his political practice that some communists came to doubt, especially given Labour's support for renewed repression in India. A conspiracy trial of left-wing Indian intellectuals and editors at Cawnpore inaugurated a new phase in the containment of the Indian press, accompanied by the harassment and detainment of the left's best-known personalities. Defense committees based in Britain raised funds for the Cawnpore defendants in an effort to resist and expose the treachery of a "progressive" British Labour government.[25]

Saklatvala was elected to Parliament as a communist in 1924, and held his seat until 1929, a testament to his independent popularity rather than the élan of the communist party, his notoriety and stature in India assured by his parliamentary presence. His biographer Mike Squires recorded the revealing *Daily Graphic* account of the 1924 contest:

> If Saklatvala returns to the House across the river it won't be because North Battersea is seething with communism. The Parsee might be Svengali, or an Indian fakir with a knowledge of black magic. He wields a magnetic influence over his audience that verges on hypnotism. I met a Battersea charwoman yesterday who was almost in tears because she lived on the wrong side of the street and couldn't vote for Saklatvala. And I saw excited women waving his handbills and actually kissing his portrait painted on them.[26]

In 1925 Saklatvala led a fight in the House against government-hired strike-breakers in India and continued his activism with the Indian Seamen's Association, the Seafarers Union, and various Indian student groups. The Workers Welfare League and British trade unions also raised some money for Indian strikers, but Saklatvala's vision of a seamless front of Labour, ILP and communist supporters united in solidarity with Indian workers foundered; the nationalists sought him out, but not enough common ground was established. He used the arena of the Commons to condemn repression and economic strife in India:

> I pay homage to the British spirit of hypocritical statesmanship. . . . We are debating here as if the Bengal ordinances were never promulgated, as if the shooting of Bombay operatives during the cotton strike had never taken place, as if a great strike of thousands of railway workers is not even now going on in the Punjab . . . as if a great controversy is not raging, not only with the people of India, but with the people all over the world, whether British imperialism, whatever its past history, is at all permissible to exist now for the benefit of the citizens of Great Britain herself. Is there a single British man or woman today, is there a person in any country in Europe, in any of the backward countries, in the Balkan states, in any of the small nations which are not yet so fully developed as Great Britain, who would tolerate for one day a power so despotic and arbitrary as the crown, under the imperial system, is insisting upon enjoying in India?"[27]

Saklatvala did not abandon his labor militancy in the United Kingdom and was sentenced to two months in the Wormwood Scrubs prison during the events of the British general strike of 1926. He was the first of many communists, nearly a quarter of the party's members, arrested under the Emergency Powers Act of 1920, a measure enforced for nine months in its first extensive use.

Saklatvala made a lecture tour of India in January 1927. He was one of only three Indians ever to have served in the British Parliament, and the mayor of Calcutta regarded him with impassioned promise: "Brother, though you were born in wealthy surroundings, you have been from your youth a true friend of the poor, the suffering and the sorrowing. Whether in India, or in Europe— Brother, you are essentially a citizen of the world. Castes and creeds, color and sex, continents and countries, do not affect you at all." Saklatvala cautioned against a liberal paternalism, urging militant students "not to go as external and superior preachers or welfare workers or advisors, but as one of them," when they approached workers in factories, mines and villages.[28] He brought a comprehensive knowledge of the European applications of communist orthodoxy and a powerful oratorical style to his engagements with bedrock followers of nationalism. On this proselytizing mission, he also brought funds with him for dispersal in India.[29]

Saklatvala addressed the mayor of Calcutta: "You have proven to the world that you are not such stupid unintelligent citizens who swallow everything that imperial press and imperial statesmen are saying against the communists." He spoke of municipal improvement in Madras: "We, who see disease, human starvation and moral degradation, are struggling to restore a world to human dignity, a humanitarian civilization and right of men and women to lead a happy, beautiful, healthy and pleasurable life." Over three months, he met with groups of Hindus and Muslims and his meeting with Gandhi resulted in a published exchange between the two.[30] He visited communist agent Allison, and Spratt and R. S. Nimbkar, who would become Meerut trial defendants. Saklatvala was refused entry into Egypt, and upon his return to London, his Indian passport was cancelled by the British government under a ban upheld by Foreign Secretary Arthur Henderson under the second Labour government of 1929. British intelligence viewed Saklatvala's activities as seditious, but also noted his caution in his dealings with the self-styled communists whom he encountered in India. His differences with M. N. Roy were evident. Roy condemned Gandhi out of hand, while Saklatvala saw Gandhi as a formidable and worthy debating partner, not wishing to appear disloyal in matters involving the Comintern.[31] Saklatvala's vision of Soviet life was emphatically inclusive of the central Asian republics. His separation from India, an absence that lasted through the 1920s until his death in 1936, shaped and disturbed his understanding of domestic Indian developments, steering his communism far away from the immediate challenges of domestic Indian politics. Saklatvala's participation in Münzenberg's 1927 Brussels conference of the League against Colonial Oppression (which became the LAI) brought him into contact with Nehru. He accompanied the British delegation that included Labour party pacifist George Lansbury, communist leader Harry Pollitt, ILP leader James Maxton, ex–Colonial Office renegade Reginald Bridgeman, and Labour MP Ellen Wilkinson. While communist Clemens Dutt served as the British representative to the Comintern, both Saklatvala and Nehru sat on the LAI executive, in a brief effort at unity.[32]

When Saklatvala returned to Britain, the CPGB published his exchange of letters with Gandhi. He criticized Gandhi's opposition to machinery, physical science, material progress and western art, and decried Gandhi's unwillingness to countenance the Marxist insistence upon industrialization as a key to the abolition of poverty. Saklatvala recounted Gandhi's call for a defense of Britain during the South Africa conflict, as the "the mess you made with some young Indians in London, drawing them into some direct or indirect service of war."[33] He challenged Gandhi's method of resistance:

> You are preparing the country not for mass civil disobedience but for servile obedience and for a belief that there are superior persons on earth and Mahatmas at a time when in this country [India] the white man's prestige is already a dangerous obstacle in our way. Politically, this cause is ruinous and from a humanitarian point of view, its degenerating influence appears to me to be a moral plague.[34]

Saklatvala's invocation of notions of "degeneration" and infection reflected the nineteenth-century legacy of utilitarianism found in Marx and the Fabian-style proponents of eugenics. His confidence in industry and his admiration for science made him impatient with what he perceived as the weakness and passivity of a moral campaign that did not seek a transformation of the material world.

In reply, Gandhi adopted a posture of reflection, agreeing that he deplored the greed of modernity. Gandhi wrote that he was *grateful* for the Tata family legacy of charity. He enjoyed his popularity in the West, even despite western immorality:

> Comrade Sak swears by the modern rush. I wholeheartedly detest this mad desire to destroy distance and time, to increase animal appetites and to go to the ends of the earth in search of their satisfaction.... Tata is benevolent. This annoys Sak.... I enjoy the affect of thousands of English men and women and in spite of unqualified condemnation of modern materialistic civilization, the circle of European and American friends is widening.

Gandhi's final definitive retort—candid and clear, distanced him from the arguments of the socialist or communist left. "I do not hold capital to be the enemy of labor."[35] Saklatvala would remain committed to debate, some of it intensely hostile, with the nationalists and the Gandhi movement through his interaction with noncommunist Indians in London.

The Simon Commission

In the summer of 1927 Saklatvala initiated all five of his children into the Zoroastrian faith. The Indian and British press covered the event. Saklatvala invited Labour and Tory MPs to the ceremony, explaining that the decision to indulge these practices, was "due entirely to the peculiar position of his people and of a purely domestic character."[36] Sarah Saklatvala reportedly spoke of the responsibility that she felt toward her father-in-law in continuing the family's traditional ties. Saklatvala kept his Tory friends and had lifetime friendships with Labour MPs like George Lansbury who was vilified by the communists; he kept firm ties to some of his Indian comrades as well, traveling to meet Nehru in Moscow. While he was in the Soviet Union, Parliament appointed the Simon Commission to investigate the Indian government, without a single Indian among its members. When he returned, Saklatvala rose in the House of Commons to oppose the Commission, and to seek more recognition for Nehru and the Indian Congress.

> You are sending out this commission, not to unify religions, not to produce touchability, not to drive away superstition and ignorance with learning and literature, not to drive away slavery by giving political rights to the people but ... to find out how the British nation can tell lies to the world at large, and hypocritically pretend that the British are carrying out their trust in India.[37]

Saklatvala penned an open manifesto to the Indian Congress after the British government imposed its ban on his travel. "The might of tyrants holds me away from my countrymen. Many have tried this trick before, to save their ill-gotten empires but no one yet has really succeeded." He condemned British imperial rule, and praised the Soviets.

> British rule in India means a standing curb on Egypt, Iraq, Persia and Afghanistan. . . . British rule in India means a constant unseen war upon the rapid development of the masses in all the nations of Europe and America. If by a magic touch the British empire were to be sovietized and the conquered races under her control set free, there would be not only real peace and prosperity for the liberated races, but there would be a sudden jump in the economic, social, political and cultural development of the human race. . . . the problem . . . is a world problem . . . of freeing all of humanity from a militarist civilization that it may build a new era of genuine equality, fraternity and liberty.[38]

Saklatvala's "British Imperialism in India: A World Menace," published in 1928, continued in this vein. "The British Empire brings the Negro, Arab and Hindi slave labor in the production of cotton though the backdoor. Britain spreads her empire not only in the rich cotton fields of India but even in Rhodesia, Mesopotamia [and] Sudan."[39]

Future prime minister Clement Attlee was one of two Labour-party members to serve on the Simon Commission. The meetings convened by the LAI in Attlee's East End Limehouse constituency witnessed calls for Attlee to step down. The ILP welcomed these protests, suggesting that the Simon Commission had a unifying effect on a skittish opposition in Britain as it did in India. The Congress party and Nehru condemned the Commission, and the Muslim League and Hindu parties also opposed it. Indian demonstrators greeted the Commission members wherever they ventured, from the moment of their arrival on February 3, 1928. By October they were chanting "Simon, go back." Lady Kathleen Simon accompanied her husband for part of the journey; there were no women commission members. The Naga Hills District head and the chiefs of the region, near Burma, welcomed Sir John Simon at Kohima, where officials presented ladies' petticoats and bodices to Lady Simon.[40] A labour meeting in Ford's Road, Bombay, demanded "Simon go back. No representation. No Commission," and the crowd burned effigies of the Conservative Prime Minister Stanley Baldwin, Secretary of State for India Lord Birkenhead, Sir John Simon, and Labour leader Ramsay MacDonald. In Peshawar, ten thousand demonstrators carried black flags. Hindus, Sikhs, and Muslims marched through the city singing nationalist songs and demanding a boycott of the "purely white" Commission as it was termed. Nehru joined the demonstrators at Lucknow and suffered a head injury at the hands of the police. Here the cry was "Shame, Simon, go back. Down With Imperialism."[41] Black kites flew amid rising balloons.

A demonstration in Hyde Park greeted Simon when he returned to London. The Congress party, the All India (Muslim) League, and the Workers Welfare League united for the occasion. Saklatvala led the forces, but police halted the procession before it reached Victoria Station, striking down its banner. There was an attempt at *Satyagraha*, a nonviolent gesture of resistance and defiant solidarity with Civil Disobedience in India. One banner cut to the chase, declaring "To hell with the Simon Commission."[42] Bob Lovell, who would host Ada Wright on Fleet Street in 1932, was arrested under the banner of the London district committee of Class War Prisoners' Aid, along with several Indian activists.[43]

In September German communist leader Ernst Thälmann visited Battersea following Saklatvala's own trip to Berlin. There he met with communist Reichstag members and debated party policies. In January 1929, after the British government banned the LAI from meeting in London, Münzenberg planned to convene the group in Cologne. When the British delegation disembarked at Ostend on the way to the LAI meeting, the Belgian authorities arrested them as aliens with no right to pass through to Germany, refusing to honor the visas of any of their number who had traveled to the Soviet Union. They detained Saklatvala, Reginald Bridgeman, James Maxton, and A. J. Cook of the Miners' Union and confiscated their passports, tickets, and luggage.[44]

In March 1929 police swarmed through many neighborhoods in India, rounding up a group of trade-union activists and communists, including workers and intellectuals, Hindus and Muslims—soon known as the "Meerut Prisoners." This moment led to a global campaign that attempted to popularize the doctrines and programs of this eclectic group of radicals, most of whom were communists. Both the establishment and left presses carried news of their plight, reaching hundreds of thousands of their fellow Indians, as well as groups of observers and activists in the West. The Meerut campaign sought to garner sympathy and stimulate interest in British imperialism's injustices in ways that no issue other than antislavery had done since the South African War of 1899–1902. The communists orchestrated the Meerut campaign and, in its first phases, successfully reached some liberals and socialists, trade unionists and students as Scottsboro did, engaging dozens of metropolitan participants. In late April 1929, just after the Meerut arrests, the House of Commons resounded with chants of "Down with the Simon Commission" and "Down with the Government" followed by "Down with Imperialism . . . Release Indian Comrades," and "Down with the Government that has starved the miners," in a reference to the domestic aftermath of the British General Strike of 1926. A woman protestor tried to clasp the rails of the gallery, leaflets in hand. As the guards removed her, red flags flew from the spectator benches and the air filled with chants.[45] Her arrest portended months and years of activism around the case, carried out by communists and noncommunist advocates, often led by the London LAI members. Ada Wright's Fleet Street escort, Bob Lovell, was again one of those arrested along with her.[46]

The Round Table talks continued in London as the Meerut Trial began, having opened in November 1930 in the aftermath of the conflict surrounding the Simon Commission's report. Saklatvala was emphatically opposed to the Round

Table and spoke in Parliament on the subject: "Between slavery and freedom there is no middle course as a transition from slavery to freedom can never be attained by general measures."[47] But when he failed to receive even tacit Labour and trade-union support in the 1929 electoral contest, he lost his parliamentary seat in Battersea. Nehru wired him one hundred pounds for a campaign that was lacking in innovation. Saklatvala wrote, resignedly, "I practically repeat the same anti-capitalist and anti-imperialist out and out socialist program as in my election addresses of 1922, 23 and 24."[48] The loss was hard to accept, and it posed the tough question of how far the CPGB would go in providing an arena in which he could articulate his concerns for India, a question that shadowed the final decade of his life.

Saklatvala's political space narrowed when Nehru signed the Delhi Manifesto in November 1929. Gandhi inspired this attempt to seek dominion status for India in exchange for an end to civil disobedience. The Manifesto also called for a reciprocal amnesty and freedom for political prisoners. Chattopadhaya wrote from Berlin to protest against the document as a "betrayal of the Indian masses." Bridgeman did the same.[49] The government never made India a dominion, but Nehru's work with the LAI ended in the wake of this episode. In January 1930 Nehru wrote to the secretariat of the LAI. "I am afraid you have not the least notion of conditions in India and yet you do not hesitate to lay down the law for us. The National Congress [Indian Congress] has welcomed your League and has agreed to cooperate with you but it cannot tolerate outside interference of the kind you have been carrying on."[50] The argument over the Indian polity seeking accommodation with the British was symbolized by the Delhi Manifesto. It mirrored conflict in the broader international left and affected the Indian left in many ways. Meantime, Indian communist M. N. Roy was in Germany, writing *Revolution and Counterrevolution in China*[51] and involved with a dissenting faction of German communists led by Heinrich Brandler and August Thalheimer. His engagement with them led to the severing of ties between Roy and the Comintern. Roy traveled to China with British communist trade-unionist Tom Mann and French communist intellectual Jacques Doriot, returning to India in 1930. His ties with official communism ended just as the Meerut Trial came to prominence. The defendants sought to revive a spirit of unity among anti-British, anticolonial activists, in a context in which both Gandhi and Nehru had recently sought compromise with an increasingly repressive government and empire, and the communist movement of which many were a part, experienced schism.

MEERUT: ACTIVISM ON TRIAL

"*The Meerut Trial: Facts of the Case*," was published in 1929 by the defense committee. It traced the events leading up to the government's decision to

Figure 4.2. "Heavy police guard for Gandhi," depicting Mahatma Gandhi's escort of detectives at the port of Folkestone, England, 1931. He attended the first Round Table talks, among other visits and public commitments, on his last trip abroad (*New York World-Telegram and Sun Newspaper Collection*, Library of Congress).

round up the defendants, pointing both to the "unprecedented loss of strike days" endured by the mill owners during the recent disturbances, and to the arrival of the Simon Commission. There were strikes in the spring of that year at the Tata works, involving employees from railway men to street cleaners. Several died in street action. The April 1928 Bombay textile strike over speed-ups and wage reductions enhanced the authority of the Girni Kamgar Union, whose leaders faced ten-year sentences.[52] In the summer, thirty jute-mill strikers went to prison and their organizers were among the Meerut defendants. Sympathy strikes violated the Trades Dispute Act, and the Public Safety Act forbade any British trade-union supporter of Indian workers from supporting his comrades on strike, stipulating that the communists be expelled from India. On November 17, 1928, members of the Hindustan Republican Association, modeled on the Irish Republican Army, shot and killed a Lahore police officer. Militant activist Sardar Bhagat Singh escaped, but was implicated in this assassination. In April 1929 he and two others threw bombs onto the floor of the Indian Legislative Assembly. Their arrests led to the discovery of bomb factories at Lahore and at Saharanpur, and they were charged in what came to be called the Lahore Conspiracy Case. The defense claimed them as "war crimi-nals" and one defendant fasted until death. Singh and two others were exe-cuted. When the Indian Congress met at Karachi a few days later, it expressed fury with Gandhi over his limited acceptance of the struggles of others in the aftermath of this case. Those sentenced in this wave of repression included na-tionalist leaders and workers. The British Labour government enacted the Press Sedition Bill at the same time, restricting free speech, and affecting all oppositionists. The arrests and roundup of the militants tried at Meerut came in the wake of these events.

In April 1929 H. G. Haig, home secretary to the government of India, wrote to Langford James, a barrister and first prosecutor in the Meerut Trial.

> From the political point of view it would be an advantage to be able to convince in general as early as possible that Communism is not the kind of movement that should receive the sympathy of Nationalists. The opposition to the Public Safety Bill has created [an] artificial and false atmosphere, and we want to set that right as soon as possible.[53]

The orders came to move against the defendants. Defendant Shaukat Usmani recalled the day.

> With Warwickshire Regiment spread all over Bombay, with special concentration where the labor leaders were residing, with the police—mounted and on foot—to be seen everywhere in the labor areas and other parts of Bombay city, the Govern-ment swooped down and arrested all the well-known Bombay labor leaders in the early hours of March 20, 1929. And what happened in Bombay, had happened all over the capital cities of India. It was a drama enacted simultaneously all over the country.[54]

Pramita Ghosh wrote that the case "involved almost the entire leadership of the young Communist and trade union movements of the country."[55] When the authorities seized the defendants, demonstrations erupted in Calcutta and Lahore. The Calcutta *Amrita Bazar Patrika* (an English-language daily) mused, "will not the world think that the communists have all but conquered India?" The next day, Nehru issued a condemnation of the arrests, and Gandhi offered to visit the defendants in jail, intimating that the government did not intend "to kill Communism [but] . . . to strike terror."[56] The Meerut defendant Philip Spratt's candid account of the trial reported that a rumor circulated that the mill owners' association had demanded the prosecutions.[57]

The decision to hold the longest and most costly legal proceeding in British imperial history in the army garrison town of Meerut—one hundred miles from Delhi and fifteen hundred miles from Calcutta and Bombay—immedi-ately backfired. The locale conjured up the horrific repression that had followed the 1857 Indian Mutiny, and was chosen because it had been the scene of a 1928 conference attended by a group of the defendants. The trial took place in

"Garden House," the bungalow of Major General Sir Edmund Ironside, who had distinguished himself in the international campaign waged against the Russian revolution of 1917 and led British forces in Iran in the early 1920s. The defendants were charged with conspiring "to deprive the King Emperor of his sovereignty over British India," and their indictment disparaged the activities of the Comintern in India. It stated that defendants had pursued "armed revolution" to replace India by Soviet republics in a global endeavor. Descriptions of the inner workings of the Comintern implied that the Comintern and the British communist party had controlled the prisoners' activities from above. The indictment identified several Comintern affiliates, including the Profintern (of Red Trade Unions), the Pan Pacific Trade Union, the LAI, and the Young Communist League. These entities had allegedly organized in the failed defense of the American anarchists Sacco and Vanzetti. The defendants had reportedly communed with "foreigners," including Chattopadhyaya and Agnes Smedley, Bob Lovell, Münzenberg, Pollitt, Saklatvala and Tagore. The names of foreign agents were divided between "A" and "B" lists. The second group were deemed "undesirables" forbidden to enter India, and included Palme Dutt, Harry Pollitt, Saklatvala, Tagore, and the Scots communist Helen Crawfurd. As historian Devandra Singh observed, "the prosecution defined communism within the Indian context," as a conspiratorial movement, promoted and fostered from Moscow and the West. R. S. Nimbkar read the defense statement, accusing the prosecution of portraying Communist goals as extralegal and committed to "historical processes and changes in which legal systems and penal codes [were] only byproducts."[58]

But the "Meerut prisoners" were not all of the same persuasion, making their mutual plight more politically complicated. Communists had never been so closely identified with trade unionists and nationalists. Though there were breakdowns in the comradely internal unity of the legal defense, the defendants endured an enforced collective existence that evoked sympathy for all, even from supporters who felt a sense of doctrinal kinship only with some of them. In a ploy to link the conspiracy with British activism, the government arrested the communist Philip Spratt, the Marxist journalist Lester Hutchinson, and the engineers' union leader and communist B. F. Bradley. Like Spratt, Hutchinson left a highly readable account of the trial. He considered the entire affair "a product of the Government of India's chronic anti-Bolshevik neurasthenia" and described his fellows:

> Besides myself there were two other Europeans in the barrack: Philip Spratt, a young Cambridge graduate, and B.F. Bradley, an engineer and a member of the AEU [Amalgamated Engineering Union] whom I had already met before. I was introduced to many I had never met before, including D.R. Thengdi, an old man of sixty-five and a former president of the All-India Trades Union Congress; Mr. Kishore Lal Ghosh, a lawyer and journalist from Calcutta; V.S. Mukerjee, a homeopathic doctor

Figure 4.3. "Twenty-five of the Meerut prisoners taken outside the jail. Back row (left to right): K. N. Sehgal, S. S. Josh, H. L. Hutchinson, Shaukat Usmani, B. F. Bradley, A. Prasad, P. Spratt, G. Adhikari. Middle row: R. R. Mitra, Gopen Chakravarty, Kishori Lai Ghosh, L. R. Kadam, D. R. Thengdi, Goura Shanker, S. Banerjee, K. N. Joglekar, P. C. Joshi, Muzaffar Ahmad. Front row: M. G. Desai, D. Goswami, R. S. Nimbkar, S. A. Dange, S. V. Ghate, Gopal Basak" (*Daily Worker*, March 21, 1931) (courtesy of *Morning Star*, reproduced by the kind permission of the Syndics of Cambridge University Library).

of Gorakhpur, who cultivated a beard in the style of Lenin and a paunch like Falstaff's; Sohan Singh Josh, a gigantic Sikh from Amritsar, the ferocity of whose exterior belied his mild disposition; and Kedar Nath Sehgal, a middle-aged politician from Lahore, who had spent most of his life in prison, and who wore black habitually as a sign of mourning for his country's slavery. The others were mostly trade unionists or members of the Workers' and Peasants' Party, the majority of whom I had never previously met. It was an international gathering of Hindus, Mohammedans and Europeans. The Sikhs were in a minority of one, and there was one Parsee, S.H. Jhabvala, who was fond of describing himself as the "father of fifty trade unions."[59]

The accused included the trade-union federation secretary of Bengal, most members of the executive of the Bombay textile workers' union, eight members of the All-India Congress Committee, and the executive of the communist rank-and-file All India Workers and Peasants Party. They included S. A. Dange, former Socialist editor of the *Amrit Bazar Patrika* of Bombay, and veteran workers' leader D. R. Thengdi, a nationalist and former representative to the LAI. Thengdi arrived in England in the 1890s to study engineering at Manchester and joined the Fabian Society in 1896. In the twenties he became a nationalist and Indian Congress party supporter. In a show of solidarity during the Meerut Trial, the LAI asked Thengdi to replace James Maxton for a brief stint as its president. Defendant K. N. Joglekar also attended the LAI 1927 Brussels congress led by Münzenberg. The remarkable Shaukat Usmani not only visited Russia in 1920, but fought in the Civil War there. He was a defendant in the Cawnpore trial that preceded Meerut. G. M. Adhikari had joined the

German communist party and had known Chattopadhyaya in Berlin.[60] Mir Abdul Majid had joined the Turks in 1920 to fight for the reinstitution of the Islamic Khalifat, and went from Turkey to Russia. A. A. Alwe, who had been a Bombay cotton textile worker from age twelve, was also present in the dock. Defendant Ameer Haidar Khan had left India years before, jumped ship in the United States, and worked in an auto plant where he joined the communist party. He traveled to Moscow and back to India where he worked for General Motors in Bombay until his arrest.

Philip Spratt's father was an elementary schoolteacher and a Baptist. His older brother died at Paschendaele. He ran with a group of "heretics" at Cambridge in the early twenties; among their number were the future economist Maurice Dobb and the West End filmmaker Ivor Montagu, a Scottsboro signatory and a central figure in the mock Reichstag fire trial. Spratt recalled himself as an advocate of an "ethical nihilism" in those years. Communism appealed:

> In its first years the British party had contained a number of intellectuals of some distinction—[Sylvia] Pankhurst, [Raymond] Postgate, [Ellen] Wilkinson . . . et al . . . together with a crowd of sandal wearers, all-wool fanatics, anti-vaccinationists and so forth of the type which gathered around the pre-1914 socialist movement. . . . by the time I joined most of the intellectuals and cranks had dropped out.[61]

The party assigned Pratt to work as a mole in the Labour Research Department, a think tank attached to the Labour party. He often sat with an Indian coworker who organized lascar seamen. The department sent communist materials like the *Negro Worker* for distribution in the colonies, but the comrades' etiquette bespoke the party's awkward internal tensions. Spratt's Jewish colleague would not sit with their Indian colleague: "The Brahmin out-Brahmined and by a slum-bred Jewess . . . Whatever we may have felt, all of us, middle-class communists, and some non-communists, knew better than to admit such a feeling. Those were the days, of course, before the Comintern had begun to stress the race, color and colonial questions." Spratt met Clemens and Palme Dutt in his early party days. Their sister worked at the offices of the League of Nations Union, and Spratt learned from M. N. Roy of the Dutt brothers' Bengali father, a doctor, and their Swedish mother, whom Roy found very beautiful. Spratt met Saklatvala in the House of Commons before his departure for India on party assignment. He toured Delhi, Aligarh, and other points with Saklatvala in 1928, but, significantly, Saklatvala failed in his attempts to introduce Spratt to useful allies.

> I recalled afterwards that [Clemens] Dutt had shown by his tone either contempt or dislike of Saklatvala, and Allison [the Scots communist miner sent to India and later deported] confirmed the possibility of a rivalry for the leadership of the forthcoming Indian party between him and the Dutt brothers. If any such rivalry existed, it is unnecessary to say that the Dutts won.[78]

Spratt encountered many nationalists upon his arrival in India and acknowledged that there was not much he "could teach them about imperialism."[62] He
met the communist activist Percy Glading, a former Woolwich Arsenal employee, later imprisoned for spying for Moscow, and the independent Indian
Marxist C. G. Shah. These contacts would merit Spratt his place among the accused at Meerut.

Lester Hutchinson had attended Edinburgh University with a young woman
member from the Chattopadhyaya family. They performed together in a student production of Tagore's *Red Oleanders*, his first exposure to Indian sensibilities. Hutchinson made his way to Berlin as a budding journalist and traveled
on to India. His mother's sympathetic involvement with the communist movement in the north of England was a stimulus to his activism and he met Ben
Bradley soon after his arrival on the subcontinent: "It is not easy to land in
India. The Government of India is very particular and takes many precautions
to prevent undesirables and especially political undesirables entering the country. They are not more thorough at Ellis island."[63]

During this time, there were as many as 23,000 political prisoners in India,
many of whom had been picked up in raids and in house searches, beaten, and
incarcerated without trial. Displays of military force accompanied arrests, and
the courts often refused to grant bail. The leaders of India's social movements
routinely faced imprisonment, but rank-and-file workers and militants did as
well, and many under more onerous conditions, without the shield of celebrity.
Some were suicides. The Meerut defendants were initially handcuffed, brought
to mosquito-filled cells, and required to undertake nine hours of manual labor
daily. At first, the authorities forbade them letters or interviews and visits from
relatives. They witnessed the whipping of young male prisoners.[64]

Hutchinson and the others arrested in the first raids were "roped, handcuffed and paraded through Meerut" and their lodgings ransacked.[65] The police found American writer Upton Sinclair's muckraker novel, *The Jungle,* in
Bradley's Bombay flat; its damning discovery appeared in the court record.[66]
Hutchinson's mother and other relatives often complained of the defendants'
prison conditions, and these complaints ultimately resulted in changes. Spratt
recalled "for some weeks I was unable to read, write or talk." But he later felt
that they all "lived well within the yard" where they could consort and con-
verse, and where they received better food than that of other prisoners. Spratt
found the *Daily Worker*'s statements that they were emaciated "disconcerting"
and in "contrast with the facts," but there were those who were unwell during
the long period of imprisonment, and the prominent defendant D. R. Thengdi
died of illness while incarcerated.[67] Prisoners from lower social backgrounds
surrounded the Meerut accused. The Meerut defendants were outraged at the
treatment of others, but their defense strategy relied upon a notion of special
entitlement and celebrity. Indeed, they were neither "ordinary" nor "common"
prisoners. Even before the trial started, in a remarkable political intervention,

defendant Shaukat Usmani challenged none other than Sir John Simon's parliamentary seat at Spen Valley, Yorkshire, from his jail cell, underlining the relative prestige of the defendants—he was behind bars and yet capable of mounting a propagandistic electoral campaign a continent away, in which a fellow
communist acted as his proxy in England.[68]

In June 1929 James Maxton demanded more rights for the Meerut prisoners
from the Labour secretary for India Wedgwood Benn. The second Labour
government had just come to power and would not take responsibility for earlier Conservative-party decisions to try the defendants before a judge instead
of a jury. James Maxton had just been expelled from the LAI, but was a staunch
defender of the Meerut campaign. If the new secretary of state for Labour had
exercised his right to switch to a trial by jury, Maxton admonished, Labour
would have had Liberal-party support in doing so.[69] Wedgwood Benn was not
moved. On December 10, 1929, the writer H. G. Wells and others issued the
first major protest letter independent of communist intervention, in the *Manchester Guardian*. It was signed by Harold Laski and R. H. Tawney of the LSE
and the Rev. Walter Walsh, and it referred to the trial as a "strike-breaking
prosecution," protested against the decisions to deny the defendants bail, to refuse a jury trial, and to forsake a more central location for the trial, and suggested that these decisions abjured the "elementary rights of British citizens."
The *Guardian*'s lead editorial on December 29 identified the trial's "most disturbing feature . . . [as] the vague charge of conspiracy, not acts."[70]

Revolution on Trial

The trial of the Meerut prisoners finally began at the end of January 1930. It
lasted for three years, commencing before the outbreak of Scottsboro and ending just as Hitler took power in Germany. The government's chief prosecutor,
Langford James, boldly framed the prosecution in terms of an abject anticommunism. He mentioned Saklatvala early in his oration, announcing that he had
been an active force among Indian students in London. James's indictment of
the Communist defendants was an effort to divide them from the nationalist
sympathizers in the dock.[71] He quipped that the communists thought of Pandit
Motilal Nehru, the head of the early legal defense team and Nehru's father, as "a
dangerous patriot" and regarded the younger Nehru as "a tepid reformist," and
Mahatma Gandhi as "a grotesque reactionary." There was a roar of laughter in
the dock when James tried to define their Bolshevism: "You do not love your
country, you are anti-country, you are anti-God, you are anti-family, in fact you
are anti-everything which a normal man considers decent." From the outset,
the prosecution used divisive rhetoric that sought to pit communism squarely
against the presumed values of an "independent" and more pliable nationalism.
But this ploy failed before a devoted and intensely curious audience: "The youth

of Meerut were also keen to see these leading figures and hear the proceedings in this case. A large number of students, *vakils* (lawyers), and politically conscious people, thronged to the place of the trial."[72]

There was an internal debate among the members of the defense team over how to address the prosecution's charges. One option was to disavow ties to the Comintern and to contend that the policy of Indian communists in their own country was an autonomous one.[73] In the period leading up to the trial, the CPI's relationship with Moscow had been strained, M. N. Roy's departure from the Comintern forming an important element of that tension. Nevertheless, Lester Hutchinson and other defendants were still members of the CPI. Instead, the defense chose to deny that there had been an attack upon the king and to assert that the defendants' real foe was imperialism. The defense team's informal pretrial notes reveal a propagandistic intention: "[The] case is not a conspiracy of a few men. Objective conditions are what determine historical events. Hence develop our conception of these events. . . . trace the development of capitalism." The defense did not wish to portray the Comintern as a puppeteer, manipulating its national sections and lacking a sure footing in the world trade-union movement. Its affiliates were "not just post offices of the Comintern."[74] The notes suggest that they planned to focus on an analysis of the global situation. "White terror considered historically—far more severe and continuous than Red Terror; fascism and bourgeois terror generally in Europe and America. Political oppression in India. . ."[75] From the demands of Indian labor to the global fight against political repression, the communist defendants mounted a rhetorical platform, and fashioned an argument within the conventions of their political doctrines. R. S. Nimbkar wrote the resulting *General Statement*, presented in the early stages of the trial by a group of eighteen of the accused. It criticized the political alternatives offered by Indian Congress and the Gandhi movement, promoting a Marxist vision of a future revolutionary society.[76]

Several large propositions governed the *General Statement*. The civil-disobedience campaigns had thus far shown the document's supporters that the Indian Congress could not lead the peasantry "to its political and economic emancipation" because of its dependence on the "landed and monied classes." It declared that "only the agrarian revolution against British capitalism and Indian landlordism can be the basis for the revolutionary emancipation of India." In identifying the need for an independent social movement on the land, it sought to unmask the charges of manipulation from Moscow, insisting that communism had the deepest English roots. The Chartist movement had been an inspiration to the hallowed founders:

> [T]he Prosecution have also argued that the Communist movement is entirely a product of Russian influence. This is the favorite theme of all contemporary anticommunist propaganda. But it is of course without any actual justification. If the historical

facts are examined . . . it will be found that almost all the essential ideas of modern Communism arose with the rise of modern large scale industry in England in the early years of the nineteenth century. Several of the leaders and writers of the Chartist movement (1834–48) and of even earlier periods display an acquaintance with much of Communist thought. These ideas were collected and synthesized by Marx and Engels in a way which has required no essential modification since. The working-class movement of their time was largely under their influence, and was to a considerable extent a Communist movement in the full sense.[77]

Interwar British socialism, manifested in organizations from the CPGB to the ILP, elevated the place of Chartism in its vernacular narrative of the formation of Marxist thought, insisting on Chartism's iconic role in the construction of an "independent" history of English class struggle. In one incarnation, ILP writer Reginald Reynolds, Padmore's friend, revived the 1849 Chartist Ernest Jones's prison writings on India. The sly appropriation of Chartism as a mythological point of departure for the Indian movement turned the tables on the prosecutors by establishing a link to their own domestic and imperial origins. The essential point was that local and national circumstances might shape a social movement and Chartism was an example of such a process coming to fruition. The General Statement dealt with recent times by describing a series of uprisings that formed a global pattern beginning with the Easter Rising of 1916 in Dublin. By 1930, Korea, Afghanistan, the French Mediterranean, China, Java, Indochina, and India had witnessed eruptions. Revolts gripped Latin America and the British and French African colonies, proliferating "among the South African negroes." Iraq, Arabia, Cyprus, "and even . . . such remote regions as Samoa" had experienced acute tensions. The plight of India was pictured in global terms.[78]

The Statement also sought to appeal to nationalist readers and listeners:

[A] great number of bourgeois agents of various sorts, independent humanitarians, Liberals, Theosophists, Congressmen, communalists as well as direct Police agents have been busy corrupting the movement with their various, but all counterrevolutionary ideas. At any rate we can say that if we are "outsiders" we are not the only ones.

The insistence that "foreignness" was not particular to the communists on the Indian scene, allowed the defendants to remain internationally attached while suggesting that all movements that strove for social change in India, no matter how wrong-headed, had global ties. When the document turned to the question of a social program it included the call for an eight-hour day with a six-hour working day for youth workers, and called for a minimum wage, equal pay for women, and the establishment of state health, accident and old age insurance. It demanded the abolition of subcontracting and of "caste and feudal customs" that obtained on work sites—in effect, the enactment of a socialized workers' state like that envisioned by the European and American social-democratic and left parties, and displaying many features of Soviet life.[79]

The *Statement* usurped the language of the most important social movement of its time, claiming it as its own and speaking to those who pinned their hopes upon civil disobedience.

> We oppose Mr. Gandhi and his policy, not because he stands for Independence, but because he does not stand for Independence. . . . like all religious propaganda, that of Mr. Gandhi tends to obscure class differences and in other ways have a reactionary effect. . . . it gives a particular shape to the tactics of reformism and invests them with a traditional sanctity (*Satyagraha* and the like). Exponents of Gandhism have frequently boasted that it stands between India and revolution. This is the fact, and this is the substance of our opposition to it.

The *Statement* did not shrink from the questions of the use of violent tactics and the serious use of force faced by any revolutionary movement. This was a brave gesture, given the circumstances of the trial and its potential for long sentences involving transportation to incarceration in exile. It resolutely addressed the Indian context in which nonviolence had established such a large following.

> Since the "war to end war," war, directly or indirectly waged by the Imperialist Powers, has continued, in the intervention in Russia, in Turkey, Syria, Arabia, Mesopotamia, Morocco and China . . . all the while the White Terror of the bourgeoisie has gone on a scale never before thought of. These things should be remembered when the Prosecution, the representatives of Imperialism, condemn us for contemplating the use of force.

The charge of violence was also leveled against supporters of Indian independence in Britain, and in response, the defendants accused the British political community of manipulating colonial issue for domestic ends: "[N]o doubt the case was found very useful in providing the Conservative Party in Britain with propaganda material for use in the General Election [of May, 1929] which took place two months after our arrest. The value of 'Red Scares' had been shown in the General Election of 1924." Britain's transatlantic ally did not escape the charge of hypocrisy:

> The USA is still sometimes held up as an example of freedom and democracy under Capitalism. . . . But the ruling class of this capitalist paradise wages a struggle against the working class of a ferocity which until the postwar period of intensified class struggle was to be found otherwise only in the colonies. The use by the American bourgeoisie of the law for class purposes and its disregard of its own professed principles of equality and justice, are perhaps the most cynical anywhere to be found. We may refer to the case of Sacco and Vanzetti.[80]

The *Statement* had global pretensions and analytical sweep. It was vast and exploratory. But the chief defense argument for acquittal was the simple contention that the prosecution had not heard evidence of conspiracy and British justice had been ill served.

> The prosecution have done their best to give the case an atmosphere of criminality by emphasizing "cryptic correspondence," "assumed names" and behind it all the lurid gleam of "Moscow gold." But even they have not claimed that any of these things is illegal. . . . This aspect of the case . . . has caused some perturbation among those who have not yet realized what imperialism is, and still retain their nineteenth century beliefs in our "traditional liberties." [81]

The *Statement* closed with reference to British reactions to the case, citing the letters of protest appearing in the *Manchester Guardian* in a country where the *Statement* charged that readers had "no conception as a matter of course of those two-thirds of the world which are subject to Imperialist domination." [82] The document was part of seven thousand printed pages of trial texts, and 12,500 exhibits, including the prisoners' individual testimonies, some of which appeared in the *Daily Worker*. These served to "humanize" the defendants and to get news of the trial out to the reading public on the British left and in the trade unions. Over three hundred persons offered testimony. G. M. Adhikari's statement turned the charges upside down.

> The prosecution have hurled the vilest abuse on Communism, Communists and the Communist International. . . . I . . . hurl back the charge of being criminal against human society. . . . Who are the social criminals? I ask the blood-thirsty imperialists who carried fire and swords through entire continents, who have instituted a Colonial regime of blood and terror, who have reduced the toiling millions of these continents to abject poverty, intolerable slavery and are threatening them with mass extinction as a people; or the communists, who are out to mobilize the revolutionary energies of the toiling masses of the whole world and hurl it against the wretched system based on ruthless oppression and brutal exploitation, smash it and create in its place a new one and thus save human society and its civilization from the catastrophe towards which it is undoubtedly heading? The official representatives of social criminals in this case are sitting on the Prosecution benches. [83]

K. N. Joglekar, a 1927 textile strike leader and a delegate to the LAI, candidly confessed his communism rather than see himself portrayed as a member of a secret, covenlike sect. R. S. Nimbkar attempted to reach the nationalists in his own testimony. Muzzaffar Ahmad insisted that "the terrorists have never believed in the real revolutionary social elements, the workers and peasants. . . . they are romantic idealists." Ben Bradley emphasized his own kinship to the working class—his youth as a factory worker, his service in the Great War, and his involvement in the British "Hands Off Russia" campaign of the post-1917 period, calling himself "a worker from the metropolis of the largest empire in the world." Shaukat Usmani said that the prisoners were only drops of water, that "new masses [would] rise up in their place," forming "large waves" of opposition.[84]

RELEASE THE PRISONERS!

News of the trial traveled to Britain and to all parts of Europe and the extra-European world touched by Comintern publications, but the *New York Times* also took note.[85] In Berlin and Moscow the communist leadership kept abreast of its proceedings. There was even talk of a Red Aid delegation to India to include Willi Münzenberg, who orchestrated the European campaign to support the Meerut defendants. The second Labour government in Britain, elected in 1929, allocated £750,000 for the trial expenses. It simultaneously extended the Bengal Criminal Amendment Act and in the first year of the trial, the authorities fired upon more strikers than in any previous year in Indian history, and shut down eighty newspapers. On June 13, 65 were killed and 150 wounded in riots in Peshawar. Members of the Gharwali Rifles who fraternized with protestors were arrested and tried, several receiving life sentences. Twenty-five died in an uprising of textile workers at Solapur. Indian Congress reported 15,980 arrests in May and June, and another 20–25,000 by the end of August. The British expended significant resources suppressing revolts in the northwest frontier, trying to preserve their foothold in a region that provided a base from which raids upon Afghanistan or the Soviet Union could be launched. In a pamphlet describing these circumstances, communist trade-union leader J. T. Murphy accused the Labour party of approving and supporting the Meerut prosecutions. Murphy charged Labour with hypocrisy in its condemnation of the Meerut defendants "for doing what the working class movement of this country has been urging should be done for many years, namely, organizing the Indian workers on a class basis and establishing class solidarity against capitalism between the Indian and British working class."[86]

At Meerut, political lines stiffened. The Indian Congress withdrew from the national defense team.[87] The "class against class" line, as promulgated by the Comintern's Seventh Congress in Moscow, exacerbated divisions between the Indian communists and the nationalists. The British defense campaign had its own unique dynamics and was the most committed defense of the prisoners mounted outside of India. It occurred as the Scottsboro case was breaking and as the Round Table talks approached new points of conflict; in Germany, the last period of the Weimar Republic witnessed its own Meerut campaign.

In the midst of these events, Saklatvala searched for political roles for himself. In 1931 the British communist party tried to salvage his historic parliamentary career by assisting him in seeking a seat in Glasgow, but his bid was abysmally unsuccessful. That spring, he fought his first campaign for a spot on the London County Council, running in his old constituency of Battersea North to no avail, his defeat symbolizing communist and Labour party mutual antipathy. But all the while, the Meerut agitation prevailed, and Saklatvala was one of its key figures. The campaign publicly claimed to achieve its national targets in 1930, including in parts of Scotland and Wales. In dozens of meetings, campaign supporters described the case and the plight of the prisoners, and inaugurated "Meerut Week." Central to its mission was the campaign's intent to embarrass and compromise the Labour government of 1929 "to expose the Labour Government, the jailers of Meerut, and its so-called 'left' supporters, Maxton and Nehru." George Allison, just released from prison in Scotland for his role in a strike action of the Sailors at Invergordon, Tom Mann, and Reginald Bridgeman spoke at Meerut rallies. A Bradford resident won a competition for a badge made by the Meerut prisoners of the same type as displayed in the defendants' press photos from India. United-front support meetings involved women in the Catholic Crusade in the Midlands milltowns of Burslem and Smallthorne.[88] A diverse group of trade-union bodies and popular associations passed Meerut resolutions around the country, in communist-led work that some others followed with sustained interest.

The organizers found support for their attempts to organize in the international apparatus emanating from Münzenberg's work on the Continent. African American James Ford wrote of the Comintern Negro Committee's attempts to recruit Indian seamen in Hamburg. The port militants worked two ships a week, each carrying six or ten black seamen. The German police were watchful, and Ford recalled their investigating Chinese workers. George Padmore continued to try to build up the harbor-workers' organization, his endeavors culminating in the June 1930 conference comprised of representatives from China, East India, Dakar, Japan, and the Middle East.[89] The Negro Committee's publications carried news of Meerut.[90]

The campaign circulated propaganda among troops departing the naval ports for India, calling attention to the role of the military in defending British rule. "India—the Meerut Trial—What All Service Men Should Know" warned of the upheaval that troops could anticipate upon arrival and claimed that the exploitation of Indian labor worsened economic imperial conditions at a time when the police at home in Britain were attacking the unemployed. In order to fight for their own emancipation, it reasoned, workers and army and navy recruits needed to assist those in India. The Portsmouth sailors' leaflet, "Hell Is Let Loose in India," posed a stark challenge to the recruits. "[For] workers and peasants who reject the non-violence nonsense of Gandhi . . . death no longer has any terrors. . . . Refuse to act as hangman of the Indian revolution."[91] On Whitsunday, May 2, 1931, the campaign merged its customary "Anti-Empire Day," a response to the national schools' celebration of the Empire, with a new "Meerut Day." A few days later, communist leader and textile-union activist Rose Smith shouted "Release the Meerut Prisoners" from the ladies' gallery of the House of Commons. She was part of a delegation led by the representatives of the ILP that visited Parliament to meet with three Labour party MPs, each of whom refused to take action on the Meerut case.[92] Its critics enumerated Labour's "crimes," including the use of press gangs and the outlawing of picketing in India. By 1931 more than 54,000 had been arrested in civil-disobedience actions in India. The *Daily Worker* also reported on the government repression of strikes in Gambia and Palestine and the deaths of dozens in police actions during the Egyptian elections. In Nigeria British flyers fired from the air on fifty-four unarmed women strikers. In the outrage over this episode, Colonial Secretary Sidney Webb of the Fabian Society was singled out for his role.[93]

The imperial moderates, cautious critics of empire who still defended its preservation, including future members of the Fabian Colonial Bureau, were moved by the proceedings at Meerut. Arthur Creech Jones, who would become leader of the FCB, drafted a memo in June 1931 on the trial, denying the Labour party's responsibility for the original charges against the defendants, which had been lodged by the 1924–29 Conservative government led by Stanley Baldwin. He contended that those charges set the dynamic of the trial upon its course, and enforced its length. But Creech Jones was implacably hostile to any notion of Indian agency, implying that the trial was justified:

> It is necessary to bear in mind that unlike their comrades in the West the workers in India are mainly the illiterate, and are dependent almost entirely for the organization of their trade unions upon persons who are not themselves workers. . . . [It is the] duty of any Government authority in India to see that persons are not using the workers for their own political ends.[94]

Creech Jones maintained that since 1925 there had been a significant infiltration of communists into the All India Trades Union Federation (Congress). The American ILD had sent a check to India to support those defending trade union prisoners in order to assist "the victims of British imperialism whether in Bombay, Lahore, or other cities." He saw the ILD's action as further evidence of outside influence; the Labour government of 1929, by then installed in power, returned the check to New York. But he also recorded the *Manchester Guardian*'s caustic remarks on the trial: "The whole case is a tragedy, not only for those involved but for the good name of British justice. It shows clearly that the procedure needs overhauling, and suggests even to the least suspicious that the connection between the Executive and the judiciary in India is far too close."[95]

Labour and Fabian anticommunism was matched by communist opposition to Gandhi. In June 1931 Saklatvala called for the release of those on trial at Meerut and for the cessation of imperial attacks in Burma, decrying Labour party support for Gandhi. The latest split between official communism and Congress—between Gandhism and Bolshevism—seemed irrevocable.[96] But Gandhi was a popular sensation when he visited Britain. He toured Lancashire in September, where the ravages of economic depression in the textile industry were visible and the historic relationships between India and the textile towns of the north of England complex and irreducible. The *Daily Worker* was not amused:

> After showering interviews on every journalist he met on the way, he finally arrived back in London on Saturday. Among those who welcomed him at Folkestone and played a prominent part in the later proceedings was Mr. James Marley, Labour MP for St. Pancras who last year recommended the Government use tear-gas for the dispersal of Indian demonstrations.[97]

Gandhi visited Fenner Brockway of the ILP, a central figure in the joint ILP and communist work of the Meerut Prisoners' Defense Committee. Brockway and Saklatvala coauthored a pamphlet on the trial.[98]

The Meerut campaign showed occasional inventiveness. Besides Shaukat Usmani's bid for election in Britain, Helen Crawfurd, the Scot whom the prosecution named as an undesirable at Meerut, ran for Parliament in North Aberdeen against the Labour secretary for India, Wedgwood Benn. London witnessed a passionate debate about many aspects of the Indian question during the years of the trial. In one instance, Saklatvala caused "uproar and wild disorder" when he intervened at a meeting of organizations who adopted "reformist" positions on the question of India's future, some favoring the Round Table model of discussion and compromises with elites.[99] H. H. Brailsford, a leading ILPer and India observer, was now among Saklatvala's opponents. Brailsford had always voiced some support for the Round Table talks. When radical elements in the meeting called for him to give up the chairman's seat to Saklatvala, police inspectors entered the hall.

At the close of the first year of the Round Table talks, Clemens Dutt wrote that "the landlord-capitalist control over the masses through the national Congress is no longer as effective as it was a year ago."[100] In this atmosphere of uncertainty about a new Indian settlement, the Meerut Trial enlightened British and Indian onlookers about the machinations of the British state and exposed the gap between theory and practice in the administration of imperial justice, the communist affiliation of many of the defendants notwithstanding. The *New Statesman and Nation* mocked the disingenuousness of the government's charging the defendants with conspiracy. In Britain their alleged infractions amounted to routine political activity. There were "few members of the cabinet who could not have been arrested" if subjected to the same scrutiny. "[Labour-party leader George] Lansbury was LAI president when the plot was hatched." He stated, "[A]bout half [of] India [is] indictable. . . . When European communists went out there [to India]—they displayed CP factionalism . . . quarreling bitterly often upon purely theoretical questions. . . . The farce was the platform afforded the Communist Party and their views." The prosecution was accomplishing precisely the opposite of its intentions.[101]

The Trial's *Finale*: 1932 and After

In early 1932 the *New Leader* reported an £11 million budget deficit in India and a £26 million decline in British trade, reflecting mounting domestic woes in Britain. Capital valued at £30 million had fled India. Repression had intensified appreciably. A sense of urgency had unleashed a new forcefulness of approach:

> [T]he British Government has declared war on India. . . . The British army may issue their Ordinances, arrest the Congress leaders, march their troops about the country, shoot upon prohibited meetings, imprison children—but all these ignoble devices of Terrorism cannot prevent 300 millions of Indian people from winning their freedom. . . . Britain is now engaged in the re-conquest of India. It is treating the Indian people exactly as an invading army treats an occupied territory during war. Military columns are marching through the towns and countryside. The Indian flag is hauled down from the Congress premises and the Union Jack substituted. Aerial demonstrations are being carried out in the North-west frontier.

The ILP reported the government's suppression of the Indian press, the billeting of troops and police, the banning of five hundred organizations, the institution of curfews and arrest of officials, the extension of two-year jail sentences to seven years, and the censorship and interception of mail, terming it all, "naked Repression."

> Our own problems are overwhelming, but in the midst of them we cannot forget that the terrible repression in India is being carried out by our Government in our name. . . . The National Council of the ILP views these proceedings with disgust and loathing, repudiates the Government and the political parties which are responsible for it, and calls for a united protest from the British people and a demand for the abandonment of these terrorist polices which are being pursued in their name.[102]

The ILP called for self-government and an immediate amnesty for political prisoners, including those at Meerut. Reginald Bridgeman, in his role as go-between in communist and ILP circles, attempted to shift the discussion of dissent in India away from the accusation of outside Comintern manipulation to the role of fundamental economic forces in the increasing conflicts.

> Despite the endeavor of British Imperialism to fasten the responsibility for the growing insurrectionary movement in India on the [Communist] Third International, the strikes arising from the miserable economic condition of the workers have been plainly defined in the [British government's trade union] Whitley report . . . strikes largely due in each instance to economic reasons. . . . India is revolting against British Imperialism today, although news is suppressed. The latest reports I have read

speak of the dead-stop of business in the City of Bombay and machine-gunning from low-flying British airplanes on the North-west frontier.

He called for a mobilization of all forces that opposed the current repression, and for freedom in Asia and the United States. "Mass action can win working-class freedom, can open jail doors, and can liberate the political prisoners of class justice—the Meerut prisoners, the Gharwali riflemen, the Burmese rebels, Paul and Gertrud Ruegg, the Scottsboro boys—all of whom are savagely penalized in the interests of Capitalism today."[103]

In May Münzenberg organized a public meeting in Germany on India, *Sturm über Indien*, at which he spoke alongside Saklatvala. Saklatvala wrote to one of Münzenberg's newspapers: "To the Comrades who read *Ein Morgen* I offer my sincere greetings. I want you to hear the heart cry of 900,000,000 of humanity who are oppressed [and] tortured . . . by Imperialists."[104] In Berlin Chattopadhyaya served as the LAI co-secretary with Münzenberg and attempted to build a base of support for Comintern work in India.[105] Several Indian youth organizations developed ties to the LAI, including the Bombay Presidential Youth League, the Bombay Student Brotherhood, the Bombay Youth League, and the Muslim Students Union. LAI contacts grew among Indians in South Africa, Australia, and the United States; a small, far-flung network of subscribers dotted a fragile global map. In Germany Tagore, Josef Bilé of Cameroon, and exiled anticolonial Indonesian leader Suwardi Suryaingrat were associated with Münzenberg's Red Aid campaigns.[106] In June a "Red Players" theater-troupe performance of the sketch *Meerut Prisoners* was banned at Camberwell Green in London; the police inspector threatened to "clean the whole street up," if the performance continued as planned.[107]

When Ada Wright came to Britain in July, Saklatvala and others involved in the Meerut defense campaign met her and appeared by her side. Scottsboro and Meerut were often invoked in communist propaganda as twin cases and portrayed as sharing roots in global economic despair. With Saklatvala's assistance, the London Scottsboro Committee approached Indian organizations for support. In July the Comintern Executive directed the Meerut campaign to make use of the defendants' mothers: "The two mothers of the English prisoners and public men should issue an appeal." At the request of Harry Pollitt, the Eastern Secretariat of the Comintern voted to assist with funds, to provide assistance to the prisoners, to offer a "special sum to publish a pamphlet [and] revive the campaign in Europe . . . 10,000 each in English, Urdu, Bengali and Hindustan," in the face of "growing terror and shootings."[108] Lester Hutchinson's mother, Mary Knight, who met Wright, was active in the campaign. The India Office in Whitehall reportedly received letters of protest from all over Britain. But the repression in India had many more dimensions than those reflected in the proceedings at Meerut. In a letter to the *New Leader*, one writer implored his readers to remember the overriding symbolism of the case as part of the larger independence struggle, defying the factionalism of much of the political community and pleading that the significance of the case not be diminished.

> It [Meerut] showed that this struggle had a property basis; that it was and is a class struggle; that the cause of Indian independence was and is inseparable from this struggle; that the Indian working class and peasantry were and are the real historic custodians of national liberation attainable only by striking off the fetters of private property, both British and Indian. . . . some people now suggest [that] Meerut . . . has lost its special significance because of the mass arrests that have accompanied the terrorist campaign against the masses of India. . . . [This] is entirely wrong.[109]

Lester Hutchinson issued the pamphlet *Meerut, 1929–32* from his prison cell. It was published by the Manchester Meerut defense committee and written in an evocative, autobiographical style. He described his time spent in Germany and the economic forces that had radicalized German workers. His affiliation with the LAI had brought friendships with comrades from Java, Indochina, Syria, and India. He described his trip to India and his first meeting with Ben Bradley. Hutchinson did not mention his mother's prior activism, and his story appeared as the life of an adventurer-convert. His later work *Conspiracy at Meerut*, was written in the same, ingenuous style.[110]

In November 1932, the veteran activist Thengdi died a prisoner. His passing signaled the intolerable length of the trial, the threats to health posed by incarceration, and the indignity of death under such circumstances. As the final stages of the verdict and sentencing approached, there were rallies in London addressed by Tom Mann, Bridgeman, and the Trinidadian oil workers' leader Adrian Cola Rienzi. In November, in a typical provincial event, one of dozens organized throughout Britain by the various local defense committees, the Forresters Hall at Dundee featured an evening of revolutionary songs in which the Dundee Workers Theater Troop performed *Meerut*. "For this sketch a prison front with two cells showing was erected on the platform. The effort of the group made a great impression on the audience and brought home very forcibly the terrible character of the imprisonment imposed on our comrades in Meerut Prison," its melodramatic style appealing to an audience accustomed to the variety stage.[111]

In December the Comintern directed the CPGB to "raise the connections [with Meerut] established through the Scottsboro campaign . . . [and] get [from Saklatvala] all names and signatures of Indian persons (staying in England or in India) for this case."[112] At a 500-person-strong London LAI meeting, held in Memorial Hall, Farringdon, Saklatvala spoke of the conditions faced by Indian workers, using images of African slavery so often invoked in Scottsboro defense work. The Meerut prisoners had fought against such conditions. Railway workers were paid nineteen shillings a month for fourteen-hour working days. Employers in the jute industry drew dividends ranging from 30 to 90 percent of their intake.

He also challenged the notions of "slavery" that were being applied in the debate about forced labor camps in the Soviet Union. The numbers of vocal opponents of the camps were growing in Britain and he derided them as critics who profited from imperialism: "These people who were drawing such dividends were now holding meetings in Albert Hall against slave labor in Russia." He dismissed as the ravings of financial parasites and hypocrites, the various practices and structures known as the Gulag, and the Stalinist forced collectivizations that had already taken over 1 million lives. Communist and other advocates of the Soviet Union in the West remained committed to presenting Soviet society as a land without terror in which "correct" police methods and "justified" incarceration served a better good. They did not believe that the Soviet Union should be scrutinized as if it were a Western capitalist and imperialist state. Their global analysis of the needs of imperialism in the Indian subcontinent provided the overarching context for Meerut and an angle from which to justify the defense of Soviet external and internal policies. Comintern statements on Arab movements, for example, emphasized Britain's use of Iraq, Palestine, and Egypt "to defend the approaches to India, to prepare for a war against the USSR, and to extend the spheres of influence East."[113] The Daily Worker cited the remarks of the former Labour prime minister Ramsay MacDonald, now the leader of the 1931 coalition National Government, as evidence of Britain's present ambition: "Let us come into power . . . and I will put a stop to all the nefarious activities of that body [Comintern] not only in India but throughout the colonial East."[114] In India, defendant Shaukat Usmani's mood darkened to despair, and his health declined after a visitor to the Meerut jail brought the news that two of the Indians who had been with him in Moscow had been executed by the Soviet authorities.[115]

In the wake of Hitler's accession to power in 1933, the Nazis pursued a murderous campaign of repression against the German Left. The communists shifted focus from the campaigns in support of the Scottsboro and Meerut defendants to the support of "German relief." In London, Münzenberg's associates mounted the mock trial of the Reichstag Fire defendants. The sentencing, appeals, and final proceedings of the Meerut Trial occurred almost simultaneously to those of the Reichstag Fire Trial in Leipzig and its "mock" event in London. In the United States, African American communist Angelo Herndon faced his jail sentence for instigating riots in Atlanta. Events in China escalated, and Bernard Shaw, Agnes Smedley, and Madame Sun Yat-Sen traveled with others to observe events in Shanghai, where Japan had invaded in January. Indian organizations abroad met in greater numbers than ever before, as expatriates became more concerned about developments at home, even if their actions had little impact on events in India. In one episode, a memo in support of the Meerut prisoners from the Japanese section of the New York ILD arrived in London, sent by a group of Japanese and Chinese American workers who met to declare their support for the campaign.[116]

Figure 4.4. "Speakers' Corner." Saklatvala speaking about the Reichstag fire, Hyde Park, London, September 24, 1933, reportedly calling for the release of the suspects being held in Germany (GettyImages).

The first announcements of the Meerut Trial's outcome on the wires carried the words of Prosecutor Yorke, who stated that "the progress of the conspiracy" had resulted in the establishment of the workers' and peasants' parties, exemplified by the leading role that the Girni Kamgar Union and Bombay CPI members played in the 1928 textile strikes.

> The fact that the revolution was not expected actually to come to pass for some years seems to me to be no defense whatsoever. No one expects to bring about a revolution in a day. It is in the light of all the above facts that I have endeavored to assess the relative guilt of the different accused in this case and to "make the punishment to fit the crime."[117]

The defendants individually received sentences of transportation for life, transportation for five or ten years, or sentences of "rigor imprisonment," a term of hard labor in incarceration.

Labour party leader and pacifist George Lansbury described the terms as "savagely severe," as if defendants on trial in the United Kingdom had been sent to jail simply for being members of the CPGB.[118] The liberal *Manchester*

Guardian derided the notion that the prisoners themselves had dictated the length of the trial.

> They were kept in prison for nearly four years: the argument that it was their own obstructive methods which kept them there is no more relevant than the similar argument used in the Sacco and Vanzetti case in the United States. . . . What one can believe is that if the Indian authorities wished to give an unexampled advertisement of Communism in India this tortuous pursuit of young hotheads, with their chatter, their schoolboy codes in secret ink, their reading parties pouring piously over the works of Stalin, was the best way to set about it . . . [and the] evidence of a capacity to see specters in the night.[119]

Saklatvala's statement on the verdict was very different:

> By savage and appalling sentences, after a monstrous trial, the British Raj in India has proclaimed to her 350 million conquered slaves that henceforth the study of the mighty triumph of Communism in the USSR, which in seven brief years has put to shame the inhuman results produced by 150 years of British rule in India, will be visited upon the heads of Communists in India with a revengeful ruthlessness.
>
> Anyone daring to propound the true blessings of Communism to workers in India will be looked upon as a conspirator against the King of England, the deity and god incarnate representing modern Indo-British capitalism. . . . several British publicists—almost everyone a notorious anticommunist—had visited India and had written from India, openly confessing that the whole trial was absolutely void of all reality.

He referred to the low wages of Indian home workers and industrial workers, grounds for agitation and organizing. In the early months of 1933, Saklatvala used the pages of the *Daily Worker* to record detailed stock dividend tables showing the profit margins reaped by British firms, noting with incredulity that a labor investigation conducted by Ellen Wilkinson, and others who traveled to India, had supposedly uncovered no "profit-mongers." He published the financial data of the Bengal coal companies, taken from the pages of the journal *Capital*. The ILP and the Glasgow Trades Council lobbied the Scottish Trades Union Congress to take action around the verdict. A coalition including the engineers' union (ASE), the Friends of the Soviet Union, and the National Unemployed Workers Movement joined together to call for the dismissal of the sentences.[120]

Saklatvala continued to write about the imperial economy, conferring responsibility for the Meerut proceedings on those whom he saw as directly engaged in economic exploitation and its political consequences:

> More than any other capitalist section of India, the textile mill owners are largely responsible for the foul persecution of the Meerut prisoners whose leadership had commenced to give very effective protection to the poor, illiterate cotton and jute

workers, working under one of the worst forms of exploitation in the world. . . . In spite of all the despicable efforts of the Tory and Labour Governments to describe it as a super-imposed Moscow conspiracy . . . in the perfectly genuine, natural and very necessary effort of the Indian workers to seek their emancipation under effective Communist leadership, the facts stand out clearly that the Indian textile workers were engaged in resisting one of the worst forms of economic and political oppression known in the world . . . .Who have been the oppressors of Indian labor for the last two generations? They have been not only capitalists of both races, but British managers, foremen, engineers, superintendents, onlookers and technical heads have also assisted the capitalists in overcoming the colored colonial labor.[121]

Saklatvala invoked his own family, as he had done in his exchange with Gandhi years earlier. "It is notorious that the Saklatvala family in Bombay is as flourishing capitalists as any British counterpart of theirs. They believe in 'kindness to animals' but they abhor the idea that labor should dare to fight capitalism as their inveterate foe."[122]

After the sentencing and before the defendants' appeals began in March, the Meerut Prisoners' defense committee issued *For the Meerut Prisoners: Against Imperialist Terror*, by French communist writer Romain Rolland. The pamphlet described the global context of the trial:

... an Imperialism of money, which transcending all the national antagonisms and conflicts, dominates the international policy of the great Empires . . . a state of siege reigns secretly or openly in Bengal as well as in Annam [Vietnam], in Batavia [Jakarta], at Hanoi and at Peshawar . . . In May of 1932, there were 80,000 prisoners in British India, whose only crime had been to follow the watchword of non-violence of Gandhi and of the Indian National Congress.[123]

Rolland wrote of the "monstrous trial" at Meerut.

English liberalism is not only powerless to repair the verdict, it is even incapable of conceiving either the illegal proceedings which have become current or the exceptional laws which the imperialist terrorism of Great Britain applies to six-sevenths of the people of the empire, to one-sixth of the population of the globe.[124]

Rolland's pamphlet and the attempt to organize a global mobilization at the time of the appeals engaged new interest in the Meerut campaign. By May 1930, groups like the South Suburban Co-operative in London were giving money for the Meerut cause, and the donors included Labour party members. The defendants joined the ranks of many other thousands of Indian political prisoners. K. N. Joglekar's wife wrote to the *New Leader* in July 1933 of the transfer of her husband and the others from the "A" wing of the prison to the "C" class.

There are no proper arrangements for washing clothes, and consequently they are always full of fleas and lice. They are not even allowed toothpaste, soap, oil or shaving materials. "C" class prisoners are not expected to read. . . . They are not allowed to purchase paper or books. Each three months they may write and receive one letter and have one visit from relatives.[125]

On August 4, 1933, the courts announced the results of the Meerut appeals, eliciting both relief and vindication. These sentiments were not lost on those in Britain seeking justice for prisoners of fascism in Germany. The court granted many commutations, and most sentences were reduced to a year. Nine of the twenty-seven defendants were freed, among them Lester Hutchinson, and all others received reduced sentences—Bradley's sentence was reduced from ten years to one, and Spratt's from twelve years to two; the *New York Times* reported that at that point the estimated cost to India of the trial was £120,000.[126] Hutchinson recalled the proceedings:

> There was a large crowd assembled to hear the judgement. I was present after having packed my belongings expecting to return to jail in the evening. . . . But as the chief Justice read the judgement, the general feeling of depression was changed to one of utter astonishment. The sentence of transportation for life was reduced to three years. . . . all the rest including myself were either acquitted or released on the imprisonment they had already undergone. . . . I was now blandly told that I had committed no offense against the law. . . . Rather ungratefully, my only thought as I left the building a free man was that I was now unemployed. I had been a Meerut accused so long that I had begun to regard it as a profession.[127]

The left press in Britain applauded the decisions, but soberly reminded the celebrants that the German prisoners deserved the same treatment. Wilhelm Volk was beheaded at Hamburg for his anti-Nazi activity and Paul Hoffmann died of wounds inflicted by storm troopers, their deaths announced ten days after the Meerut appeals. In Woodstock, Alabama, three African Americans awaiting trial were lynched.[128] In London George Padmore began to use Jomo Kenyatta's address as his own; his time as a Comintern leader and German prisoner had come to an end. Arnold Ward wrote to William Patterson, in New York, to say that there had not been a single London meeting called on colonial issues, not even one provoked by the "shootings in Palestine." He listed all the possible instigators: Ward's own Negro Welfare Association, the ILD, the CPGB, the Friends of the Soviet Union, the Indian Policy Group, the left Minority Movement among trade unionists, the LAI, the communist-supported journal *Labour Monthly*, and the Unemployed Workers Movement, reporting, "and yet nothing doing so comrade where do I come in comrade write us a line and cheer us up. Let's know about Scottsboro and also Ada Wright."[129]

MEERUT MEDITATIONS

The Meerut Trial exposed the hypocrisies of British imperial justice. There was one set of rules and procedures that seemed to apply to those who might have been prosecuted at home for their views, but were not, while those in the most valued British colony, in possession of the selfsame literature and holding many of the same ideas as their counterparts in Britain—including support for an end to British rule—had endured years of incarceration. In one context, as in the case of Saklatvala, one was an MP for a time. In the other, one spent the same number of years imprisoned. The trial not only defined the basic precepts of Indian communism as it was articulated and understood by its adherents in the early 1930s, but it also shut that movement down for a significant period by immobilizing its key leaders: "A Party leader admitted that Meerut smashed the crude beginnings of the CPI and wiped away the entire all-India leadership."[130] In both respects, the trial secured communism's rhetorical and practical authority under fire, especially when the judge singled out the 1928 strike wave and the critical role taken by communists. Meerut established some celebrity for Indian communism and defeated at least one of the purposes of the prosecution who sought not only to demobilize but to discredit and bury the movement. Though the CPI was rendered illegal, its notoriety was enhanced. Hutchinson reflected upon the impulse to prosecute and its deleterious results for the British authorities: "It was, however, too late to turn back. . . . Men were kept in prison without having been convicted until it became a public scandal, lawyers waxed fat, the world changed, men died and were born, and the Meerut conspiracy case went on its futile way as if seeking to rival Tennyson's brook."[131]

In 1936 Nehru wrote about the allure of the trial and the power of its global context. "The younger men and women of the Congress, who used to read Bryce on Democracies and Morley and Keith and Mazzini, were now reading, when they could get them, books on socialism and communism and Russia. The Meerut conspiracy case had helped greatly in directing people's minds to these new ideas, and the world crisis had compelled attention."[132] Philip Spratt claimed, "we had done what most young men wanted to do and but for the Mahatma would have done."[133] Hutchinson recalled that he and others made a train journey under guard to seek bail at the court at Allahabad during their years in prison: "Strangers entered our compartment and discussed with us topical questions with the deference due to political martyrs; and we basked in the sun of their approval and delivered ourselves of oracular and sometimes sweeping statements."[134]

In the trial's aftermath, Nehru confided that "The Meerut Case Defense Committee did not have an easy time with the accused. There were different kinds of people among these, with different types of defenses, and often there was an utter absence of harmony among them."[135] His father presumably supplied him with information during the elder Nehru's time as leader of the defense. This discordant feature of the Meerut Trial beckoned comparison with the Scottsboro case, in which communists and anticommunists took years to build what remained an unstable front outside of the courtroom, rather than inside among the nonpolitical defendants. Lester Hutchinson widened the charge of hypocrisy leveled at the British government over Meerut to include its transatlantic allies: "President Roosevelt himself is reported to have interested himself in the case, although this, in view of the notorious prosecution of innocent men in America, is an example of the pot calling the kettle black."[136]

On the face of it, the prosecutions at Meerut and Scottsboro had two fundamental similarities. The defendants in both were almost entirely persons of color though the three white prisoners in Meerut also constituted a critical difference. In each case, no clear evidence was presented to support the charges leveled against the accused. In neither case were the defendants guilty as charged, though the Meerut prisoners were indeed those whom the court identified as purveyors of political activism. While the Meerut defendants' political sympathies were clear, they were not conspirators in the treasonous terms set forth in the indictment. Most of the Meerut defendants were released after a relatively short period of time. The Scottsboro defendants served a total of 130 years in jail. The Jim Crow South was proving less maneuverable for nine African American youngsters than was the longest trial in British imperial history for thirty-six mostly communist, mostly Indian defendants. In related developments, Meerut and Scottsboro were celebrated as antifascist causes yet Nazi thuggery increasingly found many of its victims in the streets, not in the courtrooms or the jail cells awaiting trial. The Reichstag Fire Trial was an early exception.

The Labour party may have pressured the National Government to let its guard down when the time of the Meerut appeals finally came. The colonial state, and parliamentary opinion could see their strategies backfiring. Panic had promoted the trial in the first place. A "coterie of Communist leaders had gained a powerful following in the working class neighborhoods." Historian Chandavarkar stressed the relative distance of Indian Congress from the trade unions in comparison to the street-level actions associated with the Meerut defendants. The prosecutors feared that the nationalists, their "main enemies," were infatuated with Soviet appeals to their desires for independence from Britain, while Nehru's political background and his inclinations, which other sectors also embraced, contributed to government anxiety.[137] The Meerut trial came before Nehru's increasing disenchantment with Soviet internal repression; it served to enhance rather than detract from the appeal of the Soviet model.[138] The *Manchester Guardian* expressed a common view. "There was also a general impression that the Meerut prisoners had been convicted in connection with activities devoted to improving the conditions prevailing among the lower orders in India."[139] In London the Labour party's *Daily Herald* called the trial "one of the greatest judicial scandals in the empire." The court testimony contained an exposé of conditions in the country that incensed independent radicals and liberals in Britain and elsewhere. The government's preoccupation with a murky possibility of revolutionary conspiracy at the expense of the promulgation of reform, was polarizing. Even the unidentified "Comrade

Bell's" report from Britain to the Comintern insisted on the need for a youth organization in India, and for more internal party education about the issues related to the trial:

> We have in many cases a very sentimental approach to this question . . . [counting the] figures of terrific poverty which exists in Ireland, India and the rest and the terrible oppression and lack of freedom. . . . such an approach simply strengthens the hatred of the masses and does not realize its objective. . . . [We] need instead the knowledge and clear understanding that British imperialism draws wealth and strengthens the chains which bind the working class in this country, from India. . . . [We need] a clear understanding of working class emancipation . . . a real anti-imperialist movement, real anti-imperialist feeling.[140]

The establishment journal of foreign policy, the *Round Table*, assumed the pernicious influence of communism when it assessed the trial. Imperial Britain needed "more definitive legislation against Communism."

> [T]hat the sterilization had only temporary effects is evident, not only from the theoretical vaporings of such leaders as Nehru but also from the obvious and increasing attraction toward communism of Indian youth, of labor, and of the left-wing of the Congress, and of terrorists. Observers of England or other countries where the urge towards communism is offset by an intelligent appreciation of its inherent dangers and its inevitable reactions, by civic experience and by a well-founded faith in the beneficence of constitutional progress, can have little conception of India's receptivity to communism.[141]

Meerut exposed the fatuousness of liberal imperialism. It thrust the defendants into the consciousness of the adherents of the much larger nationalist social movements, straight to the heart of interlaced experience and memory that was successfully attracting hundreds of thousands, and ultimately millions, to its banners in India. Even with this greater visibility, Philip Spratt felt that he and his comrades had not behaved properly toward the other defendants who were not their political cadre: "We were not frank with them." They, in turn, did not like Spratt and the other communists. He recalled his name appearing first on the list of defendants. "Race snobbery," as he put it, led the authorities to rank him before others in a concession to the uniqueness of his and Bradley's and Hutchinson's presences. He felt the comrades had been "compelled" to criticize the nationalists even despite the achievements of civil disobedience and that in so doing "they looked silly." One of their lawyers told them in the early days of the case that "communists did not understand India." Spratt never left his adopted country, nor did he remain a Marxist and drifted instead into publishing writings on India as viewed through the lens of psychoanalysis: "Reading Gandhi I began to see what he may have meant."[142] Lester Hutchinson, the fellow traveler who left the fold only slowly and in England, wrote of Meerut in its immediate aftermath, "It began as sensational melodrama. . . .

although the climax was obscure, the interval between the climax and the end was so long that bathos was inevitable."[143]

Aftermath: Revelations

In early 1934 eight hundred people reportedly showed up in London to greet Ben Bradley upon his return from Meerut after his release from custody. Lester Hutchinson was among them, and he spoke about the great poverty of India. "This meeting should not be merely for the reception of people who were unfortunate enough to get into prison in India, or for the release of those still in prison. It should be turned into a demonstration of the solidarity of the British working classes with the Indian working classes." For the rest of the thirties, Ben Bradley would remain a communist spokesman on Indian affairs. He told a tale of intrigue. "On the 23rd I boarded a train to go to Bombay. When I got down from the train at Grant Road Station, Bombay, two CID [Criminal Investigation Department] police officers . . . who had been traveling on the same train with me, ran after me and informed me that I was under arrest." After the first few weeks on the stump in Britain, Bradley claimed that the repression in India "surpasse[d] the terror in Germany and Austria,"[144] seizing rhetorical ground that would quickly disappear under his feet as the conditions faced by white Europeans shifted and worsened. The contest between imperialism and fascism as twin evils, groups of coconspirators who had fallen out among themselves, consumed the broad racial politics of the rest of the decade. It confounded anticolonial politics, lessening their immediacy and influence. Just after the Meerut appeals, Saklatvala tried a second time for a seat on the LCC; in an anticommunist climate fueled by Labour's hostility, he failed to win election in Battersea once more. But the Reichstag Fire campaign agitation quickly galvanized him and his fellow communists, embracing others in Liberal and Labour circles, and exemplifying the changing priorities for mobilization.

In April 1934 fifty thousand Bombay textile workers went out on strike against wage cuts and rationalization, demanding equal pay, a minimum wage, rent reductions, and trade-union recognition. Extensive repression followed, and the government accused the communists of playing leading roles. In London a series of support meetings passed resolutions of solidarity with the strikers, and seventy thousand workers again poured from the Bombay mills after a May Day demonstration. M. N. Roy's forces swelled the numbers of strikers in a united front. The former Meerut defendant Joglekar was injured in a violent confrontation with the police. The strike days witnessed "fraternization between Hindus and Muslims" and by mid-May, fully thirty-one mills were still shut.[145]

Saklatvala was bound for Moscow. His pilgrimage to the Soviet Union, spent partly in the company of Scots communist William Gallacher and CPGB leader Harry Pollitt received the attentions of the press. Saklatvala betrayed a hint of the private meaning that he attached to the trip: "Now Russia is a wonderful place, but new Soviet Asia even more so."[146] His itinerary revealed his passions—Tashkent, Fergana, Stalinabad [Dushanbe, Tajikistan], Ashkabad, Baku, Batoum, Erivan, and Tifis (Tbilisi). At each stop, he ceremoniously delivered resolutions of support, exchanging greetings and promoting a diplomacy of his own making. Long after his death, his daughter and biographer Sehri Saklatvala remarked that "He had made copious notes on his tour but sadly they have all been lost to us."[147] But some of the material that she referred to lay in Saklatvala's hidden party stash. A long private memo made its way into the archives of the Comintern. He mused about this trip and expressed his doubts about the efficacy of the British party's work on colonial and imperial issues, complaining that he had suggested to the party that a prominent Indian lawyer be brought in on the Reichstag Fire Trial campaign.

> However, nothing happened and a purely European Communism was got up and it has become the object of derision among certain colonial circles. The Indians and Africans naturally feel that the example of such an additional popular trial might be used as a wholesome check against British imperialist trials in their own countries, but they are kept out of contact with such international activities. These small things have a big effect, and in India among a certain section of Indian youth internationalism has come to be disbelieved in, and Italian and German fascism are taken as good examples of intense nationalism.[148]

Saklatvala confessed to his fear of an "overt nationalistic tendency" in himself, unbefitting a communist. But his trip to the Soviet Union had convinced him of the legitimacy of his concerns. Racism was endemic and had to be fought:

> I had heard adverse comments about Negroes and Indians [in England] but on the whole I have always felt that it was want of due ability and right conception on their part that was responsible. After traveling international and autonomous regions [in the Soviet Union], I find that the Party policy in Great Britain ought to have been different, and the resentment of the colonials, though exaggerated, and unnecessarily hostile, is one that is natural and has to be foreseen by good Communists.[149]

These remarks expose an inner Saklatvala with many doubts and criticisms, whose preoccupations revolved around the CPGB's treatment of fellow Indians and blacks. While he did not voice such views publicly, his steady participation in numerous public meetings of expatriate and Indian advocacy organizations and his friendships across the political spectrum had always indicated his inclusiveness and his rejection of a closed, inbred party life. These documents equally reveal his misplaced confidence in the Soviet model of race relations, and the degree to which he, like many Indian revolutionaries, saw the Soviet central Asian experiment as a model for India.

Figure 4.5. "Happy Children of Soviet Kazakhstan" appeared with Labour MP Jennie Lee's "Just Back from Russia," in the ILP's *New Leader*, March 27, 1936, p. 2. The article recounts Lee's third trip to the Soviet Union (reproduced by kind permission of the Syndics of Cambridge University Library).

New developments in Soviet nationalities policies occurred in the thirties and were visible at the time of Saklatvala's last visit. The Soviet planners designated certain peoples of the republics more "culturally backward" than the advanced Germans, Poles, and Finns or even those ethnicities in the tier "below" them: Russians, Belorussians, Ukrainians, Jews, Georgians, and Armenians. These more "backward" peoples, including the "Greeks, Kazhaks, Chinese and Koreans, Kurds, Mongolians, Persians, Turkmen, Tatars, Uzbeks, Roma, Chechens, [and] Eskimos" were supposed to benefit from social policies devised both to address their respective literacy and educational levels and to combat the "presence of the oppression of women, religious fanaticism, nomadism, racial hostility, clan vengeance . . . and [a] dearth of cadres in soviet construction." Even if Saklatvala was not an enthusiast of the hierarchical caste system of 1930s Soviet racial doctrine, he felt the need to address the historic dilemmas of central Asia and what he perceived as Soviet progress toward such goals made a deep impression upon him as a communist and as an Indian.[150]

Saklatvala's meditations also reveal the depth of his feeling of bitterness toward the party's decisions in the Reichstag Fire campaign, and party members' racial attitudes more broadly. Saklatvala was a high-ranking loyalist among the small group of Asian communists in the West, and coming after a tour of the Soviet Union, his comments assumed the imaginative quality of a final testament. A colleague recalled Saklatvala collapsing on the Russia trip; he knew that he was ill. On August 31, 1934, a month after his return, he had agreed to dedicate a new bust of Lenin at the Marx Memorial Library in Clerkenwell. But he suffered a heart attack from which he never recovered.

FASCISM AND THE HOPES FOR INDIA

The Second Brown Book of the Hitler Terror and the Burning of the Reichstag began to circulate just after Saklatvala returned to London from Russia.[151] In August 1934 the Kirti Kisan party (worker-peasant party) in India began to gain ground and the government unleashed further repression on textile strike leaders, including the Meerut defendant George Adhikari and his brother. Both were transported under the General Powers Act and found themselves in a region of India unknown to them, cut off from political activity. In 1935 the Seventh Congress of the Comintern greeted the new and more intensive period of global repression by inaugurating the "united front against fascism." "The British Parliament promulgated the Bengal reform legislation that enfranchised a sixth of the Indian population, bringing the electorate to 30 million. Indian Congress won victories in the subsequent election, and electoral reform stirred a wider political debate about the rights of a colonized people. The British communists called the 1935 Act, the "Slavery for India Bill," yet its passage provided an unparalleled occasion for public discourse.[152] In January, rioting shook Kolhapur State. The ILP's Fenner Brockway wrote to a friend about the prevailing atmosphere in India: "Suspicion alone detains people. . . . some of the *détenus* have been in concentration camps for six years."[153] The conflict between a strategy of a negotiated, evolutionary path toward greater independence and the call for a quick and clear response to continued repression dominated nationalist, liberal, socialist, and communist debate until war overshadowed all. Nehru's centrality in Indian politics grew, even in the eyes of his critics on the British and Indian Left. He allowed Clement Attlee and others in the Labour party to intercede to gain his release from prison in India.[154]

Saklatvala spoke before the Coloured Seamen's Association in South Shields, a group he had known over the course of many years, whose members lived in racially diverse port-side neighborhoods. His attention remained fixed upon his fellow colonial subjects, and "purely European communism," as he phrased it, did not consume him. The extensive campaign for the release of the German communist leader Ernst Thälmann, being held by the Nazis, provoked Saklatvala to write to the *Daily Worker* in August 1935 from his home in St. Albans Villas, Highgate. The Berlin Penal Conference had confronted the Nazi jurists' assertion that the German concentration camps were rehabilitative and retributive.

Dear Comrade,

One reads this morning the healthy news of British visitors to the International Penal Congress at Berlin . . . demanding the liberation of untried prisoners like Ernst Thälmann. This is in keeping with the new spirit of international moral pressure against great wrongs done by governments who presume to have freedom of action for internal affairs regardless of moral opinion abroad. This is splendid. But may I point out that it is of utmost urgency and moral importance that British lovers of freedom supervise and criticize the conduct of their own rulers in India and other colonies? Government heads, like dictators in fascist Italy or Germany, or like the Viceroy of India, like to make their task easy by placing political opponents in the prison cells, even without any trial and plausible excuses, for such an action can always be found abundantly.

Are not the British friends who are making such noble efforts for giving publicity to the oppressive and unjust imprisonment of Thälmann aware that at this moment the British Viceroy of India is holding in prison in Bengal and other parts of India nearly 100 persons who have not been tried, and are even not intended to be tried, and held in prison for a few months to a few years? I appeal to the returning British delegates from the International Penal Congress to take up the question of *détenus* and other prisoners in India as an urgent and solemn duty, and I also trust the goodwill and support of your paper in such a campaign—Yours fraternally[155]

Saklatvala had expressed his frustrations privately in the memorandum about his Soviet sojourn, but now these sentiments appeared in the open air of the London street corner at a time when the communist press had a sustained readership in the thousands. As if to underline the point, and make the same global connections, Harold Laski introduced Hutchinson's *Conspiracy at Meerut* with a similar plea that forms the epigraph of this chapter.[156]

Nehru sympathized with this effort to link colonial oppression with the fate of the European continent. In March 1935 as he waited by his wife's bedside, he wrote to his sister, Vijaya Lakshmi, from Switzerland, asking for his German grammar books: "Two days ago I heard Hitler on the radio. He was speaking at Nuremberg. I could not understand what he said but the frequent cheers were impressive."[157] Months later, he wrote of the German peasants and their children whom he saw on the roads near his wife's second hospital. They said "Heil Hitler" to him, and a "forest of huge swastikas" greeted him.[158] After a visit with writer and Meerut activist Romain Rolland, Nehru and his daughter Indira arrived in London to a rapturous and unprecedented reception.[159] Nehru's prison memoir had just been published. He requested special copies for German exiled dramatist Ernst Toller, ILP leader J. F. Horrabin, Padmore's friend Reginald Reynolds, Fenner Brockway, Harold Laski, and Krishna Menon of the India League—covering many points of view on the Indian activist spectrum. Nehru held many meetings under the public eye. They included sessions with the All India Women's Association leadership, Lady Simon's colleague Gilbert Murray, Liberal politician H.A.L. Fisher, and labor and social historian G.D.H. Cole— many of whom moved in circles that had embraced the Scottsboro campaign. In Paris, Nehru visited writers André Malraux and André Gide, the latter a signatory of an Anglo-French, anti-Hitler petition of early 1933.[160]

Saklatvala's death on January 13, 1936, elicited tributes across the British political community while India mourned him. The Bombay Municipal Corporation adjourned its council session early. Gandhi's secretary sent a missive on his behalf, while the former Meerut prisoner Purand Chand Joshi read the last message that Saklatvala had sent to India—a plea for unity and the pursuit of the Communist-conceived united front. Labour leaders Lansbury and Attlee spoke of him as a parliamentary friend, intimating that his time in the House had been one of alliances and collabouration rather than iconoclasm. Trade-union leaders Ben Tillett of the dockworkers and H. H. Elvin, with whom Saklatvala had worked in the National Union of Clerks before 1919, alluded to Saklatvala's permanent break with radical trade unionism for communism. Reginald Bridgeman spoke of his life "sacrificed . . . in [the] struggle for the freedom of India from foreign domination." Willie Gallacher, his traveling companion on the last Soviet trip, said that his was a legacy that bound "the toilers of Britain and of the colonial countries together." The Irish militant Pat Devine reminded his readers that Saklatvala had been the only MP to vote against Irish partition in 1923. An unnamed Negro Welfare Association leader, presumably Arnold Ward, magnanimously claimed it had been "a great shock to the Negro peoples throughout the world to learn of his death."[161]

On January 20, Zoroastrian priests presided at Saklatvala's funeral. On the day of his cremation, the first of many memorials was held in Farringdon, at which Harry Pollitt, Tom Mann, Bridgeman, and K. S. Bhatt spoke. Pollitt focused on Saklatvala's attraction to central Asia. He recalled that in Turkestan, Kazakhstan, and the Trans-Caucasian territories, "for weeks he was wildly greeted by tens of thousands of people freed from the yoke of Tsarism. . . . 'Oh, Harry, what my people could do in India,' he said, 'if only they were as free as my comrades in those autonomous republics of the USSR.'" His parliamentary colleague Reginald Bishop noted that Saklatvala had refused the offer of the undersecretary of state for India under a Labour government, a concession as noble as it was self-sacrificing. "Those who only knew Saklatvala as a propagandist knew but part of the man. He had an amazing range of knowledge. He knew the cotton and metallurgical industries from A to Z. He would have been a tremendous organizing asset to Socialist Britain," adding that Saklatvala had never held any stocks in his family's Tata industries given his disdain for inherited wealth. The Comintern commemorated him. Nehru wrote a tribute from Austria for the *Daily Worker*.[162] Trade-union memorial letters poured forth, testimony to Saklatvala's record of service in the streets of Battersea.

Ten months later Nehru delivered a presidential address to the fiftieth session of the Indian Congress–movement meeting at Faizpur, Bombay Province. Its publication in Britain's *Daily Worker* signaled a united-front overture.

> Our problem of national freedom, as well as of social freedom, is but part of this great world problem. Even during these last eight months vast changes have come over the international situation. In Europe, Fascism has been pursuing its triumphant course, introducing an open gangsterism in international affairs. We have seen Abyssinia succumb to it. We see today the horror and tragedy of Spain. How has Fascism grown so rapidly? To understand this, one must seek a clue in British foreign policy. This policy has been one of consistent support of Nazi Germany. We find British imperialism inclining more and more toward the Fascist Powers, though the language it uses, as is its old habit, is democratic in texture and pious in tone.... The Government of India Act of 1935, the new Constitution, stares at us offensively, this new charter of bondage which has been imposed on us.... The elections must be used to rally the masses to the Congress standard.[163]

Nehru marked out the clear stratagem of seeking electoral power. Indian Congress would wield this weapon in the remaining years before the war. He spoke aggressively of the British state and of its sympathies, his language stronger than Saklatvala's and his world outlook larger. He sketched the rough design of a position that Padmore and others articulated each in his own way, as war approached. This position assumed that empire wrought havoc for the peoples of the colonial world, not in the first instance as adversaries of European fascism, but as canon fodder in a coming war effort. Nehru and others would now attempt to forge a rhetoric and vision of internationalism that the Comintern did not muster or desire. The "national interests" of the Soviet state were dictated by other concerns.[164]

In August 1957 Meerut defendant S. H. Jhabvala published a succinct and pointed statement of Saklatvala's legacy in the conflicts between advocates of Indian independence and communism.

> Who roused India first to a consciousness of Communism? ... Who gave the first impetus to the Congress to shift its angle of thought towards economic freedom and win the country an unchallenged position as the builder of Peace in the world? Shapurji Saklatvala.... whereas Gandhi interpreted *Swaraj* as India remaining as a Dominion under British suzerainty, Saklatvala wrenched away India to the Soviet Union.[165]

Jhabvala further suggested that the British had savored the early debate between Saklatvala and Gandhi when such friction damaged the movement for independence. But Saklatvala's concern for a special communism for India also won him no favors among CPGB theoreticians. In the 1930s, R. P. Dutt wrote of Saklatvala: "Within the Communist Party his gifts as a speaker and his devotion to the cause were appreciated, but his understanding of the Marxist and Leninist doctrines was not considered adequate for a leader. He was a most attractive personality and spoke with remarkable fluency and distinction." In 1969 Dutt contributed an introduction to one of the biographies of Saklatvala at this later time, sentimentalizing him.

> During subsequent years, long after his death, when I traveled over the country on propaganda, and stayed in workers' homes in all parts of the country, I came to know how dearly his memory was cherished. In the conventional histories which now abound of Britain and the British Labour movement during this period, the academic chroniclers may not be aware of his role. But in the hearts of working class families all over Britain his memory lives and is honored.[166]

By the mid-thirties, the British Left was already committed in great numbers to "German relief" work and to Spain. The first anniversary of Saklatvala's death in 1937 was marked by a Battersea celebration of his life, the life of the fallen communist writer Ralph Bates killed in Spain, and the International Brigades. His wife, Sarah Saklatvala; Palme Dutt; Krishna Menon; and a representative from the Swaraj League addressed the crowd. Stafford Cripps's Socialist League and the ILP were fully represented, attesting to the public enthusiasm for the Spanish Republic that Indian nationalists and British socialists shared with the communists. The short-lived Unity Campaign between communists, the ILP, and the Labour party was in sway.[167] Two days later, 30 million Indians went to the polls. Ben Bradley took the occasion to lambaste the Indian constitution:

> [It is] not an advance towards democracy, rather does it tighten the dictatorial control of British imperialism.... In Bengal, over 2000 youths are in concentration camps, many of them have been there for seven and eight years without trial, and are likely to remain there indefinitely.... In 1936 suppression of civil liberties grew to an enormous degree.... Repressive measures are used to prevent any move of the Colonial peoples to extract themselves from the morass.... the demand of Hitler and his henchmen for the return of the colonies becomes more and more insistent. General Göring demands of Great Britain the return of the "swag"—as one bandit to another.[168]

In March Krishna Menon wrote about the elections in India for *New Leader*, describing the stance taken by the left wing of the Indian Congress in the wake of the provincial legislative contests in which Congress secured a stunning majority. In India the Congress socialists were preparing a one-day strike against what Nehru termed the imposed "Slave Constitution," and planned to fan out to build local assemblies at the village level in the effort toward the eventual calling of a large constituent assembly, "the *Grand Panchayat*," for which they fought, and which, Menon believed, would "terminate Imperialism in India." The Congress workers' agitation would "make a large contribution to the fight against World Fascism and War and the liberation of the working classes in the 'ruling' country."[169]

The Indian Congress had earlier failed to win any Muslim legislative seats in national contests, despite the provision for communal proportional representation; Congress victories among Muslims were at the provincial level. But Nehru claimed that Congress's grassroots work had uncovered "the same anti-imperialist spirit" in rural areas as among urban Hindu supporters. "Where we went to the masses direct, we won overwhelmingly." When Nehru arrived in London in April, he emphasized the implacable, antidemocratic quality of British foreign policy rather than engaging in a critique of the Indian Congress: "The forces that move it [British policy] have nothing to do with democracy; they are friendly to the development of the Fascist Powers." When the nationalist Subhas Chandra Bose became the new Indian Congress president, British communists found themselves in tacit support of a leader with a very different political perspective than Nehru's. Bose had left Cambridge for the Indian Civil Service and was imprisoned for the first time in 1921. He was president of the All-India Trades Union Congress during the Meerut Trial. His third prison term broke his health, and in 1933, he was permitted to leave India to seek medical assistance in Europe. In 1935 he published *The Indian Struggle, 1920-34*, in which he remained equivocal on the issue of the relationship between nationalism and fascism. In 1938 Palme Dutt questioned him about this matter in an interview for the *Daily Worker*. Bose explained, "Fascism had not yet started on its imperialist expedition, and it appeared to me as merely an aggressive form of nationalism."[170] Here lay a fundamental problem of the movement toward independence, not just in India, but throughout the imperial world. The question of whether to be antifascist could quickly become "whether to support the Allied War effort" or, in another guise, the question of whether to defend the actions or policies of the Soviet Union.

In 1938 Nehru again traveled to visit his daughter Indira, the future Prime Minister, at Oxford. He was now the foreign editor of his own newspaper and was anxious to be away from conflict in India.[171] Nehru's popularity in Britain was enhanced by his embrace of the Spanish Republic. He traveled from Marseille to Barcelona, accompanied by Krishna Menon, visiting the International Brigades, including an American unit of volunteers: "There Nehru had a lively chat with a Negro comrade, a sergeant and commander of his section. Who said color bar?" Nehru spoke hopefully with British communist William Rust as he departed.

I have been very greatly moved by my visit, and retain many a vivid impression: chiefly, that there is not the faintest chance of the Republic being crushed. . . . In India, we have followed the struggle afar off although actually our people have been mostly interested in China's fight for freedom. But after my experiences here I feel that Spain's fight for independence, like ours is bound to triumph, and that in the future both countries, free and independent, will be able to co-operate for the good of the world.

Figure 4.6. "Nehru and Indira" in London, June 23, 1938. On his far left is the Indian nationalist leader Krishna Menon, and on his immediate left, his daughter, the future Indian prime minister, Indira Gandhi (GettyImages).

He returned to London and spoke at an India League meeting that featured Paul Robeson and others—Stafford Cripps, Palme Dutt, and Ellen Wilkinson. Publisher Victor Gollancz chaired a Left Book Club gathering in his honor that brought three thousand people to the Queen's Hall. Nehru reportedly insisted that "they could not meet the menace of Fascism unless they took into account imperialism: no true anti-Fascist could ignore imperialism, as some of them tried to do." In the audience "were large numbers of Indians in national costume." The collection went to an India medical-aid unit going to China. At the end of June, Nehru spoke about the centrality of India to the global political crisis:

> Fundamentally the people of India are anti-Fascist Not in the same sharp way, of course, that we are here in the West, because the issues there are not so immediately actual.... the Indian people are opposed to the foreign policy of the British National Government and cannot tolerate to be associated with it.... In the first place, our aim is independence and the Indian people will not participate in a war that is not of their own choosing.... Fascism can only be successfully defeated in war if the popular anti-Fascist forces are really in control, in the leadership.... Thus ... we in India would be facing a problem very similar to that which the really anti-Fascist forces in Britain itself would be facing—the problem of ensuring that the war was being

conducted in a really anti-Fascist, democratic and thus anti-imperialist-manner. And our struggle for freedom would assist in solving this problem.[172]

Nehru threw down the gauntlet, and he was joined by ardent supporters of both socialism and national independence: "The Anti-Fascist British people should realize that it is not possible to conduct the anti-Fascist struggle successfully, if the anti-imperialist struggle is ignored. It is no more impossible to do that than it is to condemn the Fascist bombing of open towns in Spain and China while tolerating British bombing on the North-West frontier of India."[173] He made the same argument in an interview conducted by Fenner Brockway for *New Leader*, published two days later.

[T]he Indian people cannot but note the difference when British citizens are bombed in Spain and when Indian people are bombed on the North-West Frontier. . . . I do not say that the bombing in India is comparable . . . but the same principle is involved. Perhaps if British people will think over this point they will realize why in India we cannot regard the British Government as a symbol of democracy and cannot become enthusiastic about fighting for it in a war for democracy against dictatorship.[174]

Nehru addressed one thousand delegates at the London conference on "Peace and Empire" in mid-July, chaired by Viscount Robert Cecil, an architect of the League of Nations and Lady Simon's colleague in the Anti-Slavery Society.

[N]o one can afford to think of superficial remedies. . . . Nor can we think of an empire masquerading in terms of a commonwealth of nations. . . . such a commonwealth must be based on a world order and on peace and freedom for all peoples. . . . our problem, therefore, is to work for the independence of all subject peoples, not to make them narrow-minded nationalist units, but free partners in this larger order.[175]

He turned provocatively to the problem of racial exploitation in Spain and the inability of the Republican forces to address the dilemma of the Moorish troops recruited by Franco:

[T]here was delay in dealing with the Moors in Spanish Morocco, and the forces of reaction misled them and exploited them to their own advantage. So also delay elsewhere may have disastrous consequences when the crisis ripens or war comes. The subject peoples are no longer docile and capable of being used to suit the purposes of imperial powers.[176]

Finally, he spoke of the disruptions and instability in Palestine, where tensions between Arabs and Jews living in the British mandate were manifest.

In Palestine today we see a horrible struggle and the very imperialism that created this problem posing as an arbiter. We shall not have peace there through imperialism. . . . Every decent person sympathizes with the Jews in their terrible misfortunes and wishes them well. They have rights in Palestine which must be recognized and protected. But we must recognize that Palestine is essentially an Arab country and the present struggle is a struggle for independence.[177]

Nehru had an avid social life on these trips, befitting his celebrity and pre-sumed political future. In the face of the most urgent prewar crisis for Britain, he spent a weekend at Stafford Cripps's country house where he was inter-viewed by the hopeful Labour party leadership. He attended the Unity Theater in London with Labour MP Susan Lawrence, and saw Robeson perform.[178] He also visited the aging Fabian founders Sidney and Beatrice Webb. On a week-end at Lord Lothian's Aylsham, Norfolk residence, Nehru was joined by the Lord and Lady Astor and General and Lady Ironside—the couple whose for-mer bungalow had served as the courthouse for the Meerut Trial.[179] Nehru wrote to his sister, "the fact of the matter is that world events and especially the possibility of India not cooperating in a war, have shaken up people. This pros-pect is a most disturbing one and even die-hard Tories now talk rather vaguely of independence for India."[180] He traveled to Paris for the International Peace Campaign's meeting on the "Bombing of Open Towns," attended by the Span-ish Civil War heroine La Passionaria, Dolores Ibarruri, and he addressed the conference on the subject of the German bombing of Spain, before traveling on to Prague, Budapest, and significantly, Munich.[181]

Upon Nehru's return to London, he was engulfed by "Chamberlainism." Crowds stayed in churches all night long during the Munich Crisis. In Octo-ber, after the invasion of Czechoslovakia, Nehru observed, "India has followed this tragic drama of betrayal with intense interest. From long experience her people have learned not to trust the promises of the British Government and yet recent developments in British foreign policy have amazed and shocked them." Britain, Hitler, and Mussolini had all spoken of "self-determination." Yet, he said, "it is not peace, but continuous conflict, blackmail—the rule of violence, and ultimately war."[182]

A one-day strike involving 200,000 workers gripped Bombay a month later, the greatest single day of labor action since 1928–29. The police opened fire on the strikers, and the protests spread through several other parts of the coun-try. The Indian government now faced a situation in which the Indian Con-gress membership in Sind, for example, had risen from 8,500 to over 24,000, with Muslims forming a majority of the new recruits. The United Provinces boasted a million and a half adherents. Nehru continued to comment on for-eign affairs as the domestic conflict intensified. Early in 1938 he condemned Britain's recognition of the Franco government: "The Indian people emphati-cally dissociate themselves from the policy of the British Government," and he returned to speak to the Indian Congress in March 1939 on Britain's betrayal of Czechoslovakia and Spain, "the murder of democracy."[183] He traveled to Hanoi and China that August, stayed with Chiang Kai-shek and Madame Chi-ang, and met Nelson Johnson, the U.S. ambassador. Nehru wrote rapturously of the need for freedom for all the countries of Asia and Africa. He sent ad-vanced copies of his latest book to the Roosevelts; Paul Robeson's wife, Eslanda; Roger Baldwin of the ACLU, and Du Bois. The linguist and translator of Tagore,

Edward Thompson, father of the postwar historian, also received a copy at Bledlow, Buckinghamshire; Nehru kept his many councils.[184]

The lingering impact of the death of Kamala Nehru, in 1936, at Lausanne colored Nehru's reflections on the era: "Munich was a shock hard to bear and the tragedy of Spain became a personal sorrow to me. As these years of horror succeeded one another, the sense of impending catastrophe overwhelmed me, and my faith in a bright future for the world became dim." He recalled that he had increasingly perceived all of the crises as a single global dilemma.[185] The moderate forces that had made up the Indian Congress shifted, and the Congress expressed its broad sympathy for anti-imperial China, Abyssinia, Palestine, and Spain. The world was soon at war. But in the middle of the thirties, Nehru had written to his sister of the nationalist moment and of its power and its sources of strength. He identified "its single greatest reason" for coming into being as a sentiment that could be shared by all Indians who experienced British rule—the "racial inequality [Britain] took for granted and the system of segregation that maintained it."[186] In this belief, he had a deep bond with Saklatvala's views as expressed in the memoranda written months before the latter's death. The will to end this organization of society had led them both into the circles of European communism and had at the same time distanced one privately and the other publicly from a full assimilation, even apart from their official political differences. If Saklatvala had lived, he would have been sorely tested by the events of the later thirties. Nehru found his words. He found the rhetorical means to posit a struggle against empire as an essential cornerstone of antifascism. Most in the West did not share his outlook in the thirties, but global fascism was not defeated without the spilling of colonial blood.

Nehru and George Padmore shared the view that anti-imperialism was an intrinsic part of an antifascist worldview. Both were wrong about the coming contest. The other empires did not fall as Germany and Italy fell, nor did the vast Soviet empire ever become the leader of the "darker races" that Indian activists as different as Nehru and Saklatvala had hoped for. But the pronouncement that "no true antifascist could ignore imperialism" remained as a lightning rod for the "Quit India" movement, and as a curse upon the immediate aftermath of war. Imperialism lay as a great behemoth upon the antifascist democrats. They had not yet been recruited in large numbers to the banner that called for its overthrow. For them, the antifascist struggle was a separate and urgent one; it was a European problem, a problem largely of the West and the Anglo-Saxon world; it was just and noble to protect others from the fascist peril. The foretelling of liberation and of the dangers of democracy's persistent imperial ambition required the uncommon visionary eyes of the prophet.

Chapter 5

DIASPORAS: REFUGEES AND EXILES

The air in London was suffocating. . . . Fritz Kortner and Johanna Hofer, Oscar
Homolka and many others were furiously learning English. However the Allies
had permitted the Germans to rebuild their fleet, Mosley and his followers pa-
raded in the streets and Berthold told me that watching such a demonstration
Fritz Kortner had exclaimed, "My next screen test will be in Chinese!" . . . [Lon-
don] was filled with German refugees. . . . Everyone hoped to go to Hollywood or
New York, and was waiting for a visa to the USA.
  —*Salka Viertel, Dorchester Hotel, 1932*

I do not know what I was to be charged with. There are thousands of people in
concentration camps today who do not know what they are charged with."
  —*Ernst Toller, Mock Reichstag Fire Trial, 1933*

How he survived them they could never understand:
Had they not beggared him themselves to prove
They could not live without their dogmas or their land?
  —*W. H. Auden, from Diaspora*

ON JANUARY 24, 1933, in the first days following Hitler's assumption of
power, a statement calling for assistance to German refugees appeared in London. Its signers included the French writer André Gide, the filmmaker Ivor
Montagu, and the trade unionist and Labour MP John Jagger.[1] A month later,
the aid organization Workers International Relief, issued an appeal on behalf
of its centers in Germany.

[Workers are being] fed and organized to continue the fight against fascism. . . . Socialist and Communist meetings and newspapers are suppressed, working-class organizations proscribed, and raids and suppressions carried out against the more
open-minded sections and press of the German people. Against the Jews the methods
of the Tsar are being used. . . . Nor is the attack confined to political organizations.

The signatures of writer Louis Golding, Helen Crawfurd, sexologist Havelock
Ellis, Henry Nevinson, Harry Pollitt, Sylvia Pankhurst, Carmel Haden Guest,
physicist Hyman Levy, and Shapurgi Saklatvala all appeared on the statement—
a largely but not exclusively communist group in outlook and commitment.

These signatories, along with Padmore's close friend the ILP writer Ethel Mannin, and Ellen Wilkinson, met to form the British German Relief Committee for the Release of the Victims of the Fascist Terror (hereafter, "Relief Committee") in order to "raise opposition to fascism" and to engage in "materially assisting the victims of the present rule in Germany." Isobel Brown, an indefatigable communist activist, served as one of its secretaries. Many noncommunists as well as "Jewish speakers," appeared on the platform at the group's demonstration in Hyde Park a week later. The proceeds from Paul Robeson's April performances in Eugene O'Neill's *All God's Chillun' Got Wings* went to the Relief Committee and were publicized in the communist and ILP press. ILP leaders James Maxton and Fenner Brockway pledged their support to the Committee's efforts, now fully under way. Its early statements bear the names of many who had been advocates of the Scottsboro and Meerut defendants.[2]

In June its sister organization, the American National Committee to Aid the Victims of German Fascism, circulated a transatlantic appeal signed by Sylvia Pankhurst and anthropologist Franz Boas, the refugee artist Louis Lozowick, and the writers Lincoln Steffens and Langston Hughes, among others. In the call for a meeting to be held at the New School in New York on June 29, the group's membership anticipated the postwar civil rights movement, boasting the signature of the renowned preacher Adam Clayton Powell, Sr., of Abyssinian Baptist Church, whose son would represent Harlem in the U.S. Congress in years to come.[3]

The Scottsboro defendants had mostly dropped out of sight, the news of their case appearing intermittently in the press. In the weeks and months following January 1933, the German and Austrian governments arrested thousands of Europeans, many of them communists and socialists, both Jews and non-Jews. They fled from Berlin to the Saar, Prague, Paris, and from all these points to London. They moved on from London to New York and Los Angeles, and from Berlin and other points in Europe to British-ruled Palestine. In these new demographic and political circumstances, those who continued to link antifascism with opposition to American racism wrote and spoke of the hypocrisy of American, British, and European policy toward "people of color."[4] But most found new images and languages in their advocacy of "German refugees" whose "racial" identity was of ethnic, religious, and cultural origin— "racial" in the vernacular of the time, but also "European," and in the case of the Jews, "Semitic." The left chose a language of "German relief" in order to encompass political refugees in the first order of those meriting assistance, a designation that very clearly did not signify Jews alone, or Jews as a prominent sector of refugee work. While this large and inclusive category of "German" seems at first glance less prejudicial than the official government refugee category of "racial" or "economic" victim, all were fraught with elements of anti-Semitic prejudice, and the government category of "refugee" did not explicitly imply assistance to victims of political persecution.

The nine young Scottsboro defendants all survived the war, five of them as convicts, while many of their European supporters suddenly faced death, themselves the objects of state violence that swept them into suspicion and conflict as they ran. They boarded trains, shifted apartments, and relinquished children, livelihoods, property, and well-being. Some had met Ada Wright, while many others had simply paused to glance at her, to listen to her, or to read a leaflet or buy a Scottsboro letter stamp in the summer of 1932. She was part of their story. The American South's lynchings bespoke medieval torture for its victims; those facing Nazi terror joined their ranks. The aftermath of the Reichstag Fire, the wrath of the Nazis and the Comintern, and even a hanging in the south of France awaited the small group who knew Ada Wright firsthand while for millions of others, the Blitzkreig lay ahead.

REFUGEES AS POLICY

The left's mobilization in support of European refugees occurred alongside many larger, parallel efforts undertaken by humanitarian and Jewish organizations. In 1933, with the first reports of increased repression arriving from Germany and Austria, Lionel and Guy de Rothschild, assisted by the leading Anglo-Jewish families, established the Central British Fund for German Jewry, which became the Council for German Jewry in 1936, and the Central Council for Jewish Refugees in 1939. The Anglo-Jewish community leadership drew upon the "breadth of liturgical spectrum" among Jews with "widely-diverse loyalties" in creating a relief network, assuring the government that no one would enter the United Kingdom as a "charge on the public."[5] The British authorities and volunteer-advocates classified those seeking entry as either "economic refugees" or "racial refugees." They understood Czech Jews as victims of "persecution . . . motivated by racial and economic motives rather than political animosity," invoking what they perceived as a *racial* designation. This provided a basis for "devaluing the Jews' claims to asylum."[6] Both the official and the informal acceptance of a language of "race" to describe Jews blurred the political and religious distinctions among them and tended toward the racial classification scheme that the Nazis themselves erected, albeit for different purposes. Jews' victimhood was officially condemned by the British as a matter of refugee policy, while it was sought and furthered by the Nazis. As the circles of refugee advocates expanded, an often unacknowledged debate about the notions behind classification simmered, its issues unresolved by the voluntry groups or policymakers.

Deeper distinctions in the official classification system indicated the limits of Government assistance. Britain accepted an estimated one in ten applications from Jews for asylum between 1933 and the outbreak of war. Before 1934 only two or three thousand European refugees made their way to Britain, a number

Figure 5.1. "Nazi Salute." Members of the German swim team give the Nazi salute during the playing of the German national anthem at the Port of London Authority swimming club's *Annual Open-air Gala* at Milwall Cutting, South West India Docks, London, July 1, 1933 (GettyImages).

fewer than those who sought passage to Palestine or to the United States in the first years of the Reich.[7] Only in 1939, as a consequence of the events of the Nazi persecutions of Kristallnacht, November 9–10, 1938, and the parliamentary activism in its aftermath, did Britain finally agree to admit those without the visible means and connections required of refugees in the early thirties. The merchant banker Otto Schiff had erected a temporary refugee shelter in London's East End in March of 1933; by 1939 all refugees passed through a joint refugee center at Bloomsbury House (the former Palace Hotel), which handled a thousand people a day.[8]

By the end of 1937 only 5,500 of the 154,000 refugees fleeing Nazi Germany had entered Britain from among their possible destinations. But 74,000 Germans and Austrians had arrived by 1939, after the restrictions were lifted, constituting between 10 and 15 percent of all refugees who fled Germany between January 1933 and October 1941; 90 percent were of German-Jewish origin.[9] Many of those who came to Britain were transmigrants who planned to or were forced to move on to another host country. The last waves of refugees to arrive in Britain included the *Kindertransport* passengers; the first group of children reached Harwich in December 1938. Ten thousand children came on

Figure 5.2. "Jewish Protest." A rabbi leads a procession of forty thousand Jews through London, from Stepney in the East End to a demonstration in Hyde Park in central London, against the persecution of Jews in Nazi Germany, July 20, 1933 (GettyImages).

these trains, 75 percent of whom were Jewish. After April of 1939, a fifty-pound sterling deposit was required of each child.[10] By 1941 official refugee status had been extended to 55,000 German and Austrian refugees, and many who stayed through the war were infirm, elderly, or very young.[11] Eighty thousand Austrian, German and Czech refugees remained in Britain during the war, fifty thousand of whom stayed until at least the 1950s.[12]

By October 1939, 400,000 of 680,000 Jews had left Germany, Austria, and Bohemia for all points outside.[13] Most of those who remained in Europe perished. The official response of Britain to the refugee question was obstinate and complacent, and the parliamentary debate indicated an absence of foresight and knowledge alongside prejudice in the perception of the crisis on the Continent. But there were also those in many different kinds of organizations who tried from the first moments to bear witness and to attempt the impossible mass rescue of Jewish victims, while others sought to assist the mass of "political" victims of the Reich.

Those refugees of all backgrounds who did manage to get to Britain encountered a mixed response to their presence. Some were on the German or Austrian left and found their politics at issue. The communists remained critical of capitalist "Jews with money." A 1933 Relief Committee leaflet stated that in Europe, "the hand full of Jewish bankers and Bourse speculators are spared, while . . . Jewish workers" faced persecution, mixing a Marxist "class analysis" with the common anti-Semitic prejudices of the day to convey a simplistic and inaccurate picture of events and policies inside Nazi Germany.[14] The British left were in many instances hostile to the Zionest project in Palestine and to the British mandate. The communists and the ILP called for Jewish and Arab workers to band together, condemning the persecution of Arab and Jewish militants. As late as 1937 the LAI opposed Jewish immigration to Palestine in the name of the "protection of more backward races."[15] Yet in sharp distinction to the government, the communists and others on the left also advocated an "open door" policy for refugees; they did not champion wealthier Jewry, but defended their rights all the same.

Even a figure like the progressive journalist Vernon Bartlett, later a critic of appeasement and Munich, published a book for the popular reader on Naziism in 1933 that disparaged East European Jewry, describing the Galician immigrants to Germany as the "most backward section of the Jewish race." Based upon visits to Krakow and Kishinoff, he wrote, "I should be tempted to agree, were I in power in Germany, to limit the immigration [into Germany] of these people very strictly indeed . . . not because I felt anti-Jewish. . . . they have lived so long under oppression that their standard and their methods of living would undermine the standard of life of my own people."[16]

EXILES, PARIS, AND MÜNZENBERG

"Wartime London was the center of a shadow world whose name was exile," especially for those who remained active in anti-Nazi circles once they arrived. One group of refugees included members of the German Social Democratic Party in exile (SOPADE), whose leaders fled from Prague to London. The British government disliked their activities, while their relations with their ostensible political partners in the Labour party were compromised by English xenophobia and an official Labour party culture of hostility toward the organizational left. One hundred active Social Democratic Party members remained in London along with two hundred or more exiled German communists.[17] The exiled lawyer Franz Neumann found the overall political scene alienating, and the politics at the London School of Economics "disagreeable." He moved on to the United States like many others.[18] France was the first destination of Jews

and non-Jews who fled Germany and Austria in 1933, most of whom were political victims of the Reich whose names appeared on wanted lists and who
anticipated imminent arrest. Others sought refuge in Czechoslovakia, the Netherlands, and the Saar. Paris was a closer and more cosmopolitan destination
than London, and the French refugee policy was more lenient than Britain's.
Twenty-five thousand refugees entered France almost immediately after the
Nazi seizure of power, of whom 85 percent were Jews. A half million veterans
of the Spanish Civil War swelled the number of displaced foreigners, many in
camps run by the French state.[19] In 1938, with the fall of Czechoslovakia,
France imposed greater restrictions on entry, and there was a revival of anti-
Semitism, which some observers attributed to the influx of refugees of whom
30,000 remained in 1939.[20] Some 3,000 central European social-democrats and
3,500 communists found their way to France before the Daladier government
interned enemy aliens under fifty years of age in the weeks before the German
invasion of France.[21] Many non-Jews were suspected of being Nazi spies and
when they expressed hope for an eventual and triumphal return to Germany,
the surveillance lavished upon them increased.

Parisian exile was central to the movements in thought and action that lie at
the heart of this narrative. The flight of Germans who knew and worked with
others in these pages completes the portrait of the decade. The career of Willi
Münzenberg as impresario of communist campaigns in Europe came to an
abrupt end with the announcement of the burning of the Reichstag, or so it
seemed. But he "revisited" Germany many times after 1933 through the means
of the print culture of a variety of antifascist efforts, directed from Paris. The
Brown Book of the Hitler Terror, published by his Parisian entourage in cooperation with their colleagues in London, provided the first early evidence of Nazi
atrocities to the greater public, despite its flaws, inaccuracies, and fantastical
accounts of Nazi decadence and conspiracy. Copies were smuggled back across
the borders into Germany.[22] The international exile journal, *Die Zukunft* (the
Future), Münzenberg's last publishing effort, also attempted to reach back into
Germany to spread its hopeful vision of a new country without Nazism, a vision that sought to escape the inevitability of war and the stench of Stalinism,
and to strike out against both through a coalition of liberal allies. Münzenberg,
formerly the most infamous of communist propagandists, courted Churchill,
Anthony Eden, and many figures of the British Labour, Liberal, and Tory es-
tablishments. The story of his life in exile is one thread linking Scottsboro to
Munich.

The burning of the Reichstag on February 27, 1933, unleashed a heightened
and furious period of Nazi repression against the German left. A disillusioned
ex-communist Dutch vagrant was perceived as the most likely culprit, and the
regime placed immediate blame upon the German communist party (KPD),
the fire providing the perfect pretext for a widespread and vicious manhunt.
Within seven months, fifty thousand communists, socialists, trade unionists,

intellectuals, pacifists and fellow travelers had been arrested in Germany, five or six hundred of whom were executed before the end of July.[23] On February 28, the government passed the Emergency Decree for the Protection of People and the State, and in March they arrested communist party leader Ernst Thälmann, who was subsequently the center of the vigorous and unsuccessful international campaign for his release. The arrest, imprisonment, and deportation of George Padmore from Hamburg occurred in this context.

Until 1935 the Reich identified the first waves of "refugees" as political subversives—their activism, not their religious, "ethnic," or "racial" backgrounds being the crucial identifying factor. The authorities entered the names of those who left Germany legally into a register, discrediting them at the moment of departure. They removed their rights to citizenship, and the Gestapo often followed them outside of the country as did the German Foreign Office. Some individuals were chosen for special public denunciation. The government announced the "denaturalization" of the writers Lion Feuchtwanger, Heinrich Mann, and Ernst Toller; the social-democrats Rudolf Breitscheid and Philipp Scheidemann; and the communists Heinz Neumann, Wilhelm Pieck, and Münzenberg. More than ten thousand persons were condemned to statelessness.[24] Any who returned from exile after January 15, 1934, were immediately incarcerated. Münzenberg fled with his wife and partner Babette Gross, also a KPD member.[25] Gross later told a riveting story of their flight into exile.[26] During the hours immediately after the Reichstag fire, she and Münzenberg traveled across Germany to Saarbrücken assisted by social-democratic police. Gross intrepidly returned to Berlin in order to secure their funds that were stashed there. She distributed pay to the staffs of their defunct Soviet-backed publications and grabbed enough for herself to set up in Paris.

There was a formidable community of sustained advocates of refugees in France that, until 1940, allowed the members of exiled European communities considerable breathing space. Though the French government exhibited many failings, the French communists, socialists, and groups like the League of Rights of Man and the Citizen, and members of the Catholic left continuously agitated for refugee rights. French-based aid agencies were markedly and visibly more political than in England, mirroring the greater strength of the organized and established French left where both socialists and communists led mass parties; the British communists were more sectarian than their French counterparts, and the French socialists more left leaning than the British Labour party. The activist bodies included the socialist Mateotti committee with ties to Labour party circles in London, and the Sécours Rouge, the French Comintern aid agency. French communists were less interested in the problem of anti-Semitism than other groups, and loathe to identify individual Jews qua Jews as victims of fascism.

The "influence of individuals and groups" affected the status of committed political refugees, and an increasingly elaborate web of persons and information emanated from the camp system within the Reich.[27] Münzenberg was a large player in this network that extended throughout Europe, spread copiously to London, and reached across the Atlantic. Both French and German security agencies took interest in his arrival in their midst.[28] He had made friends in France before 1933, and he and Gross quickly fashioned a life for themselves and for their associates.[29] He moved quickly to spearhead the World Committee for the Victims of German Fascism, whose first signatories included the British former naval commander and Labour member of the House of Lords Lord Marley (Dudley Leigh Aman), who served as its president and wrote the introduction to *The Brown Book of the Hitler Terror and the Burning of the Reichstag*.[30] This was the same organization that issued the first appeals for German relief that surfaced in London, and Lord Marley's involvement assured its growth, legitimacy, and sustenance there.

THE REICHSTAG FIRE TRIAL: 1933–34

One of the first large German Relief Committee gatherings in support of refugees and against terror was held at Essex Hall in May 1933. The Labour party's international secretary, William Gillies, was in attendance as a spy and depicted Lord Marley as chairman, leading the meeting with fairness; there had been "no limit to the parties" present. But he also saw the committee as former MP Ellen Wilkinson's "front," noting that Trotskyists attended, and that a communist who spoke had recently been released from prison. (Wilkinson lost her parliamentary seat in 1931.) An unidentified former KPD Reichstag deputy addressed the crowd while the meeting's sponsors recruited members of the audience to attend a conference on antifascism in Paris.[31] Individual Labour-party members appeared on the platforms of the Relief Committee. In June the Committee sponsored an event at Kingsway Hall featuring the exiled German writers Toller and Egon Erwin Kisch. Wilkinson, Maxton, Pollitt, Lord Marley, the Socialist League's E. F. Wise, Bertrand Russell, and Saklatvala were also present.[32] The crowd of 2,500 donated over two hundred pounds, and telegrams arrived from French writer Henri Barbusse, Franz Boas, and several American communist leaders. Meanwhile, Gillies contacted the European socialists of the Second International, and they confirmed his findings. "Our information is that in practice, the work of this Committee benefits Münzenberg's WIR (Workers International Relief)." The communists, they said, were avowedly "exploit[ing] it, " and its resources reportedly went to "fund fugitives in Saarbrücken" where Münzenberg and his supporters, including Wilkinson, had indeed organized shelters for many exiles.[33] Wilkinson made a trip to Saarbrücken and published the pamphlet *Feed the Children* under the imprint of the Relief Committee.

Barbusse's, Romain Rolland's, and Lord Marley's names appeared on the Committee's logo, but so did those of the eminent American social worker Jane Addams, scholar and jurist John Dewey, and birth-control advocate Margaret Sanger, their inclusion indicative of Münzenberg's self-styled "united front" politics and his transatlantic reach. The Committee made distinctions among those for whom it served as advocates, illustrating the problem of a hierarchy of victimhood shared with all communities of supporters. "This war is a war of extermination," Wilkinson wrote, contending that political refugees faced a "separate problem" from others, and claiming that Jews were cared for by "their kith and kin." She cited the work of a Parisian Jewish relief agency as a case in point. In this respect, Wilkinson understood Nazi policy as a devastating attack on human lives, but assumed that the brunt of the assault would fall upon the Reich's *political* enemies. The Relief Committee was committed to the problem of the relief of "worker-refugees. . . . fascism is the last stand of capitalist imperialism."[34] The perception of the "Jewish problem" as separable from the dilemma faced by other refugees misrepresented the large numbers of Jews who were part of the political left, as well as replicating the invidious categories conceived by the governments involved—British, French, and Nazi.[35]

William Gillies continued to shadow his opponents, writing to London Labour party boss Herbert Morrison of communist partisanship. "Thälmann is not the only prominent political prisoner in Germany. He is the Communist leader. . . . our friends look after theirs."[36] In February 1933 James Maxton debated the British fascist leader Oswald Mosley. Maxton's colleagues in the leadership of the London ILP articulated a basis for common agreement on a set of issues with the London communist party leaders, including support for "[a]ll possible assistance to the struggles of the colonial peoples and for the release of all class war prisoners, particularly of Meerut prisoners," as some of the latter were still incarcerated. But the Trades Union Congress and the Labour party both refused to sign this motion of unity.[37] In June, Maxton, Saklatvala, and Bertrand Russell appeared together again at Kingsway Hall; Gillies reported that Saklatvala was greeted with "a great ovation." Barbusse, Münzenberg, American playwriter Elmer Rice, and Rabbi Benjamin Goldstein, a Scottsboro signatory and activist from Alabama, all extended written greetings to the meeting. Isobel Brown delivered a "stirring and effective appeal for funds," as Gillies attested. Maxton and Pollitt both spoke, but Gillies concluded that a majority of those in attendance were communist sympathizers.[38] In October the Relief Committee held a London Conference on the Hitler Victims. Wilkinson read a eulogy for the KPD founding member Clara Zetkin, spoke of the growth of the diverse "unity committees" involving the left and the Labour party throughout England, and reported on her children's home project in the Saar.[39] Her presence was a sign of dissent from the prohibitions imposed by the Labour party leaders on their supporters, and of the interventionist commitment of the Socialist League, the dissenting Labour organization led by Labour MP Sir Stafford Cripps.[40]

The staging of a "mock trial" in London, coinciding with the Nazi trial of four defendants in Leipzig accused of setting the Reichstag fire (German Ernst Torgler, and Bulgarians Georgi Dimitroff, Vasil Tanev, and Blagoi Popov), occurred at the suggestion of the exiled Czech communist and Münzenberg associate Otto Katz (aka André Simone), a central author of the *Brown Book of the Hitler Terror*, who joined Münzenberg in Paris in 1933.[41] Beginning on September 14, 1933, the Relief Committee staged the event in a room of the Law Society in the Strand. They tried the accused in a mock proceeding complete with witnesses, evidence, and jurists. The home secretary, none other than Sir John Simon, intervened at the eleventh hour in order to try to forbid their use of the appointed room, claiming that the Committee was in violation of government protocol, but the Law Society refused his request. The night before the mock trial was to begin, after Simon failed to persuade the Law Society to cancel it, the immigration authorities detained Otto Katz as he arrived at London Airport, ordering him back to Paris. Katz telephoned Ellen Wilkinson and was able to brief his colleagues for the trial while awaiting deportation. In this way, the mock trial's organizers called Simon's bluff—the Home Secretary could not risk exposure over his mistreatment of Katz by forbidding Katz the right to make contact with his colleagues.[42]

The communist filmmaker Ivor Montagu recalled that the key players in the mock trial had first met months before in Ellen Wilkinson's flat. They included Isobel Brown, whom he recalled as "comfortable but never placid, a rock, [a] fine organizer and the greatest fund-raising orator [he had] ever known," and Frederick Voight, the former *Manchester Guardian* Berlin correspondent, who had fled to England thwarting an assassination attempt on his life. Montagu felt that this effort had to be "a research in the passionate discovery of the facts." Their brief was to examine evidence "independently," in lieu of the German government allowing the defendants to appoint their own legal counsel in Leipzig. In September, D. N. Pritt, K.C., and a second English lawyer, Neil Lawson, had attempted unsuccessfully to act as Torgler's lawyers in the lead-up to the mock trial. Montagu reported that the Nazis sought to identify the mock trial's financial sponsors. A Nazi-appointed lawyer approached Katz in Paris to ask who was behind the London event; Katz replied in an audible whisper, "A group of English lords."[43]

Wilkinson and Montagu officially convened the mock trial. The only British member of its "legal officers" was Pritt, who presided over the "court," though Sir Stafford Cripps, the former British solicitor-general, brought the spectacle to order on opening day.[44] Pritt was not a communist, but he and his wife had journeyed to the Soviet Union in the 1932 delegation that included Richard and Naomi Mitchinson. He was, with Cripps, a Socialist League member, and he later became an apologist for the Moscow Trials, proceedings which he traveled

REICHSTAG ARSON INQUIRY—OPENING SESSION
Back Row (second from left) GARFIELD HAYES (U.S.A.), DR. BAKKER-NORT, (Holland), D. N. PRITT, K.C. (England), VALD HUIDT (Denmark), M.P. VERMEYLEN (Belgium).

Figure 5.3. "Reichstag Arson Inquiry—Opening Session. Back Row (second from left) Garfield Hayes [*sic*] [Hays] (USA), Dr. [Betsy] Bakker-Nort (Holland), D. N. Pritt (England), Vald Huidt [*sic*] [Huidt Vald] (Denmark), M. P. [Maître Pierre] Vermeylan (Belgium)." The jurists convened to "try" the Reichstag fire accused in the "mock trial" held at the Law Society offices off the Strand, London, including Arthur Garfield Hays, D. N. Pritt, Betsy Bakker-Nort, Vald Huidt, and Maître Pierre Vermeylen (*Daily Worker*, London, September 15, 1933) (courtesy *Morning Star*, reproduced by kind permission of the Syndics of Cambridge University Library).

to observe firsthand. He assisted the International African Service Bureau in the later thirties and would have met Padmore in that context, an irony given Pritt's proximity to organized communism. Pritt recalled the mock trial:

> We had to meet the strong hostility of the British Government, which was pressed by the Nazi Government to prohibit the Enquiry. . . . it wanted to be friendly and "appeasing" to the Nazis; it feared the Soviet Union, and was always seeking to build up enemies against it, and the Nazis were a perfect weapon for the purpose.[45]

Arthur Garfield Hays, the American Jewish attorney who had worked with Clarence Darrow in the Scopes "evolution" trial in Tennessee and was active in the Scottsboro campaign, was among the group of international jurists who helped to author its concluding legal opinions. He was contacted by a lawyer for the CPUSA, yet he stated, in retrospect, "None of the members of the Commission was either Communist or Nazi; all were lawyers. . . . there was a vast body of evidence obtainable from German refugees which would not be available to a German court."[46] In his memoirs, Pritt claimed that one mounted a legal case and defended clients "to propagate one's political point of view,"[47] but

Montagu remembered him as "a courageous advocate largely non-political, who had almost fumbled his way toward socialism as accorded with his ideas of rightness and justice." Pritt later contributed an Introduction to the second edition of the *Brown Book*.[48]

The Labour party observers at the mock trial included Gillies, who was always looking for an opportunity to unveil an ultraleft conceit. He wrote to Herbert Morrison that the MPs in attendance were "victims," who had come at the instigation of Lord Marley and Ellen Wilkinson.[49] Garfield Hays identified H. G. Wells, George Lansbury, Saklatvala, and Ernst Toller as among those in the audience, and Toller also served as a witness. Otto Katz helped to recruit witnesses from Europe to testify. Rudolf Breitscheid, a former Reichstag socialist leader, and the former police president of Berlin Albert Grzesinski were among the noncommunist participants who came to London as witnesses in the mock trial. The German communist Wilhelm Koenen entered the country illegally and was sequestered from the public during his appearance, as he and his supporters feared collusion between British and Nazi authorities. The organizers planted decoys to distract spies.[50] The panel of international jurists arrived at a set of "official findings" based on the testimony of Koenen and others who spoke against the Nazi regime. They identified Dutch anarchist Marinus van der Lubbe as the only arsonist among the defendants in Leipzig and an *opponent* of the communists, insisting that an underground passage that connected the Reichstag with the offices of the deputies was the route that the perpetrator had taken, pointing to the political advantages accruing to the Nazis from the fire.[51] They released their findings just as the Leipzig trial opened, to dramatic effect. The philosopher George Caitlin, husband of Vera Brittain, was among the observers at the Leipzig court and he journeyed to Moscow thereafter. German defendant Torgler bargained a plea without implicating others, and was summarily jailed.

The Leipzig trial was a shambles in which the brilliant Bulgarian communist and Comintern leader Georgi Dimitroff even managed to compromise Hermann Göring, who made a brief appearance. Van der Lubbe was tried separately, convicted of the arson, and beheaded on January 10, 1934. The British communist Dorothy Woodman and the writers Anabel Williams-Ellis and Catherine Carswell visited and cared for Dimitroff's mother and sister before the humiliated German authorities let the remaining defendants flee to asylum in the Soviet Union after the court failed to convict them.[52] In June 1933 the *Daily Worker* announced a new Nazi scheme under the heading "Plans Made to Lynch Nazis's Victims," charging that the Nazis had planted a "lynch mob" to seize the defendants from the courtroom.[53]

A public campaign in Britain, launched around the Leipzig trial, widely reported the dramatic proceedings in the German court. The London region ILP protested against the absence of a proper defense team. In January 1934 a demonstration in Kingsway demanded the release of the Leipzig prisoners. Rallies in Sheffield and Glasgow reportedly each drew more than 1,500 supporters. Lord Marley expressed his solidarity with a similar event held that day in Boston, Massachusetts, and announced the publication of 250,000 copies of the *Brown Book of the Hitler Terror*, voicing his hopes that these protests had done something to "check atrocities ... perhaps some [perpetrators were] driven underground." He made available visas for the Soviet Union and France to those suffering repression, though neither destination offered long-term safety for many exiles.[54] During the next month, Marley journeyed to the United States, where the philosopher John Dewey and other supporters of the relief work, attended a banquet in his honor.[55] A new petition against Hitler appeared in London, bearing the names of economist Maynard Keynes, Bertrand Russell, Leonard and Virginia Woolf; writers E. M. Forster, Siegfried Sassoon, H. G. Wells, Winifred Holtby, and Storm Jameson; Julian Huxley, Charlotte Despard, George Caitlin, and Vera Brittain; philanthropist Sebohm Rowntree; Labour party trade-union leader Ernest Bevin; and the women's suffrage leaders Frederick and Emmeline Pethick-Lawrence. These were a mixed group of liberals, Labour party supporters, and fellow travelers, and their petition celebrated the begrudging Leipzig verdict and the release of Dimitroff and his fellows, treating the rout at Leipzig as a validation of their own views.[56]

A newly formed, London-based Dimitroff Committee issued an appeal for assistance for Dimitroff's mother, and included among its signatories Scottsboro Defense Committee chair Lascelles Abercrombie. In March 1934 its organizers asked Eleanor Rathbone, with whom some had worked in the early Scottsboro committee, to become its vice president. Rathbone wrote to Frederick Pethick-Lawrence. "I am in full sympathy with the object. ... I cannot promise any assistance in raising funds, both from lack of time and because I am already so deeply committed to other objects," and indeed, she was largely absent from the early refugee-assistance gatherings and became more active only after 1937.[57] The staging of the mock trial assisted the success of the *Brown Book of the Hitler Terror* and served as a model of cooperation for the left and liberals that was re-created, however imperfectly, in campaigns and coalitions that followed. For Münzenberg, the mock trial served as a template for his chosen work in Paris for the remainder of the decade. "In the battle for public opinion ... Münzenberg was the clear victor. ... he was able to sit back and watch the Nazis incriminate themselves simply by failing to disprove his accusations."[58]

In various guises, Münzenberg sought to bring the most established and respected voices of liberalism to bear upon fascist duplicity, right up until 1939. If he did this solely to gird his own loins, it proved an unsuccessful strategy of self-protection. At this early point, he was still a communist, working under the direction of the Comintern and its agents, as well as being monitored by them, and the mock trial was also a defense of communism as a means to discredit fascism. Anson Rabinbach points to it and the *Brown Book*'s publication as diversions from facing up to the need to develop an urgent, critical perspective on the failure of German communists to thwart fascism's rise to power.[59] Its staging could hardly bring new recruits to the now-exiled KPD, but it enhanced the work of the fellow travelers around the British communist party and its web of front groups, especially the German Relief Committee. The "clean face" of antifascism was discernible in the mock trial. Its propaganda was rhetorically shorn of an anti-imperial or anticolonial language, and as Saklatvala had recalled it, "a purely European Communism was got up."[60] It and the publication of the *Brown Book* brought celebrity to Münzenberg far from Berlin and Moscow. The new era of antifascist politics added new dimensions to the various languages of advocacy being used to describe and defend "racial victims" in the terms in which the left chose to portray them. Even though the communist-led efforts increasingly focused work upon "political" and European victims, the news of anti-Semitic terror, "racial" terror as it was understood, proliferated. As the former French president, the socialist Léon Blum said in 1933, "This is the beginning of racist terror. Our comrades in Germany were indeed right to fear as the supreme danger the combination of the racist organization and the government apparatus in the same hands."[61] Meantime, at least the Nazi supporters had not forgotten Münzenberg's anticolonial commitments and accused him of wishing to foment race war. In October 1933 a Dutch fascist paper invoked the record of his propaganda and his use of front organizations:

> He tries with the aid of apparently humanitarian organizations to incite colored, colonial peoples against European colonial administrators. . . . It is grotesque that Münzenberg . . . has found admirers among the political and cultural elite of Europe, among those, that is, against whom he actively foments "hatred" on the part of colored peoples in the Far East.[62]

Here, Münzenberg's past activity was brought to bear upon the incipient debate about anticolonialism and antifascism. The fascists sought to draw supporters who feared colonial movements for freedom. But many on the left feared losing a broader base by invoking an allegiance to colonial liberation, and tacitly moved toward defense of empire instead, or, simply forsook the question. Still others were ordinary Europeans, of social-democratic or even conservative and religious leanings, who opposed fascism on the grounds of its threat to their existence and its moral bankruptcy, not as an incipient threat to colonial subjects' lives per se.

In the left's pursuit of the "truth behind the Reichstag Fire," van der Lubbe, first accused of arson by the Nazis, was hounded as a homosexual, the drive to uncover evidence of his enigmatic social life unrelenting. Writer Klaus Mann wrote critically of this preoccupation. "We are not very far from identifying homosexuality with fascism. . . . the antifascist press places the words 'murder and pederasts' alongside each other almost as often as the Nazi press does the words 'Jews and traitors.'" This coupling appeared in many other narratives of Nazi "degeneration."[63] In 1933 the *Negro Worker* referred to the "openly admitted neurotic perverts and drug fiends as Captain Goehring and Roehm and Hitler, who openly declare that they are out to exterminate Jews, Negroes and all other peoples who do not belong to the so-called Aryan race." The *New Leader* published materials derived from the *Brown Book*, citing van der Lubbe's connections to Hitler's chief of staff Ernst Röhm. "It has been definitely established that Röhm was a homo-sexual and that van der Lubbe introduced to him by [Nazi doctor] Bell was on his list of young men."[64] The Paris Münzenberg circle sought to promote what Rabinbach terms a "virile innocence" contrasting itself to the insalubrious practices of the Nazis. This claim constituted another kind of hypocrisy, as Münzenberg and his exiled comrades enjoyed a fast and sexually complicated lifestyle in Paris.[65]

Communist critics and writers continued to describe the violent repression of fascism as a form of "white terror," interchanging this usage with the "terror" that imperialists used against colonial inhabitants. "White" was not contrasted to Jew or to "black" per se, but to the *redness* of Bolshevism; its terminological origin lay in the use of "white Russian" to identify the czarist armies of the Russian Civil War. But Nazis also appeared as "white terrorists" in this lexicon, and their inclusion in the diseased and degenerate "terror" regime of the West was a rhetorical ploy that reinforced the notion of a bifurcated world of revolutionary and counterrevolutionary players. Jews, blacks, and the colonized were victims of "white terror," while antifascists were both felled and fought on behalf of those who could not defend themselves. The British ILD Executive wrote in June of 1933 that white terror was linked to colonial terror "more particularly cruel on the seats of imperial war," and referred to the seventy-three American "Negro workers" lynched in 1932, citing repression in China, El Salvador, Bolivia, Chile, Cuba, Argentina, and India. "Terror [was] going on under the hypocritical appearance of a 'civilizing mission.'"[66]

In January 1934 Harry Pollitt reported that

> the Communist Party [of Britain] . . . played a leading part in the development of activities of such united front movements as anti-war, anti-fascist, anti–Means Test, the German Relief Campaign, and in connection with the Reichstag trial campaign, and undoubtedly many sections of Labour party workers have been won for participating in these campaigns.[67]

But this month also witnessed the International Conference for the Relief of German Jews in London, a formidable gathering of many agencies representing mainstream Jewish life, including the Board of Deputies, the Joint Foreign Committee, the Anglo-Jewish Association, the Refugee Committee Allocations Committee, the English Zionist Federation, the Consultative Committee, Chaim Weizmann's Jewish Agency, the American Jewish Congress, the Alliance Israelite Universelle led by Jules Braunschweig, the Consistoire Central des Israélites en Bulgarie, the Jewish Colonization Association, and the Parisian Comité National de Sécours aux Réfugiés Allemandes Victimes de L'Antisémitisme.[68] The distance grew between the secular mobilization of center-left British opinion on behalf of relief for "political victims" and the increasing sense of urgency and organization among Jewish bodies whose purpose was to assist the vast majority of real and potential refugees. Both were internationally connected, but in very different ways, even despite the parallel affiliations of some individuals in flight.

The ILP also maintained an international network on behalf of the leftist social-democrats of the German Socialist Workers' Party (SAP), prisoners being held in Dresden in early 1934. At this time, a majority of ILP branches polled favored collaboration with the communists on specific issues: support for the Meerut defendants, German relief, the celebration of May Day, opposition to the Means test, demands for housing, protests at air pageants, and some joint electoral activity.[69] The ILP rank-and-file were less wary than Maxton himself of collaboration with communists, and there was a protest against the removal from the London ILP divisional council of members who supported Comintern affiliation. Though Maxton's views prevailed, fascism was a potent force for spontaneous, street-level unity, and his deep and justified doubts about the Soviets were less common than the enthusiasm generated for a broad antifascism in the wake of the first flush of rage against the Third Reich.

In June 1934 the Comintern's Anglo-American Colonial and Negro Committee, shorn of Padmore, received news that the Alabama court had upheld Haywood Patterson's and Clarence Norris's convictions. It called for an intensified Scottsboro campaign and for member sections to protest against "lynch terror and Scottsboro in the USA with Thälmann and fascist terror in Germany and Austria." The American ILD was instructed to organize daily picketing of the White House, linking Scottsboro to Thälmann. But a month later, there had not been a single response from member sections abroad on the Scottsboro issue. France was the only section with a "functioning Colonial Department," yet a branch of the strongest remaining communist party outside of the Soviet Union was credited with holding only four sessions with Indian students. The existing contacts with Palestine and Syria were "not good." The Profintern "red trade union" work was not faring well.[70] There were many proposals for reorganization as the colonial work of the Comintern foundered.

At the end of June 1934, SPD lawyer Kurt Rosenfeld, maverick Welsh labour leader Aneurin Bevan, Willi Münzenberg, and Babette Gross traveled to the United States on behalf of Thälmann under the auspices of the Münzenberg affiliate, the World Aid Committee for the Victims of German Fascism. Though Münzenberg had been refused entry into Britain for the mock Reichstag Fire Trial, he and the others traveled freely to America. On this remarkable trip, Münzenberg spoke at German workers' clubs in the American Northeast and across the Midwest, and addressed communist-led rallies at Madison Square

Garden and the Bronx Coliseum, predicting the imminent overthrow of Hitler. Writers Sinclair Lewis and Malcolm Cowley appeared with him at points on the journey. In a New York appearance for a lawyers' organization, Münzenberg "declared that the new Germany which would rise from the ruins of Hitlerism would be . . . a nation erected by the cooperation of workers, peasants and intellectuals." The *Berliner Tageblatt* referred to Münzenberg as "one of the most brilliant propagandists on earth," and noted that "he was seeking to create political trouble in the US, in the context of labour unrest."[71] Bevan's presence is especially interesting as he was not widely associated with the communist front groups or the communist party; his involvement is another forceful example of Münzenberg and his friends' ability to cultivate important allies in Britain at a time when they were still associated with the Comintern. Their arrival was the occasion for a demonstration in front of the German embassy in Washington, and the American ILD published *The Sonnenberg Torture Camp* by "An Escaped Prisoner" jointly with Münzenberg's Workers International Relief.[72]

On August 22, 1934, the anniversary of the executions of Sacco and Vanzetti, London communists celebrated a Thälmann–Scottsboro–[Angelo] Herndon Day in London. The French Scottsboro campaign briefly experienced new vigor.[73] In October Scottsboro protests were inaugurated in South Africa and Australia.[74] But as the Comintern withdrawal from anticolonial work and propaganda grew, the willingness to devote time and effort to non-European causes flagged. The attention to Scottsboro lessened as violence on the European continent increased, and the broad design of Soviet foreign policy focused on the possibilities of accommodation with the allied nations of the West.

REFUGEE ACTIVISM

The several hundred German-Jewish and Austrian-Jewish refugees[75] of the political left who came to London between 1933 and 1939 arrived in a country that still permitted most forms of political dissent. But the Nazi regime monitored British-based protests against the imprisonment of the German counterparts of the British left and trade-union militants. *Der Angriff*, the Nazi paper that derided Ada Wright's visit to Germany, kept a correspondent in London until the war. The German press was quick "to expose" the Jewish background of some of the leaders of refugee and relief work, like Harold Laski, while the *Völkischer Beobachter* identified Ellen Wilkinson as a "half-Jewess."[76] The Nazi government hoped Britain would "restrain" refugee political activity and made this known through diplomatic communiques, providing lists of persons whom they wanted followed from the ports of entry, a practice that may have spurred Padmore's "shadows." The participants in exile activism were from diverse political backgrounds, linked in many instances to Münzenberg's operations in

Paris. Political and cultural organizations sprang up like the German Peace Movement led by socialists Gerhard Seger, Franz Neumann, and entrepreneur David Yaskiel, whose British International News Agency published the second edition of the *Brown Book of the Hitler Terror* in 1934 with the new introduction by D. N. Pritt.[77]

Many in the exile political community were prepared to work with German communists in Britain, even if they had many differences with Stalinist ideas and policies.[78] Among the activists was Heinrich Fraenkel, a former journalist who acted as a translator at the Reichstag Fire mock trial.[79] The League for Civil Rights, the Free German Youth, and New Beginning, had communist support.[80] Communist playwright Ernst Toller was involved in the mobilization around Spain, and German agents monitored his 1935–36 speaking tour of Britain, reporting upon it in memos sent on to Berlin.[81] Activist exiles joined many noncommunist British political circles as well. Stefan Zweig's Free German League of Culture included among its members Presidents Oskar Kokoschka and Berthold Viertel, and the antislavery and Scottsboro advocate Gilbert Murray; David Grenfell, MP; Julian Huxley and the writers J. B. Priestley, Storm Jameson, and Wickham Steed.[82] The historian Marian Berghahn concluded that as small as the German communist contingent was, it exercised considerable leadership over many others, gathering around the household of Fred Uhlmann and continuing to recruit new arrivals to its projects. Other important formations included Kurt Hiller's Club 43 and the Group of Independent German Authors.[83] Hiller was a critic of the Soviet Union and in 1939 broke with the communist-leaning New Beginning. The cabaret Four and Twenty Black Sheep grew from those around the photo montage artist John Heartfield (the former Helmut Herzfeld), who contributed his brilliant stylus to Scottsboro.[84]

The Labour party's reception of their "brothers and sisters" among the German and Austrian socialists remained chilly—fraught "with suspicion and misunderstanding."[85] The recent German movement's failure to defeat fascism did not inspire confidence, and the political exiles were regarded as "representatives of an exhausted political system."[86] Exiled Jews and the broader refugee community encountered "xenophobic restrictionism and the liberal hospitality traditional . . . in British politics."[87] Franz Neumann's alienating political experience at LSE from 1933 to 1936, where he studied under Harold Laski and the Hungarian sociologist Karl Mannheim, led to his immigrating to America.[88] President Franklin Roosevelt was more progressive than Stanley Baldwin or Neville Chamberlain; New York and California trumped London, and the ample previous record of American immigration of both Jews and non-Jewish Central Europeans and Russians suggested the presence of a greater cosmopolitanism across the Atlantic. A "burst of jazz" greeted exiled German writer Otto Regler when he visited the United States to raise money for Spain.[89] At the same time, there were ample disincentives to remaining in Britain. In May

1936, finally bowing to the earlier wishes of former German ambassador
Hoesch (then deceased), a group of MPs traveled to Germany, "the first occasion on which English politicians and MPs from the Labour Party . . . expressed
the desire to become personally acquainted with social questions in Germany."
The British government still deemed it "inopportune" to take action against
Nazi organizations in the United Kingdom. A reversal of this policy was post-
poned when the future German foreign minister Joachim von Ribbentrop visited London that year, where members of the Cunard family were among his
hosts. In March 1937, despite queries from MI-5 about national security, the
Cabinet delayed unequivocal action until the coming August.[90]

Thousands of refugees also remained in Britain, the politics of both British
and German left and labor circles having little influence on them, many with
little choice about whether to stay or to go. Those in the mainstream of Jewish
refugee life were centered in the neighborhoods of north and northwest London. Apart from the Jewish Aid Committee and Council for German Jewry (or
German-Jewish Aid Committee), Sidney Warburg founded Self-Aid in 1938,
a specifically German-Jewish organization, which searched for avenues that
allowed refugees to come to reside permanently in Britain.[91] The Christian
Council for Refugees, the German Emergency Committee, the Friends' Campaign for Refugees and Aliens, the Society for the Protection of Science and
Learning, the International Student Service, WILF, the Inter-Aid Committee for
Children from Germany, and the Labour party all assisted mainstream refugee
immigration. The LNU ran the Save the Children Fund, led by disarmament
figure Philip Noel-Baker, who reported on Kristallnacht in the Commons.[92]
But the interaction between this Jewish relief apparatus and left exiles, both
Jews and non-Jews, was strained. Jews were increasingly understood to be central victims of fascism by the organized left, yet many on the left remained un-
interested in their Jewishness at best, still construing much of relief propaganda
in national terms as pleas for assistance to "Germans and Austrians." The Jewish organizations, in turn, pointedly strove for an apolitical image in which the
line between ignoring and suppressing politics was permeable. Thus the Free
Austria Movement and the Free German League of Culture, both with many
Jewish members, had no representatives in the Anglo-Jewish organizations.[93]
When Scottsboro and German relief activist Carmel Haden Guest died in 1937,
after her son David was killed fighting in Spain, her surviving son Peter chose
to have a Jewish service with an officiating rabbi, explaining, "I knew Carmel
had the lowest opinion of various religious connections of ours . . . but I also
know that with anti-Semitism what it is here at the moment, Carmel would ten
times rather have put that flag up than give currency to any misconception."[94]

In 1938 William Gillies concluded that Jewish organizations had not wanted
responsibility for those identified as political refugees and "were anxious to
dissociate themselves from any suspicion of revolutionary or communist sympathies."[95] The Labour party attempted to inhibit its members from interacting

Figure 5.4. "Paul Robeson." Robeson performs at the *20th Century German Art Exhibition* at the New Burlington Galleries, London, August 3, 1938, in aid of refugee artists. Max Beckmann's triptych *Temptation* is in the background (Hudson/GettyImages).

with communists and Gillies prohibited Labour members from joining the Relief Committee, the Workers' International Relief, and the European Workers' Anti-Fascist Congress. No one from these organizations could be admitted to Labour party membership.[96] Gillies also cautioned about the negative effect that increased immigration would have upon trade-union perception. "It would be difficult to convince trade unionists out of employment that they would eventually benefit." In 1938 Gillies wrote of the need to rationalize the refugee crisis and to calm the public.

> The main need is to "put across" the economic truths . . . anti-alien prejudice is unfortunately easily aroused and requires to be counteracted . . . Even people of liberal views sometimes tend to take a short-sighted sectional view of the problem. Thus they mistakenly give tacit approval to doctrines of nationalism and even racialism.[97]

He worked with Quaker Margery Fry, the sister of the artist Roger Fry, in refugee relief efforts. Gillies gave her many French socialist contacts, but his Labour partisanship surfaced repeatedly in his approaches to the refugee issues.[98] In 1936 he reported on his inquiries into the activities of a refugee who approached the Labour party several times, "a penniless Austrian Social Democrat, has . . . appeared in London on three different missions. . . . I am convinced that the connecting link is Münzenberg."[99] The divisions in the British political community, like those that Europeans brought with them, subverted unity among antifascists and contributed to conflict over the "most deserving" victims fleeing, enduring, or perishing in the Reich's terror. The government lacked enthusiasm for many of the refugees and was involved in the surveillance of others. In the years leading to appeasement and Munich, these factors combined to help stall the very assistance that antifascist organizers of all hues desired, in consonance with the sheer impossibility of ever taking in all who sought asylum—a number utterly unfathomable to those in government and antifascists, alike.

MÜNZENBERG IN PARIS

Münzenberg's life in France was a complex sojourn in the Continental political quicksands of 1933–39.[100] He had to negotiate the shift in French communist activities consequent upon the Anti-War Congress of 1932 in Amsterdam, at which Ada Wright was present, which ushered in an era of attempted coalition and collaborative activism that was very different from his past practice.[101] He was the oldest Bolshevik-era veteran and leader, still operating in Western Europe in Comintern and left circles in the era of the Moscow trials.[102] The Comintern policy of soliciting allies in the establishment governments of the West, and the internal domestic French political situation, both contributed to the new directions adopted by the French communist party (PCF) in the mid-1930s—the years of Münzenberg's exile in Paris. The French party was increasingly "bypassed" in Moscow's search for Western allies, a picture that conforms to Padmore's insistence that the Comintern was abandoning many local and colonial struggles in favor of a grander geopolitics of Soviet preeminence and self-preservation.[103] Stalin "viewed the Comintern with contempt."[104]

The failure of the 1935 counterplebiscite in the Saar region, a project of the socialists in which ethnic Germans were asked to reject governance by the Reich, ended the rescue and exile work that had been going on in the border region involving not only Münzenberg and Gross, but Ellen Wilkinson. He and Gross traveled twice to Moscow from Paris, where Gross claimed they were shocked at the sight of a forced labor camp.[105] But this was not enough to propel Münzenberg away from the Comintern; its support made his lifestyle possible. Instead, he mourned the reduction in his allowance. By 1935 exiled communists in Moscow were disappearing. This unsettling information reached Gross and Münzenberg, yet Münzenberg remained on the politburo of the exiled KPD organization awhile longer, loyal to Moscow, and even writing to Stalin on his own behalf as he began to fear excommunication.[106] As Léon Blum's Popular Front government rose to power in France, Münzenberg was more than once forced to reassess his direction. The Franco-Russian military agreement of 1935 sat very poorly with German communists whose massive defeat hardened attitudes against mutual cooperation between SPD and KPD survivors.[107]

In June 1935 a London gathering at Trafalgar Square featured George Allison, the trade-union militant who had been active in India before the Meerut Trial. He appeared with Ivor Montagu and others. The rally called for "Friendship with the German People. Not With the Hitler Government of Terror and War." Fascism came "from above" in this formulation, and it was a line that Münzenberg shared. The rich were fascism's key supporters and this outlook supposed that defeatism, an unwillingness to fight for the Nazis, could still grip German workers.[108] By late 1936 London liberals and independent radicals had mobilized their own, independent antifascist apparatus, including the British Anti-Nazi Boycott group, and the British Non-Sectarian Anti-Nazi Council, boasting Norman Angell, Herbert Morrison, and Eleanor Rathbone.[109] In 1937 a new, meteoric attempt at a Unity Campaign began, involving the ILP, the communists, and Cripps's Socialist League. Cripps, Richard Mitchison, James Maxton, Fenner Brockway, and Palme Dutt were among the members of the three negotiating teams.[110] In late 1937 the ILP leadership drafted resolutions supporting the Popular Front and the struggle against imperialism, and in favor of resisting war and opposing Japanese imperialism in China.[111] The ILP summer-school topics for 1938 reflected the consciousness of the last days before Munich. There were classes on "the American situation," France, Austria, and the POUM.[112]

British antifascism looked to France, where Blum's Popular Front government made the possibilities for action seem greater than in the cold political climate of the Second National Government at Westminster. But most French refugees were much less fortunate than Münzenberg's well-heeled circle, especially as economic conditions had worsened in 1934 and 1935. Gross acted as proprietor of the Moscow-financed Éditions Carrefour publishing concern, the French publisher of the *Brown Book of the Hitler Terror*.[113] In July 1936 Münzenberg joined the consultative commission of eight that advised the French government on refugee issues, created in part to identify Nazi agents. Its members included German socialist Albert Grzesinski, who had testified at the mock trial in London, as well as Jewish, Quaker, and refugee representatives from other sectors. But Münzenberg's membership lasted only a few months.[114] In his inner sanctum, he continued to rely upon Otto Katz and Arthur Koestler. Koestler had joined the German communist party in 1931, and was a correspondent for the Ullstein press during the early thirties. Koestler also worked for the British *News Chronicle* in Moscow, Paris, and Zurich, and was in the press corps covering the Moscow trials. His base in Paris was the Free German Library established by Münzenberg and others as a response to the Third Reich's book-burning campaign; it served as a documentation center on what was going on inside Germany.[115] Koestler and Katz helped to form the Committee for the Preparation of a German People's Front, created to bring together the top socialist and communist leaders in exile, but the socialists had an ambivalent response to its negotiating sessions that occurred at the Hôtel Lutetia from 1935.[116]

Münzenberg's membership in the exiled KPD executive continued while intellectuals of liberal or left persuasions were coming into the orbit of his small, ecumenical People's Front. On December 21, 1936, seventy signatories issued a "call to the German People," including writers Lion Feuchtwanger, Toller, and Stefan Zweig, and communist leaders Wilhelm Pieck and Walter Ulbricht—the future East German prime minister—along with Münzenberg. Future West German chancellor Willy Brandt signed for the dissident socialist SAP (the allies of Britain's ILP), and several social-democrats attached their names. The declaration spoke "against war and autarchy and for peace and cooperation." The group protested against injustice in the Reich and entered the controversy provoked by the 1936 Berlin Olympics.[117] But this alliance ultimately expelled Ulbricht, and Münzenberg resigned or was expelled.

In August 1936 Bolshevik leaders Grigory Zinoviev and Lev Kamenev were executed in the Soviet Union. The news of their deaths was a deep blow for Münzenberg, who had been their rebel protégé and beneficiary. In October Gross and Münzenberg visited Moscow again, where they saw Gross's exiled sister Margarete Buber-Neumann and brother-in-law Heinz Neumann.[118] The Soviets tried to persuade Münzenberg to remain there, and he was asked to appear before the Comintern security body, the infamous International Control Commission, but he fled to France instead, deeply suspicious of such a meeting. He may have written a statement of support for Zinoviev's execution in order to "buy" his visa.[119] The Comintern's lurch away from collaborative politics during 1933–34 rendered Münzenberg's French coalition work on a smaller scale useless to him, unsupported as it was by Moscow.[120] Münzenberg, surely in fear for his life, retreated to a chateau at Châtenay-Malabry south of Paris, the home of exiled Russian Menshevik supporters. By January Bolshevik leader Karl Radek; Buber-Neumann's husband, Heinz Neumann; and Münzenberg's friend from the Russian embassy in Paris, Marcel Rosenberg, had all been arrested in Moscow. Another attempt to bring all the exiled groups together in Paris foundered in April 1937. There was tension over the Moscow trials and disunity among factions. The group committed to the Hôtel Lutetia negotiations could not reaffirm its mission.[121] In the summer of 1937, Münzenberg tried to form a Deutsches Freiheits Partei in France among German exiles including writer Heinrich Mann, exiled newspaper editor Leopold Schwarzchild, and journalist Georg Bernhard.[122]

But Münzenberg finally abandoned the circles and the offices of the communist party even despite his expulsion at the hands of the Comintern, though he initially refused to acknowledge this outcome.[123] In July he placed notices in a Russian exile paper, and stated that he had still not broken with the Comintern. But he was formally expelled on October 27, 1937, and only able to hang onto his fragile membership in the KPD in exile. In May 1938 the exiled German KPD executive followed suit, and that autumn, he wrote to his closest friends of his departure from organized communism.[124] Meanwhile, Arthur Koestler traveled to Spain as a journalist, where he was imprisoned at the risk of his life. Koestler's *Spanish Testament*, published in 1937, reached George Orwell who released *Homage to Catalonia* in 1938, exposing a wider readership to the realities of Soviet treachery in Spain.[125]

During the late thirties, many individual communist refugees and former communists still populated France. The International Brigade members who had departed the fighting fronts of the Spanish Republic were the former members of a five-thousand-strong German contingent, 90 percent of whom were communists. A third had come as volunteers directly from inside Germany, and many from exile in France. Two thousand of these *brigadistas* died in battle. The survivors were held in French internment camps at Gurs and other locations. They relied upon the mercy of the French government, which adopted a noninterventionist position on Spain.[126] Münzenberg opened up lines to these veterans and their newly formed exile groups. There was a growing belief in France and elsewhere that the Russians had betrayed the Republicans in Spain. Former communists who had gone over to the anti-Stalinist POUM, had not forgotten Münzenberg from his days of celebrity as a militant KPD orator and Reichstag deputy, and their plight became central to his life's final efforts in France. Münzenberg was still a Leninist when he left the Comintern, and did not attack the Soviet Union in print. But he made known his break with Stalin for posterity, during the short life of the eclectic, broad-front, antifascist, pro-Spain journal *Die Zukunft*, first issued on September 29, 1938, two weeks after Munich, from offices in the rue de Faubourg St. Honoré.

Languages of Assistance

> My sister Paula is in a panic. . . . If only they could get out. Jacob Heyner, (B's publisher) arrived emaciated after eight weeks in a Gestapo prison, also his seventeen year old daughter. Camil Hoffmann helped to free them through some foreign Embassy. Here in England an incredible indifference. Some papers are openly anti-Semitic. Only the Quakers perform miracles of helpfulness. Have my friends Christopher Isherwood and Wyston Auden arrived in Santa Monica?[127]

In the compounding crises of the later thirties, many pressures bore down upon the language and actions of British refugee activism. The numbers fleeing the Spanish Civil War to Britain increased, the Poles clamored to expel their "excess Jews," and the Italians passed racial laws endangering the many thousands of Italian Jews living under Mussolini's rule. Arab hostility to advancing Jewish immigration to Palestine exacerbated guerilla attacks and labor disputes in the mandate, while Jewish-British tensions in the region grew to boiling point. The hope that the Empire might accommodate vast numbers of Jews and others fleeing central Europe remained as a chimera throughout the discourse of the refugee question: "The refugees had to be readily assimilable into the white population," a racial standard that allowed many colonies to claim that they could not receive transfers, while Whitehall categorized other territories as unfit to receive those seeking asylum.[128] William Gillies stated that candidates for such immigration schemes had to be "assimilable types from those countries to similar stock and outlook to Britain."[129] Those refugees who were both "white" and "Western European" in appearance and sensibility were best tolerated. The governor of Kenya opposed the plan to send Jews there: "A Jewish enclave of this kind would be an undesirable feature in a colony which . . . should be developed on lines predominantly British." Only "Nordic Jews" were appropriate in his view, and Germans and Austrians were subsequently selected for agricultural work, with a ceiling set at 150 in September 1938. The West Indies, British Honduras, and British Guiana were removed from the transfer list on the grounds that there were too many people there already.[130] India accepted more Jews than did other colonies,[131] while white settler communities resisted the refugee influx in many territories. The eleven thousand whites already in northern Rhodesia sat "encamped in a vast uninhabited and undeveloped territory and like dogs in the manger refuse[d] to allow anyone else to enter it."[132]

Eleanor Rathbone was one of several key figures slowly moving to the center stage of refugee advocacy within the political establishment.[133] She served as secretary of the Parliamentary Committee on Refugees, chaired by Lord Marley, who had served Münzenberg from the earliest days of the Paris–London–New York axis of communist relief work. Her chief parliamentary ally was Josiah Wedgwood MP, and the *Manchester Guardian* often served as a sounding board for her views. Rathbone rhetorically sought to link Nazi internal policy with the purported imperial ambitions of the Reich. Hers was not a voice speaking out against empire per se, but a voice raised against the Nazification of mandates or colonies, a policy that she condemned as racist, and she also articulated a notion of hierarchy in which nonwhite, non-Europeans were categorized as more vulnerable than Jews. In 1933 she wrote, "Well, if Germany is not disillusioned, we are. Who can doubt that its foreign policy if it dared to show its hand, would be in full keeping with its internal policy? To permit any measure of re-armament to such a Germany would be lunacy and to give a share in Mandates would be a crime against any colored race affected."[134]

In reply to a correspondent who questioned the assumption that Germany would necessarily treat colonial peoples in worse ways than Britain did, Rathbone replied, "the theory of racial superiority and of what is justifiable in the treatment of races judged inferior which has taken such strong roots in Germany do seem to make it clear that their treatment of subject peoples less well able to protect themselves than the Jews would be very ruthless."[135] Yet in 1935, at the parliamentary elections where she again stood for her combined universities seat, Rathbone appeared more flexible, intimating that there might be some grounds for the transfer of British territories under controlled circumstances: "The transfer of mandates and extension of the mandatory system should only be considered with due regard to the welfare and wishes of native populations, who must not be treated as pawns in an imperial or profit-seeking game."[136]

Rathbone spoke and wrote so much on "rescuing the perishing" that the pundits dubbed her "the perishing Miss Rathbone."[137] She had a global thrust. Her friend Margery Fry recalled that Rathbone's charges included "Little girls suffering from cruel ceremonies in Africa ... hungry refugees in Europe ... Polish people."[138] In addition to her belated and scant involvement in communist-led German relief work, Rathbone seriously indulged united-front work with the communists in the National Joint Committee for Spanish Relief."[139] In May 1937, after the Nazi bombing of the Spanish market town of Guernica, Rathbone addressed a meeting of this body and spoke of her communist colleague: "As for Isobel Brown, I expect most of you know and are anticipating perhaps painfully the part she will play in this meeting. Give generously."[139] Her approach to the diplomacy of the era differed with that of Lord and Lady Simon. "If the League had stood firm over Abyssinia, neither Italy nor Germany would have dared so much in Spain."[140] In May of 1937, four thousand Basque children were allowed into Britain, the children of "only the very respectable" Republicans.[141] The Simons were among the noted visitors to their camp.

Rathbone worked with Violet Bonham Carter on the Non-Sectarian Anti-Nazi Council but was never brought into the Focus Group ("Focus in Defense of Freedom and Peace") comprised of Winston Churchill's trusted intimates and collaborators from across the political spectrum, a group that prominently included Bonham Carter.[142] Churchill could not have regarded Rathbone as clubbable, nor especially useful as an Independent MP, lacking in hard party ties as she was, though she supported him in Parliament in the context of the struggle against appeasement.[143] Many Focus Group members, including Bonham Carter, contributed to Münzenberg's *Die Zukunft* while Rathbone did not. Rathbone sought to avert race war and to inspire and preserve Britain and the Empire as reforming and civilizing entities. She warned of the possibility of a fascist-backed Arab mobilization, and was familiar with the dilemmas of Palestine.[144] Her sense of maternal rescue was strong; she wrote of the "backwardness of Arab women" and of the limitations faced by women in Africa as compared to the "ample opportunities given to Jewish women to participate in the magnificent experiment of building a National Home."[145]

Rathbone sought to forge policy allowing refugees across the Empire to avoid intense concentrations that might ignite racist sentiment. Increasingly, she and others who shared her views fought fiercely for "their Empire" versus that of the Reich. She became particularly involved in debate about assistance to Sudeten Germans and German refugees in Czechoslovakia, emphasizing their *political* persecution. Here, the distinction between the "racial" persecution of Jews, and the "racial" exploitation potentially faced by colonial peoples under the Reich were not confused with the "political" repression faced by the Czechs.[146] In a reply to Rathbone during the House debate, Sir Samuel Hoare stated that more refugees might be let in to Britain, application by application, depending on the "capacity of the voluntary organizations to undertake responsibility for their maintenance and establishment in this country without involving a displacement of British labor." But Rathbone pressed further, claiming that they were in "imminent danger." She subsequently pled for the temporary maintenance of Czech refugees by the government, and was rebuffed by Sir John Simon, who stated that there was no hope of altering the policy of requiring private funds rather than government subsidies in the Czech case. Rathbone persisted, and continued to press for help for refugees after the onset of the war. Her parliamentary committee was not formed until very late in the refugee crisis, but it fought valiantly for recognition and a more inclusive and urgent policy, with little success in terms of numbers, given the lateness of the hour. Her biographer Susan Pedersen concludes,

> large schemes had failed—the Spanish Republic lay in ruins, Eastern Europe's last democracy had been crushed in the Nazi fist—but the knowledge that she had helped to bring a few threatened Spanish Republicans, a few German social democrats and a few Czech Jews to safety was comfort of a kind.[147]

The notion of the refugee-in-transit as an agent of political unrest was in part "created" by the interwar-period insistence that transferring "native" populations was wrong, that it catered to suspicion and prejudice, and that even European ethnic groups, not unlike colonial subjects, belonged in the regions and nations where they habitually resided. The League supported this idea, and historian Louise London contends that in so doing, it rendered the "refugee" a destabilizing element and persona. In her view the Nazis took this concept to a radical extreme. Britain and France finally challenged some of the objections to ethnic transfers at the Munich Conference of 1938 in their rush to see ethnic Germans moved back across established borders. The concomitant expulsion of Jews from Germany and Austria, if not from Czechoslovakia, was also accepted by the Allies at that table. Thus, by 1938 "the international community was generally resigned to the Jews' permanent expulsion" in an about-face of the posture they had adopted at Versailles. Child refugees, for example, could be anglicized. There could be a humane process of reabsorption. This was a distinctively British assertion of ethnic goals along lines certainly articulated more compassionately than the Nazi policy of forcing the "purification" of the population by other means. But a paradox surrounding those who supported the League and condemned Munich was that it was in part the League that had *opposed* the rational transfer of condemned populations, while it was Munich that legitimated it, de facto. Britain helped Germany deport the Czech Jews after Munich—the efforts of Rathbone, Gillies, and others to prevent their expulsion to no avail. The British did not behave at that moment as the political opponents of the Germans. Tory MP and First Lord of the Admiralty Duff Cooper was willing to allow some Czech communists to be included among those assisted, but he favored limiting their number.[148] Some hundreds of thousands on the European continent took the last advantage given them and most others perished. The League's intransigence on the issue of the sanctity of the nation-state limited its sympathy for populations at risk who were increasingly stateless. There was certainly a British impulse to assist foreigners who were victims of unfair persecution, but it collided with a desire to limit the inclusion of these selfsame foreigners in the nation-state. Even after 1938, policy continued to reflect these conflicts.

On November 21, 1938, in the aftermath of Kristallnacht, Lord Noel-Baker introduced a motion in the House to express "profound concern" and to develop "a common policy" for refugees, in cooperation with other nations, including the United States, acknowledging the aspirations of Jewish patriotism, and admitting the Jews to a stature of "Europeanness" and "Britishness," which served to justify assistance to them and to frustrate the charge of alien betrayal or conflict of interest.

> Nothing is more certain than that it is no crime, no disloyalty, no treason of the Jews which has brought this fate upon them. We have good cause in this country to know the great services which the Jews have rendered to our nation. . . . Members will not forget the Jewish contribution to the building of the Empire . . . their five Victoria crosses. . . . Their services to Germany were certainly not less. . . . Throughout the world, they have made . . . an immeasurable contribution to . . . all that makes civilization worthwhile. . . . only when they were driven from their posts in 1933 [did we see] clearly how great a part of what we call the German genius, was really the genius of the Jews.[149]

In hindsight, this discussion demonstrated the severe limitations of the parliamentarians' apprehension of the proportions of the impending crisis. In response to Kristallnacht, Conservative MP Samuel (Hugh) Hammersley called for Palestine to take "50,000 additional immigrants," while Liberal MP Geoffrey Mander reported that there were 5 million Jews living in the "nations to the East," speculating that in some places, "particularly in Poland, the Jewish question is becoming very serious indeed, and we may have very large numbers of these persons on our hands as well." He added, emphatically, "It really will not do for us to tell other nations, possessing the enormous empire that we do." In late November he suggested that temporary camping facilities might assist in Belgium or Holland; James Maxton replied, "It is hardly camping weather just now." Conservative MP Herbert Butcher, like many others, continued to debate the criteria for entry into Britain, positing "good character" and "robust health" as possible standards.

> Either the refugees are a burden which, for very shame of our common humanity, we are compelled to shoulder, or, alternatively, they are a definite and positive asset, the

value of which is temporarily forgotten in certain countries, the rulers of which are blinded by fear, by untenable and untested theories of *race and political culture* and the true position that religion should occupy in the State [author's emphasis].

Conservative MP Archibald Southby ventured that "One of the difficulties in finding a solution of the problem is that many of the people from Germany are . . . not suitable for work on the land. They are people of business occupation. Great assets they will be, to the countries which are able to absorb them." Maxton protested against the slowness with which the Czech requests were being treated, citing the case of a Jewish socialist colleague whose visa was finally granted, only to be withdrawn. "The getting of these people away from danger point is a matter of urgency, and the merit of the individuals can be looked into after their bodies are safe." Ribbing those who supported the maintenance of "international capitalism," he took aim at the use of Jewish stereotypes and the treatment of refugees as business investments: "The type of problem we are confronting . . . should not be confronted from the point of view of how we can exploit the Jewish people, but of how we can give them the same opportunities in the world as we have ourselves. That is perhaps not a guarantee of perfect security or of the certainty of being able to earn a livelihood." In November 1938 Neville Chamberlain rose:

> As regards the colonial Empire, it must be remembered that, although covering a great extent of territory, it is not necessarily capable of the immediate absorption of large numbers of refugees. Many of our Colonies and Protectorates and our Mandated Territories in East and West Africa contain native populations of many millions, for whom we are the trustees, and whose interests must not be prejudiced. Many large areas, which at present are sparsely populated, are unsuitable either climactically or economically for European settlement.[150]

Conservative Samuel Hoare spoke in the House about the need to confront the "groundswell of opposition to refugees." Churchill's cousin Lord Londonderry and Admiral Sir Barry Domvile had both had dealings with von Ribbentrop and were among those who saw refugees as "Marxists." In May 1939 immigration to Palestine was limited to 75,000, unless the Arabs consented to a larger number. Meanwhile, Walter Guiness (Lord Moyne), who chaired the Royal Commission on the West Indies, protested against too much reliance on that region, predicting an "outcry" amid the "fear" of refugees being sent there.[151] In the aftermath of Munich, there were attempts to test the limits of refugee policy. In June 1939 the peace and civil liberties activist Elizabeth Acland Allen applied for visas for eight Spanish Civil War veterans held in camps in southern France. Rathbone was involved in this effort.[152]

As the discourse around the refugee questions grew more prolific, the problems of categorization and competing notions of victimhood remained. Never was there a single category of acceptable refugee. Campaigns for each potential group of beneficiaries: political dissenters, Jews, Czechs, Basques, Spanish citizens—even if these were overlapping identities—competed for support and for parliamentary and government recognition. Racial politics played a formidable role in delivering notions of victimhood. Those subjected to the exigencies of colonial policy in the Caribbean, India, or elsewhere in the Empire were not understood as commensurate with those fleeing fascism. But neither were the enemies of fascism perceived or treated as a single constituency. Prejudice fed policy, while much that was to happen in the European theater of war remained unanticipated. Profound sympathy for the Reich's imminent victims in their millions was uncommon and unexplored in the late 1930s, and the competing political agendas were large.

Die Zukunft: The Last Intervention

Willi Münzenberg and his colleagues conceived the Parisian-based journal *Die Zukunft* as a kind of opposition paper "above party"—a last effort at collaboration among exiles and their allies before the German invasion of France.[153] In November 1938 Münzenberg wrote to Guy Menant, a French *député* and former undersecretary of state, about his plans for the publication.

> We are not proposing a journal concentrating on German or Austrian emigration as such, the scope of the paper being essentially European. . . . As for the editorial tendencies of the paper, these lean towards [*sic*] totalitarian dictatorship, be it Bolshevik or Fascist. . . . The editorial board is endeavoring to develop a positive program which proves that there exists in the German-speaking lands a peaceful and democratic alternative to Hitlerian imperialism.

He added that he saw *Die Zukunft* as an important platform for men of status and position in the Anglo-Saxon and French worlds who were interested in events on the European continent. "The paper rigorously abstains from any interference in the domestic policies of the democracies."[154] Arthur Koestler led *Die Zukunft's* original editorial staff, which included the writer and social scientist Manès Sperber; the prominent Catholic exile and former editor Werner Thormann; and the literary critic and philosopher Ludwig Marcuse who was also the former editor of the liberal Berlin journal *Vossische Zeitung*. *Die Zukunft's* benefactor was Münzenberg's friend the Swedish banker Olaf Aschberg, who left Berlin for Paris before 1933.[155]

Otto Katz remained a communist in the face of Münzenberg's departure and expulsion from the Comintern and he visited London on behalf of *Die Zukunft*, where his affiliation may have been hidden. Katz also sought funds in Hollywood, using his alias "André Simone." *Die Zukunft* had many English contributors, and the task of translating their essays was a major preoccupation of its editors. The English-language writers hailed from many strata of the establishment political community, but very rarely from the organized or communist left. The journal's executives included the general secretary of the Fabian Society, John Parker MP.[156] Some of the contributors had assisted in Koestler's release from Spain, including press baron Walter Layton, proprietor of the *News Chronicle* who first sent Koestler into Spain as a reporter. Violet Bonham Carter, Lady Astor, and the Duchess of Atholl all wrote for the journal, and Atholl contributed the introduction to Koestler's *Spanish Testament*. Koestler, Katz, and Münzenberg turned to Koestler's British supporters for help with *Die Zukunft*'s London operations. During the summer of 1938, Koestler vacationed in Sanary-sur-Mer where historian Ernst Kantorowicz, Heinrich Mann, novelist Arnold Zweig, Ernst Toller, Austrian writer Robert Neumann, and Ellen Wilkinson were all guests at the home of Lion Feuchtwanger, indicating an ornate set of connections between the journal, the Reichstag Fire mock trial, the exile community, and the Socialist League.[157]

Some French socialists offered Münzenberg financial support for the new journal, but he made no headway among his former communist comrades. Manès Sperber recalled, "If he had harbored the hope that the intellectuals he had recruited for the cause would follow suit, he quickly had to resign himself to the fact that none of his former *compagnons de route* would have anything to do with him."[158] Koestler recalled *Die Zukunft* as "stillborn" and stale and left the journal after three months of extensive involvement. Yet his biographer David Cesarani asserts, "it was a rallying point for disillusioned Communists and anti-Fascists of all hues. The paper was loosely tied to the Deutsches Freiheits Partei and together they represented one of the first attempts to create a progressive, anti-Stalinist and anti-Fascist politics for Europe."[159]

Münzenberg's recent and notorious communist credentials did not seem to have alienated his more moderate supporters and writers. These included literary figures like H. G. Wells and former *Daily Mail* editor Edward Montagu Compton MacKenzie; the Marxist writer Max Beer; the journalist, editor, and historian Henry Wickham Steed; the *New Statesman* editor Kingsley Martin; the *Economist* editor Graham Hutton; and political figures like Alfred Duff Cooper, Lord Robert Cecil, and Herbert Morrison, who all appeared in its pages in the first year of *Die Zukunft*'s two-year run. From Norman Angell to Violet Bonham Carter to John Heartfield, the leading humanitarians, anti-appeasement politicians, as well as many antifascist creative artists and literary figures both British and German, were contributors or subscribers.[160] The British contributors comprised a mostly liberal-minded but establishment group, with strong League of Nations and antislavery connections among them. Most were *not* Scottsboro signatories and were outside the loop of the ILP and communist fellow-traveler circles, and much closer to the upper circles of government; some, like Steed were strong anticommunists and even anti-Semites, while others, like Beer had socialist and *marxisant* backgrounds. Morrison was a Labour party leader.

Many of the British contributors wrote on issues of foreign policy and diplomacy, trying to suggest a unity of purpose between the "English people" and, as Wickham Steed referred to it, "The True Germany." Steed described Hitler as betraying the "best elements" among the Germans.[161] Duff Cooper wrote of the empathy the English felt for Germans in the face of repulsive Nazism, greeting "the appearance of a German-language publication devoted to events in areas where intellectual freedom is still respected."[162] The repeated premise was that Hitler's policy was aimed at Europe and Europeans, and was un-German, and in this respect, there was an echo of the communist line that the "German people," or German proletariat per se, were not the enemy. A characteristically British establishment and Germanophile cultural affinity informed these arguments. Harold Nicolson and Arthur Koestler wrote on English "character" and German "temperament" in paired articles; Herbert Morrison published "An Open Letter to the German People."[163] They shared an absence of confidence in the Munich mindset, Cooper writing that Chamberlain had wandered "too far down the road to capitulation."[164] In October 1938 Max Beer wrote "Thank God war was prevented, but the peace rests on a tragic misunderstanding."[165]

Die Zukunft considered policies toward the colonies and mandates as they emerged in the diplomatic arena. In late 1938 Kingsley Martin wrote that it was "still possible to save Spain," and that rearmament was the best guarantor of freedom from fascism.[166] Others offered history lessons on democracy, as in Lord Robert Cecil's "The Foundations of the English Constitution." There were statements of lofty principle, like Scots Liberal-party leader Archibald Sinclair's contribution to a series of identifications of walks of life, entitled "We English Liberals." He wrote, "We Liberals support social justice without regard to race, religion or class. Internationally, we support the friendship of nations, and oppose anything that would prevent the free movement of people, goods and capital."[167]

After founding the journal, Münzenberg went to see Nehru at the Swiss sanitarium in the Black Forest where Kamala Nehru lay dying. Babette Gross reported that Nehru told Münzenberg that he simply wanted to be interned in prison in India rather than forced to choose sides in an impending war. The only surviving contribution from anyone of color to *Die Zukunft* is Nehru's "India Speaks to the German People," which appeared in November 1938. In expressing his anti-imperialism, Nehru contended that he and others in the Indian national movement opposed imperialism and National Socialism at the same time. In so doing, they opposed the violence of the Nazis *and* British imperial policy, a divisive force incapable of defeating fascism. Instead, Nehru advocated a united progressive front against "evil . . . war and . . . violence." India's intransigence in the face of the British offered an example for the Germans in their struggle against Hitler, "and to all peoples who want[ed] to struggle against a superior force." Nehru insisted that Indians had no contempt for the English people or for any other people.[168]

Klaus and Erika Mann, members of the *Die Zukunft* circle, represented the particular strand of Continental exile culture that was neither pro-Soviet nor centrist, but of the critical, socialist left. Klaus Mann had acted as an emissary for the Soviet writers in the West and attended the 1934 Writers' Congress in Moscow; his greatest work *Mephisto*, was published in 1936.[169] Writers were a key constituency of the journal, and its literary ambitions were considerable. Among its writer contributors was the former publisher Ludwig Feuchtwanger, poet Theodor Kramer of the Neue Sachlichkeit movement, and Stefan Zweig, the most translated of all the exiled writers, who worked with *Die Zukunft* in Paris. They were joined by the editor Manfred George reporting from New York, H. O. Simon from Johannesburg, the London journalist Vernon Bartlett (who also wrote for the African American press), and the historian Emmanuel Mousnier of the Catholic antifascist group L'Esprit, whose communal base was in Châtenay-Malabry, the hamlet near Robinson where Münzenberg had also sought refuge, whence the historian Marc Bloch was later seized by the Nazis.[170] *Die Zukunft* claimed to speak for "all who believe in the fellowship of men, and in the necessity of organized community life between nations and individuals."[171] It advocated the principle of nontyrannical nations having the right to defend themselves, and opposed war, calling instead for peace and the promulgation of free constitutions.

Die Zukunft boasted ties to the Labour-inspired New Commonwealth Institute and the Fabian Research Bureau in London, and pledged to supply statesmen and journalists with "reliable material" on the events taking place on the Continent from offices in the Anglo-Continental Press Agency in the Strand. Its Fabian thrust aligned it with the moderation of official imperial reform currents in London. Its commitment to information gathering and documentation had also characterized the work of exposé surrounding the *Brown Book of the Hitler Terror*, though *Die Zukunft* was a far less sensational or propagandistic publication. Letitia Fairfield, the sister of writer Rebecca West, held literary and social evenings for the journal in her London home. The "Friends of *Die Zukunft*" had its headquarters in the Theobald Road, and its editorial offices in Bayswater. Wilhelm Wolfgang Schütz was *Die Zukunft*'s London editor, a member of German socialist exile circles. He was involved in the YMCA and Fabian activity and well connected with the milieu that Münzenberg now addressed. As a young journalist, Schütz also contributed to those publications whose editors had ties to *Die Zukunft*, including the *Contemporary Review*, the *New Statesman and Nation*, and the *Spectator*. He was an active member of PEN, the writers' international civil rights association, a lifeline between writers and journalists in Paris, London, and New York.[172] Key London contributors and those who assisted in the inner circle of the journal included Koestler's friend the "red" Duchess of Atholl, the first woman Scots MP, who traveled to Spain with Rathbone and Wilkinson and resigned her seat over Munich, never to be reelected. The League of Nations secretary Noel-Baker, the Hungarian film producer Alexander Korda, and the journalist Arthur Cummings, who covered the Leipzig Reichstag Fire trial of 1933, were all associated with *Die Zukunft*. Cummings was the most widely read political columnist in the nation and an avid opponent of appeasement. Conservative MP Duff Cooper's recruitment to *Die Zukunft* was a serious coup for Münzenberg. If Cooper wavered on compromise with the Italians, he was nevertheless a strong opponent of Hitler who also resigned his parliamentary seat over Munich and was subsequently re-elected. Harold Nicolson MP, another contributor, recalled that Cooper "regarded as barbarous all extremists of the Right or the left."[173]

Still, this pantheon of establishment figures did not allow Münzenberg to shirk his image and reputation as a leading communist. London financial magnate Horace Samuel approached Koestler in late 1938 to demand that *Die Zukunft* publish a disclaimer against communism, citing all the organizations with which Münzenberg had been associated.[174] Archibald Sinclair sent a clipping containing these accusations to Paris, writing that "every newspaper or person is accused nowadays of communism or war-mongering, if it refuses to believe that the Munich line is the road to salvation."[175]

During *Die Zukunft*'s short life, Münzenberg and his collaborators regularly appealed to leading Western statesmen, including Churchill and Roosevelt, through extensive correspondence. Their solicitous letters portrayed the group of exiled Germans as united against Hitler and in possession of authoritative information on the world of the Reich. The editors approached Labour party and trade-union leaders like Walter Citrine, David Dubinsky of the American garment trades' union (ILGWU), and Tory leaders like Anthony Eden. Ludwig Marcuse continued his editorial work for *Die Zukunft* in his American exile. ACLU leader Roger Baldwin remained a contact after his involvement in the Scottsboro campaign and the mock Reichstag Fire Trial. *Die Zukunft* had global ambitions. There was a French section, and an unidentified "German-African" party approached Münzenberg. In 1938 William Gillies researched the widening web connecting *Die Zukunft* to Labour party figures, identifying Isobel Brown and the anarchist Monica Whately, who was active in the feminist social policy Six-Point Group with Helen Fletcher and George Lieber of *Die Zukunft*. They had ties in turn with Rathbone, Hope Simpson, and Josiah Wedgwood, all refugee advocates. Gillies had always pursued the links between communists and Labour party members, but by the end of the decade the multiple and overlapping affiliations transcended his earlier maps of surveillance.[176] *Die Zukunft* was also represented by Guenther Anders and Oskar Maria Graf in the United States.[177] There were hosts of local subscribers in each country where a German, and very often German-Jewish constituency of recent exiles or residents of long-standing, sustained interest.

The London group of subscribers included many exiles and émigrés of prominence on the German and Austrian left from both socialist and communist circles, including writer and homosexual rights advocate Kurt Hiller, Hans

Gottfurcht of SOPADE (the exiled SPD), and Herta Gotthelf, a member of the Spartacus uprising of 1919, who had worked with Ernst Toller. Helene Stöcker, the leader of the Sexual Reform League, was a veteran of Münzenberg's early LAI.[178] Other subscribers were exiled journalists like Rudolf Olden. Czech caricaturist Walter Trier illustrated the German edition of Twain's *Huckleberry Finn* just before his exile. He published in the English literary magazine *Lilliput* from 1937 to 49 and provided hundreds of antifascist drawings to the London dailies, including the *Picture Post*.[179]

Toller, a critical figure of the political literary community, was both author and dramatist. He was imprisoned for his part in the German revolution of 1918–19 and, after his release, visited London as a guest of the ILP, where he first met Ellen Wilkinson, Fenner Brockway, and George Lansbury. In 1927 Toller helped to found the League against Colonial Oppression with Münzenberg and Nehru. He and Rudolf Olden served as official PEN delegates in Britain. Like Klaus Mann, he attended the 1934 Congress of Soviet Writers and helped to establish the German Freedom Library before arriving in the United Kingdom in 1935. His friends included Kingsley Martin, Wickham Steed, Harold Laski, and D. N. Pritt. The ILP maintained its illegal network of assistance for Germans underground through Toller. But his view of his fellow exiles and of his fellow Jews was unsparing, reflecting another strand of prejudice not uncommon on the left. He wrote to Ludwig Marcuse, "The émigrés of 1933 are a confused collection of those exiled by chance—including many Jews who are Nazi *manqués*, weaklings with vague ideas, paragons of virtue whom only Hitler prevents from being swine, with very few men of conviction among them. German, all too German."[180] In May of 1939, Toller attended the large PEN conference in New York and committed suicide in his hotel room. It was not his first American sojourn; he had toured the country in 1931 and written against lynching.[181]

Academics were among the prominent British exiles who subscribed to *Die Zukunft*, and like other professionals, they often had advantages under the British alien entry criteria that obtained until just before the war. Kurt Rothschild, a professor of political economy in Vienna, came to the United Kingdom in 1938 where he pursued an internationally recognized career as an economic theoretician. The mathematician Hans Ludwig Hamburger arrived in 1939. But despite this roster of subscribers and the caliber of many whose work appeared in the journal's pages, Manès Sperber recalled that, "The influence of *Die Zukunft* on émigrés and others outside their circles could not readily be ascertained, yet none of us considered abandoning it. . . . almost all other German publications [in Paris] were overtly or covertly Communist." He reported the confusions surrounding Münzenberg.

It was common knowledge that *Die Zukunft* was published by Münzenberg, and thus certain people suspected it of being Communist, though most people understood that it was, on the contrary, the organ of a loosely-connected group of former communists who wished to remain neutral toward the Comintern only until Fascism was defeated.[182]

Münzenberg continued to try to organize a small political formation of exiles in Paris, calling his new salon group the Friends of Socialist Unity. In London he and his agents approached nearly every faction that opposed fascism, including the anti-Munich Tories, tapping the "mainstream" representatives of British intellectual political culture on behalf of German exiles who were themselves considerably more progressive than many in England who were now acting as their unwitting advocates through their contributions to the journal. His compass moved to the parliamentary arena, where Münzenberg tried to leverage official foreign policy; Babette Gross's recollection that he sought ties in "politically interested circles" is a transparent understatement.[183] Münzenberg wrote to writer and dramatist Jean Giraudoux in January 1939 of his commitment to "the question of exiles, victims of political, religious and racial persecution in the countries of Central Europe."[184]

From their headquarters along the Dutch border at Münster, the Gestapo monitored Paris in the final months before the German occupation. They regarded *Die Zukunft* as a "mouthpiece" for dissenters.[185] When the Spanish Civil War Republican front finally collapsed in March 1939, German refugees retreated across the Pyrenees to join their comrades interned in the French camp at Gurs. The Münzenberg circle was allied with People in Distress, a committee active in this camp among internees, some of whom became *Die Zukunft* readers and devotees of Münzenberg in his new political guise.[186] They knew of him both from the European world before 1933, and from the exile culture that contributed so much to Spain.[187] Many were experiencing the revelations of Stalinist misdeeds and became open to a new politics of unity across a broad anti-Stalinist left, even though it was far too late. On May 3, 1939, Münzenberg wrote to Gardner Jackson of the American Labor Non-Partisan League and the Washington, D.C., Civil Liberties Union, referring to *Die Zukunft* as the "European tribune for all oppositional movements" and eschewing the "economic royalists" of Europe (Sir John Simon, British foreign secretary Samuel Hoare, French foreign minister Georges Bonnet, and others), "still in the respective cabinets." He called for the "collaboration of democratic allies of world-wide prestige . . . from the Catholics to the extreme left."[188] Was Münzenberg seeking a visa? The contact names who appeared on his internal list included philosopher Otto Neurath in Holland, playwright and poet Bertolt Brecht in Scandinavia, theologian Karl Barth and writer Emil Ludwig in Switzerland, and Helene Stöcker in London.[189] The journal's wider subscription and correspondence pool boasted contacts on each continent, befitting the scope of Münzenberg's lifelong activities.

Figure 5.5. Refugee members of the Republican International Brigade of the Spanish Civil War, reading *Die Zukunft* in the French internment camp at Gurs, near the Pyrenees, in 1939. The photo was sent to Münzenberg by mail; he also received letters and petitions from camp readers, thanking him for his oppositional, anti-Stalinist newspaper. Many of *Die Zukunft*'s Gurs readers were former German communists, now internees on the eve of the German invasion and the fall of France (courtesy of the *Archives Nationales de France*).

In June 1939 Münzenberg once again wrote to a group of world leaders on the situation inside Germany, trying to attract attention in a "confidential" effort "to select authentic and carefully checked information in appropriately condensed form."[190] On June 10, 1939, his colleague Louis Gibarti wrote to Maynard Barnes, first press secretary to the American embassy in Paris with a confidential report for U.S. Secretary of State Cordell Hull and Secretaries Harold Ickes and Henry Morgenthau, enclosing a questionnaire that had been devised in February that year, asking haltingly, "Does your Excellency suppose that the USA will continue its efforts and interest for the positive solution of the refugee question, in spite of handy caps of various character?" Gibarti received a letter from Churchill's private secretary on June 16, 1939, thanking him for his last missive and enclosure, stating that Churchill "would be very glad to receive further communications" from him.[191]

On August 23, 1939, came the announcement of the Nazi-Soviet pact and, a week later, the German invasion of Poland. France and Britain declared war on Germany on September 1. *Die Zukunft* pled, "Peace and freedom must be defended against Hitler and Stalin."[192] Münzenberg, Gross, and their associates anticipated internment. The Daladier government required that Germans under fifty turn themselves in to the French authorities. Münzenberg, just fifty, continued to lobby for his own protection and for the rescue of his closest colleagues. Some Germans detained at the camp at Le Vernet, where there were many internees still loyal to the German communists, reportedly spread the call for "defeatism"—nonsupport to the Allies in the face of the Nazi-Soviet pact. *Die Welt*, published from Stockholm under Walter Ulbricht's editorship, issued a call: "Anyone who intrigues against the friendship of the German and the Soviet people is an enemy of the German people and will be branded as an assistant of British imperialism."[193] This language signaled disarray and dénouement for any remaining hopes for the broad unity of German exiles, and Münzenberg refused its challenge. On September 21, 1939, he wrote to a French government minister on behalf of the nine hundred German communists being held at Gurs, stating that many were no longer supporting a communist line.[194] In October he wrote to French secretary of the interior M. A. Berthoin about the Saar's "breakaway communist movement" in existence since 1936, claiming that it was now part of the "friends of a united socialist Germany," his small salon formation. In this letter and others, Münzenberg continued to seek redress for internees in the French camps. He portrayed himself and those for whom he wrote as anti-Stalinists.[195] That same month, a day before he contacted Léon Blum, Münzenberg wrote to Churchill, asking him to help him get an interview with the journalist Albert Thomas who was stationed at the Maginot Line.[196]

In January 1940 Münzenberg and his colleague, the former communist trade unionist, Walter Oettinghaus, sent a letter of indignation to Nell Black, an associate of Spanish Civil War relief activists in London. They had obtained Black's address from Paul Eduard Koch, an internee among the Spanish volunteers at Gurs, Ilot B. Koch had written to Wilfred Roberts, chair of the National Joint Committee for Spanish Relief Work, "expressing his astonishment concerning the continuous support the 'Stalinists' are getting from the English Relief Committee [for Spain], while the Socialists of the *Ilot B* are not getting anything in spite of their evident need for help." They asked if Black might talk to Roberts in order to "bring about an equitable distribution of relief for all." Koch's complaint signaled the need "to desire and accomplish a radical separation from the Stalinists." After the Stalin/Hitler pact, Ilot B had become a "purely democratic and anti-Stalinistic camp." Yet, the Spanish Relief Committee, they complained, was in the hands of the communist party, and each of forty communist internees had recently been given pounds sterling by the English committee. More than 160 interned Germans and Austrians still needed help. Münzenberg had come full circle, his own past organization now an object of his outrage. The letter was signed, "Friends of the Socialist Unity in Germany . . . French/German Union," Münzenberg's last logo.[197]

In February 1940 Münzenberg managed to meet Sefton Delmer, a leading British journalist visiting the Maginot Line. Jean Giroudoux's freedom radio station was broadcasting readings of *Die Zukunft*'s articles, and in late February, *Die Zukunft* declared "all of these refugees thus thought they were doing their duty and proving that they were indeed the enemies of Hitler, by fighting for Spain: socialists, communists, Jews and the minority parties—all of them were already in Africa," referring to those who had fled to French centers of exile like Dakar. The invasions of Denmark and Norway followed in April, and Holland, Belgium, and Luxemburg fell to the German army in May. The last issue of *Die Zukunft* appeared on May 9, 1940, the day before the first incursion that led to the fall of France and French surrender on June 12.[198]

Chapter 6

A THIEVES' KITCHEN, 1938–39

Towards all peoples of whatever race the British have built up a characteristic attitude of cultivated aloofness, but most Britons, irrespective of social status, display an added aversion to peoples of darker skin. It is this racial egotism and national arrogance which has created a conflict between the British and colored peoples of the Empire.... Few Negroes, in England, I imagine, have not passed through the bitter experience of looking for apartments and being told constantly, "We do not take colored people." In five weeks of flat-hunting the writer learned to find his way competently about London.

   —*George Padmore,* The Crisis, *1938*

I haven't much to say about Negroes. I know that the popular conception of them as a lazy, throat-cutting, fried chicken eating race is wrong but I do think that they are different from the white races—less civilized if you like. I suppose the Tropics are not the place to look for a Leonardo, an Einstein or a Farraday—but I don't think that means they are intellectually inferior. The policy of the white races has always been to exploit the negro, but now that they are getting some measure of Freedom and the benefits of Western culture, they are proving that though they may be backward, there is no reason, given good conditions, why they shouldn't play a very important part in the world.

   —*Mass Observer, housewife, age thirty-nine, near Olney, Yorkshire, 1939*

In november 1937 the fearless Padmore purportedly returned to Nazi Germany. The *Chicago Defender* published his remarkable, if unverified report from Hamburg:

Four years ago I was arrested by the Nazis and deported from Germany for criticizing Hitler's treatment of Negroes from the former German African colonies.... I have recently made a tour through Germany from Holland to Sweden, during which I have had the opportunity to meet and speak with many Jewish leaders and to discuss the "Jewish" problem. For obvious reasons, I shall not mention names, but I am able to say that the position of the Jews under the Nazi regime is as bad as the conditions of the Negroes in the Southern States of America and South Africa.

He described the use of "drastic anti-Semitic methods of terrorism" and the dispatch of fascists to America and South Africa in order to study the methods applied toward blacks in each region, since the Nazis considered Jews to be the "same 'inferior race' as colored people." He reported on the moves toward confining Jews in ghettoes, and the German government's sanction of acts of repression committed by the local police. Padmore explained the new regulations that allowed the expulsion of Jews from towns if they were accused of criminal activity: the right to refuse Jews lodging, holiday accommodation and restaurant meals, and the refusal to serve Jews in shops and small businesses. "Jews may be refused admittance to public baths, libraries and reading rooms."[1] The pattern that Padmore identified was familiar to his African American readers, and this outlook informed the larger analytical framework that he elaborated in the years after his Comintern affiliation. He posed the question of whether the world was headed for "Fascist or Democratic Imperialism."[2] The history of anti-Semitism and the pre-history of the Holocaust were joined with other histories of racial politics, their discursive and practical connections commonplace to the persons whose names fill these pages.

TRADING COLONIES AND PEOPLES

Padmore threw himself into his writing in the later thirties, and much of it was about diplomacy and foreign policy. He always touched upon the lives of populations of color, ruminating on their fate in the coming war. His involvement in the International African Service Bureau and in the many activities surrounding the Italian invasion of Abyssinia enshrined Padmore in a network of black activists and intellectuals who saw this issue as a touchstone for black global solidarity and as a portent of the attitude that imperial statesmen would take toward colonies and mandates in the approach to war.[3] Spain also posed the issue of international solidarity. Franco's use of Moorish troops fanned racial prejudices; news cartoons of wanton, menacing Moors expressed increasing outrage at British neutrality, and Padmore sought to interpret these images in the context of wider imperial racial attitudes.[4]

The debates over whether to defend Abyssinia and Spain bordered on the impulses to appease fascism. The various attempts to placate, "buy off," or otherwise trade and deal with the German ambition for colonies, and the consequences of this ambition for "other races" had a strong place in appeasement discourses, even though the final deals that were cut with Hitler did not encompass the trading of colonies. The British political community was more willing to contemplate "colonial transfers," the return of German colonies lost at Versailles, the redefinition of the mandate system, and other schemes for barter and buyout, than were the Germans prepared to take the bait.[5] There was some German interest in repossessing Tanganyika, where there were pro-Nazi German settlers, but the British were not as interested in parting with this territory as they were in other cases. Hitler stated that the "Jewish press" had emphasized the claim for lost colonies in an effort to "stir hatred" for Britain among Germans.[6] *Mein Kampf* characterized the claim for colonies as a "Jewish swindle." Historian Woodruff Smith explained that "Naziism from the late 1920s onward was *primarily* an imperialist ideology . . . a comprehensive imperialist policy to be implemented by stages . . . [with] a schedule of imperialist expansion."[7] During 1938 and 1939, the debate about the viability and desirability of colonial transfers absorbed Padmore. He acknowledged that "Ukraine [was] of greater interest to Hitler than the colonies,"[8] but he and others feared a war between Nazi imperialism and British imperialism in which colonial peoples would be mere cannon fodder. Nehru expressed this fear in his essay in *Die Zukunft*, though both he and Padmore took a strong antifascist line.[9] They also recognized the leverage and power of colonial armies to avert a global Armageddon and used the vision of this overwhelming force as a polemical tool.

In *Mein Kampf*, Hitler wrote of Germany's need for land in Europe, chastising France for its *"negrification* . . . we can already speak of an African state arising on European soil," and of the "developing European-African mulatto state," resulting from racial mixing in France. He praised Germany for refraining from the use of colonial troops in Europe in the Great War, and after.[10] When the Nazis spoke of *Lebensraum*, they meant a place to expand on the continent of Europe, for Germans and those of German "ethnic" origin. Forging new settlements in lands whose climates and populations were not only hostile, but geographically distant, was less palatable and a more cumbersome proposition than moving next door into adjacent weaker territories, including those that had been part of an earlier Reich or made weaker by Allied disinterest or Soviet complicity. Whatever came in the way of the acquisition of space and the quality of life lived in that space became expendable for the Nazis. This direction of thought and action was predicated both on the anti-Semitism that so maliciously and violently dispensed with Jews, and on the presumption of a racial order in the rest of the "nonwhite" world, especially in Africa. Some of the British appeasers accordingly pinned their hopes on the possibilities for accommodation with Germany in Africa. In the end, the Germans did not wish to advance there through negotiation, to spread there in large numbers as settlers, or to fortify territories militarily. Instead, Hitler may have envisioned a temporary division of labor in which the British managed some of the more difficult regions and peoples to his advantage. In Southwest Africa, a mandate under South African rule, Nazi supporters were sharply admonished by the Germans to "show proper courtesy to their British hosts."[11] When Hitler finally moved to consider a colonial transfer agenda, it was at British bidding and in order to placate his own avid imperial interest groups. Lords Halifax and Lothian articulated several propositions that interested Hitler as talks progressed, Halifax having served as viceroy of India, 1926–31, while Lothian had served in South Africa and India. "The British had shown that they seriously considered colonial concessions." The Germans had mentioned colonial transfers, "with less unanimity or enthusiasm, than might have been expected." Finally, in March 1938, just before Austria's annexation by Hitler, Prime Minister Neville Chamberlain made an offer. He placed the colonies of other League of Nations member states on the block, despite Sir John Simon's admonition in Parliament on November 16, 1938, that "His Majesty's Government are not contemplating the transfer of any territories under British administrations. . . . In this matter His Majesty's Government must, of course, give full attention to the views of the populations of any territory concerned."[12]

What then did the British make of the various bids to barter "their" colonial peoples? The most ardent defenders of empire after Hitler's assumption of power were often Nazism's bitter enemies. This paradox hangs over any clear assessment of the thirties. The left wished to perceive the two positions as incompatible, but the fact they that were not is a key to the outcome of the war, and all of empire's critics from Nehru to Padmore had to reckon with this realization—from nationalists to internationalists. Eleanor Rathbone did not favor reducing the proportion of the "British" domestic population as a means of strengthening the Empire, and supported a hegemonic, white, British domestic presence: "While welcoming a moderate reduction of population in these overcrowded islands, we may question whether it is good for the world that the proportion of the white races to the colored and of the Anglo-Saxon race to all others should steadily diminish."[13] In 1937 she commented on the Italian presence in Abyssinia, fearing Italy's and Germany's Mediterranean and Middle Eastern ambitions as harbingers of race war: "When a Fascist power is firmly established on the southern borders of France and at the gate of the Mediterranean, how long shall we be able to resist those demands for African colonies, those aspirations for leadership in a great Pan-Islamic rising, which Hitler and Mussolini are even now troubling to conceal?" The job of Britain was to contain and to control, not to relinquish. Rathbone ridiculed the peace lobby, eschewing their unwillingness to defend lands that were not "their own". James Maxton and a large section of the ILP had opposed any armed combat to assist Abyssinia. Rathbone found this position untenable: "Everyday saved for peace! But has it been saved for peace? Not for the unhappy people of Abyssinia, Spain or China . . . whom we taught to depend on the League and whom the League has abandoned."[14]

Kingsley Martin, the editor of the *New Statesman and Nation*, testified in the mock Reichstag Fire Trial as a supporter of the early antifascist mobilization and was a contributor to *Die Zukunft*. But he was no opponent of empire, writing of Britain's resistance to the measures that the League took against Italy as acts of imperial resignation. It would have sustained Britain's global position to fight against Italy's advances:

It is the British imperialists who in order to destroy the League have been led by the wily Mr. Baldwin into endangering British control of the Mediterranean, the route to

India, and her strategic position in Egypt and the Sudan, and indeed throughout the whole Near East. . . . British Imperialists hated the League more than they loved the Empire.[15]

The writer and anticolonial activist Leonard Barnes, in many respects the most important of the critics of empire who remained independent of the organized left, took the notion of white racial superiority to one of its logical conclusions. Writing in the National Peace Council's *International Affairs* in 1938, he recalled the Hitler-Halifax conversations of the previous November 30, 1937, after which Lord Halifax reported that they had made "a preliminary examination . . . of the colonial question in all of its aspects." Barnes quipped, "Instead of conceding Europe to save the colonies, as was feared in some quarters, the British Government now looks like making colonial concessions in the hope of saving Europe," given that the Nazis were opposed to Britain's offer of a mandate reshuffle. He challenged British racial attitudes in a very different way from Rathbone. For Barnes, war might offer understanding, equality, and the abandonment of imperial ambition. It was not enough to be more benevolent imperialists than the Nazis.

> It is a grave psychological blunder, though one frequently committed in discussion of the colonial question, to make use either of the argument that colonies are of no particular economic value, or of the argument that the racial doctrine of the Nazis is so repulsive that no responsibility for non-Aryan colonial populations can be permitted to them. . . . if the colonies are good for us they are good for Germany; if they are bad for Germany, they are bad for us. . . . however much some of us may dislike Nazi race theory, the leading principles of that theory do in fact form the mainspring of conduct for Europeans in their relations with dark-skinned races in every colony in the world. There is no firm ground for discriminating between Briton and German when it comes to color prejudice.[16]

In late 1938 the socialist geographer J. F. Horrabin wrote to the *Manchester Guardian*:

> We have no right to regard the British Empire as "based on principles superior to the Aryan blood theory" of the Nazis. There is no difference whatever between the racial theory of discrimination operating throughout the whole of the British African possessions especially in the Union [South Africa] and the racial discrimination of Hitler's Germany. . . . Still less can we condemn German or Italian expansion while glorying in the fruits of British expansion over three centuries and five continents. . . . And if we are expecting the subject peoples of the empire to rally to the support of British capitalist democracy against Nazi dictatorship we are letting ourselves in for some surprises.[17]

This last prophecy was central to Padmore's problematic and it eventually proved fallible. But at this early stage, a potent ingredient in the debate about the status of the colonies was the fear of alienating colonial troops from the war effort; the negotiations that lay ahead, between Britain and her opponents in India on India's participation in the war, embodied that fear. The failure of Stafford Cripps's 1942 "mission" to India, and the ensuing division over support for the Allied war effort, with or without independence, was accompanied by resistance, continual and often massive repression in India, and the imprisonment of the Congress leaders and of Gandhi. Both the "Quit India" movement and Subhas Chandra Bose's fifth column "Indian National Army" actions influenced outcomes.[18]

During the 1930s some British parliamentary leaders like former colonial secretary and Conservative MP Leo Amery were opposed to the break-up of any territory in the Empire and convinced that Hitler would ultimately seek a new colonial empire, even if his ambitions were initially focused upon Europe. Others, like Neville Chamberlain, believed that the mandates, as distinct from the colonies, were not part of the Empire, and were transferable.[19] The Covenant of the League stated that the Central African mandated territories were "at such a step" in their degree of backwardness that the mandatory power must handle all their administration. This led empire defenders like Amery to take a very strong, protective stance toward Nazi ambitions as he understood them, albeit in a deeply racial-paternalistic framework.[20] In May 1936, 118 MPs, including Tories Winston Churchill, Harold Nicolson, and Brendan Bracken, formed a watchdog group led by Churchill's son-in-law MP Duncan Sandys to make sure that the Empire was protected in any forthcoming negotiations. A diarist recalled that the question of colonial transfers was "always coming up at parties" during 1936.[21]

Members of both left and right were opposed to transferring colonies or mandates to Germany, and many across the political spectrum were committed to avoiding another war. In 1937 Rathbone spoke against the "working classes and the intelligentsia" who would not fight for the Empire.[22] When Neville Chamberlain's September 1938 Munich trip temporarily assuaged the public's fears of war in Britain, Naomi Mitchison wrote to the writer Aldous Huxley saying that the right thing would have been to pressure and confront Chamberlain not to give in to Hitler. Even had there been a war, she and her like-minded friends ought to have turned upon the British government and "substituted another government by violence." But she allowed that only "a small minority" would have wanted this and Huxley would not have been among them. She describe the war panic that hit London and the "cowardice" that seemed to surface: "*That* is what we with our anti-war propaganda have done; we've just made people afraid, so that everyone was enormously relieved to think that Nazi methods had won again and it was only Czecho-Slovakia which was being done in." She wrote that many communists were more warlike in their contempt for the Nazis than the pacific Labour party advocates like herself. Yet a *News Chronicle* poll indicated that people were more willing to fight on behalf of the colonies than for Czechoslovakia. Mitchison pled for a new patriotism, fostered by the shame she felt not just over Chamberlain's and Hitler's recent actions, but over Abyssinia and the failure to prevent the invasion there.[23] Virginia Woolf wrote with remorse at what was proclaimed as the new day. "We were all to live on apples, honey and cabbage. . . . How all will worship C[hamberlain] now; but in five years time we may be saying we ought to have put him, Hitler, down. . . . But now we can't help being glad of peace."[24]

The question of whether to support colonial transfers inevitably overlapped with the question of whether the Empire was worth defending. Those who would become the Fabian Colonial Bureau, many presently members of the Labour Party Advisory Committee on International Questions, included Leonard Barnes and Charles Roden Buxton.[25] In 1938 Buxton expressed views grounded in an economic appraisal of the Empire's value: "Labor questions and the various questions related to them overshadow the whole of the Colonial Empire." A month later Roden Buxton wrote to Labour MP and future Chancellor Hugh Dalton about the kind of Realpolitik involved in the sustenance of empire. He was not a quitter; people would not like losing the Empire, making its loss an electoral hindrance.

> But I start on the assumption that the shedding of Empire is not a practical proposition on the grounds of: a) sentiment b) strategy c) power politics d) accessibility to certain natural resources (copper, tin, gold, oil, etc.) e) investment fields f) in many cases the people concerned would not, in the conditions of the modern world, welcome it . . . . retention . . . would be conditioned by the larger problem of European appeasement.[26]

Roden Buxton's controversial support for appeasement was not typical of the future Fabian Colonial Bureau or Labour party brains trusts. The Empire reformers among this diverse policy group included those who foresaw the acquisition of civil liberties and subject rights in the colonies as prerequisites for the retention of empire, and most were opponents of appeasement. Norman Leys articulated the extreme reform view: "This matter of racial discrimination that lies under every problem in British Africa, has been obscured and confused by the false idea that Africans today lead lives of their own in which such things as the franchise and higher education are incongruous." With prescience, he pointed to the threats of settler "armed resistance" in Rhodesia, Kenya, and South Africa.[27] White South Africans perceived the Italians and French "Latins" raising black armies to challenge white rule in Africa from their respective empires: "The dominion elite made the implementation of the principles of rational self-determination—the redrawing of state boundaries on racial not strategic grounds—synonymous with the preservation of peace."[28] Norman Leys pled for Britain not to "repeat India," and warned of resistance to rule. "In East Africa every educated African is conscious that color bars thwart his own personal advancement. Our country's choice is not between leaving them alone and dealing with them. It is between their deliberate removal and their being torn down, by violence and in disorders in which much besides color bars, that is of value, will perish."[29] Leys conferred upon colonial subjects more potential for action than mere "victims" could possess, yet his fears of violent racially inflected disorder suggested that he believed that the educated could unleash the more "primitive" emotions of the masses if the British failed to offer the appropriate concessions. His fears were similar to those expressed by Eleanor Rathbone.

The African American press thundered its outrage at the idea that the Europeans might concede colonies to Hitler, whether Hitler wanted them immediately or not. "Britain Ready to Give Colonies to Hitler" by Padmore appeared in the *Chicago Defender* on April 1938 and included remarks by Vernon Bartlett that supported Padmore's analysis of diplomatic discussions on the fate of Togoland, the Cameroons, and Ruanda-Urundi. Padmore signaled a willingness on Britain's part to contemplate their use "in order to appease the imperialistic appetite of the Nazi dictator, who, together with Mussolini, is the greatest enemy of the darker races. Everywhere African and other colonial students here are discussing the future of the Dark Continent."[30]

SOVIET SYMPATHIES AND ANTIPATHIES

Attitudes toward the Soviet Union influenced the outlooks of those debating the fate of empire on the eve of the war. Most people in positions of power, and large sections of the left, looked the other way when facts about Moscow's failings and her punitive and repressive actions against her own people surfaced over time.[31] Moscow did not viciously purge the communist parties of Britain and America, but in Spain and among German exiles in France and other places where KPD refugees fled, communists and other left militants disappeared from the streets, their elimination part of a larger policy of purging and, in many instances, murdering identifiable enemies within and without.[32] Both Nazi agents and NKVD assassins lurked. The revelations of Orwell and others about Spain exposed Stalinist treachery, but there was still a spirit of displacement and diversion among British onlookers. The fascination with the Soviet example in the face of economic deprivation at home often "won over" rank-and-file trade unionists and intellectual party workers alike. CPGB leader Harry Pollitt confessed, "I have noticed many comrades coming to the Lenin School [in Moscow], who in England could talk simply and clearly to the workers—[they] go back speaking a foreign language."[33] The communist party was a more desirable commitment for intellectuals and middle-class supporters than for workers, and the British party remained very much weaker and smaller as compared to the mass parties of the Continent. But it had the capacity to bring many workers into the fold in the period of the party's largest recruitment on record during the thirties and the war, its numbers climbing from

10,000 members in the early thirties, to over 55,000 after 1939, even if the typical rank-and-file recruit did not remain a member for more than a few years. "It had a significant purchase on a range of social movements, notably including several trade unions and the interwar unemployed."[34]

Others apart from the communists watched Russia intently. They visited and observed. Beatrice Webb and her husband, Sidney, were enamored of Stalinist state planning; she recorded the news of the Moscow trials as a "nasty shock," finding British reactions to policies undertaken in India and Ireland more seemly: "We did not talk about it, or revel in reviling our victim." After all, the USSR had "just emerged from the Middle Ages."[35] Virginia Woolf used similar language to describe a visit with John Maynard Keynes's Russian wife, Lydia, though she was less complacent than Webb: "Lydia like a peasant woman, wringing her hands, on a stool. . . . It is a terrible age. This refers to the Russian spy trials, which reflect the middle ages. A veil of insanity everywhere: & what's to be done save keep pegging round one's little plot?"[36] When Leon Trotsky was assassinated by Stalin's agents in Mexico, Webb remarked on the implications of his death for the Fabians' statist vision, finding it "so damaging to the expectations of our 'New Civilization.'" Parliament had rebuffed James Maxton's attempts to offer Trotsky asylum in the United Kingdom.[37]

The establishment's anticommunism fueled the fellow travelers' embrace, even affecting the views of liberal skeptics. Eleanor Rathbone, who had flinched from a close identification with Scottsboro and the early "German Relief Committee," still decried the wealthy middle and "upper classes" who "didn't like Fascism, but [who] disliked it much less than Communism or even pale pink socialism." Why not cooperate with the Soviet Union? She noted that Winston Churchill and his people were "not converted to administration of the USSR. [There is] much that [they] may legitimately fear and dislike there. But as our opponents tell us, [we have] no right to refuse co-operation because we dislike [the soviet] internal system, provided that [it poses] no menace to ourselves."[38] In a 1940 pamphlet Rathbone expressed sympathy for the political victims of fascist repression, suggesting that Jews were less committed as sufferers. "Political prisoners are enduring worse things than the Jews with greater valiancy, because they are sustained by their political faith. They chose danger." This was a strange appeal, since Rathbone had been much less active in the early years of refugee politics when the movement involved many of her friends and associates. In this pamphlet Rathbone expressed displeasure with the government's choice of catering to those of greater means, conveying the most typical of anti-Semitic prejudices in her critique of policy. She wrote that those then being admitted were "the wrong type of Jew—the flashy, middle class, including the unsuitable aspirant for domestic service who throws up his job as soon as it has secured for her a permit of entry."[39]

Rathbone remonstrated the Soviets on their September 1939 murderous deportations of Poles in the eastern zones of the Reich.[40] Churchill and his closest supporters, who did not tolerate Bolshevism or Sovietism in any form ultimately dealt with the Soviet Union when Britain's defense required it. They opposed appeasement but not every goal of the appeasers: "Chamberlain's and Churchill's objectives were identical. Both intended to preserve the independence of Britain and its Empire." By 1935 Churchill saw the German question and the imperial question as inseparable; his chosen allies had to agree. He sought accommodation from those on the center to left who saw his usefulness in terms of his willingness to pull Tories over into a center-left coalition. Münzenberg's *Die Zukunft* recruited an impressive group of writers from Churchill's milieu. But before Munich, Churchill lacked a sufficiently large angle of vision and did not act as he could have on Japan, Abyssinia, or Spain until it was far too late. After Neville Chamberlain's visit to Hitler at Bad Godesberg, Churchill's criticism of him arose, in the moment, more than it did as part of a dogged struggle against the events that made the visit possible. When the Germans occupied Prague in March 1939, hindsight helped to increase the authority of Churchill's views.[41]

While the Germans did not "take the Soviets seriously," Churchill, who had equivocated on both the defense of Abyssinia and of Spain, was slow to accept the need for "unity with the Soviets." For Churchill, this path was "difficult to reconcile with British ideals." Historian D. C. Watt maintained that the United States posed an obstacle to antifascist mobilization in several parts of the world and did not seek to oppose the "Arab revolt" of the late thirties in Palestine or to check Japan's and Turkey's ambitions. Watt found Roosevelt "unreliable" and "hostile to European colonialism," despite his superior racial attitudes. He could not accept a reform-minded imperial Britain remaining a world power on a grand scale, and this slowed the pace of Allied unity in the face of the appeasers.[42]

Some in Britain agonized publicly over the news of incarceration, disappearances, and the failure to install democracy in the Soviet Union. William Gillies and Herbert Morrison of the Labour party responded to the Soviet Union's doctrines and policies by avoiding or forbidding political interaction with communists. In a related decision, the Labour leaders did not and could not support arms for Spain. Those who dissented from Soviet actions also broke with communist organizations, despite the communist attempts at political coalitions in various phases of the thirties. James Maxton, Fenner Brockway, and many in the ILP chose this path. Skeptics and progressive opponents of the Soviet Union abounded in the thirties and they included Leonard and Virginia Woolf, Bertrand Russell, and the NAACP hierarchy in the United States, who remained in contact with, for example, the Trotskyist Magdeleine Legendre Paz, Leon Blum's associate, who had hosted Ada Wright at the Salle Wagram. Many of communism's most cogent critics were not liberals but those squarely on the left, like Paz. At this writing, a photograph of Paz hangs in the first room of the French barracks at Auschwitz, a memorial to those who ardently fought fascism in France.

Figure 6.1. "Appeasement . . . specially drawn for the 'New Leader' by
Joseph Southall," February 3, 1939.
The noted painter Southall (1861–
1944) was a Quaker and an ILP
member in the late 1930s. The image
appeared alongside an article analyzing the aftermath of the Munich
agreement and weighing the imminent possibility of war's outbreak
(courtesy of George Barrow for the
estate of Joseph Southall; reproduced by kind permission of the
Syndics of Cambridge University
Library).

George Padmore did not fail to expose what he saw as the self-interested
machinations of the Soviet Union, and claimed that the Soviets shared much
ground with the imperialists as the war approached. Padmore sat in the visitors' gallery of the House of Commons, taking notes for his satirical and brilliant commentary, his crisp, pedagogical pieces instructing the popular readers
of the *Chicago Defender*, the *Pittsburgh Courier*, and *The Crisis*. He did not appear in the pages of *Die Zukunft*, and there is no trace of his correspondence in
the files of the newspaper seized by the French police at the time of the German occupation. One wishes in vain to know if Padmore and Münzenberg
ever met between 1933 and 1939 when they were often so near each other in
Paris. His former comrades in and around the CPGB in some instances remained loyal to the party. In 1965 Reginald Bridgeman wrote to Palme Dutt,
whose brother Clemens he had known since the Brussels conference of 1927,
regarding his hope of publishing a short history of the LAI. Bridgeman suggested that Clemens was best qualified to attempt such an effort. "He would be
able to deal with the thorny questions of Willi Münzenberg, and the support
which the League received from the USSR." Bridgeman conceded that basic

source materials documenting the work of the LAI had disappeared, noting that the LAI had supplied documents as a framework for questions asked in Parliament by sympathetic MPs that formed a backbone of its history and gave it purpose and a legacy: "I destroyed a good slice of the League's archives during the 1939-45 war, many individuals in different countries being identified with the various aspects of its work, but I could contribute notes on the struggle for freedom [in] Africa, E.S. and W., the Negro struggles, Indonesia, Abyssinia, the Meerut Conspiracy case, and so forth."[43]

Fellow travelers and party members, among workers and mandarins alike, who supported communist party platforms and were caught up in campaigns from Scottsboro to the Jarrow marches on behalf of the unemployed in Britain, remained sympathetic to Soviet communism in the face of the Stalin-Hitler pact of August 1939, until its end in June of 1941, even if they did not defend the new course enthusiastically. Others despaired in the face of what they saw as final proof of the betrayal of the Spanish Republic.[44] But the spirit of coexistence between the West and the Soviet Union found its fullest expression after Stalin was forced back into the arms of the Allies. In 1941, four days after the launch of operation Barbarossa, the communist physicist Hyman Levy wrote to Kingsley Martin, chastising the New Statesman and Nation of which Martin was editor for not being more open to political dialogue among "antifascists."

> There are many intelligent people—and I include myself among them—who just refuse to believe that the Soviet policy had any taint of what has been called by you appeasement, but who have seen in it a most intelligent mode of meeting the menace of Nazism . . . not out of loyalty to the CP or to the USSR but actually because they read the evidence this way. . . . It has been the inability to make the assumptions I mention that has led to those stupid attacks on Marxists as being amoral. It is a damned lie. My ethics and morals are as good as those of anyone else.[45]

This view was not at all incompatible with a communist defense of Britain's empire in wartime, and in this respect some of the softness toward the Soviet Union found its counterpart in hostility to Neville Chamberlain, the Munich negotiator, shared among communists and anticommunists once the Soviet Union "rejoined" the Allies. Martin, who believed that Hitler, Stalin, and Japan represented "a new totalitarian ideal," later wrote that support for Chamberlain in 1938-39, was support for "Hitler's domination of Europe, the end of the British Empire and Chamberlain's acceptance of a little England with a status like that of a Scandinavian country."[46] But the notion of the defensible empire, fighting twin totalitarian states, was not accepted by leading anticolonial opinion on the eve of the war; opposition to appeasement was not enough for all.

In the spring of 1938 Padmore sat in the gallery of the House of Commons as it debated the West Indies Royal Commission (Moyne Commission). His seatmate was Arthur George Murchison Fletcher, whose heretical views on colonialism in the Carribean helped to expose conditions there to the British

The Colonial Workers Revolt

Figure 6.2. "The Colonial Workers Revolt," whose caption began with: "The workers in the West Indies are seething with revolt," and ended with a call to demonstrate in solidarity with "victims of Imperialism," appeared in the middle of a lead article in the ILP's the *New Leader* on May 20, 1938, entitled "Bombers for Capitalism." The article challenged British policy in the Caribbean, but like the text around it, maintained a fidelity to the ILP pacifist and anti-re-armament stances (reproduced by kind permission of the Syndics of Cambridge University Library; *Upsurge* by J. W. Harcourt, published by John Lane in 1934, was noted, but did not display the image).

public and had just cost him his appointment as governor-general of Trinidad, where he had served since 1936. Padmore reported that James Maxton offered "the most trenchant and devastating attack delivered from the floor of the House of Commons against vested interests in the colonies."[47] In July Nehru presided over the London Conference on Peace and Empire attended by 620 delegates and 400 visitors. The Conference condemned what it called the "redistribution of colonies," calling for the extension of basic democratic rights to the territories of the Empire, posing this demand in the face of the deadly clashes between strikers and the military across the Caribbean and in India.[48] Two months later Padmore wrote in *The Crisis*, "On the eve of the opening of the Empire Exhibition in Glasgow, which Lord Elgin, the [exhibition] president, informed the King and Queen represented a glorious contribution to the peace and prosperity of the peoples of the Empire, the Jamaica police were shooting and bayoneting native workers for daring to demand a living wage."[49] The Glasgow exhibition shared ties to the planners of the New York World's Fair of 1940, who visited Glasgow and later celebrated Empire Day in honor of Britain, in New York. In Glasgow one pavilion featured the reenactment of the labor process on the rubber plantations of Liberia, depicting the gathering of raw materials for Firestone's plants in Ohio.[50] A year later, in the pages of *The*

Crisis, Padmore protested against the tightening of restrictions on labor and dissent in imperial Africa:

> Colored Americans have a moral obligation to stand back of these Negro workers and peasants in their struggle to ward off the tightening up of the "democratic" imperialist yoke. . . . these same people were in the forefront of the struggle on behalf of the Scottsboro Boys and Angelo Herndon. Now is a splendid opportunity for Afro-Americans to show their solidarity with their brothers in Africa.[51]

His was a challenge that did not defer the anticolonial struggle to another moment, that asserted its timeliness rather than its marginality.

A RACE INQUIRY: 1939

Those British "mass observers" who contributed to a Mass Observation project (MO) inquiry in the months after Munich offered commentary that demonstrated the distance between the kind of vision articulated by strong anticolonialists and those in Britain's literate, lower middle class, who were drawn to MO and its ethnographic pursuits. In August 1939 MO issued a special directive on "Race." Over four hundred mass observers chose to fill out the directive's questionnaire. Each stated his or her name, age, gender, marital status, place of residence, and occupation.[52] They were asked, among other questions, "How do you feel about Negroes? Write down the first thing that comes into your head." Participants also ranked a list of "races" with whom they would "prefer the British to collaborate," including some "national" groupings—identified as the "French, Americans, Italians, Irish, Poles and Russians," and others—the Jewish, Asiatic, Scandinavian, and Negro "races." They ranked ten foreign leaders, including Hermann Göring, Stalin, and Roosevelt, on the basis of the "greatest respect" due them. A series of short questions probed whether the writer would want to be seen in public with a Negro, to shake hands with a uniformed Nazi, or to borrow a Jew's clean handkerchief. They were asked to react to terms—*French, Germans, Negroes*, and, *cannibals*, and to state whether the crucifixion of Christ had any "racial implications."[53]

The complexity of their answers and speculation about the wider patterns that they reveal are not the subjects of this study.[54] Nevertheless, a sample of the replies serves as a signal of the anxieties that were common among the cohort of participants in MO in the late thirties, on the eve of war. Many of those responding reacted to the term "Negro" as an explicit reference to African Americans, whom they portrayed in their questionnaires as a needy and expressive part of humanity, worthy of pity: " Negroes. Slaves. An oppressed and subject race exploited by the white man. I think of their songs so full of pathos, nostalgia, bewilderment and longing. I remember the form in which their deeply moved souls have turned in their religion," wrote a Lancashire chemist, aged thirty-one. A woman teacher from Watford wrote of her associations with America, and of solutions to the country's dilemmas.

> The thought of Negroes makes me very sad. The slavery of the American negroes. The cruelty of the slave trading and the shipment of slaves to America in the early days, the cruelty as described in *Uncle Tom's Cabin* and the still continuing news of lynching in America—these are uppermost in my mind when I see or hear the word "Negroes," listen to Negro spirituals, or hear of people like Paul Robeson. There is something pathetic in the gaiety of their dancing and singing. . . . The lynching of Negroes should be stopped, very forcibly if necessary. . . . all Negroes should be sent back to Africa. . . . Old Negroes who prefer to stay in America should be protected in special areas. Europeans in Africa who cannot or will not work with and for the Africans could be sent to America to take the place of the repatriated Africans.[55]

The mass observers differed in their perceptions of the smell and hygiene of Negroes. Jazz, film, and entertainment were commonly mentioned as "Negro" domains.[56] Some expressed "repugnance" while others were ashamed of such a feeling, pointing to the irrationality of their own views. Their reactions were sometimes inflected with notions of raw sexuality, physicality, physical difference, and foreignness: "Hot music which they [Negroes] . . . render in most violent and absurd forms, the grosser the cacophony of sound the greater the attraction to women and cissyfied men. Generally speaking Negroes repulse me." A single, twenty-three-year-old resident of Gower Street in Bloomsbury was the subwarden of an international students' club: " [Negroes are] one of the most charming and cheerful sets of people—Friendly, intelligent, with their great failing, in many, being women and often . . . homosexuality, a failing which is very much encouraged and pandered to by the sort of white women they meet."[57]

Most referred to the problem of racial inferiority, imagining or experiencing Negroes as "simple" and intellectually inferior, or, conversely in the case of an adamant minority of respondents, strongly asserting their innate equality. Several wrote of the untapped potential of Negroes that was ready to be launched through education, or of the suspicion that educated Negroes were not representative of the race as a whole and were those who had made it across the Atlantic to Britain when most could not have done so.[58] Many recalled Negroes displaying qualities of physical beauty, joyfulness, and strong emotions. These characteristics connoted a kind of equality within difference, but more often suggested an overexcitability, a childlike sense of melodrama, or the will to entertain an audience and to see humor in pathos.[59]

Some observers leaped to a discussion of the Empire, writing about Africans rather than American Negroes. These included a reservist Military officer: "They are just niggers. . . . [I have] been in the South African war." A retired woman in her early fifties, living in northwest London had been there as well: "I have lived in a Black Country [South Africa]. I look upon negroes as animals, without the fidelity of a dog." Some also thought that "Negroes" belonged in

Africa, and were "better" there, meaning more suited to being there and belonging there. One observer wrote that the Negro should "inhabit a tract or country of his own and govern himself under some sort of mandate. Otherwise, they become like Paul Robeson and adopt communism."[60]

Many respondents wrote about racial mixing in Britain, expressing opposition to intermarriage, even though they were not asked about this issue. Some stated that they did not wish to be seen with Negroes (they were asked about this) and others opposed interactions like mixed boxing. A twenty-one-year-old bank clerk from Surrey expressed outrage: "[Negroes are] all right in jazz bands and Africa but nowhere else. Negresses disgust me and whenever I see a white woman and a colored man I feel like shooting both." A twenty-two-year-old salesman from Yorkshire wrote, "I feel that [Negroes'] association with white women is revolting, but I have nothing against them as a class, and I have every sympathy with them as regards the treatment which is meted out to them by the Americans."[61]

A minority expressed opposition to American racial policies, the color bar, and the treatment of American Negroes. A solicitor's clerk from Sowerby Bridge, wrote: "I feel well-disposed towards them. Bad treatment of Negroes—particularly American lynchings—fills me with disgust at . . . my supposedly civilized fellow men, and pity for the unfortunate possessor of a dark skin." Yet a Sheffield clerk voiced his opposition to both oppression and notions of equality. "The way Negroes were exploited during the slavery period, [and] more recent lynchings and Ku Klux Klan activities, make very bad reading on the debit side of the white man's record. . . . I cannot get away from the feeling that negroes are better in a secondary position. . . . mixed marriages to my mind are a tragedy." A sanitary inspector from Stockport, one of many who mentioned Robeson, wrote of conflicted sensations: "I feel kindly disposed toward them. I have a jumble of thoughts linking up with the 'Old South' and the plantations: huge, ebony Negroes laughing and carefree—Paul Robeson. Then I think of racial discrimination in the US, of lynching and 'Jim Crow' restaurants and roped off seats in trams and buses." A Camberwell clerk was critical of "anti-Negro" sentiment but held anti-Semitic views: "They are denied . . . all so-called rights of 'democracy'. . . . Feeling in Great Britain is definitely against them. America who condemns Jew-baiting condones negro-lynching," adding "both Jews and religion make me sick." Other critics of American policies defended Jews: "'Color-bars' I believe are inhuman, and the USA treatment of Negroes seems to me as loathsome as the German treatment of Jews." A printing engineer from Surrey wrote of "[Negroes who were] harmless, friendly people—[who] only go wrong in the face of industrialization, as in the USA, and bitter opposition—e.g. KKK and Scottsborough. I suppose they react to opposition the same way that Jews do—[they] become clannish and surly."[62]

One respondent questioned the humanity of Negroes: "While deploring the American attitude to blacks, I myself deep down do find it hard to believe that people with black skins, woolly hair, and odd faces can be human." Yet she found Harlem and jazz "fascinating" and "women friends report[ed] un-asked, when they see the Cotton Club, etc., that they feel the same." There were men who wrote longingly of black women, identifying "the groups of negroes one sees in Charing Cross Rd near Leicester Square. . . . negro women . . . sometimes attract me strongly. . . . [I feel] sympathy for [the] tremendous struggle they have had and are having in [the] USA to get something like equality with whites." A single clerk from Newport, aged twenty-six, was ardent in his openness, defiant in his candor: "Quite sincerely, and in spite of the sinister meaning a psychologist might read into such a statement, I can visualize myself falling in love with a negress. If I did, I wouldn't hesitate about marrying her." In Newport he observed mixed couples whose children seemed happy. The London scene provided furtive contact and some experimentation: "In the environment of London Night-Clubs, drink, etc.—[one sees Negroes] mostly . . . poor and frequently out-of-work . . . cadging and spongeing . . . it is much more direct and unabashed than in Whites. [T]he women of these surroundings . . . [are] generally of a happy and straightforward disposition. . . . [they] are not mercenary, and are in happy contrast to their white counterparts." The author identified himself as thirty-seven and independently wealthy.[63] A woman wrote, "I like their looks but I don't think I would sleep with one—unless it was Paul Robeson."[64]

Still others pitched the need for tolerance more than pity. Some conceded that they had never met a black person and relied upon literary, journalistic, or film portrayals, several expressing awkwardness in the face of unfamiliarity rather than prejudice. There were those who engaged in interracial political activities; a small number claimed a left-wing political affiliation or strongly hinted at one, including a single, twenty-four-year-old chemist from Harrow who thought Stalin the leader most worthy of respect: "I think Negroes are mainly very charming people—at least those I have met have been. And as a member of the League of Coloured Peoples, I have probably come into contact with more of them than the average Englishman." He supported collaboration with the Russian, Jewish, and Negro "races," and found the French "not so reliable" and the Germans "joylike" at Christmas, with a "tendency to hysterical brutality." Some of his views were more common than others: "[The Negroes'] overflowing *joie-de-vivre* makes a great tonic after the solemn grimness of most of the white people of our industrial civilization. . . . [They are] capable of developing an artistic way of life. . . . given proper chances they would be able to compare favorably with white men intellectually." One name-dropper boasted, "I am not amused by their stupidity as invented and portrayed on screen and admire Paul Robeson, Stepin Fetchit, Fats Waller, [the] Mills Bros., Bill Robinson, Nina MacKinney, Langston Hughes, Joe Louis, George Padmore and one or two more." A young Welsh teacher, familiar with the lingo, confessed, "For me the associations of the word are—folklore . . . slavery, America, Robeson, [and the] colonial question. I cannot really conceive [of] a Negro as an individual (of whom I could write a short story). As yet, they only appear as factors in folk-lore or politics."[65]

Scottsboro signatory and writer Naomi Mitchison was one of the mass observers who responded to this directive. She identified herself as a forty-one-year-old married writer living in Hammersmith, and in her celebrity as a privileged author from a prominent family, was atypical of the group of respondents: "I got a feeling of immediate friendliness and charm and attraction, due to my association of colored students at American universities, negro share-croppers, etc. Possibly Paul Robeson has something to do with it. If I think more the immediate impression would wear off, but the first idea is of friendliness." She added a cautionary note: "In all cases I would hesitate about, say, encouraging any of my children to a mixed marriage, either with another nationality or race, but on grounds of social expediency only, not of any innate difficulty. I have seen a good deal of this in practice."[66]

Mitchison also referred to her political activism as a brake on the unconditional acceptance of others: "Germans? Prussians, Saxons, refugees, Nazis? I am bored with Germans because I have to deal with so many refugees and talk so much German, which I am not very good at. Possibly the Germans are slower and stupider than the French, or will be when they have quite got rid of their Jews, but even that is a very tentative generalization."[67] Public ritual begot private prejudice. Conflicted sentiments and misalliances were as much a part of activist political culture as they were of the "high politics" of the era.

POSTSCRIPT: DEATH, AND THE GERMANS

The French guards at the internment camp Le Vernet, where Münzenberg was held prisoner as an enemy alien, let their charges walk away when they heard that the fearsome German army was advancing upon France in June of 1940. Münzenberg was buoyant as he strolled out of the camp en route to Marseille, his departure another escape in the nick of time. But a hunter discovered his decomposed body months later, a noose and rope around his neck, far from any scene of Nazi violence. Münzenberg's death in the French countryside between Lyons and Grenoble, almost certainly at the hands of Stalin's NKVD agents, was a sign of the Comintern's travesties in the face of German advances and the failure of the West to prevent them. The murdering of its own most adept and successful former propagandist and organizer in the West paralleled the hunting-down of Trotsky and many of his family and supporters, and the former Red Army commander's assassination in Mexico. Münzenberg's brother-in-law Franz Neumann, whom he and Gross had seen for the last time in

Moscow, died in the Gulag; Gross's sister Margarete Buber-Neumann was a long-time Soviet prisoner who left a memoir that is an important source on life inside the Soviet camps.[68]

Münzenberg's *Die Zukunft* is either unknown or unconsidered by most historians of communism and the European left. It was a futile effort at political integrity when the clock had run out, and a last daring challenge to the Comintern, even if its first purpose may have been to cultivate enough interested parties in high places to guarantee its editors a safe harbor away from France. For the Scottsboro campaigners, the antifascist militants, and the Reichstag trial defendants' advocates who were still alive and in a position to hear of his passing, Münzenberg was someone who had supplied enough funds, enough spirit, and enough inspiration at various moments in the thirties to be mourned. His time spent with Lenin in Zurich and his connections to the Bolshevik revolutionaries of 1917, his links to the *Spartacus* uprising and the German 1920s meant that the news of his death elicited loss or jubilation. His execution at the hands of the Stalinists could not have come as a surprise to readers of *Die Zukunft*, even if they were somehow unaware of Münzenberg's communist background. What is surprising and unrecorded in British biographies, memoirs, and parliamentary histories, are the number and identities of his British contributors who hailed from the highest echelons of Conservative, Labour and Liberal circles—including those who sat with Churchill in his weekly salon near Victoria Station, before he assumed power with the downfall of the appeasers.[69]

Babette Gross managed to reach London from the internment camp at Gurs near the Pyrenées. Arthur Koestler was luckier and better connected than Münzenberg. He was released from French custody in January 1940 at Le Vernet, after the Duchess of Atholl and others mounted an extensive campaign in Britain on his behalf. His estranged wife, Dorothea, had seen Anthony Eden and R. G. Vansittart, the Foreign Office head. Koestler's final arrival in Britain came after a stint with the French Foreign Legion. He was imprisoned at Pentonville jail in London upon arrival, as an illegal alien. He published *Darkness at Noon*, his celebrated anticommunist testament from his cell.[70] Koestler's career in Britain as a science writer was complemented by his fame as a "right turned" communist. He famously wrote that he and his comrades had "been wrong for the right reasons" in the 1930s.[71] In 1983 he committed suicide in the face of serious illness. Otto Katz, with whom Koestler had plotted the mock Reichstag Fire Trial, coedited the *Brown Book*, and organized the early issues of *Die Zukunft*, remained a communist and fled to the Soviet Union; he was executed in the Rudolf Slanksy "conspiracy" trials in Prague in 1952.[72]

Some London exiles who were active in the *Die Zukunft* circles were interned in Britain as aliens during the war; others went to work for the war effort. The jurist Otto Kahn-Freund advised the British government propaganda division and the wartime Labour party.[73] Peter Ihle was among those who went to work for the BBC. Still others were successful in their quests to go to the United States. The political writer Rudolf Olden came to the New School for Social Research through Latin America. Stefan Zweig and his wife, Charlotte, took their own lives in Brazil in 1942. Helene Stöcker died in New York City in 1943; Rudolf Breitscheid died, along with KPD leader Ernst Thälmann, in Buchenwald in 1944. Heinrich Mann followed his nephew, Klaus Mann, as a suicide in 1949. In the wider circles of the former *Die Zukunft* adherents lay many connected to the anti-Nazi war effort. Richard Crossman, who had helped Koestler enter Britain, headed the Political Warfare Executive, the secret propaganda division of the British government, while MI5, the military intelligence security service, took charge of the vetting of German communist and socialist members and former activists who were interned in Britain or captured as prisoners of war. Declared anti-Nazis were placed in special, separate camps. One hundred and forty-five of these "refugee volunteers" died in the Blitz, while more than nine thousand others enlisted and saw military service.[74]

Some London exiles chose to return home at the war's end. In 1945 Berthold Viertel signed the Declaration for a Democratic Germany with theologian Paul Tillich and returned to Germany to work for the BBC, directing the first German productions of Tennessee Williams's *Streetcar Named Desire* and the *Glass Menagerie*.[75] Heinrich Fraenkel, who had spoken out against the Nazi-Soviet pact, went to work in the occupied zone as a film censor after the war, serving as a correspondent for the *Manchester Guardian* and the *New Statesman and Nation*. The traces of this fractured and temporary community lay across the European continent and the Atlantic, and also across North London. The racial politics of the 1930s united many as undesired refugees; antifascism provided them with a fleeting common creed.

POSTCRIPT: THE ENGLISH

Lascelles Abercrombie, a literary critic and the first Scottsboro defense-committee secretary, collaborated with Virginia Woolf on several petitions in support of the Spanish Republic and died in 1938. Woolf committed suicide in July of 1941, three years after her nephew Julian Bell was shot while driving an ambulance in Spain, where he died. Death struck many others soon after 1945. Rathbone died in January of 1946. Her fellow parliamentarian James Maxton succumbed to lung cancer in the same year. George Padmore's wreath card was among those honoring Maxton in death and Padmore wrote of him in his autobiography: "Maxton's memory will ever be cherished by Africans and peoples of African descent as the Wilberforce of his generation."[76] Münzenberg's collaborators in the mock Reichstag Fire Trial, and the British establishment figures whose bylines appeared in *Die Zukunft* were flung across the postwar political community. After V-E Day, *Die Zukunft* contributor Alfred Duff

Cooper became the British ambassador to France. Attorney D. N. Pritt was expelled from the Labour party for defending the Soviet attack upon Finland in 1939, but was reelected to the House of Commons after the war, his Marxism-Leninism notwithstanding. Pritt worked with Richard Crossman in Parliament, and with the left-wing Labour MP Lester Hutchinson, the former Meerut Trial defendant, who was expelled from the Labour party for refusing to support the NATO Treaty, and who ran unsuccessfully for reelection as an ILP candidate in 1950. In 1952 Pritt served as legal counsel for those accused in the Mau-Mau rising in Kenya, including Jomo Kenyatta, his former colleague in the IASB. He was presidential professor at the University of Ghana until the overthrow of Kwame Nkrumah in 1965.[77] Leonard Barnes, the interwar left-liberal critic of imperialism, served government as a Labour party-appointed advisor on post-war colonial policy.

Luminaries like George Bernard Shaw and Arthur Koestler opposed the formation of an anti-imperialist league, when it was proposed by Fenner Broadway in 1945. Shaw wrote to Brockway,

> When does a Commonwealth become an Empire? and *vice versa*? Are we to back the tribes who will every stranger against ourselves in north west India? Against Russia in North Persia? As we backed the Danakil savages of Abyssinia against Italy? Every case is different. Slogans are useless. My advice is Drop it.[78]

Koestler likewise responded to Brockway that he could not support an anti-imperialist league.

> If I were pinned down in a debate to say whether I wished the British to clear out of Egypt, Iraq, Transjordan and Palestine, I would have to say no—A weakening of the, already loose knit of the British Empire and Commonwealth, without coordinated anti-imperialistic activities within the rival powers, seems to me to increase the danger of upsetting the precarious balance. . . . I hope you won't think I have gone Tory.[79]

The independence movements that emerged in Britain's empire after the war, drew adventurers and socialists to them—Padmore and Pritt to Ghana, and Naomi Mitchison to Botswana, where she became an advocate of health services and municipal reform. Her description of an early 1960s visit to West Africa is reminiscent of her outlook on the American South and the Soviet Union, thirty years earlier. She recorded a visit to a dance held at Federal University College, Ibadan:

> For a time I sat at a table watching the dancing, admiring the completely easy rhythm of moving bodies. The young dancers held one another loosely, often leaving go entirely, so that each danced separately, abstracted, making their own hand movements in beautiful time. Occasionally a man would be dancing alone, showing off a little,

Figure 6.3. Naomi Mitchison (1897–1999), Scots writer and activist, in 1997, who lived on the Mull of Kintyre from 1939 until her death, traveling between Scotland and Botswana in the postwar era (courtesy of the photographer, Murdo Macleod).

but with nothing cissy about it. Many of the young men were wearing what has come to be adopted as national costume: a handsome robe of figured cotton over short cotton trousers, or sometimes heavily embroidered white. A few were in correct western clothes, a dozen or so in fancy dress, many with paper hats; it all fitted in. The girls again wore anything from the pink organdie and rhinestones of Europe to their own handwoven cottons in lovely, soft deep colors . . . [80]

Mitchison's commitment to a postcolonial service ethic—a secular mission of enlightenment in the midst of new global alignments—insisted upon a voyeurism toward Africans that she had displayed toward African Americans in the thirties.

POSTSCRIPT: PADMORE AND NEHRU

When war came, Padmore remained vigilant: "The second world war has begun. Already Africans, Indians, West Indians, and other colored races are being appealed to, and in the French colonies conscripted, as cannon fodder for the bloody holocaust which threatens to drown the world in blood and bring misery, ruin and devastation on a scale undreamt of." He denied that the war was being fought for democracy, and though he expressed sympathy for the Polish workers and peasants who were suffering at the hands of the Germans, he was doubtful of a war to "save a Fascist state from Fascism." For Padmore, Neville Chamberlain's schemes at Munich had amounted to "a midsummer night's dream." His central grievance remained his contention that the Allies had designated some of the world's peoples for freedom, and others for continued exploitation. "Justice like freedom is indivisible."[81] In a contribution to *The Crisis*, Padmore invoked Nehru's words: "The better international system to which the British Prime Minister referred was meant only for the people of Europe, but not for Asia."[82] The Gestapo captured his friend Garan Kouyate. Historian Eve Rosenhaft has established that Kouyate arrived at the Mauthausen concentration camp in Austria in September, 1943, and died there in July, 1944, reportedly of a heart attack. For his part, Nehru, who had lost a friend to the Terror in Russia, adopted the Indian communist party's line on the war between 1939 and 1941 arguing that is was a "purely imperialist venture on both sides," and defending and explaining the Nazi-Soviet pact.[83] Nehru served time in prison in India until December 1941, and again from 1942 to 1945. The British used aerial bombing against the "Quit India" movement in 1942 even after Nehru ceased to advocate resistance against the colonial power. He was released from prison in the aftermath of V-E day and, ten years later, as the Indian president, opened the historic Bandung Conference in Indonesia in an effort to "bring the non-European world together." His keynote address championed nonalignment and coexistence with both capitalist and communist worlds.[84] When W.E.B. Du Bois turned eighty, Nehru wired his greetings to the Hotel Roosevelt in New York City, scene of the birthday celebration.[85]

Both Padmore and Du Bois had made their way to Ghana after the fledgling 1945 Pan-African Congress at Manchester University. Padmore introduced Du Bois to the assembled as the father of Pan-Africanism, and Du Bois took the opportunity on this trip to Britain to visit his old friends H. G. Wells and Harold Laski, a year before Wells's death.[86] The Manchester delegates included representatives of the West African Students Union, and the Negro Welfare Association. The International African Service Bureau's delegation was headed by Padmore, who represented his birthplace of Trinidad and Tobago; Ras Makonnen; Amy Ashwood Garvey; South African writer Peter Abrahams; and Kwame Nkrumah. I.T.A. Wallace-Johnson of Sierra Leone, freed from his imprisonment for sedition in East Africa, which had been prompted by his work on behalf of the Scott-bsoro defendants, was in attendance, as was Jomo Kenyatta, his country's future president. The redbrick modesty of the building, and the relative smallness of the gathering, did not defeat this auspicious assemblage of freedom fighters. The imprint of the 1930s was indelible and irreducible, the war now past. Padmore became ill in Ghana a decade before Du Bois's passing. When he returned to England for medical care in 1959, only two years after arriving in Africa for good, he fell into a deeper illness from which he did not recover and died in the place where he had lived for the greatest number of years of his life, but where he had by his own admission felt the least accepted. Indeed, no country had con-tained him, nor had any national political culture absorbed the largeness of his ideas. Across the Atlantic, the Mediterranean, and the African continent, per-haps bemused by his outliving so many others with whom he had struggled as an activist, Kenyatta prevailed until 1978, surviving Padmore by twenty years.

Postscript: Scottsboro Outcomes

The United States receded as a focus of antiracist fervor for many who had found it so fascinating and so objectionable during the early years of the 1930s. Hitler was more ominous, closer, and more dangerous to Europeans than Jim Crow. Still, there had been a kind of comparative logic that affected the judge-ment of many who chose the Soviet or another "socialist" model over the American model, the New Deal offering insufficient reason to do otherwise. A former British communist who left the party in 1956 told this author that when young British activists looked across the Atlantic in the 1930s, they saw a deeply hypocritical, economically wounded and exploitative society, and across the Volga, a more equitable experiment. In this evasive perception of the Soviet Union, even the Stalin-Hitler pact was justified as a defense of a state that the British or U.S. leadership, might have been prepared to sacrifice in its own in-terests.[87] The journalist Robert Dell, one of those most involved in the publica-tion of the London edition of the *Brown Book of the Hitler Terror*, reported on streetwise encounters that revealed his own sense of contradiction in a series of "American Impressions" appearing in the *Manchester Guardian* in 1936. One was entitled "New Orleans: Relics of France and Spain; the Color Problem."

> The prejudice is almost universal. . . . My cabman was a strong supporter of President Roosevelt and distinctly left in his tendencies, but he declared that the Negroes were an inferior race who must be kept in their place but at the same time kindly treated. The cabbie was violently anti-Nazi. . . . I pointed out to him that anti-Negro prejudice was as much a form of Hitler's "racism" as the antisemitic prejudice, and that Hitler had actually used it against the US in a violent speech. He was not convinced.[88]

When the war ended, America became suspect on many of the same grounds that it had been before the war: racism, naked capitalism, moral vacuity, and imperial ambition. For many others, the United State was the most preferred shelter. The mandarins were always in contact with their prodigals there. Mitchison wrote bluntly to Leonard Woolf, bereft of his wife: "In some ways it is a lost world; everything has changed since then. I'm not sure she would have liked the present set-up. One has to do a lot of re-adjustment, not always very well. And so many people are dead. Or in America, which comes so much to the same thing."[89]

From 1935, in an application of a version of the Popular Front strategy, the U.S. Scottsboro defense, and likewise its partners in the United Kingdom and in Europe, had incorporated their former political opponents into the wide coalitions that marked the later years of the campaign. The ACLU, the NAACP, and the ILD worked jointly in the U S. The contention that the domination of the campaign by the communists lessened its impact is counterfactual. Their presence surely could have been strengthened and sustained by earlier cooperation. They made the case more of a priority than any other organization did and for longer, but they too could not see it to the bitter end. McCarthyism, the Cold War, and the persistence of Jim Crow all bore down when the defendants were released, escaped, were rearrested for other crimes, and were again released in the North. The third set of trials occurred in 1936–37. The courts declined to review the convictions of the five defendants who remained incarcerated in their wake. Four were paroled in 1943 and 1950, a full nineteen years after the train made its stop in Paint Rock and its hidden passengers alighted into the hands of their captors. In 1948 Haywood Patterson, most vilified and rendered most notorious in his imprisonment, escaped from a chain gang and fled to Detroit.

Ada Wright died in Chattanooga in 1965, in the same year as Dr. Du Bois. She died at home, Louis Engdahl's picture framed by her bedside in the small white house near what is now Martin Luther King, Jr., Boulevard, the old East Ninth Street. Alabama Judge James E. Horton, whose decision in the defendants' favor meant that he would never hold public office again in Alabama, died in Tennessee in 1973, where he had fled to work for the Tennessee Valley Authority. Ada Wright's younger son Leroy did military service but was not buried with military honors in segregated Chattanooga. Instead, his grave lies by his mother's in a small, hilly, overgrown African American cemetery near Missionary Ridge. Before his release in 1943, her older son Andy wrote to Roy Wilkins from prison—the same Roy Wilkins who wrote a 1940 editorial on Scottsboro in *The Crisis* and marched on the bridge at Selma.[90] But neither son died a martyr of the Civil Rights era. The police reported that Leroy shot himself and his wife dead in his New York City apartment. The Wright family members went by train all the way North to identify his body. Without enough funds to stay in a hotel, they spent the night in a car and took the body back to Chattanooga by train, burying Leroy by his mother, where his brother would also lie.

CONCLUSION

At the close of the Second World War, the peoples of Western Europe—who were hard put to govern or even feed themselves—continued to rule much of the non-European world. This unseemly paradox, whose implications were not lost on indigenous elites in the European colonies, had perverse consequences. To many in Britain, France or the Netherlands, their countries' colonies and imperial holdings in Africa, Asia, the Middle East and the Americas were balm for the suffering and humiliations of the war in Europe; they had demonstrated their material value in that war as vital national resources.

—*Tony Judt,* Postwar

[T]he end of colonialism has traditionally been explained primarily in terms of the economic emasculation of the colonial powers by the Second World War. At least one further reason may be suggested—a change in collective consciousness that took shape as a result of the ideological struggles of mid-century. After the war against Hitler's racism, the inherent right of white men to rule the rest of the world was decreasingly defensible to European consciences. All the empires resisted decolonization, though some did so with greater energy than others.

—*Bernard Wasserstein,* Barbarism and Civilization

[T]he Empire had stood alone against the truly evil imperialism of Hitler. Even if it did not last for the thousand years that Churchill hopefully suggested that it might, this was indeed, the British Empire's "finest hour." Yet what made it so fine, so authentically noble, was that the Empire's victory could only have been Pyrrhic. In the end, the British sacrificed her Empire to stop the Germans, Japanese and Italians from keeping theirs. Did not that sacrifice alone expunge all the Empire's other sins?

—*Niall Ferguson,* Empire

Much of this story of contact and of the exchange of ideas between British socialists and colonial radicals, as well as among the latter, is almost impossible to recover. . . . [It is] outside the boundaries of formal politics—in private meetings, personal friendships, brief encounters of various sorts, leaving no written records. . . . [Oral histories] cannot hope to reconstruct the pattern as a whole.

—*Stephen Howe,* Anti-Colonialism

IN MAY OF 1940, when Winston Churchill rose to defend his assumption of political and military power in the face of Munich's treacherous sacrifices, he posed the future of Britain under fascism in indelible terms. Without the coming struggle, he said, "We should become a slave state." The vernacular of the "Camptown Races," of the blackface minstrel tradition, pervaded early twentieth-century British and European culture—the slavery of antiquity was reenacted in Nazi ambition, but embodied in the American experience. Even when progressives sought to champion the oppressed or to challenge racism and social injustice, they deployed the very images that Hollywood and the traveling entertainers promoted. Those born in slavery, like the visitor to Edinburgh in 1937—Bishop William Heard—or the grandchildren of slaves, who included Ada Wright, George Padmore, and Louis Armstrong, were often seen by Europeans as symbols of that institution: worthy of pity but unfit to act as agents of their own destinies. The Scottsboro case involved not only communism's embrace—an adoption that saved the lives of the defendants in the racist South—but also the invocation of communism's own racial attitudes and racial vernaculars, all endured by black witnesses who themselves were "in the know," and aware of the tenor of thought and articulation that surrounded them. In the 1950s Padmore wrote, "Politically-minded Negroes despised the opportunism of the British communists, who during the Popular Front period of the thirties, simply looked upon the Africans as 'backward, unsophisticated tribesmen.'" This kind of prejudice carried over into the left's attempts to address colonial and imperial questions. Communists like almost everyone else, were prepared to relegate anti-imperialism to the back burner; as the decade passed, they had the force of Stalin's foreign policy as a ready inducement.[1]

In 1932 Ada Wright journeyed through a world laden with racial codes. Committed activists articulated an antiracist and antifascist politics while their casual presumptions and ways of speaking and writing flowed from that larger, racially inflected cultural vernacular, its presumptions hovering over Wright.[2] But her presence in Britain and Europe also tested these understandings—the knowledge of what she looked like, who her sons were, and how she spoke—influencing judgments in new directions even when much was lost in translation. Many others of color were highly visible agents of dissent in the heart of the national and imperial structures that denied their importance or agency, including the structures of organized political formations like the British Labour and Liberal parties. Many among the white British majority, like the Mass Observers, had opinions of "Negroes," even if they were not deeply preoccupied with the Empire.[3] The American South provided a dramatic and visceral imaginary and resonated for common people as much or more than Africa or India.[4] A majority of Europeans who knew of the United States may well have opposed lynching and abject Southern racial violence. As they entered the next decade of war and global capitalism's resurgence, this objection resonated. The era of "decolonization" witnessed the reconfiguration of anti-imperialist and anticolonial forces in tandem with the establishment and refinement of many mediating organizations of global control, from the organization of the Nuremberg trials to the UN Charter and the Cold War alliances of NATO and the Warsaw Pact. Efforts to oppose the racial violence of wartime merged with a legacy of fighting Jim Crow.[5] Arthur Creech Jones, of the Fabian Colonial Bureau, polemically called for international trusteeship status to be conferred upon African Americans.[6]

In watching and commenting upon these events, George Padmore's eyes stayed wide open. He did not submit to a second-class status in European left political circles, and he could not lead as a black man shorn of the Comintern apparatus; instead he made his mark as a journalist and interventionist. He was quicker than most of his contemporaries, and his ambitions and prodigious energy made many people uncomfortable but no more so than for his message. His short life was a speeding bullet of daring and verve—"Gwine to run all night, gwine to run all day." His absence from more powerful, active duty in politics affected the design of the 1930s; hence the ILP supporters who tried to get him to run for Parliament.[7] Padmore was a causal force unspent, restricted, and proscribed. His life and writings, steeped in the data from Geneva and parliamentary publications, bore witness to the possibilities missed *for his fellow Europeans*—his adopted neighbors, be they émigrés, refugees, or poor migrant maritime workers—not just for the hope for freedom on the African continent and in the Caribbean.[8] His story cannot be removed from that of the Comintern collapse, and it links that collapse to the imperial and racial aspirations of the Soviets and their agents and sympathizers. But it also shows the tenacity of dissent, and avant-garde reflection, and the fluidity of "fellow traveling." It begs the necessity of decentering communism in understanding the era and of countenancing heterogeneous contemporary opinion.

The ILP's provocative journal the *New Leader*, in which Padmore played a greater editorial role as the war approached and ensued, and the African American press across the Atlantic in which he and others wrote, engaged public discourse on the Moscow trials, the threat of colonial transfers, Munich, and the problem of war as imagined from the perspectives of the world's majority of Asian, African, and Latin American peoples. In wartime, Padmore continued to differentiate himself from the dominant trends of the British antifascist left, remaining in a corner with some of the ILPers. In the lead-up to war Padmore emphasized the British appetite for appeasement but also the League of Nations' betrayals—the thieves' kitchen. Unlike his former comrade Münzenberg, Padmore forswore the Comintern in a departure "to its left," forming alliances based upon a perceived need for global anti-imperial solidarity, while Münzenberg sought out anticommunist liberals and anti-appeasement Tories in the United Kingdom, asking them to contribute to *Die Zukunft*, which supported a fictive, parliamentarist "new Germany," shorn of Nazi terror. Padmore was critical, intransigent, and urgent in his business, laboring under the slogan "Hands off the colonies." He challenged conscription, the BBC's use of the term "nigger" in its broadcasting (though it was a term later used in the

House of Commons), and the segregation policies of the British military services, bemoaning the absence of black representatives to the International
Labour Organization.[9] He did not wait for Ghana, and continued to soar. After
the Manchester Pan-African Congress of 1945, he went to Accra to work with
Kwame Nkrumah in the final chapter of his extraordinary life, his aspirations
for a new global order still largely a matter of journalistic expression rather
than a lived international vision coming to fruition before his eyes. He did not
conform to the picture of colonial elites (whom he called colonial quislings)
suddenly awakened to national consciousness, and derided that image: "We
are not narrow nationalists."[10]

Lady Kathleen Manning Simon was both canny and unwitting, her pursuits
offering an argument for the duplicities of liberal humanitarianism when har-
nessed to a perilous and supremacist foreign policy. Antislavery was a successful British interwar social movement that galvanized thousands across Britain,
a long and luxurious hangover from the rites of the nineteenth century. It was
expansive, inclusive, and salving. There was clear exploitation to document
and oppose, and the movement educated thousands, furthering some forms of
antiracism and appeals for imperial reform. Importantly, it also allowed breathing space for capitalism and for the thieves' kitchen—the diplomatic failures of
the League and Locarno. It did not disavow the "successes" of Ramsay Mac-
Donald's visit to Berchtesgaden and what followed and culminated in Munich, in which Sir John Simon played such a profound architectural role.[11] Like
Scottsboro or Meerut, though the communist-inspired campaigns were smaller
and different in Britain, Lady Simon's vintage antislavery activities changed
outlooks and promoted a rudimentary racial justice but could not solve the
problems that they identified. Their legacy was a form of righteous, journalistic
witness, and advocacy from above that invoked the motifs of nineteenth-century
melodrama. Forms of slavery, discovered and identified across a large modern
topography, remain the movement's sustenance to this day.[12]

Britain's empire rendered many liberals stark naked, but Lady Simon and Sir
John Simon posed as august agents of what would now be termed human
rights, while simultaneously providing back-handed support to Mussolini, using
the issue of "slavery" as a prop with which to court fascism. The plea for rights
was manipulated in the service of a foreign policy that led to the institution of
Nazi slave labor on the European continent and the deaths of tens of thousands
of Ethiopians. In another sphere, the prospect of colonial transfers, a significant feature of the British ambition at Munich, was debated and challenged
with the same ferocity expended upon events like the passage of the Nuremberg laws, the latter only tentatively understood as part of a more murderous,
emergent Nazi racial policy. Opposition to colonial transfers was embraced by
empire supporters as well as critics of empire, but it was Hitler's own disinterest in bargaining stolen colonial land for peace that finally resolved this feature
of Munich's racial politics. It was as potent an example of British notions of

superiority as was the sympathetic judgment rendered by Lord Halifax and the British negotiators on Hitler's desire to repatriate Sudeten Germans. In 1938, Lord Runciman wrote to Neville Chamberlain:

> I have much sympathy . . . with the Sudetan [*sic*] case. It is a hard thing to be ruled by an alien race; and I have been left with the impression that Czechoslovak rule in the Sudetan [*sic*] areas . . . though not actively oppressive and certainly not "terroristic," has been marked by tactlessness, lack of understanding, petty intolerance and discrimination, to a point where the resentment of the German population was inevitably moving in the direction of revolt.

The Germans were considered "racial equals" by the British. In March 1939 Viscount Halifax spoke in the House of Lords: "The world will not forget that in September last Herr Hitler appealed to the principle of self-determination in the interests of two million Sudetan [*sic*] Germans. That principle is one which the British Empire itself has been [*sic*] erected, and one to which we felt obliged to give weight in considering Herr Hitler's claim—now rudely contradicted."[13]

Shapurji Saklatvala's prominence in mainstream British political culture, the Meerut Trial's notoriety among activists and readers of a broadly interested press, and Nehru's growing prewar metropolitan presence all offered evidence of the centrality and importance of the Indian case as an element of 1930s racial discourse in Britain. Many metropolitan narratives underestimate the implication of Western communism, liberal sentiment, and street interest in India in the 1930s. While the attitudes of British sympathizers of the Meerut prisoners or activist independence supporters in Britain bore little upon India's immediate outcomes during the war, the knowledge of these events played a role in a widening domestic racial consciousness and were among the many challenges to colonial paternalism of the era. Saklatvala and Nehru were not the first Indian parliamentary officeholders or touring politicians in Britain, but they enjoyed the great popular interest equally given no other Indians apart from Gandhi in the twentieth-century metropole. Saklatvala and his projects represented the penetration of information, propaganda, and celebrity in electoral and extraparliamentary activism, even though he was regarded as a lesser intellect and a dilettante in some communist circles, and derided by the leading communist theoretician Palme Dutt. Saklatvala and Nehru were both committed to lodging fervent complaints within the halls of power. Saklatvala's interracialism, national concerns, and steadfastness in politics, from his younger antipoverty socialism to his promotion of multiracial sovietism, exemplified the complexity of trying to reconcile communist orthodoxy with anticolonialism. The Meerut Trial heightened communism's appeal for some in India and persuaded its external onlookers of the brutalities of British rule, but it also showed the resilience of the imperial state under duress, and its ability to recoup from a wrong-headed, backfiring prosecution. This resilience did not last, and the rehabilitation and survival of most of the Meerut defendants increased anti-imperialist sentiment in India, while demonstrating the futility of punishing unsubstantiated "terrorism" as a means to prod the larger public into renewed support for the imperial presence—a route to self-justification at home.

"German relief," and the world the refugees made in London, occupied a rich space within which Münzenberg and his associates attempted to proselytize *Die Zukunft*, and its utopian program. The deep networks and surprising interconnections that the story of that publication reveals suggest that "antifascism" was a very large gambit in which Churchill's staff could keep distant council with the Comintern's most flamboyant and notorious West European ex-comrade. Münzenberg understood that not all fascist opinion was global in its vision, and not all antifascists opposed empire or imperialism—in fact *most* did not. Although many involved in antifascist activity increasingly challenged Nazi racial policies, or the racial connotations of Mussolini's ambitions and aggression in North Africa, most would not have identified opposition to "racism" or to global racial injustice as a defining feature of their antifascist beliefs, or extended the map of the perpetrators to all imperialists.[14] In this mix, race was redefined for the moment as a "German problem" for British and European activists. They themselves never resolved just how far their advocacy of Jews and opposition to anti-Semitism extended, or how far their support for all refugees ran. These were matters upon which liberals and the left were divided. In July 1939 *New Leader* published "Should the Refugees Fight for Britain?" by "a German Socialist," which pled for a "German working class . . . overthrow of the German dictatorship," not the British government's war effort:

> Many bourgeois Jews and other bourgeois refugees who had to leave their country for other than political reasons share the view that they must "support" British democracy against Hitler's barbarism. These people never see this suppression of colonial people by British "democracy." . . . just as the emigrated Jewish bourgeoisie find their way over national and racial differences to their own class, so will the refugees belonging socially and politically to the proletariat.[15]

In sharp distinction to those who advocated the liberation of the colonial world and continued to do so up to and after the declaration of war in Europe, most antifascists saw the struggle against fascist rule in Italy, Spain, and Germany—and subsequently, the territories invaded by the Axis powers—as their primary central focus. They increasingly saw these struggles as including the *defense* of empire as they perceived the growing German threat to British, French, and Dutch possessions. They would not have entertained Padmore's slogan "Hands Off the Colonies." Nor did all anti-imperial, colonially based movements or Anglo-American advocates of those movements see the easy resolution of their anti-imperial ambitions in terms of the victory of the Allies—these differences created specific fault lines. In India important sections of the left and nationalist leadership spent considerable periods of time incarcerated during the war. Padmore sought support for Senegalese efforts against the

Vichy regime in France as he sought to combine anticolonial and antifascist programs.[16] Special pressures existed for nonwhite populations of colonial subjects, refugees, or migrants without diplomatic representation, trapped in Europe when war was declared and states occupied.[17]

Opposition to both imperialism and fascism were in certain ways irreconcilable. Opponents of both saw fascism as a form of imperialism, as racist, but also saw imperialism as an equally malevolent force. W.E.B. Du Bois's trip to Nazi Germany on a fellowship and his involvements in Japan; Nehru's and Gandhi's visits to Italy and Germany; and the Indian nationalist Subhas Chandra Bose's eventual defection to Japan in his fight against the British in Asia were all features of the ambiguities over what actions to take in the face of multiple agendas, and which powers to support—even if most remained antifascist. Padmore's line was more visionary. If India and the colonies were freed in wartime, he reasoned,

> The world would be electrified by a change of policy which would turn the slogan of "Democracy" into living reality—into the struggle of free peoples, regardless of race, for their common rights against a menace felt by all. Thereby also would be nullified the activities of Nazi and fifth column agents.[18]

The American Nuremberg trials prosecutors had to acknowledge the Jim Crow practices of their country as an element of immediate postwar, antifascist hypocrisy. At the London Conference to prepare for the trials, Justice Robert H Jackson stated,

> We have some regrettable circumstances at times in our own country in which minorities are unfairly treated. We think it is justifiable that we interfere—only because the concentration camps and the deportations were in pursuance of . . . an unjust or illegal war in which we become involved. We see no other basis on which we are justified in reaching the atrocities which were committed inside Germany . . .[19]

How do the portraits drawn above cast the decade in a new light? The multiracial network of varied political and religious persuasions whose members engaged the racial politics of the 1930s was a chaotic, often broken, sometimes duplicitous one. After the war, masses of people passed from British rule, some with the blaring bugle and lowered flag, but others in the tumult that enveloped many zones of Asia, Africa, and the Caribbean; the death toll in partition and the vicious British counterinsurgency campaign in Malaya being early cases in point. In the American theater the postwar civil rights movement, and the black-Jewish alliance that lay near its center, aggressively confronted Jim Crow. But these postwar patterns were bound up with the interwar era that preceded them. This is more than just an issue of a simple historical blindspot and more than a compensatory reconstruction.[20] As new archival openings occur and older collections are newly interrogated, a conceptual leap is possible, offering a holistic and more complete account of the era in which the racial politics of the 1930s becomes an irreducible element of the understanding of the decade as a whole.

The role of the Soviet Union remained a potent factor in the lives of many political actors in this era. The Moscow trials were known and debated in their time. The London press carried regular reports of them; *New Leader* and other publications raised the deepest questions about their legitimacy, and people left the communist party because of them. Not all waited until 1956 or 1968; for many, there was already sufficient evidence to depart the circles of the party in the thirties, and the heroic Russian war effort did not bring them back. The treatment of many of the nonwhite members of the communist party hierarchy, including George Padmore and Saklatvala, were part of communism's inherent failures, not a side act to the central Soviet state's repressive apparatus. The sacrifice of struggles like those in Spain, scene of the murderous last days of factional warfare in Barcelona, mirrored the treatment of the anticolonialists and their followers. Many party members of all racial backgrounds also remained among the outspoken antiracists of their day—in Britain, Europe, the United States, and elsewhere, yet Soviet policy explicitly favored a series of negotiations with the imperial powers and serious trade relationships with the United States; the Comintern could not and did not seek to undermine these potential or real alliances by contributing to their subversion in the mid- to late thirties. After the Stalin-Hitler pact, Operation Barbarossa thrust ardent communists back into the camp of the Allies, and the prewar pattern of celebrating Soviet achievement superseded a critique of the Russian use of terror in many contexts. This hubris was sustained at Nuremberg and went hand in hand with the unspoken cooperation exercised in the "nonmention" of Jim Crow by Allied prosecutors.

Journalist Robert Dell contended at the war's outset that the Russians forged the Stalin-Hitler pact as a response to their being excluded from the table at Munich. But it was not just in the sphere of foreign policy that the Soviet apparatus was committed to policies that did not challenge and indeed furthered injustice. It should not come as a surprise that a state prepared to incarcerate millions of its own people unto death, in the exercise of what was often an ethnic-based policy of repression, should have dealt as it did with some of the activist leaders of color who emerged in the thirties. The exile communities that formed in Europe in the face of fascism (Münzenberg's circle was one, but there were many others) in turn ceased to see Moscow as a force for antifascism and desperately mounted alliances with liberals, even though it was too late. *Both* Munich and the Stalin-Hitler pact cemented their worst fears—to be sold out by the Allies and by their former Moscow bosses. Padmore was not the only one to lapse.

The deep ironies of 1930s racial politics were not resolved by the war, contrary to Ferguson's suggestion above. Retribution upon the British was not so easily had. The tenacity with which white Rhodesians, South Africans, and many other Empire settlers strove to maintain their rule brought repression, civil and regional wars, and the wasted lives of a postwar generation. Britain only hesitatingly relinquished her grip, sometimes in the face of overwhelming force or, as at Suez, in the face of abandonment by her overlords among nations. Historian Tony Judt cites Labour party leader Herbert Morrison, a close ally of William Gillies in the 1930s, describing the granting of independence to the colonies as tantamount to giving "a child of ten a latch-key, a bank account, and a shotgun."[21] He was a member of the wartime government and a member of Attlee's 1945 Labour government, a regime that Padmore jibed "owed more to Kipling than to Marx."[22]

For those portrayed within who lived on after the war, the 1930s never escaped reference. When Nehru spoke at the Non-Aligned Bandung conference of 1955, he eulogized a long-deceased former German communist whose 1929 League against Colonial Oppression conference lay among the ruins of an earlier multiracial moment—Willi Münzenberg—before a curious and in many cases unknowing audience. In 1960 we find the Ghanaian President Kwame Nkrumah speaking at Harlem's Hotel Theresa with Malcolm X on the reviewing stand. On the same trip he met with Nehru in Manhattan's Hotel Carlyle, affirming the link between the Pan-Africanist and the U. S. civil rights movements. President Jomo Kenyatta greeted Thurgood Marshall in Kenya in 1963 while ILP leader Fenner Brockway hosted Coretta Scott King in London in 1970, two years after her husband's assassination. But many others who appear in these pages did not outlive the war or its immediate aftermath. The "Scottsboro boys'" collective 130 years in prison extended beyond the war for some of them. It is a deep historical irony, right at the heart of the matter, that they survived in incarceration longer than did most of their leading defenders across the waters.

What joins Scottsboro to Munich? The centrality of racial thinking helped to define the transatlantic political culture in which both events occurred, one at the end and the other at the start of a decade that led to global war. The Scottsboro defendants were regarded as pariahs by Southern society, and the status quo sought to uphold their prosecutions, unfair and unjustified as they were. Their supporters saw the righteousness of their plight and many opposed the South's segregationist practices. In Britain the censor of the American South sometimes stretched to a condemnation of imperial and colonial practices. The dilemma of the later thirties, in terms of expressly racial politics in the British imperial context, bore within it the reification of notions of racial superiority like those that fed Jim Crow among Americans: there was an appetite for exchanging nonwhite peoples and their stolen lands for a European peace, and there was a sympathy for the racial ethnocentrism of German national and ethnic claims upon central Europe that were expressions of racial values. These were manifestations of regarding a people as expendable, as unworthy of advocacy, as less deserving, and as unequal. The sacrifice of the rights and the lives of Jews and many other Europeans lay in the balance of this acquiescence to Hitler's claims. The contention that "race" in its many manifestations cannot be separated from the logic and design of the era is not a new proposition. When the imperial and racist designs of the Munich decisions were exposed, not just by Padmore or Nehru but by many other critics and opponents, the defense of empire seemed the only logical response for most in the Anglo-American and Allied world. The ultimate defense of the Soviet Union fit neatly into the package, once Hitler's invasion of the Soviet Union rendered Stalin's engagement with Germany moot.

The opponents of empire to whom this narrative is most committed lost the weight of the argument in the face of fascism. They hovered in the interstices of decisions they did not influence or necessarily support, remaining critical witnesses. The rise of anticolonialism in the postwar era bore the imprint of their intentions, but fascism took a large toll upon those who had spent the better parts of their lives in the maze of 1930s politics. These endless lists of names, the number of meetings, the petitions and posters and marches and conferences dazzle, yet the triumph of fascism and the victory of the Allied empires in the war, the preservation of Jim Crow for two more decades, the new and brutal American theaters of war that erupted in the 1950s and 1960s owed a great deal to the "other side" of the racial politics of the 1930s, as did the much longer lists of victims in their millions. The present global culture bears witness to the uneven legacy of that time.

The post-1945 outcomes reflected the tensions that beset the relationships in the 1930s. When movements for national liberation grew in Asia, Africa, and Latin America in the years after the war, amid other projects of imperial reform, many liberals and social-democrats were deeply divided over whether to offer them support. The mobilization against the European fascisms was far more pronounced than the support for "Third World" anticolonialism after 1945. The U.S.-led anticommunist project that followed the war helped to reconstitute the British and European left into several camps. In Britain, and in each society of the Continent, varied forms of accommodation and dissent arose in the transitions from 1945 to 1956, and in 1968 and the aftermath of 1989. In the postcommunist world of the new century, one can conjure up heroes and heroines but the trail of betrayal and death is also wide. Tearing the grass away from the stones on the path that leads from Scottsboro to Munich lengthens the journey from Munich to Nuremberg, from Scottsboro to Selma and all the trails that crossover in between. Through the back roads and the necessary detours, we come upon our own time, its unresolved dilemmas now more visible from afar.

CHRONOLOGY

1927

League against Colonial Oppression convened at Brussels. Jawaharlal Nehru, Ernst Toller, George Lansbury, Palme Dutt, Roger Baldwin, K. N. Joglekar, Clemens Dutt, Jomo Kenyatta. Chattopadhyaya, Henri Barbusse, Harry Pollitt, Fenner Brockway, Garan Kouyate, and founder **Willi Münzenberg** attend (Feb.). **Shapurji Saklatvala** tours India.

1928

Sir John Simon, accompanied by **Lady Kathleen Manning Simon**, leads British Parliament's Simon Commission to India; members greeted by protests (Feb.). Sixth Congress of the Comintern convenes in Moscow (July–Sept.). Textile workers' strike engulfs Bombay.

1929

Police sweep through Indian neighborhoods, arresting militants who become Meerut Trial defendants (March). British second Labour government, elected in May, bans League against Imperialism from meeting in London. LAI meets in Frankfurt. **George Padmore,** William Pickens, Jomo Kenyatta, James Maxton, Reginald Bridgeman, and Garan Kouyate attend (July). **Lady Simon** publishes *Slavery*. Second wave of Bombay textile strikes.

1930

Meerut Trial opens in India. **Padmore** meets Asian Communists on Moscow visit, makes only prewar trip to Africa, and hosts Hamburg First International Conference of Negro Workers. Kenyatta and Kouyate attend (July). **Lady Simon** and Sir John Simon tour North America (Aug.). First Indian Round Table talks convene in London (Nov.–Jan., 1931).

1931

Scottsboro defendants arrested and convicted in Alabama (March–April). **Padmore** speaks on Scottsboro in Leningrad (July). British National Government elected (July). Kenyatta returns to London from Moscow; rooms with Paul Robeson (Aug.). Second Indian Round Table talks convene; Gandhi attends, visiting Romain Rolland in Marseille en route (Sept.–Dec.). Japan invades Manchuria (Sept.). World Congress of Red Aid convenes in Berlin (Oct.). **Padmore** meets Nancy Cunard in Paris.

1932

Naomi Mitchison visits Soviet Union and encounters Langston Hughes and Loren Miller. **Ada Wright** and Louis Engdahl disembark at Hamburg and travel through Europe, Britain, and the Soviet Union (May–Oct.). Cunard travels to the United States. **Münzenberg** organizes Meerut demonstrations in Germany. **Wright** attends Hamburg Harborworkers Conference called by **Padmore** (May); meets **Saklatvala**, Bridgeman, Arnold Ward, Bob Lovell in London (July); attends Amsterdam Anti-War Congress, as do **Münzenberg** and **Saklatvala** (Aug.); and attends Moscow International Red Aid Congress addressed by **Padmore**. Miriam Sherman hears **Padmore**'s speech, encounters Hughes in Moscow, and escorts **Wright** back to the United States after Engdahl's death (Oct.) D. A. Thenghi dies while standing trial at Meerut (Nov.). British Independent Labour party disaffiliates with British Labour party, holds Sheffield unity talks with CPGB. **Padmore** speaks on Scottsboro in London. Third Indian Round Table talks convene in London (Nov.–Dec.). Meerut Trial ends.

1933

Hitler assumes power in Germany. Japanese occupy Shanghai. **Münzenberg** and Babette Gross flee Germany to Paris. First London call for German refugee assistance issued. (Jan.) Meerut sentences handed down in India. (Feb.) **Padmore** arrested in Hamburg, released two months later, deported to The United Kingdom. British Labour rejects CPGB coalition offer. Decatur, Alabama court convicts Scottsboro defendants; Judge James E. Horton overturns jury (June). Meerut Trial appeals decisions announced (July). Central British Fund for German Jewry established. Mock Reichstag Fire Trial held in London, directed from Paris by **Münzenberg**, Otto Katz, Koestler. Garfield Hays and D. M. Pritt among its "judges" (Sept.). Scottsboro convictions handed down (Nov.–Dec.). William Wilberforce Centenary begins.

1934

Comintern officially expels **Padmore** (Feb.). Nancy Cunard publishes *Negro* anthology. Wilberforce Centenary reaches apogee in London (August). USSR joins League of Nations (Sept.). **Münzenberg**, Gross, Ellen Wilkinson, and Aneurin Bevan tour United States with World Aid Committee for the Victims of European Fascism (March). Conviction of Scottsboro defendants Norris and Patterson upheld in U.S. courts (June); stays of execution granted. Indian Girni Kamgar union boasts sixty thousand members. British circulation of the **Münzenberg** circle's *Brown Book of the Hitler Terror*. **Saklatvala** makes final sojourn to Soviet Union.

1935

U.S. Supreme Court defies southern Scottsboro convictions (April). Franco-Soviet pact signed (May). British Government of India Act enfranchises 30 million, one-sixth of population (Aug.). Seventh Congress of Comintern held in Moscow. (July–Aug.) Hunger marches in U.K. (Aug.–Oct. 1936). Nehru joins Kamala Nehru in Switzerland (Sept.). Italy invades Abyssinia (October).

Tories retain leadership in U.K. General Election (Nov.). Hoare-Laval pact signed (Dec.) NAACP joins Scottsboro defense case in United State (Dec.).

1936

Edward VIII ascends throne (Jan.) **Saklatvala** dies (Jan.). Patterson convicted in The United States (March). German reoccupation of the Rhineland (March). Spanish Civil War begins (July). Bolshevik veteran leaders Zinoviev and Kamenev executed in Moscow (Aug.). **Münzenberg** and Gross make last journey to the Soviet Union (Oct). Largest London antifascist demonstration (Oct). **Padmore** sees Cunard off to Spain in Paris. Socialist League, CPGB, ILP attempt new Unity Campaign in Britain. Abdication of Edward VIII (Dec.).

1937

Spain at war. Moscow trials continue (Jan.) Ralph Bunche sails to England from United States (Feb.). Indian Congress party sweeps national elections (March). London formation of International African Service Bureau. FDR makes conciliatory gestures toward Italy (April). German bombing of *Guernica* (April). Coronation of King George VI (May). **Simons** visit U.K. camp for Basque refugee children (May). Bunche visits Paris Exposition (June). Strikes spread in Trinidad (June). **Münzenberg** announces resignation from the Comintern (July). Courts free four Scottsboro defendants; other convictions upheld (Aug.). Bishop William Heard denied hotel room in Edinburgh (Aug.). Comintern and KPD-in-exile expel **Münzenberg** (November). **Padmore** claims surreptitious return to Germany as journalist; meets Jewish leaders. John Harris tours the American South with African American sociologist Charles Johnson.

1938

First number of **Münzenberg's** *Die Zukunft* published in Paris (Feb.). Germany annexes Austria into Third Reich in *Anschluss*. Moscow trials continue (March). Léon Blum's Popular Front government falls in France; Daladier government assumes power (April). **Padmore's** "Britain Ready to Give Colonies to Hitler" appears in *Chicago Defender* (April). Robeson visits Spain (May). Scottsboro defendant Clarence Norris's death sentence commuted to life (July). British representatives sign agreement with Hitler at Munich (Sept.). Bombay witnesses largest single day of strikes since 1920s (Nov.). Kristallnacht grips Germany (Nov.). France imposes greater restrictions upon aliens (Nov.). Five remaining imprisoned Scottsboro defendants denied pardons (Nov.). First *Kindertransport* trains arrive in United Kingdom. Nehru travels to Britain and Europe, visits Spain.

1939

Scottsboro defendant Patterson convicted in a retrial (Jan.). Germans invade Prague (March). Nehru travels to Hanoi and China (Aug.). Nazi-Soviet pact signed (Aug.). Germans invade Poland. Britain declares war on Germany

(Sept.); 400,000 of 680,000 Jews have left Germany, Austria, and Bohemia. CPGB calls war "unjust."

1940

Last issue of *Die Zukunft* (May). Churchill becomes British Prime Minister (May). France falls to Germans (June). Trotsky assassinated in Mexico by GPU agent (Aug.). Nehru imprisoned in India (Oct.). **Münzenberg**'s remains discovered in French countryside (Oct.).

NOTES ON SOURCES

In the spring of 2007 the National Gallery in Washington featured an exhibition that subsequently moved to the Guggenheim Museum in New York, entitled *Foto: Modernity in Central Europe, 1918–1945*, curated by Matthews Witovsky. The Yale literary critic Peter Demetz contributed an Introduction to its catalogue, and dozens of researchers across Europe are thanked for tracing the images. I passed through rooms filled with graphic design and art photography, searching for references to the wartime Hungarian regime and the German invasion. Just before encountering a very few works devoted to the Holocaust, I paused near some of the only expressly political images in the show. One was Lajos Vajda's *Tolstoy and Gandhi*, an undated collage featuring photo cut-outs of the principals, flanked by a few other strangers' mounted faces and bodies in skewed disorder characteristic of the genre—one of these was Lenin's.

I stopped short in sudden recognition of the face of an African American woman—it was a clipped head-shot of Ada Wright at the very bottom of the canvas. Wright was banned from Hungary and much of Eastern Europe during the summer of 1932. I was both pleased to see her there and reminded of the disappearance of the very history to which I had committed the last fifteen years of my life. The exhibition catalogue offered no relief. It explained that Vajda left Budapest for Paris in 1929 (where Wright, of course, had spoken), identifying only the work's namesakes and the bust of Lenin. Vadja was a pacifist and the catalogue simply states that "other emissaries of peace inhabit the lower half of the composition." No one seeing this work in recent times seems to have left any note of Ada Wright's presence, secure in the presumption of her anonymity or unable to imagine how to find out who she was.

The central methodological core of this book is reflected most visibly in the ways in which sources not usually linked are brought to bear upon one another. In some instances, the sources are previously unrecorded, as in some of the Comintern files material, but in other instances, well-established biographies, memoirs, diaries, letters, parliamentary, and private paper collections are revisited in new ways. In this respect, the text engages a hybrid of materials whose selection is driven by the retelling of a series of 1930s mostly known "racial-political" narratives, newly organized around the lives of the individual activists at center stage. Many strands of the story are incomplete in archival terms, and the hope is that this exploration will tempt other scholars to take up the individual parts and renovate them, explore them, and recalibrate them in deeper and different ways. James Hooker's short biography of George Padmore, for example, remains the central standard source on Padmore's life partly because no one has linked other kinds of sources to a major new study, or explored the very sources that Hooker himself suggested or identified in his time. And many other biographers, like those of James Maxton or Stafford Cripps, were unaware of Padmore's existence when they wrote their works.

The materials on individuals of a biographical nature are diverse, some hagiographical, while others constitute conventional scholarship, but for conceptual reasons, the connections made in this text are often missing in these works, as some of my endnotes state. Reconstructing them has required testing the biographical narratives against both known and new sources. Future researchers can make full use of the new edition of the *Dictionary of National Biography.* The files of the Communist International provided one starting point for my doing so, and not simply for those individuals previously unquestionably associated with communist organizations. In this respect, the Comintern archives must be seen as useful to a range of investigations of different kinds of political commitments. Despite the new systems of access to *selected* Comintern material that have grown up since my trips to Moscow, and most notably the online materials (http://www.comintern-online.com/) and those available in several international work stations, like the one at the Library of Congress (http://www.loc.gov/rr/ElectronicResources/full_description.php?MainID=1108), the best way to use the Comintern materials, especially for a non-Russian speaker, is to visit RGASPI in Moscow (http://www.rgaspi.ru/).

Apart from the linguistic and practical problems that this option poses and, at this writing, the increasing level of racial attacks in the city that researchers must consider, the original index of the CI materials is not organized in ways that readily make connections that we might term "transnational," an irony given the CI's ostensible purposes. Most materials are based upon the *national* or *regional* principle of organization that guided CI activity, and they require that the researcher have a complex knowledge of CI linguistic and organizational practices and norms. The researcher must be prepared to seek out the interrelationships between CI Secretariats, and in some instances simultaneously look for the supranational organizations, like the "Negro Bureau," LAI, Profintern and Lenin school. No institutional or web-based selection of documents known to me (including the *selected* Tamiment Library [http://www.nyu.edu/library/bobst/research/tam/] and LOC collections [http://www.loc.gov/rr/mss/]) has achieved the breadth of purchase that encompasses these problems, so it is not unusual to find only half of a given correspondence available in collections apart from Moscow's. A solution can lie in the preparation of a research design informed by a full orientation in CI history, the seeking out of a Russian-based translator and documents liaison, and the intrepid will to look for interconnections in places where logic would take one, rather than submitting to the outlook of the Comintern itself, per se. These are unresolved problems for future research that ideally will involve multilingual groups of scholars. I also note that many restrictions and discrepancies in access still apply to CI and related files. Nevertheless, the materials that are available are in many instances staggering, the actual telegrams sent to New York from the South when the Scottsboro case broke being one example, or the exit interviews conducted with each departing International Brigades recruit to the Spanish Civil War, another. Couriers brought documents for valorization, guidance, censor, and safe-keeping from all over the world; the collection is exciting and challenging and will continue both to thrill and to dismay many kinds of historians for years to come, as it snakes its way into larger, international public view.

Mercifully, many other important collections are more easily organized for the types of inquiries this book is committed to, though ingenuity in interrogation is still required. These include the Amsterdam International Institute of Social History's (http://www.iisg.nl/) materials on the League against Imperialism, and the recently reconstituted Labour History and Archive Study Center's (http://www.archiveshub.ac.uk/inst/labhist.shtml) materials on the Labour party and the CPGB, among them the revealing collection of papers of Labour international czar William Gillies. Gillies monitored the left so copiously that his files are a rich source on 1930s non-BLP radical dissent in Britain. There are also Meerut Trial and Reichstag Fire Mock Trial materials at LHASC. The U.S. Department of Justice, whose files are held in the U.S. National Archives in Maryland, monitored international dissent in liaison with the State Department, and this text has not engaged surveillance materials released to the British National Archives at Kew, which could enhance or challenge findings noted here. The Independent Labour Party collection at the LSE archives (http://www.lse.ac.uk/library/archive/Default.htm) provides a third arena for organizational inquiries and can be read alongside the complete set of New Leader for the thirties. There are few microfilm copies that contain the issues of New Leader for the later thirties because of an early oversight in filming; the Cambridge University Library is one holder of a full folio edition. There is another full set of bound volumes buried in the Adams building of the Library of Congress.

My use of the files of the NAACP at the LOC, and the papers of the Anti-Slavery Society and Lady Simon, at Rhodes House, Oxford, which signal the complex courting of liberals and socialists by the anticommunist, antiracist black leadership of the 1930s illustrates the need to link unsuspecting sources in transatlantic sets. This also applies to materials on Ralph Bunche's sojourn and his commentary on his London contacts. These sources address what is an underestimation of the parallel Euro-Anglo-American liberal and socialist dissenting activity that ran alongside communist agitation, and the commensurate nonrecognition of significant black participation in these networks. The Moscow trials and the Gulag were hardly hidden by these individuals or their publications, private and otherwise. A larger discursive formation than "world communism" emerges from this linkage. The African American press is a deeply compelling source for such European and global networks of this period, as well as a source of rich cultural commentary. Its potential use is virtually limitless in the light of past neglect. *International African Opinion* offers a rich vantage point on London and the imperial context, in related ways.

Materials housed in the excellent research library at the United States Holocaust Memorial Museum, and the Paris police materials contained in the F7 files at the *Archives nationales* in Paris, provide opportunities to expand our understandings of the interrelationships between prewar histories of Jewish and non-Jewish migration and immigration, and their connections to liberal and left operations in Britain, the United States, Europe, and beyond. The lists of subscribers to Münzenberg's *Die Zukunft*, held in F7, constitute an example of the significant convergence of these histories; the evidence of the paper's South African contributors, another.

Finally, the text engages cultural sources of the era to convey an impression of "racial vernacular." The left and liberals were purveyors of language and representation in many forms, and shared an orientation with the general public that deployed racial imagery ubiquitously. This is a fruitful area for future investigation, and the researcher must expect to find offensive and stereotypic portrayals in great numbers. But the task in part is to map ambiguity, impulse, and cultural contradiction rather than simply to underline existing racism, the latter inevitably part of such disclosure. This applies broadly to all sources from the era under discussion here. Plays, poetry, film, photographs, cartoons, travelers' accounts, and materials like those housed in the records of *Mass Observation (http://www.massobs.org.uk/index.htm)* are invaluable tools for the historian concerned with racial politics and wider sensibilities, and they comprise spaces where he or she will intersect relevant literary-historical and cultural studies endeavors.

NOTES

INTRODUCTION

1. Peter Cain and Tony Hopkins, *British Imperialism 1688–2000*, 2nd edition (London: Longman, 2001), 85. See also, Nicholas Owen, *The British Left and India: Metropolitan Anti-Imperialism, 1885–1947* (Oxford: 2007) 2–5.

2. *Chicago Defender*, August 14, 1937, 1. The *Defender*'s London office noted that such exclusion from hotels was also common in Paris, where white American tourists made the same demands. See also William Henry Heard, *From Slavery to the Bishopric in the AME* (New York; Arno Press of the *New York Times*, 1969); *New York Times*, August 8, 1937, 29; and August 9, 1934. Temple served as Archbishop of Canterbury from 1943 until his death in 1944. See John Kent, *William Temple: Church, State and Society in Britain, 1880–1950* (Cambridge: Cambridge University Press, 1992) and Temple's anti-fascist *Christianity and the Social Order* (New York: Penguin, 1942) and *The Church Looks Forward* (New York: Moorehouse-Gorham Co., 1942), which includes Stafford Cripps, "The Challenge of Christianity," 26–35.

3. *Simon to Du Bois*, February 28, 1938, in Hebert Aptheker, ed., *The Correspondence of W.E.B. Du Bois, Vol. II, Selections, 1934–1944* (Amherst: University of Massachusetts Press, 1976), 159–60. John Simon received correspondence from a London hotel proprietor á propos of the Heard coverage, advising him that such practices were prevalent in London shops and other Edinburgh hotels, citing the cases of Asian clients. See, MSS Brit. EMP. S. 25 Bremner to Simon, August 9, 1937, University of Oxford, Rhodes House, Lady Simon Papers (LSP).

4. Heard, op. cit., 60.

5. See, James A. Miller, Susan D. Pennybacker, and Eve Rosenhaft, "Mother Ada Wright and the International Campaign to 'Free the Scottsboro Boys,' 1931–34," *American Historical Review*, April 2001, 387–430.

6. George Padmore, *Pan-Africanism or Communism?: The Coming Struggle for Africa* (New York: Ray, 1956).

7. Gerhard Hirschfeld, ed., *Exile in Great Britain: Refugees from Hitler's Germany* (Leamington Spa, England: Berg, 1984), 2.

8. World Committee for the Victims of German Fascism, *The Brown Book of the Hitler Terror and the Burning of the Reichstag,* (London: Gollancz, 1933).

9. The rally was at Queen's Hall, July 6, 1938. See *Daily Worker*, July 9, 1938.

10. Gordon Brown, *Maxton/Gordon Brown* (Edinburgh: Mainstream, 2002, 2nd edition). Important works include Peter Clarke, *Hope and Glory: Britain, 1900–2000, 2nd edition, Penguin History of Britain* (London: Penguin, 2004) and *The Cripps Version: A Life of Sir Stafford Cripps, 1889–1952* (London: Penguin, 2003); R.A.C. Parker, *Churchill and Appeasement* (Papermac, 2001); Roy Jenkins, *Churchill: A Biography* (London: Macmillan, 2001); and, Susan Pedersen, *Eleanor Rathbone and the Politics of Conscience* (New Haven: Yale, 2004).

11. See Stephen Howe, *Anti-Colonialism in British Politics: The Left and the End of Empire, 1918–1964* (Oxford and New York: Oxford University Press, 1993); Penny M.

Von Eschen, *Race against Empire: Black Americans and Anticolonialism* (Ithaca, NY: Cornell University Press, 1997); Paul B. Rich, *Race and Empire in British Politics* (Cambridge and New York: Cambridge University Press, 1990); Vijay Prashad, *The Darker Nations: A People's History of the Third World* (New York: The New Press, 2007), and Owen, op.cit. For a critique and survey of the historiography of colonialism, see Fred Cooper, *Colonialism in Question: Theory, Knowledge and History* (Berkeley: University of California, 2005).

12. See Peter Fryer, *Staying Power: The History of Black People in Britain* (London: Pluto, 1984); Laura Tabili, *"We Ask for British Justice"* (Ithaca, NY: Cornell University Press, 1994); Paul Gilroy, *The Black Atlantic: Modernity and Double Consciousness* (London, 1993), *After Empire: Melancholia or Convivial Culture?* (London: Routledge, 2004), *Postcolonial Melancholia* (New York: Columbia, 2005), and *Black Britain: A Photographic History* (London: Saqi, 2007); the *Newsletter of the* Black and Asian Studies Association (Institute of Commonwealth Studies), passim; and, Brent Hayes Edwards, *The Practice of Diaspora: Literature, Translation and the Rise of Black Internationalism* (Cambridge: Harvard University Press, 2003).

13. See, e.g., Mark Naison, *Communists in Harlem during the Depression* (Urbana: University of Illinois, 1983); Robin D. G. Kelley, *Hammer and Hoe: Alabama Communists during the Great Depression* (Chapel Hill: University of North Carolina Press, 1990); Dan T. Carter, *Scottsboro: A Tragedy of the American South* (Baton Rouge: Louisiana State University, rev. ed., 1979); and the standard work, James Goodman, *Stories of Scottsboro* (New York: Pantheon, 1994). Glenda Gilmore, *Defying Dixie: The Radical Roots of Civil Rights, 1919–1950* (New York: W. W. Norton, 2008), documents the role of the CPUSA in the lives of activists in the American South. James A. Miller, *Remembering Scottsboro: The Legacy of an Infamous Trial* (Princeton: Princeton University Press, 2009), pursues the case as manifested in literary and other sources.

14. See, e.g., Harvey Klehr, John Earl Haynes, and Fridrikh Igorevich Firsov, *The Secret World of American Communism* (New Haven: Yale, 1995); Kevin McDermott and Jeremy Agnew, *The Comintern: A History of International Communism from Lenin to Stalin* (New York: St. Martin's, 1997); Mark Solomon, *The Cry Was Unity: Communists and African-Americans, 1917–1936* (Jackson: University Press of Mississippi, 1998); Eric Arneson et al. "Up for Debate," *Labor: Studies in Working-Class Histories of the Americas*, vol. 3, #4, Winter, 2006; and Walter T. Howard, ed., *Black Communists Speak on Scottsboro: A Documentary History* (Philadelphia: Temple University Press, 2008).

15. See, esp., Eric D. Weitz, *Creating German Communism, 1890–1990: From Popular Protests to Socialist State* (Princeton: Princeton University Press, 1997); Wendy Goldman, "Stalinist Terror and Democracy: The 1937 Union Campaign," *American Historical Review*, vol. 110, no. 5, December 2005, 1427–53; and *Terror and Democracy in the Age of Stalin: The Social Dynamics of Repression* (Cambridge: Cambridge University Press, 2007).

16. Shaw to Brockway, August 1933, The Papers of Fenner Brockway, Churchill Archive Center, Cambridge, FEBR Box, #12.

17. On Comintern control, see Robert Service, *Stalin: A Biography* (Cambridge: Harvard University Press, 2005) 286, 380, 387; on Stalin's war against the ranks of the Comintern and the POUM, 389, and *Comrades: A History of World Communism* (Cambridge: Harvard University Press, 2007), chapter 9; and, on the expansion of mass terror, see Service, *Comrades*, chapter 31, passim. On popular participation in the terror, see

Wendy Goldman, op. cit., passim. The NKVD seized roughly 1.5 million persons be-tween 1937 and 1938, of whom 200,000 were released and three quarters of a million perished. See also Orlando Figes, *The Whisperers: Everyday Life in Stalin's Russia* (New York: Metropolitan, 2007); and Lynne Viola, *The Unknown Gulag* (Oxford: Oxford University Press, 2007). On the CPGB, see E. J. Hobsbawm, *Interesting Times: A Twentieth-Century Life* (New York: Pantheon, 2002); and for the results of an important oral history project, see Kevin Morgan, Gideon Cohen, and Andrew Flinn, *Communists and British Society, 1920–1991* (London: Rivers Oram, 2007), passim.

18. "The Communist Jonah," *Pittsburgh Courier*, June 23, 1934; July 7, 1934.

19. See Tony Judt, "The Last Romantic" *New York Review*, vol. 50 #10, November 20, 2003. For Rathbone's appearance on the program for the 1937 Second National Congress of Peace and Friendship with the USSR, where she chaired a session on "Soviet Planning, " see Labour History Archive and Study Center (LHASC), LP ID/CI/51/7, and *Daily Worker* (London, and hereafter), February 23, 1938, for Rathbone's appearance at an "Eden-Chamberlain" discussion sponsored by the Left Book Clubs.

20. George Padmore, *Africa and World Peace with a Foreword by Stafford Cripps* (London: Secker and Warburg, 1937), 270.

21. See, Gilmore, op. cit., passim, for a related narrative.

22. See, e.g., Patrick K. O'Brien, "Britain's Economy between the Wars: A Survey of Counter-Revolution in Economic History," *Past and Present*, #115, 1987, 114:

> In the wake of global war and the failure of the great powers to reconstruct international eco-nomic institutions which might have facilitated a resumption in world trade at traditional rates of growth, Britain's structural problems intensified. Of course there remains a legitimate debate on how far the diplomatic policies pursued by the government of the world's senior trading na-tion were conducive to the reconstruction of an efficient international economic system.

CHAPTER 1. ADA WRIGHT AND SCOTTSBORO

The epigraphs are taken from: LHASC, *The Labour Party Songbook: Every-Day Songs for Labour Festivals* (London: The Labour Party, 1933). Song 30, 7; Song 34, 8. See also, Stephen Collins Foster, *Plantation Melodies* (J. Knight and Co., 1888); C. A. White, *I'se Gwine Back to Dixie: Companion to Old Home Ain't What It Used to Be* (Boston: White, Smith and Co., 1874).

LHASC, Workers Music Association Songsheet "Doo-Dah-Day" (London: Marston Printing, n.d.), also featured "Sovietland" and "Let Him Go. Let Him Tarry." The Work-ers' Music Association was founded in 1936 by Dr. Alan Dudley Bush, who joined the communist party in 1935. See Alan Dudley Bush, *Music in the Soviet Union* (London: Workers' Music Association, 1943).

1. Ivan H. Browning, "Across the Pond," *Chicago Defender*, May 24, 1930, 10.

2. Eugene Pottier, "Internationale," in *Chants révolutionnaire* (Paris: Dentu, 1887); Alain J. Locke, "Sterling Brown: The New Negro Folk-Poet" in *Negro: Anthology Made by Nancy Cunard, 1931–1933* (London: Nancy Cunard at Wishart and Co., 1934, re-printed New York: Negro Universities Press, 1969), 115. Locke wrote following James Weldon Johnson, "Preface," *The Book of American Negro Poetry, Chosen and Edited, with an Essay on the Negro's Creative Genius* (New York: Harcourt, 1931), xl–xli.

3. "Great Gobbet," *Time*, May 25, 1931, vol. 17, 25.

4. *Daily Mail*, "Color Bar Not Lifted," 13.

5. Jennie Lee, *This Great Journey: A Volume of Autobiography, 1904–45* (London: Macgibbon and Key, 1963), 117.

6. Jennie Lee, "Uncle Tom's Cabin: A Picture of Life in Carolina," *New Leader*, March 11, 1932, 3.

7. Lee, *This Great Journey*, 119, 120.

8. Sylvia Townsend Warner, "Folk Songs from America," *New Statesman and Nation*, vol. 5, 1932–33, 262. See Claire Harman, *Sylvia Townsend Warner* (London: Minerva, 1989), 84–85,179–82.

9. National Library of Scotland (NLS), Naomi Mitchison Papers (NMP), Acc.10899, Russian diary, 216–17. See also Naomi Mitchison, *You May Well Ask: A Memoir, 1920–40* (London: Gollancz, 1979), 187–205; Jenni Calder, *The Nine Lives of Naomi Mitchison* (London: Virago, 1997), 111. See, David Mikosz, ed., Langston Hughes, *A Negro Looks at Soviet Central Asia* (Moscow and Leningrad: Cooperative Publishing Society of Foreign Workers in the USSR, 1934) (Bishkek: Al Salam Printhouse, 2006), passim; and Langston Hughes, *I Wonder as I Wander* (New York: Hill and Wang, 1956), 74, 95. On Hughes and Miller, see Arnold Rampersad, *Life of Langston Hughes, Vol. I, 1902–1941* (Oxford, 2002), chapter 10, passim.

10. Ibid., NLS, NMP, 218. See Langston Hughes, *Scottsboro Limited: Four Poems and a Play in Verse* (New York: Golden Stair Press, 1932).

11. "Trial of Mrs. Barney," *Star*, July 4, 1932, 1.

12. "Acquittal of Wealthy Parasite," *Daily Worker*, July 7, 1932, 1.

13. See Miller, Pennybacker, and Rosenhaft, op. cit., passim. Fn. 1 contains historiographical material on the case, 388.

14. *Daily Worker*, June 2, 1931. *"Negro Lads Framed-Up for Death."*

15. James W. Livingood, *A History of Hamilton County, Tennessee* (Memphis: Memphis State University Press, 1981), 341–44; Livingood interview with author, Chattanooga, February 1998. See Mark Curriden and Leroy Philipps, Jr., *The Turn of the Century Lynching That Launched a Hundred Years of Federalism* (New York: Faber and Faber, 1999). African American Ed Johnson's conviction was overturned in 2000, after ninety-four years.

16. See V. Fields, G. Ricks, S. Horton, *Precious Memories '88, 1850–1950* (Chattanooga: Chattanooga Afro-American Museum, 1988), passim.

17. Schomburg Center for Research in Black Culture (SC), International Labor Defense (ILD) Papers, Reel 2, 0705 0731, *Legal Correspondence*, Statement of Douglas MacKenzie, "Report on Stephen Roddy," April 26, 1931.

18. See Doris Faber, *Printer's Devil to Publisher* (New York: Julian Messner, Inc., 1963), 37–8, chapter 7. Ochs died in Chattanooga in 1935.

19. RGASPI 515/142/1996, *Johnson to John Williamson* (Organizational Department, Central Committee), July 22, 1930, 15. In instances where an RGASPI file is cited without a document title, date, or page number, the reader may assume that most of, or a portion of the file in question broadly pertains to the material in the text where the endnote appears. In other instances, a reference may be incomplete because the file was incomplete when consulted or reproduced.

20. Ibid., Johnson to Williamson, May 10, 1930, 6.

21. Ibid., July 23, 1930, 23.

22. Ibid., *Johnson to Darcy*, August 27, 1930, 45.

23. Ibid., *Johnson to Weiner*, September 2, 1930, 50: "Finally let me out a county line with warning that if I ever came back to Jefferson County I would be shot on sight." Those who picked him up told Johnson that they were instructed not to make arrests, "but to drive us out or kill us."

24. Ibid., 515/1/3027, *Martha Hall to Secretary, Central Committee*, 122.

25. See, Miller, Pennybacker, and Rosenhaft, op. cit., 392–94.

26. RGASPI, 515/142/2285, *Tom Johnson to Earl Browder*, April 14, 1931, 22.

27. Ibid., *Tom Johnson to Hathaway*, April 15, 1931, 28.

28. LOC, Papers of the NAACP, Scottsboro Series, Part I: D69, file folder 12, "Confidential excerpts from report to the national office from Mr. William Pickens, Field Secretary, NAACP," June 12, 1931.

29. RGASPI 539/4/54, 97.

30. The unidentified photograph of a lynching that appears on the front cover of the *Negro Worker*, November–December 1932, vol. 2, nos. 11–12, was also circulated by lynching afficionados as "evidence" of the spectacle, and as popular Americana. See, James Allen et al., *Without Sanctuary: Lynching Photography in America* (Santa Fe, NM: Win Palms, 2000), plate 31, "The Lynching of Thomas Shipp and Abram Smith, August 7, 1930, Marion, Indiana."

31. RGASPI 534/3/546, 131–36.

32. For the most recent account of Münzenberg's work during the Weimar Republic, see Sean McMeekin, *The Red Millionaire: A Political Biography of Willi Münzenberg, Moscow's Secret Propaganda Czar in the West* (New Haven: Yale University Press, 2003), part II, passim.

33. See, e.g., Francis Beckett, *Enemy Within: The Rise and Fall of the British Communist Party* (London: Merlin, 1995), chapters 3–4; James Eadon and David Renton, *The Communist Party of Great Britain Since 1920* (Hampshire and New York: Basingstoke, 2002), chapter 2, passim. The party membership, as distinct from its front groups, was down to 2,500 in 1930. In the thirties, the National Unemployed Workers' Movement grew to 50,000 members. CPGB membership peaked at the close of the thirties, reaching over 17,000, when the sharp "class line" in the party's politics was most muted, and its trade-union work weakest, 36, 42, 57, 62.

34. *Resolution of the Secretariat of the International Red Aid on IRA Work among Negroes*, November 3, 1930, in *10 Jahre Internationale Rote Hilfe* (Berlin: MOPR Verlag, 1932) 193–98.

35. RGASPI 539/2/474, 97.

36. Ibid., 539/2/488, 58.

37. *Lattimour et al., to the President of the United States*, March 11, 1932, U.S. Department of Justice Central Files (USDJ), no. 158260–46; *DePriest to Hoover*, April 2, 1932; *Nugent Dodds to DePriest*, April 6, 1932. On Bricktop, see Edwards, op. cit., 64, 66, 79, 99–100.

38. *Gould to Gray*, USDJ, April 6, 1932.

39. On the global Scottsboro campaigns, see RGASPI 500/1/16, 88–89, 105–106; 539/2/474, 77–86, 97–100; 593/2/488, 85–86, 100, 114; 539/9/501, 4; 542/1/46, 1–2, 7–10; 542/1/51, 10. See also Richard H. Frost, *The Mooney Case* (Stanford: Stanford University Press, 1968).

40. *Cole to Secretary of State*, February 18, 1932. USDJ. See also *Skinner to Secretary of State*, April 18, 1932 from the U.S. legation to the Soviet Union.

41. Mark Naison, op. cit., 60–61.

42. *Morris to C. A. Appeil*, April 26, 1932. USDJ.

43. *Daily Worker*, May 2, 1932.

44. *FBI Director to Robert F. Kelley*, May 3, 1932, USDJ, memo 61–7041–4. See also *Oslo report*, July 18, 1932, which refers to a State Department memo of May 9, 1932 (File no. 811, 4016, Scottsboro/62) used in "transmitting copies of the decisions of the Supreme Court of Alabama," and discusses Wright's visit to Norway.

45. Interview material in the possession of the author, Chattanooga, 1998–2003.

46. RGASPI 539/5/54, 99, 95.

47. Ibid., 515/1/3017, *Desmond to Engdahl*, May 23, 1932, 129; *Engdahl to Desmond*, May 28, 1932, 130–31.

48. Ibid., *Engdahl to Red Aid (IRA) Berlin*, June 1, 1932, 155.

49. See Fryer, op. cit., chapter 10; Hakim Adi, *West Africans in Britain, 1900-60: Nationalism, Pan-Africanism and Communism* (London: 1984), 2–88; Tabili, op. cit., passim; Anne Spry Rice, "Imperial Identity in Colored Minds: Harold Moody and the League of Coloured Peoples, 1931–50," *Twentieth-Century British History*, vol. 13, no. 2, 2002, 356–83; and David Killingray, "Harold Moody and the League of Colored Peoples," in Bill Schwarz, ed., *West Indian Intellectuals in Britain* (Manchester: Manchester University Press, 2004), 51–70.

50. RGASPI 495/154/425, August 16, 1930.

51. Anne Chisholm, *Nancy Cunard, a Biography* (New York: Penguin, 1981), 237–42; Lois Gordon, *Nancy Cunard: Heiress, Muse, Political Idealist* (New York: Columbia, 2007), 163–66.

52. RGASPI 534/3/668 *Ford to Padmore*, 67–68. On Cunard's importance to the era, see Jane Marcus, *Hearts of Darkness: White Women Write Race* (New Brunswick; Rutgers University Press, 2004), chapter 5, passim.

53. LOC, Papers of the NAACP, Part I: D 70, file folder #8, *Cullen to White*, July 25, 1931.

54. Ibid., *Fletcher to White*, July 24, 1931; *White to Fletcher*, August 5, 1931.

55. See *Daily Worker*, August 15, 1931, August 29, 1931. "Wells Opposes Negroes' Sentence," *New York Times*, September 6, 1931, cites an NAACP report of the letter.

56. LOC, Papers of the NAACP, part I: D71, file folder #10, *Moody to White*, November 24, 1931. Moody notes that Arthur Garfield Hays, who appeared later in the Mock Reichstag Fire Trial, was involved in the Scottsboro defense. Olivier was a Fabian Society member.

57. Ibid., file folder #7, *Moody to White*, December 12, 1931; See Walter White, "The Negro and the Communists," *Harper's Monthly* 164 (December 1931) 62–72.

58. RGASPI 534/7/50, *Ward to Padmore*, December 30, 1931, 189. Alexander Macauley Jabavu (1885–1946) was a South African trade-union leader, son of the Cape liberal J. T. Jabavu. The Saunders identity is unknown and presumed a misspelling.

59. Ibid., *Ward to Padmore*, December 8, 1931, 182.

60. RGASPI 534/3/754, *Headley to Padmore*, March 7, 1932, written from the International Seamen's Club, 162.

61. RGASPI 515/1/3016.

62. RGASPI 534/3/755, *Ward to Padmore*, April 6, 1932, 30; *Wallace-Johnson to Padmore*, 53. Padmore's desire to recruit Africans to communism was explicit. See *Padmore to anon.*, May 11, 1932, 68–69.

63. *Everyman*, April 14, 1932; *Daily Mirror*, May 4, 1932.

64. *Daily Worker*, May 10, 1932.

65. John M. Kahl, "First World Unity Congress of Water Transport Proletarians Held at Altona, Near Hamburg, Germany, on May 21, 1932," refers to "Instructions from Department of State, dated May 2, 1932, USDJ, No. 800.00B-International of Seamen and Harbor Workers/27," 2, 5.

66. RGASPI 539/3/1096, records a worker's "murder . . . by police while protesting," May 17, 1932, 42.

67. Ibid., 534/3/755 *Ward to Padmore*, May 11, 1932, 72–73; *Padmore to Ward*, May 17, 1932, 89.

68. Ibid., *Ward to Padmore*, May, 1932, 100 and overleaf. Rienzi was an East Indian oil workers' trade-union organizer from Trinidad; his fellow countryman Ashford Sastri Sinanan was an East Indian lawyer and politician.

69. Reginald Bridgeman, "The Scottsboro Trial: Seven Negro Boys Condemned to Death in America," *New Leader*, June 17, 1932.

70. RGASPI 534/7/50, *Ward to Padmore*, 93 and overleaf. Barbour James was a civil servant from Guyana who was transferred to Gold Coast and came to live in London, where he was a cofounder of the LOCP. His family was a prominent part of small Edwardian "black bourgeoisie." See Jeffrey Green, *Black Edwardians: Black People in Britain, 1901–1914* (London and Portland, Oregon: Frank Cass, 1998), 70–73, 266–67. Carmel Haden Guest was on the Scottsboro Committee; Hare and Birch were unidentified, though Reg Birch was a trade-union militant and CPGB leader married to Dorothy Lawson Birch, a school teacher. Dorothy C. Hare was a noted London physician during the 1930s.

71. Ibid., *Ward to Ford (Hamburg)*,141. He refers to: Lady Kathleen Simon; Labour MP for Yorkshire Charles Roden Buxton (1875–1942); and Lord Robert Cecil (1864–1958) of the Anti-Slavery Society and International Peace Campaign, who was the Nobel Peace prize recipient for 1937; and African American actor Beresford Gale.

72. National Archives, United Kingdom (NA), *Alfred F. Thraves to Sir John Simon*, May 13, 1932, A3038.

73. Ibid., FO 371/1/15875, paper 3038, 25.5 and cosigned, 25.6. Marcus cites the contents of U.S. State Department files on Cunard that record dissatisfaction with Wright's visit. She does not indicate the source of these complaints, which were leveled against Wright being given a valid passport and Cunard being permitted to enter the country. See Marcus, op. cit., 139–40.

74. *Daily Worker*, July 29, 1932, 2.

75. See Goodman, op. cit., 394. The U.S. Supreme Court agreed to review the convictions in May 1932, before Wright's journey, and reversed seven of the nine convictions in November 1932, leading to the Decatur, Alabama, trial of June 1933.

76. *Daily Worker*, July 29, 1932, 2; June 30, 1932, 1. Hijli Detention camp, a notorious institution in Kragpur, India, was a base for British counterinsurgency, imprisonment, torture, and death.

77. *Daily Mail*, June 30, 1932, 8.

78. *North London Recorder*, July 1, 1932, 10.

79. *Daily Worker*, July 1, 1932, 2; July 4, 1932, 2.

80. *Willesden Chronicle*, July 8, 1932.

81. Louis Golding, "Nine Niggers on a Train: The Color Problem in America," *Dundee Free Press*, July 8, 1932, 3. "Ten Little Injuns," by Septimus Winner, appeared in London

1868 followed by Frank Green's "Ten Little Niggers" a music-hall song, in 1869. Agatha Christie took the title for her *Ten Little Niggers* (London: Harper, Collins, 1939), which later appeared as *Ten Little Indians* (New York and Los Angeles: Samuel French, 1946). She staged "Ten Little Niggers" at the St. James Theater in London in 1943, but the New York production at the Broadhurst, in 1944, was entitled, "Ten Little Indians." Six film productions followed, including *Zehn kleine Negerlein* (Germany, 1969), and *Desyat' Negrityat* (USSR, 1987).

82. *Fifeshire Advertiser*, July 9, 1932.

83. *Daily Worker*, July 5, 1932, 1.

84. *Glasgow Evening News*, July 6, 1932.

85. *Daily Worker*, July 4, 1932, 2. Power had been in New York lecturing in 1930, as had Laski in 1931; Laski was a friend of the ACLU's Roger Baldwin. Tawney had been at Rugby with Archbishop William Temple. In 1912 Tawney became a director of the Ratan Tata Company (Saklatvala's family firm), which endowed LSE to study and address "poverty and destitution." See Anthony Wright, *R. H. Tawney* (Manchester: Manchester University Press, 1987), 8; Maxine Berg, *Eileen Power: A Woman in History* (Cambridge: Cambridge University Press, 1996), 158, 163; and Isaac Kramnick, *Harold Laski: A Life on the Left* (New York: Allen, Lane, Penguin, 1993), Chapter 13.

86. *Daily Worker*, July 7, 1932, 2; September 15, 1932.

87. RGASPI 534/3/756, 90.

88. "A Pigmy Princess," *Irish Times*, July 6, 1932.

89. *Daily Worker*, July 8, 1932, 4.

90. Golding, op. cit., *City and East London Observer*, July 9, 1932.

91. *Daily Worker*, July 9, 1932, 7.

92. Ibid. See Hugh Murray, "Letter to the Editor," *American Historical Review*, vol. 107, #1, February, 2002, 340, on the CPGB's inflation of reported numbers.

93. RGASPI 534/3/756, *Ward to Padmore*, 7.

94. RGASPI 534/3/756, 29; see George Padmore, *The Life and Struggles of Negro Toilers* (London: RILU magazine for the International Trade Union Committee of Negro Workers, 1931).

95. RGASPI 534/3/756, 58.

96. RGASPI 515/1/2222, 15.

97. *Hoffman Phillips to Secretary of State*, USDJ, July 18, 1932.

98. Ibid., *US Legation, Copenhagen to Secretary of State*, July, 1932. The article referred explicitly to American writer Theodore Dreiser's arguments. See "An Open Letter to the Governor of Alabama," *Labor Defender*, June 6, 1931, 108–109.

99. Ibid., USDJ *Frank A. Keller to Secretary of State*, August 19, 1932.

100. James R. Hooker, *Black Revolutionary: George Padmore's Path from Communism to Pan-Africanism* (New York and London: Praeger, 1967), 142, fn. 19, cites Cunard, "Scottsboro and other Scottsboros," in *Negro*, op. cit., 260.

101. LHASC, LP/ID/CI/4i.

102. LSE archive, ILP/8/1932/54, "Report and Manifesto of the World Anti-War Congress at Amsterdam, August 27–29, 1932."

103. *Daily Worker*, July 7, 1932; RGASPI 495/72/218, 37–39.

104. Black served Alabama in the Senate from 1926–37, and on the Court from 1937 until 1971.

105. RGASPI 539/2/474, 121. See *American Consulate, Ghent, to Secretary of State*, USDJ, August 26, 1932, on Wright's arrest in Gilly. Engdahl was arrested in Ghent. Reports of protests in Seville reached the USDJ on the same day. See, *Irwin Laughlin to Secretary of State*, USDJ, August 26, 1932.

106. LOC, Papers of the NAACP, Box D-72 (16) *Paz to White*, June 25, 1932 and translation of same, 49-52. Magdeleine Legende Paz (1889-1973) was a Trotskyist Left Oppositionist who left the French communist party and became its critic in the 1920s. See Paz, *Frére Noir* (Paris: E. Flàmarion, 1930) and *Femmes à Verdre* (Paris: Reider, 1936). Cunard reports on Paris Scottsboro actions, *Negro*, op. cit., 259. Poet Jacques Prévert was involved with the theater company Octobre, which performed in cafes and factories, and included *Sauvez les nègres de Scottsborough* in its repertoire in 1933. See Alain Viala et al., *Le théâtre en France des origines à nos jours*, "Les remises en question contemporaines (1887-1997)" (Paris: Presses Universitaires de France, 1997), 418. I am indebted to Philip Nord for this reference.

107. RGASPI 515/1/3016 describes a meeting at Delft, addressed by Wright and several Indonesian activist speakers, 71.

108. RGASPI 539/4/54, 97-99.

109. Ibid., September 25, 1932, 153-53; *Daily Worker*, September 8, 1932, September 24, 1932.

110. RGASPI 539/3/1096, September 25, 1932, 154-55.

111. Southern California Library for Social Studies and Research, Los Angeles (SCLS), "Family Papers donated to SCL by Miriam Brooks [Moore] Sherman," Miriam's notebook on trip to World Youth Congress in Moscow, November, 1932, and interview with the author, Los Angeles, 2002. Stassova (1872-1967) unusually survived the era.

112. See, e.g., Weitz, *Creating German Communism*, chapters 2, 5.

113. Ben Pimlott, *Labor and the Left in the 1930s* (Cambridge: Cambridge University Press, 1977) is a critical portrait of the divisions among and between Labour and the left parties, 1-4, 194-202.

114. Southern California Library for Social Studies and Research (SCLS), "Family Papers," op. cit., November 13, 1932.

115. Ibid., November 16, 1932.

116. Interview with the author, Los Angeles, 2002.

117. *Assistant Director of the FBI to Dodds*, September 24, 1932, USDJ.

118. Naison, op. cit., 74.

119. See, Miller, Pennybacker, and Rosenhaft, op. cit., passim.

120. RGASPI 542/1/53, vol. 1 no. 2, 68, 78.

121. *Daily Worker*, August 8, 1931.

122. "Scottsboro Boys Appeal from Death Cells to the Toilers of the World," *Negro Worker*, May 1932, cited in Philip S. Foner and Hebert Shapiro, eds., *American Communism and Black Americans: A Documentary History, 1930-34* (Philadelphia: Temple, 1991) 292-93.

123. Cunard, ed., op. cit., *Negro*, 115.

124. *Pittsburgh Courier*, "They Shall Not Dine," May 19, 1934. See John Wexley, *They Shall Not Die* (New York: Knopf, 1934), and "Scottsboro Case on Stage Recalls 'Uncle Tom's Cabin,'" *Chicago Defender*, March 3, 1934.

125. See LSE archives, Low Collection, "Low and Terry Bump Off the Old Year," *Evening Standard*, December 31, 1932, 7, depicting a snake charmer's accomplice: "Treat a negro kindly and you can do almost anything with him."

126. *Daily Worker*, May 3, 1930.

127. See, e.g., LHASC LP/ID/CI/1/35ii, "Workers of the World Unite," *Daily Worker*, April 29, 1933, 3, in which otherwise naked black and Chinese workers sport loin clothes; American and European workers are clothed.

128. Locke, in *Negro* op. cit., after Johnson, op. cit., xxxviii, xl–xli. See also Michael Pickering, "Race, Gender and Broadcast Comedy: The Case of the BBC's *Kentucky Minstrels*," *European Journal of Communication* 9, September 1994, 311–33.

129. On Armstrong's reception, see Jim Godbolt, *A History of Jazz in Britain, 1919–50*, (London: Quartet Books, 1984), chapter 6.

130. RGASPI 539/3/1096, 160–61 overleaf.

131. See, RGASPI, 515/142/2285, 22–40, passim.

132. RGASPI 542/1/53, 75–78.

133. *Daily Worker*, October 8, 1932.

134. Goodman, op. cit., 118–240. This episode is a focus of Barak Goodman and Daniel Anker's award-winning documentary, *Scottsboro: An American Tragedy* (New York: Social Media Productions, Inc., 2000, 2001).

135. Interview with Lloyd Brown, London, 1998.

136. SC, Papers of Richard B. Moore, Box 6 (2) *Bates to Moore*, July 8, 1933.

137. Walter, White, *A Man Called White* (New York: Arno Press, 1969), 126.

138. RGASPI 515/1/4074; 33, cites *Labor Defender* (July 1937), 6. See Robert C. Cotrell, *Roger Nash Baldwin and the ACLU* (New York: Columbia, 2000). Baldwin was a friend of Walter White and a member of the LAI, who privately acknowledged the legitimacy of the communists' campaign, 163.

139. Cotrell, op. cit., 162.

140. David Levering Lewis, *W.E.B Du Bois, Vol. II: The Fight for Equality and the American Century* (New York: H. Holt, 2000) records that Du Bois approached the Anti-Slavery Society for help in securing a venue for the 1921 Pan-African Congress, which Walter White also attended, 30. Garfield Hays attended the 1921 Congress, and served as a "judge" in the Mock Reichstag Fire Trial.

141. See White, op. cit., 96–97, and LSP, Brit. Em. MSS S25, K22, *White to Simon*, November 7, 1934.

142. Lewis, op. cit., 40, 111–13. Attendees included the former Jamaican governor-general Sydney Olivier, writer H. G. Wells, political journalist and Africanist Norman Leys, and the former prime minister and Labour leader Ramsay MacDonald, who joined the National Government.

143. *Daily Worker*, July 23, 1932.

144. White, op. cit., 68–69.

145. LOC, Papers of the NAACP, part 6, Box D-72, *Paz to White*, June 25, 1932, including clippings from *Le Populaire, Économique et Social*. Maurice Paz (1896–1985) was also a leading Left Oppositionist who broke from the PCF.

146. Ibid., *White to Paz*, September 20, 1932.

147. Ibid., Part 6, Box D-76, "The Farce Is Halted," editorial, *Birmingham Post*, August 24, 1932.

148. *Daily Worker*, June 30, 1932, 1; July 5, 1932, 2.

149. Oliver Elton, *Lascelles Abercrombie, 1881–1938* (London: Milford, 1939), 23–24.

150. Lascelles Abercrombie et al., *Revaluations: Studies in Biography by Lascelles Abercrombie, Lord David Cecil, G. K. Chesterton* (London: Oxford, 1931).

151. RGASPI 542/1/43; *David Abercrombie to John Lonsdale*, November 14, 1991, in possession of John Lonsdale to whom I am indebted for this reference.

152. "Unfair Trials in the US: Two Notorious Cases: Political and Racial Bias," *Manchester Guardian*, August 22, 1932.

153. See RGASPI 539/2/474.

154. "The Scottsboro Case," *The Week-end Review*, LSP, Mss. Brit. Emp. 525, K22.

155. Eugene O'Neill, *The Emperor Jones* (New York: Boni and Liveright, 1921); Martin B. Duberman, *Paul Robeson* (New York: Knopf, 1988), 123–25, 158–59. Cunard and Robeson fell out in 1935, 191.

156. See Nancy Cunard (Hon. Organizer, Scottsboro Defense), to "97 newspapers in the British Isles, and 10 News Agencies," dated March, 1933, issued from 66 Chandos St., Strand, and published, by the *Daily Worker*, March 16, 1933. Pound met Cunard through her mother, Lady Cunard. See John Tytell, *Ezra Pound, the Solitary Volcano* (Chicago: Ivan R. Dee, 1987), 128, 202. Riding, Cunard, and the Woolfs all knew each other through the Hours Press. See Tytell, 220, and Elizabeth Friedmann, *A Mannered Grace: The Life of Laura (Riding) Jackson* (New York: Persea Books, 2005), 170. J. B. Priestley wrote of his 1930s visit to New Orleans in *Rain upon Godshill* (New York: Harper, 1939), 71.

157. RGASPI 542/1/61, 28–29; Hatch appeared in the London gossip and entertainment column of the 1930s African American press. See "Across the Pond," *Chicago Defender*, April 1, 1931. "Scottsboro Defense Committee: Appeal," April, 1934 (London: 4 Parton Street, WC1) lists the committee members. Gladys White may have been the performer and spouse of Walter White, signaling the NAACP's direct involvement in the British campaign in 1934.

158. Nancy Cunard, "New Directions" in Ford, ed., op. cit., 112. See also LSE archives, E. Rickword, *War and Culture: The Decline of Culture under Capitalism* (London: 1936), 1934/34, with a cover photograph depicting public book-burning in Berlin in May, 1933. Rickword was also a lover of Cunard's. See Gordon, op. cit., 67, 172, 176, 281.

159. RGASPI 515/1/3373, *Ward to Patterson*, June 19, 1933, 29, *Patterson to Ward*, n.d., 30. On Rathbone, see John McIlroy, "The Establishment of Intellectual Orthodoxy and the Stalinization of British Communism, 1928–33," *Past and Present*, vol. 192, #1, 2006, 187–230.

160. *Negro Worker*, Feb–March, 1933. Isaac Theophilus Akunna Wallace-Johnson (1895–1965) was born in Sierra Leone. See Leo Spitzer and LaRoy Denzer, "I.T.A. Wallace-Johnson and the West African Youth League," *International Journal of African Historical Studies*, part I, vol. 6, no. 3, 1973, 415–52, which mistakenly identifies Independent MP Eleanor Rathbone as a member of the Labour party's left wing; Rathbone assisted Wallace-Johnson in the 1930s.

161. RGASPI 495/154/512, March 17, 1933. See also Hull University archives, Brynmor Jones Library, ILD Press Service Report, Africa meeting, DCL/108/17a.

162. LHASC, LP/ID/CI/39/16.

163. LHASC, LP/ID/CI/18/31 *Morrison to Gillies*; LHASC ID/CI/8/44 William Gillies, *The Communist Solar System: The Communist International* (London: Labor Party, 1933). See Bernard Donoughue and G. W. Jones, *Herbert Morrison, Portrait of a Politician* (London: Phoenix, 2001), which states that Morrison was the pamphlet's author, 277.

164. *Daily Worker*, July 9, 1933; "Program of the Scottsboro Defense Gala" (London: Utopia Press, 1933). Ivan H. Browning, "Across the Pond," *Chicago Defender*, April 19, 1930, 5, refers to Gale as founder of the first London Elks lodge, along with Ike Hatch. Both Gale and his wife were from Philadelphia. "Black Bottom Johnny" was a black dancer who played the West End and especially Soho; see Godbolt, op. cit., 189. Godbolt cites Dunbar's published narrative of racial discrimination as a London musician, and Ken Johnson's late thirties career, 189, 127.

165. LHSAC LP/ID/CI/34/3(ii).

166. Ibid., LP/ID/CI/15/4.

167. See Pimlott, op. cit., 5; Eadon and Renton, op. cit., 36–37, 48–49.

168. Ibid., LP/ID/CI/26/77. In 1934 Herbert Morrison attacked Harold Laski, Ellen Wilkinson, Lord Marley, and Aneurin Bevan for their involvement in Willi Münzenberg's Relief Committee for the Victims of Fascism. See, Donoughue and Jones, op. cit., 227.

169. RGASPI 534/3/895 *Ward to Patterson*, November 14, 1933, 122.

170. Eugene O'Neill, *All God's Chillun Got Wings, and Welded, by Eugene O'Neill* (New York: Boni and Liveright, 1924); "All God's Chillun," *New Leader*, December 8, 1933, 8–9.

171. Cunard, op. cit., passim. See Marcus, op. cit., 128–31; 137–40.

172. See "Cunard Anthology on Negro Is Issued," *New York Times,* February 17, 1934, which mentions Cunard's treatment of Scottsboro.

173. Hertz founded the Council on Christians and Jews with Archbishop of Canterbury, William Temple, in 1942. He was educated in New York City, and had worked in South Africa before coming to London.

174. Cunard, op. cit., iii. See, also, Edwards, op. cit., 313–14, on Cunard's dealings with Kouyate. For a portrait of Marseille, where Kouyate was also involved, see Yaël Simpson Fletcher, "City, Nation, and Empire in Marseilles, 1919–1939" (Ph.D. dissertation, Emory University, 1999), esp. 301–306.

175. Ibid., Cunard, *Negro*, iii–iv; "Harlem Reviewed," 75.

176. Ibid. Pauli Murray (Reverend Dr. Anna Pauline Murray), "From three Thousand Miles on a Dime," 90–93; Cunard, "A Reactionary Negro Organization," 145–46; W.E.B. Du Bois, "Black America," 48–52; Walter White, "The Negro and the Supreme Court," 152–58; George Schuyler, "Black Civilization and White," 784–88. On Murray's life and work as an attorney and priest, see Gilmore, op. cit., chapters 6, 8.

177. Ibid., James W. Ford, "Communism and the Negro," 281–87 William Pickens, "Furies of Florida," 178–79; Zora Neale Hurston, "Characteristics of Negro Expression," 39–46. On Hurston, see Claudia Roth Pierpont, "The Measure of America: The Anthropologist Who Fought Racism," *New Yorker*, March 8, 2004, 48–63.

178. See Henry Crowder, *As Wonderful as All That?: Henry Crowder's Memoir of His Affair with Nancy Cunard, 1928–1935 with the Assistance of Hugo Speck* (Navarro, CA: Wild Trees, 1987); Cunard, *Negro*, ii; Henry Crowder, "Erred," in *Negro*, 386–88.

179. Iris Tree, "'We Shall Not Forget' for Nancy Cunard" in Hugh Ford, ed., *Nancy Cunard: Brave Poet, Indomitable Rebel 1896–1965* (Philadelphia: Clinton Book Co., 1968), 22. On Cunard's self-representations, others' photographic representations of her, and observations on her sexuality, see Marcus, op. cit., 126–29, 132–36, 144–47.

180. *Left Review*, no. 7, April 1935.

181. Nancy Cunard, "Glimpses of the Twenties" in Ford, op. cit., 46.

182. Ibid., Nancy Cunard, "New Directions," 102.

183. Ibid., Raymond Michelet, "Nancy Cunard," describes a 1931 trip as a "a tour of all the ethnographic museums, which had particularly rich holdings in African cultures," 128.

184. Ibid., Janet Flanner, "Nancy Cunard,"88.

185. William Carlos Williams, "The Colored Girls of Passenack—Old and New" in Cunard, *Negro*, 93–96. She stayed with Williams in Rutherford, New Jersey, on visits in 1931 and 1932. See Chisholm, op. cit., 175. Pound was their mutual friend. See Tytell, op. cit., 296.

186. Cunard, *Negro*, "Portrait of Vena," 538; "Ike Hatch," 327; "George Padmore," 814; George Padmore, "Pass Laws in South Africa," 807–809; "How Britain Governs the Blacks," 809–13; "White Man's Justice in Africa," 813–17; "Ethiopia Today," 612–18; "Johnstone Kenyatta," 803; B. N. Azikiwe, "Liberia: Slave or Free," 780–83.

187. "Negro Anthology Banned by Trinidad as Suspicious," *New York Times*, April, 13, 1934, reports its banning by the governor and an Executive Council with two Negro members. See also *Pittsburgh Courier*, April 21, 1934, 2, "Nancy Cunard's *The Negro* is banned."

188. W. J. Strachan, in Ford, op. cit., 276.

189. *Daily Worker*, May 10, 1934.

190. Ibid., August 18, 1934. Marcus Garvey married Amy Jacques in 1922. She remained in Jamaica when Garvey himself moved to London in 1935, where he died in 1940.

191. Scottsboro Defense Committee, "'We Were Framed!' The First Full Account Published in England of the Trials of the Nine Scottsboro Boys" (London: 1934), DBN/25/21A.

192. Wexley, op. cit.

193. *Times* (London), June 29, 1934, 15; July 10, 1934. See Goodman, op. cit., 394.

194. *J. Garner (Secretary, Old Trafford, ILP) to President Roosevelt*, USDJ, July 12, 1934; *M. H. Whetworth (Secretary, Women's Cooperative Guild, Rochdale) to President Roosevelt*, USDJ, December 7, 1934.

195. Ibid., *Ross to Roosevelt*, from the High School for Girls, Wellington, Salop, November 20, 1934.

196. See Pimlott, op. cit., chapters 8 and 9; McDermott and Agnew, op. cit., chapters 3 and 4.; Paul Corthorn, *In the Shadow of the Dictators* (London: Tauris, 2000), chapters 5 and 6.

197. Goodman, op. cit., 241–46; Naison, op. cit., 104–105, 132–34.

198. Henry Lee Moon, "A Negro Looks at Soviet Russia," *Nation*, vol. 138, no. 3582, February 28, 1934, 244. I am indebted to the late Lloyd Brown, likely one of the rally's speakers, for this reference. Moon went to work for the *Amsterdam News* in 1931 and to the Soviet Union in 1932 on the film trip that included Langston Hughes; he served as NAACP director of public relations, 1948–64. See Langston Hughes, op. cit., chapter 3; Langston Hughes, *A Negro Looks at Soviet Central Asia*, op. cit., passim.

199. On Lee and Mitchison, see Lee, *The Great Journey*, 20. They attended at least one meeting in common. See also Jennie Lee, "Slaves—White and Colored," *New Leader*, March 15, 1935, 2; Calder, op. cit., 135–38; Norman Thomas, "The Plight of the Share-Cropper" (New York: League of Industrial Democracy, 1934), which "includes a report of a survey made by the Memphis Chapter."

200. NLS, NMP, Acc. 10882.

201. Ibid., *Mitchison to Maya* n.d., circa 1934–35, NLS, NMP. Acc. 454914. On Zita Baker's first marriage to Oxford biologist and eugenicist John R. Baker, see Michael G. Kenny, "Racial Science in Social Context: John R. Baker on Eugenics, Race and the Public Role of the Scientist," *Isis* 95, 2004, 394–419, esp. 405–406. She was also the lover of Mass Observation founder Tom Harrisson. Zita Baker later married Richard Crossman, postwar Labour party leader and *New Statesman* editor. See Richard Crossman, *The God That Failed* (New York: Bantam, 1964), to which Louis Fischer, André Gide, Arthur Koestler, Ignazio Silone, Stephen Spender, and Richard Wright contributed.

202. Manuscript drafts and corrected typescripts, *You May Well Ask*, NLS, NMP. Acc. 7219, 18–20. Howrah District is near Calcutta.

203. RGASPI 539/4/7, November 23, 1934; 41.

204. *Patterson to Roosevelt*, USDJ, December 9, 1934.

205. LOC, Papers of the NAACP, Park 1, C159, Feb.–Nov., 1935. *Rathbone to Mitchison*, January 14, 1935.

206. Ibid., *Walter White to Rathbone*, March 8, 1935.

207. World Committee for the Victims of German Fascism, op. cit.; *Daily Worker*, May 24, 1935.

208. *Daily Worker*, June 26, 1934; October 22, 1934.

209. Paul Peters, *Stevedore, a Play in Three Acts, by Paul Peters and George Sklar* (New York: Covici, Friede, 1934); see Martin B. Duberman, *Paul Robeson* (New York: Knopf, 1988), 634; and Jeffrey C. Stewart, ed., *Paul Robeson Artist and Citizen* (New Brunswick: Rutgers University Press), xxviii.

210. Nancy Cunard, "Stevedore in London," *The Crisis*, August 1935, 238.

211. Nancy Cunard, "Paris Sees Gala Demonstration to Aid Ethiopian Independence," *Pittsburgh Courier*, December 28, 1935, 3.

212. Stanford Robinson, *Plantation Songs, 2d Selection, Arr. for Baritone Solo and Chorus of Mixed Voices with Pianoforte Acc. [Words and Melodies Partly] by Stephen C. Foster* (London and New York: Curwen, n.d.); *L'il Liza Jane . . . Old Slave Song Freely Paraphrased by L. Murray* (London: Ascherberg, Jopwood and Crew, 1960).

213. *The Crisis*, December, 1935, 369; Goodman, op. cit., 395.

214. *The Crisis*, ibid.

215. "Persecution of the Jews . . . " *Times*, February 7, 1936, "Britain and the Spanish War," *New Statesman and Nation*, vol. XII, no. 287, August 22, 1936, 250–51, "The Vortex in Spain: Issues of the Conflict," *Times*, August 19, 1936, as cited in Jeffrey Cooper, *A Bibliography and Notes on the Works of Lascelles Abercrombie* (Hamden, CT: Archon Books, 1969). Signers included: Norman Angell, C. Day Lewis, E. M. Forster, Leonard and Virginia Woolf, Julian Huxley, and Charlotte and J.B.S. Haldane (Naomi Mitchison's brother and sister-in-law).

216. *Daily Worker*, August 2, 1937; Paul Robeson, "Minstrel Man," by Langston Hughes, LOC recording, H.M.V. B8604.

217. SC, ILD Papers, Reel 6, Box 5, 0303, folder C72, Wright family correspondence, *Wright to Baron*, November 20, 1936.

218. Ibid., *Wright to Baron*, Jan. 9, 1937; *Baron to Wright*, Jan. 16, 1937.

219. *Times,* February 3, 1937, 13.

220. Goodman, op. cit., 395.

221. *Times*, June 13, 1937, 15–16; June 23, 1937, 15.

222. Ibid., July 26, 1937.

223. See Goodman, op. cit., esp. chapters 15–18.

224. *Chicago Defender*, "Freed Youths Go Shopping in Brooklyn," August 4, 1937, 10.

225. SC, ILD Papers, Reel 6, Box 5, folder C72, Wright Family Correspondence, *Lucile Wright to Liebowitz*, July 27, 1937.

226. *Daily Worker*, August 28, 1937, 24.

227. Ibid., January 29, 1937; February 13, 15, 1937; May 1938, 34–35. Robeson also spoke alongside Mme. Sun-Yat Sen at the Royal Opera house in support of peace in China. On David Guest, see Carmel Haden Guest, ed., *David Guest, a Scientist Fights for Freedom (1911–1938): A Memoir* (London: Lawrence and Wishart, 1939). See, also, David Levering Lewis, "Paul Robeson and the USSR," in Stewart, op. cit., 217–34.

228. Nancy Mitford, *The Pursuit of Love* (London: Penguin, 1945, 1952), 113–14. I am indebted to John Lonsdale for this reference.

229. *Pittsburgh Courier*, June 11, 1938, 24. See, also, H. G. Wells, *The New American, the New World* (New York: Macmillan, 1935); D. N. Pritt, *The Autobiography of D. N. Pritt Part I: From Right to Left* (London: Lawrence Wishart, 1965), chapter 5, passim.

230. See Goodman, op. cit., 396–97.

231. SC, ILD Papers, Reel 6, Box 5, Folder C72, Wright Family Correspondence, *Wright to Baron*, November 28, 1939.

232. *Forward*, June 25, 1932.

233. Golding, op. cit., 3.

234. Elizabeth Lawson, *Scottsboro's Martyr—J. Louis Engdahl* (New York: International Labor Defense, 1932), 4.

235. RGASPI 534/3/756, 6–7.

236. RGASPI 539/3/309, 85; 539/3/309, 23, 42. On the communists and WASU, see, RGASPI 495/100/985. On the LOCP, see LOC, Papers of the NAACP Papers, Part 6: D-71, *Moody to White*, November 24, 1931, and Part 1: D-71, File Folder #10, December 12, 1931.

237. On African American responses to Abyssinia, see Naison, op. cit., 155–58, 174–76, 195–98, 262.

238. Roy Wilkins, a 1935 Scottsboro activist, became a leading postwar civil rights leader. See RGASPI 515/1/3933, 17, and Roy Wilkins, *Standing Fast: The Autobiography of Roy Wilkins* (New York: 1982), 107, 108, 113, 151–60.

239. See Miller, Pennybacker, and Rosenhaft, op. cit., 428, fn. 134, passim.

240. Interviews in author's possession.

241. See SC, ILD Papers, Reel 6, Box 5, 0303, folder C-72, Wright family correspondence, passim.

242. On the banning of U.S. jazz musicians, see Godbolt, op. cit., 21, 116–21.

CHAPTER 2. GEORGE PADMORE AND LONDON

1. See Hooker, op. cit., chapter I, passim. This account relies on Hooker, Padmore's only biographer, who consulted many sources but had no access to Comintern documents, or other recently released archives of the 1930s that were in turn available to historian Woodford McClellan who made unique use of German materials, as below. See also Bill Schwarz, "George Padmore," in Bill Schwarz, ed., *West Indian Intellectuals in*

Britain (Manchester and New York: Manchester University Press, 2003), 132–52; Joyce Moore Turner, with the assistance of W. Burghardt Turner, *Caribbean Crusaders and the Harlem Renaissance* (Urbana: University of Illinois Press, 2005), chapter 7, passim; and Ani Mukherji, "The International Trade Union Committee of Negro Workers: A Report from the Moscow Archives," Rodney Worrell, "George Padmore, the COMIN-TERN and the Liberation of Black People," and Matthew Quest, "George Padmore's, and C.L.R. James's *International African Opinion*"—unpublished papers of the symposium on *Anti-Colonialism, Marxism and Black Liberation: Early Twentieth-Century Black Radicalism*, Brown University, 2008.

2. The claim that Williams was Padmore's uncle appears in Ras Makonnen, *Pan-Africanism from Within* (London: Oxford University Press, 1973), 100.

3. SCLS, Sherman, op. cit., and interview with Miriam Sherman, Los Angeles, 2002; RGASPI 542/1/46, 36.

4. Nnamdi Azikiwe, *My Odyssey: An Autobiography* (New York: Praegar, 1970), "Nurse to Azikiwe" (1927), 138–39; chapters 6 and 8, passim.

5. Hooker, op. cit., 8.

6. International Institute for Social History, Amsterdam (IISH), League against Colonial Oppression, "Agenda of the Congress against Colonial Oppression and Imperialism, Brussels, Feb. 10, 1927," and "Honorary Presidents and Executive Committee." The latter included: Jawaharlal Nehru, Sengalese activist Lamine Senghor, the NAACP's William Pickens, German activist Alfons Goldschmidt, Roger Baldwin of the ACLU, and Julio Antonio Mella, a founder of the Cuban communist party. See, also, Prashad, op. cit., 16–24.

7. Fenner Brockway of the ILP, was its first chairman, who was first elected to Parliament in 1929. See William Knox, *James Maxton* (Manchester: Manchester University Press, 1987), 146.

8. See IISH, League against Imperialism and for National Independence, "Affiliated Organizations and Sympathizing Organizations" (Berlin: Internationale Sekretariat, July 1929), which lists the Indian National Congress, the African National Congress, the ACLU, the Garveyite UNIA, the NAACP, and a host of Asian, Latin American, and Middle Eastern political and trade union bodies, in addition to its European affiliates. See also IISH, LAI, "The Colonies and Oppressed Nations in the Struggle for Freedom: Resolutions Adopted by the Executive Committee . . . " (Berlin: International Secretariat of the LAI, 1931), passim.

9. Hooker, op. cit., 13. On the LAI factions and the British left, see Knox, op. cit., 102–15.

10. See, Edwards, op. cit., chapter 5, passim. On Kouyate, see Turner, op. cit., 195–213.

11. Turner, op. cit., traces Otto Huiswoud's sojourn to Moscow, his rejection as head of the Negro Committee in favor of Padmore, and his directorship of Profintern work among blacks, 187–95. For Padmore's understanding of the Profintern, see, Padmore, *The Life and Struggles*, op. cit., 121–26. See also Mukherji, op. cit., passim.

12. Hooker, op. cit., reports on his Moscow life, and on the Pollitt meeting as rumor, 15–16. On the lifestyle of expatriate black Comintern agents, see Turner, op. cit., chapter 7, passim.

13. Woodford McClellan, "George Padmore and the Hamburg Conference: Some Background," 5–6, cites RGASPI, 534/3/450, 50–51; 534/4/330, 10. This paper was presented at "The Life and Times of George Padmore: Black Radicalism in the Twentieth

Century," University of the West Indies, St. Augustine, October 2003. Padmore also wrote to critic George Schuyler that he had come to West Africa just as Schuyler was leaving Liberia, though Schuyler visited in early 1931. George S. Schuyler, *Black and Conservative* (New Rochelle: Arlington, 1966), 208, cites *Padmore to Schuyler*, December 5, 1932. Schuyler arrived in Liberia February 11, 1931, "By the way, I was in the West Coast just at the time when you were saying goodbye to the lone star of Liberia."

14. McClellan, ibid., 6, cites RGASPI 534/3/490, 29–31.

15. Andrei M. Pegushev, "The Unknown Jomo Kenyatta" in *Egerton Journal*, vol.1, no. 2, 1996, 174. Hooker, op. cit., 24, cites R. W. Howe's report of a secret visit by Padmore to South Africa, a claim Hooker could not substantiate and which is absent from McClellan.

16. See Woodford McClellan, "Africans and Black Americans in the Comintern Schools, 1925–34," *International Journal of African Historical Studies*, 26 (2), 1993, 371–90; "Black *Hajj* to 'Red Mecca': Africans and Afro-Americans at KUTV, 1925–1938," in Maxim Matusevich, *Africa in Russia, Russia in Africa: Three Centuries of Encounters* (Trenton, NJ: Africa World Press, 2007), 61–83; and Turner, op. cit., 191.

17. Hooker, op. cit., 19–21, and Turner, op. cit., 193–94.

18. John Callaghan, *Rajani Palme Dutt, a Study in British Stalinism* (London: Lawrence and Wishart, 1993), identifies Brussels as Dutt's home base in 1934, 146.

19. McClellan, "Africans and Black Americans," 6, fn. 35, cites RGASPI 534/4/330, 12 with the clipping, "Ban on Negro Congress."

20. "A Report of Proceedings and Decisions of the First International Conference of Negro Workers at Hamburg, Germany, July 1930," (International Trade Union Committee of Negro Worker: Hamburg, 1930), 21, 23.

21. On the early Pan-African Congresses, see Lewis, *W.E.B. DuBois, Vol. I: Biography of a Race* (New York: Henry Holt), 248–51, 567–69; and Lewis, vol. II, op. cit., 109–15.

22. RGASPI, 534/3/740, 66–73. The delegates included U.S. miners and needleworkers red trade union representatives, South Africans Albert Nzulu and Moses Kotane, and a member of the Jamaican Trade and Laborers Union. McClellan, "George Padmore and the Hamburg Conference," 7, fn. 39, cites RGASPI 534/3/490, 25, in which South African communist delegate E. S. "Solly" Sachs observes, "[M]ost of them were . . . by no means Communists. . . . They were very backward. . . . Instead of drawing them into the movement in Germany, or . . . starting a discussion . . . for fourteen days they wasted their time running around Berlin." Sachs, a garment workers leader, was expelled from the South African party in 1931. On Nzulu, see also Turner, op. cit., 209.

23. RGASPI 534/3/740, 66–73. McClellan, "George Padmore and the Hamburg Conference," fn. 44, 12. RGASPI 534/390/25 cites delegate Sachs's further complaint that they received "a pile of resolutions . . . written in a mechanical way. . . . they were not even discussed or read before the delegates."

24. In the *Negro Worker*, Padmore criticized African American sociologist Charles Johnson and his correspondent George Schuyler of the *Pittsburgh Courier* for their stances on Liberia. The Comintern alluded to these writings at the time of Padmore's expulsion from its ranks. See George Padmore, *American Imperialism Enslaves Liberia* (Moscow: Contrizdat, 1931). See the *Communist*, February, 1931.

25. Jan Valtin, *Out of the Night: Memoir of Richard Julius Krebs Alias Jan Valtin* (Edinburgh and Oakland: AK Press/Nabat, 2004), 308–309; Hooker, op. cit., chapter 2, passim; Turner, op. cit.,193–97.

26. See Turner, op. cit., 187–88. See also RGASPI 495/155/98, 1–16.

27. See IISH, *W. Münzenberg and V. Chattopadhyaya to Friends*, March 3, 1931.

28. RGASPI 534/3/756, *Bridgeman to Padmore*, December 9, 1931.

29. Hooker, op. cit., 19.

30. RGASPI 534/3/668, 96, *Padmore to Ford*, November 16, 1931. See, also, Turner, op. cit., 197.

31. Padmore, *Life and Struggles*; 7.

32. Ibid., chapter 1, passim.

33. Ibid., 6, 51, 34. Albert Londres, *Terre d'ébène: la traite des noirs* (Paris: Albin Michel, 1929), recounts a trip through Dakar, Niger, Gabon, and Congo-Océan.

34. Londres, *Terre d'ébène*, 80–81, 87, 126.

35. RGASPI 538/1/12, 4; 51–57. German communist Clara Zetkin; artist John Heartfield, British communist Harry Pollitt; American writers Upton Sinclair, John Dos Passos, and Theodore Dreiser; sculptor Kathe Kollwitz; French writer Henri Barbusse; and Russian Maxim Gorki attended. McMeekin, op. cit., 240–51, describes the Red Aid operations, their Soviet sources of finance, and their demise in the face of organizational and political chaos as 1933 approached.

36. RGASPI, 534/3/754, 1.

37. Ted Crawford, Barry Buitekant, Al Richardson, eds., *C.L.R. James and British Trotskyism*, interview with Richardson, Clarence Chrysostom, Anna Grimshaw, June 8, and, November 16, 1986, London (http://www.workersrepublic.org/Pages/Ireland/Trotskyism/clrjames.html), 3. See comments on James's ILP entry, "The Trotskyists decided to go into the ILP and I went with them," 1. Hooker, op. cit., fn. 26, cites Ivar Oxaal's report that James was asked to come to hear a "great Negro Communist" speak.

38. RGASPI, 534/3/754, 136–37, *Padmore to Bridgeman*, February 26, 1932.

39. RGASPI 534/3/754, 186, *Padmore to Comrades*, 186. March 24, 1932. On Bilé, see R.J.M. Aitken and E. Rosenhaft, "Politik und Performance. Deutsch-Afrikaner in Berlin der 20er und 30er Jahre," in Ulrich Van der Heyden and Joachim Zeller, eds., *Macht und Anteil an der Weltherrschaft: Berlin und der deutsche Kolonialismus* (Münster: Unrast-Verlag, 2005), 271–27; Robbie Aitken, "From Cameroon to Germany and Back via Moscow and Paris: The Political Career of Joseph Bilé (1892–1959), Performer, 'Negerarbeiter' and Comintern activist," *Journal of Contemporary History* 43 (2008), 597–616.

40. Padmore commented that Otto Huiswoud, the CPUSA leader from Dutch Guiana (Surinam) was no longer in Russia and suggested that this compromised his own ability to leverage funds. Indeed, Turner, op. cit., 200, states that Huiswoud and his wife, Hermie, traveled to Europe in February 1932, which conforms to Padmore's movements. Turner is the daughter of the West Indian, New York City–based communist Richard B. Moore, an important figure in Scottsboro.

41. Turner, op. cit., 195, fn. 23 cites RGASPI, 534/3/669, 145.

42. *Manchester Guardian*, March 16, 1932; *Le Monde*, March, 28, 1932. See RGASPI, 534/3/754, 200, 201.

43. RGASPI 534/3/755, *Padmore to anon.*, May 11, 1932, 68–69.

44. RGASPI 534/3/754 *Ward to Padmore*, n.d., 200.

45. Hooker, op. cit., 28. Padmore also wrote to George Schuyler of a recent trip to the United Kingdom on behalf of Scottsboro. See, Schuyler, op. cit., 209.

46. RGASPI 534/3/755 *Padmore to Maxton*, June 1, 1932, 165; *Maxton to Padmore*, June 23, 1932.

47. Hansard, *Parliamentary Debates*, House of Commons, June 1, 1932, vol. 335/1150–51.

48. RGASPI 534/3/756 *Ward to Padmore*, August 4, 1932, 61.

49. RGASPI 534/7/50, *Ward to Padmore*, 93.

50. Ibid., *Brown to Padmore*, July 10, 1932, 26.

51. Ibid., *Ford to Padmore*, 172.

52. Ibid., *Ward to Padmore*, July 16, 1932, 31; Sherman, op. cit.

53. Ibid., *Ford to Padmore*, 172.

54. See Hooker, op. cit., 27–28; fn. 23, 142 cites *Cunard to Hooker*, November 1964.

55. RGASPI 542/1/54, 92, *Padmore to Comrades*, September 14, 1932, 92.

56. See Padmore, "American Imperialism Enslaves Liberia," op. cit.

57. I am especially indebted to Woodford McClellan for stressing the other side of this dualism, and the role of accommodation assumed by the United States in 1933.

58. RGASPI 542/1/54, 80, 92; 542/1/56, *Hans to Chatto*, January 21, 1932.

59. On the "Sheffield Council of Action," see Knox, op. cit., 110, and Pimlott, op. cit., 79.

60. Adi, op. cit., 79.

61. RGASPI 534/3/895, 100–16, *Padmore to comrades*, March 6, 1933. "We shall establish a base for distribution via Marseilles, Rouen, Cardiff and London, together with New York." But he added that New York was "not interested in this work," and that from England, the paper would be shipped to Jamaica, Sierra Leone, and South Africa. Padmore remained listed as editor through March–April, 1933, and that issue bears his marks. Turner, op. cit., 197–98, states that he was arrested at the end of 1932, citing RGASPI 534/3/895, 126–29, which contradicts Padmore's own subsequent testimony.

62. *Negro Worker*, "Fascist Terror against Negroes in Germany," vol. 3, no. 4–5, April–May, 1933, 1.

63. Ibid., 5; "The Scottsboro Case," ibid., 8–15.

64. *Negro Worker*, June–July 1933, "United Front against Fascism," vol. 4, no. 6–7, 30–31.

65. Ibid.

66. *Daily Worker*, July 9, 1933, and LHASC, *Program of the Scottsboro Defense Gala*.

67. RGASPI 542/1/58, 37 and passim. For an account of Padmore's expulsion, see Turner, op. cit., 198–200; 209–13. The *Étoile nord-africaine*, founded in 1926, was a small Algerian, anti–French Empire organization with communist ties. See Rosenberg, op. cit., 143, 194, 208.

68. Isaac Theophilus Akuna Wallace-Johnson, 1894–1965. See "A Scottsboro Meeting on the Gold Coast, West Africa," reprinted from the *Times of West Africa*, Accra, Gold Coast, *ILD Press Service*, March 17, 1932, DCL/108, 17a.

69. One English translation of Lenin's description of the League is: "an alliance of robbers, each trying to snatch something from the others," in V.I. Lenin, *Collected Works*, vol. 31 (Moscow: Progress Publishers, 1966), 323. The rendering "thieves kitchen" was common in Trotskyist circles.

70. Adi, op. cit., 87–88, fn. 75.

71. Schwarz, op. cit.,137.

72. See George Shepperson, " 'Pan-Africanism' and 'pan-Africanism': Some Historical Notes," *Phylon 23* (Winter 1962), 346–58.

73. For further accounts of the four congresses that preceded the Manchester Congress of 1945, see David Levering Lewis, *W.E.B. Du Bois*, vol. II, op. cit., 37–49,108–17, 208–11.

74. Peter Abrahams, *The Black Experience in the Twentieth Century: An Autobiography and Meditation* (Bloomington: Indiana University Press, 2000), 39; Ras Makonnen (G.T.N. Griffith), changed his name in honor of Abyssinia; see Makonnen, op. cit., 103.

75. Padmore, in Cunard, *Negro*, op. cit., passim.

76. See Edwards, op. cit., chapter 5, passim.

77. Hooker, op. cit., 39–40, cites *Padmore to Du Bois*, February 17, 1934. See also Edwards, op. cit., 246–27, and chapter 5, passim.

78. George Padmore, *How Britain Rules Africa* (London: Wishart, 1936). Hooker, op. cit., 33. On Paris, see 39–41. See Turner, op. cit., 212–13.

79. Padmore, *Pan-Africanism or Communism?*, op. cit.

80. Hooker op. cit., cites the testimony of Padmore's nephew Malcolm Luke, and ILP leader C. A. Smith, 32; fn. 31, 143.

81. Interview with John Saville, Hull, 1998.

82. Hooker, op. cit., 31–34.

83. See Turner, op. cit., 209–14.

84. *Padmore to Schuyler*, Dec. 5, 1932, in Schuyler, op. cit., 208.

85. RGASPI 495/155/102, 128, "c/o G. Kenjotta [*sic*], 95 Cambridge St., London SW."

86 See Turner, op. cit., 214–17.

87. *Negro Worker*, October–November, 1934, *frontispiece*. See Turner, op. cit., 216–17.

88. Makonnen, op. cit., 120.

89. See Ian Bullock and Richard Pankhurst, eds., *Sylvia Pankhurst: From Artist to Anti-Fascist* (New York: St. Martin's, 1992), chapter 6, passim; Richard Pankhurst, *Sylvia Pankhurst: Artist and Crusader* (London: Paddington Press, 1979), esp. 196. On Cunard's involvement with Ethiopia and Pankhurst, see, Gilbert, op. cit., 206–11, 223.

90. Hooker, op. cit., 42–43. Others included Fenner Brockway and F.A. Ridley of the ILP; Walter Goldwater, a former CPUSA member and book dealer; and Willis N. Huggins, a leading African American advocate for Ethiopia. See, e.g., Ethel Mannin, "The Englishman Abroad," *New Leader*, March 18, 1932, 16.

91. Reginald Reynolds, *My Life and Crimes* (London: Jerrold's, 1956), 116–17. The biblical allusion to David's cave refuge also connotes a move to retreat in dissent, for the purpose of repositioning. Reynolds refers to the Popular Front turn of the Comintern.

92. On Jones, see ibid., 118–20. Mannin and Padmore were godparents to Jones's son.

93. See, e.g., Makonnen, op. cit., chapter 8, passim; Von Eschen, op. cit., 7, 11. Amy Ashwood Garvey (1897–1969) was Marcus Garvey's first wife.

94. Conversation with Dorothy Thompson, Worcester, England, 1998.

95. Adi, op. cit., 77, 80.

96. Hooker, op. cit., refers to the argument of George Padmore, *Africa and World Peace*. See, also, George Padmore, "Ethiopia and World Politics," *The Crisis*, May, 1935, 138–57.

97. RGASPI, 495/30/1034, 14.

98. *Bridgeman to Hooker*, September 22, 1964 in Hooker, op. cit., 44.

99. *Liberty and Democracy Leadership Manifesto*, Glasgow City Archives and Special Collections, James Maxton Papers (JMP), TD 956/28/38. See Knox, *James Maxton*, 115–16; Pimlott, op. cit., 90–91; Corthorn, op. cit., chapter 1, passim.

100. Hooker, op. cit., 37; Homer Smith served as Moscow correspondent for the *Chicago Defender*. See also Gilbert, op. cit., 205–206.

101. RGASPI 495/155/98, 1.

102. Ibid., and, *The Crisis*, no. 10, October 1935, 315.

103. RGASPI 495/155/98, 2.

104. Crawford et al., eds., op. cit., 4.

105. RGASPI 515/1/3482 *Ward to Patterson*, n.d., 1.

106. See, e.g., *Negro Worker*, vol. 5, no. 6, June 1935, frontispiece, where "Woodson," alias of Huiswoud, appears as editor, and Arnold Ward as a contributing editor.

107. RGASPI 495/155/102, 129–30.

108. Ibid., *Ford to Patterson*, September 17, 1935, 253.

109. See esp. Turner, op. cit., 195, 209, 213.

110. See, George Padmore, *American Imperialism Enslaves Liberia*, "Liberia . . . shows us that Negro capitalists will exploit other Negroes." He called, for "delivering the final blow to the whole system of imperialism," through black and white united workers' struggle, 5–6, 46.

111. "Miss Cunard said that Padmore 'used to laugh much about their lamentable outlook,' but was prepared to write the way the Negro press wanted," citing *Cunard to Hooker*, February 15, 1965, in Hooker, op. cit., 54.

112. George Padmore, "Ethiopia and World Politics," *The Crisis*, May, 1935, 138–39.

113. George Padmore, "The Mississippi Racket in Africa," *The Crisis*, July 1935, 214.

114. "Soviet Russia Aids Italy," *The Crisis,* October, 1935, 305.

115. Hooker, op. cit., 44–45. See also National Peace Council, *Peace and the Colonial Problem* (London: National Peace Council, 1935). Arnold Ward, Saklatvala, Bridgeman, the Anti-Slavery Society leader John Harris, and C. Roden Buxton were all in attendance. See also, e.g., Leonard Barnes, *Caliban in Africa: An Impression of Colour-Madness* (London: Gollancz, 1930) and *The Duty of Empire* (London: Gollancz, 1935); William M. Macmillan, *Bantu, Boer and Briton: The Making of a South African Native Problem* (London: Faber and Gwyer, 1929) and *Complex South Africa, an Economic Footnote to History* (London: Faber, 1930).

116. Hooker, op. cit., 45, 47. Menon was the future postwar Indian defense minister. See Owen, op. cit., 230. On the Swaraj League, see Owen, 268–670, and on the India League, chapters 7–8, passim.

117. George Padmore, *Africa and World Peace* (London: Frank Cass, 1937, 1972).

118. Hooker, op. cit., 30, cites *New Leader*, November 13, 1936.

119. Crawford et al., op. cit., 3–5; See, Corthorn, op. cit., chapter 2, passim.

120. See, e.g., Naison, op. cit., 155–58, 174–76, 195–96, 262.

121. Padmore, *How Britain Rules Africa*.

122. Ibid., v, James Russell Lowell, "Stanzas sung at the anti-slavery Picnic in Dedham, on the anniversary of West-India Emancipation, August 1, 1843," in, *Poems by James Russell Lowell in Two Volumes*, vol. 1 (Boston: Ticknor and Fields, 1849), 206: "They are slaves who fear to speak, For the fallen and the weak."

123. Padmore, *How Britain Rules Africa*, 386, 393, 395. The National Peace Council had strong League connections and its liberal leadership was active in the milieux of the Nobel Prize, international pacifism, and interwar relief organizations.

124. Ibid., 395–96; 3, quoting the *Manchester Guardian Weekly*, June 1, 1934.

125. Ralph Bunche, "Britannia Rules the Africans," *Journal of Negro Education*, vol. 6, no. 1, January, 1937, 75–76. See also Bunche, *A World-View of Race* (Washington, DC: The Associates in Negro Folk Education, 1936), chapter 3, passim.

126. UCLA Library, *Ralph Bunche Diary* (RBD), March 24, 1937. Hooker, op. cit., 50, cites George Padmore, "Hands Off the Protectorates" (International African Service Bureau: London) July–August 1938.

127. Hooker, op. cit., 50.

128. Ibid., 48. See also, Schwarz, op. cit., 146, and fn. 48.

129. Padmore, *Africa and World Peace*.

130. See Jung Chang with Jon Halliday, *Madame Sun Yat-Sen*: Soong Ching-Ling (New York: Penguin, 1986), 67–78. Mme. Sun Yat-Sen worked with Agnes Smedley, the partner of LAI co-leader, Virendranath Chattopadhyaya, a key Comintern figure of interwar Europe. She was recruited to act as a communist agent in China. See Niroda K. Barooah, *Chatto* (Oxford: Oxford University Press, 2004), chapters 7–10; Ruth Price, *The Lives of Agnes Smedley* (Oxford, New York: Oxford University Press, 2005), esp. 219–33, and the obituary of Smedley's friend from 1930s Shanghai, "Ruth Werner," *New York Times*, July 23, 2000.

131. Padmore, *Africa and World Peace*, ix–xi. Peter Clarke, *The Cripps Version*: *The Life of Sir Stafford Cripps, 1889–1952* (London: Allen Lane, Penguin, 2002), makes no mention of this, and Clarke is unaware of Cripps's involvement with Padmore or Padmore's identity, simply positing, "There is, in fact, impressive evidence of Cripps' personal freedom from racial prejudice. This can be found not only in his public declarations or in private incidents like his well-meaning attempt to break down the slight 'color bar' that he found on his ship home from Jamaica in 1938." See, also, Corthorn, op. cit, passim, esp. chapters 6 and 7, which mention C.L.R. James, but—following suit—make not a single mention of Padmore.

132. Padmore, *Africa and World Peace*, "Introduction," ix–x, 1.

133. SC, Ralph Bunche Papers, "General Correspondence" Box 10b, *Padmore to Bunch*, April 4, 1937; *Padmore to Bunche*, 1937 n.d., mentions the *Pan African Federation for the Defense of Africans and People of African Descent*, the *Pan-African Book Agency*, and the *Pan-African Speakers' Bureau*, as related entities.

134. RBD, April 13, 1937.

135. Ibid., 1937, n.d. See also, Brian Urquhart, *Ralph Bunche, An American Life* (New York, London: Norton, 1993), chapter 4: "England, 1937"; Charles P. Henry, *Ralph Bunche: Model Negro or American Other?* (New York and London: New York University Press, 1999), 77–83.

136. RBD, April 29, 1937.

137. Ibid., April 25, 1937. See, Reginald Reynolds, *The White Sahibs in India: An Examination of British Rule in India* (London: Secker and Warburg, 1937). See Reynolds, *My Life and Crimes*, 141–43. Nehru wrote the foreword. Saumyendranath Tagore was the grandson of the poet and philosopher Rabindranath Tagore, a Scottsboro signatory. On Reynolds's involvement with Indian affairs, see Owen, 223–24, 248–49.

138. See, e.g., David Low and Terry (H. Thorogood), *Evening Standard*, "The Patriots," July 26, 1936, "Rebel Leader: What a pity-if only we had enough Moors and riff-raff to wipe out the Spanish people, we could save Spain," in LSE, archives, *David Low Papers*.

139. RBD, May 2, 1937.

140. RBD.; The POUM (*Partido Obrero de Unificación Marxista*) was the Trotskyist-influenced Workers' Party of Marxist Unification of the Spanish Civil War. See Reynolds, *My Life and Crimes*, 127–28, 140, 212.

141. RBD, May 2, 1937. On MacDonald and Snowdon, see Fenner Brockway, *Inside the Left* (London: Allen and Unwin, 1942) 218; Corthorn, op. cit., Chapter 1, esp. 12–13.

142. Ibid, May 2, 1937; July 24, 1937. See also May 16, 1937, and May 29, 1937.

143. Ethel Mannin, *Privileged Spectator: A Sequel to "Confessions and Expressions"* (London: Jarrold's, 1946), 117. The Colonial Liberties Group corresponded with Ralph Bunche. SC, Ralph Bunche Papers, Colonial Liberties Group, *Longridge Rd., Earl's Court to Bunche*, n.d., lists the group's members, including the Countess of Warwick, Mannin, and ILP writer Kitty Lamb. The group "embodied" the Society for International Studies. The Countess was also associated with her neighbor in Little Easton, Essex, the Scottsboro signatory H. G. Wells. See House of Lords, Parliamentary Archives, BLU/1/21/WARW.1–25.

144. RBD, June 3, 1937.

145. Schomburg Center, Papers of Ralph Bunche, General Correspondence, box 106, *Padmore to Bunche*, July 27, 1937; Picasso's *Guernica* was on display in Spain's pavilion at the Exposition, which sought to foster world peace and was the occasion for significant protest, travel, and mobilization. Both Nazi Germany and the Soviet Union had pavilions.

146. Ibid., *Padmore to Bunche*, August 23, 1937.

147. George Padmore, "Abyssinia—the Last of Free Africa," *The Crisis,* May, 1937, 134–56.

148. George Padmore, "Abyssinia Betrayed by the League of Nations," *The Crisis,* June 1937, 166.

149. Ibid., 167, 168, 180, 188.

150. "March against Capitalism this May Day" *New Leader,* April 29, 1938, 1.

151. See Trevor Williams, "What the Empire Is"; Reginald Reynolds, "The Road to Empire: How Britain Won and Keeps India"; "British Govt. is also 'Imperialist Aggressor': How 100,000 square miles were added to empire last year, Tribes terrorized by aerial bombings";"Says a British Imperialist"; Kitty Lamb, "African Empire Is Slave Colony"; Fenner Brockway, "Has Hitler Anything to Teach Our Ruling Class?"; "Conservative MP on Bombing in India"; George Padmore, "Colonial Fascism in the West Indies," in *New Leader* April 29, 1938, and Jomo Kenyatta, "Africa: Hitler Could Not Improve on Kenya," *New Leader,* May 20, 1938.

152. Hooker, op. cit., 46–47. See Louis Aragon et al., *Authors Take Sides on the Spanish War* (London: Left Review, 1937). *New Leader,* May 20, 1938; and, Hooker, *Bridgeman to Hooker*, September 22, 1964, 144, fn. 17.

153. Adi, op. cit., 80.

154. Louis Aragon et al., op. cit.

155. Hooker, op. cit., 46; see also, Lois Gordon, op. cit., 231–32.

156. Louis Aragon et al., op. cit.

157. Hooker, 41–42, 54; see the *Rhodesia-Nyasaland Royal Commission Report of 1939* Cmd. 5949 (London: H. M. Stationery Office, 1939). The High Commission Territories became contemporary Botswana, Lesotho and Swaziland.

158. See, e.g., George Padmore, "Colonial Fascism in the West Indies." See also Thomas Holt, *The Problem of Freedom: Race, Labor and Politics in Jamaica and Britain, 1832–1938*, "Epilogue" (Baltimore: Johns Hopkins, 1992), passim.

159. Hooker, op. cit., 53.

160. Ibid., cites the *Chicago Defender*, July 23, 1938.

161. See FCB 2/7, 30, December 20, 1938. This committee included Stafford Cripps, Arthur Creech Jones, and Charles Roden Buxton. See also *West Indies Royal Commission Report*, Cmd. 6607 (London: H. M. Stationery Office, 1945).

162. This was the name of an IASB manifesto, see Hooker, op. cit., 53. See Owen, op. cit., chapter 8, passim.

163. See chapter 6 below.

164. See Crawford, op. cit., in which C.L.R. James discusses recruiting Ballard to the Marxist group of the ILP, 2. Guérin later experienced and wrote about the postwar American civil rights movement.

165. FCB, Mss. Brit. Emp. S 365, FCB 2/7 (87). *International African Opinion*, vol. 1, 99, which cites the Colonial Office report on *Colonial Students in Britain*, 1939.

166. Adi, op. cit., 80.

167. "Editorial: An Open Letter to West Indian Intellectuals," *International African Opinion*, May–June, 1939, 1.

168. Ibid., 2.

169. Ibid., 3.

170. See, e.g., "Editorial: Hitler and the Colonies," *International African Opinion*, vol. 1, no. 5, November, 1938, 2–3; "Editorial: An Open Letter to West Indian Intellectuals," 1–3. See also Hooker, op. cit., 56–57.

171. Padmore, *From Communism to Pan-Africanism*, "Author's Note," xv; "Foreword," xxiii–xxiv.

172. Ibid., 126, 293, 109, 303, 342.

173. Ibid., 342, 306.

CHAPTER 3. LADY KATHLEEN SIMON AND ANTISLAVERY

The epigraph is taken from: Graham Greene, *Journey without Maps* (1936, 1961), 68–69.

1. Padmore, *Pan-Africanism or Communism?*, 303.

2. On eighteenth-century opposition to slavery, see Christopher Leslie Brown, *Moral Capital: Foundations of British Abolitionism* (Chapel Hill: University of North Carolina Press, 2006); and Stephen Farrell, Melanie Unwin, and James Walvin, eds., "The British Slave Trade: Abolition, Parliament, and People," *Parliamentary History*, supplement 2007, passim. On the later era, see Suzanne Miers, *Slavery in the Twentieth Century: The Evolution of a Global Problem* (Lanham, MD: Rowan and Littlefield, 2003), chapters 8–17; Kevin Grant, *A Civilized Savagery: Britain and the New Slaveries in Africa, 1884–1926* (New York: Routledge, 2005), chapters 1 and 5, passim; and, "Human Rights and Sovereign Abolitions of Slavery, c. 1885–1956," in Kevin Grant, Philippa Levine, and Frank Trentmann, *Beyond Sovereignty: Britain, Empire and Transnationalism, c. 1880–1950* (Macmillan: New York, 2007), 80–102. Sir John Simon became a Society vice president in 1928 and served in the British Cabinet as foreign secretary, 1931–35; home secretary, 1935–37; and chancellor, 1937–40.

3. Miers, op. cit., chapters 13 and 14, passim. On the importance of trusteeship, see Grant, 15–21, 171, chapter 5, passim.

4. Miers, op. cit., 301 and 313, fn. 4, citing correspondence between Pankhurst and Anthony Eden, foreign secretary, and Foreign Office documents. Meirs concludes that the F.O. relished the raw divisions among antislavery advocates.

5. See Grant, op. cit., chapter 5, passim. Micheline R. Ishay, *The History of Human Rights from Ancient Times to the Globalization Era* (Berkeley: University of California Press, 2004), 174–211; and Paul Gordon Lauren, *The Evolution of International Human Rights* (Philadelphia: University of Pennsylvania Press, 2003), chapters 3 and 4, passim.

6. David Dutton, *Simon: A Political Biography of Sir John Simon* (London: Aurum, 1992), 325.

7. John Allsebrook Simon, 1st viscount, *Retrospect: The Memoirs of Viscount Simon* (London: Hutchinson, 1952), 121.

8. Dutton, op. cit., 56.

9. Ibid., 326; 340, fn. 14.

10. See *LSP*, MSS Brit. Emp. s. 25, K 13/1, E.N.A., "Lady Simon on Indian Women," n.d.

11. See, *Report of the Indian Statutory Commission . . . Presented by the Secretary of State for the Home Department to Parliament by command of His Majesty* (London: H. M. Stationery Office, 1930), Cmd. 3568. See also Owen, op. cit., 158–69.

12. On the Society's history, see, Mike Koye, "The Development of the Anti-Slavery Movement After 1807," in Ferrell et al., eds., op. cit., 237–51, and especially Grant, op. cit., 159–66.

13. LSP, MSS. Brit. Emp. s 25 K13/1 *Times*, May 3, 1927. Bonham Carter was the daughter of the wartime Prime Minister H. H. Asquith and a great friend of Winston Churchill's. See, also, Miers, op. cit., chapter 6, passim.

14. LSP, ibid., *Times*, October 17, 1927; January 2, 1928.

15. Lady Kathleen Simon, *Slavery, with a Preface by John Simon* (London: Hodder and Stoughton, 1929), vii–viii, ix.

16. Ibid, 2.

17. See Frederick Cooper, Thomas C. Holt, and Rebecca Scott, *Beyond Slavery: Explorations of Race, Laborer and Citizenship in Post-Emancipation Societies* (Chapel Hill and London: University of North Carolina Press, 2000), 5–11.

18. Simon, *Slavery*, 33–34.

19. See, Miers, op. cit., Chapter 6, passim.

20. Harriet Beecher Stowe, *Uncle Tom's Cabin* (New York: Dover, 2005). In February 1928 the manager of the Pavilion Theater approached Simon for help in promoting the film version of *Uncle Tom's Cabin*. She attempted to get Prime Minister Stanley Baldwin to view it, who begged off. "Cannot go to a film . . . even in so good a cause as yours." (LSP, *Stewart to Simon*, February 18, 1928; *Baldwin to Simon*, February 1, 1928). A correspondent recalled a version performed in London in 1874 at Princess's Theater with a cast of three hundred ex-slaves. On Sudan, see Miers, op. cit., 153–6.

21. Simon, *Slavery*, 82.

22. Padmore, *American Imperialism*, op. cit., 22.

23. For the wider context, see Miers, op. cit., chapters 11–12, passim, especially on Burma, 126–28, 152–53, and Nepal, 188–89. See, also, Katherine Mayo, *The Isles of Fear: The Truth about the Philippines* (New York: Harcourt, Brace, 1925); and Owen, op. cit., 224–25.

24. See, Miers, op. cit., 143–49; Grant, *A Civilized* Slavery, chapter 4, passim, and 162–63.

25. See, Miers, op. cit., 137, 168.

26. Simon, *Slavery*, 185. See also Charles Roden Buxton, *The Exploration of the Colored Man* (London: Anti-Slavery and Aborigines Protection Society), 17.

27. Ibid., Simon, 195–226.

28. Ibid., 231.

29. "Lady Simon's Great Book—Slavery. What the Press Says," *Anti-Slavery Reporter and Aborigines' Friend* (hereafter, ARAF), January, 1930, 161.

30. Ibid., *Daily News*, 162.

31. LSP, MSS. Brit. Emp. s. 25 K3/1 *White to Simon*, January 18, 1930.

32. "Quarterly Notes, Lynching in the U.S." ARAF, April 1930, 2–3.

33. See Grant, *Civized Savagery*, 141–55. Lady Simon's *Slavery* extended the evangelical approach common in the preceding century of antislavery agitation.

34. LSP, MSS Brit. Emp. s. 25 K2, *Locke to Simon*, July 9, 1930.

35. LSP, ibid., *Locke to Simon*; Alain Locke, ed., *The New Negro: An Interpretation* (New York: A. and C. Boni, 1925).

36. LSP, ibid., *Simon to Locke*, July 11, 1930.

37. See, Francine Hirsch, *Empire of Nations: Ethnographic Knowledge and the Making of the Soviet Union* (Ithaca, NY: Cornell University Press, 2005), 13–17, 254, 296–97, for an understanding of Soviet ethnic policy, 1924–34, the "encouragement of people to articulate their identities in official 'national' terms," 17.

38. ARAF, "The Native in Parliament," October 1930, 118–19; "Nigeria: Execution of Natives," 142; "Fiji (Franchise)," 146; "Child Adoption in Ceylon," April 1930, 50.

39. LSP, MSS. Brit. Emp. s. 25 K13/1 *Welfare of Africans in Europe War Fund*, 1930. See, e.g., ARAF January 1930, 164.

40. On Roden Buxton, see Victoria De Bunsen, *Charles Roden Buxton: A Memoir* (London: G. Allen and Unwin, 1948), esp. chapter 10. On Cecil, see Miers, op. cit., 123–24 and Grant, op. cit., 160–65.

41. See Susan Pennybacker, "Changing Convictions: London County Council Black-coated Activism between the Wars," in Rudy Koshar, ed., *Splintered Classes: Politics and the Lower Middle Class in Interwar Europe*, (Holmes and Meier, 1990), 97–120.

42. LSP, MSS. Brit. Emp. s. K25 13/1 "Negroes at Livingstone's Tomb," *Bath Herald*, May 5, 1930. On conditions in Hong Kong, and the fate of *mui tsai*, girls sold by their parents to wealthier families, see Miers, op. cit., 157–61.

43. LSP, ibid., "Christianity and Slavery," *Manchester Guardian*, May 7, 1930. On practices in Sudan, see, Miers, op. cit., 153–57; 183–8, and Grant, op. cit., 164–66.

44. LSP, ibid. "Christianity and Slavery."

45. LSP, ibid., Cornelia, "Lady Simon Sounds Clarion Call for New Crusade," circa August 22, 1930. See Harriet Martineau, *Views of Slavery and Emancipation; from "Society in America"* (New York: Piercy and Reed, 1837).

46. LSP, ibid. "US Help Asked against Slavery by Lady Simon: Condemns America for Tolerating Lynchings," *Chicago Evening Post*, August 23, 1930.

47. LSP, MSS. Brit. Emp. s. K22 "Sheriff's Fears Permitted Indiana Lynchings," *World*, August 24, 1930. See Miller, Pennybacker, and Rosenhaft, op. cit., for an image of U.S. lynchings on the cover of the *Negro Worker*, November–December 1932, 407.

48. LSP, MSS. Brit. Emp. s K13/1 "America Asked to Aid in Move to Ban Slavery," *Christian Science Monitor*, September 5, 1930; "Happy Chicago," *Manchester Guardian*, September 17, 1930.

49. LSP, MSS. Brit. Emp. s. 25 K13/1 "New York Women Are Once More Stirred by Anti-Slavery Talk," *New York Sun*, September 8, 1930.

50. LSP, "Happy Chicago"; Marc Connelly, *The Green Pastures, a Fable Suggested by Roark Bradford's Southern Sketches, 'Ol' man Adam an his chillun'* (New York: Farrar and Rinehart, 1930).

51. LSP, "Happy Chicago."

52. See "The Liberian Commission," ARAP, January, 1931, 9–10. See, Miers, op. cit., 140–41, 188.

53. LSP, MSS, Brit. Emp. s. 25 K13/1 "Picanninies in Pawn," *News Chronicle*, October 16, 1930; Miers, op. cit., 140–43.

54. See LSP, MSS Brit. Emp. s. 25 K13/1 "Slavery in British Empire ... Russian Camps," *Oxford Mail*, February 21, 1931; "Another Slavery Inquiry," *Sunday Times*, January 11, 1931; "Russia and Forced Labor," *Manchester Guardian*, January 27, 1931; "'Slave Labor In Russia, Heated Debate,'" *Manchester Guardian*, November 21, 1930; "Prison Timber Camps of Russia," *Morning Post*, January 10, 1931. See, also, Hansard, *House of Commons*, vol. 259/81–90.

55. *Out of the Deep: Letters from Soviet Timber Camps, with an Introduction by Hugh Walpole* (London: G. Bles, 1933). See also Sir Alan Pim, *Report on Russian Timber Camps* (London: E. Benn, 1931); Anne Applebaum, *Gulag: A* History (London: Penguin, 2003), 75.

56. Victoria De Bunsen, *op. cit.*, 114–15. On Mitchison's trip, see chapter 1, above. See Charles Roden Buxton, *In a Russian Village* (London: Labor Publishing, 1922) on his travels with the Labour party delegation to the Soviet Union in the Civil War era.

57. LSP, MSS. Brit. Emp. s. 25 K13/1 "Prison Timber Camps of Russia," *Morning Post*, January 1931.

58. LSP, ibid., "Russian Atrocities: the Limitations of Human Pity," *Time and Tide*, March 14, 1931, 309–10.

59. See, e.g., LSP, ibid., "Parliament: Labour under the Soviet: Alleged Slave Condition," *Daily Telegraph,* November 21, 1930; "Prison Timber Camps of Russia: Anti-Slavery Society Decides to Investigate," *Morning Post*, January 10, 1931; "Slavery in British Empire; Sir John Simon on World Problem; Russian Camps," *Oxford Mail*, February 21, 1931, Quartaly Notes: "Russian Timber Camps, ARAF, July 1931, 74–75.

60. "Review": *The Race Problem in Africa*, ARAF, October, 1931, 163. See Charles Roden Buxton, *The Race Problem in Africa* (London: Hogarth, 1931).

61. See "Slave Trade and Slavery in Abyssinia," in "Annual Report, 1930," ARAF, April 1931, 52–53.

62. Ibid., "Labour in Abyssinia," 10–11.

63. LSP, MSS Brit. Emp. s. 25, K 3/3, *Harris to Simon*, May 5, 1931. See Miers, op. cit., chapter 15, passim.

64. See "Abyssinia," ARAF, January 1933, 125; League of Nations, "Report of the Slavery Commission of the League of Nations" (about: a series of League publications VI. B, Slavery 1932, VI.B1), 124.

65. Ibid., "Report of the Slavery Commission," 123.

66. "The League of Nations and Slavery" ARAF, July 1930, 156–57; *Leader: Slaves in Abyssinia, Times*, April 7, 1932.

67. Anne Olivier Bell, ed., *The Diary of Virginia Woolf* (New York: Harcourt, Brace, 1983), vol. 4, 1931–35, October 5, 1933, 182–83. Leonard Woolf described Buxton as "a good man . . . mentally and emotionally a nineteenth century non-conformist Liberal . . . never completely at home in the twentieth-century Labour Party," 182–83, fn. 5.

68. "Lynchings in the United States," ARAF, April 1930, 2: "Lynching in the United States," ARAF, January, 1932, 182–83. "The excuse that lynching prevents outrages on white women will not hold, for less than a quarter of the victims since 1890 were accused of such offenses. . . . Lynching . . . is directly connected with poverty and lack of education . . . [and] highest in sparsely settled areas." Since 1889, there had been almost 3,700 lynchings, the greatest number occurring in Georgia.

69. Ibid., January, 1931, 3; LSP, MSS. Brit. Emp. s. 25 K22 "Negro Lynched" *Morning Post*, January 13, 1931; *Peltier to Lady Simon*, January 16, 1931.

70. LSP, MSS. Brit. Emp. s. 25 K13/1 "Lady Simon's Conversion," 1931.

71. Ibid. See also, Aptheker, ed., *Simon to Du Bois*.

72. LSP, ibid., "Last of Slavers' Victims," *Times*, December 6, 1931.

73. For an Islamic cleric's response to the radio show, see, LSP, *Dard to Simon*, May 22, 1932.

74. Rhodes House, Oxford, Anti-Slavery and Aborigines Society Papers, MSS Brit. Emp. S22 G484, *Notes for Lantern Slide Lecture, 1932*; See, also, Eldon Rutter, *The Holy Cities of Arabia* (London, New York: G. P. Punam's Sons, 1928). On the use of lantern slides in related campaigns including Congo Reform, see, Grant, *Civilized Savagery* chapters 1 and 2, passim.

75. LSP, MSS. Brit. Emp., s. 25 K13/1 *Finchley Press*, April 22, 1933.

76. LSP, ibid., fragment, November 3, 1932.

77. LSP, ibid., "The Scottsboro Case." See chapter 1.

78. LSP, ibid., "Condemned Negroes' Appeal in USA," *Times*, October 11, 1932.

79. LSP, ibid., "Seven Youths to Die," *Times*, October 11, 1932.

80. "Convict Labor in the US" ARAF, January 1933, 134.

81. Dutton, op. cit., cites interview with Roger Makins, Lord Sherfield, May 19, 1986, 325.

82. LSP, MSS, Brit. Emp. s. 25 K22 "Mob of 2000 Lynch Wounded Negro," *Star*, December 5, 1932. Pres. Herbert Hoover appointed the commission in 1929 to investigate criminal activity, and much of its work revolved around Prohibition.

83. LSP, MSS Brit. Emp. s. 25 K 3/3. *MacLeod to Simon*, May 10, 1933. See, Ronald Gow, *Gallows Glorious: A Play in Three Acts* (London: Gollancz, 1933).

84. LSP, MSS Brit. Emp. s. 25, K3/2, *Frost to Simon*, July 26, 1933.

85. For the dual approach that petitioners of the Simons took, see LSP, ibid., *Boon (Lewisham League of Nations Union) to Lady Simon*, August 30, 1933. The writer invited her to his branch's International Dress Ball, noting that if she were to speak on her international work it would have a great influence. There were seventy thousand electors in Lewisham, and the LNU had two thousand members. Boon asked if Sir John Simon could also come; it would "make the task of working for international good will easier." The branch sent its younger members to Geneva to observe the League.

86. "League of Nations and Slavery," ARAF, January 1934, 144–45. See Miers, op. cit., 217, and chapter 14, passim.

87. "Lady Simon at Barry," ARAF, July 1933, 56–57.

88. Ibid., "The Annual Meeting," 78.

89. LSP, MSS Emp. s. 25, K3/4. *Simon to Churchill*, May 8, 1933; *Churchill to Simon*, May 17, 1933; *Simon to Churchill*, May 24, 1933; *Churchill to Simon*, June 7, 1933. See Harriet Beecher Stowe, *Uncle Tom's Cabin* (London: Dent, 1919 [1909]) Everyman's Library.

90. "Lady Simon at the Minerva Club," ARAF, July 1933, 58.

91. "Lady Simon at Cardiff" ARAF, July 1933, 55.

92. Ibid., "The Catholic Commemoration," 58.

93. LSP, MSS. Brit. Emp. s. 25 K13/1 "The Anti-Slavery Centenary, 1833–1933," *Cleakheaton Guardian*, April 21, 1933. See Miers, op. cit., 72–74; 100–102.

94. LSP, ibid., "Slavery: The Centenary of Abolition and Emancipation, 1933–34," *Spectator*, May 12, 1933.

95. LSP, ibid., "Freedom of Slaves" *Times* (London), July 9, 1933; Reginald Coupland, *The British Anti-Slavery Movement* (London: Frank Cass, 1933, 1964), 184–85.

96. LSP, ibid., Henry W. Nevinson, "Why We Honor the Name of Wilberforce," July 21, 1933. See Angela V. John, *War, Journalism and the Shaping of the Twentieth Century: The Life and Times of Henry W. Nevinson* (London: Tauris, 2006), 42–59, and, Henry Nevinson, *A Modern Slavery in Angola, San Thomé and Principe* (London: Harper, 1906).

97. ARAF, October 1933, 99.

98. "Centenary Celebrations," ibid., 96–97, cites *Leeds Mercury*, July 23, 1932.

99. LSP, MSS., Brit. Emp., s. 25 K13/1, "Fighting Slavery for One Hundred Years," *News Chronicle*, April 12, 1933.

100. "Lady Simon in Brazil" ARAF, August 9, 1933, 131.

101. LSP, *Du Bois to Simon*, September 26, 1933. On the first three Pan-African Congresses, see Lewis, vol. II, op. cit., 37–49, 109–17. On Du Bois's subsequent resignation from the NAACP, see Lewis, vol II, op. cit., 335–37. See also LSP, MSS, Brit. Emp., s 25 K1 *Du Bois to Simon*, February 11, 1938, informing her of his resignation as editor of *The Crisis*.

102. LSP, MSS. Brit. Emp. s. 25 K22 "Great Exodus of Negroes Begins," *Daily Express*, December 1, 1933.

103. LSP, ibid., "Maryland Lynching: Arrested Men Released," *Times*, December 1, 1933.

104. LSP, "Great Exodus."

105. LSP, "Maryland Lynching."

106. "Georgia Nigger" ARAF, January 1934, 175. See John Louis Spivak, *Georgia Nigger* (New York: Warren and Putnam, 1932).

107. ARF, January 1934, 175; see World Committee for the Victims of German Fascism, op. cit.

108. "Overseas Meetings; Sierra Leone" ARAF, April 1934, 36–37; October 1934, 104.

109. LSP, MSS. Brit., Emp., s. 25 K13/5 "Negro Emancipation Meetings at St. Botolph's Church," typescript notes, July 31 and August 1, 1934.

110. LSP, MSS Brit. Emp., s. 25 K13/1 "Midnight Scene Marks Hundred Years of Freedom," *News Chronicle*, August 1, 1934.

111. LSP, ibid., "Midnight Peal of Bells," August 1, 1934; "St. Botolph's Bishopsgate, EC: Commemoration of the 100th Anniversary."

112. LSP, ibid., "Descendants of Freed Slaves" *Daily Mail*, circa July, 1934.

113. LSP, "Midnight Scene, op. cit.

114. LSP, MSS. Brit. Emp. s. 25 K13/1 "Sir John and Lady Simon," July 30, 1934. The Anglo-Irish Treaty of 1921 created the Irish Free State, but helped to provoke Civil War.

115. LSP, "Midnight Scene, op. cit.

116. Isaiah 61:1–2: "The Spirit of the Lord is upon me, because he has anointed me; he has sent me to preach glad tidings to the poor, to heal the broken in heart, to proclaim liberty to the captives, and recovery of sight to the blind; to declare the acceptable year of the Lord, and the day of recompense; to comfort all that mourn."

117. LSP, "Midnight Scene," op. cit.

118. LSP, MSS. Brit. Emp. s. 25 K 13/1 "Slave Freedom Centenary," July 31, 1934, and "100 Years of Freedom," August 1, 1934.

119. LSP, ibid., "A Hundred Years Ago Today," August, 2, 1934, cites Simon in the *Times*.

120. LSE Archives ILP/8/1934/4, Charles Roden Buxton, "Impressions of Liberia: A Report to the League of Coloured Peoples" (London: League of Coloured Peoples, 1934).

121. "Mansion House Meeting," ARAF, January 1935, 138–40; "Centenary of Emancipation in Cape Town," ARAF, April 1935, 3.

122. Fryer, op. cit., 234.

123. "Lynching in the United States" ARAF, July 1934, 96. The failed Wagner-Costigan bill was sponsored by Sens. Robert F. Wagner of New York and Edward Costigan of Colorado. Both were Democrats, but FDR would not support the bill, fearing the loss of Southern support for his reelection.

124. LSP, MSS Brit. Emp. s. 25, K22. *White to Simon*, November 7, 1934.

125. LSP, MSS Brit. Emp. s. 25 K 3/1. *Simon to White*, December 4, 1934. See Jacquelyn Dowd Hall, *Revolt against Chivalry: Jessie Daniel Ames and the Women's Campaign against Lynching* (New York: Columbia, 1979).

126. LSP, MSS Brit. Emp. s. 25, K22. *Ames to Simon*, November 10, 1934, mentions that she sent Simon the Association's "A New Public Opinion" and "Are the Courts to Blame?" See also, MSS. Brit. Emp., s. 25 K 3/1 *Simon to White*, December 4, 1934; op. cit. *Simon to Ames*, MSS Brit. Emp. s. 25 K22, January 22, 1935, states: "I lived in both Georgia and Tennessee, and though I am happy to say that I was never witness to any mob riot against colored people, yet I saw how much they were regarded as something less than human. . . . I know the difficulty of the whole question, but lynching is a disgrace to any country which calls itself civilized."

127. LSP, MSS. Brit., Emp., s. 25 K13/1, "Abolition of Slavery: Lady Simon at Bedford," *Bedfordshire Standard*, July 14, 1933.

128. LSP, *Simon to Ames*, January 22, 1935.

129. Her other American correspondents included WILF leader Emily Balch, Mrs. Harry Emerson Fosdick, former Colorado senator and industrialist Simon Guggenheim, banker and philanthropist George Foster Peabody, Alaskan congressman James Wickersham (of the Commission), and African American writer James Weldon Johnson.

130. LSP, *Simon to Ames*, January 22, 1935. Ames replied judiciously, "Since I am not only of the South but in the South, it scarcely behooves me to claim a conscience for the South, let alone to claim whether or not it has been aroused," MSS Brit. Emp. s. 25, K22. *Ames to Simon*, February 14, 1935. A month later, Simon's secretary wrote to Ames, "She thanks you so much for your letter and wishes me to say that since she lived in the South in her youth, she has always been very strongly opposed to such methods of

carrying out the law as this abomination called lynching," LSP, *Simon to Ames*, March 6, 1935.

131. Simon, *Retrospect*, from a note he wrote just after his trip, 202. Niall Ferguson, *The War of the World: Twentieth-Century Conflict and the Descent of the West* (London and New York: Penguin, 2006), 319. See chapters 9–10, passim.

132. Simon, *Retrospect*, 203.

133. Ibid., 203–204; 211–14, and Dutton, op. cit., 203.

134. See, e.g., George Padmore, "Ethiopia and World Politics," *The Crisis*, May 1935, 138.

135. Mark Pottle, ed., *Champion Redoubtable: The Diaries and Letters of Violet Bonham Carter* (London: Weidenfeld and Nicolson, 1998), 186.

136. See, Clarke, *The Cripps Version*, 60–67, and chapter 2, above. See Corthorn, op. cit., 44–45, 72, 79–85.

137. Simon, *Retrospect*, 212–13.

138. See, Grant, *Civilized Savagery*, 10.

139. "Redistribution of Colonial Territories" ARAF, January 1936, 155; see also Rich, op. cit., 82–85.

140. ARAF, Janaury 1935, 156.

141. "Slavery in Abyssinia" *Harris to Hoare*, November 8, 1935, and *Peterson to Harris*, November 20, 1935, ARAF, April 1936, 2–3.

142. "Slavery in Abyssinia," ARAF, January 1936, 133, cites the *Times*, November 11, 1936. "It was admitted that once again slave owning and slave raiding were largely responsible for the war."

143. Simon, *Retrospect*, 214.

144. ARAF, January 1936.

145. Hansard, Parliamentary Debates, *House of Lords*, vol. 99/629; 99/627. See Noel Noel-Buxton, "Slavery in Abyssinia, the Trade in Negroes," *Times*, April 7, 1923.

146. See, e.g., G. C. Baravelli, *Abyssinia: The Last Stronghold of Slavery* (London: British-Italian Bulletin, 1936).

147. ARAF, April, 1936.

148. LSP, MSS. Brit. Emp., s. 25 13/5, "Abyssinia."

149. See Hansard, *House of Lords,* vol. 80/911–38.

150. See, Greene, op. cit., 121–28.

151. See Miers, op. cit., 230, and chapter 15, passim.

152. LSP, MSS. Brit., Emp., s. 25 K13/5, "The Abyssinian Question," *Suffolk and Essex Free Press*, May 21, 1936. On Sudan, see Miers, op. cit., 153–56. "The Abasement of Abyssinia," *Freethinker*, May 3, 1936.

153. LSP, MSS Brit. Emp. s. 25, K1. *Fisher to Simon*, February 3, 1936.

154. "The Annual Meeting" ARAF, July 1936, 71–73; 76, 81. Lytton led the League's expedition in Manchuria.

155. "Italy and Abyssinia," ARAF, October 1936, 165–67; Hansard, *House of Commons*, vol. 314/1644. See, also, Pedersen, *Eleanor Rathbone*, 273–77.

156. Ibid., "Italy and Abyssinia," 166–67; Hansard, *House of Commons*, vol. 314/1457–58. Ormsby-Gore was past undersecretary of state for the colonies (1922–29) and the future colonial secretary (1936–38).

157. "Italy and Ethiopia," ARAF, October 1936, 130.

158. LSP, MSS. Brit. Emp., s. 25 K13/5, "The Case for the Negro: Mr. C.L.R. James a Spirited Champion," *Colne and Nelson Times*, March 16, 1935.

159. LSP, MSS Brit. Emp. s. 25 K13/1.

160. LSP, MSS. Brit. Emp. s. 25 *Treatt (Halperin Productions, California) to Simon*, June 9, 1936; *Halperin to Simon*, June 8, 1936. See *Simon to Du Bois. Cape to Cairo* (London: Wardour Films, 1929). William Faulkner wrote "Slave Ship," (20th Century Fox, 1937).

161. LSP, ibid., K13/5, "5 Years of 'Hate' Case Reopens Tomorrow," *Sunday Dispatch Cable*, January 19, 1936.

162. LSP, MSS. Brit., Emp., s. 25 *Garvey to Simon*, October 10, 1936.

163. LSP, ibid.

164. RBD, op. cit., February 4, 1937.

165. Hansard, *House of Commons*, vol. 308/1120, vol. 317/853–54, 1025. See also Tabili, op. cit., chapters 6 and 7, passim.

166. Ibid., Hansard, *House of Commons*, vol. 308/1120.

167. See Fryer, op. cit., 299–316; Tabili, op. cit.,132–39.

168. FCB, MSS. Brit. Emp. s. 23, "The Moral Aspect," 2.

169. Hansard, *House of Commons*, vol. 317/853.

170. Ibid., vol. 317/1021.

171. Ibid., Vol. 317/853–1023, 1025.

172. LSP, MSS. Brit., Emp., s. 25 K13/5 John Harris, "In the Cotton Belt," *Manchester Guardian*, September 21, 1937.

173. See Aptheker, ed., *Simon to Du Bois*.

174. "The Annual Meeting" ARAF, April 1938, 29.

175. "Abyssinia" ARAF, April 1937, 31. Hansard, House *of Commons*, vol. 321/778. See Hansard, Parliamentary Papers, 1904, vol. 62, Cd., 1933, on the British investigation into the Congo atrocities.

176. "Abyssinia" ARAF, April 1937, 31, for Simon's report of July 30, 1937, and Hansard, *House of Commons*, vol. 321/779.

177. "Abyssinia" ARAF, April, 1937, 31, and Hansard, *House of Commons*, vol. 321/779.

178. *Roberts and Harris to Signor Grandi*, March 11, 1937, in "The Massacre in Adis Ababa," ARAF, April 1937, 39.

179. "Abyssinia," ARAF, April 1937, 36, and Hansard, *House of Commons*, vol. 321/2544.

180. LSP, MSS. Brit., Emp. s. 25 K13/5 Sir John Harris, "Fair Play for Britain's Black Subjects," *Daily Herald*, June 9, 1937.

181. Ibid.; see also "The Kenya Highlands" ARAF, April 1937; Miers, op. cit., 137, and Frederick Cooper, "Conditions Analogous to Slavery: Imperialists and Free Labour Ideology in Africa," in Cooper et al., eds., op. cit., 120. See also 120–26.

182. See, also, Adi, op. cit., 72, for a related statement issued in 1938.

183. Hansard, *House of Commons*, vol. 333/411.

184. LSP, MSS. Brit. Emp., s. 25 K13/5 "Get your Mind Clear about This Colonies Business," December 3, 1937. See, also, John Harris, *Germany's Lost Colonial Empire and the Essentials of Reconstruction* (London: Simpkin, Marshall, 1917) for his earlier views, 80–88.

185. ARAF, April 1938.

186. *Lytton et al. to Chamberlain*, February 17, 1938. "Transfer of Colonial Territories" ARAF, April, 1938, 3–4, citing Hansard, *House of Lords*, February 17, 1938; February 21, 1938.

187. "The Question of Colonies," ARAF, July 1938, 75–76, cites Philippa Fawcett, *The Colonial Problem: Some Facts and Figures* (League of Nations Union, n.d.). Fawcett came from a leading suffrage family and had served as a schools reformer in South Africa and at the London County Council.

188. "Abyssinia," ARAF April 1938, 15. Hansard, *House of Commons*, vol. 332/2.

189. Dutton, op. cit., 254.

190. Hansard, *House of Commons*, vol. 332/1868; vol. 333/411.

191. LSP, MSS Brit. Emp. s. 25, K1. *Du Bois to Simon*, May 2, 1938. Du Bois was reading Africanist Margery Perham and *Round Table* journal founder Lionel Curtis's work on South Africa, and corresponding with Bronislaw Malinowski and Harold Laski. See Margery Perham and Lionel Curtis, *The Protectorates of South Africa: The Question of Their Transfer to the Union* (London: Milford, 1935). On Du Bois's 1936 German trip as recipient of an Oberlander Trust fellowship, when he also visited China, Japan, and Hawaii, see Lewis, op. cit., vol. II, chapter 11, passim.

192. See LSP, ibid., K13/5 "African Students Will Flock to Camden Square," *St. Pancras Gazette*, July 15, 1938. In 1939 the Colonial Office issued a report on colonial students and the need for them to have more supervision. See *International African Opinion*, May–June 1939, vol. 1, #7 in Rhodes House, FCB 2/7 (87). Rhodes, the African adventurer, entrepreneur, and politician died in 1902; his will established the trust.

193. LSP, ibid., *West Africa*, July 30, 1938.

194. LSP, ibid., "Opening of 'AFRICA HOUSE,' Camden Square," typescript, July 9, 1938.

195. LSP, ibid., Gwen Edwards, "Lady Simon, and Her Work for Colored Races," *Jamaica Standard*, August 31, 1938. See also LSP, MSS. Brit. Emp. s. 25, K1. *Edwards to Simon*, July 25, 1938.

196. Hansard, *House of Commons*, vol. 338/1116 for Henderson; vol. 337/203 for Rathbone. See, also, vol. 338/2188–9, for Rathbone, Henderson, and Lt. Col. Fletcher on question of Africans drifting into Italian territories, and their fate.

197. Woolf was a member from 1929 with Charles Roden Buxton, Labour politician Hugh Dalton, trade-union leader Ernest Thurtle, and Labour party international czar William Gillies. In the late thirties, the committee included Leonard Barnes, Buxton, Labour MP John Benn, medic and Liberal MP Haden-Guest, Labour MPs Arthur Creech Jones and Fabian Sidney Webb; Sydney Olivier, Labour MPs Tom Williams, Clement Attlee (later, Prime Minister), Susan Lawrence, Herbert Morrison, and Ellen Wilkinson. Woolf, Haden Guest, and Williams had direct connections to the Scottsboro defense, despite Gillies' censure. Williams helped to host Ada Wright at the House of Commons in 1932.

198. *Harris to Woolf et al.*, September 12, 1938, University of Sussex Library, LWP, IG3.

199. Simon, *Retrospect*, 253–54.

200. Great Britain Foreign Office, *Documents on British Foreign Policy, 1919–1939*, edited by E. L. Woodward and Rohan Butler (London: H.M. Stationery Office, 1946–), #113, 1938, *Appendix: A Documentary Anthology of the Crisis*, comments by Lord Walter Runciman, Chamberlain's emissary to Czechoslovakia, 204.

201. LSP, MSS. Brit. Emp., s. 25 K13/5, "Nazi Press Storms at Atrocity Stories about India and Palestine," *Evening News*, November 15, 1938. Herschel Grynszpan, a German Jew from Hanover, was forced out of Germany along with his family. Fifteen thousand Polish Jews also fled. In 1936 he went to France, and planned to assassinate the German ambassador, but instead shot vom Rath, in October 1938. The events of November 9–10, 1938, known as Kristallnacht, followed.

202. LSP, MSS. Brit. Emp. s 25 K13/5, "U.S.: Hideous Crimes," *Evening News*, November 15, 1938, refers to U.S. radio broadcasts of the previous day, citing the words of Democratic Senator William H. King of Utah; "A New Phase in Germany," *New York Times*, November 15, 1938.

203. "Colonies and Mandated Territories" ARAF, January 1939, 124–25; Hansard, *House of Commons*, vol. 341/146.

204. Ibid., ARAF, 124–25; ibid., Hansard, vol. 341/491–3.

205. ARAF, 124; ibid., Hansard, vol. 341/848.

206. Ibid., Hansard, vol. 341/848-9.

207. LSP, MSS. Brit. Emp. s 25 K13/5, "Yellow Badges Must Be Worn by Jews," *Daily Express*, November 24, 1938.

208. ARAF, 1938, 113–14, citing Hansard, *House of Commons,* November 26, 1938.

209. See E. D. Morel, *The Black Man's Burden* (London: National Labor Press, 1920), and Grant, op. cit., chapter 5, passim.

210. *Lytton et al., to Chamberlain*, December 6, 1938, "Germany and Colonial Claims," ARAF, April 1939, 2.

211. "Debate in the House of Commons," ARAF, April 1939, 5–6; Hansard, *House of Commons*, December 7, 1938.

212. Ibid., ARAF, 6; Hansard, December 7, 1938. MacDonald was Ramsay MacDonald's son.

213. "Abyssinia," ARAF April 1939, 14–15, citing Hansard, *House of Commons*, February 1, 1939.

214. Dutton, op. cit., 275.

215. R.A.C. Parker, op. cit., portrays him as a central and consistent advocate of the appeasement of Hitler, 210–12.

216. LSP, MSS Brit. Emp. s. 25, K 3/1, *Harris to Simon*, April 4, 1939.

217. LSP, ibid., K13/5, "Fight against Slavery: Africans and West Indians at Centenary Luncheon," *Bath Chronicle and Herald*, April 12, 1939; *News Chronicle*, "Fighting Slavery for 100 Years," April 12, 1939.

218. "Politics and the Negro: Slavery in the Colonies," *International African Opinion*, May–June 1939, 14.

219. Dutton, op. cit., 325–26.

220. LSP, MSS. Brit., Emp., s 25, *Simon to Storr*, December 22, 1938.

CHAPTER 4. SAKLATVALA AND THE MEERUT TRIAL

The epigraph is taken from: Lester Hutchinson, *Conspiracy at Meerut* (New York: Arno, 1972), 8.

1. See especially Mike Squires, *Saklatvala: A Political Biography* (London: Lawrence and Wishart, 1990), chapters 5–8; Panchanan Saha, *Shapurji Saklatvala, a Short*

Biography (Delhi: People's Publishing, 1970); and Sehri Saklatvala, *Fifth Commandment: A Biography of Shapurji Saklatvala* (Calcutta: National Book Agency, 1996).

2. See, e.g., Benjamin Zachariah, *Nehru* (London: Routledge, 2004), chapters 3–4.

3. See Judith M. Brown, ed., *The Oxford History of the British Empire, Volume IV: The Twentieth Century* (Oxford: Oxford University Press, 2001), 193; Anil Seal, ed., *Decline, Revival and Fall of the British Empire: The Ford Lectures and Other Essays by John Gallagher* (Cambridge: Cambridge University Press, 1982), xv.

4. John Gallagher, "The Decline, Revival and Fall of the British Empire," in Seal, ed., *op.*, 100, 108.

5. For a wide-ranging discussion of anti-imperialist politics in interwar Britain that focuses primarily on Labour party activity and the London left, see Owen, op. cit., chapters 4–8, passim.

6. See Barbara D. Metcalf and Thomas Metcalf, *A Concise History of India* (Cambridge: Cambridge University Press, 2002), 166, 167; and Mahadev Haribhai Desai, *A Righteous Struggle* (Ahmedabad: Navajivan Publishing House, 1951), iv; 183.

7. Metcalf and Metcalf, op. cit., 183.

8. See, *e.g.* Barooah, op. cit., chapters 5 and 8, passim.

9. M. N. Roy, *M. N. Roy's Memoirs* (Bombay and New York: Allied, 1964), 492.

10. Shaukat Usmani, *Historic Trips of a Revolutionary (Sojourn in the Soviet Union)* (New Delhi: Sterling Publishers, 1977), 4.

11. Kalplana Dutt, *Chittagong Armoury Raiders: Reminiscences* (Bombay: People's Publishing, 1945), 1–13.

12. Rajnarayan Chandavarkar, *Imperial Power and Popular Politics* (Cambridge: Cambridge University Press, 1998), chapter 5, passim.

13. Jawaharlal Nehru, *An Autobiography, with Musings on Recent Events in India* (London: John Lane, 1936, 1962), 241, 341, 528, 528 (1); 364. See Owen, op. cit., 185–86 and 214, on Gandhi's 1931 visit.

14. Chandavarkar, op. cit., 176.

15. Metcalf and Metcalf, op. cit., 195–96.

16. Judith Brown, "India" in Brown and Louis, op. cit., 423–32.

17. Sheri Saklatvala, op. cit., 9.

18. See Emily C. Brown, *Har Dayal, Hindu Revolutionary and Rationalist* (Tucson: University of Arizona Press, 1975), chapters 1–2, 4–6; Som Nath Aggarwal, *The Heroes of Cellular Jail* (Patiala: Publication Bureau, Punjabi University 1995), chapters 5–7; and especially Barooah, op. cit., 3–5, and chapters 1–5, passim. On Brussels, see Prashad, op. cit., 16–30. On Indians in New York City, see Vivek Bald, "Lost in the City: Spaces and Stories of South Asian New York, 1971–1965" in *South Asian Popular Culture*, vol 5., no. 1, April 2007, 59–76, and "Overlapping Diasporas, Multiracial Lives: South Asian Muslims in U.S. Communities of Color, 1880–1950," *Souls*, 8(4), 3–18, 2006.

19. Squires, op. cit., 6–12.

20. Ibid., 14, cites the recollections of Spittam Cama, 33, fn. 1. Cama attended St. Xavier's College in Bombay, with Saklatvala. See Squires, op. cit., 2.

21. Ibid., 19–33. On the early CPGB, see, e.g., Francis Beckett, op. cit., chapter 1, passim.

22. See LHASC, CP/IND/MISC/10, Helen Crawfurd, manuscript memoir, 252–54. See also Owen, op. cit., 215–16.

23. Dharani Goswani, "Impact of the October Revolution." See, also, McClellan, "Africans and Black Americans," and Philip Spratt, *Blowing Up India: Reminiscences and Reflections of a Former Comintern Emissary* (Calcutta: Prachi Prakashan, 1955), 34.

24. Usmani, op. cit., 53.

25. Sibnarayan Ray, ed., *M. N. Roy, Philosopher-Revolutionary: An International Symposium and Selection of Documents with a Detailed Chronology of Roy's Career,* 2nd ed., (Calcutta: Renaissance Publishers, 1984), "Statement of Remittance from Foreign Suspect Sources Reported to Have Been in India during the Period, 1922–28 inclusive . . . ," *Indian Defense Committee, London, for Cawnpore Defense*, L22.

26. *Daily Graphic*, October 20, 1924, cited in Squires, op. cit., 87.

27. Saha, op. cit., 12, citing Hansard, *House of Commons*, vol. 186/705–19.

28. Saha, op. cit., 50, 36.

29. S. Ray, ed., *M. N. Roy*, 81. Ranen Sen, a leading Indian communist, recalled, "I heard a speech from Saklatvala, who, apart from having been a Communist, was a member of the British Parliament. He gave several speeches in Calcutta, which inspired us [students in the National Revolutionary Party].We decided to procure a good number of Marxist literatures. . . . some of us, after reading them, decided to join the Communist movement." *Ranen Sen: Looking Back to 75 Years as a Communist* (http://www .calonline.com/cal/alaap/ranen.html).

30. Saha, op. cit., 50, 52; Appendix 1, contains the Gandhi-Saklatvala exchange, 69–95.

31. Meerut prisoner George Adhikari recalled that when Saklatvala came to Bombay he told the press that he would not associate with a communist party that did not possess Comintern authority. See George M. Adhikari, "The Comintern Congresses and the CPI," *Marxist Miscellany*, #2, January, 1971, 19.

32. On Brussels, see McMeekin, op. cit., 196–201; Prashad, op. cit., 16–30.

33. Saha, op. cit., Appendix 1, 69. See also Owen, op. cit., 184–86.

34. Saha, op. cit., 75.

35. Ibid., 77–78, 80.

36. Squires, op. cit., 128.

37. Sehri Saklatvala, op. cit., 335.

38. Saha, op. cit., Appendix 3, 93.

39. Shapurji Saklatvala, "British Imperialism in India: A World Menace," *Imperialist Review*, vol. 1, no. 1, July 1928, 27.

40. S. R. Barkshi, *Simon Commission and Indian Nationalists* (New Delhi: Munshiram Manoharlal Publishers, 1976, 1977), 10. See also Owen, op. cit., 158–70.

41. Barkshi, op. cit., 64, 100.

42. Ibid., 120.

43. Lovell and Wright appear in the front cover photograph of this text.

44. Squires, op. cit., 173.

45. Barkshi, op.cit. 120.

46. See Owen, op. cit., 212–16, for a CPGB internal view of the campaign's obstacles,

47. Hansard, *House of Commons*, 1929/1387–8, cited in Barkshi, op. cit, 120.

48. Squires, op. cit., 102.

49. Usmani, op. cit., See also Barooah, op. cit., 263–66.

50. Barooah, op. cit., 266

51. M. N. Roy, *Revolution and Counter-Revolution in China* (Westport, CT: Hyperion, 1973).

52. National Meerut Prisoner's Defense Committee, "The Meerut Trial, Facts of the Case" (London, 1929), 2–3.

53. Ray, ed., op. cit., "Haig to James," Home Department Political Branch, *Draft D-O Letter No. D 347*, April 29, 1929.

54. Usmani, op. cit., 106, citing his retrospective narrative in the *Bharat Jyoti*, July 5, 1964, and *Radiance*, July 19, 1964.

55. Pramita Ghosh, *Meerut Conspiracy Case and the Left Wing in India* (Papyrus: Calcutta, 1978), 65.

56. Devendra Singh, *Meerut Conspiracy Case and the Communist Movement in India, 1929–35*, (Research India Publication: Meerut, 1990), 86, 77, 79.

57. Philip Spratt, *Blowing Up India: Reminiscences and Reflections of a Former Comintern Emissary* (Calcutta: Prachi Prakashan, 1955), 47.

58. Singh, op. cit., 48, 47, 61; 65, citing "The Joint Statements."

59. Lester Hutchinson, op. cit., 67.

60. G. Adhikari, "Speech," in Ali Ashraf and G. A. Syomin, *October Revolution and India's Independence* (Sterling: New Delhi, 1977), 38–39.

61. Spratt, op. cit., 22.

62. Ibid., 23, 36, 38.

63. Hutchinson, op. cit., 16.

64. Ghosh, op. cit., 16–22.

65. Ibid., 102.

66. LHASC, CP/IND/BRAD/2/5, *Individual Case Brief and Preliminary Notes for the General Case for Appeal*.

67. Spratt, op. cit., 47, 49.

68. "Red Jailed in India Commons Aspirant," *New York Times*, May 6, 1929.

69. See "What we Think," *New Leader*, June, 1929; July, 1929, 9–10.

70. *Manchester Guardian*, December 10, 1929; December 29, 1929.

71. Ghosh, op. cit., 142.

72. Singh, op. cit., 53, 52.

73. LHASC, CP/IND/BRAD/2/5, "Suggestions in Regard to Defense" 1, #1a, #1b.

74. Ibid., 1, 1 (General) a, and 2, 3 (International Trade Union Movement and India).

75. Ibid., 2, 7 (White Terror Considered Historically).

76. Raghunath Shivaram Nimbkar, *Communists Challenge Imperialism from the Dock* (Calcutta: National Book Agency, 1967). *The general statement of eighteen communist accused*, e.g., 194–95.

77. Ibid; 218–19.

78. Ibid., 24–25; Reginald Reynolds, "The Road to Empire: How Britain Won and Keeps India," cites Jones's "The Revolt of Hindustan," *New Leader*, "Empire Special" April 29, 1938.

79. Nimbkar, 220, 233. The Theosophical Society was founded in New York in 1875 to pursue metaphysics and spirituality. Its Indian leader was the former London trade union leader and women's advocate Annie Besant, who maintained ties to Indian nationalism and the Indian Congress.

80. Ibid., 268–70; 280–81; 305. The use of anti-Bolshevik accusations assisted a Conservative victory in 1924; 293–94.

81. Ibid., 306.

82. Ibid., 307.

83. L. P. Sinha, *The Left-wing in India, 1919–47* (Muzzaffarpur: New Publishers, 1965), 236–37.

84. *Daily Worker,* January 27, 1931; July 31, 1931.

85. See "Red Arrests in India Draw Commons Query," *New York Times*, March 22, 1929; "Reds' Application Fails," July 17, 1929; "Rebel Trials Opens in India," February 1, 1930.

86. J. T. Murphy, "The Labour Government—an Examination of Its Record" (1930), 60. On repression in Bengal, see "Viceroy Acts to End Terrorism in Bengal; Courts May Suspend Right to Public Trial," *New York Times*, December 1, 1931.

87. Sinha, op. cit., 248.

88. *Daily Worker*, March 17, 1930, 2; April 18, 1931; April 12, 1931. The Catholic Crusade was founded by Scottsboro signatory Conrad Noel. Its opposition to Stalinism ultimately drew it away from the CPGB after years of supportive advocacy.

89. RGASPI 534/3/668. For a more diminished view of the Meerut campaign's achivements, see Owen, op. cit., 212–16.

90. RGASPI 534/3/668.

91. RGASPI 495/100/1073, "India: the Meerut Trial: What All Servicemen Should Know."

92. *Daily Worker*, May 6, 1931. Smith worked in China from 1960 until her death in Beijing in 1985. See Graham Stevenson, "Biographies . . . graham.thewebtailor.co.uk/archives/00089.html.

93. Ibid., May, 1931. On Gambia, see Arnold Hughes and David Perfect, "Trade Unions in the Gambia," *African Affairs*, October 1989, 88:24–25. Palestine witnessed one of a series of general strikes in 1931.

94. FCB, Creech Jones 1/5, "Memorandum on the Meerut Case," June 25, 1931, 2.

95. Ibid., 3, "The Meerut Trial," *Manchester Guardian*, June 10, 1931, 8.

96. RGASPI 495/154/459, August 8, 1931.

97. *Daily Worker*, September 14, 1931. See James D. Hunt, *Gandhi in London* (New Delhi: Promilla and Co., 1978), chapter 7, passim, esp. 207–11. See also Owen, op. cit., 185–86, 214.

98. RGASPI 495/100/717, 10, 16–19.

99. *Daily Worker*, November 30, 1931.

100. Ibid.

101. "Meerut Conspiracy Case," *New Statesman and Nation*, vol. 2, July–December 1931, 161.

102. *New Leader*, January 26, 1932.

103. Ibid., February 26, 1932; March 18, 1932. Soldiers from the 18th Royal Gharwali Rifles had refused to fire on a Muslim crowd at Peshawar in April 1930, and seventeen of them were given harsh punishments and prison sentences. The rebellion against the British in Burma met with severe repression; Paul and Gertrud Ruegg were militants imprisoned by the Chinese nationalists, their plight another Comintern cause.

104. RGASPI 542/1/44.

105. Barooah, op. cit., chapter 8, passim.

106. RGASPI 542/1/51, 3–9, 30–35, 44–45, 53, 56, 64–71, 101. Suryaningrat was the former Ki Hajar Dewantoro. On Bilé, see Aitkin, op cit.

107. "Stop Press; Police Ban Sketch," *New Red* Stage, June/July 1932, in *The Meerut Conspiracy Trial*, Working Class Movement Library, www.wcml.org.uk/internat/meerut.htm.

108. RGASPI 534/3/754.

109. *New Leader*, October 1932.

110. Lester Hutchinson, *Meerut, 1929–32* (Manchester: Manchester Meerut Defense Committee, 1932), and Hutchinson, op. cit., passim.

111. "Workers' Theatre Gives *Meerut*," *Daily Worker*, November 23, 1932. For the full text of the sketch, see www.wcm/.org.UK/www-bin/www-tails. See also Charlie Mann's "How to Produce Meerut," at the same site.

112. RGASPI, 495/154/479, December 27, 1932.

113. Ibid.

114. *Daily Worker*, December 29, 1932.

115. Spratt, *Blowing Up India*, 41–42.

116. RGASPI 495/154/479, January 5, 1933; on Smedley's journey, see Price, op. cit.

117. LSE archives, ILP 1933/2, *British in India: Meerut Conspiracy Case Specially Written by a Barrister-at-Law with an Introduction by Romain Rolland* (London: Meerut Prisoners' Release Committee, 1933), 5.

118. *Times*, July 18, 1933.

119. *Manchester Guardian*, January 17, 1933, cited in Ghosh, op. cit., 155–56.

120. *Daily Worker*, January 18, 19, 20, 23, 1933.

121. Ibid., February 18, 1933.

122. Ibid.

123. Romain Rolland, "For the Meerut Prisoners; Against Imperialist Terror," http://www.wcml.org.uk/internat/meerut.htm, first published in *L'Humanité*, March 18, 1933, as cited in David James Fisher, *Romain Rolland and the Politics of Intellectual Engagement* (Berkeley: University of California, 1988), chapter 7, fn. 34.

124. Ibid., Rolland.

125. "Cruelty in India," *New Leader*, July 28, 1933. Her letter appeared alongside a letter of M. N. Roy's sent from Allahabad Prison.

126. "Nine Freed in India as Plot Trial Ends," *New York Times*, August 4, 1933.

127. Hutchinson, *Conspiracy*, 181–82.

128. *Daily Worker*, August 14, 1931.

129. RGASPI. 534/3/895, *Ward to Patterson*, November 14, 1933.

130. Sinha, op. cit., 238.

131. Hutchinson, *Conspiracy*, 81. See Alfred, Lord Tennyson, "The Brook": "I slip, I slide, I glance . . . For men may come and men may go. But I go on forever."

132. Nehru, op. cit., 361. See James Bryce Bryce (1838–1922), *The American Commonwealth* (New York: Macmillan, 1910, 1912). John Morley (1838–1923) was a Liberal party politician and biographer, and Giuseppe Mazzini (1805–1872), the Italian independence leader.

133. Spratt, op. cit., 51.

134. Hutchinson, *Conspiracy*, 134.

135. Nehru, op. cit., 189.

136. Hutchinson, *Conspiracy*, 81.

137. Chandavarkar, op. cit., 164; 73, 164.

138. See Zachariah, op. cit., 104.

139. Sinha, op. cit., 238.

140. RGASPI 495/154/523, August 23, 1933.

141. *Round Table*, no. 349, 1933, 142.

142. Spratt, *Blowing Up India*, 50, 53, 57. See Philip Spratt, *Hindu Culture and Personality: A Psychoanalytic Study* (Bombay: Manaktalas, 1966).

143. Hutchinson, Conspiracy, 82.

144. *Daily Worker*, January 30, February 5, March 30, 1934.

145. *Bombay Chronicle* in *Daily Worker*, May 24, 1934. See also April 26, May 3 and 5, 1934.

146. *Daily Worker*, July 26, 1934.

147. Sehri Saklatvala, op. cit., 413.

148. RGASPI 495/100/938, 208. The exact provenance of the memo is unknown.

149. Ibid.

150. Terry Martin, *Affirmative Action Empire*, 178.

151. World Committee of the Victims of German Facism, op. cit.

152. See *Daily Worker*, August 9, 11, 21 August, 1934 and January 10 and 12, 1935.

153. FBP, Brockway to N., February 16, 1935.

154. See Zachariah, op. cit. 76.

155. *Daily Worker,* August 27, 1936. For a brief summary and comment on the 1935 Berlin Penal Congress, see the unsigned review of Jan Simon Van der Aa, *Proceedings of the XIth International Penal and Penitentiary Congress Held in Berlin, August, 1935* in *Journal of Criminal Law and Criminology (1931-1951)*, vol. 29, no. 6 (Mar.-Apr., 1939), 925-26.

156. Hutchinson, *Conspiracy*, 8.

157. Nayantara Sahgal, ed., *Before Freedom: Nehru's Letters to His Sister* (New Delhi: HarperCollins, 2000), March 10, 1935, 163.

158. Ibid., September, 1935, 173.

159. Ibid., 183. Rolland was an early biographer of Gandhi, who had visited him in Switzerland four years earlier, and a close associate of Tagore's. See R. A. Francis, *Romain Rolland* (Oxford: Berg, 1999), 137. Rolland had just returned from a visit to Stalin.

160. Sahgal, ed., op. cit., November 2, 1935, 187-88, 191, 194, 195; December 20, 1935, 196.

161. *Daily Worker*, January 18, 1936.

162. Ibid., January 20, 1936.

163. Ibid., December 31, 1936.

164. See, e.g., Zachariah, op. cit., 107.

165. S. H. Jhabvala, "Shapurji Saklatvala, the Trail-Blazer of Communism in India," *BLITZ newsmagazine*, August 17, 1957.

166. LHASC, CP/IND/DUTT/19/7; May 1, 1969. See Owen, op. cit., chapters 8 and 9, passim, for a full treatment of the events that occurred at the outbreak of war and immediately thereafter.

167. See, Pimlott, op. cit., chapter 8, passim; and Corthorn, op. cit., 111-62.

168. *Daily Worker,* February 22, 1937.

169. Ibid., March 26, 1937. Congress won a clear majority in Madras, Central Provinces, Bihar, Orissa, and United Provinces. It won pluralities in Bombay, Assam, and North-West Province. See the Digital South Asia Library http://dsal.uchicago.edu/reference/schwartzberg/pager.html?object=260&view=text, VII. C.5 "Major Elections, 1920-45."

170. *Daily Worker*, March 29, April 10, 1937; January 24, 1938; Subhas Chandra Bose, *The Indian Struggle, 1920-34* (London: Wishart, 1935).

171. Zachariah, op. cit., 94.

172. *Daily Worker*, June 19 and 20, 1938, 2.

173. Ibid.

174. *New Leader*, July 1, 1938.

175. *Daily Worker*, July 27, 1938.

176. Ibid.

177. Ibid.

178. Sahgal, ed., op. cit., July 22, 1938, 263; June 25, 1938, 255; July 2, 1938, 257.

179. Ibid., July 2, 1938.

180. Ibid., July 22, 1938, 263.

181. Zachariah, op. cit., cites British intelligence reports that reveal that Nehru visited the Nazi leadership and undertook political conversations with them, but states, "the sources ruled out Nehru's responding to any overtures the Nazis might have made towards him because of his honorable anti-fascist credentials," 95.

182. *Daily Worker*, October 20, 1938.

183. Ibid., December 9, 1938; February 27; March 12, 1939.

184. Saghal, ed., op. cit., September 19, 1939; See Edward Thompson, *You Have Lived through All This, an Anthology of The age* (London: Gollancz, 1939).

185. Nehru, *Autobiography*, 599, 601.

186. Saghal, ed., op. cit., 4.

CHAPTER 5. DIASPORAS: REFUGEES AND EXILES

The epigraphs are taken from: Salka Viertel, *Kindness of Strangers* (New York: Holt Reinhart, 1969) 202. Homolka was a famed Austrian actor who went to Los Angeles in 1937; Sir Oswald Mosley was the leader of the British fascists. Kortner and Hofer, actors and a married couple, returned to Austria in 1947. Viertel's husband and correspondent, Bertheld Viertel, was a stage director and author associated with Karl Kraus's Viennese satirical journal *Simplicissimus*. He went from Paris to the Little Theatre in London, and began to do English language productions in 1939. His residence permit was not renewed and he left again for Los Angeles in May of 1939, where the couple had resided intermittently since 1932.

Richard Dove, *He Was a German: A Biography of Ernst Toller* (London: Libris, 1990), 208. See also "Fenner Brockway and Ernst Toller: Document and Drama in *Berlin-letzte Ausgabe!*," in *German Life and Letters*, vol. 38, issue 1, 45, October 1984.

W. H. Auden, *Collected Poems*, edited by Edward Mendelson (New York: Vintage, 1991) 300–1; see, also, "In Memory of Ernst Toller," 249–50.

1. RGASPI 539/3/309, 23.

2. *Daily Worker*, March 24, 31, 1933; April 1, 1933; April 8, 1933. See also "Help for Victims of Fascism," *New Leader*, April 14, 1933. The *New Clarion* reviewed the O' Neill production. "He puts [in] all the pathos of the uncomprehending child, the weakness of the negro, bullied and oppressed by the white man, and the strength of man fighting for the dignity and rights of his race," March 25, 1933, LHSAC ID/CI/7/27ii.

3. RGASPI 495/30/941, 39, 45.

4. For the contemporary vernacular use of this term see, e.g., I.T.A. Wallace-Johnson, *Daily Worker*, March 22, 1937.

5. Eva Mitchell, "Introduction," *Archives of the Central British Fund for World Jewish Relief, 1933–60* (1989), 2, 12.

6. Louise London, *Whitehall and the Jews: 1933–48* (Cambridge, UK: Cambridge University Press 2000), 272.

7. Ibid., 131; Marion Berghahn, *Continental Britons: German-Jewish Refugees from Nazi Germany* (Oxford, UK: Oxford University Press, 1988), 75.

8. Mitchell, op. cit., 2.

9. Gerhard Hirschfeld, ed., op. cit., 2.

10. Berghahn, op. cit., 110.

11. Hirschfeld, ed., op. cit., 2.

12. Berghahn, op. cit., 76.

13. Ibid., 72.

14. RGASPI 495/30/941, 36.

15. Hull University Archives, Brynnor Jones Library, The Papers of Reginald Francis Orlando Bridgeman, *British LAI report*, 1937, DBN 25/21A. See also "Our View of It," and I. Itz'haki, "Why British Imperialism Doesn't Want More Jews in Palestine," *New Leader,* July 21, 1939.

16. Vernon Bartlett, *Nazi Germany Explained* (London: Gollancz, 1933), 112.

17. Anthony Glees, "The German Political Exile in London" in Hirschfeld, ed., op. cit., 83; See Patrik von zur Mühlen, "Exile and Resistance," in W. Benz and W. Pehle, eds., *Encyclopedia of German Resistance to the Nazi Movement* (New York: Continuum, 1997), passim. Louise London discusses the exclusion of political militants at the British Channel passport offices, a policy deriving from practices of the 1920s (London, op. cit., 20). Tory MP Alfred Duff Cooper stated that communists had "been weeded out [from amongst the] refugees," London, 41.

18. Berghahn, op. cit., 122.

19. Vicki Caron, *Uneasy Asylum: France and the Jewish Refugee Crisis, 1933–1942* (Stanford: Stanford University Press, 1999), 2.

20. See Jean Lacouture, *Léon Blum* (New York: Holmes and Meier, 1982), 206–207.

21. Von zur Mühlen, op. cit., 91.

22. See Anson Rabinbach, "Staging Antifascism: The Brown Book of the Reichstag Fire and Hitler Terror," *New German Critique, 193*, vol. 35, no. 1, Spring 2008, 97–126, passim. Rabinbach is completing *Staging Anti-Fascism, 1933–90* on the role of Münzenberg, Otto Katz, Koestler, and others, in the writing and distribution of the *Brown Book*, and the orchestrating of the mock trial. On the historiographical disputes concerning the burning of the Reichstag, see Fritz Tobias, *Der Reichstagsbrand: Legende und Wirklichkeit* (Rastatt: G. Grot'sche Verlagbuchhandlung, 1962), 97. On Münzenberg in Paris, the *Brown Book*, and related events, see Arthur Koestler, *The Invisible Writing* (London: Hutchinson, 1954, 1969), 244, and chapter 18, passim.

23. John P. Fox, "Nazi Germany and German Immigration to Great Britain," in Hirschfeld, op. cit., 36–37.

24. Ibid., 41–42; 48. Feuchtwanger was a German-Jewish novelist and playwright (not the biblical scholar Ludwig Feuchtwanger).

25. See Babette Gross, *Willi Münzenberg, a Political Biography* (East Lansing: Michigan State University Press, 1974), passim. Gross joined the KPD in 1920. Stasi and Comintern papers, and the French police files, were unavailable or unknown to Gross.

26. See McMeekin, op. cit., part 3, passim, which relies upon Gross for its narrative of this period of Münzenberg's life.

27. Caron, op. cit., 9. On the treatment of the non-European immigrant population, see Rosenberg, op. cit. passim.

28. Caron, 20. The Nazi Ministry of the Interior contacted the French Foreign Office regarding the presence in France of socialist Rudolf Breitscheid and Münzenberg, fn. 46.

29. Gross, op. cit., 239–326, passim; McMeekin, op. cit., chapters 15, 16.

30. World Committee for the Victims of German Fascism, op. cit.

31. LHSAC, LP/ID/CI/26/7i–iii. Wilkinson was reelected to Parliament in 1935, representing Jarrow. See Ellen Wilkinson, *The Terror in Germany* (London: British Committee for the Relief of the Victims of German Fascism, n.d.); Ellen Wilkinson and Edward Conze, *Why Fascism* (London: Selwyn and Blount, 1934); and Betty D. Vernon, *Ellen Wilkinson, 1891–1947* (London: Croom Helm, 1982), 158–83.

32. *Daily Worker*, June 30, 1933. See also Koestler, op. cit., 283, 285.

33. LHSAC, LP/ID/CI/26/14i–ii, *Adler to Gillies*, July 3, 1933. See also Koestler, op. cit., 328–32.

34. Ellen Wilkinson, *Feed the Children: What Is Being Done to Relieve the Victims of the Fascist Regime* (London: British Section, *International Committee for the Relief of the Victims of German Fascism,* n.d.). See also Vernon, op. cit., 158–59.

35. On Jews, Jewishness and British communism, see Morgan et al., eds., op. cit., 185–87, 189, 191, 192, 195–96.

36. LHSAC, LP/ID/CI/12/12, *Gillies to Morrison*, June 20, 1934. He told Morrison that £1,000 had been sent to Germany for communist use.

37. LSE archives, ILP, 9/60, February 23, 1933, "Basis for Common Agreement," London District Committee, CPGB, and London Divisional Council, ILP, 2.

38. LHSAC, LP/ID/CI/26/16i. Elmer Rice's *Judgement Day: A Melodrama in Three Acts* (New York: Coward-McCann, 1934) took the Reichstag Fire Trial as its inspiration.

39. RGASPI 495/30/937.

40. On early "unity" attempts involving the Socialist League of which Wilkinson was a member, and the Labor party; see, esp., Corthorn, op. cit., chapters 1–2.

41. Katz was involved with London German exiles before 1933. See Viertel, op. cit., *B. Viertel to S. Viertel*, October 7, 1932. "Otto Katz (Czech Communist) has arrived in Berlin from Moscow." At this early point, Katz tried to persuade Viertel and his wife to move to Moscow, 181. See Rabinbach, op. cit., 106, 114–15 on Katz; 114–20 on the London mock trial; and 121–26 on the Leipzig trial. Koestler attributes the mock trial idea to Münzenberg, identifying Katz as the chief writer of the *Brown Book*. See Koestler, op. cit., 244, and on Katz, 255–57, 399, 406–407, 446, 450, 493–94.

42. LHSAC CP/IND/MONT/2/5, Ivor Montagu, *Memories of the Counter-Trial* 1965, 9, 10.

43. Ibid., 3–4. Morgan et al., eds., op. cit., calls Montagu the "most plutocratic and least self-conscious" of British communists, 159, 8. For Katz's Paris negotiations, and the role of the Nazi legal defense, see Rabinbach, op. cit., 116–17. See also "Reichstag Prisoner's Defense," *Daily Worker,* September 12, 1934.

44. Pritt took up commercial law before the Great War, working in Berlin. His allegiances shifted from Tory to Liberal after the war, and in 1935 he was elected Labour

MP for Hammersmith North. See D. N. Pritt, vol. 1, op. cit. 36, 42–80, passim; "Reichstag Fire Inquiry Begun," *Daily Worker*, September 15, 1933. See Bartlett, op. cit., 160; Eadon and Renton, op. cit., 65.

45. Pritt, op. cit., 56.

46. See Hooker, op. cit., on Pritt's IASB involvement, 47–48. See "Stars to Aid Scottsboro Boys," *Chicago Defender*, February 10, 1934, 13; Arthur Garfield Hays, *City Lawyer* (New York: Simon and Schuster, 1942), 339, 344, chapter 13, passim; and Rabinbach, op. cit., 114, 117.

47. E. T. Williams and Helen M. Palmer, eds., *The Dictionary of National Biography, 1951–60*, 692, citing D. N. Pritt, op. cit., part 3, *The Defense Accuses* (London: Lawrence and Wishart, 1966).

48. Montagu, op. cit., 6; see World Committee for the Victims of German Fascism, *The Reichstag Fire Trial. The Second Brown Book of the Hitler Terror* (London: John Lane, 1934).

49. LHSAC, LP/ID/CI/12/13, *Gillies to Morrison*; Garfield Hays, 349.

50. Montagu, op. cit., 10–12.

51. *The Burning of the Reichstag* (London: *Relief Committee for the Victims of German Fascism*, 1933), 2–3; Rabinbach, op. cit., 97–101, 119–26.

52. Montagu, op. cit., 16, LHSAC LP/ID/CI/9/31; Gillies mentioned that Leonard Woolf and Vera Brittain were bound up in the mock trial defense, LP/ID/CI/9/29. On the trial, see Koestler, op. cit., 237–42, 249, 258–59, 242–43.

53. *Daily Worker*, June 22, 1933, 1; Montagu, op. cit., 15.

54. RGASPI 539/4/7, January 3, 1934; "London ILP and Reichstag Trial," *Daily Worker*, September 19, 1934. See also "Foreign Counsel for Leipzig," on a petition signed by leading European socialists, *Daily Worker*, September 20, 1933.

55. RGASPI 495/30/997, 103; 495/30/999, 8.

56. RGASPI 539/3/309, 48–52.

57. RP XIV 2.6 (1–10), *Pethick-Lawrence to Rathbone*, March 27, 1934. Her name does not appear on a list of vice presidents, LHSAC LP/ID/CI/12/13. On Rathbone's refugee work, see Pedersen, op. cit., part 4, passim, which does not mention the Scottsboro Defense Committee, the Relief Committee, or the Dimitroff Committee.

58. McMeekin, op. cit., 269. See also Koestler, op. cit., 242–43.

59. See Rabinbach, op. cit., 106.

60. RSGAPI, 495/100/938, 208.

61. Lacouture, op. cit., 219.

62. *Telegraph*, October, 1933, cited in Gross, op. cit., 253.

63. Andrew Hewitt, *Political Inversions: Homosexuality, Fascism, and the Modernist Imaginary* (Stanford: Stanford University Press, 1966), 1, cites Klaus Mann, "Homosexuality and Fascism," in *Die neue Weltbühne*, 1934, 130–37. See Rabinbach, op. cit., 112–13, for a discussion of these sources. On the *Brown Book*, see McMeekin, op. cit., 265–66.

64. *Negro Worker*, vol. 3, #2, April–May 1933, 7; "Who Fired the Reichstag?" *New Leader*, September 15, 1933.

65. Rabinbach, "The Culture of Antifascism," unpublished manuscript, Princeton University, 20.

66. "On Fascist Reaction and Increasing White Terror" (*International Labour Defense*: June, 1933), 5–6, LHSAC CP/IND/MONT/4/11, 7, 9.

67. LHSAC, LP/ID/CI/7/36, *Imprecor*, January 30, 1934.

68. Archives of the Central British Fund World Jewish Relief, 1933–60, reel 4, file 19, "International Conference of Relief of German Jewry," London, October 20–November 1, 1933, "Attending Organizations."

69. LSE archives, ILP 3/24, NAC Minutes, February 10–11, 1934, 1; Corthorn, op. cit., 33–35.

70. RGASPI, 539/4/7, June 29 and July 9, 1934.

71. See "Hitler debacle seen by ex-Reich leaders," *New York Times*, July 8, 1934; Gross, op. cit., 270–71; "Red Leader Sees German Revolt," *New York Times*, July 7, 1934; "Radical Gain Here Forecast in Reich," *New York Times*, August 23, 1934; "Communists Here Denounce Hitler," *New York Times*, July 28, 1934. Bevan attended an anti-Nazi dinner with former German justice Kurt Rosenfeld, German writer Annabel Williams-Ellis, and others. See "Anti-Nazi Dinner Today," *New York Times*, June 28, 1934.

72. RGASPI 539/4/7, August 23, 1934, 22.

73. Ibid. See also Koestler, op. cit., 328–32.

74. RGASPI 539/4/7. See also ibid., October 11, 1934.

75. For biographical and political information on exiles and refugees, see Werner Röder, et al., *International Biographical Dictionary of Central European Emigrés, 1933–45*, vols. 1–3 (New York: K. G. Sauer, 1999); and *Displaced German Scholars: A Guide to Academics in Peril in Nazi Germany during the 1930s* (San Bernardino, CA: Borgo Press, 1933).

76. LHSAC, LP/ID/CI/29.14i, *Völkischer Beobachter*, September 22, 1934.

77. Fox, "Nazi Germany . . . " in Hirschfeld, ed., op. cit., 51, 53, 50. A former social-democratic *Vörwarts* editor was a Nazi informer among the German exiles in London. In September 1934, pacifist documents were sent to the Reich's Ministry of the Interior and the Gestapo, fns. 70, 71. See James J. and Patience P. Barnes, *The Life of Hans Wosemann, 1895–1971* (Westport: Praeger, 2001), and Charmain Brinson, "The Gestapo and the German Political Exiles in Britain during the 1930s: The Case of Hans Wosemann and Others," *German Life and Letters*, 1998, 51(1), 43–64 (22).

78. Glees in Hirschfeld, op. cit. Viktor Schiff, Heinrich Fraenkel, Adele Schreiber-Krieger, Otto Lehman-Russbuldt, Leopold Ullstein, and Irmgard Litten were all prepared to work with the KPD in exile; the latter included Hans Fladung, Hugo Gräff, Emmy Koenen, and Artur Becker. Walter Loeb and Curt Geyer joined the Labour party, 92, 93.

79. Heinrich Fraenkel originally worked for the Ullstein press. Key exile activists included Willi Eichler, Erwin Schoettle, Richard Löwenthal, Susanne Miller, Erich Brost, and E. F. Schumacher, ibid., 90.

80. Lothar Kettenacker, "The Influence of German Refugees on British War Aims," in Hirschfeld, ed., op. cit., 19.

81. Fox, "Nazi Germany . . . " in Hirschfeld, op. cit., 52. See Morgan et al., eds., op. cit., for an account of Toller speaking in halting English at a 1937 public meeting, 106–107.

82. *AN* F7 15123 Alf Evans to *Die Zukunft*, July 2, 1939.

83. Berghahn, op. cit., 150.

84. See Lisa Appignanesi, *The Cabaret* (New Haven: Yale University Press, 2004). Heartfield came to London in 1938 from Czechoslovakia, but his brother's work permit application was denied, so they moved on to the United States in 1939.

85. Hirschfeld, ed., op. cit., 3.

86. Ibid., Kettenacker, "The Influence of German Refugees," 4.

87. Hirschfeld, ibid., 5.

88. Berghahn, op. cit.,122. Social thinker Franz Neumann was the former SPD leader from Upper Silesia and the Berlin attorney for the building laborers' union. He worked with Max Horkheimer at the New School in New York from 1936.

89. Gustav Regler, *The Owl of Minerva* (New York: Farrar, Strauss, 1959).; Koestler, op. cit., 285, 299.

90. Fox, "Nazi Germany . . . " in Hirschfeld, ed., op. cit., 52, 79. Niall Ferguson mistakenly refers to Nancy Cunard as among the family hosts of Ribbentrop. See Ferguson, *War of the World*, 339.

91. Berghahn, op. cit., 150.

92. Mrs. Roden Buxton and a Friends delegation visited Foreign Secretary John Simon to discuss Norwegian asylum proposals. See A. J. Sherman, op. cit., 54. Antislavery and League of Nations advocates Lord Robert Cecil and Gilbert Murray visited Simon, 54, fn. 88. For Noel-Baker's speech, see Hansard, *House of Commons*, 341/1428–1440, November 21, 1938.

93. Berghahn, op. cit.,155. Historian Eric Hobsbawm describes his 1930s youth as an émigré communist, and central-European Jew, who was also a British subject (and not a refugee). His family's secular world and communist activity rarely encountered organized Jewry. Family gatherings and brushes with older, East End Jewish communists were his limited, common Jewish experiences. See E. J. Hobsbawm, op. cit., 117.

94. LHSAC, CP/IND/MONT/8/9, *Annual Report of the Society for Cultural Relations with the USSR.* Isobel Brown was with her at her death. Rabbi Kokotek of the liberal Jewish synagogue in St. John's Wood Road officiated at the funeral.

95. LHSAC, WG/REF/1/67, "Labour Party memo on refugees from Germany and Austria," December, 1938.

96. LHSAC, WG/REF/43iiii.

97. LHSAC, WG/REF/1/67, "Labour Party memo on refugees from Germany and Austria," December, 1938.

98. See, e.g., *Gillies to Fry*, LHSAC, WG/REF/1i.

99. *Gillies to Middleton*, January 9, 1936, LHSAC, LP/ID/CI/72/2iii.

100. Among the most compelling accounts for English language readers are Caron, op. cit.; Julian Jackson, *The Popular Front in France: Defending Democracy, 1934–38* (Cambridge, UK: Cambridge University Press, 1988); Kevin McDermott and Jeremy Agnew, op. cit.; and, Eric Weitz, op. cit.

101. See, Jackson, op. cit., on the Amsterdam conference, and the Salle Pleyel movement, 25–27.

102. McMeekin, op. cit., chapter 15, passim.

103. Jackson, op. cit., 32; Agnew and McDermott, op. cit., 123–25; 127.

104. Jackson, op. cit., 35.

105. Gross, op. cit., 263; McMeekin, op. cit., 273; Koestler, op. cit., 328–32.

106. McMeekin, op. cit., 292.

107. See Koestler, op. cit, 314–15.

108. LHSAC LP/ID/CI/26/10/iii.

109. RP XIV 2.6 (1–16).

110. LSE archives ILP 3/25 *A Survey of the Party Position*, "The Strength of the Party," 1–12; December 11–12, 1937, 3, *Draft Resolutions*; ILP8/1936/1–12, *Unity Campaign of 1937*. For a study of the failure and import of the unity campaigns, see Corthorn, op. cit., Chapters 5–7.

111. LSE, ILP December 11–12, 1937, 3.

112. The POUM was the anti-Stalinist Republican left party and paramilitary formation in Spain.

113. Gross, op. cit., 246–50; McMeekin, op. cit., 263, 266, 277, 287.

114. Caron, op. cit., 128.

115. See, *AN*, F7 15131 #1, "International Antifascist *Archiv und Deutsches Freiheits bibliotek*," including Heinrich Mann; Koestler, op. cit., 19, 56–57, 228; chapter 18, passim, 283, 285, 299, 308.

116. Jackson, op. cit., 32. Gross, op. cit., 283; McMeekin, op. cit., 280–83, 285, 289.

117. von zur Mühlen, op. cit., 138.

118. See Margarete Buber-Neumann, *Under Two Dictators* (New York: Dodd, Mead, 1950), ix–xiii. Buber-Neumann's first husband was the son of theologian Martin Buber.

119. For versions of this trip, see Gross, op. cit., 290, and McMeekin, op. cit., 286. McMeekin's only reference for his contention that this letter was written is Gross, yet he disputes her story, which does not mention a denunciation of Zinoviev. This author gives McMeekin the benefit of the doubt.

120. Jackson, op. cit., 32.

121. Von zur Mühlen, op. cit., 96.

122. See, *AN* F7 15132, Folder 4, on the German Liberty party whose newsletter included an essay by Scottsboro advocate Alfons Goldschmidt, "A Scientist Looks at Germany." See Gross, op. cit., 300, and McMeekin, op. cit., 290–91. *Die Zukunft* announced Goldschmidt's death in Mexico; see "Death of Goldschmidt," January 19, 1940. Münzenberg failed to keep Mann in his immediate entourage after his expulsion from the Comintern, and from 1937 Mann instead worked with Schwarzchild on the Bund Free Press.

123. McMeekin, op. cit., 294.

124. *Posledniy a Novosti*, July 26, 1937, as cited in R. N. Carew-Hunt, "Willi Münzenberg" in D. Footman, ed., *St. Anthony's Papers*, no. 9 (London: Chatto and Windus, 1960), 83, 85. Carew-Hunt cites a public statement that appeared in *Deutsche Volkszeitung*. See also Gross, op. cit., 300–10.

125. Mark Levene, *Arthur Koestler* (New York: F. Ungar, 1984) 16; Arthur Koestler, *Spanish Testament*, with an introduction by the Duchess of Atholl (London: Gollancz, 1937); George Orwell, *Homage to Catalonia* (London: Secker and Warburg, 1938).

126. Von zur Mühlen, op. cit., 96.

127. Viertel, op. cit., 225, *Salka Viertel to Berthold Viertel*. Camil and Irma Hoffman died in Theriensenstadt.

128. London, op cit., 45.

129. LHSAC, WG/REF/1/67, 11.

130. Sherman, op. cit., 106, citing FO 371/22534 w12288/104/98, June 18, 1938, 135, 109.

131. London, op. cit., 186.

132. Sherman, op. cit., 189.

133. See Pedersen, *Eleanor Rathbone*, op. cit., chapters 14, 15, passim.

134. RP XIV 2.6 (1–16), *Times*, April 11, 1933.

135. RP XIV 2.6 (1–16), *Rathbone to Flenely*, June 3, 1933.

136. RP XIV 3.3 (1–40). "Combined English Universities Parliamentary Elections, 1935."

137. London, op. cit., 208; Eleanor Rathbone, "Rescue the Perishing" (London: National Committee for Rescue From Nazi Terror, 1943).

138. RP XIV.3.92–108, "For the Fourteens," BBC Home Service for Schools.

139. Pedersen, *Eleanor Rathbone*, 430, fn. 40. Pedersen questions the significance and implication of Koestler's emphasis upon the National Joint Committee's ties to the unnamed "Comintern propaganda chief for Western Europe, based in Paris," though Koestler was clearly and accurately referring to Willi Münzenberg. Koestler, *Invisible Writing*, 256, 294–95.

140. RP XIV.3.35–58, May 7, 1937, *National Joint Committee for Spanish Relief.*

141. London, op. cit., 159.

142. RP XIV 2.6.1–16, *British Non-Sectarian Anti-Nazi Council*; RP XIV.3.3 (1–40), *Bonham Carter to Rathbone*, February 9, 1945. On the Focus Group, see Roy Jenkins, *Churchill* (London: MacMillan, 2001) 493–97, 541–42; Bonham Carter, op. cit., 187–98.

143. Parker, op. cit., 171.

144. See RP XIV.3.35–58, International Peace Council Conference, Caxton Hall, October 22, 1937.

145. Ibid., RP XIV.3.3 (1–40), *Combined English Universities Parliamentary Elections, 1935.*

146. Hansard, *House of Commons*, vol. 340/369–70, November 3, 1938. Her terms were "Sudeten-German and German refugees of anti-Nazi opinions now in Czechoslovakia" (369). See also, 340/34–5, November 1, 1938.

147. See, Pedersen, *Eleanor Rathbone*, chapters 15, 16, passim; 304. See Hansard, *House of Commons*, vol. 336/380 (9), May 18, 1938, for Rathbone's insistence that the government form a "definite British policy toward refugees." She pressed for an international conference on "political refugees" (336:834/22) and for the formation of a parliamentary committee (336:834/47); queried work permit and cost issues (336:835/26); and pressed for a Dominion committee (336:836/48), May 23, 1938. Chamberlain told her that her demand for a revolving loan six months' later was "premature" (336:1317/30) November 21, 1938.

148. London, op. cit., 281; see 276–81, passim; 156, 159. William Gillies objected to cooperation with Nazi agents and took exception to British assistance to Czech Jews, 156.

149. Hansard, *House of Commons*, vol. 341/1428, 1432–33, November 21, 1938.

150. Ibid., vol. 341/1442, 1445, 1449, 1451, 1452, 1459, 1461, 1314.

151. Sherman, op. cit., 216, 232, fn.

152. London, op. cit., 165–66, cites *Minutes, Visa Committee*, June 23, 1939, PRO HO 294/52.

153. See, e.g., Manès Sperber, *Until My Eyes Are Closed with Shards* (New York: Holmes and Meier, 1994) 136–37; 144–45.

154. *AN* F7 15123 *Münzenberg to Guy Menant*, November 9, 1938.

155. McMeekin, op. cit., 296–97. McMeekin does not indicate any use of those French police files in the *Archives Nationales* F7 that specifically contain the materials and

apparatus of *Die Zukunft*, its correspondents, editors, and subscribers. Koestler also identifies writer Paul Sering (aka Richard Lowenthal) and Julius Steinberg as *Die Zukunft* founders; Koestler, *The Invisible Writing,* 454, and see chapter 38, passim.

156. *Die Zukunft*, July 28, 1939.

157. David Cesarani, *Arthur Koestler: The Homeless Mind* (New York: Free Press, 1999) cites the recollections of Ludwig Marcuse, 151.

158. Sperber, op. cit., 136–37.

159. Cesarani, op. cit.,152.

160. See, for example, *AN* F7/15124 *Koestler to Atholl*, October 11, 1938, and *Atholl to Koestler*, October 31, 1938, which list a host of individuals involved with *Die Zukunft* in Britain; on Sigmund Freud's presence, see Koestler, *The Invisible Writing*, 497.

161. Wickham Steed, "The True Germany: Message to *Zukunft*," *Die Zukunft*, October 12, 1938. (All titles and quotations appear in translation from the German).

162. Ibid., Duff Cooper, "The English People Feel."

163. Harold Nicolson, "English Temperament and German Character," *Die Zukunft*, November 25, 1938; Arthur Koestler, "German Temperament and English Character," *Die Zukunft*, November 25, 1938; Herbert Morrison, "An Open Letter to the German People," *Die Zukunft* December 2, 1938. Morrison's involvement is especially striking in light of his close ties to Gillies and to Labour's past surveillance of Münzenberg.

164. Duff Cooper, op. cit.

165. Max Beer, "Foreign Policy Review," *Die Zukunft,* October 12, 1938.

166. Kingsley Martin, "The True Danger," *Die Zukunft*, October 28, 1938.

167. Lord Robert Cecil, "The Foundations of the English Constitution"; Archibald Sinclair, "We English Liberals," *Die Zukunft*, November 25, 1938.

168. Jawaharlal Nehru, "India Speaks to the German People," *Die Zukunft*, November 4, 1938. Not all issues of the journal have been recovered. The sole English-language issue, planned and edited by Koestler, does not appear in the facsimile edition and this author has found no copy of it.

169. Klaus Mann, *Mephisto* (New York: Penguin, 1983).

170. *AN* F7 15123 *George to Münzenberg*, May 3, 1940. George edited *Aufbau*, the German-language New York weekly that focused on issues of Americanization and the immigrants. See H. O. Simon, "What Is South Africa's Position?" and "Hitler in South Africa," *Die Zukunft*, June 3, 1939; Vernon Bartlett, "America and Russia Must Be Won," *Die Zukunft*, June 9, 1939.

171. *Die Zukunft*, July 28, 1939.

172. Werner Röder et al., *International Biographical Dictionary* op. cit.

173. Williams and Palmer, eds., *Dictionary of National Biography, 1951–60,* "Alfred Duff Cooper," 250.

174. F7 15123, *Samuel to Koestler*, November 2, 1938; November 5, 1938, enclosure, *News and Reviews*, 3, November 15, 1938.

175. F7 15123, *Sinclair to Münzenberg*, November 15, 1938, states with reference to Munich, that it is "unwise for a newspaper printed by foreigners in the English language and imported into England to take such a sharp and aggressive line. *Quod licet jovi . . .* (*What is permitted Jupiter is not permitted a cow*), though he still thought it a good idea to quote from Neville Chamberlain's speech. He may have referred to the lost, sole English-language issue of *Die Zukunft*.

176. LHSAC, WG/REF/43iii, *Gillies to Adler*, LSI, December 1938.

177. Graf was a writer, a Catholic of communist background who had worked in both Vienna and the Soviet Union, and a supporter of the 1934 Saar proclamation. He emigrated to the United States in 1938, where he died in 1967. Anders was a Jewish writer and the former spouse of Hannah Arendt; both were students of Edmund Husserl and Martin Heidegger before the war. He went to Paris in 1933 and to New York from 1939 to 1942, finally settling in Los Angeles.

178. See Atina Grossmann, *Reforming Sex: The German Movement for Birth Control and Abortion Reform, 1920–1950* (New York: Oxford University Press, 1995).

179. See Claire Nelson and Walter Trier, *The Jolly Picnic: Ten Little Negroes, A New Version* (London: Sylvan Prese, 1944).

180. Dove, op. cit., 210.

181. See Ernst Toller, *Which World, Which Way?: Travel Pictures from America and Russia* (English version by Herman Ould) (London: Sampson, Low, Marston, 1931), for his portrayal of lynch-law cases, and the Tom Mooney case.

182. Sperber, op. cit., 144.

183. Gross, op. cit., 314–16. See AN F7 15123 *Koestler to Anglo-German publisher*, November 11, 1938, which mentions Robert Cecil, Archibald Sinclair, Harold Nicolson, Sigmund Freud, and Mann.

184. *AN* F7 15123 *Münzenberg to Giroudoux*, January 17, 1939.

185. Gross, op. cit., 317.

186. *AN* F7 15125, Folder 1d, contains photos that readers sent from Gurs, in which they are seen holding up *Die Zukunft* before the camera. One of these appears in this text, figure 5.5.

187. AN F7 15132, 1a *Die Zukunft to Isabelle* [*sic*] *Brown*, March 15, 1939: "The underground militants of our Party remember thankfully the outstanding role played by the Communist Party of Great Britain." Here, Münzenberg referred to the CPGB antifascist work, part of his past activist transatlantic network.

188. *AN* F7 15124, May 3, 1939, *Gardner Jackson to Münzenberg*; *Münzenberg to Jackson*, June 10, 1939, contains notice of a publication by the fascist Union Franco-Allemand. Secretary Harold Ickes placed a note of greeting on Jackson's letter. (See, also, F/7/15124, January 13, 1939, *Gardner Jackson to Münzenberg*: "swell job," and a statement that the president was adopting such positions; *Sumner Welles to Gardner Jackson, for Louis Gibarti*, January 24, 1939, and *Ickes to Gibarti*). Louis Gibarti had associations with Jackson during the Sacco and Vanzetti campaign. *Die Zukunft* planned an American issue to include Theodore Dreiser, Fiorello La Guardia, Arthur Garfield Hays, and John L. Lewis. Münzenberg saw La Guardia and Hays on his trip to the USA in 1934.

189. *AN* F7 15131 (8g).

190. *AN* F7 15127, 1d; June 9, 1939. *Jean Giraudoux to M. Pezet*, vice president of the *Commission Affaires Étrangères*, October 27, 1939, describes Münzenberg's operation:

> The contacts between the exiled democrats from Central Europe and the political and intellectual circles of the Western powers were established in October 1938, and based on the most extensive collaboration between the different political tendencies (Catholic, Socialist or Liberal) ... M. having become a ferocious adversary of the Stalinist regime and the Communist Internationale.

The file mentions Germaine Paz for the "International Bureau of the right of asylum and aid to political refugees," and in the UK—Norman Angell, Stafford Cripps, Margaret Lansbury, and Gilbert Murray.

191. AN F7 15123 *Gibarti to Barnes*, June 10, 1939; *Hill to Gibarti*, from Chartwell, June 16, 1939; *Gibarti to Churchill*, August 3, 1939, in which Churchill is congratulated on his Commons speech the previous day. On Gibarti's subsequent "defection" to the American FBI, see Price, op. cit., 7-8; 419-20, fns. 26-28 (483). Gibarti unmasked the 1930s European Comintern networks in FBI interviews conducted in 1951.

192. *Die Zukunft*; Gross, op. cit., 319.

193. Gross, op. cit., 321, cites *Die Welt*, February 6, 1940.

194. *AN* F7/15124; *Münzenberg to Monsieur le Ministre*, September 21, 1939, tells of communist strength in the preceding days of the underground movement. He said he had recruited militants to a "united socialist formation." At Gurs, the former Republican recruits to Spain, included nine hundred KPD Germans who had volunteered for Spain, two hundred of whom went over to Münzenberg before the Hitler/Stalin pact, and another four hundred who did so afterward. He bemoans the French police for not distinguishing among the politics of exiles and says that he was working with the SPD executive. He sent the letter with Gross, asking for a day upon which she might return to pick up a reply. This may well have been written to M. Stefan Osusky, Minister of Czechoslovakia at Paris, or Gaston Palewski, *Chef de Cabinet du Ministre des Finances*. (See, also, *AN* F7 15123, *Internees at Gurs to Münzenberg*, December 26, 1939.)

195. F7 15124, *Münzenberg to Berthoin*, October 6, 1939; see, especially, *Münzenberg to Blum*, October 13, 1939.

196. Ibid., *Münzenberg to Churchill*, October 12, 1939.

197. *AN* F715125 B folder, *Münzenberg and Oettinghaus to Black*. See also *Koch et al. to Münzenberg*, December 26, 1939, signed by several dozen internees of Gurs. For a communist report on poor conditions in the camps, see "Camp Horrors Worse than War," *Daily Worker*, February 21, 1939, 4.

198. Denis Sefton Delmer, born in Berlin of Australian parents, was the *Daily Express* correspondent in Berlin 1928-33. He was friendly with Ernst Röhm, and the first reporter to interview Hitler in the Brown House in Munich; he walked through the Reichstag with him at the time of the fire of 1933. The Foreign Office suspected Delmer of being a German agent, but he worked for the FO in the war. He reported from Paris and from Spain in 1936, then Poland, and again from Paris in 1940. See *Delmer to Zukunft, Zukunft to Delmer*, and *Weimer Germany: Democracy on Trial* (London and New York: Macdonald American Heritage), 1972, 117-18: "But Hitler just said, 'Evening, Delmer,' and that was my ticket of admission," 118.

CHAPTER 6. A THIEVES' KITCHEN: 1938-39

The epigraph is taken from: George Padmore "Abyssinia Betrayed by the League of Nations," *The Crisis*, June 1937, 168, citing V.I. Lenin's use of "thieves kitchen" to describe the League of Nations. For one English translation of Lenin's description of the League as "an alliance of robbers . . . ," see, V. I. Lenin, *Collected Works*, vol. 31, op. cit., 323.

George Padmore, "A Negro Looks at British Imperialism," *The Crisis*, December 1938, 396-97.

Mass Observation Archive (MO), University of Sussex, *1939 Race Directive*, 1362.

1. "Hitler Will Treat Jews Like Blacks: Adopts South African Methods to Deal with Problem," *Chicago Defender*, November 13, 1937, 24.

2. George Padmore, *Africa and World Peace* (London: 1937), 270. As early as 1930, William Wilson, an activist associate of Padmore's, released a memo on behalf of the International Conference of Negro Workers in which he referred to the "1924 holocaust fought for democracy." January 9, 1930. RGASPI 495/155/86, 27.

3. See Von Eschen, op. cit., 11–17.

4. See LSE archives, Low Collection, "Low & Terry" (David Low and H. Thorogood), "The Patriots," July 24, 1936, *Evening Standard*, 1936, in which the pro-France "Rebel Leader" says, "What a pity—if only we had enough Moors and riff-raff to wipe out the Spanish people, we could save Spain." See George Padmore, "Hitler, Mussolini in Africa," *The Crisis*, September 1957, on the use of Moorish troops, and "How Britons Beat Moors," *Daily Worker*, January 18, 1937.

5. The Germans surrendered Tanganyika, South-West Africa, Togoland, and the Cameroons at Versailles. South-West Africa became a South African mandate. Tanganyika and part of Togo went to Britain with part of the Cameroons going to Britain and "Cameroun" to France, though a German administrative presence remained in one region. Martin Gilbert and Richard Gott, *The Appeasers* (London: Phoenix, 2000), reports that two-thirds of *Daily Mail* readers supported the return of colonies to Germany, 94. See Peter J. Beck, "Searching for Peace in Munich Not Geneva: The British Government, the League of Nations, and the Sudetenland Question," in Igor Lukes and Erik Goldstein, eds., *The Munich Crisis, 1938: Prelude to World War II* (London and Portland, OR: Frank Cass, 1999), 279, on Neville Chamberlain taking the colonial question much more seriously than did the Germans.

6. Gilbert and Gott, op. cit., 91.

7. Adolf Hitler, *Mein Kampf*, trans. Ralph Mannheim (Burton: Houghton Mifflin, 1943), Woodruff D. Smith, *The Ideological Origins of Nazi Imperialism* (New York: Oxford, 1986) 235, 241, 250. In its third stage lay the acquisition of Mittelafrika and parts of South America, 252.

8. George Padmore, "Hitler, Mussolini and Africa," *The Crisis*, September, 1937, 274. Padmore refers to the Baltic German and Nazi theorist Alfred Rosenberg's expansionist ambitions.

9. Nehru, "India Speaks of the German People."

10. Adolf Hitler, op. cit., 138–40, 645.

11. Gilbert and Gott, op. cit., 94. John Lukacs, *Five Days in London May 1940* (New Haven: Yale University Press, 1999), quotes Churchill's remarks on May 17, 1940, "If Herr Hitler was prepared to make sense on the terms of the restoration of the German colonies and the overlordship of Central Europe, that was one thing. But it was quite unlikely that he would make any such offer," 151. See also chapter 5, passim.

12. Gibert and Gott, op. cit., 103, See, also, 99–107; 105; *Hansard*, House of Commons, vol. 341, 849/45, November 16, 1938.

13. RP XIV.3.3 (1–40), "Combined English Universities, Parliamentary Elections, 1935," October 29, 1935.

14. RP XIV.3.35–58, International Peace Campaign Conference, Caxton Hall, October 22, 1937.

15. University of Sussex archives, Kingsley Martin papers, Box 28/3, "On Abyssinia," 27. See also Kingsley Martin, "The Actual Risk to One's Self," *Die Zukunft*, November 4, 1938. Martin was a friend of Ernst Toller. See Dove, op. cit., 211.

16. FCB, 2/3, item 34. Leonard Barnes, "The Colonial Question," *International Affairs*, 1938, 7.

17. J. F. Horrabin, *Manchester Guardian*, October 24, 2938.

18. See Owen, op. cit. chapters 8 and 9, passim.

19. Gilbert and Gott, op. cit., 97. See Leopold C.M.S. Amery, *The German Colonial Claim* (London and Edinburgh: W. R. Chambers, 1939). Amery opposed the German ambition: "the Nazi centers are obsessed by the dream of a Colonial empire to be won at our expense and will not lightly abandon it," 186.

20. Amery, ibid., 189, and chapter 10, passim.

21. Gilbert and Gott, op. cit., 99.

22. RP XIV.3, 35–58, "Failure to observe the minorities treaties of the League," March 24, 1938.

23. NLS, NMP, op. cit., *Acc. 8185, Mitchison to Huxley*, October 17, 1938.

24. Woolf, in Bell, ed., op. cit., Saturday, October 1, 1938, 177–78.

25. In 1929 the Labour Party Advisory Committee on International Questions included: Leslie Haden-Guest, Arthur Creech Jones, Norman Leys, Sydney Olivier, Sidney Webb, Tom Williams, M.P., Leonard Woolf, Clement Attlee, Hugh Dalton, Ellen Wilkinson, and Herbert Morrison. Many were Scottsboro signatories, but others like Herbert Morrison would never have signed on to a "communist front" petition. See LWP, ID/C "Minutes of the Advisory Committee in International Questions," January 1929.

26. FCB 2/3, 53, "Notes in View of Debate on Colonial Office Estimates," June 14, 1938; *Roden Buxton to Dalton*, July 30, 1938.

27. LWP, Labour Party ID2a, Norman Leys, "The Labour Party's Colonial Policy," Private and Confidential No. 205B, June, 1939, 1–2.

28. Michael Graham Fry, "Agents and Structures: The Dominions and the Czechoslovakia Crisis," September, 1938, in Lukes and Goldstein, eds., op. cit., 311. South Africa, in particular, sought financial compensation from Germany for Southwest Africa.

29. LWP, Leys, op. cit., 3. See also Norman Maclean Leys, *The Color Bar in East Africa* (London: Hogarth Press, 1941).

30. George Padmore, "Britain Ready to Give Colonies to Hitler," *Chicago Defender*, April 9, 1938, 24. See also I.T.A. Wallace-Johnson, "Give No Colonies Back to Germany," *Daily Worker*, March 22, 1937: "Has Herr Hitler forgotten his remarks about Jews, Negroes and people of color when the arrangements for the Olympics were on foot?" Bartlett was elected to Parliament in November 1938.

31. See Walpole op. cit.; Applebaum, op. cit.; Morgan et al., eds., op. cit., 211–14, 218–25, 229; Raphael Samuel, *The Lost World of British Communism* (London: Verso, 2006), chapters 3 and 4.

32. See McDermott and Agnew, op. cit., 146. "Nearly all [Communist] parties suffered, but the worst affected were those that were illegal—the German, Yugoslav, Hungarian, Italian, Bulgarian, Finnish and Baltic parties." On Spain, see 139–42.

33. RGASPI. 495/72/208, 31–32.

34. Morgan et al., op. cit., 14, viii.

35. Norman and Jeanne MacKenzie, eds., *Diary of Beatrice Webb* (Cambridge: Harvard, 1982–85), August 28, 1936, 375.

36. Bell, ed., op. cit., Thursday, March 10, 1938, 129.

37. MacKenzie, eds., op. cit., August 25, 1940, 460–61. On Maxton, JMP TD 956/28/15, *Evening Standard*, May 5, 1934.

38. RP XIV, 3, 35–58, "Failure to Observe the Minorities Treaties," *National Committee on Peace and Friendship with the USSR*, September 30, 1938; See, also, Pedersen, *Eleanor Rathbone*, 225.

39. Eleanor Rathbone, "A Summary of the Refugee Problem" (London: Taylor, 1940), 3, 9.

40. Pedersen, *Eleanor Rathbone*, 228. See Keith Sword, *Deportation and Exile of Poles in the Soviet Union, 1939–48* (London: Macmillan, 1996).

41. Parker, op. cit., 262, 190.

42. Donald Cameron Watt, "Could Anyone Have Deterred It?" *Times Literary Supplement*, December 22, 2000, 9. The "Arab revolts" of 1936–39 began with a general strike. The British were asked to end the immigration of Jews to the region, to stop land transfers to Jews, and to form a new government.

43. Ibid., 307; DBN, *Bridgeman to Dutt*, July 13, 1965.

44. See Corthron, op. cit., 212–16.

45. University of Sussex archives, KMP, "Letters," *Levy to Martin*, June 26, 1941. Levy left the CPGB in 1957. See Morgan et al, eds., op. cit., 211–16, 218–23, 229, and, on Levy, 84, 185, 196.

46. Corthron, op. cit., 215, and KMP 28/ 1, "British Foreign Policy in the 1930s," 8.

47. George Padmore, "Parliament Upset by the West Indies," *Chicago Defender*, April 1938; Moyne Commission, op. cit.

48. "Conference on Peace and Empire," *Daily Worker*, July 1938.

49. George Padmore, *The Crisis*, September 1938, "Labor Trouble in Jamaica," 287.

50. See "Link to Peace Seen in World's Fairs," *New York Times*, June 13, 1939.

51. George Padmore, "Fascism Invades West Africa," *The Crisis*, October 1939.

52. See Tony Kushner, *We Europeans? Mass-Observation, "Race" and British Identity in the Twentieth Century* (Hampshire, England: Ashgate, 2004), and esp., "Mass-Observation, Beyond the Opinion Poll? The Mass-Observation Directive," 109–29; 299 men and 141 women responded. See also Nick Hubble, *Mass-Observation and Everyday Life: Culture, History, Theory* (Basingstoke, Hampshire, 2006); Caleb Crain, "A Critic at Large": "Surveillance Society: the Mass-Observation Movement and the Meaning of Everyday Life," *New Yorker*, September 11, 2006, 76–82; and Susan D. Pennybacker, "Mass-Observation Redux" in *History Workshop Journal*, 64 (1) 2007, 411–19.

53. University of Sussex, Mass Observation , *Directive on Race* (MO), June, 1939.

54. See Kushner, op. cit.; Hubble op. cit.,, Crain, op. cit., and Pennybacker, "Mass Observation," op. cit.

55. MO, June, 1939, #1194 and 1048. For notions of pity emanating from a sense of exploitation or oppression, see, 1013, 1057, 1079, 1135, 1176, 1208, 1287, 1312, 1327, 1578, 1600, 1630, 1632, 1992, 2007, 2008, 2019, 2062, 2064, 2065, 2070, 2075, 2097, 2150, 2164. All citations are examples taken from an unsystematic search of the majority of the questionnaires filed in response to this directive; most respondents were males. None indicated that they were nonwhite; some were Jews.

56. On smell and hygiene, see 1109, 1264 ("They do not stink."), 1299,1457 ("They stink . . . loathe any physical contact with them"), 1483, 2056, 2098, 2116. On music and black achievement in jazz, sports, entertainment and film portrayals, and personalities, the most commonly cited categories among the responses, see 0343, 1040, 1057, 1098,

1167, 1183, 1198, 1200, 1264, 1267, 1286, 1287, 1304, 1353, 1433, 1460, 1490, 1551, 1554, 1557, 1600, 1630, 1632, 1656, 1988, 2004, 2007, 2008, 2047, 2054, 2076, 2094, 2116, 2118, 2125, 2181, 2193.

57. For expressions of repugnance, revulsion or negativity, including the category of being "uncivilized," see 1057, 1063, 1247, 1260, 1264, 1313, 1316, 1529, 1554, 2007, 2034, 2056, 2098, 2106, 2157, 2181, 2957. For expressions of shame, remorse, and self-reproach, see 1013, 1183, 1562, 1974, 2062, 2145; 1616; 2111.

58. Many perceived inferiority as an innate quality. See 1014, 1054, 1078, 1085, 1099, 1135, 1184, 1198, 1287, 1299, 1300, 1312, 1375, 1411, 1460, 1512, 1529, 1628, 2007, 2019, 2062, 2070, 2076, 2077, 2097, 2107, 2118, 2125, 2145, 2150, 2164, 2196, 2202. Others assumed innate equality between the races. See 1287, 1992, 2064. On education as a means to "achieve" equality, see 1208, 1265, 1383, 1628, 2055, 2062, 2158, 2164. On "the cream" of African Americans crossing to England, see 1264.

59. On pleasing characteristics that could demean or appear exotic, see 1019, 1078, 1200, 1267, 1287, 1632, 2004, 2007, 2019, 2032, 2041, 2054, 2066, 2093, 2166, 2181.

60. MO, 1457. 1. For largely derogatory imperial associations, see 1124, 1142, 1198, 1477; 1014. On "Negroes" belonging in Africa, extending to being "better there" or "better-off there," see 1098, 1320, 1483, 1628, 1968, 2007, 2111, 2059, 2155, 2157; 1551.

61. For opposition to intermarriage, see 1019, 1112, 1330, 1247, 1289, 1362, 1457, 1477, 1483, 2038, 2041, 2059, 2074, 2089, 2094, 2111, 2137, 2191. On boxing, see 1656; 2094; 2089.

62. On opposition to Jim Crow, and U.S. policy, see 1019, 1085, 1167, 1176, 1208, 1224, 1287, 1304, 1375, 1541, 1630, 1992, 2049, 2065, 2171; 2075; 2074; 1327; 1304; 1498, a single male, publisher's employee from Ealing; see also, 1149, 2171; 1988.

63. MO, 1085; 1988; 2081; 1122; 1200.

64. 2052.

65. See MO, 1287, 1167, 1494, 2008, 2060; 1227, 1383, 1494, 1578; 1130; 1167, a single, twenty-six year old male weighbridge attendant from Birmingham; 1633.

66. MO, 1351.

67. 1534.

68. Appelbaum, op. cit., 151, 153–54, 182, 190, 256–57, 284–85, 360. See Buber-Neumann, op. cit. On the terror of 1934–38, in which 2.5 million were arrested and in which more than 680,000 people were executed for "counter-revolutionary crime," and the debate surrounding it, see Wendy Z. Goldman, *Terror and Democracy*, which argues that "repression was a mass phenomenon, not only in terms of the victims it claimed, but also in terms of the perpetrators it spawned," 5, 7 and Introduction, passim. See also Koestler, *Invisible Writing*, 108–109, 255, 496, 497, fn. 1.

69. See Jenkins, op. cit., and Lynne Olson, *Troublesome Young Men* (New York: Farrar, Strauss, and Giroux, 2007), passim, in which many *Die Zukunft* British contributors appear.

70. Cesarani, op. cit., 171. Others who assisted were Harold Laski, Vernon Bartlett, Sir Peter Chalmers-Mitchell, and Wickham Steed.

71. Koestler, *Arrow in the Blue* (New York: Macmillan, 1970), 274.

72. *Viertel to Viertel*, October 7, 1932: "Korda introduced me to British Gaumont and . . . Otto Katz (Czech Communist) has arrived in Berlin from Moscow." Viertel, op. cit., 181.

73. See Sauer, op. cit., vol. 2.

74. Francis L. Carsten, *German Refugees in Great Britain, 1933–1945: A Survey,*" in Hirschfeld, op. cit., 23–25.

75. Viertel, op. cit.

76. Padmore, *Pan-Africanism or Communism?*, 304, 342. See JMP, TD956/11/11 for Padmore's card. Cooper, op. cit., 342, cites "The Vortex in Spain: Issues of the Conflict," signed by Abercrombie and Woolf, 128.

77. See Pritt, *The Defense Accuses*, passim.

78. FEBR, *Shaw to Brockway*, December 1, 1945. Shaw disparaged the northern Afar people of the Danakil Ethiopian desert.

79. Ibid., *Koestler to Brockway*, December 9, 1945.

80. NLS, NMR "Women of West Africa," Acc 10772, 10, n.d.

81. George Padmore, "The Second World War and the Dark Races," *The Crisis*, November, 1939, 327.

82. George Padmore, "Democracy: Not for Colored Races," *The Crisis*, January 1940, 13.

83. Zachariah, op. cit., 107, cites *Nehru to Gandhi*, January 24, 1940. See also 104.

84. See, G. M. Kahin, *The Asian-American Conference* (Ithaca, NY: Cornell University Press, 1956), 64–72.

85. Lewis, op. cit., vol. II, 560.

86. Ibid., 501. Lewis also describes Du Bois's side collaboration with Walter White and Padmore's move to relocate the conference from London to Manchester, 512.

87. See Koestler, *Invisible Writing*, 474, and Morgan et al., eds., op. cit., 211.

88. *Manchester Guardian*, February 22, 1936.

89. University of Sussex archives, Leonard Woolf papers, *Mitchison to Woolf*, November 22 194–, n.d. IQ3C.

90. SC, ILD papers, Reel 5, Box 5, May 9, 1943.

CONCLUSION

The epigraph are taken from: Tony Judt, *Postwar: A History of Europe since 1945* (New York: Penguin, 2005), 278 and Bernard Wasserstein, *Barbarism and Civilization: A History of Europe in Our Time* (Oxford: Oxford University Press, 2007), 461.

Ferguson, *Empire*, 363.

Howe, op. cit. , 25.

1. Ferguson, *The War of the World*, op. cit., 381; Padmore, *Pan-Africanism or Communism ?*, op. cit., 126. See Morgan et al, op. cit., pp. 212–19, 224–5.

2. See Anson Rabinbach, "Antifascism," in John Merriman and Jay Winter, eds., *Europe—Since 1914—Encyclopedia of the Age of War and Reconstruction* (Europe) (New York: Charles Scribner, 2006), for a summary of the many forms and meanings of "antifascism."

3. See Bernard Porter, *The Absent-Minded Imperialists*, vii, viii, and chapter 1, passim.

4. See, e.g., Kushner, op. cit., 112.

5. See, e.g., Lauren, op. cit., chapters 6–8, and Kevin Grant, "Human Rights and Sovereign Abolition of Slavery, c. 1885–1956," in Grant et al., op. cit., 94–99.

6. See R. M. Douglas, "An Offer They Couldn't Refuse: The British Left, Colonies, and International Trusteeship," in Elizabeth Bishop, R. M. Douglas, and Michael D. Callahan, eds. *Imperialism on Trial*, op. cit., 141.

7. Hooker, op. cit., 46.

8. See Susan Pedersen on the mandates and League of Nations, as sources of knowledge. "The Meaning of the Mandates System: An Argument," in *Geschichte und Gesellschaft*, Heft, 2006, 32, 4, 560; "Internationalist Practice and the 'Spirit of Genevia'" in *European Studies Forum*, Spring 2007, 37:1, 14–18; and "Review Essay: Back to the League of Nations," *American Historical Review*, October, 2007, 1091–117.

9. "Hands off the Colonies," *New Leader*, February 25, 1938; Hooker, op. cit., 59–60, 67.

10. Hooker, op. cit., 61.

11. See Robert Dell, *Geneva Racket* (London: R. Hale, 1941), 279.

12. See, e.g., International Labour Organization, "A Global Alliance against Forced Labour," International Labour Conference 93rd session, 2005, Report I (B), (Geneva, ILO, 2005); "Stop Firestone's Exploitation and Cruelty" (www.stopfirestone.org); and, Kwame Anthony Appiah, "A Slow Emancipation," *New York Times*, March 18, 2007, 15–17.

13. See Grant in Grant et al., eds., op. cit., for related material. Great Britain Foreign Office, op. cit., vol. 113, 1938, Appendix A, "Excerpt from Lord Runciman's Report to the Prime Minister," 204. Vol. 116, 1939, "Statement in the House of Lords by Viscount Halifax, Secretary of State for Foreign Affairs," March 20, 1939, 603.

14. See Rabinbach, *Staging Fascim*, on the large "antifascist conference" in Amsterdam in 1932, which had a strong rhetorical focus on imperialism as "the enemy," before Popular Front era "antifascism" came to the fore, 104.

15. "Should the Refugees Fight for Britain?" *New Leader*, July 7, 1939, 5.

16. See Hooker, op. cit., 60.

17. See e.g., Rosenberg, op. cit., Epilogue.

18. Hooker, op. cit., 66, cites George Padmore and Nancy Cunard, *White Man's Duty* (London: W. H. Allen, 1942), 48.

19. See, Michael Marrus, ed., *The Nuremberg War Crimes Trial, 1945–46: A Documentary History* (Boston: Bedford, 1997), 44–45, and "Minutes of the London Conference for the Preparation of the Trial," July 23, 1945, 45.

20. See Cheryl Lynn Greenberg, *Troubling the Waters: Black-Jewish Relations in the American Century* (Princeton: Princeton University Press, 2006). On the issue of historical continuity, see Gilmore, op. cit., 1–12.

21. Judt, op. cit., *Postwar*, 280, from a statement made in 1951.

22. Hooker, op. cit., 88.

GLOSSARY

Glossary of selected names and terms, identified in relation to their use in this text. Readers will find further identifications in the Abbreviations, Endnotes, and Chronology.

Abdication Crisis — King Edward VIII assumed the English throne upon the death of George V (1865–1936), in January 1936. In November 1936 he sought to marry an American divorcee, Wallis Simpson. The Cabinet upheld the Church of England's prohibition against the remarriage of those divorced; the "crisis" inhered in this decision, prompting the king to renounce the throne in December. His brother George VI (1895–1952) replaced him. Edward married Mrs. Simpson, and as Duke and Duchess of Windsor, they visited Hitler at Munich in March 1937.

Abyssinia — The Italian army under the fascist leader Benito Mussolini (1883–1945), invaded the northern African Christian kingdom of Abyssinia ("Ethiopia") in October 1935, seizing the capital Addis Ababa in May 1936 and forcing Emperor Haile Selassie (1892–1975) from his throne and into exile; Selassie resided in Bath, England, from 1936 to 1941.

Antislavery — Following upon agitation including the formation of the Committee for Abolishing the Slave Trade, founded in London in 1787, the British Parliament banned the slave trade in its colonies and on British ships in 1807. William Wilberforce (1759–1833), parliamentarian and evangelical Christian (1759–1833), and others, fought for the abolition of slavery itself in the British colonies; the Abolition of Slavery Act of 1833 was passed three days before his death. It is his centenary, coinciding with the Act's passage, that was celebrated in 1933. The 1823 Anti-Slavery Society was succeeded by the British and Foreign Anti-Slavery Society in 1839. Its merger with the Aborigines Protection Society resulted in the organization in which Lady Kathleen Manning Simon, John Harris, and others served as leaders in the 1930s.

Anti-War Congress, Amsterdam — A gathering supporting a struggle for world peace, attended by three thousand organizations representing twenty-seven countries, including groups like the Fellowship of Reconciliation, the Women's International League for Peace and Freedom (WILF), and pacifist organizations that had large followings in the aftermath of the Great War, as well as supporters of anti-imperialism and anticolonialism. Saklatvala, Münzenberg, and Ada Wright were in attendance.

Reginald Bridgeman (1884–1968) — A former diplomat with an aristocratic family background, Bridgeman became a fellow traveler of the communist left and a member of the LAI. His short diplomatic career in Europe and Teheran, including visits to India and Iraq, led him to pursue Middle East questions as a radical. He was also active in Chinese issues from the 1920s. As secretary of the LAI during the Meerut campaign years (1929–1933), he helped to host Ada Wright in London and chaired the Fleet Street press conference when she was photographed with Bob Lovell. Bridgeman ran unsuccessfully for Parliament as a left-wing independent; his LAI affiliation caused the Labour party to drop him as a candidate and he was expelled from the Labour party in 1940.

British Empire — The complex system of colonies, protectorates (both dominated and controlled by the British), and Dominion territories was extended to include various mandated territories yielded by Germany and the Ottoman Empire to Britain and France in the peace negotiations at Versailles, and then held under the auspices of the League of Nations. The largest British possession, India, was the scene of tumultuous struggle in the 1930s (see below), while the promulgation of the Statute of Westminster in 1931 allowed the "white" settler Dominions independence, with Canada in the lead. Ireland experienced the aftermath of the Civil War and partition of the 1920s. Saudi Arabia and the Iraq mandate achieved independence in 1932, Egypt in 1936. The mandate in Palestine experienced acute conflict in 1937, and the West Indies witnessed uprisings and labor revolts on the eve of the war. Some mandated African territories changed hands in the thirties, coming under Dominion control, as in Southwest Africa's transfer to South Africa, where the extended abridgment of the rights of the African majority in both territories foretold the coming Apartheid era.

British Government — Prime Minister Stanley Baldwin's Conservative government of 1924–29 was succeeded by Ramsay MacDonald's First Labour Government of 1929–31, followed by the coalition "National Government" of 1931, a rightward-leaning amalgam of Conservative and breakaway Liberal and Labour MPs, again led by MacDonald. The second "National Government" of 1935–40 was first led by Stanley Baldwin, followed by the appeasement advocate Neville Chamberlain, who represented Britain at the Munich Conference of 1938. A wartime coalition government led by Winston Churchill came to power in 1940. The leading parties of the 1930s were the Conservative or Tory party, formed in the 1830s; the Liberal party, also formed in the 1830s, though each had older roots, and the Labour party, founded in 1900. The Independent Labour party was founded in 1893 and had various ties to the Labour party, though it alternately sought relationships with the communist party of Great Britain, founded in 1921. The Fabian Society of utilitarian socialists remained closer to Labour. Sir Stafford Cripps and other ILP dissenters formed the Socialist League in 1932, which was dissolved in 1937. A 1936 "Unity Campaign" sought to build an ILP, CPBG, Socialist League electoral block to challenge the political right. The Labour renegade Sir Oswald Mosley founded the British Union of Fascists in 1932.

Fenner Brockway (1888–1998) — leader of the ILP, who served as its chairman, 1931–33; general secretary, 1933–39, and editor of *New Leader*, 1931–46. He was an ILP MP in 1929 and 1931, and a Labour MP from 1950 to 1964, when he was an ardent advocate for domestic civil rights legislation. Brockway was born in Calcutta, was a conscientious objector during the Great War, and often visited India in the interwar years.

Ralph Bunche (1904–1971) — The grandson of a slave, Bunche grew up in Los Angeles. He taught at Howard University where he met first met George Padmore, and visited Africa in 1932–33 as a doctoral candidate at Harvard. During 1936–38, he worked at the LSE and at the University of Cape Town, visiting Padmore and his circle in London. He was active in the U.S. civil rights movement and served the United Nations in many capacities in the postwar era, receiving the Nobel Peace Prize in 1950 for his work in the Middle East.

China — The "Hands Off China" campaigns that began in 1925 thrust the issue of "colonial revolution" onto a world stage. In April of 1927 nationalist forces under Chiang-kai Shek invaded Shanghai, murdering hundreds of communist and other militants and provoking deeper conflict between communists and nationalists, as well as various Comintern interventions from Moscow. The plight of the Chinese left became a key radicalizing force in Britain and the West, leading into the 30s. In April 1931, the Japanese invaded the province of Manchuria, prompting agitation and a boycott of Japanese goods. In 1932 Japan sent troops to Shanghai, disrupting Chiang's anticommunist endeavors. In 1933 the Japanese declared the former Manchuria, "Manchuko," a state unrecognized by the League of Nations, but afforded recognition in 1934 by Nazi Germany, fascist Italy, and several right-wing Latin American regimes. The Chinese communist party defied the nationalists and began the Long March. Frustrated by Chiang's moves, Japan finally declared war on China in 1938.

Comintern — The "Communist," or Third International (1919–1943), based in Moscow, followed after Karl Marx's First International (1846–1872), and the Socialist International, formed in 1889, which remained in existence thereafter. The onset of the Russian Revolution of 1917 and the series of failed left-wing attempts at revolution elsewhere, 1919–23, (Münzenberg was a leader of the most significant, German conflict), fostered the consolidation of a stronger, centralized apparatus, especially after Lenin's death in 1924, until 1928. The CI was at first led by former Bolsheviks and, in principle, was responsible for steering the course of its national member sections (communist parties in other states) and supranational organizations toward world revolution. Multilingual congresses and plenums were held involving representatives, and cadre from member sections did residencies in Moscow and helped to form secretariats to direct work and maintain a voluminous apparatus of documents for review and scrutiny. From 1928 to 1933, under Stalin, the CI entered the socalled "Third Period" pursuant on the Comintern sixth Congress (1928) resolutions, and took a radical, militant, and critical posture toward all noncommunist movements of the left, crucially, in Germany. The switch to a "Popular Front" orientation at the CI's 7th Congress (1935) led to attempts to form coalitions with liberal and other left parties while Soviet foreign policy appeased capitalist states and regimes in several instances; this occurred in the same era as the Terror (1936–37) and the Moscow Trials (1936–38). Stalin dissolved the CI in 1943. This text concerns the German KPD (founded, 1918), Indian CPI (founded 1920 and CPI [Marxist], founded 1925), French PCF (founded 1920), American CPUSA (founded, 1919), and British CPGB (see below), as well as CI-sponsored organizations, including Soviet MOPR, Münzenberg's European "Red Aid," the U.S., British, and European ILD bodies, the LAI, Padmore's Hamburg-based "Negro Committee" (ITUCNW), as well as the Red Trade Union body, the Profintern. Comintern support for member sections and organizations included funds, personnel, espionage (including the means of assassination), and the use of a vast propaganda apparatus. Its archives are housed in RGASPI, in the former Marx-Engels-Lenin Institute near Red Square.

Communist Party of Great Britain — Founded in 1920, the CPGB weathered many fraught periods of relations with the Labour party, and Labour ultimately disavowed CPGB members and the party from affiliation with it. In 1922 Saklatvala was elected as one of two openly CPGB members in Parliament. The events of the General Strike of 1926 thrust the CPGB into greater prominence in the wider labor movement, and Saklatvala was the first militant jailed as a strike support leader. Attacks upon the Labour party and the ILP characterized CPGB work during the "Third Period" (1929–32), and the party's involvement in red trade union (Profintern) policy led it to attempt to challenge the efforts of the Trades Union Congress on the shop floors.

In this context, its relative success in the National Unemployed Workers' Movement and the hunger marches of the day won it adherents among some workers, intellectuals, and students. In the Popular Front era, the party widened its approach to non-CPGB leftists, Labour party supporters and liberals, and led important confrontations with the BUF. In 1939 Stalin and the CI adopted a "peace" stance toward the war in keeping with the agreements of the Molotov-Ribbentrop pact (see below), and did not reverse that stance until 1941. This text concerns many CPGB-sponsored and-linked organizations, and individual members and "fellow travelers," including Arnold Ward's Negro Welfare Association, the Meerut prisoners' defense groups, the Scottsboro defense groups, and the LAI. Rajani Palme Dutt (1896–1974) was the party's leading theoretician and the founder of its journal *Labour Monthly*. Harry Pollitt (1890–1960) served as the party's general secretary from 1929 until 1956. The *Daily Worker,* its daily organ, was founded in January 1930.

French Government — The Third Republic (1870–1940) was led by a Popular Front coalition government of the PCI, the French Socialist Party (SFIO) (see below), and the radical socialists, in the mid-1930s. Ada Wright came to Paris under President. Édouard Herriot (radical, 1932). The Popular Front was in power from 1936 to 1938, twice led by socialist Léon Blum, who had welcomed Wright to Paris. Blum was in power during the General Strike of May and June 1936. Édouard Daladier (Radical socialist) returned to office from 1938 to 1940 and it was his government that required German "aliens" to report for internment, including Gross and Münzenberg. During the 1930s the French ruled an empire of over 12 million persons, second only in population to that of the British. France fell to the Germans in June of 1940.

Marcus Garvey (1887–1940) — Born in Jamaica, Garvey was the founder and leader of the Universal Negro Improvement Association (UNIA), which sought, unsuccessfully, to send large numbers of people of African descent to Africa, including to Liberia. He founded the Black Star shipping line and the newspaper *Negro World*, and appeared with a petition before the League of Nations in 1928. Garvey built a 4 million member movement based in Harlem in the 1920s, the largest single African American organization in the United States of its time. He lived in London from 1912 to 1914, and from 1935 until his death, never seeing Africa. He first married fellow Jamaican Amy Ashwood Garvey (1897–1969), a cofounder and leader of the UNIA, and then married her friend and associate, the journalist Amy Jacques Garvey (1895–1973), in 1922. The former was involved in WASU in London, and was a jazz cabaret proprietor there. She was a founder of the IASB with Padmore and others, and an organizer of the 1945 Manchester Pan-African Congress.

German Government — The Weimar Republic under the 1919 Constitution, was inaugurated in the wake of the German revolutions of 1918–19, which followed upon the cessation of the Great War, and Germany's defeat. The far left Spartacist uprising was suppressed in these revolutions, and the coalition government that emerged was a compromise between pro-capitalist, Christian centrist, and moderate socialist parties (see below). The KPD had a legal existence under Weimar, but the global splits between socialists and communists, combined with the dire economic circumstances of the widening Depression, and the impositions faced by Germany as dictated by the Versailles Treaty, served to enhance the position of the far-right Nazi party (National-Socialists). In January of 1933 the German president Paul von Hindenburg (1847–1934) acceded to Nazi pressure to yield the German chancellorship to Adolf Hitler, an Austrian war veteran and former house painter; Hindenburg served out his term until death (1925–34) as the Nazis readily consolidated power in their exclusive hands. In late February the Reichstag fire occurred, blamed upon the communists; the accused included the Bulgarian Comintern official Georgi Dimitroff (1882–1949); all were acquitted except the Dutch defendant Marinus van der Lubbe (1909–1934) who was executed, and pardoned in 2008.

Langston Hughes (1902–1967) — A leading poet, playwright, and literary figure of modern American culture, Hughes was of African American and Native American descent and grew up in the country's Midwest. He traveled to Europe and West Africa in 1923–24, living in Paris for a time. In 1932 he toured the Soviet Union with a group of African American activists who were part of a failed film project. It was on this trip that he and Loren Miller encountered Naomi Mitchison, and on his further travels that year to the Caucasus region, he met and journeyed for a time with Koestler in Turkmenistan. Miriam Sherman also saw him in Moscow that year. In 1937 Hughes reported on the Spanish Civil War for the *Baltimore African-American* and, in 1938, expressed sympathy for the Moscow trials. He denied ever joining the CPUSA and lived and died in New York City.

Indian Government — Britain ruled over five hundred different jurisdictions in India before the war, of different forms of internal government. The oppositional Indian National Congress party, or "Indian Congress" or "Congress party," was founded in 1885 and grew to over 15 million members in the 1930s. After the bitterly challenged visit of the Simon Commission (1927–28), Congress called for Britain to confer dominion status on India. Mohandas K. Gandhi (1869–1948) left India in 1888 to receive legal training in London. He returned in 1915 after a transformative time spent in South Africa, and launched the civil-disobedience campaign in 1930, during the period of the Meerut prosecution, only departing India once more in his life, for London, in 1931, when he attended the First Round Table talks. Jawaharlal Nehru (1889–1964), son of the barrister and politician Motilal Nehru (1861–1931), was educated at Oxford, served as Congress president in 1929–30, and spent all but four months of 1931–35 in prison in India for his activism. He journeyed to Britain and Europe in 1935, where his wife died in Switzerland in 1936. The British Parliament passed the Government of India Act in 1935, extending the franchise, and Nehru was reelected Congress president in 1936 and 1937, and returned to Britain in 1938. In 1939 the radical nationalist leader Subhas Chandra Bose was expelled from Congress though he served as its president from 1938 until his expulsion; he later worked in tandem with the Japanese toward a British defeat in the war. Gandhi called for Britain to "Quit India" in 1942, and Nehru's support for this demand earned him a prison sentence from 1942 to 1945. India was granted independence in 1947, and the partition of the country into the future Indian Republic and the state of Pakistan ensued, an event that cost over 3 million lives. Gandhi was assassinated in Delhi in 1948. Nehru was elected the country's first prime minister in 1946. He was a leader of the global Non-Aligned Movement that held a historic conference in Bandung, Indonesia, in 1955, at which Nehru eulogized his prewar associate Münzenberg.

C.L.R. James (1901–1989) — A radical socialist-humanist writer and activist born in Trinidad, James came to live in Lancashire in 1932, joined the Labour party, and worked in part as a cricket sportswriter and as a contributor to the *Manchester Guardian*. He moved to London in 1933 and was there reunited with Padmore, assisting in the work around Abyssinia (see above) and the formation of the IASB. He became a follower of the former Red Army leader and Russian revolutionary theoretician Leon Trotsky, and led a faction of Trotsky's supporters in and out of the ILP. They became part of a larger tendency, the Revolutionary Socialist League, in 1938, and James departed for a tour of the United States undertaken by his comrades there, returning first to the United Kingdom in 1953, and then to Trinidad, then moving again to London where he died in Brixton, leaving a prolific corpus of political and literary production.

League of Nations — Founded in 1919, based upon a covenant provided for in the Versailles Treaty, the League had as many as fifty-eight member states in the midthirties, but failed to prevent war in Abyssinia and Spain, and could not prevent German rearmament and the outbreak of WWII. The United States never joined because of Senate Republican party opposition, Germany departed in 1933, and the Soviet Union joined in 1934, dismaying critics like Padmore. The attempt to partition Abyssinia that the British minister Samuel Hoare and the French representative Pierre Laval attempted to broker in secret failed when it reached the public in 1935 (Hoare-Laval); Emperor Haire Selassie addressed the League in Geneva in 1936 on his kingdom's behalf. This text also engages the work of the ILO and the League's Slavery Commission, and the work of the Mandates Commission that divided fourteen territories between the powers at Versailles, launching them on ostensible roads to independence. Only Iraq achieved that goal before the postwar period. Robert Cecil, a Tory MP and Nobel Peace Prize winner, was the most active British architect of the League, and president of its rank-and-file organization in Britain, the League of Nations Union (LNU).

Mass Observation — A mass opinion, mass anthropological and ethnographic project, still in existence, that was founded in London in 1937 by Tom Harrisson, Charles Madge, and Humphrey Jennings, to survey attitudes about British life and politics, international news and local custom, and to do so systematically over time, with a large group of "mass observer" volunteers and diarists. Many such people came forward and stayed with the project for years, some sending in daily diaries. Others volunteered for individual surveys like the 1939 survey of racial attitudes discussed in this text. MO began with a special focus on the aftermath of the Abdication Crisis (see above), and did intense work in Bolton, Lancashire, on provincial life and thought. Its archives represent one of the richest extant sources on ordinary, streetwise opinion in the 1930s of any population, the self-selected status of the volunteer participants and the politics of MO's organizers notwithstanding.

James Maxton (1885–1946) — A former Scots schoolteacher and teachers' union organizer who became the most important leader of the ILP. Maxton joined the ILP in 1904, and served a long prison term during the Great War for sedition. He remained a pacifist, representing a Glasgow district in the Commons from 1922 until his death and was recognized by friends and foe as a highly skilled and effective force in Parliament. He served as ILP chair from 1926 until 1931, and from 1934 to 1939. He engineered the ILP's break with Labour (see British Government, above) in the 20s especially after his own militant action and what he saw as Labour's betrayal of the General Strike of 1926. He loathed the onset of another war, leading him to take many contrary positions, including his surprising and infamous support for Chamberlain's attempts at appeasement (see Munich below).

Naomi Mitchison (1897–1999) — A Scots writer and poet who was from the wealthy and prominent land-owning Haldane family, and the sister of the acclaimed biologist J.B.S. Haldane. Mitchison served as a nurse in the Great War and married barrister and future Labour MP, G. R. Mitchison (1894–1970), a wartime officer. In 1932 she traveled to the Soviet Union, where she encountered Langston Hughes (see above). Her writing included controversial work on rape and abortion and novels set in antiquity. She was a "fellow traveler" of the left who visited the United States in the 30s under the aegis of the American Socialist party. After 1939 she and her husband were most active in the Scots isles, where their house on Kintyre, Carradale, served as a beacon for her work in local government, and her home away from Africa, where she became deeply involved in postindependence Botswana. Eugenics, feminism, sexuality, and the birth control movement were among her interests and causes.

Molotov-Ribbentrop Pact — Also known variously as the Non-Aggression Pact and the Stalin-Hitler Pact, this treaty was signed by German foreign minister Joachim von Ribbentrop and his Soviet counterpart Vyacheslav Molotov in August of 1939. The pact declared that neither country would invade the other or make war upon the other, and each vowed to uphold neutrality should the other be attacked, and to refrain from agreements or coalitions involving any powers seeking war with the other. Underlying protocols, denied thereafter, allowed for the subsequent invasions and division of Latvia, Estonia, Romania, Lithuania, Poland, and Finland in which only the Finns retained their sovereignty in a successful counter struggle. The CI ordered the member sections in the West, notably in Britain and France, to adhere to the Pact's implications, demanding that the CPGB and PCF membership oppose war and support a peace platform when WWII was first declared, a measure that affected levels of rank-and-file loyalty in many instances. The Germans benefited immensely from Soviet weapons and armaments, and freely moved operations into Soviet territory under the pact. Hitler then reneged upon its provisions and invaded the Soviet Union in June of 1941.

Moscow Trials — A series of "show trials" held in the Soviet Union in which Stalin's political opponents, including veteran Bolshevik leaders of the 1917 Revolution, were eliminated through the use of forced confessions followed by life imprisonment and execution, notably Zinoviev, Kamenev, and Radek. Red Army officials were also tried and convicted. The trials occurred between August 1936 and June 1937 and had wide international press coverage, including in the communist and ILP press in Britain. Münzenberg's protectors in Moscow and the founder of the Comintern Bukharin were among those tried and executed. The trials occurred in the context of the "Terror" of 1937–38 (also known as the "Great Purges") in which large scale liquidations, cleansings, trials, and fingering procedures that led to population transfers, labor deployments, and changes in bureaucratic leadership swept through the Soviet Union, also part of Stalin's strategy to consolidate and maintain effective discipline, loyalty, and submission in a system of rewards and punishments, economic rationalization, and forced collectivization leading to millions of deaths. The "Gulag" penal system served as a dimension of this wider process of repression, in which 18 million people served prison sentences in labor camps between 1929 and 1953, more than 1.5 million of whom died in incarceration, tens of thousands of whom were executed in 1937–38. Gross's sister, Buber-Neumann, was among those who survived to write about the era, while her brother-in-law perished.

Munich Agreement— Germany annexed Austria in the Anschluss in March 1938. With the threat to Czechoslovakia looming, a strong antiwar attitude in Britain, and a long-term appetite among some in the British political community for the pursuit of "appeasement" vis. Hitler, Prime Minister Neville Chamberlain visited Hitler at Berchtesgaden on Sept. 15 and 16, 1938, and Bad Godesberg on Sept. 22, to discuss German ambitions. Nationalist activists among the Sudeten Germans in Czechslovakia—German-speaking former inhabitants of the dissolved Austro-Hungarian Empire many of whom were pro-Nazi—had sought independence from the Czechs since Versailles. The strategic position of the Sudetenland led Hitler to support this demand, and promote pro-German agitation there; acquiescence to it lay at the crux of the Munich agreement, signed in that city on September 29, 1938. Hitler, Chamberlain, Daladier, and Mussolini were its signatories. Both Stalin and the Czech premier Eduard Beneš, were excluded from the meeting; Stalin had stated his willingness to defend the Czechs if needed. The agreement essentially gave the Germans the right to annex the Sudetenland over a period of ten days, and stipulated terms for the Czech evacuation and further terms for Polish and Hungarian minorities," and for some plebiscites, but not in areas where a "strictly ethnographical" as it was put, "determination" could be made. The Czechs were infuriated over its terms, and though Chamberlain returned to a grateful Britain to say that he had "secured peace," by March 1939, Hitler had seized all of the Czech territory and the global war was inevitable. In Britain Chamberlain had many supporters, and Hitler's hunch that many did not want an alliance with the Soviet Union proved correct at that juncture; in fact, Stalin perceived Munich as a pretext for the Ribbentrop-Molotov Pact (see above). But the group of MPs and others around Churchill, as well as voices recorded in this text, were fierce opponents of appeasement from many different quarters, even despite their anticommunism, and they expressed skepticism, doubt, and opposition to the Munich settlement, some resigning their parliamentary seats; the Czechs perceived the agreement as outright betrayal.

NAACP— The National Association for the Advancement of Colored People grew from the turn-of-the century Niagara Movement and was founded by black and white activists in 1909 in New York City. By 1920 it boasted over 90,000 members. Its purpose was to fight "Jim Crow" in all forms, the name taken from the nineteenth-century blackface character of a man dressed as a crow, and given to all the institutions and practices of the racial segregation and exploitation that characterized American life in the slavery era, and in the overturning of Reconstruction gains after the U.S. Civil War. The NAACP fought segregation in the courts, in education, and in employment, and mobilized against lynching. It ultimately participated in the later phases of the Scottsboro defense (see below), its early 1930s anticommunism a profound barrier to cooperation with the CPUSA. The NAACP also pragmatically feared guilt by association with communism. One of the most formidable and leading American intellectuals of the twentieth century, W.E.B. DuBois (1868–1963), was an NAACP founder, and founder and editor of its journal *The Crisis* from 1910 until his departure from the NAACP in 1934. (Du Bois journeyed to Japan and China in 1936, and returned to Germany on a fellowship in 1936, where he had been a student, despite his declared and continued opposition to Nazi anti-Semitism. DuBois joined the CPUSA in 1962 and died in Ghana.) The writer James Weldon Johnson (1871–1938) served as an early field secretary and then as NAACP president. Water F. White (1893–1955) became the organizational secretary in 1931 and was involved in the early rejection of the communist-led Scottsboro defense. White and Du Bois were friends and correspondents of Lady Simon's. Journalist William Pickens (1881–1954), whose parents were born in slavery, served Johnson as an assistant field secretary and became a senior officeholder.

Scottsboro Case — The nine African American defendants (Clarence Norris, Ozie Powell, Charlie Weems, Olen Montgomery, Clarence Norris, Haywood Patterson, Eugene Williams, and Roy and Andy Wright), some the grandsons of former slaves, were taken off a train and arrested in Paint Rock, Alabama, March 25, 1931, after a report of a fight among black and white hoboes traveling illegally on the line between Chattanooga and Memphis, Tennessee. Two white women dressed as men, Ruby Bates and Victoria Price, were also found, and each subsequently accused the defendants of rape, a capital offense. In hasty trials held at the county seat in Scottsboro before all-white juries, eight of the young men were sentenced to death except thirteen-year-old Roy Wright, who had a hung jury, as a sole juror did not want to execute him because of his age. Both the communist ILD and the NAACP vied with the defendants' families for the right to take the case; the NAACP withdrew when the defendants chose the ILD, which already had a base among CPUSA members working in Chattanooga and the region. In January 1932, a boyfriend of Ruby Bates produced a letter in which she said she had not been raped; she later went over to the defense, then headed by Samuel Liebowitz (1893–1978), a celebrity criminal lawyer without communist sympathies. In November the Supreme Court ruled in favor of a retrial on the grounds that the defendants had not had proper counsel in Scottsboro; they were reconvicted in a trial at Decatur in which Ruby Bates testified for the defense, but Judge James E. Horton, a former slaveowner's son, overturned the second jury's decision in March 1933. Medical evidence presented at the Decatur trial proposed that the women had not had intercourse on the night in question. In his decision Horton stated that the mood of the town would not allow a fair trial, but thereafter, convictions were upheld in November–December 1933, and Horton never again served on the bench. From the spring of 1933, the NAACP decided to support the ILD-directed defense, joining in a coalition with the ILD, the ACLU, and a committee formed by Liebowitz to build a Popular Front–style campaign, related to the earlier domestic and international campaign discussed in this text. In a landmark decision, the U.S. Supreme Court ruled in 1935 that the defendants' constitutional rights had been violated as no blacks appeared on the jury rolls whence jurors had been chosen in the previous proceedings; retrials in 1936 and 1937 still upheld the convictions. Plea-bargaining led to the release of four of the men in 1937; the remaining five either escaped or served time until the release of Andy Wright, the last defendant held, in 1950. None was ever declared innocent, but Governor George Wallace of Alabama pardoned the last living defendant, Clarence Norris, in 1976; Norris died in 1989. Altogether, the defendants served 130 years in prison.

Socialism — The Second "Socialist" International was founded in 1889, and until the splits that led to the Bolshevik party's formation, Lenin and the "Bolshevik" faction of the Russian social-democrats were members. Twenty member organizations were represented at the second International's founding. Headquartered in Brussels, the Second International member parties failed to oppose nationalist parliamentary motions and sentiment in favor of each state's government entering the Great War; this caused splits, defections, and the dissolution of the apparatus in 1916, but the international organization was revived in 1920, now a rival formation to the Leninist Third International and the Comintern (see above). Splits and fusions resulted in the formation of the Social Democratic Labor and Socialist International, which survived until 1946, and in new forms, until the present. This text engages the histories of some parties and formations that were members of, or in the orbit of, international socialism in the 1930s. These include the NAACP (see above), parts of the Bundist and Zionist movements, the British Labour party, many parts of the trade union movement, and the ILP (see above, British Government), the German Social-Democratic party (SPD, founded 1863) (see above, German Government), the French SFIO (1905–1969 and thereafter, the Socialist party; see above, French Government), and the American Socialist party (founded 1901), whose jailed leader Tom Mooney (1882–1942) was championed in the Scottsboro campaign. During the German revolutions of 1918–19, SPD leaders and generals helped to suppress the Spartacist uprising while the CI launched attacks at the socialists in the "Third Period" and sought them out for coalitions in the Popular Front era (see above, Comintern). In Spain, related schisms proved as fatal to the Republican struggle (see below) as they did to anti-Nazi mobilization in Weimar Germany.

USSR — Constituted in January 1924, the Union of Soviet Socialist Republics relied upon a federal model that combined an array of small, relatively autonomous "ethnic" entities in combination with larger "nations" that became federated socialist republics under a plan contributed to by Stalin and by Lenin just before his death. The larger entities were Belorussia, Ukraine, and the Transcaucasian region comprised of Georgia, Armenia, and Azerbaijan. Soviet Central Asia comprised a set of larger, individual republics and smaller autonomous regions. A series of transformations in "ethnic" and "national" policies ensued between 1928 and the war, which included initial trials and purges, a revival of "great Russian" notions of the progressive nature of the tsarist policy uniting the Russian empire, and a greater long-term Russo-centered understanding of Soviet internal rule. In 1938 the Russian language was required to be taught in all schools in which students learned in a "national" language as well. Yet, the notion of the Soviet Union as a group of permanent nations was also reinforced. The immutability of "race" suited a rhetoric aimed against "suspicious" nationalities, and over 1 million of these so-designated persons were driven into exile and death in the later thirties. This all occurred during an era of forced collectivization on the land, and a deeper and more pervasive development of industry and single industry centers involving transfers of population and the rationalization of the economy in the lead-up to the war. Sakalatvala, Hughes, Koestler, and other visitors to the Soviet Union, were exposed to some of the features of this complex system, and its languages of "antiracist," egalitarian propaganda. Thousands of Soviet sympathizers also moved permanently to the Soviet Union, some of them unemployed communist workers. Many did not escape the exigencies of the often murderous 1930s policies of incarceration (see above, Moscow Trials).

Spanish Civil War — A conflict between an elected 1936 Popular Front, Republican government, and a rebel force led by Gerneral Francisco Franco and mobilized from Morocco to defeat the Republic and its armies which were in turn supported by international volunteers drawn from among the exiled German left, to unemployed British miners to the American "Lincoln brigade" members who came to Spain to fight. The war lasted from July 1936 to April 1939. Italy, Portugal, and Germany supported the forces loyal to Franco; the CI and the Soviet Union gave conditional, limited material support to the Republic, encouraging deep conflict among the Republican factions, and especially violent conflict between the communist Republican supporters and members of the POUM that had ties to ex–Soviet leader, now-exiled Leon Trotsky. Spanish anarchists were also the victims of murderous communist betrayals. Particularly under these circumstances, the policy of "nonintervention" on the part of the other governments, notably those of France and Britain, sounded a death knell to the Republic. The Germans bombed the Basque market town of Guernica in 1937; in March of 1938, Barcelona, capital of the autonomous Catalan region, was bombed. The September 1938 Munich agreement assured Franco of his free hand, and the Nationalists captured Barcelona in January 1939, and Madrid in March, signaling the end of the conflict. This left thousands of Republican fighters stranded in France, where some German contingents turned to the ex-communist Münzenberg and read *Die Zukunft* in the last weeks before the Fall of France.

United States Government — Herbert Hoover (1874–1964), an engineer and a Republican, served as president from 1929 to 1933. The attorney and Democrat Franklin Delano Roosevelt (1882–1945), who led the country through World War II in a close collaboration with Churchill, served three terms as president (March 1933 until his death on April 12, 1945). From 1933 to 1938, he led the legislative struggle to launch the New Deal social welfare programs and economic policies that sought to bring the country out of the Depression that began in 1929, and sought relief from the subsequent recession of 1937.

BIBLIOGRAPHY

I. ARCHIVAL SOURCES

Archives Nationales (Paris)
  F Series, *Versements des Ministères et des Administrations qui en Dépendent*
  Police générale
  F7 15123–15128, 15131–2
Churchill Archives Center, University of Cambridge
  The Papers of Fenner Brockway
Hull University, Brynmor Jones Library
  The Papers of Reginald Francis Orlando Bridgeman
  Archives of Liberty (Formerly the National Council for Civil Liberties)
Hulton Archive-GettyImages, Paddington, London
International Institute for Social History, Amsterdam
  Papers of the League against Colonial Oppression
  Papers of the League against Imperialism
Labour History Study Centre, Central Lancashire University
  Papers of the Communist International
  Papers of the British Labour Party, International Department
  Papers of Ben Bradley, Rajan: Palm Dutt, Ivor Montagu, and William Gillies
Library of Congress
  Papers of the NAACP
London School of Economics Archives
  David Low Papers
  Independent Labour Party Archives
  National Peace Council Papers
The Mitchell Library, Glasgow
  Papers of James Maxton
National Library of Scotland
  Naomi Mitchison Papers
Russian State Archive of Socio-Political History, Moscow
  Archives of the Communist International
  Fonds 495, Executive Committee of the Communist International (ECCI)
        500 Caribbean (Central american) Bureau of the ECCI
        515 CPUSA
        534 Red International of Labour Unions (Profintern)
        538 International Workers Relief
        539 MOPR
        542 LAI
Schomburg Center for Research in Black Culture, New York Public Library
  Papers of the International Labor Defense
  Papers of Ralph Bunche
U.K. House of Lords, Parliamentary Archives

U.K. National Archives, Kew Gardens
  British Foreign Office Papers
University of California at Los Angeles Library
  Brian Urquhart Collection on Ralph Bunche
University of Liverpool
  Papers of Eleanor Rathbone
University of Oxford, Bodleian Library of Commonwealth and African Studies at
  Rhodes House
  Anti-Slavery Society Papers
  Fabian Colonial Bureau Papers
University of Southern California: Library for Social Studies and Research
  Family Papers of Miriam Brooks [Moore] Sherman
University of Sussex Library
  Mass Observation Archive
  Papers of Leonard Woolf
  Papers of Kingsley Martin
U.S. Holocaust Memorial Museum
  Archives of the Central British Fund for Jewish Relief
U.S. National Archives
  Department of Justice Central Files

II. GOVERNMENT PUBLICATIONS (UK)

Great Britain, Foreign Office, edited by E. L. Woodward and Robert Butler, *Documents on British Foreign Policy. 1919–39*. London: H. M. Stationery Office, 1946.
Hansard, Parliamentary Debates, House of Lords
  Parliamentary Debates, House of Commons
Colonial Students in Britain, Colonial Office Report. London: H. M. Stationery Office, 1939.
Correspondence and Report from his Majesty's Consul at Bona Respecting the Administration of the Independent State of the Congo 1904, vol. 62, ed 1933.
Report of the Indian Statutory Commission . . . Presented by the Secretary of the State for the Home Department to Parliament by Command of His Majesty, Cmd. 3568. London: H. M. Stationery Office, 1930.
Rhodesia-Nyasaland Royal Commission Report of 1939, Cmd. 5949. London: H. M. Stationery Office, 1939.
West Indies Royal Commission Report, Cmd. 6607. London: H. M. Stationery Office, 1945.

III. INTERVIEWS

Interview material in the possession of the author, anonymous participants, Chattanooga, Tennessee, 1998–2003.
Lloyd Brown, London, England, 1998.
James Livingood, Chattanooga, Tennessee, 1998.

John Saville, Hull, England, 1998.
Miriam Sherman, Los Angeles, California, 2002.

IV. CONTEMPORARY SOURCES

Periodicals and Newspapers (England, unless stated otherwise)

Amsterdam News (New York City)
Anti-Slavery Reporter and Aborigines' Friend
Bath Chronicle and Herald
Bedfordshire Standard
Birmingham Post (Alabama)
Chicago Defender (Illinois)
Chicago Evening Post (Illinois)
Christian Science Monitor (Chicago, Illinois)
City and East London Observer
Cleakheaton Guardian
Colne and Nelson Times
Controversy
Crisis (Atlanta, Georgia)
Daily Express
Daily Graphic
Daily Mirror
Daily Telegraph
Daily Worker
Die Zukunft (Paris)
Evening News
Everyman
Fifeshire Advertiser
Glasgow Evening News (Scotland)
Forward (Scotland)
L'Humanité (Paris)
International African Opinion
Irish Times (Dublin)
Journal of Law and Criminology
Leeds Mercury
Left Review
Manchester Guardian
Le Monde (Paris)
Morning Post
Negro Worker (Hamburg, Copenhagen)
New Leader
New Statesman and Nation
New York Sun (New York)
New York Times (New York)
News Chronicle
North London Recorder

Oxford Mail
Pittsburgh Courier (Pennsylvania)
Le Populaire, Économique et Social (Paris)
Round Table
Spectator
St. Pancras Gazette
Star
Sunday Dispatch Cable
Times
Time and Tide
Völkischer Beobachter (Berlin)
The Week-end Review
Willesden Chronicle
The World

Books and articles

Abercrombie, Lascelles. *Revaluations: Studies in Biography by Lascelles Abercrombie, Lord David Cecil, G. K. Chesterson*. London: Oxford, 1931.

Abrahams, Peter. *The Black Experience in the Twentieth Century: An Autobiography and Meditation*. Bloomington: Indiana University Press, 2000.

Adhikari, George M. "The Comintern Congresses and the CPI," *Marxist Miscellany*, #2, January, 1971.

Amery, Leopold C.M.S. *The German Colonial Claim*. London: Edinburgh: W. R. Chambers, 1939.

Aptheker, Herbert, ed. *The Correspondence of W.E.B. Du Bois*, vol. 2, selections, 1934–54. Amherst: University of Massachusetts Press, 1976.

Aragon, Louis, et al., *Authors Take Sides on the Spanish War*. London: *Left Review*, 1937.

Auden, W. H. *Collected Poems*. Edited by Edward Mendelson. New York: Vintage, 1991.

Azikiwe, Nnamdi. *My Odyssey: An Autobiography*. New York: Praeger, 1970.

Baravelli, G. C., *Abyssinia: The Last Stronghold of Slavery*. London: British-Italian Bulletin, 1936.

Barnes, Leonard. *Caliban in Africa: An Impression of Color-Madness*. London: Gollancz, 1930.

———. *The Duty of Empire*. London: Gollancz, 1935.

Bartlett, Vernon. *Nazi Germany Explained*. London: Gollancz, 1933.

Bell, Anne Olivier, ed. *The Diary of Virginia Woolf*. New York: Harcourt, Brace, Jovanovich, 1980.

Bose, Subhas Chandra. *The Indian Struggle, 1920–34*. London: Wishart, 1935.

Brockway, Fenner. *Inside the Left*. London: Allen and Unwin, 1942.

Bryce, James Bryce. *The American Commonwealth*. New York: Macmillan, 1912 [1910].

Buber-Neumann, Margarete. *Under Two Dictators*. New York: Dodd, Mead, 1950.

Bunche, Ralph. "Britannia Rules the Africans." *Journal of Negro Education*, vol. 6, no. 1, January 1937.

———. *A World View of Race*. Washington, DC.: The Associates in Negro Folk Education, 1936.

Bush, Alan Dudley. *Music in the Soviet Union*. London: Workers Music Association, 1943.

Buxton, Charles Roden. *The Exploitation of the Colored Man*. London: Anti Slavery and Aborigines Protection Society, 1923.

———. "Impressions of Liberia: A Report of the League of Coloured Peoples." London: League of Coloured Peoples, 1934.

———. *In a Russian Village*. London: Labour Publishing, 1922.

———. *The Race Problem in Africa*. London: Hogarth, 1931.

Christie, Agatha. *Ten Little Indians, etc. (a new edition of "Ten Little Niggers")*. New York and Los Angeles: Samuel French, 1946.

———. *Ten Little Niggers*. London: Harper, Collins, 1939.

Connelly, Marc. *The Green Pastures, A Fable Suggested by Roark Bradford's Southern Sketches, O'l' man Adam an his chillun'*. Farrar and Rinehart: New York, 1930.

Coupland, Reginald. *The British Anti-Slavery Movement*. London: Frank Cass, 1933.

Crawford, Ted, Barry Buitekant, and Al Richardson, eds. *C.L.R. James and British Trotskyism*. Interview with Richardson, Clarence Chrysostom, Anna Grimshaw. http://www.workersrepublic.org/Pages/Ireland/Trotskyism/clrjames.html, London, 1986.

Crossman, Richard. *The God That Failed*. New York: Bantam, 1964.

Crowder, Henry. *As Wonderful as All That?: Henry Crowder's Memoir of His Affair with Nancy Cunard, 1928–1935 with the Assistance of Hugo Speck*. Navarro, CA: Wild Trees, 1987.

Cunard, Nancy. *Negro: Anthology Made by Nancy Cunard*. London: Nancy Cunard at Wishart, 1931–33. Reprinted, New York: Negro Universities Press, 1969.

Curtis, Lionel. *The Protectorates of South Africa: The Question of Their Transfer to the Union*. London: Milford, 1935.

DeBunsen, Victoria. *Charles Roden Buxton: A Memoir*. London: G. Allen and Unwin, 1948.

Delmer, Sefton. *Weimar Germany: Democracy on Trial*. London and New York: Macdonald American Heritage, 1972.

Dell, Robert. *Geneva Racket*. London: R. Hale, 1941.

Digital South Asian Library. http:/dsal.uchicago.edu/reference/schwartzberg/pager.html.

Dreiser, Theodore. "An Open Letter to the Governor of Alabama." *Labor Defender*, June 6, 1931.

Du Bois, W.E.B., "Black Reconstruction: An Essay Toward a History of the Part Which Black Folk Played in the Attempt to Reconstruct Democracy in America, 1860–68," edited by David Levering Lewis. Oxford: Oxford University Press, 2007 [1935].

Dutt, Kalplana. *Chittagong Armoury Raiders: Reminiscences*. Bombay: People's Publishing, 1945.

Edgar, Robert R., ed. *An African American in South Africa: The Travel Notes of Ralph Bunche*. Athens: Ohio University Press, 1992.

Elton, Oliver. *Lascelles Abercrombie, 1881–1938*. London: Milford, 1939.

Fawcett, Philippa. *The Colonial Problem: Some Facts and Figures*. London: League of Nations Union, 1938.

Fields, V. G. Ricks, and S. Horton. *Precious Memories 88, 1850–1938*. Chattanooga: Chattanooga Afro-American Museum, 1988.

Foner, Philip S., and Herbert Shapiro, eds. *American Communism and Black Americans: A Documentary History, 1930–34*. Philadelphia: Temple, 1991.

Ford, Hugh., ed. *Nancy Cunard: Brave Poet, Indomitable Rebel, 1896–1965*. Philadelphia: Clinton Book Co., 1968.

Foster, Stephen Collins. *Plantation Melodies*. J. Knight and Co., 1888.

Garfield-Hays, Arthur. *City Lawyer*. New York: Simon and Schuster, 1942.

Goswani, Dharani. "Impact of the October Revolution," graham.thewebtailor.co.uk/archives/000089.html.

Gow, Ronald. *Gallows Glorious: A Play in Three Acts*. London: Gollancz, 1933.

Greene, Graham. *Journey without Maps*. London: Heineman, 1936.

Gross, Babette. *Willi Münzenberg, a Political Biography*. East Lansing: Michigan State University Press, 1974.

Guest, Carmel Haden. *David Guest, a Scientist Fights for Freedom, 1911–1938*, London: Lawrence and Wishart,1939.

Harris, John. *Germany's Lost Colonial Empire and the Essentials of Reconstruction*. London: Simpkin, Marshall, 1917.

Heard, William Henry. *From Slavery to the Bishopric in the AME*. New York: Arno Press of the *New York Times*, 1969.

Hitler, Adolf. *Mein Kampf*. Trans. Ralph Manheim. Burton: Houghton Mifflin, 1943.

Hobsbawm, E. J. *Interesting Times: A Twentieth Century Life*. New York: Pantheon, 2002.

Howard, Walter T., ed. *Black Communists Speak on Scottsboro: Documentary History*. Philadelphia: Temple University Press, 2008.

Hughes, Langston. *A Negro Looks at Soviet Central Asia*. David Mikosz, ed. Moscow and Leningrad: Cooperative Publishing Society of Foreign Workers in the USSR, 1934, and, Bishkek: Al Salam Printhouse, 2006.

———. *I Wonder as I Wander*, New York: Hill and Hughes, 1956.

———. *Scottsboro Limited: Four Poems and a Play in Verse*. New York: Golden Stair Press, 1932.

Hutchinson, Lester. *Conspiracy at Meerut, 1929–1932*. London: George Allen and Unwin, 1935; New York: Arno, 1972.

———. *Meerut, 1929–32*. Manchester: Manchester Meerut Defense Committee, 1932.

Jahre Internationale Rote Hilfe. Berlin: MOPR Verlag, 1932.

Johnson, James Weldon. *The Book of American Negro Poetry*. New York: Harcourt, 1931.

Koestler, Arthur. *Arrow in the Blue*. New York: Macmillan, 1970.

———. *The Invisible Writing*. London: Hutchinson, 1954, 1969.

———. *Spanish Testament*. London: Gollancz, 1937.

The Labour Party, *The Communist Solar System: the Communist International*. London: Labour Party, 1933.

The Labour Party Songbook: Everyday Songs for Labor Festivals. London: The Labour Party, Transport House, 1933.

Lawson, Elizabeth. *Scottsboro's Martyr—J. Louis Engdahl*. New York: c. International Labor Defense, 1932.

League of Nations, "Report of the Slavery Commission of the League of Nations," League Publications VI.B; slavery VI.B1, 1932.

Lee, Jennie. *The Great Journey: A Volume of Autobiography 1904–45*. London: Macgibbon and Key, 1963.

Lenin, V. I. *Collected Works*, vol. 25. Moscow: Progress Publishers, 1966.

Leys, Norman Maclean. *The Color Bar in East Africa*. London: Hogarth Press, 1941.

Locke, Alain, ed., *The New Negro: An Interpretation*. New York: A. and C. Boni, 1925.

Londres, Albert. *Terre d'ébène: la Traite des Noirs*. Paris: Albin Michel, 1929.

Lowell, James Russell. *Poems by James Russell Lowell in Two Volumes*, vol. 1. Boston: Ticknor and Fields, 1949.

MacKenzie, Norman and Jeanne, eds. *Diary of Beatrice Webb*. Cambridge: Harvard University Press, 1982–85.

Macmillan, William M. *Bantu, Boer and Briton: The Making of a South African Native Problem*. London: Faber and Gwyer, 1929.

———. *Complex South Africa, an Economic Footnote to History*. London: Faber, 1930.

Makonnen, Ras. *Pan-Africanism from Within*. London: Oxford University Press, 1973.

Mann, Klaus. *Mephisto*. New York: Penguin, 1983.

Mannin, Ethel. *Privileged Spectator: A Sequel of "Confessions and Expressions."* London: Jarrold's, 1946.

Marrus, Michael, ed. *The Nuremberg War Crimes Trial, 1945–46: A Documentary History*. Boston: Bedford, 1997.

Martineau, Harriet. *View of Slavery and Emancipation: From "Society in America."* New York: Piercy and Reed, 1837.

Mason, Mark. *Ten Little Niggers Polka* [sound recording, The British Library], 1869.

Maxton, James. "Liberty and Democracy Leadership Manifesto," Mitchell Library, n.d.

Mayo, Katherine. *The Isles of Fear: The Truth about the Philippines*. New York: Harcourt, Brace, 1925.

"The Meerut Trial: Facts of the Case," National Meerut Prisoner's Defense Committee, London, 1929.

Mitchison, Naomi, *You May Well Ask: A Memoir*. (National Library of Scotland) London: Virago, 1997.

Mitford, Nancy. *The Pursuit of Love*, 2nd ed. London: Penguin, 1958.

Moon, Henry Lee. "A Negro Looks at Soviet Russia," *Nation*, vol. 138, no. 3582, February 28, 1934.

Morel, E. D. *The Black Man's Burden*. London: National Labor Press, 1920.

Murphy, J. T. "The Labour Government—an Examination of Its Record." London: Modern Books, 1930.

Nehru, Jawaharlal. *An Autobiography, with Musings on Recent Events in India*. London: John Lane, 1962 [1936].

Nelson, Claire, and Walter Trier. *The Jolly Picnic: Ten Little Negroes, A New Version*. London: Sylvan Press, 1944.

Nevinson, Henry. *A Modern Slavery in Angola, San Thomé and Principe*. London: Harper, 1906.

Nimbkar, Rashunath Shivaram. *Communists Challenge Imperialism from the Dock: The General Statement of 18 communist accused*. Calcutta: National Book Agency, 1967.

O'Neill, Eugene. *All God's Chillun Got Wings and Welded*. New York: Boni and Liverright, 1924.

———. *The Emperor Jones*. New York: Boni and Liverright, 1921.

Orwell. George. *Homage to Catalonia*. London: Secker and Warburg, 1938.

Padmore, George. *Africa and World Peace with a Forward by Stafford Cripps*. London: Secker and Warburg, 1937.

————. *American Imperialism Enslaves Liberia.* Moscow: Centrizdat, 1931.

————. *How Britain Rules Africa.* London: Wishart, 1936.

————. *The Life and Struggles of Negro Toilers.* London: RILU Magazine for the International Trade Union Committee, 1931.

————. *Pan-Africanism or Communism?: The Coming Struggle for Africa.* New York: Ray, 1956.

————. and Nancy Cunard. *White Main's Duty.* London: W. H. Allen, 1942.

Paz, Magdeleine Legende. *Femmes á Verdre.* Paris: Reider, 1936.

————. *Frére Noir.* Paris: E. Flamarion, 1930.

Peace and the Colonial Problem. London: National Peace Council, 1935.

Perham, Margery, and Lionel Curtis. *The Protectorates of South Africa: The Question of Their Transfer to the Union.* London: Milford, 1935.

Peters, Paul. *Stevedore: A Play in Three Acts, by Paul Peters and George Sklar.* New York: Covici, Friede, 1934.

Pim, Sir Alan. *Report on Russian Timber Camps.* London: E. Benn, 1931.

Pottier, Eugene. *Internationale,* in *Chants révolutionnaire.* Paris: Dentu, 1887.

Pottle, Mark, ed. *Champion Redoubtable: The Diaries and Letters of Violet Bonham Carter.* London: Weidenfeld and Nicholson, 1998.

Priestley, J. B. *Rain upon Godshill.* New York: Harper, 1939.

Pritt, D. N. *The Autobiography of D. N. Pritt: Part One: From Right to Left.* London: Lawrence and Wishart, 1965.

————. *Part Three: The Defense Accuses.* London: Lawrence and Wishart, 1966.

Program of the Scottsboro Defense Gala. London: Utopia Press, 1933.

Rathbone, Eleanor. "Rescue the Pershing." London: National Committee for Rescue from Nazi Terror, 1943.

Ray, Sibnarayan. ed. *M. N. Roy, Philosopher-Revolutionary: An International Symposium and Selection of Documents with a Detailed Chronology of Roy's Career,* 2nd ed. Calcutta: Renaissance Publishers, 1984.

Regler, Gustav. *The Owl of Minerva.* New York: Farrar, Strauss, 1959.

"A Report of Proceedings and Decisions of the First International Conference of Negro Workers at Hamburg, Germany, July 1930." Hamburg: International Trade Union Committee of Negro Workers, 1930.

Reynolds, Reginald. *My Life and Crimes.* London: Jerrold's, 1956.

————. *The White Sahibs in India: An Examination of British Rule in India.* London: Secker and Warburg, 1937.

Rice, Elmer. *Judgement Day: A Melodrama in Three Acts.* New York: Coward-McCann, 1934.

Rickword, Edgell. *War and Culture: The Decline of Culture under Capitalism.* London: 1936.

Robinson, Stanford. *L'il Liza Jane . . . Old Slave Song Freely Paraphrased by L. Murray.* London: Ascherberg, Hopwood and Drew, 1960.

————. *Plantation Songs,* 2d selection. Arr. For Baritone Solo and Choir of Mixed Voices with Peianoforte acc. [words and melodies partly] by Stephen C. Foster. London and New York: Curwen, n.d.

Rolland, Romain. "For the Meerut Prisoners: Against Imperialist Terror," from *L'Humanité,* www.wcml.org.uk/internat/meerut.htm, March 18, 1933.

————. *Release the Prisoners,* London, n.d.

Roy, M. N. *Revolution and Counter-Revolution in China*. Westport, CT: Hyperion, 1973.

———. M. N. *Roy's Memoirs*. Bombay and New York: Allied Publishers, 1964.

Rutter, Eldon. *The Holy Cities of Arabia*. London, New York: G. P. Putnam's Sons, 1928.

Sahgal, Nayantara, ed. *Before Freedom, 1909–1947: Nehru's Letters to His Sister*. New Dehli: Roli Books, 2004.

Saklatvala, Shapurji. "British Imperialism in India: A World Menace." *Imperialist Review*, vol. 1, no. 1, July 28, 1928.

Samuel, Raphael. *The Lost World of British Communism*. London: Verso, 2006.

Schyuler, George. *Black and Conservative: The Autobiography of George S. Schyuler*. New Rochelle, NY, Arlington House, 1966.

Scottsboro Defense Committee. "Scottsboro Defense Committee: Appeal," London: 1934.

Sen, Ranen: *Looking Back to 75 Years as a Communist*. http://www.calonline.com/cal/alaap/ranen.html

Simon, John Allesbrook. *Retrospect: The Memoirs of Viscount Simon*. London: Hutchinson, 1952.

Simon, Lady Kathleen. *Slavery, With a Preface by John Simon*. London: Hodder and Stoughton, 1929.

Sperber, Manès. *Until My Eyes Are Closed with Shards*. New York: Holmes and Meier, 1994.

Spivak, John Louis. *Georgia Nigger*. New York: Warren and Putnam, 1932.

Spratt, Philip. *Blowing Up India: Reminiscences and Reflections of a Former Comintern Emissary*. Calcutta: Prachi Prakashan, 1955.

———. *Hindu Culture and Personality: A Psycho-Analytic Study*. Bombay: Manaktalas, 1966.

"Stop Press: Police Ban Sketch," *New Red Stage*, in *The Meerut Conspiracy Trial*, Working Class Movement Library, www.wcml.org.uk/internat/meerut.htm, June/July 1932.

Stowe, Harriet Beecher. *Uncle Tom's Cabin*. London: Dent, 1919 [1909].

———. *Uncle Tom's Cabin*. New York: Dover, 2005.

Temple, William. *Christianity and the Social Order*. New York: Penguin, 1942.

———. *The Church Looks Forward*. New York: Moorehouse-Gorham Co., 1942.

Thomas, Norman. "The Plight of the Sharecropper." New York: League of Industrial Democracy, 1934.

Thompson, Edward. *You Have Lived through All This: An Anthology of the Age*. London: Gollancz, 1939.

Toller, Ernst. *Which World, Which Way: Travel: Pictures from America and Russia* (trans. by Herman Ould). London: Sampson Low, 1931.

Usmani, Shaukat. *Historic Trips of a Revolutionary (Sojourn in the Soviet Union)*. New Delhi: Sterling Publishers, 1977.

Valtin, Jan. *Out of the Night: Memoir of Richard Julius Krebs Alias Jan Valtin*. Edinburgh and Oakland: AK Press/Nabat, 2004.

Viertel, Salka. *Kindness of Strangers*. New York: Holt Reinhart, 1969.

Vinogradov, Anatolik. *The Black Consul*. London: Gollancz, 1935 [1934].

Walpole, Hugh. *Out of the Deep: Letters from Soviet Timber Camps with an Introduction by Hugh Walpole*. London: G. Bles, 1933.

Wells, H. G. *The New American, the New World*. New York: Macmillan, 1935.

Wexley, John. "They Shall Not Die." New York: Knopf, 1934.

White, C.A. *I'se Gwine Back to Dixie: Companion to "Old Home Ain't What Is Used to Be."* Boston: White, Smith and Co., 1874.

White, Walter. *A Man Called White.* New York: Amo, 1969.

———. "The Negro and the Communist." *Harper's Monthly* 164, December 1931, 62–72.

Wilkins, Roy. *Standing Fast: The Autobiography of Roy Wilkins.* New York, 1982.

Wilkinson, Ellen. *Feed the Children: What Is Being Done to Relieve the Victims of the Fascist Regime.* London: British Section, International Committee for the Relief of the Victims of German Fascism, n.d.

———. *The Terror in Germany.* London: British Committee for the Relief of Victims of German Fascism, n.d.

———. and Edward Conze. *Why Fascism ?* London: Selwyn and Blount, 1934.

Winner, Septimus. "Ten Little Injuns: Comic Songs and Chorus." London: 1868.

World Committee for the Victims of German Fascism. *The Brown Book of the Hitler Terror and the Burning of the Reichstag.* New York: Knopf, 1933.

———. *The Reichstag Fire Trial, the Second Brown Book of the Hitler Terror.* London: John Lane, 1934.

Films

Cape to Cairo. London: Wardour Films, 1929.

Slave Ship USA. Twentieth Century Fox, 1937.

Zehn kleine Negerlein. West Germany: 1969 [1954]; Russian version *Desyat' Negrityat,* 1954.

Sound Recording: Paul Robeson, "Minstrel Man" by Langston Hughes, H.M.V. B8604.

V. SECONDARY SOURCES

Books and Articles

Adi, Hakim. *West Africans in Britain: Nationalism, Pan-Africanism and Communism.* London: Lawrence and Wishart, 1988.

Aggarwal, Som Nath. *The Heroes of Cellular Jail.* Patiala: Publication Bureau: Punjabi University, 1995.

Aitken, R.J.M. "From Cameroon to Germany and Back via Moscow and Paris: The Political Career of Joseph Bilé (1892–1959), Performer, 'Negerarbeiter' and Comintern Activist." *Journal of Contemporary History* 43 (2008), 597–616.

——— and E. Rosenhaft. "Politik und Performance. Deutsch-Afrikaner in Berlin der 20er und 30er Jahre," in Ulrich Van der Heyden and Joachim Zeller, eds., *Macht und Anteil an der Weltherrschaft: Berlin und der deutsche Kolonialismus.* Münster: Unrast-Verlag, 2005.

Allen, James, *et al. Without Sanctuary: Lynching Photography in America.* Sante Fe, NM: Win Palms, 2000.

Appignanesi, Lisa. *The Cabaret.* New Haven: Yale University Press, 2004.

Applebaum, Anne. *Gulag: A History of the Soviet Camps.* London: Penguin, 2003.

Ashraf, Ali, and G. A. Syomin. *October Revolution and India's Independence.* Sterling: New Delhi, 1977.

Bald, Vivek. "Lost in the City: Spaces and Stories of South Asian New York, 1917–65," in *South Asian Popular Culture*, vol. 5, no. 1, April 2007.

———. "Overlapping Diasporas, Multiracial Lives: South Asian Muslims in U.S. Communities of Color, 1880–1950," *Souls Journal*, New York, 2006.

Barkshi, S. R. *Simon Commission and Indian Nationalists*. New Delhi: Munshiram Manoharlal Publishers, 1977.

Barnes, James J., and Patience P. Barnes, *The Life of Hans Wosemann, 1895–1971*. Westport, CT: Praeger, 2001.

Barooah, Niroda K. *Chatto*. Oxford: Oxford University Press, 2004.

Beckett, Francis. *Enemy Within: The Rise and Fall of the British Communist Party*. London: John Murray, 1998.

Berg, Maxine. *Eileen Power: A Woman in History*. Cambridge: Cambridge University Press, 1996.

Berghahn, Marion. *Continental Britons: German-Jewish Refugees from Nazi Germany*. Oxford, UK: Oxford University Press, 1988.

Brinson, Charmain. "The Gestapo and the German Political Exiles in Britain during the 1930s: The Case of Hans Wosemann and Others." *German Life and Letters*, vol. LI, no. 1, January 1998.

Brown, Christopher Leslie. *Moral Capital: Foundations of British Abolitionism*. Chapel Hill: University of North Carolina Press, 2006.

Brown, Emily C. *Har Dayal, Hindu Revolutionary and Rationalist*. Tucson: University of Arizona Press, 1975.

Brown, Gordon. *Maxton/Gordon Brown*. Edinburgh: Mainstream, 2002.

Brown, Judith, ed. *The Oxford History of the British Empire*, vol. 4: *The Twentieth Century*. Oxford: Oxford University Press, 2001.

Bullock, Ian, and Richard Pankhurst, eds. *Sylvia Pankhurst: From Artist to Anti-Fascist*. New York: St. Martin's Press, 1992.

Cain, Peter, and Tony Hopkins. *British Imperialism 1688–2000*, 2nd ed. London: Longman, 2001.

Calder, Jenni. *The Nine Lives of Naomi Mitchison*. London: Virago, 1997.

Callaghan, John. *Rajani Palme Dutt: A Study of British Stalinism*. London: Lawrence and Wishart, 1993.

Carew-Hunt, R. N. "Willi Münzenberg," in D. Footman, ed., *St. Anthony's Papers*, no. 9. London: Chatto and Windus, 1960.

Caron, Vicki. *Uneasy Asylum: France and the Jewish Refugee Crisis, 1933–1942*. Stanford: Stanford University Press, 1999.

Carter, Dan T. *Scottsboro: A Tragedy of the American South*, rev. ed. Baton Rouge: Louisiana State University Press, 1979.

Cesarani, David. *Arthur Koestler: The Homeless Mind*. New York: Free Press, 1999.

Chandavarkar, Rajnarayan. *Imperial Power and Popular Politics*. Cambridge: Cambridge University Press, 1998.

Chang, Jung, with Jon Halliday. *Madame Sun Yat-Sen: Soong Ching-Ling* New York: Penguin, 1986.

Chisholm, Anne. *Nancy Cunard: A Biography*. New York: Penguin, 1981.

Clarke, Peter. *The Cripps Version: A Life of Sir Stafford Cripps, 1889–1952*. London: Allen Lane, 2002; Penguin, 2003.

———. *Hope and Glory: Britain, 1900–2000*, 2nd ed. *Penguin History of Britain*, London: Penguin, 2004.

Cooper, Frederick, Thomas C. Holt, and Rebecca Scott. *Beyond Slavery: Explorations of Race, Laborer and Citizenship in Post-Emancipation Societies.* Chapel Hill and London: University of North Carolina Press, 2000.

———. *Colonialism in Question: Theory, Knowledge and History.* Berkeley: University of California Press, 2005.

Cooper, Jeffrey. *A Bibliography and Notes on the Works of Lascelles Abercrombie.* Hamden, CT: Archon Books, 1969.

Corthorn, Robert. *In the Shadow of the Dictators.* London: Tauris, 2000.

Cotrell, Robert C. *Roger Nash Baldwin and the ACLU.* New York: Columbia University Press, 2000.

Crain, Caleb. *A Critic at Large*: "Surveillance Society: The Mass-Observation Movement and the Meaning of Everyday Life." *New Yorker.* September 11, 2006.

Curriden, Mark, and Leroy Philipps, Jr. *The Turn of the Century Lynching That Launched a Hundred Years of Federalism.* New York: Faber and Faber, 1999.

Desai, Mahadev Haribhai. *A Righteous Struggle.* Ahmedabad: Navajivan Publishing House, 1951.

Donoughue, Bernard, and G. W. Jones. *Herbert Morrison, Portrait of a Politician.* London: Phoenix, 2001.

Douglas, R. M., Michael D. Callahan, and Elizabeth Bishop, eds., *Imperialism on Trial*: *International Oversight of Colonial Rule in Historical Perspective.* London, MD: Lexington Books, 2006.

Dove, Richard. *He Was a German: A Biography of Ernst Toller.* London: Libris, 1990.

———. "Fenner Brockway and Ernst Toller: Document and Drama in *Berlin-letzte Ausgabe!*" *German Life and Letters*, vol. 38, issue 1, 45–56: October, 1984.

Duberman, Martin. *Paul Robeson.* New York: Knopf, 1998.

Dutton, David. *Simon: A Political Biography of Sir John Simon.* London: Aurum, 1992.

Eadon, James, and David Renton. *The Communist Party of Great Britain since 1920.* Basingstoke: Palgrave, 2002.

Edwards, Brent Hayes. *The Practice of Diaspora: Literature, Translation and the Rise of Black Internationalism.* Cambridge: Harvard University Press, 2003.

Faber, Doris. *Printer's Devil to Publisher.* New York: Julian Messner, Inc., 1963.

Farrell, Stephen, Melanie Unwin, and James Walvin, eds. "The British Slave Trade: Abolition, Parliament and People." Edinburgh: Edinburgh University Press for the Parliamentary History Yearbook Trust, 2007.

Ferguson, Niall. *Empire: How Britain Made the Modern World.* London: Allen Lane, 2004 [2003].

———. *The War of the World: Twentieth-Century Conflict and the Descent of the West.* London and New York: Penguin, 2006.

Figes, Orlando. *The Whisperers: Everyday Life in Stalin's Russia.* New York: Metropolitan, 2007.

Fisher, David James. *Roman Rolland and the Politics of Intellectual Engagement.* Berkeley: University of California, 1988.

Francis, R. A. *Romain Rolland.* Oxford: Berg, 1999.

Friedmann, Elizabeth. *A Mannered Grace: The Life of Laura (Riding) Jackson.* New York: Persea Books, 2005.

Frost, Richard H. *The Mooney Case*. Stanford: Stanford University Press, 1968.

Fry, Michael Graham, "Agents and Structures: The Dominions and the Czechoslovak Crisis, September, 1938." in Igor Lukes and Erik Goldstein, eds., *The Munich Crisis, 1938: Prelude to World War II*. London and Portland, OR: Frank Cass, 1999.

Fryer, Peter. *Staying Power: The History of Black People in Britain*. London: Pluto, 1984.

Ghosh, Pramita. *Meerut Conspiracy Case and the Left Wing in India*. Papyrus: Calcutta, 1978.

Gilbert, Martin, and Richard Gott. *The Appeasers*. London: Phoenix, 2000.

Gilmore, Glenda. *Defying Dixie: The Radical Roots of Civil Rights, 1919–1950*. New York: W. W. Norton, 2008.

Gilroy, Paul. *After Empire: Melancholic or Convivial Culture*. London: Routledge, 2004.

——. *The Black Atlantic: Modernity and Double Consciousness*. London: Verso, 1993.

——. *Black Britain, a Photographic History*. London: Saqi, 2007.

——. *Postcolonial Melancholia*. New York: Columbia University Press, 2005.

Godbolt, Jim. *A History of Jazz in Britain, 1919–50*. London: Quartet Books, 1984.

Goldman, Wendy. "Stalinist Terror and Democracy: The 1937 Union Campaign." *American Historical Review*, vol. 110, no. 5, 1427–53, December 2005.

——. *Terror and Democracy in the Age of Stalin*. New York: Cambridge, 2007.

Gordon, Lois. *Nancy Cunard: Heiress, Muse, Politics Idealist*. New York: Columbia University Press, 2007.

Grant, Kevin. *A Civilized Savagery: Britain and the New Slaveries in Africa, 1884–1926*. New York: Routledge, 2005.

——, Philippa Levine, and Frank Trentmann. *Beyond Sovereignty: Britain, Empire, and Transnationalism, c. 1880–1950*. Macmillan: New York, 2007.

Green, Jeffrey P. *Black Edwardians: Black People in Britain, 1901–1914*. London and Portland, OR: Frank Cass, 1998.

Greenberg, Cheryl Lynn. *Troubling the Waters: Black-Jewish Relations in the American Century*. Princeton: Princeton University Press, 2006.

Grossmann, Atina. *Reforming Sex: The German Movement for Birth Control and Abortion Reform, 1920–1950*. New York: Oxford University Press, 1995.

Hall, Jacquelyn Dowd. *Revolt against Chivalry: Jessie Daniel Ames and the Women's Campaign against Lynching*. New York: Columbia, 1979.

Harman, Claire. *Sylvia Townsend Warner*. London: Minerva, 1989.

Henry, Charles P. *Ralph Bunche: Model Negro or American Other?* New York and London: New York University Press, 1999.

Hewitt, Andrew. *Political Inversions: Homosexuality, Fascism, and the Modernist Imaginary*. Stanford: Stanford University Press, 1996.

Hirsch, Francine. *Empire of Nations: Ethnographic Knowledge and the Making of the Soviet Union*. Ithaca: Cornell University Press, 2005.

Hirschfeld, Gerhard, ed. *Exile in Great Britain: Refugees from Hitler's Germany*. London: Humanities Press, German Historical Institute, 1984.

Holt. Thomas. *The Problem of Freedom: Race, Labor, and Politics in Jamaica and Britain, 1832–1938*. Baltimore: Johns Hopkins, 1992.

Hooker, James R. *Black Revolutionary: George Padmore's Path from Communism to Pan-Africanism*. New York and London: Praeger, 1967.

Howe, Stephen. *Anti-Colonialism in British Politics: The Left and the End of Empire, 1918–1964*. Oxford and New York: Oxford University Press, 1993.

Hubble, Nick. *Mass-Observation and Everyday Life: Culture, History, Theory*. Basingstoke and New Hampshire: Palgrave, Macmillan, 2006.

Hughes, Arnold, and David Perfect. "Trade Unions in the Gambia." *African Affairs*. October, 88: 24–5, 1989.

Hunt, James. *Gandhi in London*. New Delhi: Promilla and Co., 1978.

International Labor Organization, "A Global Alliance against Forced Labor," International Labor Conference 93rd Session, 2005, Report I (B). Geneva: International Labor Organization, 2005.

Ishay, Micheline R. *The History of Human Rights from Ancient Times to the Globalization Era*. Berkeley: University of California Press, 2004.

Jackson, Julian. *The Popular Front in France: Defending Democracy, 1934–38*. Cambridge, UK: Cambridge University Press, 1988.

Jenkins, Roy. *Churchill: A Biography*. London: Macmillan, 2001.

Jhabvala, S. H. "Shapurji Saklatvala: The Trail-blazer of Communism in India." *BLITZ Newsmagazine*, August 17, 1957.

John, Angela. *War, Journalism and the Shaping of the Twentieth Century: The Life and Times of Henry W. Nevinson*. London: Tauris, 2006.

Judt, Tony. "The Last Romantic." *New York Review*, vol. 50, no. 10. November 20, 2003.

———. *Postwar: A History of Europe since 1945*. New York: Penguin, 2005.

Kelley, Robin D. G. *Hammer and Hoe: Alabama Communists during the Great Depression*. Chapel Hill: University of North Carolina Press, 1990.

Kenny, Michael G. "Racial Science in Social Context: John R. Baker on Eugenics," *Race and the Public Role of the Scientist. Isis 95*, 2004.

Kent, John. *William Temple: Church, State and Society in Britain, 1880–1950*. Cambridge: Cambridge University Press, 1992.

Khain, G. M. *The Asian-American Conference*. Ithaca: Cornell University Press, 1956.

Killingray, David. "Harold Moody and the League of Colored Peoples." In Bill Schwarz, ed. *West Indian Intellectuals in Britain*. Manchester: Manchester University Press, 2004.

Klehr, Harvey, John Earl Haynes, and Fridrikh Igorevich Firsov. *The Secret World of American Communism*. New Haven: Yale University Press, 1995.

Knox, William. *James Maxton*. Manchester: Manchester University Press, 1987.

Kramnick, Isaac. *Harold Laski: A Life on the Left*. New York: Allen Lane, Penguin, 1993.

Kushner, Tony. *We Europeans? Mass-Observation, "Race" and British Identity in the Twentieth Century*. Hampshire, England: Ashgate, 2004.

Lacouture, Jean. *Léon Blum*. New York: Holmes and Meier, 1982.

Lauren, Paul Gordon. *The Evolution of International Rights*. Philadelphia: University of Pennsylvania Press, 2003.

Levene, Mark. *Arthur Koestler*. New York: F. Unger, 1984.

Lewis, David Levering. *W.E.B. Du Bois: The Fight for Equality and the American Century, 1919–63*, vol. 2. New York: Henry Holt, 2000.

———. *W.E.B. Du Bois: Biography of a Race, 1818–1919*. New York: Henry Holt, 1993.

Livingood, James W. *A History of Hamilton County, Tennessee*. Memphis, TN: Memphis State University Press, N: 1981.

London, Louise. *Whitehall and the Jews, 1933–1948: British Immigration Policy, Jewish Refugees, and the Holocaust*. Cambridge: Cambridge University Press, 2000.

Lukacs, John. *Five Days in London May 1940*. New Haven: Yale University Press, 1999.

Marcus, Jane. *Hearts of Darkness: White Women Write Race*. New Brunswick: Rutgers University Press, 2004.

Martin, Terry. *The Affirmative Action Empire: Nations and Nationalism in the Soviet Union, 1923–39*. Ithaca: Cornell University Press, 2001.

McClellan, Woodford. "Black Hajj to 'Red Mecca': African and Afro-Americans at KUTV, 1935–1938." in Matusevich, Maxim, ed., *Africa in Russia, Russia in Africa: Three Centuries of Encounters*. Trenton, NJ: Africa World Press, 2007.

——. "George Padmore and the Hamburg Conference: Some Background." Presented at The Life and Times of George Padmore: Black Radicalism in the Twentieth Century, University of the West Indies, St. Augustine, October 2003.

——. "Africans and Black Americans in the Comintern Schools, 1925–34." *International Journal of African Historical Studies*, 26(2), 1993.

McDermott, Kevin, and Jeremy Agnew. *The Comintern: A History of International Communism from Lenin to Stalin*. London: Macmillan, 1996.

McIlroy, John. "The Establishment of Intellectual Orthodoxy and the Stalinization of British Communism, 1928–33." *Past and Present*, vol. 192 (2006), 187–230.

McMeekin, Sean. *The Red Millionaire: A Political Biography of Willi Münzenberg, Moscow's Secret Propaganda Czar in the West*. New Haven: Yale University Press, 2003.

Metcalf, Barbara D., and Thomas Metcalf. *A Concise History of India*. Cambridge: Cambridge University Press, 2002.

Miers, Suzanne. *Slavery in the Twentieth Century: The Evolution of a Global Problem*. Lanham, MD: Rowan and Littlefield, 2003.

Miller, James A., *Remembering Scottsboro: The Legacy of an Infamous Trial*. Princeton: Princeton University Press, 2009.

Miller, James A., Susan D. Pennybacker, and Eve Rosenhaft. "Mother Ada Wright and the International Campaign to Free the Scottsboro Boys, 1931–40." *American Historical Review*, 387–430, vol. 106, no. 2, April 2001.

Mitchell, Eva. "Introduction." Archives of the Central British Fund for World Jewish Relief, 1933–60 [United States Holocuast Memorial Museum], 1989.

Morgan, Kevin, Gideon Cohen, and Andrew Flinn. *Communists and British Society, 1920–1991*. London: Rivers Oram, 2007.

Mukherji, Ani. *The International Trade Union Committee of Negro Workers: A Report from the Moscow Archives*. Symposium on Anticolonialism, Marxism, and Black Liberation, Africana Studies, Brown University, 2008.

Murray, Hugh. "Letter to the Editor," *American Historical Review*, vol. 107, #1, 2002.

Naison, Mark. *Communists in Harlem during the Depression*, 2nd ed. Urbana: University of Illinois, 1983.

Newsletter of the Black and Asian Studies Association. London: http://www.blackandasianstudies.org/.

O'Brien, Patrick. "Britain's Economy between the Wars: A Survey of Counter-Revolution in Economic History." *Past and Present*, 115 (1): 107–30, 1987.

Owen, Nicholas. *The British Left and India: Metropolitan Anti-imperialism, 1885–1947* (Oxford: Oxford University Press, 2007.

Oxford Dictionary of National Biography [electronic resource]. Oxford; New York: Oxford University Press, 2004–. www.oxforddnb.com.

Pankhurst, Richard. *Sylvia Pankhurst: Artist and Crusader.* London: Paddington Press, 1979.

Parker, R.A.C. *Churchill and Appeasement.* London: Macmillan, 2000.

Pedersen, Susan. *Eleanor Rathbone and the Politics of Conscience.* New Haven: Yale University Press, 2004.

——. "Internationalist Practice and the 'Spirit of Geneva'" *European Studies Forum,* 37:1, Spring 2007, 14–18.

——."The Meaning of Mandates System: An Argument," in *Geschichte und Gesellschaft,* 32, 4, 60, 2006.

——. "Review Essay: Back to the League of Nations," *American Historical Review,* vol. 112, no. 4, October 2007, 1091–117.

Pegushev, Andrei M. "The Unknown Jomo Kenyatta," in *Egerton Journal,* vol. 1, no. 2, 1996.

Pennybacker, Susan."Changing Convictions: London County Council Blackcoated Activism between the Wars," in Rudy Koshar, ed. *Splintered Classes: Politics and the Lower Middle Class in Interwar Europe,* New York: Holmes and Meier, 1990.

——. "Mass Observation Redux," in *History Workshop Journal,* 64 (1), 2007, 411–19.

Pickering, Michael. "Race, Gender, and Broadcast Comedy: The Case of the BBC's Kentucky Minstrels, *European Journal of Communication,* vol. 9, no. 3, 311–13, September 1994.

Pierpont, Claudia Roth. "The Measure of America: The Anthropologist Who Fought Racism." *New Yorker,* vol. 80, March 8, 2004.

Pimlott, Ben. *Labour and the Left in the 1930s.* Cambridge: Cambridge University Press, 1997.

Porter, Bernard. *The Absent-Minded Imperialists.* Oxford: Oxford University Press, 2004.

Prashad, Vijay. *The Darker Nations: A People's History of the Third World.* New York: The New Press, 2007.

Price, Ruth. *The Lives of Agnes Smedley.* Oxford, New York: Oxford University Press, 2005.

Quest, Matthew. "George Padmore and C.L.R. James' *International African Opinion.*" Symposium on Anticolonialism, Marxism and Black Liberation. Africana Studies, Brown University, 2008.

Olson, Lynne. *Troublesome Young Men.* New York: Farrar, Strauss, and Giroux, 2007.

Rabinbach, Anson. "Staging Antifascism: The Brown Book of the Reichstag File and Hitler Terror." *New German Critique,* vol. 35, no. 1, Spring 2008.

——. "The Culture of Antifascism," unpublished manuscript, Princeton University, 2006.

——. "Antifascism," in John Merriman and Jay Winter, eds., *Europe since 1914: Encyclopedia of the Age of War and Reconstruction.* New York: Charles Scribner, 2006.

Rampersad, Arnold. *Life of Langston Hughes,* vol. I, 1902–41. Oxford, England: Oxford University Press, 2002.

Rice, Anne Spry. "Imperial Identity in Colored Minds: Harold Moody and the League of Colored Peoples, 1931–50." *Twentieth-Century British History,* vol. 13, no. 2, 2002.

Rich, Paul B. *Race and Empire in British Politics.* Cambridge and New York: Cambridge University Press, 1990.

Röder, Werner. *Displaced German Scholars: A Guide to Academics in Peril in Nazi Germany during the 1930s.* San Bernardino, CA: Borgo Press, 1933.

——. et al. *International Biographical Dictionary of Central European Emigrés, 1933–45*, vols. 1, 3, New York: K. G. Sauer, 1999.

Rosenberg, Clifford. *Policing Paris: The Origins of Modern Immigration Control between the Wars*. Ithaca and London: Cornell University Press, 2006.

Saha, Panchanan. *Shapurji Saklatvala: A Short Biography*. Delhi: People's Publishing, 1970.

Saklatvala, Sehri. *Fifth Commandment: A Biography of Shapurji Saklatvala*. Calcutta: National Book Agency, 1996.

Schwarz, William. "George Padmore," in William Schwarz, *West Indian Intellectuals in Britain*. Manchester and New York: Manchester University Press, 2003.

Seal, Anil, ed. *Decline, Revival and Fall of the British Empire: The Ford Lectures and Other Essays by John Gallagher*. Cambridge: Cambridge University Press, 1982.

Service, Robert. *Comrades: A History of World Communism*. Cambridge: Harvard University Press, 2007.

——. *Stalin: A Biography*. Cambridge: Harvard University Press, 2005.

Shepperson, George." Pan-Africanism and 'Pan-Africanism': Some Historical Notes." *Phylon*, vol. 23, no. 4 (Winter), 346–58, 1962.

Singh, Devendra. *Meerut Conspiracy Case and the Communist Movement in India, 1929–35*. Meerut: Research India Publication, 1990.

Sinha, L. P. *The left-wing in India, 1919–47*. Mazzaffarpur: New Publishers, 1965.

Smith, Woodruff D. *The Ideological Origins of Nazi Imperialism*. New York: Oxford, 1986.

Solomon, Mark. *The Cry Was Unity: Communism and African-Americans, 1917–1936*. Jackson: University Press of Mississippi, 1988.

Spitzer, Leo, and LaRoy Denzer. "I.T.A. Wallace-Johnson and the West African Youth League." *International Journal of African Historical Studies*, vol. 6, no. 3 (1973), 413–52.

Squires, Mike. *Saklatvala: A Political Biography*. London: Lawrence and Wishart, 1990.

Stevenson, Graham. *Biographies*. Graham.thewebtailor.co.uk/archives/000089.html.

Stewart, Jeffrey, ed. *Paul Robeson Artist and Citizen*. New Brunswick: Rutgers University Press, 1998.

"Stop Firestone's Exploitation and Cruelty." *www.stopfirestone.org*.

Sword, Keith. *Deportation and Exile of Poles in the Soviet Union, 1939–48*. London: Macmillan, 1996.

Tabili, Laura. *We Ask for British Justice*. Ithaca: Cornell University Press, 1994.

Tobias, Fritz. *Der Reichstagbrand. Legende und Wirklichkeit*. Rawstatt: G. Grot'sche Vrlagbuchhandlung, 1962.

Turner, Joyce Moore, and W. Burghardt Turner. *Caribbean Crusaders and the Harlem Renaissance*. Urbana: University of Illinois Press, 2005.

Tytell, John. *Ezra Pound, the Solitary Volcano*. Chicago: Ivan R. Dee, 1987.

Urquhart, Brian. *Ralph Bunche, an American Life*. New York, London: Norton, 1993.

Valtin, Jan. *Out of the Night: Memoir of Richard Julius Krebs Alias Jan Valtin*. Edinburgh and Oakland: Ak Press/Nabat, 2004.

Vernon, Betty D. *Ellen Wilkinson. 1891–1947*. London: Croom Helm, 1982.

Viala, Alain, et al. *Le Théâtre en France des origines à nos jours: "Les remises en question contemporaines. 1887–1997."* Paris: Presses Universitaires de France, 1997.

Viola, Lynne. *Unknown Gulag*. Oxford: Oxford University Press, 2007.

Von Eschen, Penny M. *Race against Empire: Black Americans and Anticolonialism*. Ithaca: Cornell University Press, 1997.

Von zur Mühlen, Patrik. "Exile and Resistance." In Wolfgang and Walter H. Pehle, eds., *Encyclopedia of German Resistance to the Nazi Movement.* New York: Continuum, 1997.

Wasserstein, Bernard. *Barbarism and Civilization: A History of Europe in Our Time.* Oxford: Oxford University Press, 2007.

——. *Britain and the Jews of Europe, 1939–45.* London: Leicester University Press, 1999.

Watt, Donald Cameron. "Could Anyone Have Deterred It?" *Times Literary Supplement.* December 2, 2000.

Weitz, Eric D. *Creating German Communism, 1890–1990: From Popular Protests to Socialist State.* Princeton: Princeton University Press, 1997.

Williams, E. T., and Helen M. Palmer, eds. *The Dictionary of National Biography, 1951–60.* London: Oxford University Press, 1971.

Worrell, Rodney. "George Padmore, the Comintern and the Liberation of black people," Symposium on Anticolonialism, Marxism and Black Liberation, Africana Studies, Brown University, 2008.

Wright, Anthony. *R. H. Tawney.* Manchester: Manchester University Press, 1987.

Zachariah, Benjamin. *Nehru.* London: Routledge, 2004.

Film

Goodman, James, and Daniel Anker. *Scottsboro: An American Tragedy."* New York: Social Media Productions, Inc., 2000, 2001.

Thesis

Fletcher, Yaël Simpson. "City Nation, and Empire in Marseilles, 1991–1939." Ph.D. Dissertation, Department of History, Emory University, 1999.

INDEX

Page numbers in italics refer to illustrations.